General Editor's Introduction

Asbury Theological Seminary Series in World Christian Revitalization Movements

This volume is published in collaboration with the Center for the Study of World Christian Revitalization Movements, a cooperative initiative of Asbury Theological Seminary faculty. Building on the work of the previous Wesleyan/Holiness Studies Center at the Seminary, the Center provides a focus for research in the Wesleyan Holiness and other related Christian renewal movements, including Pietism and Pentecostal movements, which have had a world impact. The research seeks to develop analytical models of these movements, including their biblical and theological assessment. Using an interdisciplinary approach, the Center bridges relevant discourses in several areas in order to gain insights for effective Christian mission globally. It recognizes the need for conducting research that combines insights from the history of evangelical renewal and revival movements with anthropological and religious studies literature on revitalization movements. It also networks with similar or related research and study centers around the world, in addition to sponsoring its own research projects.

Professor Richie's research in developing a Pentecostal theology of religions relies on the classical Pentecostal tradition of pneumatological testimony, linked to a propensity for creativity in deploying that perspective in engaging interreligious encounter and dialogue appropriate for the twenty-first century. It is to be noted that this classical tradition of pneumatological testimony has historical precedence in the federal tradition of Reformed Pietism, rooted in Cocceius, which gave impetus for a range of proto-Pentecostal initiatives in the early eighteenth century. With this important study, that honored tradition is implicitly reclaimed to occupy its rightful place in providing a basis for interreligious dialogue in this century. In its scope and content, this study demonstrates congruence with the mission of the Center in its engagement of movements of revitalization in global Christianity, thereby advancing our research objectives.

J. Steven O'Malley
Director, Center for the Study of World Christian Revitalization Movements, Asbury Theological Seminary
General Editor, The Asbury Theological Seminary Series in Christian Revitalization Studies

The Pentecostal and Charismatic Sub-Series

Of all the renewal traditions that have engaged the theological landscape, the Pentecostal Movement has undoubtedly made the most significant impact since it emerged at the turn of the twentieth century. Starting as a revival in a small African-American congregation on Azusa Street in Los Angeles, California, the movement soon swept the world, establishing itself in more than forty countries in the first three years. One hundred years later Pentecostalism has grown to an estimated 500 million global adherents or approximately twenty-five percent of all of Christendom. In the same manner that Wesleyanism burst beyond the bounds of Methodism to embrace an interdenominational holiness movement following the American Civil War in the nineteenth century, Pentecostalism transcended denominational lines in the form of the Charismatic Movement during the second half of the twentieth century.

This sub-series is designed to explore the historical, theological and intercultural dimensions of these twin twentieth-century Restorationists traditions from a global perspective. In this volume Tony Richie draws deeply on these interrelated dimensions to develop a Pentecostal theology that articulates a powerful challenge for the need for Pentecostals to be engaged in interfaith dialogue and provides an effective strategy for implementation. Over fifty years ago, David Duplessis, then General Secretary of the World Pentecostal Fellowship, justified his approaching the World Council of Churches (at the time anathema to most of the Pentecostal leadership) by quoting the prophet Joel, "In the last days I will pour out my spirit upon all flesh," and adding, "not just Pentecostal flesh." Sometimes he would also add and "not just Christian flesh." In this volume, Richie builds upon the work of Amos Young, Veli-Matti Kärkkäinen and others to provide the theological foundation to undergird Duplessis' prophetic challenge to the Pentecostal movement.

D. William Faupel
Sub-Series Editor

Speaking by the Spirit:
A Pentecostal Model for Interreligious Dialogue

Tony Richie

*Asbury Theological Seminary Series in
World Christian Revitalization Movements in
Pentecostal/Charismatic Studies, No. 6*

EMETH PRESS
www.emethpress.com

Speaking by the Spirit: A Pentecostal Model for Interreligious Dialogue

Copyright © 2011 Tony Richie
Printed in the United States of America on acid-free paper

All rights reserved. No part of this book may be reproduced, or stored in a retrieval system or transmitted in any form or by any means, electronic, mechanical, photocopying, recording, scanning or otherwise, except as permitted by the 1976 United States Copyright Act, or with the prior written permission of Emeth Press. Requests for permission should be addressed to: Emeth Press, P. O. Box 23961, Lexington, KY 40523-3961. http://www.emethpress.com.

Library of Congress Cataloging-in-Publication Data

Richie, Tony.
 Speaking by the Spirit : a Pentecostal model for interreligious dialogue / Tony Richie.
   p. cm. -- (Asbury Theological Seminary series in world Christian revitalization movements in Pentecostal/Charismatic studies ; no. 6)
 Includes bibliographical references (p.   ).
 ISBN 978-1-60947-014-2 (alk. paper)
 1. Theology of religions (Christian theology) 2. Pentecostal churches--Doctrines. 3. Christianity and other religions. I. Title.
 BT83.85.R53 2011
 261.2--dc22
                        2010054247

Contents

Abbreviations vii
Foreword by Amos Yong xi
Acknowledgements...xiii

Introduction 1

Part One: Laying the Foundation

Chapter 1: Religious Pluralism from a Pentecostal Perspective................. 11
Chapter 2: Current State of Pentecostal Theology of Religions................. 43
Chapter 3: Interreligious Dialogue through a Pentecostal Lens.................79

Part Two: Framing the Structure

Chapter 4: The Paradigmatic Story of Pentecostal Testimony 129
Chapter 5: Testimony as a Resource for Interreligious Dialogue...............163

Part Three: Passing Inspection

Chapter 6: Representative Objections to Pentecostal Involvement......... 203
Chapter 7: Future Pentecostal Engagement with
                Non-Christian Religions... 239
Conclusion..281
Afterword by Cheryl Johns...295
Appendix..297
Bibliography.. 312
Scripture Index...349
General Index...351

Abbreviations

Journals and Periodicals

ABS	*American Behavioral Scientist*
AJ	*Asbury Journal*
AJPS	*Asian Journal of Pentecostal Studies*
AJS	*American Journal of Sociology*
ATJ	*Asbury Theological Journal*
CD	*Current Dialogue*
Charisma	*Charisma & Christian Life*
CHB	*Christian History & Biography*
COGE	*Church of God Evangel*
CPCR	*Cyberjournal of Pentecostal-Charismatic Research*
CT	*Christianity Today*
EJ	*Enrichment Journal*
Ekklesia	*Ekklesia: A New Way of Thinking*
EPTAB	*European Pentecostal Theological Association Bulletin*
EQ	*Evangelical Quarterly*
ERT	*Evangelical Review of Theology*
ET	*Expository Times*
IBMR	*International Bulletin of Missionary Research*
IRM	*International Review of Mission*
JAAR	*Journal of American Academy of Religion*
JEPTA	*Journal of European Pentecostal Theological Association*
JES	*Journal of Ecumenical Studies*
JETS	*Journal of Evangelical Theological Society*
JPT	*Journal of Pentecostal Theology*
JSSR	*Journal for the Scientific Study of Religion*
JSup	*Journal of Pentecostal Theology Supplement Series*
PE	*Pentecostal Evangel*
Pneuma	*Pneuma: The Journal for the Society for Pentecostal Studies*
PR	*Pneuma Review: The Journal of Ministry Resources and Theology for Pentecostal and Charismatic Ministries and Leaders*
PT	*Political Theory*
Refleks	*Refleks: med karismatisk kristendom i fokus*
RFIA	*Review of Faith & International Affairs*

SC   Social Compass
SJT   Scottish Journal of Theology
TCS   Theory, Culture & Society
TF   Thinking Faith: The Online Journal of the British Jesuits
TJ   Trinity Journal
WTJ   Wesleyan Theological Journal
WUNT   Wissenschaftliche Untersuchungen zum Neuen Testament
USCH   U. S. Catholic Historian

Commentaries, Collections, Handbooks, Dictionaries, Etc.

ACCS   *Ancient Christian Commentary on Scripture,* T.C. Oden, gen. ed (Downer's Grove: InterVarsity, 2002).
ANF   *Ante-Nicene Fathers* (Peabody, MA: Hendrickson, 1999 ed.).
BDT   *Baker's Dictionary of Theology,* eds. E.F. Harrison, G.W. Bromiley, and C.F.H. Henry (Grand Rapids: Baker, 1960, 1987).
BTDB   *Baker's Theological Dictionary of the Bible,* ed. Walter A. El well (Grand Rapids: Baker, 1996).
CWJW   *The Complete Works of John Wesley* (The Wesleyan Heritage Collection; Ages Software, Inc. Rio, WI: 2002)
EDT   *Evangelical Dictionary of Theology,* ed. W. Elwell (Grand Rapids: Baker, 2001)
EHHC   *Eerdmans' Handbook to the History of Christianity,* ed. Tim Dowley (Grand Rapids: Eerdmans, 1988)
FLBCNT   *Full Life Bible Commentary to the New Testament,* eds., F.L. Arrington, R. Stronstadt (Grand Rapids: Zondervan, 1999)
GDT   *Global Dictionary of Theology,* eds. W.A. Dryness, V.M. Kärkkäinen (Downer's Grove, IL: InterVarsity 2008)
NHCT   *New Handbook of Christian Theology,* eds. D.W. Musser & J.L. Price (Nashville: Abingdon, 1992).
NIBC   *New International Biblical Commentary,* OT editors, R.L. Hubbard, Jr., and R.K. Johnston/NT editor, W.W. Gasque (Peabody, MA: Hendrickson).
NIBD   *Nelson's Illustrated Bible Dictionary* (Nashville: Thomas Nelson, 1986).
NICNT   *New International Commentary on the New Testament,* gen. ed. F.F. Bruce (Grand Rapids, MI: Eerdmans).
NIDPCM   *New International Dictionary of Pentecostal Charismatic Movements* (Grand Rapids: Zondervan, 2002).
NPNF   *Nicene/Post-Nicene Fathers* 1 (Peabody, MA: Hendrickson, 1999 ed.).
NT   New Testament

NWDCS	*New Westminster Dictionary of Christian Spirituality,* ed. Philip Sheldrake (Louisville, KY: Westminster John Knox Press, 2005).
OT	*Old Testament*
Strong's	*Biblesoft's New Exhaustive Strong's Numbers and Concordance with Expanded Greek-Hebrew Dictionary* (Copyright © 1994, 2003 Biblesoft, Inc., International Bible Translators, Inc.).
TDNT	*Theological Dictionary of the New Testament,* G. Kittle and G. Friedrich, eds., *Theological Dictionary of the New Testament,* trans. and abridged by G.W. Bromiley (Grand Rapids: Eerdmans, 1985, 1990).
TWOT	*Theological Wordbook of the Old Testament* (Copyright (c) 1980 by The Moody Bible Institute of Chicago)
WBC	*Wycliffe Bible Commentary* (Electronic Database. Copyright © 1962 by Moody Press).
WNONT	*Wesley's Notes on the New Testament,* John Wesley (Rio, WI: Ages Software, Inc., 2002).
WNOT	*Wesley's Notes on the Old Testament,* John Wesley (Rio, WI: Ages Software, Inc., 2002).

Organizations

NAE	National Association of Evangelicals (USA)
NCC	National Council of Churches (USA)
PFNA	Pentecostal Fellowship of North America
PCCNA	Pentecostal Charismatic Churches of North America
WCC	World Council of Churches (Geneva, Switzerland)

Foreword

When I first ventured as a pentecostal into this arena of theology of religions and interreligious dialogue with my dissertation over ten years ago, it was a relatively lonely endeavor. To be sure, many of my pentecostal colleagues urged me on (although quite a few did so only in private conversations) and this itself was encouraging simply because it reflected that others were aware of the challenges at hand, even if none were willing to jump into the fray. I thus felt blessed when a few years after the publication of my dissertation, Tony Richie introduced himself to me at a Society for Pentecostal Studies annual meeting as someone who had resonated with what I was trying to do as a pentecostal theologian. I immediately recognized this Church of God pastor and aspiring scholar as a fellow pentecostal sojourner and confidant. Here was someone who could grapple with the most difficult theological issues in these areas, but yet translate them – as if he had the gift of interpretation of (strange academic) tongues, even! – to lay pentecostal audiences. As I came to see, in Tony Richie's ministry, an inclusivistic and pneumatological theology of religions actually "preached" to the churches!

Over the next few years, Tony read and critically interacted with my published work and we exchanged ideas and discussed his own writings, many of which have been published as essays and articles in a variety of scholarly and ecclesiastical venues – including one co-authored book chapter as well. At least in part as a result of our collaboration, Tony has continued to heed to call of the Spirit to develop his own constructive theology of interreligious encounter, which is the book you hold in your hands. I am very pleased with this thorough, expansive, creative, and carefully considered work. With *Speaking by the Spirit*, Tony has taken pentecostal theology of religions and theology of interfaith encounter and dialogue to a wholly new level, sublating all that has gone before him (including my own work, I am ecstatic to report) in articulating – testifying about, to be precise – a powerful theology of witness in a pluralistic world. Beginning with our joint work over the years as representatives of the Society of Pentecostal Studies to the National Council of Churches of Christ Interfaith

Commission and now culminating with the completion of this volume, I feel a sense of having passed the theology of religions mantle on to this capable fellow pentecostal brother and theologian. As this volume shows, the topic is in capable hands. May the Spirit of God accomplish that which this book bears witness to, even in ways that exceed its human author's expectations and prayers.

—Amos Yong
　J. Rodman Williams Professor of Theology
　Regent University School of Divinity

Acknowledgements

Although acknowledging the aid of others in such an endeavor this study is part of academic protocol, and is appropriate enough, and indeed would be not only impolite but incredibly egocentric to either shy away from doing so or to suppose it not authentically applicable, in the present case it seems especially apropos. I am assured that this endeavor would not have come to effective fruition without the positive and profound influence of several others besides me. First, and most, often I had a sense of divine guidance and assistance, and although I cannot and would not testify to infallibly following these, I know that the glory for this endeavor and whatever fruitfulness it may enjoy is due to the God of the spirits of all human beings, and to his Son and Spirit working away all the while. However, I am also fully conscious that it has its faults and failings and that these are due to my own faults and failings.

Second only to God, I am ever grateful to the most supportive partner in marriage and in ministry that my most ardent prayers could ever hope would be mine to affectionately enjoy. I am convinced that not only this project but many another endeavor would either not have been possible or at least would not have been productive without Sue's undoubted love and undaunted loyalty. Further, my children (Josh, Kimberly, Kathy, Shannon) and grandchildren (Elizabeth, Abigail, Robby, Jerrod), have not always (or maybe ever) understood what all the fuss was about, but they too have been unflinchingly faithful in their encouragement nevertheless. The same may be said for my precious spiritual family, New Harvest Church of God in Knoxville, TN, dearly beloved brothers and sisters who have been more of a blessing to their pastor than they will ever begin to comprehend. I must also acknowledge my parents, Reverend Andrew and Carolyn Richie, who passed on to me their rich heritage of "full gospel" faith. Many other dear friends (like Raymond Hodge, e.g.) have offered more encouragement than they probably know but would be too numerous too mention.

Certainly, the expertise and encouragement of Larry Wood (Asbury Theological Seminary), Graham MacFarlane and Max Turner (both of London School of Theology), and Mark Cartledge (Birmingham University) have been essential to this endeavor—particularly in its earlier development as a PhD dissertation. Of course, I am sincerely grateful for Bill Faupel's (Wesley Theological Seminary) insightful editorial work in bringing this manuscript into its present published form. In my own thought as a theologian, I am deeply indebted to those pioneers in Pentecostal theology of religions that have boldly gone before me, especially Amos Yong (Regent University) and Veli-Matti Kärkkäinen (Fuller Seminary). Many of my teachers at Pentecostal Theological Seminary, including Hollis Gause, French Arrington, Steve Land, Rickie Moore, Jackie and Cheryl Johns, Chris Thomas, David Beatty, David Franklin, and others, have made their mark on my faith and life in a way that is frequently refracted throughout the pages of this book. Finally, the commitment to scholarship of the Society for Pentecostal Studies that included engaging the Interfaith Relations

Commission of the National Council of Churches of Christ (USA) provided much-needed impetus and inspiration and eventually led to working internationally with the World Council of Churches on interfaith issues.

Hallelujah! Thank you all!

Introduction

The present study focuses on developing a Classical Pentecostal theology of religions that utilizes their tradition of testimony as a pneumatological paradigm for interreligious encounter and dialogue. In a word, it suggests that for Pentecostals their historic practice of personal testimony as a public form of Spirit-inspired speech may serve both as a justification for and as a foundation of a specifically Pentecostal approach to developing interfaith conversations, that is, for formal and informal discussions with adherents of non-Christian religions, in certain contemporary contexts.

Orientation of the Present Research

In the Conclusion of this volume I share a brief testimony of how I became personally involved in Pentecostal theology of religions and interfaith dialogue on a doctoral level eventually leading to the present volume. What it does not tell is my personal faith journey regarding Christianity and the religions. It seems appropriate to share that story here. Perhaps readers will gain some helpful insight into me and my work as it follows in this volume. A "P. K. [preacher's kid]," I was raised in a Pentecostal home.[1] In fact, I am a third generation Pentecostal. My paternal and maternal grandparents were among the early mountain folk baptized in the Holy Spirit in southern Appalachia. Yet as a young adult I fought mightily with agnosticism and later flirted with religious pluralism. But the roots of the seeds of faith planted in my spirit by my parents during childhood ran far deeper than I had ever suspected. I was perennially dissatisfied. I was always seeking, never finding.

Finally, I experienced a rather difficult but dramatic conversion bringing me to full faith in Jesus Christ as my Lord and Savior. At last! I had found "the peace of God which surpasses all comprehension" (Pp. 4:7 NASV). After a protracted period of seeking, I also experienced an especially important sanctifying moment, including a closer walk with Christ in the fruit of the Spirit, and an empowering infilling of the Holy Spirit, accompanied by the practice of speaking in tongues and other spiritual gifts. In the ensuing years, which included affiliating with the Church of God (Cleveland, TN), responding to the call to ordained ministry and the pastorate as well as the process of education, specifically theological training, I have continued to sense that the issue of how Christians relate to the religions, always important, has steadily become paramount. More specifically, I have had a sense of divine direction leading me deeply into the area of Pentecostal theology of religions. The present work is part of a journey of faith attempting to respond obediently to what I sense as God's calling for me at this time.

However, as Amos Yong also shares in his Foreword to *Speaking by the Spirit,* pursuing Pentecostal theology of religions can be a lonely endeavor. It can be a daunting task too. In fact, not only interreligious issues but even ecumenism, in the sense of intra-Christian relations, has sometimes been a special challenge for Pentecostal believers. Yet Vinson Synan suggests Pentecostal ecumenism began in the postwar period. Pentecostals had been disfellowshiped by organized fundamentalism in 1928, but relations improved after World War II with evangelicals who were more moderate.[2] By 1942, the National Association of Evangelicals (NAE) admitted Pentecostals. Pentecostals in the United States later organized their own ecumenical groups, such as the Pentecostal Fellowship of North America (PFNA), now the Pentecostal Charismatic Churches of North America (PCCNA). These groups also cooperated with the Pentecostal World Conference, first convened in Zurich, Switzerland in 1947. A South African Pentecostal minister who immigrated to the United States, David du Plessis, became the most important ecumenical voice in Pentecost after the outbreak of the neo-Pentecostal or Charismatic Renewal movement.[3] According to Synan, by 1980 Classical Pentecostals "had grown to be the spearhead of the largest and fastest growing family of Christians in the world."[4] However, Synan also stresses that, "there is only one outpouring of the Spirit in the latter days," although its "streams" flow through different "channels" such as Classical Pentecostalism, "neo-Pentecostalism", or "Catholic charismatic renewal."[5]

Walter Hollenweger, however, argues for a view of Pentecostalism as an early ecumenical movement that failed in its original vision.[6] He suggests, "The purpose of the Pentecostal movement was to reconcile the different Christian denominations."[7] Dogmatic barriers were to be overcome in an experience of the living Spirit of God. When the immediately expected eschaton did not occur, dogmatic and ethical differences, along with an emerging necessity for ecclesiastical polity, brought fragmentation instead of unification. Hollenweger insists Pentecostals have so far refused to face "this unfaithfulness to the original vision of an ecumenical revival movement which would take in all churches."[8]

Perhaps Pentecostalism may be viewed as a movement that may have missed its early unlimited ecumenical mission but settled later for a limited ecumenical ministry. In any case, its admittedly ecumenical impulse has a checkered history, one which Pentecostals themselves may not fully comprehend. Remaining to be seen is the future ecumenical course of the movement. However, Warrington optimistically notes that it has had greater dialogical readiness and cooperative ecumenical willingness in recent years.[9]

In any case, for me the ecumenical impulse latent but dormant within Pentecostal spirituality and theology arguably extends, with careful qualifications of course, to interreligious relations as well—that is to say, to interreligious encounter, dialogue, and cooperation. Thus, I find myself a pretty much traditional Classical Pentecostal exploring Pentecostal theology of religions. This dialectical dimension between continuing identification with traditional Pentecostalism and ongoing exploration of the newly developing field of Pentecostal theology of religions adds an essential dynamic to my work. Wherever this journey may, in God's providence, lead, I admit I am finding the trip fascinating!

Argumentation of the Present Research

To begin with, this study examines the contemporary setting of cultural diversity and religious plurality that is fast becoming typically descriptive of a world increasingly characterized by globalization with focus on issues involving Pentecostals, especially with its strong heritage of evangelism and missions, generally conservative ethical and theological history, and undeniable multicultural variety. Its context is the US but its conversation is global. My research explores the supreme importance of intentional (vs. confrontational) interreligious encounter and dialogical partnership (vs. scapegoating tendencies) among the religions. Further, it explores the historic and current status and insights of Classical Pentecostal theology of religions as foundational for the task of interreligious encounter and dialogue. Some key figures and developments are highlighted. Themes of continuity and creativity, that is, faithfulness to the Pentecostal past and relevance for the Pentecostal present and future are examined. I consider the Pentecostal sectarian past as an "icon" through which it may link into its original identity, but not as an "idol" by which it is eternally bound. What emerges out of this research is that a fairly inclusive theology of religions flows rather naturally out of the Wesleyan-Arminian roots of the Holiness heritage into Pentecostalism.

Methodologically this study draws on biblical, theological, and practical resources of a Pentecostal and pneumatological theology of religions (always Christological and ecclesiological) to provide a praxis approach for actual interreligious encounter and dialogue. Hence the subtitle stresses a theology "*for* interreligious dialogue." Also, the title "Speaking *by* the Spirit" further suggests, in addition to the usual or traditional themes of *confession* and *proclamation* (basic values of confessional and evangelical Christianity), the Holy Spirit's voice may also be authentically heard in a process or experience of interreligious dialogue and encounter through the Pentecostal tradition of *testimony*. Thus the resources of an already established belief and practice within Pentecostalism are mined for developing a model of interreligious encounter and dialogue with familiarity and specificity.

Testimony, especially "Pentecostal" testimony, differs from creedal or dogmatic confession, on the one hand, and from evangelistic proclamation on the other hand. Pentecostal testimony is primarily a grateful public sharing of God's gracious work in one's own life to the glory of God. Testimony is a telling of the story of God's words and acts in one's own life. But Pentecostal testimony is not necessarily primarily evangelistic or conversionary, or even didactic or instructive, strictly speaking, so much as it is an invitation for others to join in joyfully expressing thanksgiving for another's divine blessings—though sometimes it may have such consequences dependent upon listeners' free participatory response of faith. In other words, I ask whether Pentecostal testimony may provide some important assistance in today's challenge of interreligious dialogue—at least for Pentecostals themselves. If Pentecostal testimony is also considered Holy Spirit inspired and empowered speech, in some ways parallel to but distinct from glossolalia or prophecy, theological and practical ramifications may be even more noteworthy. The Spirit's participation in the testimonial/dialogical process is of crucial significance. Possibly testimony provides Pentecostals with a category to engage religious others in respectful yet unreserved speech.

Further, one of the great benefits of Pentecostal testimonial services is that everyone listens to everyone else "giving" their testimony (as traditional nomenclature has it). Therefore, although perhaps not always immediately evident, a kind of conversational-dialogical process does indeed occur. And this conversation, because it is not primarily creedal or evangelistic but doxological, helps avoid the pitfalls and problems common to complex interfaith encounters. Arguably, a testimony model can give dialogue participants clear guidelines about why they are involved and what is expected of them.

Finally, this research addresses possible scriptural, theological, and practical objections to its thesis and outlines demographic and political contexts for its application. Emphasis is on demonstrating feasibility and plausibility rather than erasing all ambiguity or achieving irrefutability. However, the burden of proof is thus shifted to challengers—especially any who may simplistically assume that Pentecostalism and interreligious dialogue and encounter are inherently incompatible.

Overview of the Present Research

The basic thesis explored and developed in this study is that Pentecostal pneumatology not only provides space appropriate for interreligious encounter and dialogue but also actually inspires and empowers it, and that testimony specifically provides paradigmatic structure and substance to the same. The title, *Speaking by the Spirit: A Pentecostal Model for Interreligious Encounter and Dialogue*, informs regarding its general approach. It signals an intentional effort to maintain fidelity to historic Classical Pentecostalism while using it as a fount out of which to draw deliberate resources for what will be presented as a pressing contemporary need regarding interreligious encounter and dialogue. The distinctive Pentecostal tradition of testimony will be explored as a possible paradigm for engaging religious others in encounter and dialogue in a manner that is true to Pentecostal Christian faith and values. Essentially this process will entail developing a pneumatological theology of interreligious dialogue. In other words, the role of the Holy Spirit in and through testimony applied to conversation with religious others will be central to this project.[10]

While Pentecostals have already done some first rate work on theology of religions, including pneumatological approaches,[11] in depth exploration of and application to the dialogical task has not occurred. I know of none that explores or develops the Pentecostal tradition of testimony for that purpose.[12] The present proposal would therefore encourage original discussion and action. I am personally involved in formal interreligious encounter and dialogue at some fairly sophisticated levels.[13] Therefore, I wish to help myself and others, hopefully, both academically and practically, through this intensive study. An overarching assumption of this work is that contemporary Pentecostal theology of religions (as well as other theological themes) calls for approbation and integration of values of *continuity* and *creativity*.[14] Hereby faithfulness to the movement's conception joins forces with a vision for its maturation.[15] In other words, this study will make an effort to build faithfully on the original ethos of the Classical Pentecostal movement even while attempting to develop effectively a contemporary approach to interreligious encounter and dialogue appropriate for the times. Therefore, not only the aim but also the approach of the present work is critical and original.[16]

One may observe a certain serial or sequential development in the unfolding of the chapters of this study. I attempt to capture the progressive interrelatedness of this project through a three-part descriptive arrangement based on the idea of a carpenter erecting a building.[17] Part One, "Drawing up a Blueprint and Laying a Foundation," announces preparatory work. As in carpentry, this is in large part planning but also in an important way a beginning of the work. First, the chapter after this Introduction, Chapter 1, will assess the contemporary setting of cultural diversity and religious plurality that is fast becoming typically descriptive of a world increasingly characterized by globalization with focus on issues involving Pentecostals. Second, Chapter 2 will explore the historic and current status and insights of classical Pentecostal theology of religions as foundational for the task of interreligious encounter and dialogue. Some key figures and developments will be highlighted. Chapter 3 provides an in depth study of the nature of interreligious encounter and dialogue itself in preparation for applying testimony as a paradigm to its praxis.

Part Two, is "Doing Framing and Finishing Work," and announces the constructive part of the project. As in carpentry, this involves getting up the basic supportive structure and making the inside as attractive and presentable as possible. Chapter 4 does an in depth study of the nature of Pentecostal testimony in preparation for its application to interreligious encounter and dialogue processes. Then, Chapter 5 finally brings together the theological and practical insights gleaned from the preceding chapters to present a proposal for how testimony can serve paradigmatically for Pentecostal engagement of religious others and involvement in interreligious dialogue. Part Three, "Passing Inspection and Making Code," signals follow up work. As in carpentry, a certain standard of excellence is necessary for an inhabitable edifice. Builders depend on others for final approval of their work. This section attempts some self-evaluation in anticipation of final evaluation by readers. Chapter 6 attempts to anticipate and answer possible objections to the proposal of the previous chapter utilizing Pentecostal testimony as a paradigm for interreligious encounter and dialogue. Chapter 7 envisions possible future directions Pentecostal theology of religions, in the context of interreligious encounter and dialogue in a religiously pluralistic society. Finally, the Conclusion summarizes and presents some specific conclusions derivative from this overall study. That is, it attempts to first draw together the main lines of the study and, second, to point the way forward. (Of course, the Introduction and Conclusion transcend the 3-part structure and have overall application.) Thus, I sincerely hope to achieve a substantive contribution that is genuinely open to ensuing conversation.

Conclusion/Summary

Ultimately, the present work draws on biblical, theological, and practical resources of a Pentecostal and pneumatological theology of religions (always faithfully christological and ecclesiological) to provide a praxis-oriented approach for actual interreligious encounter and dialogue. The desire is for the Holy Spirit's voice to be heard authentically in a process or experience of interreligious dialogue and encounter through the Pentecostal tradition of testimony for the glory of God. In order for that to happen, dialogue participants must "speak by the Spirit." My own testimony involves experience that may serve as an example of journey into interreligious encounter and dialogue. Whatever may be learned through the added analytical information (hopefully) acquired in this study should serve to give attention to what kind(s) of model(s) or paradigm(s) may be discerned and practically applied for Pentecostals (and others?) resulting from progress (if any) on utilizing testimony in interfaith dialogue. I propose that exploring and exploiting Pentecostal testimony as a basis of and model for engagement in interreligious encounter and conversation does indeed represent an original and critical contribution to the theory and praxis of interfaith dialogue today.

Notes

1. For more on Pentecostalism, see the Appendix to this volume, "Introducing (but Not Necessarily Explaining) Pentecostalism."

2. H. V. Synan, "Classical Pentecostalism," *NIDPCM* (Grand Rapids: Zondervan, 2002), 553-55 (554-55).

3. For more on this astounding Pentecostal ecumenist, see R. Howard, "David du Plessis: Pentecost's Ambassador-at-Large," *The Spirit and Spirituality: Essays in Honor of Russell P. Spittler*, ed. W. Ma and R.P. Menzies (New York: T & T Clark, 2004), 271-97.

4. Synan, "Classical," 554-55. Excellent full-length histories of Pentecostalism in the United States and the world include V. Synan, *The Holiness-Pentecostal Movement in the United States* (Grand Rapids: Eerdmans, 1971) and W.J. Hollenweger, *The Pentecostals* (London: SCM, 1972/Peabody: Hendrickson, 1988). More recently, see A. Anderson, *An Introduction to Pentecostalism: Global Charismatic Christianity* (Cambridge: Cambridge University Press, 2004). For an informative overview of the more recent Charismatic Renewal or neo-Pentecostal movement, including helpful comparisons and contrasts with the older Classical Pentecostalism, see R. Quebedeaux, *The New Charismatics II: How a Christian Renewal Movement Became Part of the American Religious Mainstream* (San

Francisco: Harper & Row, 1976, 1983). Cf. also to R.P. Spittler, ed. *Perspectives on the New Pentecostalism* (Grand Rapids: Baker, 1976).

5. Synan, *In the Latter Days: The Outpouring of the Holy Spirit in the Twentieth Century* (Ann Arbor: Servant, 1974), ix.

6. Hollenweger, *Pentecostals,* 505.

7. Hollenweger, *Pentecostals,* 505. K. Warrington, *Pentecostal Theology: A Theology of Encounter* (New York: T & T Clark, 2008), adds that divisiveness among themselves has not helped Pentecostals foster ecumenical relations with other Christians, 170. Interestingly, an important early Pentecostal, Frank Bartleman, taught that implications of Pentecostal Spirit baptism include "growth in spiritual power, simplicity, and unity." See A. Cerillo, Jr., "Frank Bartleman: Pentecostal 'Lone Ranger' and Social Critic," Goff and Wacker's *Portraits,* 105-22 (116).

8. Hollenweger, *Pentecostals,* 506. Worth remembering is that Hollenweger made this charge in 1972 (though reprinted in 1988).

9. Warrington, *Encounter,* 170-71. Although still wary, some Pentecostals are exhibiting increasing openness to dialogue and cooperation with the WCC (172-75) and Roman Catholicism (175-78). For Warrington, though there are many obstacles, the way forward for Pentecostal ecumenical engagement seems plausible (178-79).

10. Much may be said for doing theology of religions and interreligious dialogue in close conversation with religious others. See *Hermeneutical Explorations in Dialogue: Essays in Honor of Hans Ucko,* eds. A. Rambachan, A. R Omar, and M.T Thangaraj (Dehli: ISPCK, 2007). This focus on unique Pentecostal contributions is by no means a fracas with such visions, but an effort to enter that conversation with a clear conception of self identity.

11. E.g., standing out is the work of A. Yong: e.g., "Whither Theological Inclusivism? The Development and Critique of an Evangelical Theology of Religions," *EQ* 71:4 (October 1999), 327-48, *Discerning of the Spirit(s): A Pentecostal-Charismatic Contribution to the Christian Theology of Religions* JSup 20 (Sheffield: Sheffield Academic, 2000), *Beyond the Impasse: Toward a Pneumatological Theology of Religions* (Grand Rapids: Baker, 2003), *Hospitality and the Other: Pentecost, Christian Practices, and the Neighbor* (Maryknoll: Orbis, 2008). Also see V.M. Kärkkäinen's considerable output: e.g., "Toward a Pneumatological Theology of Religions: A Pentecostal-Charismatic Inquiry," *IRM* 91: 361 (2002), 187-98, *An Introduction to Theology of Religions: Biblical, Historical, & Contemporary Perspectives* (Downer's Grove: InterVarsity Press, 2003), *Trinity and Religious Pluralism: The Doctrine of the Trinity in Christian Theology of Religions* (Burlington: Ashgate, 2004), "How to Speak of the Spirit among Religions: Trinitarian 'Rules' for a Pneumatological Theology of Religions," *IBMR* 30:3 (2006): 121-27.

12. Obviously, so-called testimonials are sometimes included as part of the dialogue process by various traditions. E.g., see "Testimonies from a Multifaith Hearing on Conversion, Lariano (Italy), May 12-16, 2006" in *CD* 50 (February 2008), 20-37. However, a close look suggests both that these traditions often understand testimony in quite diverse ways, not only from Pentecostals but from each other, and that even so testimony is not usually actually in any way paradigmatic for dialogue. Nevertheless, see M.L. Tan-Chow, *Pentecostal Theology for the Twenty-First Century* (Burlington, VT: Ashgate, 2007), 162-64.

13. E. g., I am a Society for Pentecostal Studies liaison to the Interfaith Relations Commission of the NCC (USA). I am also a Pentecostal representative to the Inter-Religious Dialogue and Cooperation of the WCC (Geneva, SW) and to the Commission of the Churches on International Affairs, on the interreligious dialogue task group, also of

the WCC. I have participated in national and international dialogue ecumenically with Protestants and Roman Catholics and interreligiously with representatives from Judaism, Islam, Hinduism, Buddhism, Sikhism, and African indigenous religions such as Yoruba. Furthermore, I have engaged in conversation with Native Americans and African Americans regarding their unique religious heritage and relationship with Christianity.

14. This idea has been variously phrased. P. Tillich speaks of progress as a maturing of existing potentiality coupled with a new moment of fresh opportunity, a *kairos* time Cf. 'The Decline and Validity of the Idea of Progress' in *The Future of Religions* (New York:: Harper & Row, 1966), 64-79 (75-79). H. Küng, in *Theology for the Third Millennium: An Ecumenical View* (New York: Anchor Books, 1990), talks about a '*double movement*' involving '*centripetal*' or 'back to the sources' and '*centrifugal*' or 'out to open sea' orientations or '*a theology from the perspective of Christian origins and the Christian center, against the horizon of today's world*' (105-106; original italics).

15. An intriguing use of a developmental metaphor for the maturation of the Pentecostal movement may be seen in C.B. Johns, "The Adolescence of Pentecostalism," *Pneuma* 17 (Spring 1995), 3-18.

16. As will be seen, typically those who emphasize the history of Pentecostalism assume it results by default in an exclusivist posture regarding interreligious understanding while those who emphasize contemporary contexts inclining toward more inclusivist postures assume that is something of a departure from Pentecostalism's historic identity. One of the underlying aspects of this study is its critique of such common assumptions to argue for both continuity and creativity in interreligious encounter and dialogue.

17. Inspiration for this analogous arrangement arises from my father, Rev. Andrew Richie, who for many years served as a bi-vocational minister, a full-time preacher and part-time carpenter. Consequently, in our youth my younger brother Tim and I spent many a strenuous hour as "carpenter's helpers." For the present purposes, I intend it to help map out the developing argument and its various components.

PART ONE: LAYING A FOUNDATION

Chapter 1

Religious Pluralism from a Pentecostal Perspective

Introduction

The present chapter will assess the contemporary context of religious pluralism in terms of both problem and opportunity. Focus is on religious pluralism in the sense of the reality of the different faiths and their adherents co-existing in close proximity in contemporary society. Surveying the fact of religious pluralism today inevitably involves critical interaction with pluralist philosophy as an ideology more or less affirming and embracing multireligious culture. First, this chapter will look at the crisis coming out of globalization: the unprecedented bringing together of people of different faiths into close and at times uncomfortable or crisis related contact. Then, it will look at a variety of suggestions for ways of addressing this crisis effectively. It utilizes a wide array of resources, but includes Pentecostal critiques, especially in a final section. The next chapter will focus more on specifically Pentecostal approaches to theology of religions.

The Problem Examined[1]

Terminological and Ideological Definitions

Terminological. The term "pluralism" is often used in three senses, as Ninian Smart explains.[2] First, it expresses that an actual plurality of religions and other beliefs and practices exists in the world. Second, it identifies a pluralistic political system allowing the free exercise of diverse religious and political practices and beliefs. Third, and most significant for this study, pluralism often references a theory of religions and worldviews affirming that all religions ultimately point to the same reality or verity.[3] Smart further subdivides pluralism into categories of "realistic" and "regulative" pluralism.[4] Realistic pluralism supposes that, "all religions are so many different paths to, or versions of, the one Truth." Regulative pluralism understands the religions as having different beliefs and values but insists that they are historically evolving "toward a common truth."⁵ Popular alternatives to pluralism are some form of exclusivism, which insists that only a particular religion experiences revelation or possesses truth, all others being certainly false or suspiciously demonic, or inclusivism, which sees truth in other faiths but asserts the priority of a specific faith.⁶ Leading exclusivists have included Karl Barth and Hendrick Kraemer, leading pluralists John Hick and Wilfred Cantrell Smith, and, historically, a leading inclusivist was Nicholas of Cusa.⁷ More recently, John Wesley and C. S. Lewis were perhaps two of the best-known inclusivists.⁸ Smart opines that inclusivism probably will remain the most attractive option for a majority of various traditions, though he thinks especially so for more liberal-minded Christians.⁹

Other, that is, non-Christian, religions may also be pluralist. For example, the Dalai Lama, of Tibetan Buddhism, says, "I believe that all the major world religions have the potential to serve humanity and to develop good human beings." He adds, "I always say it is better to follow one's traditional religion, because by changing religion you may eventually find emotional or intellectual difficulties." Furthermore, "We must therefore appreciate that potential which is in each religion, and respect those who follow them." He is sure that "Since there are different types of people in the world, we need different types of religion."¹⁰ Other religions may also be inclusive. For example, Islam has at times advanced an inclusivist view based on its recognition of Jews and Christians as "People of the Book".¹¹ The Koran quotes Allah saying, "If the People of the Book accept the true faith and keep from evil, We will pardon them their sins and admit them to the gardens of delight" (Surah 5:65). The Koran also says, "Some there are among the People of the Book who truly believe in God, and in what has been revealed to you and was revealed to them" (Surah 3:198; cf. 3:110, 5:55-82).¹² This inclusivist tradition has inspired contemporary Muslim scholars such as A. Rashied Omar and Mohammad Al-Sammak actively to promote interreligious dialogue and cooperation.¹³ For centuries, Roman Catholicism may have been the most exclusive religious organization on earth. However, many contemporary Catholics, especially since the Vatican II Council, have become quite inclusive.¹⁴

Ideological. John Hick is an important and influential British philosopher of religion who has, among other things, contributed significantly to developing the ideology of religious pluralism. He is in fact the most influential if most controversial proponent of radical religious pluralism today.¹⁵ Once a conservative evangelical Christian, he shifted dramatically to liberal and pluralistic views due to his observations of cultural diversity and studies of religious epistemology.¹⁶ Hick maintains an active website promoting his books and teachings.¹⁷ Though a complex thinker and prolific writer, Hick has helpfully summed up briefly his major ideas on religious pluralism in an energetic dialogue with conservative critics called *Four Views of Salvation in a Pluralistic World*.¹⁸

Hick first recounts his personal testimony of gradual conversion from conservative ideology to liberalism. He thus eventually arrives at religious pluralism. As he explains it, this transition occurred as he encountered intellectual doubts brought about by formal philosophical training. He nonetheless argues for an intellectual appropriation of the Christian faith. Yet he came to be particularly guided by a critical view of the inspiration and authority of Scripture, including the New Testament confession of Christ. At this point, he began to face the challenge of other religions. Interaction with adherents of other faiths brought him to a, for him at that time, startling awakening. In his own words,

> I soon realized something that is obvious enough once noticed, yet momentous in its implications. This is that although the language, concepts, liturgical actions, and cultural ethos differ widely from one another, yet from a religious point of view basically the same thing is going on in all of them, namely, human beings coming together within the framework of an ancient and highly developed tradition to open their hearts and minds to God.[19]

Hick realizes that there are other legitimate responses to the diversity and similarity which he encountered, that is, broadly speaking, either exclusivism or inclusivism. However, admittedly based on "personal experience and observation" he adopted the pluralistic hypothesis.[20]

Hick, however, does not fail to offer further arguments supporting pluralism.[21] First, he argues for the moral equality of the religions. That is, he felt that he had found, more or less, an equal level of moral sensibility and development in other major world religions, as he knew in his own Christianity.[22] Secondly, Hick argues that "the phenomenon of salvation" be viewed not through strictly Christian lenses, but redefined as a gradual transformation from self-centeredness to a radical new orientation centered in God that is merely differently conceptualized and expressed. Then it becomes obvious, at least to him, "that salvation is taking place within all of the world religions". Accordingly, he thinks it logical "to conclude that not only Christianity, but also these other world faiths, are human responses to the Ultimate."[23] Thirdly, he argues from epistemological premises that pluralism is a philosophical explanation of religious phenomena. In other words, reality, whether environmental or religious, is interpretive experience, and involves relative human factors capable of explaining both differences and similarities.[24] Finally, Hick argues that the preceding means God should be thought of and spoken of as "the Ultimate, the Real, the Transcendent, Ultimate Reality"—though he usually shortens his phraseology to simply "the Real". The Real (or God) is therefore understood in distinct senses as that which exists as It is in and of Itself and as It is experienced by humans. Again, this distinction allows for relativity and variety in the world religions. In sum:

> The hypothesis is that in order to account for the existence of the different religio-cultural totalities that we call, in rough historical order, Hinduism, Judaism, Buddhism, Taoism, Confucianism, African primal religion, Christianity, Islam, Sikhism, as apparently more or less equally effective contexts of salvation/liberation, we have to postulate an ultimate transcendent reality, the source and ground of everything, that is in itself beyond the scope of human conceptuality but is variously experienced, and therefore variously responded to in life, from within these different religious totalities.[25]

Hick adds that worship is not offered to the Real directly, which is incomprehensible as It is in and of Itself, but indirectly to one or the other of the various manifestations in the different faiths. Each religion is therefore allowed to remain more or less unchanged, except that, it opens itself up to dialogue with others and "winnows" out of its own tradition exclusivist claims to superiority.[26]

> However, Hick admits that there are immense implications of the pluralist hypothesis for Christianity.[27] Deeply rooted in Christianity's belief system ultimately arising out its doctrine of the Incarnation with all of its implications is a claim to uniqueness that runs counter to religious pluralism. Contra conservative varieties of Christianity, he questions the Incarnation as being a doctrine Jesus himself did not teach and as being so paradoxical as to be nonsensical.[28] Hick boldly proposes resolving this impasse between religious pluralism and tradition orthodox Christianity by totally reinterpreting the Incarnation to make it fit with his hypothesis. The incarnation of God in Jesus Christ is seen as a metaphor of his openness and obedience to God in God's acting in and through him. Of course, the doctrines of the Trinity, the atonement, and even the practice of prayer must be radically revised to agree with this metaphorical vision of the Incarnation. Hick candidly concludes that, "Unlike the traditional doctrines, all this is compatible with religious pluralism."[29]

Interreligious Competition and Suspicion

Martin Marty, an American Lutheran religious scholar, is a foremost analyst and activist regarding intersections of politics and religion on the national and international levels. In a recent book, *When Faiths Collide*,[30] he argues that, "The collisions of faiths, or the collisions of peoples of faith, are among the most threatening conflicts around the world in the new millennium." Essentially, this dangerous situation exists, Marty thinks, because people of different faiths frequently divide themselves and others into competitive and suspicious groups of "belongers" and strangers. They thus become a menace to each other and to others surrounding them.[31] Demonization of religious others, or "monster making", often follows, leading to conflict and even violence, because of the tragic instinctive tendency to view other faith communities as menaces.[32] Historically, the religions have exhibited exclusivist and hostile proclivities arising out of fear of the unfamiliar other. Consequently, interreligious contact becomes conceptualized in terms of a battle for survival.[33] Moreover, the impulse to convert or to proselytize the other can often become a mercurial component of this competitive scenario.[34] Tragically, this "survival of the fittest" battle between rival belief systems may engulf others far beyond the respective faiths involved.[35]

Religious Fundamentalism and Violence

Today, as Marty notes, globalization has made neighbors of strangers, but many, especially of the fundamentalist type religious persuasion, react with conflict. The all-too-easy availability of advanced weaponry makes antagonism between radical faith communities into a frightening face off with potentially worldwide repercussions.[36] Fundamentalists, those with radical, rigid understandings of religious tradition and sacred texts, react as if in violent self-defense to any perceived compromise of or encroachment on their faith turf.[37] In such settings, enmity and hostility toward those of another faith can seem a necessary expediency. In this light, Marty's discussion of "lethal theology" is chilling. Some actually believe in killing in God's name. A few put it into practice.[38] Accordingly, faiths collide and collide with catastrophic consequences.

The September 11, 2001 terrorist attack by radical fundamentalist Islamic terrorists on the United States exemplifies Marty's assessment of faiths in collision.[39] He refers to this event as the "intrusion of murderous fanaticism" and "the activity of murderous strangers".[40] Unfortunately, it also brought ill-deserved suspicion on the moderate Muslim majority in America and in the world, in the process contributing to the cyclical potential for further collisions of faiths.[41] Pre-and post-September 11 ignorance of Muslims, coupled with misinformation about complex Islamic understandings of concepts such as jihad, further exacerbates the issue and occasionally erupts into violent interactions. Furthermore, psychological fallout, an intensification of fear of the stranger, from September 11 has made taking the risk of hospitality even more difficult while also making it ever more pertinent.[42] However, remembering that, even fundamentalists do not always turn violent and that violent fundamentalism is not confined to Islam or to any other single religion, but shows up, often unexpected and unwelcome, in the history of all major religions, is helpful for placing the problem of terrorism in context.[43]

Discovering America Again

In a stunning study Harvard comparative religions scholar and pluralist advocate, Diana Eck, challenges other Americans to open their eyes to the remarkable religious changes remaking America today.[44] Even the architectural landscape, now dotted with mosques and temples alongside churches and synagogues, has dramatically changed.[45] Eck observes that the people of the United States "now form the most profusely religious nation on earth"; but, this religiosity is no longer the traditional Protestant, Catholic, Jew varieties of faith. Rather, it encompasses and even embraces Hindus, Buddhists, Muslims, and many other religions.[46] She traces this startling development to the 1965 Immigration and Naturalization Act reversing earlier strictures on immigration. In the decades since America has experienced an unprecedented influx of immigrates, many of whom brought their non-Judeo-Christian religions with them.[47] The bare fact of so many people of such different faiths in close proximity can lead to difficulty—even to interfaith violence. [48]

Moving from Fear to Violence

Eck approaches the problem of interfaith conflict and violence from a somewhat different perspective than Marty. She relates numerous incidents of outbreaks of interfaith violence. Though she speaks of "the fear of the foreign" and "the desecration of the different", she insists we are actually "afraid of ourselves". America is changing and some Americans simply do not like it. They are afraid of what "we" are becoming, of what is happening to "our" country.[49] In a scary "prophecy," prior to September 11, 2001, she predicted, "the religious controversies of America are just beginning."[50] Eck observes people reacting (or over-reacting) when the increasing religious plurality of America make a visible difference. This reflex reaction occurs, for example, when different religious groups appear as people of different races, with different customs, dress, and so on. Then there is the long history in America of stereotypes and prejudice regarding other religions further fueling distrust and suspicion.[51] Sometimes heated efforts occur to keep groups out of certain neighborhoods in which they planned to build prominent religious facilities. Vandalism against sacred property and hate crimes against worshipers are becoming more common. Tensions over religious appearance and practice in the work place occur often. Even the courts have become centers of technical disputation over acceptable legal limits of expressing religious diversity and plurality.[52]

The Rise of Religious Violence

Mark Juergensmeyer, Professor of Sociology and Director of Global and International Studies at the University of California in Santa Barbara, has studied the startling and seemingly counterintuitive relationship between terrorism and religion in depth. Of the terrorist attacks on the United States September 11, 2001, he asks, "How could religion be related to such vicious acts?"[53] Before answering, he notes that it is a question not limited to 9/11.

> It is a question that has arisen with alarming frequency in the post-Cold War world. Religion seems connected with violence everywhere. Since this book was first published, religious violence has erupted among right-wing Christians in the United States, angry Muslims and Jews in the Middle East, quarrelling Hindus and Muslims in South Asia, and indigenous religious communities in Africa and Indonesia. Like the activists associated with Osama bin Laden, the individuals involved in these cases have also relied on religion to provide political identities and give license to vengeful ideologies.[54]

Juergensmeyer concludes that "this dark alliance" between religion and violence is not simply due to political strategy. Rather, "these acts are forms of public performance".[55] In other words, they are "symbolic statements aimed at providing a sense of empowerment to desperate communities."[56] Religion plays a crucial role by providing moral justification for killing and by providing a scenario of cosmic war. Significantly, he states that, "Violent ideas and images are not the monopoly of any single religion."[57] Christian, Jewish, Muslim, Hindu, Sikh, and Buddhist have all at times provided resources for violence.[58] Moreover, religious violence is rising dramatically. Juergensmeyer suspects that an intense reaction to and resistance to modern globalization is behind the rise. He is careful to offer the caveat that globalization does not necessarily cause religious violence, but to clarify those inappropriate responses to it may be part of the problem nonetheless.[59] Significantly, terrorism is most often a corporate act.[60] Apparently, many of those who resort to using religious violence are attempting to defend and promote a narrow worldview that is perceived as being threatened with alteration or even extinction through the ever-widening reach of contemporary globalization of cultures.[61]

There are of course important differences between the approaches of Juergensmeyer, Marty, and Eck. For example, contrary to Marty, Juergensmeyer rejects the notion that fundamentalism is at fault in religious violence. He finds explanations in "current forces in geopolitics and in a strain of violence that may be found at the deepest levels of religious imagination."[62] It matters much whether one considers religious violence to be a distortion of or intrinsic to true religion. Yet for all of that, practically speaking, Juergensmeyer's analysis welds well with the ideas of Marty and Eck. Essentially, the increasing complexity of contemporary culture, including the disturbingly prevalent experience of religious diversity and pluralism, sometimes results in intense paranoia. In extreme cases, violence between the faiths or their adherents is the outcome. Considering current trends in global cultures indicating the unlikelihood that globalization may be realistically overcome, that is successfully reversed or at least resisted in making further inroads, a frightening vision of ever-intensifying conflict between the faiths is not an unreasonable supposition. Obviously, rising religious pluralism is an inescapable component of this complex crisis.

High Stakes at the Interreligious Dialogue Table

Controversial but perennially popular Catholic ecumenical theologian from Tübingen University in Würtemberg Hans Küng lays before the religious world a frightening view of what is at state in interreligious relations in a contemporary pluralistic world. In a chapter titled "No World Peace without Religious Peace",[63] he explains why interreligious dialogue must go on. First, because increasingly closely linked lives requires us all to become better acquainted. In addition, it helps promote better self-understanding too. Moreover, it has both local and global implications for the public good.[64] For Küng, there is little doubt that "peace in the world very much depends on peace among the various religions."[65] Ecumenism, in the broadest sense of interreligious relations, connects significantly to world peace. Ecumenical theology has the potential to contribute moral and spiritual resources where religious strife is spilling over into the political realm. The religions need to do their duty for world peace. That requires dialogue with one another. To the extent that religion and religions have a share in provoking violent strife in the world, they also share in a responsibility in promoting peace.[66] Rather than engaging in irrelevant theological quibbling, positive interreligious encounter and dialogue are keys to the life and health of the entire planet.

The Opportunity Explained[67]

Overcoming Collision through Hospitality

Marty's proposed contribution to a solution for alleviating escalating conflict between religious strangers is for one party or the other to move beyond conventional tolerance to risk hospitality to one another.[68] Hospitality reaches out to the stranger. It makes the religious stranger welcome. Conversation and interplay, though "full of risk", must follow.[69] For Marty, tolerance is better than its opposite, intolerance, but still ultimately anemic. He advises "a move toward hospitality, not tolerance, as an instrument or means of dealing more justly and with more potential of satisfying the interest of the faiths in collision and those who surround them and are affected by their interactions."[70] Hospitality, Marty explains, conveys a domestic portrait of a biblical and practical way of relating between hosts and guests that is polite and respectful. Thus, it is an ideal model for overcoming "belonger" and "stranger" conflicts.[71]

A Modest Pluralist Paradigm

Significantly, Marty's vision of interfaith hospitality requires adopting "a pluralist policy." The pluralism Marty prescribes is a "modest pluralism" that is primarily "civil" or "political" in perspective. However, it is inevitably "a religiously informed civic pluralism".[72] In short, he wants to allow room in the public square for different faiths to co-exist without co-option. He wishes to avoid or downplay religious wrangling over theological issues. He prefers to make a "bid for conversation more than argument".[73] Nevertheless, Marty does eventually reluctantly face philosophical and theological issues as a matter of integrity, mostly as an overview of major positions and their supporting arguments.[74] He attempts to form his proposal in a way that could have broader appeal and, therefore, broader impact. Theoretically, one could co-exist peacefully with religious others without pronouncing ultimate judgment on issues of salvation and truth. Yet one wonders if this mutual acceptance could not easily deteriorate into the tolerance he eschews rather than developing the hospitality he espouses.[75]

Realistic Limits and Hopeful Beginnings

Marty argues that a primary difference between tolerance and hospitality is that tolerance can remake or reshape the other into an acceptable, that is, familiar or similar, image while hospitality requires acknowledging that the other, the stranger, really is different.[76] Those who practice hospitality risk losing the privileges of the "belongers", but win the strangers as friends. Marty is not naïve enough to suppose that a little friendliness will achieve the "utopian notion" that the world's religions will resolve all their differences. He thinks that unrealistic. Conversation has its limits.[77] However, risking hospitality, welcoming, the stranger, and starting the conversation are worthwhile beginnings.[78] Hospitality can encourage conversation that invites belonger and stranger, host and guest, to be on equal terms with "no referee or determiner of a winner". Mutual enrichment can freely occur. Mutual safety can be assured.[79] Yet hospitable interreligious dialogue need not, in fact, ought not, avoid addressing the hard questions. Christians do their dialogue partners no favor by failing to remain open and upfront about their belief and practice.[80] Yet Marty admits that engaging one another in conversation earlier rather than later is crucial to its effectiveness. Sometimes things can get so bad that it takes a lot more than table talk to straighten them out.[81] For an obvious example, there is no way dialogue with Al Qaeda, indefatigable perpetrators of terrorism, is a viable option.[82] Rather than causing us to give up on dialogue with religious others, this frank admission out to spur us to engage one another before potentially irreversible and irreconcilable differences do develop. A sort of realistic optimism (or optimistic realism) surfaces and serves Marty here. He concludes:

> Faiths will continue to collide, but those individuals and groups that risk hospitality and promote engagement with the stranger, the different, the other, will con-

tribute to a world in which measured hopes can survive and those who hope can guide.[83]

Building Multireligious Bridges

A Radical Pluralist Proposal. Diana Eck champions a radically pluralist ideology in response to the developing reality of religious diversity and plurality in America and the world. In her opinion, a thoroughgoing pluralism is the appropriate response capable of producing and protecting harmonious and healthy co-existence in a multicultural and multireligious society. For Eck, principles of religious freedom and pluralistic faith are not only compatible but also inseparable.[84] Eck admits that she finds three general approaches to cultural and religious diversity in American history and philosophy. She analyzes these as they either do or do not exemplify the national motto of *E Pluribus Unum*, or "From Many, One". These alternative options are exclusion, assimilation, or pluralism. Exclusion simply says to those of diverse cultures and religions, "stay home" or "go home". Assimilation allows "aliens" to stay but insists they put away all that is different from existing American mores in order to "become like us." Pluralism invites them to come and to stay and celebrates with them their differences as enhancing and enriching America.[85] Eck explains that she understands pluralism as a "symphony" celebrating the beauty of difference.[86] Again, Eck admits that advocates can make arguments for each from American history and philosophy, but personally prefers the pluralist option for America's future.[87] For her it seems most consistent with the motto "From Many, One."

Practical Steps toward a Multireligious Culture. Continuing to utilize her assist from architecture, Eck explores interfaith development through the analogy of bridge building. "Bridges," she says, "are the lifelines of a society on the move." Bridges "enable us to cross the deepest gorges and widest rivers, linking the two sides with a flow of traffic." For the "new religious landscape of America", Eck explains, "We need energetic bridge builders to create a truly pluralistic society."[88] She happily and hopefully explains that even many stories of interfaith conflict or violence have "sequels and silver linings"—that is, they eventually have beneficial and positive outcomes as people come together to overcome adversity. Sometimes different faith groups become next neighbors who become partners on joint projects. Public acknowledgements, or "proclamations and parades", of America's new religious diversity is making it easier for some adherents of different faiths to enjoy common ground. Even the United States military is reaching milestones in its recognition that their personnel are religiously plural. Participation in public life is slowly becoming more a multireligious matter.[89]

Some consider the World Parliament of Religions in Chicago in 1893 the beginning of a new era in American, and indeed, in Western, history.[90] For Eck, with all its religious diversity and variety, it signals both where America has come from and where it is going.[91] Accordingly, she notes that a vibrant interfaith movement exists and continues to grow in the nation. Spiritual dialogue between faith communities is occurring, along with "not-so-random acts of kindness".[92] She imagines new communities of faith and life. She envisions a present opportunity to construct a society "without the chauvinism and religious triumphalism that have marred human history".[93] This excellent opportunity is the ideological and practical outgrowth, according to Eck, of the national founding vision of religious freedom. Though unsure where it is all going, she assures readers that, ready or not, the United States has become a religiously diverse nation and its citizens will have to deal with it one way or another.[94]

Religion as Cause and Cure[95]

Available Options

Possibly there has been a tendency to highlight the notorious and downplay the therapeutic when it comes to religion and violence.[96] Mark Juergensmeyer's sociological analysis suggests that the same religions that perpetrators of violence draw on, licitly or illicitly, for support may also provide resources for combating violent conflict.[97] Religions are "revolutionary" by nature, and are thus "capable of providing the ideological resources for an alternative view of public order." Juergensmeyer insists his work "is not a judgment against religion." Rather, it points to the power of religion in public life. As for religion itself, "many will find in it a cure for violence instead of a cause."[98] In arguing his case for religion, so to speak, Juergensmeyer reminds that precedents for violence in the major world religions are actually rare, and that those who attempt to rely on them as a basis for violence, such as in terrorism, are almost always marginal in their own religious traditions. Largely, they use violence to counterbalance their own marginality, and to experience a personal sense of empowerment.[99] The troublesome tendencies of governments to suppress or render impotent the power of religion in public life often plays into the hands of those appealing to religious sensibilities in a postmodern age for motivating dramatic action.[100]

Juergensmeyer identifies five possible outcomes to the "war on religious terrorism". First is "Destroying Violence", or simply killing off all the terrorists.[101] It seems unlikely if not impossible. Second is "Terrifying Terrorists", or making it so hard on terrorists they hesitate to act.[102] Although sometimes effective to a limited to degree, it does not work with all terrorists all the time. The third possibility is "Violence Wins", or the terrorists actually achieve their goals.[103] Usually negotiations with terrorists involve so much mutual compromise no one ends up satisfied and, as always to be expected, the more extreme only become angrier. Fourth, is "Separating Religion from Politics", or relegating religion to the moral and spiritual plane through a process of privatization.[104] Most deeply religious people are inevitably offended at what may be perceived as a "selling out" of religious values to political expediencies.[105]

Finally, Juergensmeyer discusses "Healing Politics with Religion".[106] This solution requires secular authorities to "embrace moral values, including those associated with religion."[107] This option is the opposite of secularism, the exclusion of religion from the public square.[108] Such an uneasy partnership is undoubtedly complicated and problematic but may hold the proverbial key to opening the door for peace nonetheless. Juergensmeyer insists that, even with the violence it may inspire in rare instances, "Religion gives spirit to public life" and it "provides a beacon for moral order."[109] He suggests progress may come when "some accommodation can be forged", when "some assertion of moderation in religion's passion, and some acknowledgement of religion in elevating the spiritual and moral values of public life" is possible.[110] He opines that, "In a curious way, then, the cure for religious violence may ultimately lie in a renewed appreciation for religion itself."[111]

Partners for Peace

Leaders heavily involved in dealing with religious terrorism are apparently coming to share Juergensmeyer's conclusion that within religion itself lays resources for overcoming religion related violence. Former United States Secretary of State Madeline Albright advocates increasing government understanding of religious dynamics and utilizing religious resources in dealing with volatile interfaith issues.[112] Former President Jimmy Carter emphatically appeals to spiritual values throughout his recent controversial bestseller, *Palestine: Peace Not Apartheid*.[113] Now former Secretary of State, Condoleezza Rice, articulates America's global role in defending freedom in term of religious faith. She approvingly quotes Thomas Jefferson as saying, "The God who gave us life, gave us liberty at the same time."[114] Additionally, former British Prime Minister Tony Blair, is known as one who takes his religion seriously,[115] although in a context of broadmindedness politically, ecumenically, and even with non-Christians religions.[116] Notably, Blair has expressed open ideas regarding the Abrahamic religions, and sees the world religions as a force for human unity and social activity.[117]

Of these examples of changing attitudes toward the role of religion in politics, Madame Albright especially testifies that in her experience this budding transformation is a stout reversal of traditional conventional wisdom in national and international diplomatic policy.[118] Apparently, issues of religious pluralism, including, of course, religious violence, are pressing pragmatic politicians to search and reach for new initiatives.[119] The same process seems to be occurring in theology, perhaps for partly the same, partly different reasons. At the least, Christian theology, including Pentecostal theology, needs to account adequately for the existence of other faiths, and devise a sound strategy for interfaith encounter and dialogue—as this study will propose subsequently.

However, an important difference needs noting. Albright and Carter mostly explore how religious faith and values affect the *other* in diplomatic negotiations and relations while Rice mostly argues for a right to apply her *own* religious faith and values to a specific national and international political ideology. Blair alone seems to say that *all* the religions working together is necessary for both spiritual and political stability and security. Obviously, this slight sampling of their views cannot pretend to be exhaustive. Perhaps the four views here represented are more complex than immediately appears. Nonetheless, the point bears making that participants in religiously emotive and explosive contexts must attempt to be as aware as humanly possible of both one's own and the others' faith and values and how these may or may not affect public behavior, especially violent or potentially violent behavior. That point may need stressing simply because there seems to be a certain proclivity among all humanity to judge the other more harshly while justifying oneself.[120]

Danger Signs

As for Juergensmeyer's argument about the religious imagination having both, admittedly rare, precedents for violence, and more commonly and positively, resources for curing the cause of violence, Charles Kimball provides helpful clarification. Kimball is professor of religion and chair of the department at Wake Forrest University in North Carolina. An ordained minister who received his Th. D. from Harvard in comparative religion with specialization in Islamic studies, he speaks straightforwardly to the issue of violent faith. Kimball observes that, "Religion is the most powerful and pervasive force on earth."[121] He also acknowledges that, "Religious ideologies and commitments are indisputably central factors in the escalation of violence and evil around the world."[122] To the question, "Is religion itself the problem?" he answers, "No ... and yes."[123] In short, the major religious traditions of the world that have stood the test of time have both "life affirming faith" that sustains and provides meaning, and "corrupting influences that lead toward evil and violence".[124] Discerning between religion that affirms and sustains life, and provides meaning and purpose, and that which has succumbed to corrupting influences becomes paramount.[125]

Kimball identifies five warning signs for recognizing religion gone wrong.
1. Absolute Truth Claims
2. Blind Obedience
3. Establishing the "Ideal" Time
4. The End Justifies Any Means
5. Declaring Holy War[126]

Whenever a religion, any religion, claims not only that absolute truth exists but also that it alone has absolute understanding of truth it is a warning sign that it is headed in the wrong direction. Add appeals by religious authorities for unquestioning obedience to their decrees and proclamations, intense eschatological expectations and predictions, willingness to go to any lengths to fulfill an alternative vision of reality, and, finally, a demonizing of others with a declaration of a war against them as evil personified, and the ingredients of a recipe for religious violence are frighteningly present. Though one or more of these ingredients may be present without the evil of violence following necessarily, when they are all present in combination the danger is extremely severe.

The Pentecostal Perspective Explored[127]

Critique of Pluralist Proposals

Ideological Pluralism. The pluralism of John Hick is the primary example of an ideology that actively promotes religious plurality as a form of religious faith in itself.[128] Pentecostal theologians are cognizant and highly critical of the pluralist hypothesis of John Hick. Pentecostal theologian of religions Amos

Yong asserts that in the pluralistic theology of religions of John Hick "the universal aspect of the divine relations with human beings has been emphasized to the neglect and the relativization of the christological core." Hick's theology of religions therefore "suffers" from a "christological defect". It loses "the particularity and concrete historicity of Jesus of Nazareth as the Christ."[129] Yong also identifies unfavorably the coalescence of pluralism and relativism evident in Hick's thought. He notes that pluralistic relativism is in retreat, but fairly admits that some pluralists are trying to deal with their relativism more efficiently. However, Evangelicals and others continue to be concerned about inherently relativistic and universalistic tendencies in the pluralism of Hick and others.[130]

Pentecostal ecumenical theologian Veli-Matti Kärkkäinen describes Hick's theology of religions, which he calls "Realitycentrism", as appealing only to extreme pluralists and as having "shape and content" that is "still quite vague and undefined." For him, Hick has "left behind the particular God of the Bible" for a more "generic term."[131] Kärkkäinen points out that Hick's pluralist theology of religions has taken many twists and turns over the years, and that Hick consistently tends to eschew clarity. In fact, Kärkkäinen concludes that Hick's thought on theology of religions is "dynamic to the point of bordering on internal contradiction." Furthermore, in denying the absolutist beliefs of existing religions and then replacing them with his own version of religion, he works himself into an absolutist posture that is actually against the entire pluralist idea.[132] For Kärkkäinen, the major challenge to Hick's philosophy of pluralism is whether it is actually pluralist at all. As he denies differences between religions, he effectively compresses them all into one same religion. Kärkkäinen also suggests Hick has not satisfactorily explained how one can hold to a generic view of God about whom nothing can be know but whose existence can be assumed. Finally, within the limits of language there are serious doubts about whether it is possible to the personal/impersonal divide as Hick claims.[133]

Though expressing respect for Hick and even agreement at some points, for example, regarding Hick's argument that Christian doctrines are human attempts to grasp the meaning of the Christ event rather than divine formulations, Kärkkäinen is especially perturbed at the approach to the Trinity and Christology by Hick. He therefore takes issue with Hick's contention that the doctrine of the Trinity is foreign to the New Testament, and with his subsequent radical revision of Christology. Hick bases his arguments against the divinity and uniqueness of Christ on the older, now discredited Quest for Jesus approach.[134] He also attempts to use abuses of Christology as an argument, rather than its best representation, an approach that falters when these are in view. His functional use of doctrine tends to relativism of truth claims even while he expects his own claims to be recognized as true![135] In dismissing paradoxical doctrines, Hick misses, according to Kärkkäinen, the reality of mystery in religion. Again, Hick sometimes claims the incomprehensible divine cannot be experienced and sometimes describes the Real as experienced, contradicting himself at an essential epistemological point. Hick's vague conception of the Incarnation is too weak. For it, he ditches the Trinity. He ends up with a generic God, an impersonal, that is, non-personal, being of some indefinable identity. His continued use of Christian language in such contexts is simply confusing. Kärkkäinen concludes that the pluralist theology of religions of John Hick is completely incompatible within "the contours of the classical Christian view of God as triune."[136]

Frank Macchia, a leading Pentecostal systematic theologian, also takes issue with the pluralism of John Hick.[137] He initially makes some of the same criticisms occurring elsewhere, with some additional observations and insights. However, he then makes a bold and uniquely Pentecostal move. Affirming that Pentecost (Acts 2) is about diversity of tongues and a plurality of cultures and peoples, he nonetheless uses the doctrine and experience of Spirit baptism in refuting radical religious pluralism as an option for Pentecostals.[138] Placing his critique in an ecclesiological context confronting the challenge of pluralism, Macchia rejects Hick's attempt to disassociate the Kingdom from the Church and the Church from Christ.[139] In a genuinely Pentecostal move, Macchia argues that Christ's role as the Spirit Baptizer sets him apart from all prophets, from John the Baptist, indeed from all others. Only God can give the Spirit of God.[140] Hick's difficulty with Christ's literal resurrection, for Macchia, arises out of his rejection of Jesus as the Spirit Baptizer.[141] He points out that Christ's role as Spirit Baptizer makes the link between Christ and the historical Church that Hick insists is lacking—and subsequently uses to reject the teaching of the historical Church on Christology and the Trinity.[142] The christological-ecclesiological connection is made by Christ imparting the Spirit to the Church. Hick's argument about a Church developing its own teaching for purposes of gaining power in the ancient world falls apart thus.[143]

Furthermore, Macchia argues that the very diversity and plurality that Hick attempts to establish is present in Pentecost. A particularly pertinent paragraph requires quoting in full.

> At Pentecost, the legitimate reaching for God implied in various cultures and religions expressions finds fulfillment in the grace of God revealed in the crucified and risen Christ as the one who imparts the Spirit in the latter days. Their differences and past histories are not dissolved but affirmed and granted a new loyalty and a new direction. In the process all idols are forsaken and the cultures are pruned. But the critical pruning is demanded for the church as well. Though the church is the central locus of the kingdom of God in the world, the church is also a loving fellow traveler with the world's religions while pointing them to the superiority of Christ. Spirit baptism can be developed so as to respond to Hick's critique of ecclesiastical superiority in the world but in a way that rejects his reduction of Jesus to simply one symbol of the sacred among others.[144]

Yet in Pentecost the diversity and plurality is not separated from the divine uniqueness of Jesus Christ but streams out of the unutterable uniqueness of Christ as the divine Spirit Baptizer. Out of the uniqueness of Christ arises the Spirit baptized Church as the unique representative and instrument of Christ. Yet this ecclesial uniqueness is not narrow. The Spirit baptized Church simultaneously exists in loving relationship with non-Christian religions even while pointing to Christ.[145] Therefore, Macchia's Pentecostal experience and doctrine help him achieve a balance and poise in his theology of religions absent from Hick's radical pluralism.

Practical Pluralism. The pluralism of Martin Marty is a practical attempt to deal with the collision of faiths occurring in increasingly religiously pluralistic societal settings. While he uses "civil", in terms of "civic", to describe his brand of pluralism, one might well note that it also applies in terms of civility of attitude and intent. He wants to establish harmony and peace among conflictive faiths. In other words, he wants them to be civil toward each other. As such, his primary concern is not the philosophy or theology of pluralism, as with Hick, for example. The little that he does deal with theology is as a concession to the conviction that religious people will require some theological grounding. Yet he does squarely base his poignant appeal for hospitality on the biblical tradition as well as on political practicality. Martin Marty is obviously not coming from the same reference point as John Hick. Accordingly, elements of his approach will be more acceptable for anti-pluralist Pentecostals.

Perhaps no Pentecostal will fault Marty's hopeful vision of interfaith peace.[146] His domestic model, as it were, of hospitality, with its emphasis on welcoming and conversing, may also be of solid use for resolving interreligious strife, at least that which arises directly out of the fear of the unfamiliar. Other, more difficult cases, where individuals or groups of different religions know each other well enough, but have established histories of anger and hate, as he himself admits, will probably benefit little from simple hospitality. So then, the model is useful within limits. It may be particularly useful in America and Europe, for example, where fresh interfaith encounters are occurring frequently, but less so, say, in the Middle East where entrenched animosity exists. Moreover, his broad appeal style of presentation downplaying theology could be perhaps a weakness in the eyes of Pentecostals who may be suspicious about underlying pluralist assumptions. Believing that his moderate civil pluralism is really an almost "fill in the blank" approach to theology of religions is rather difficult. For Pentecostals to accept his hospitality appeal for welcome and conversation between faiths experiencing confrontation, solid, substantive, serious theology will have to be its chief support. Moreover, Pentecostals will not expect that supportive theology to be pluralist.[147] Marty's proposal, therefore, holds positive potential for Pentecostal exploitation but only with significant adjustment.

Like Marty, only more so, Diana Eck avoids discussing theology—at least with any depth or specificity. First, she builds her exhortations to harmonious existence in a multireligious culture upon a political adage, "From Many, One", not a theological principle.[148] Second, her main weapon of persuasion, so to speak, is to recount tirelessly the increasingly religiously pluralistic environment of America. She in effect says, "This is the way it is here now so deal with it."[149] Third, she seems, in spite of some serious violence between religions, to place great faith in the inclination of ordinary people to respond positively to other people, even vastly different people, if they just get to know each other a little better. At times, this optimism comes across almost as an evangelistic invitation to "just get out there and get to know your neighbors of other faiths and things will work out all right."[150] One suspects a rather advanced ideology of pluralism underpins her exhortation, but if so, it is unspoken.[151]

Eck's approach might almost be called "anthropological pluralism." She seems to trust in the general goodness of humanity to overcome the calamity of interfaith conflict. Though, hopefully and prayerfully, there may be some truth to this confidence in her fellow man (or woman), Eck's approach, taken alone at least, is anemic. A generally vague anthropological pluralistic optimism suffers from the same malady as Marty's moderate, civil pluralism, only more so. It will work only when attached to a substantive theological paradigm that gives specificity, direction, and purpose to interfaith encounters between human beings. Pentecostals, for one, will probably not "just get out there and get to know their neighbors of other faiths" in order to see if "things will work out all right," until they have some sense of who, what, when, where, and how (not to mention, why).[152] In other words, they will require a clearly articulated theology of religions. Eck does not supply that theology. Without it, all the interfaith interaction she calls for sounds a lot like an open invitation to a pluralist party. That is not to say that bringing people together is not a good idea. One senses that it could be a good idea indeed. Yet such delicate contact can be soundly successful only when guided by (and guarded by) a carefully articulated and sophisticated theology of religions. As already indicated, for Pentecostals, that theology of religions will not be pluralism. Therefore, Pentecostals will likely be exceedingly cautious of Eck's approach, perhaps learning from her research and experience but not leaning toward her conclusions.[153]

Issues of Intense Interest for Pentecostals

Compromised Christology: Absolute and Utter Uniqueness of Jesus Christ. Several areas of particular concern stand out for Pentecostals about the general approach of the ideology of pluralism to the contemporary reality of religious pluralism. Foremost among these concerns has to do with the compromise of a high Christology, or, more plainly put, abandoning the absolute and utter uniqueness of Jesus Christ. Critics occasionally accuse Pentecostals of diminishment of Christ in preferment for the Holy Spirit.[154] It is untrue. As Pentecostal New Testament scholar and theologian French Arrington explains, Christ is at the heart of their faith and relationship with God, central to their faith, worship, and teaching. Even Pentecostal experience of the Holy Spirit is inseparably indebted to their understanding of Christ. For Pentecostals, Christ is the center and foundation of all Christian faith.[155] Moreover, the conviction of Christ's essential centrality includes avid affirmation of his preexistence and incarnation, full divinity and humanity, atoning death and literal resurrection, as well as his ascension to glory as exalted Lord and return to earth as its Redeemer and Ruler.[156]

Understandably, the tendency, differing only in degree, among pluralists to diminish or even deny the uniqueness of Christ, to make him one more divine manifestation alongside others, or to make him a myth or metaphor for God's truth and love, is problematic at best for Pentecostals. In fact, they reject it outright.[157] In my experience, they see it as a sell out of the central tenet of the Christian faith in an attempt to placate non-Christian faiths.[158] To say that Pentecostals are suspicious of pluralism is an understatement. In fact, they resent it as a reduction of the very vitality of their faith to meaninglessness and powerlessness. Pentecostals, therefore, are not at all sympathetic to pluralism.[159]

Diminished Sacred Text: Inspiration and Authority of Holy Scripture. Another concern for Pentecostals regarding ideological pluralism is its tendency to diminish the role of Scripture in Christian faith and life. All kinds of other philosophical founts seem to compete with Scripture, and often to win out over Scripture, as more acceptable authorities.[160] As Arrington observes, though Pentecostals have been called "people of the Spirit," they are also "people of the Book." Pentecostals traditionally hold fast to an emphasis on biblical focus. Though Pentecostals experience truth in many forms, such as in song, testimony, sermon, or through spiritual gifts, "all such means lead back to the Scriptures." The divine inspiration and authority of the Bible is a universal given among Pentecostals.[161] The Pentecostal concept of the Bible includes commitments to its nature as divine revelation and inspiration, an acceptable and reliable canonization process, and to the Holy Spirit's continuing illumination in human experience and interpretation.[162]

Accordingly, any philosophy or theology that diminishes, denies, or otherwise undermines the sacredness of Scripture, particularly its inspiration and authority, is *a priori* reprobate for Pentecostals.[163] This reasoning affects attitudes toward pluralism rather directly. Pentecostals are inclined to conclude that pluralists are unable to find support for their ideas through a serious biblical hermeneutic and are therefore driven to either change their views or found them in other sources.[164] Sadly, many choose other sources. Of course, this choice also often includes a redaction-revision approach to Scripture to force it into alignment with ideas really rooted in foreign soil, usually modernist liberal philosophy. Pentecostals note that liberals and/or pluralists are often much more adept at explaining what the Bible *does not* mean than what it *does* mean. They commonly call this negative hermeneutic of Scripture, "explaining it away." Pentecostals, therefore, reject outright radical religious pluralism as a fundamentally unbiblical ideology. They prefer to rely heavily on a pneumatological hermeneutic reverent of the text and its power for faith and for life.[165]

Distorted Soteriology: Nature and Necessity of Salvation. Pentecostals are concerned that high on the agenda of pluralists is redefining Christian salvation to fit categories more amicable to non-Christian religions.[166] Pentecostals take the reality of sin seriously. Evil is real. Salvation, therefore, is essential, and is a personal experience of the benefits of the sufficiency of Christ's atoning death on the cross through trusting faith in him. Salvation brings eternal life, is a way or spiritual journey throughout life, is received as a gift, and necessarily involves a lifestyle of Christian discipleship.[167] For Pentecostals, the terms and concepts of repentance, justification or forgiveness, reconciliation, adoption and regeneration, assurance, sanctification, and glorification, are indicative of real and essential aspects of salvation.[168] God's gracious provision through faith for human depravity is central to the Pentecostal worldview. Hell, or everlasting judgment and punishment, are real possibilities for human destiny making salvation all the more highly prized. Heaven also, or everlasting reward and bliss are real possibilities for human destiny making salvation all the more highly prized.[169] Pentecostal Christians, even more than some others, stress a strong pneumatological component in salvation.[170] In terms reminiscent of its Wesleyan heritage, for Pentecostalism, salvation is *via salutis* (way of salvation) more so than an *ordo salutis* (order of salvation), and is quite correctly characterized as living in the Spirit.[171] This pneumatological component of Pentecostal soteriology suggests that salvation is at the core of Christian identity and spirituality for Pentecostals.

Therefore, pluralism's efforts to redefine Christian salvation in terms of other religions or abstract philosophies, efforts usually involving a denial of the literal reality of Christian salvation as revealed in the Bible, are overtly offensive to Pentecostals.[172] That truncated "salvation," if it can still even be called such, is unrecognizable and undesirable to devout Pentecostals accustomed to rejoicing in a robust and vibrant redemptive experience.[173] Pentecostals often quote from biblical texts such as Nehemiah 8:10 or Psalm 51:12 or 1 Peter 1:8 to defend their view that salvation is a powerfully joyful experience. Even when pluralism does not redefine salvation for Christians themselves, it makes it optional to the point of being dismissive. Pentecostals believe the universality of sin necessitates the universality of salvation. Accordingly, religious pluralism tends to cut at the roots of everything Pentecostals believe and value. The radical ideology of religious pluralism is therefore not an option for Pentecostals. To choose it would be to lose their identity. Pentecostals prefer to maintain a passion for the Kingdom of God arising out of a salvific experience that has stood them in good stead.[174]

Minimized Ecclesial Mission: Christian Conversion and Evangelism Emphases. Another problematic factor for Pentecostals in ideological pluralism is the proclivity to minimize the uniqueness or significance of the Church, especially of its evangelistic mission.[175] Conversely, Pentecostals believe the Church is a divinely created institution formed by God's saving grace in Christ though progressively developed throughout redemptive history in the biblical testaments.[176] The Church does not exist for itself alone, but as a servant with a mission, the mission of the ministry of reconciliation.[177] Even more so than some other Christian bodies, Pentecostalism fervently affirms that as a divine creation the divine mission of the Church is to bear witness to the world of Jesus Christ as the only Savior.[178] No peripheral matter, this profound conviction of the mission of the Church is thought of as flowing "out of the heart of God" and "manifesting the truest and deepest nature" of the Church. Evangelism, therefore, is the task of the entire Church, arising out of Christ's "great commission" and the experience of Pentecost through the power of the constraining love of God in Christ.[179] Pentecostals, along with other Evangelicals, believe conversion is essential for salvation, and therefore feel compelled by love to present everyone with an opportunity in liberty to repent and believe.[180]

Pluralism's insistence that "all roads lead to God," implying more or less everyone will be saved so long as they devoutly follow some spiritual path, is repulsive to Pentecostals. It flies in the face of their entire faith. When pluralists begin calling for Pentecostals (and others) to cease evangelistic proclamation to adherents of other faiths of the good news of God's saving grace in Christ in order to avoid offense, they are literally challenging the very bedrock of their existential identity. Pentecostals understand themselves to be a movement distinctively and specifically raised up by God, in eschatological fervor, as a witness to the world of Jesus Christ in the mighty, miraculous power of the outpoured Spirit.[181] Their evangelistic fervor alone makes Pentecostals incompatible with the gestalt of radical religious pluralism.

Whatever options are available for Pentecostals in response to a society with an increasingly religiously pluralistic tone, an ideology of religious pluralism that compromises Christ, diminishes the Scripture, distorts salvation, and minimizes the Church's missionary task it not one of any feasible validity.

Finding A Way Forward for Pentecostals

One draws certain important conclusions and implications from the preceding overview of the problems and opportunities raised by the reality and ideology of religious pluralism and the Pentecostal critique of that context. First, an increasingly religiously plural culture is a factual reality for contemporary global society. Second, the response of ideological religious pluralism is not adequate or appropriate for the situation for Classical Pentecostals due to serious discrepancies with their traditional values, though some practical applications of moderate forms are perhaps possible. Third, however, Pentecostal dissatisfaction with pluralist responses does not release them from responsibility. Rather, the crisis of escalating interfaith violence necessitates development by Pentecostals of a proactive response authentically appropriate to their traditional beliefs and practices.

Obviously, a moral and spiritual obligation rests with all faith groups, including Pentecostals, for mitigation of current conflict.[182] A key biblical text for Pentecostals, probably due to deep roots in the nineteenth century Holiness Movement, has been Hebrews 12:14: "Make every effort to live in peace with all men and to be holy; without holiness no one will see the Lord."[183] In fact, this verse helped formed a basis for an early Pentecostal pronouncement on peace.[184] A tradition of connection between holiness and the pursuit of peace, therefore, should motivate Pentecostals to work for peace among the religions.[185] In addition, the globalization of Pentecostalism means that it is "has enormous ecumenical implications, and adherents are often on the cutting edge of encounter with people of other faiths."[186] Pentecostalism may not only have a general responsibility to engage other religions more intentionally; it may actually have a special opportunity among the members of the Christian family to do so.

Recognizing Pentecostal responsibility and opportunity regarding religious pluralism is all the more pertinent because Pentecostals on the interfaith front have sometimes themselves related to religious others "antagonistically".[187] In fact, their checkered history suggests one of the chief challenges, if not the chief challenge, for Pentecostals at this stage may consist in confronting and conquering their own hesitance and reluctance. If anything at all about the above analysis is accurate, then a symbiosis between interfaith fear and interfaith violence exists that real religion simply cannot sustain. The reality and ideology of radical religious pluralism coupled with the global context of clashing faith groups, requires Pentecostals to rise to the occasion with integrity and energy.

Conclusion/Summary

The intention of this chapter has not been that of presenting an exhaustive analysis of religious pluralism. Rather, it has aimed only to set the stage for a consideration of Pentecostal theology of religions by demonstrating the pluralist environment as a practical reality and as a philosophical ideology. A biblically, practically, and theologically informed approach to interreligious encounter, dialogue, and cooperation is appropriate for Pentecostals. Yet a Pentecostal theology of religions adequate for the contemporary task of interreligious coexistence must be faithful to its own inherent values. Faithfulness for Pentecostal theology of religions includes attention to an uncompromised Christology, an undiminished view of the inspiration and authority of Scripture, an undistorted soteriology, and a non-minimal ecclesiology. For Pentecostals, these values come together in a distinctive pneumatological framework. Here then is the challenge of Pentecostal theology of religions: to utilize its distinctive pneumatology for developing a theology of religions that effectively addresses the current situation of religious pluralism in a manner avoiding the pitfalls of pluralism that is thus faithful to Pentecostal identity and ethos. As the next chapter shows, Pentecostal theologians and thinkers have already actively begun to engage this important task.

Notes

1. This section will be in dialog with the work of Diana Eck, John Hick, Mark Juergensmeyer, Hans Küng and Martin Marty.

2. N. Smart, "Pluralism," *NHCT*, eds. D.W. Musser and J.L. Price (Nashville: Abingdon, 1992), 360-64. Of course, the entire concept of pluralism lends itself to intricate theological interpretation as well as linguistic or functional analysis. E.g., see T. Reynolds, "Reconsidering Schleiermacher and the Problem of Religious Diversity: Toward a Dialectical Pluralism," *JAAR* 73:1 (Mar 2005), 151-81.

3. Smart, "Pluralism," *NHCT*, 360.

4. Smart, "Pluralism," *NHCT*, 362.

5. Smart, "Pluralism," *NHCT*, 363-64. Sir Norman Anderson, *Christianity and World Religions: The Challenge of Pluralism* (Downer's Grove, IL: InterVarsity Press, 1970, rev. ed., 1984), theoretically distinguishes between religious pluralism (affirming multiple religions) and syncretism (integrating multiple religions) but admits practically there is often overlap, 15-16, especially in mystical religions, 38.

6. A. Yong, *Discerning of the Spirit(s): A Pentecostal-Charismatic Contribution to the Christian Theology of Religions* JSup 20 (Sheffield: Sheffield Academic, 2000), questions the viability of this popular typology but admits its heuristic value, 34. Cf. John Hick, "The Theological Challenge of Religious Pluralism," *Christianity and Other Religions: Selected Readings*, ed. John Hick and Brian Hebblethwaite (Oxford: Oneworld, 2001), who explores further complexities within each of these categories, 156-71.

7. Smart, "Pluralism," *NHCT*, 362-64.

8. On Wesley, see R.L. Maddox in "Wesley and the Question of Truth or Salvation in Other Religions," *WTJ* (27 1992), 9-29. On Lewis, see L. Summer, "Non-Christian Religions," *The C. S. Lewis Readers' Encyclopedia*, eds. J.D. Schultz and J.G. West Jr. (Grand Rapids: Zondervan, 1998), 294-95. Cf. T. Richie, "Mr. Wesley and Mohammed: A Contemporary Inquiry Concerning Islam," *ATJ* 58:2 (Fall 2003), 79-99, and "Hints from Heaven: Can C. S. Lewis Help Evangelicals Hear God in Other Religions?" *ERT* 32:1 (January 2008), 38-55.

9. Smart, 363. Cf. B.G. Smith, "Attitudes toward Religious Pluralism: Measurements and Consequences," *SC* 54:2 (2007), 333-53. Smith argues that while exposure to other religions' ideas is important in developing inclusivist views, denominational affiliation and activity are stronger factors. Furthermore, views on religious pluralism and its counterparts directly and greatly influence religious, political, and social actions.

10. The Dalai Lama, *The Four Noble Truths*, trans. Geshe Thupten Jinpa and ed. Dominque Side (London: Thorsens, 1997), 1-7 (1, 2, 6).

11. Smart, "Pluralism," 363.

12. Koran quotes are from *The Koran*, trans. N.J. Dawood, (New York: Penguin, 1956, 1999).

13. I.A.R. Omar, "Pope Benedict XVI's Comments on Islam in Regensburg: A Muslim Response," *CD* 48 (December 2006), 16-19, and M. Al-Sammak, "The Culture of Dialogue in Islam; Freedom of Choice and the Right to Differ," *CD* 48 (December 2006), 20-25.

14. Cf. A. Flannery, Gen. Ed., *Nostra aetate* in "Declaration on the Relations of the Church to Non-Christian Religions," *Vatican Council II: The Conciliar and Post-Conciliar Documents*, vol. one (Collegeville, MN: Liturgical Press, 1992), 738-42. See K. Rahner, "Jesus Christ in Non-Christian Religions," *Foundations of Christian Faith: An Introduction to the Idea of Christianity*, trans. W.V. Dych (New York: Crossroad, 1978, 2002), 311-21, and H. Küng, *Theology for the Third Millennium* (New York: Doubleday, 1987), 209-56.

15. Other influential pluralist theologians include S.J. Samartha, *One Christ, Many Religions: Toward a Revised Christology* (New York: Maryknoll, 1991), R. Panikkar, *The Unknown Christ of Hinduism* (London: Darton, Longman, & Todd, 1964, 1981), and P.F. Knitter, *Jesus and the Other Names: Christian Mission and Global Responsibility* (New York: Maryknoll, 1996).

16. See D. Cheetham, *John Hick: A Critical Introduction and Reflection* (Abingdon, UK, & Brookfield, VT: Ashfield, 2002), 1-8. Cf. G. D'Costa, *John Hick's Theology of Religions* (New York: University Press of America, 1987).

17. See http://www.johnhick.org.uk/.

18. J. Hick, "A Pluralist View," *Four Views of Salvation in a Pluralistic World*, Counterpoint Series, eds. S.N. Gundry, D.L. Okholm, T.R. Phillips (Grand Rapids: Zondervan, 1995, 1996), 27-59. Hick elucidates his ideas more in depth in *The Metaphor of God Incarnate Christology in a Pluralistic Age* (Louisville: Westminster John Knox, 1993).

19. Hick, "Pluralist," 29-39 (38).

20. Hick, "Pluralist," 39.

21. However, H. Netland, *Encountering Religious Pluralism: The Challenge to Christian Faith & Mission* (Downer's Grove, ILL: InterVarsity, 2001), insists that pluralism is based on a "pluralistic ethos" consisting of "a set of assumptions and values" (14).

22. Hick, "Pluralist," 39-42.

23. Hick, "Pluralist," 42-45 (43, 44). Interestingly, Charismatic Baptist C. Pinnock, a close associate of Classical Pentecostals, argues that Hick's pluralism is mostly a mis-

taken application of his personal experience of religious others propped up with pseudo-logic. See C.H. Pinnock, "Response to John Hick," *Four Views of Salvation in a Pluralistic World*, 60-64.

24. Hick, "Pluralist," 46-47.

25. Hick, "Pluralist," 47-51 (50). Cheetham, *John Hick,* suggests that Hick's admittedly provocative thought is ultimately tied to a vision of religious liberalism vanishing in an age of "post-liberalism" and "post-conservativism", 174-75. Indeed, according to Cheetham, Hick's overwhelming liberalism and pluralism may even eclipse the lasting value of his overall work (e.g., on epistemology, theodicy), 175-76.

26. Hick, "Pluralist," 50-51.

27. Netland, *Encountering Religious Pluralism,* insists that pluralism strikes "at the heart of Christianity" (14), provoking acute crisis regarding the "legitimacy of Christian mission" (15).

28. Hick, "Pluralist," 51-57.

29. Hick, "Pluralist," 57-59 (59). However, in consideration of Hick's "Chalcedon Defended: A Pluralistic Re-Reading of the Two Natures Doctrine," *ET* 118:3 (2006), 113-19, P. Schmidt-Leukel contends that the idea of incarnation is not a problem for a pluralistic theology of religions but rather, for him, the problem arises in an assertion of its complete uniqueness in Christ.

30. M.E. Marty, *When Faiths Collide,* (Malden: Blackwell, 2005).

31. Marty, *Collide,* 1-4 (1).

32. Marty, *Collide,* 4-11. R. Niebuhr, in *The Children of Light and The Children of Darkness: A Vindication of Democracy and A Critique of Its Traditional Defense* (New York: Charles Scribner's Sons, 1944, 1960), argued that "religious diversity remains potentially the most basic source of conflict", and that it has wide ranging cultural complexities, 125.

33. Marty, *Collide,* 13-14.

34. Marty, *Collide,* 162-65.

35. J. Stout argues that political secularism can also lead to force and violence as a means of conversion or containment regarding an opposing position, in this case, theism. See Stout, "2007 Presidential Address: The Folly of Secularism," *JAAR* 76:3 (September 2008), 533-44.

36. Marty, *Collide,* 29-35, 57-60.

37. Marty, *Collide,* 14-17. J.W. Jones, *Blood that Cries Out from the Earth: The Psychology of Religious Terrorism* (Oxford/New York: Oxford University Press, 2008), both a clinical psychologist and an authority on comparative religion, argues that research on the psychology of violence shows that several factors work to make ordinary people turn "evil." These include feelings of humiliation or shame, a tendency to see the world in black and white, and demonization or dehumanization of other people. Authoritarian religion or "fundamentalism" can be a source of such ideas and feelings, 142-70, (157).

38. Marty, *Collide,* 30, 159-61.

39. Yong, *Discerning,* notes that while Pentecostals have undoubtedly been influenced by fundamentalists, 155, 185, they have also had a tense polemic and combative relationship, 229, 291. In fact, Pentecostal spirituality may provide an alternative to fundamentalism, 227.

40. Marty, *Collide,* 2, 10.

41. Marty, *Collide,* 26. For a different view see S.P. Huntingdon, *The Clash of Civilizations and the Remaking of World Order* (New York: Touchstone, 1996).

42. Marty, *Collide,* 109-10, 133, 137. See below on Marty's proposal of hospitality.

43. Marty, *Collide*, 57-60. Latin American historical theologian J.L. Gonzalez reminds in *The Crusades: Piety Misguided* (Nashville: Graded Press, 1988) that learning from history that religious violence can sometimes arise out of sincere but sadly misdirected piety is an important lesson for avoiding a repetition in the present of past horrors such as in the Christian crusades of the Middle Ages.

44. D.L. Eck, *A New Religious America: How A "Christian Country" Has Become the World's Most Religiously Diverse Nation* (New York: HarperCollins, 2001). Cf. T.C. Muck, *Alien Gods on American Turf,* Christianity Today Series (Wheaton, IL: Scripture Press Publications, Inc., Victor Books, 1990) and W.R. Hutchinson, *Religious Pluralism in America: The Contentious History of a Founding Idea* (New Haven: Yale, 2003).

45. Eck, *New*, 1, 11, 19.

46. Eck, *New*, 5-6, 61-65.

47. Eck, *New*, 1.

48. Hutchinson argues that religious plurality was an original founding idea of the United States that has endured conflictive acceptance as it has evolved into its contemporary form. Interestingly, he lists the rise of Pentecostals, among others, as evidence of the increasingly visible religious diversity of the nation. See, *Pluralism*, 114-15.

49. Eck, *New*, 294-334 (295).

50. Eck, *New*, 294. In a subsequent edition, Eck considers that September 11 revealed the undercurrent of concerns over religious plurality in America but also finally caused the nation to focus on interreligious relations more openly and in depth. See D.L. Eck, "Preface," *A New Religious America—After September 11* (New York: HarperSanfrancisco, 2002).

51. For a discussion of how sectarianism, nationalism, and racism affect attitudes toward religious others even in developing a Christian theology of religions, see T. Richie, "God's Fairness to People of All Faiths: A Respectful Proposal to Pentecostals for Discussion Regarding World Religions," *Pneuma* 28:1 (2006), 105-19 (113-18).

52. Eck, *New*, 296-328.

53. Mark Juergensmeyer, *Terror in the Mind of God: The Global Rise of Religious Violence* (Berkeley and Los Angeles: University of California, 2001), xi.

54. Juergensmeyer, *Terror*, xi. Noteworthy is that many of his examples occur in contexts of religious plurality.

55. Jones, *Blood*, sees strong psychological components in religious violence that may be either fostered or countered by religion and religious leaders depending on their models and ideas, 157-59. However, Jones agrees with Juergensmeyer that terrorism is at least "partly a public theater performed for an audience", and therefore analyzes the role of an unwittingly complicit media, 148.

56. Juergensmeyer, *Terror*, xi.

57. Juergensmeyer, *Terror*, xii. In an earlier work on *The New Cold War? Religious Nationalism Confronts the Secular State* (Los Angeles, CA: University of California, 1993, 1994), Juergensmeyer "paints a provocative picture of the new religious revolutionaries altering the political landscape in the Middle East, South Asia, Central Asia, and Eastern Europe" (from the back cover). He subsequently expanded on that thesis and developed it in light of September 11, 2001 and subsequent events in *Global Rebellion: Religious Challenges to the Secular State from Christian Militias to Al Qaeda* (Los Angeles, CA: University of California, 2009).

58. Juergensmeyer's work is replete with specific case studies driving home this unpleasant and unpalatable point. Cf. *Terror*, 19-118.

59. Juergensmeyer, *Terror*, 4-10.

60. Juergensmeyer, *Terror*, 10-15.

61. Contrarily, Church of God Presiding Bishop R.F. Culpepper, *The Great Commission: The Solution...* (Cleveland, TN: Pathway Press, 2009), insists on connecting and identifying with peoples and their cultures, and includes dialogue as a part of that approach, 35-36, 49-50, and 161-65. For him, this is all part of "the Spirit's stretching ministry" and helps "prevent dull and stolid thinking" (169).

62. Juergensmeyer, *Terror*, 6. Cf. C. Flint, *Introduction to Geopolitics: Tensions, Conflicts and Resolutions* (New York: Routledge, 2006), 172 and 204, for surging religious and nationalist syntheses.

63. H. Küng, *Christianity and World Religions: Paths to Dialogue with Islam, Hinduism, and Buddhism* (New York: Doubleday, 1986), 440-43.

64. Küng, *World Religions*, 441.

65. Küng, *World Religions*, 441. Various authors affirm in various forms the critical importance of peace among the religions. E.g., see Francis Cardinal Arinze, *Religions for Peace: A Call for Solidarity to the Religions of the World* (New York: Random House, 2002) and J.B. McDaniel, *Gandhi's Hope: Learning from World Religions as a Path to Peace* (Maryknoll, New York: Orbis, 2005).

66. Küng, *World Religions*, 441. Cf. J.R. White, "Political Eschatology: A Theology of Antigovernment Extremism," *ABS* 44:6 (February 2001), 937-56.

67. This section will be in dialog with the work of Diana Eck and Martin Marty.

68. D.J. Good, in "Hospitality Challenges Our Restricted Vision", points out biblical and post-biblical traditions about Jesus and Abraham suggest hospitality can move well beyond the domestic setting of homemaking. See November 22, 2007 at *Ekklesia*, News Brief, http://ekklesia.co.uk/node/6336.

69. Marty, *Collide*, 1.

70. Marty, *Collide*, 66 Cf. 126.

71. Marty, *Collide*, 128-42.

72. Marty, *Collide*, 70-76, 97-98. Marty makes it plain that there are various responses for an environment of pluralism, ranging from skepticism through syncretism and relativism to pluralism itself (150-52). However, Marty, also clearly rejects any idea that all religions are really one and the same at their core (165-67).

73. Marty, *Collide*, 12. A. Toynbee, *Christianity Among the Religions of the World* (New York: Scribner's, 1957), is an example of an earlier pluralist agenda with strong political overtones, but Marty does not go nearly so far.

74. Marty, *Collide*, 149-78.

75. Interestingly, Moltmann expresses keen interest in America's "civil religion" or political philosophy. In it, he identifies "messianic overtones" with both modern and secular indebtedness to "the millenarian branch of Christian hope." He warns, however, that because of its association with "apocalyptic dualism", especially regarding "the final struggle between God and Satan, Christ and the Antichrist, good and evil," that America's "religious politics" may be at best a mixed blessing. Noting that American presidents often invoke God's blessing on their nation, for Moltmann whether God blesses America will depend on whether "America is a blessing for the peoples of the world, or their burden and curse; for one is blessed only in order to be a blessing in oneself." See J. Moltmann, *A Broad Place: An Autobiography* (Minneapolis: Fortress, 2008), 144.

76. Marty, *Collide*, 124-25.

77. Marty, *Collide*, 149, 123, 146.

78. Marty, *Collide*, 176-77. Jones, *Blood*, advises religious leaders to teach and model compassion and religious adherents to practice love and compassion, 158-62. However, he admits that religions can be ambivalent, sometimes fostering compassion

and sometimes fostering violence, 10. E.g., in the West Buddhism has a reputation for compassion but in reality has its own history of violence, 53.

79. Marty, *Collide*, 91-92, 168-69.

80. Marty, *Collide*, 164-65.

81. Yong, *Discerning*, suggests a pneumatological approach to interreligious dialogue can address serious differences, 313, but also argues for discernment, 315.

82. Cf. Flint, *Geopolitics*, 204. See Marty, *Collide*, 96, 146.

83. Marty, *Collide*, 178. Similar to Marty, Stout argues for non-theological practical partnerships between secularists and moderate theists combating the threat of plutocracy, "Folly of Secularism," 533-44.

84. Eck, *New*, 25, 69-77.

85. Eck, *New*, 29-79 (47-48). Cf. with Niebuhr's statement that, "Democracy is thus, in one sense, the fruit of a cultural and religious pluralism created by the inexorable forces of history" (*Children*, 120). However, he also said, "Democratic institutions are the cause, as well as the consequence, of cultural diversity and social pluralism" (122). Accordingly, remembering that democracy's interrelatedness with various forms of pluralism is complex rather than simple seems wise.

86. Eck, *New*, 56-59.

87. D. Bandow, *Beyond Good Intentions: A Biblical View of Politics* (Wheaton, ILL: Crossway, 1988), argues for a pragmatic prudential approach viewing the role of government not to inaugurate God's kingdom but to regulate relations among all aspects of society. As with Eck, helping harmonious relations among the religions, therefore, is a significant duty of all citizens.

88. Eck, *New*, 335.

89. Eck, *New*, 340-66.

90. R. Seager, *The Dawn of Religious Pluralism: Voices from the World's Parliament of Religions, 1893* (Peru, IL: Open Court, 1993, 1999), 10.

91. See Eck, *New*, 152-53, 366-70, and 372.

92. Eck, *New*, 377, 380-83.

93. Eck, *New*, 383. Or, one might add, where religious prejudice is not a deep-seated contributor to the problems between peoples, Flint, *Geopolitics*, 140.

94. Eck, *New*, 385.

95. This section will be in dialog with Madeline Albright, Tony Bair, Jimmy Carter, Mark Juergensmeyer, Charles Kimball, and Condoleezza Rice.

96. As H. Cobban, "Religion and Violence," *JAAR* 73:4 (Dec 2005), 1121-39, argues.

97. Niebuhr suggests three possible approaches to violence fomented by religious pluralism. He rightly rejects authoritarianism (one religion rules) and secularism (ruling religion/s out). A religious solution to this religious problem is preferable but requires great commitment to humility and charity, *Children*, 126-38. Sadly, if the religious solution is not adopted, another, lesser way will take over by default—to the detriment of democracy, 137-38.

98. Juergensmeyer, *Terror*, xii. C. Catherwood reaches similar conclusions in *A Brief History of the Middle East: From Abraham to Arafat* (New York: Carroll & Graf, 2006).

99. Juergensmeyer, *Terror*, 218-24.

100. B.A. McGraw and R. Formicola, ed., *Taking Religious Pluralism Seriously: Spiritual Politics on America's Sacred Ground* (Waco, TX: Baylor University Press, 2005), go even farther, arguing that governments (and citizens) should take not only religion but religious pluralism seriously. And D. Eck argues, in the Foreword to McGraw and Formicola, that religious freedom and the health of democracy are also involved, ix-xv. Cf. Juergensmeyer, *Terror*, 224-29.

101. Juergensmeyer, *Terror,* 233-36.

102. Juergensmeyer, *Terror,* 236-38.

103. Juergensmeyer, *Terror,* 238-40. Of course, there are those who argue for some version of conspiracy theory that do not really think there is a legitimate war on terror at all, especially for the United States. Cf. M. Chossudovsky, *America's "War on Terrorism"* (Quebec: Global Research, 2005). However, Flint, *Geopolitics,* definitely demonstrates global concern for religious terrorism's political implications, 172 and 204. See esp. 154-55 and 157-58 for the unique dilemma of the United States regarding protecting its own borders while projecting its power into others' borders in the context of its War on Terror.

104. Juergensmeyer, *Terror,* 240-43.

105. M. Siddiqui, "When Reconciliation Fails: Global Politics and the Study of Religion," *JAAR* 73:4 (Dec 2005), 1141-53, suggests that only a partnership between religions and political groups is effective for addressing global violence with both religious and political components.

106. Juergensmeyer, *Terror,* 243-49. Jones, *Blood,* also suggests that religion after all, at least non-fundamentalist religion, may be the best counter to the violence of terrorism, 157.

107. Juergensmeyer, *Terror,* 244.

108. E.S. Gaustad and L.E. Schmidt, *The Religious History of America: The Heart of the American Story from Colonial Times to Today* (New York: HarperCollins, rev. ed., 2002), suggest that while North American history certainly suggests that religion is sometimes complicit in violence, frequently religious adherents and their movements have also been "caught up in a much larger web of imperial expansion, conflict, and violence" (424 and 166).

109. Juergensmeyer, *Terror,* 248.

110. Juergensmeyer, *Terror,* 249.

111. Juergensmeyer, *Terror,* 249. M.A. Muqtedar Khan, "American Muslims and the Rediscovery of America's Sacred Ground," McGraw and Formicola, *Seriously,* 127-48, suggests a particular type of religion (not a particular religion per se), i.e., a combination of "democracy, pluralism, and cultural and religious tolerance in action," can "resolve differences peacefully" (141).

112. M. Albright, *The Mighty & the Almighty: Reflections on America, God, and World Affairs* (New York: Harper, 2006).

113. J. Carter, *Palestine: Peace Not Apartheid* (New York: Simon & Schuster, 2006).

114. C. Rice, "America's Confidence in Freedom," *RFIA* 4:2 (Fall 2002), 37-40 (39).

115. J. Rentoul, *Tony Blair: Prime Minister* (London: Time Warner, 2003), 33.

116. Rentoul, *Blair,* 351-52. Yet Blair has also been notoriously private about his own religion too, 202, 236.

117. Rentoul, *Blair,* 348. A. Seldon, *Blair* (Sidney, Australia: Simon & Schuster, 2004, 2005), says Blair saw the world religions as a force for human action and unity and that he affirmed a multi-faith view of salvation, 525, 701.

118. Albright, 3-14. Although in his Introduction to her book, her former boss, President Clinton, affirms the importance of relating to religion in political issues with religious dynamics, affirming a pragmatic and cooperative pluralism. See Albright, ix-xii.

119. However, as B.S. Turner shows in "Sovereignty and Emergency: Political Theology, Islam and American Conservatism," *TCS* 19:4 (2002), 103-19, integrating and relating political and theological concerns is a complex process to say the least. Yet a political philosophy attempting to avoid the religious realm encounters even more com-

plexities, especially in the ethical and moral realm. Cf. B.J. Shaw, "Habermas and Religious Inclusion: Lessons from Kant's Moral Theology," *PT* 27:5 (October 1999), 634-66.

120. Although Netland, *Encountering Religious Pluralism,* warns against so-called tolerance which is only politically correct thinly disguised agnosticism, relativism, and skepticism, 144-46.

121. Charles Kimball, *When Religion Becomes Evil* (New York: HarperSanFrancisco, 2002), 1. Cf. Flint, *Geopolitics,* 132, 206, and 208.

122. Kimball, *When,* 4.

123. Kimball, *When,* 5.

124. Kimball, *When,* 5, 15-40.

125. M. Volf, "Forgiveness, Reconciliation, and Justice: A Christian Contribution to a More Peaceful Social Environment," 27-49, *Forgiveness and Reconciliation,* ed., R. Helmick, S. J., and R.L. Petersen (Radnor, PA: Templeton Foundation, 2001), 27-49, argues that practicing deeply the Christian religion does not lead to violence. Only when practicing it superficially does it tend to violence.

126. Kimball, *When,* 41-185. Cf. Jones, *Blood,* on the psychology of religious violence in relation to feelings of humiliation or shame, a tendency to see the world in black and white, and demonization or dehumanization of other people, 142-70, (157).

127. This section will be in dialogue with the work of Amos Yong, Veli-Matti Kärkkäinen, Frank Macchia, and Tony Richie.

128. Pluralism is itself becoming an increasingly diverse group. E.g., S.M. Heim's *Salvations: Truth and Difference in Religion* (New York: Orbis, 1995, 1997) has the thesis of multiple ultimate ends for religions. He improves on Hick and Knitter, at least in his consistency, but pluralism still falls short.

129. Yong, *Discerning,* 46, 47.

130. A. Yong, *Beyond the Impasse: Toward a Pneumatological Theology of Religions* (Grand Rapids: Baker, 2003), 24, 109-110, 123.

131. V.M. Kärkkäinen, *An Introduction to Theology of Religions: Biblical, Historical, & Contemporary Perspectives* (Downer's Grove: InterVarsity Press, 2003), 25, 171. G. D'Costa, *Christianity and the World Religions: Disputed Questions in the Theology of Religions* (West Sussex, UK: Wiley-Blackwell, 2009), suggests pluralism, further specifically identifying Hick's brand of "unitary pluralism", is "inconsistent with orthodox Christianity and some of it is neo-Christian in its presuppositions" (9). D'Costa also suggests that although Hick's intentions are noble his thought inevitably leads to "a new form of triumphalism and imperialism, albeit of an agnostic type" (10). In fact, for him Hick demonstrates indebtedness to "agnostic liberalism" (35).

132. Kärkkäinen, *Theology of Religions,* 292-93.

133. Kärkkäinen, *Theology of Religions,* 350-51.

134. L.W. Hurtado, in *How on Earth Did Jesus Become a God: Historical Questions about Earliest Devotion to Jesus* (Grand Rapids/Cambridge: Eerdmans, 2005), gives strong historical evidentiary argumentation that Jesus was very early recognizably worshiped as divine—contra speculative hypotheses that later the Nicea of Cicea (325 AD) declared him divine and pushed their position on a reluctant but impotent Church.

135. See Yong, *Beyond,* 24, 109-110, 123.

136. V.M. Kärkkäinen, *Trinity and Religious Pluralism: The Doctrine of the Trinity in Christian Theology of Religions* (Burlington: Ashgate, 2004), 113-17.

137. F.D. Macchia, *Baptized in the Spirit: A Global Pentecostal Theology* (Grand Rapids: Zondervan, 2006), 182-90.

138. Macchia, *Baptized,* 184-85.

139. Yves Congar, *I Believe in the Holy Spirit* 3 vols. trans. David Smith (New York: Seabury, 1983), suggests that Christ and the Spirit and the Church and the Spirit "condition each other" (1:68; 2:211). One might say they are interdependently distinctive. For Congar, *The Word and the Spirit* trans. David Smith (San Francisco: Harper & Row, 1986), the eschatological element in the Spirit's work in bringing to fulfillment and consummation God's promise in Christ still "points emphatically to the tendency towards the kingdom of God which secretly inspires the history of mankind" (132). Therefore, these admittedly distinctive realities yet are not to be divorced.

140. Macchia, *Baptized,* 184.

141. Macchia, *Baptized,* 185-87.

142. Cf. J. Hick, *The Metaphor of God Incarnate Christology in a Pluralistic Age* (Louisville: Westminster John Knox, 1993).

143. Macchia, *Baptized,* 187-89. Cf. H.J. Sharkey, *American Evangelicals in Egypt: Missionary Encounters in an Age of Empire (Jews, Christians, and Muslims from the Ancient to the Modern World* (Princeton, NJ: Princeton University Press, 2008), 104, 130, and 152 on complex power relations sometimes occurring between missionaries and local and foreign entities both religious and political. At times, even benevolent use of power can become paternalistic, 205, and other altruistic agencies' struggle with appropriate power balances as well, 178. At best, power can be an ambiguous and elusive force even for well-meaning missionaries, 4-6.

144. Macchia, *Baptized,* 188. Although perhaps at times more difficult to practice in lands where Christianity is a minority confronted with strong-willed or insecure majority, Sharkey, *American Evangelicals in Egypt,* 124, 132—yet not impossible, 139, even if complicated, 144-45.

145. Macchia, *Baptized,* 190.

146. Although, as A.C. Van Gorder, *Muslim-Christian Relations in Central Asia* (New York: Rutledge, 2008), observes, some Pentecostals view interfaith encounters through a prism similar to the power encounter of Elijah with the false prophets of Baal, especially if they sense involvement from supernatural powers, 110. Even so, hospitality can sometimes be extended or at least offered from religious others toward Christians with effectiveness, 95.

147. More on this in the next chapter, as Pentecostal theologian of religions Amos Yong does indeed utilize the category of hospitality but solidly grounds it in Pentecostal theology.

148. Eck, *New,* 26.

149. Eck, *New,* 80, 142, 222.

150. Cf. Eck, *New,* 294, 355.

151. I.e., in the work here reviewed. In fact, as Director of Harvard's "The Pluralism Project", Eck openly espouses a sophisticated view of religious pluralism. She celebrates religious diversity while she advocates moving beyond it to a pluralism of informed interreligious engagement in the context of continuing commitment to one's own tradition in dialogue with others and consistent with the United States constitutional tradition of religious liberty. See D. Eck, "From Diversity to Pluralism" (revised 2006), at the project website http://www.pluralism.org/pluralism/essays/from_diversity_to_pluralism.php.

152. See Yong's advise on why Pentecostals need and should desire to develop a Pentecostal theology of religions, *Discerning,* 206.

153. Admittedly, Eck's radical liberal views and lifestyle also make it difficult for generally conservative Pentecostals to take her seriously. For example, she is an open proponent of and participant in the so-called "gay" lifestyle and same-sex marriage. Cf. J.

Bigner and R. Steitmatter, *From "Perverts" to "Fab Five": The Media's Changing Depiction of Gay Men and Lesbians* (New York: Taylor & Francis, 2009), 162.

154. E.g., J.R.A. Merrick, "The Spirit of Truth as Agent in False Religions? A Critique of Amos Yong's Pneumatological Theology of Religions with Reference to Current Trends," *TJ* 29:1 (Spring 2008), 107-25 (esp. 108, 123). Cf. V.M. Kärkkäinen, *Pneumatology: The Holy Spirit in Ecumenical, International, and Contextual Perspective* (Grand Rapids: Baker, 2002), 16-19.

155. F.L. Arrington, *Christian Doctrine: A Pentecostal Perspective Volume Two* (Cleveland: Pathway, 1993), 25-26. For Pentecostals, Jesus' uniqueness is nonnegotiable.

156. Arrington, *Doctrine 2,* 25-116.

157. E.g., H. Carpenter, "Tolerance or Irresponsibility: The Problem of Pluralism in Missions," *Advance,* 31:2 (1995), 19, and D.C. Barnes, "Is There a Difference?" *COGE,* (August 12, 1944), 6-7.

158. Cf. R.L. Gallagher, "The Holy Spirit in the World: In Non-Christians, in Creation, and Other Religions," *AJ PS,* 9:1 (2006), 17-33.

159. Cf. V.M. Kärkkäinen, "A Response to Tony Richie's 'Azusa-era Optimism: Bishop J. H. King's Pentecostal Theology of Religions as a Possible Paradigm for Today," *JPT* 15:2 (October 2007), 263-68.

160. E.g., see J.B. Cobb, Jr., *Christ in a Pluralistic Age* (Philadelphia: Westminster, 1975), 97-110.

161. Arrington, *Doctrine 1* (Cleveland: Pathway, 1993), 25-26.

162. Arrington, *Doctrine 1,* 25-83.

163. An early work by P.L. Walker, who later became General Overseer of the Church of God (Cleveland, TN), a classical Pentecostal denomination, declares that "Beyond the text of every other world religion stands the Bible ... an infallible word that is unexcelled ... no other book of any other religion compares to the divinely inspired Word of God." See *Is Christianity the Only Way?* (Cleveland, TN: Pathway, 1975), 149. Cf. M.L. Brown, "Why is Christianity the Only Way? Isn't Buddha as Good as Christ?" *PE* (July 2009), http://pentecostalevangel.ag.org/Life_QA/Religions.cfm#author.

164. A position paper on the official Assemblies of God website, "Non-Christian Religions," repeatedly insists that the inspiration and authority of the Bible and a resultant biblical worldview are the primary means of addressing other religions. See http://www.ag.org/top/Beliefs/gendoct_16_religions.cfm.

165. Cf. C.H. Pinnock, "The Work of the Holy Spirit in Hermeneutics," *JPT* 2 (April 1993), 3-23. See also F.D. Macchia, "Theology, Pentecostal," *NIDPCM,* 1120-41 (1121-23).

166. P. Copan, "Following a Unique Christ in a Pluralistic Society," *EJ* (Fall 2008), http://enrichmentjournal.ag.org/200804/200804_040_Pluralistic.cfm.

167. Arrington, *Doctrine 2,* 159. Cf. L. Sterling, Jr., "Our Only Hope in a Pluralistic World," *COGE* (December 2007), 8-9.

168. G.P. Duffield and N.M. Van Cleave, *Foundations of Pentecostal Theology* (Los Angeles: L.I.F.E. Bible College, 1983, 1987), 206-60.

169. Duffield, *Foundations,* 550-56. Cf. Arrington, *Doctrine 2,* 117-251.

170. Kärkkäinen, *Pneumatology,* 92-94.

171. See R.H. Gause, "Introduction," *Living in the Spirit: The Way of Salvation* (Cleveland: Pathway, 1980).

172. A. Orr-Ewing, "Truth or Intolerant? Are All Beliefs Equally Valid?" *EJ* (Fall 2008), http://enrichmentjournal.ag.org/200804/200804_040_tolerance_sb.cfm.

173. P. Copan, *"True for You, But Not for Me" Overcoming Objections to Christian Faith* (Bloomington, Minnesota: Bethany House, 2009), 26-31.

174. Cf. S.J. Land, *Pentecostal Spirituality: A Passion for the Kingdom* (Sheffield: Sheffield Academic Press, 1993).

175. Duffield, *Foundations,* 430, 433. Cf. D. Fink, "Critics of Conversion" (September 22, 2003), on the website of the activist group, Institute for Global Engagement, at http://www.globalengage.org/issues/articles/freedom/652-critics-of-conversion.

176. Duffield, *Foundations,* 417-20. F.L. Arrington, *Christian Doctrine: A Pentecostal Perspective: Volume Three* (Cleveland: Pathway, 1993), 166.

177. Arrington, *Doctrine 3,* 187-88. Interestingly, cf. R. Bauckham, *The Theology of Jürgen Moltmann* (Edinburgh: T & T Clark, 1996), 13-14; cf. 126.

178. See A. Lord, "Mission Eschatology: A Framework for Mission in the Spirit," *JPT* 11 (1997), 111-23, and "The Moltmann-Pentecostal Dialogue: Implications for Mission," *JPT* 11:2 (2003), 271-87; J. Sepulveda, "Reflections on the Pentecostal Contribution to the Mission of the Church in Latin America," *JPT* 1 (1992), 93-108.

179. Arrington, *Doctrine 3,* 197-99. Cf. Culpepper, *The Great Commission,* 190-91. J.R. Williams, *Renewal Theology: Systematic Theology from a Charismatic Perspective* (*RT*), three volumes in one (Grand Rapids: Zondervan, 1996), says the Church "stands constantly under the Great Commission of the risen Christ" 3:133.

180. See S.M. Horton, *What the Bible Says About the Holy Spirit* (Springfield, MO: Gospel Publishing House, 1992), 135-37. Cf. Arrington, *Doctrine 2,* 209-10. Arrington cites Acts 3:19 in support.

181. R.H. Hughes, *Church of God Distinctives* (Cleveland: Pathway, 1968, 1989), 40-62, J. Sims, *Power with Purpose: The Holy Spirit in Historical and Contemporary Perspective* (Cleveland: Pathway, 1984), 169-93, and F.J. May, *The Book of Acts & Church Growth: Growth Through the Power of God's Holy Spirit* (Cleveland: Pathway, 1990), 20-22.

182. This moral imperative seems to be the least that can be inferred from the writings of Juergensmeyer, Kimball, and Küng referenced above.

183. J.W. Adams, "Hebrews," *FLBCNT*, eds., F.L. Arrington & R. Stronstad (Grand Rapids: Zondervan, 1999), 1295-1399, argues that this text suggests the foundational importance of practical holiness in the Christian life, but focuses the pursuit of peace primarily within the Christian community, nonetheless indicative of "an objective reality tied to Christ and his redemptive death" "which makes possible harmony and solidarity in Christian community", 1382-83 (1383). However, D. Bowdle, the Pentecostal editor of C.J. Ellicott, *Ellicott's Bible Commentary in One Volume* (Grand Rapids: Zondervan, 1971, 1980), does not agree, but argues for a general charge to peace, in a context of religious persecution, without a compromise of Christian holiness, 1146. *Ellicott's* also connects Hebrews 12:14 to the beatitude of Jesus in Matthew 5:8. Similarly, D.A. Hagner, *NIBC: Hebrews* (Peabody: Hendrickson, 1983, 1990), notes that this verse integrates the goal of holiness/sanctification (*hagiasmos*) and peace with the eschatological vision, 221. I.H. Marshall, *New Testament Theology: Many Witnesses, One Gospel* (Downer's Grove: InterVarsity Press, 2004), reminds that Hebrews 12:14 occurs in a pericope concerned to confront the possibility of apostasy, 619.

184. As recorded in *The Weekly Evangel,* August 4, 1917, 6, and quoted by E. Blumhofer, *The Assemblies of God: A Chapter in the Story of American Pentecostalism* (Springfield, MO: 1989), 352-53. Cf. J. Shuman, "Pentecost and the End of Patriotism: A Call for the Restoration of Pacifism Among Pentecostal Christians," *JPT* 9 (1996), 70-96 (esp. 75-76).

185. In fact, some Pentecostals at least are convinced that their belief and practice is best true to its tradition when expressed through actively promoting justice, peace, and

reconciliation. E.g., see the Pentecostal Charismatic Peace Fellowship at http://www.pcpf.org/.

186. A. Anderson, *An Introduction to Global Pentecostalism: Global Charismatic Christianity* (Cambridge: Cambridge University Press, 2004), 15, 282-83.

187. Anderson, *Introduction,* 283. Tension with others has included not only non-Christian religions, but even other Christian expressions as well. See C.M. Robeck, Jr., "World Council of Churches," *NIDPCM,* 1213-17.

Chapter 2

Current State of Pentecostal Theology of Religions

Introduction

The previous chapter has set the pace for what follows it by establishing the reality and ideology of religious pluralism as a factor with which Pentecostals, along with other Christians, must deal forthrightly. The present chapter will survey contemporary Pentecostal theology of religions with a view toward assessing progress on preparedness for dealing with radical religious pluralism. First, it will look briefly at the foundational background for Pentecostal theology of religions in historic Christianity with special attention to its Evangelical/ Wesleyan precedents and partners. Second, it will look at major developments in Pentecostal theology of religions through leading proponents in the newly forming field, including an attempt to assess critically where Pentecostal theology of religions is at present and what may help it move forward into the future. Finally, it articulates a bold example of an approach for moving into the future intentionally and distinctively Pentecostal.

Foundational Orientation[1]

A Diverse Family

Of all contemporary Christian movements, Pentecostalism has some of the most diverse roots and branches. For example, on its official website the Church of God (Cleveland, TN), one of oldest and largest Classical Pentecostal denominations, describes itself today as Christian, Foundational, Protestant, Evangelical, Pentecostal, Charismatic, and Organized, with specific commitments to Ministry and Laity, Education, being a Caring Church, Social Concerns, Ministry to the Military, and World Missions.[2] Furthermore, although not explicitly mentioned in this list, clearly present in the official denominational history and Declaration of Faith, is its profound Wesleyan-Holiness heritage.[3] Comparison with the "16 Fundamental Truths" of the Assemblies of God, globally the largest

43

of Classical Pentecostal denominations, with international offices in Springfield, MO, reveals less reliance on Wesley but still represents the same general diversity of history, spirituality, and theology.[4] Other Pentecostal denominations share the same general diversity in history, spirituality, and theology while retaining more of the intentional Wesleyan-Holiness emphasis.[5]

As international Pentecostal historical and theological scholar Allan Anderson suggests, at the global level it becomes even more evident that identifying and describing Pentecostals and Pentecostalism is an adventure in diversity.[6] Anderson goes so far as to say that, "The Pentecostal experience of the power of the Spirit was the reason for an unprecedented flexibility on the part of its emissaries to the various cultures to which they took the Pentecostal message."[7] Noting especially the "unprecedented" nature of the "flexibility" is important. While all Christian movements may have more or less mixed contributions to their distinctive identities and momentum as movements, Pentecostalism seems to take these tendencies to unparalleled levels. A consistent though not controlling influence of North American Pentecostalism on global Pentecostalism contributes to an underlying unity with a localized diversity. Anderson thus speaks of "Pentecostalism" (singular) and "Pentecostalisms" (plural).[8]

Apparently, remembering the diverse constitution and contexts of the movement is mandatory for making sense of it. Nonetheless, chapter one of this study has already outlined that Wesleyan and Evangelical Christianity has had and still has special significance for Pentecostals. Accordingly, due to their clear preponderance of influence in forming Pentecostal identity, this study gives attention to the general historical setting of Christian theology of religions, while focusing on Wesleyan and Evangelical roots of a Pentecostal of religions before exploring how its branches grow into a specifically Pentecostal theology of religions.[9]

General Christian Tradition

Pentecostal theology of religions should first be set in the context of historic Christianity. A historical survey by Mark Noll shows that relations with other religions often have been a significant component during decisive turning points in Church history for centuries. For one thing, Judaism has exerted important and ongoing influence on Christianity, in spite of the fact that later, when in positions of power, the offspring faith has sometimes persecuted or oppressed its parent.[10] Much of Christianity's early doctrinal and creedal development is a translation of inherited Jewish concepts and terminology into those of its contemporary setting in classical Greco-Roman culture.[11] Nonetheless, Martin Luther actually published harsh denunciations and demands for violent expulsion and oppression of Jews in Germany, including confiscation of property, when he thought them a threat to Christianity—arguably precipitating a tragic prelude to and precedent for the Holocaust.[12]

Laurie Guy describes the relationship between Christianity and Judaism as characterized by complexity and ambiguity arising out of both continuity and discontinuity and sometimes degenerating into hostility.[13] In establishing a distinct Christian identity, some early Church leaders countered harmonization efforts and syncretistic systems by sharply distancing Christianity from Judaism.[14] Nevertheless, the fact that Christianity arose out of a Jewish matrix left an indelible mark upon its faith and practice, especially in its liturgy.[15]

According to Noll, quarrelling and division among North African Christians weakened Christianity and prepared the way for triumph of Islam.[16] After the seventh century, the history of Christianity cannot be fully understood apart from its interaction with or reaction to Islam.[17] The spread of Islam had an important impact on Christianity's transition from "a Mediterranean, eastern-oriented faith to an expressly European, northward looking form of religion."[18] The Crusades may tell us more about the sad internal state of Christendom at the time than anything else. Yet they have nonetheless left a horrific legacy to hurdle in relations between not only Christians and Muslims but also between Western and Eastern Christians (after all, in the Fourth Crusade the Christian capital of Constantinople was brutally plundered and pillaged too).[19]

More recently, Philip Jenkins calls Christianity and Islam "divided giants" and suggests changing balances of historical and geographical influence and presence have tended to contribute to increasing aggression in their relations.[20] Furthermore, the issue of conversions is paramount as Christians have increasingly and effectively conducted evangelism and missions in previously Muslim dominated areas, worrying many Muslims regarding the future religious landscape of their descendants.[21] Indeed, Marty suggests Christian missionary impulse has been a chief factor in many historical encounters between different religions, though American Christian sympathy for interfaith dialogue surged subsequent to World War II, especially with Jews.[22]

However, Christian missions have always had to face the fact of other religions. Many have chosen to do so in creative ways. Accordingly, Thomas Aquinas wrote apologetics for Muslims and St Francis engaged in cross-cultural evangelism.[23] Lay Franciscan Raymond Lull devised and carried out a full-fledged mission strategy among Muslims that included learning Arabic.[24] German pietists also led peaceful evangelism among Jews and Muslims, vis-à-vis former violent efforts, in the seventeenth and eighteenth centuries.[25] In the nineteenth century, indigenous Anglican missionary Samuel Ajayi Crowther stressed, in dealing with Muslims, common ground between the Koran and the Bible. Regarding attitudes toward traditional African (Yoruba) religion, he allowed a tolerant attitude toward converts among Christians.[26]

At times Christians have had a complex and controversial history of dealing with other religions as missionaries in foreign lands. For example, effective Jesuit missionary endeavors in sixteenth century Japan under the leadership of Francis Xavier sparked intense debate in Rome and Europe about proper cross-cultural evangelism techniques when he freely adapted to Japanese society in order to gain a hearing for the gospel.[27] That debate intensified (and continued for centuries) when Jesuit missionary, Matteo Ricci (1552-1610), labored intentionally to adapt to Chinese culture, even to find common ground between Christianity and Confucianism and to suggest certain aspects of Chinese ancestor veneration were not inimical to authentic Christianity.[28] This "Chinese Rites" controversy eventually helped Jesuit (and later Protestant) missionaries to hammer out a helpful cross-cultural strategy and theology for evangelism. Jesuit Jean de Brébeuf (1593-1649) very successfully spearheaded missions among the Huron Indians employing the same policy.[29]

Moreover, Noll notes that historically even Pentecostals have been involved, and have sometimes had a distinctively open-ended approach to Christian missions and contact with other religions.[30] African Zionism (early twentieth century), influenced by Andrew Murray and the charismatic restorationism of Alexander Dowie (pre/proto-Pentecostals), capitalized on aspects of traditional African religion—exorcisms of demons, ecstatic dance, and centrality of prophet-healers, as well as elaborate purification and initiation rites—put into service of a biblical and Christ-centered Pentecostal form of Christianity.[31] Noll says, "The contribution of the early Pentecostal, or Pentecostal-leaning, missionaries was critical in providing Western forms of the faith that bridged the gap to the world of African primal religions".[32]

A point of the preceding is that when Pentecostals attempt to generate creative contact with adherents of other religions they are building on solid historical ground. Accordingly, Warrington notes that today some Pentecostal scholars are beginning to call for dialogue with those of other religions.[33] More will be said about Pentecostal developments in this area in a subsequent chapter. For the time being, note that it is historically consistent that, as Warrington discusses, in Pentecostalism, though traditionally exclusivist concerning Christ, a minority are opening up to the possibility of the Spirit's work through Christ beyond the borders of the institutional Church.[34] As the subsequent section shows, more recently, the Evangelical movement has also increasingly involved itself in this effort.

The Evangelical Element[35]

As indicated earlier, Evangelicalism has exerted immense influence on Pentecostals. This influence includes theology of religions. British theologian Sir Norman Anderson has been a foundational Evangelical thinker on theology of religions.[36] His *Christianity and World Religions* has had an enormous impact on many in the movement in the United States.[37] Noting increasing interest in non-Christian religions in the West, Anderson cites several possible reasons in explanation. Improved communications with other lands, questioning of role of the West in lives of non-Western peoples, increased availability of information on popular level, and greater numbers of adherents of other religions now residing in the West are part of the explanation. Furthermore, growing disillusionment with intellectual foundations of Western society, dissatisfaction with an affluent and technologically sophisticated society, revolt against pace of life in West, barrenness of intellectual humanism, and desire to make religious education more interesting and relevant, figure into the fascination with other faiths.[38] He distrusts any syncretism that tends to downplay the importance of the historicity of Christ's incarnation, atonement, and resurrection.[39]

Anderson argues that no religion, including Christianity, is salvific, but that Christ is the only Savior.[40] The only ones actually excluded by Christianity's claims to uniqueness of Christ, however, are "those who with open eyes persist in rejecting".[41] Anderson boldly raises the possibility that,

> where the 'God of all grace' has been at work by his Spirit in the hearts of individuals from other religious backgrounds, revealing to them something of their sin and need and enabling them (as he alone can) to throw themselves on his mercy, they too may profit from this 'specific remedy' for man's spiritual sickness and this 'unique historic deed' which still stands as 'the turning point of history', but about which they have never had the opportunity to hear.[42]

Yet Anderson is discriminating to a high degree.[43] He sees John Hick as an example of compromising pluralism,[44] Hans Küng is interesting but often equivocal,[45] but Lesslie Newbigin (with expansive experience working among peoples of other religions) has a balanced posture of affirming that some in other religions may authentically experience communion with God to some extent but salvation is only and always by and through Jesus Christ.[46] He notes that mysticism often transcends the boundaries of religions but suggests some of this transcendence is due to such factors as shared philosophical background or the commonality of human nature in the subconscious realm of experience. He cautiously admits, however, that in some sense some mystics from various traditions may be recounting a shared encounter with the same reality of God that is genuine.[47]

Anderson adamantly asserts the uniqueness of Christ—in all its particularity and historicity—and criticizes Paul Tillich for sacrificing (or negating) these tenets.[48] He also criticizes the position of John Hick, saying it "with respect, seems to be a somewhat strange amalgam of heterogeneous assertions—some obviously true, some misleading, or mutually inconsistent, and some, in my view, totally unacceptable".[49] Christians must not suggest we have anything of ourselves to offer; that would be "intolerably arrogant". What we "dare to share" is what Another has graciously given to us.[50] He agrees with Hick that the teaching of Christian uniqueness implies that only through Christ can God be adequately known (citing Acts 4:12) but disagrees that this then implies that all beyond the sphere of Judeo-Christian faith are thereby excluded from "the sphere of salvation".[51]

Furthermore, Anderson incisively argues against an evolutionary pattern of religious development based on the co-existence of magic and religion and evidences of early or primitive monotheism rather than a straight line from polytheism to monotheism.[52] Yet he argues that, "the Bible as a whole represents a progressive, not a contradictory, revelation".[53] He admits that "there are, indeed, parallels to some aspects of Christian doctrine in a number of different religions," but argues "that the core and essence of the Christian faith is *sui generic*, for it is directly derived from, and essentially dependent on, the unique event to which it always looks back".[54]

Nevertheless, the uniqueness of the historical event that gave rise to Christian faith does not mean that, "God has revealed himself in no other way and at no other time."[55] Rather, Christian uniqueness is "intended to signify that the historical event on which Christianity is founded is itself without parallel, as is also—in its fullness and essential nature—the salvation which it offers and the self-disclosure of God which it enshrines".[56] Biblical references (e.g., John 10:8; 14:6; Matt 11:27; 1 John 2:23; Acts 4:12) clearly suggest that "it is *only* through Christ that any man can come to a personal knowledge of (and fellowship with) God, and *only* through his life, death and resurrection that any man can come to an experience of salvation".[57]

However, Scripture also teaches that pre-Christian Jews before the Incarnation of the eternal Christ enjoyed forgiveness and experienced communion with God through Christ (Rom 4:7f; 3:25; cf. Heb. 9:15). They had a shadow-like experience of which Christianity is the substance. Of course significant is that many pious OT characters were also non-Jews.[58] Anderson argues, quoting Scripture and Calvin, that those who have never heard the gospel are in much the same state as OT Jews, provided they positively receive the extraordinary revelation of God (dreams, vision, direct communication, as well as nature or conscience) other than only the ordinary (preaching/Word). He adamantly insists that a key point is that they come to the realization of their own sinfulness and cast themselves on the mercy of God, as they understand it; their righteousness cannot save them in any sense, only divine grace.[59] Their piety and morality, however, may be evidence of their inner condition. They nonetheless still need to hear and heed the gospel.[60]

Anderson warns against dogmatizing about the soteriological fate of individuals in other religions, recommending leaving that matter finally to a faithful Creator.[61] Regarding Jews since the advent of Christ, he argues that although the majority of Jews have probably heard of Christ their own traditional teaching and the history of Christian persecution often obscure the authentic gospel so that they may not be said to have really rejected Christ. They may be considered in the same state as pre-Christian OT Jews. Others, because of family and cultural pressures or even persecution, are perhaps secret disciples who, though losing much of the spiritual richness of in the fullness of Christian living, may not be considered non-Christian. Tragically, some Jews do willingly reject Christ and will be judged and lost for it if they do not repent. Finally, some Jews openly embrace Christ, considering themselves "completed Jews", and are indeed Christians.[62]

Anderson argues that the teaching, based on the NT, that only a few may be saved is not as explicit as at first seems obvious. First, it may refer to relative numbers not total numbers. Second, the implicit purpose of such statements seems to be motivation toward deeper discipleship. Finally, the redemptive purpose of God seems to have a corporate context, not merely individual application. Those who persist in individual rebellion are those who are lost.[63] Therefore, universalism certainly is ruled out but not universality. Anderson describes a range of common Christian attitudes toward non-Christian religions. There is religion that is a *preparatio evangelica*, with some genuine good or truth from original or general revelation though mixed more or less with falsehood, imperfection. Next is religion entirely of the Devil, demonic deception. In addition, there is religion that is the result of human aspirations for God. Christianity is the nearest approximation to highest truth as the only actual revealed religion. Anderson argues some accuracy exists in each but none is absolute.[64]

Increasingly, Evangelical works are addressing theology of religions as part of a comprehensive viewpoint. On the one hand, this enlarged (and enhanced) venue is partly due to non-Western Christian theological participation and contribution. For instance, in a book about Christian eschatology, Roland Chia, heavily informed by his Southeast Asian context, directly interacts with other religions.[65] Chia accepts an inclusive soteriology, though he bluntly and completely rejects radical religious pluralism (e.g., John Hick and Stanley Samartha) as "fundamentally flawed".[66] For another instance, James Nkansah-Obrempong suggests that African primal religions and cultural heritage have been misunderstood by Western missionaries, and ought to have been better utilized as part of a creative and constructive theological enterprise, though not without the ability to be self-critical.[67] He expresses explicit disappointment with Evangelicals for failing to deal with African religions positively, and blames it on an over-inflated fear of syncretism. Nevertheless, he sees "ethnic and religious pluralism" as among the greatest challenges for African Christianity.[68]

On the other hand, Evangelicals are certainly not unanimous regarding recent developments on theology of religions. Ravi Zacharias, though gracious, feels compelled to defend the absolute claims of the Christian message in a more exclusive manner.[69] Ramesh Richard takes an even harder line, openly insisting on everlasting Hell for those who have not personally heard the gospel message.[70] Others, like Kevin Daugherty, just seem skeptical of the whole theology of religions/interreligious relations issue.[71] Harold Netland gives one of the better discussions of Evangelical alternatives to outright inclusivism. He divides exclusivism into a harsher "restrictivism" camp and a milder one "particularism" and adopts the latter.[72] He thus still manages respect and appreciation for other religions, and a sort of agnosticism toward the possible salvation of their adherents or the unevangelized. He also has an excellent treatment relating dialogue and apologetics in Christian missions among non-Christian religions.[73]

A great deal of diversity and complexity actually exists among Evangelicals on theology of religions. Unfortunately, most of the attention focuses on the fate of the unevangelized. Admittedly, the soteriological question is an immensely important part of the discussion. However, as suggested below, it should not entirely overshadow all other issues. Nevertheless, Greg Boyd and Paul Eddy have helpfully clarified and summarized the main perspectives. They list these: no other name (the restrictivist view), God does all he can do (the universal opportunity view), hope beyond the grave (the postmortem evangelism view), and God has not left himself without a witness (the inclusivist view).[74] The wide range of options is evident.[75] This study argues that Pentecostals, though undeniably involved in and informed by the overall Evangelical discussion, ought to look specifically to their own spiritual and theological origins for guidance on developing and articulating their own views. These roots include John Wesley and those who appropriate his ideas. Understood is that many, if not most, Wesleyans are also Evangelicals. Separate consideration merely highlights their distinctive contribution.[76]

The Wesleyan Way[77]

The work of John and Charles Wesley was a significant turning point in Christian history, greatly influencing later Protestantism and Evangelicalism.[78] In particular, John Wesley was an important predecessor to Pentecostalism, and Charles Fox Parham, identified by some as the founder of the modern Pentecostal movement, was an early Wesleyan proponent of the Pentecostal Revival which itself became one of the most decisive turning points in recent Christian history.[79] Much of Wesley's uniqueness (like later Pentecostals) is traceable to his authentic integration of historic Christianity with innovative ideas and measures or practices. He insisted on testing the reality of faith through experience rather than traditional conformity; examined practical and utilitarian aspects of faith and not merely inherited truths; and, made individual decision more prominent than that which previous generations only handed down.[80] Owing to overt dependence on Wesley, these and other tendencies are also commonly characteristic of Classical Pentecostals.

Laurence Wood has superbly studied the decisive influence of John Wesley himself and through his talented lieutenant John Fletcher on subsequent Holiness-Pentecostal movements. He further asserts the relevance of Wesley/Fletcher for the contemporary ecumenical movement as well.[81] The dynamic, perfectionist, and transformational pneumatological soteriology of Wesley and his successors continue to have heavy influence on Pentecostals to the present. Even among less overtly Wesleyan Pentecostals, views on Spirit baptism and Christian spirituality owe a great deal still to the Wesleyan way. As Hollis Gause and Steve Land show, among distinctively Wesleyan Pentecostals the influence is direct and determinative.[82] The present study arises out of this denominational and theological tradition.

Less well known but increasingly relevant is Wesley's theology of religions with its implications for Pentecostal Christians.[83] British Methodist leader and scholar G. Howard Mellor well captures the nuanced nature of Wesley's response to the reality of religious pluralism in his own day. Mellor suggests, "Wesley had a very suitable stance for his theology and evangelism in a plural world," which he described as "a mixture of openness toward people and certainty of message." Wesley's sophistication in this area, however, defies easy classification. Mellor summarizes Wesley thus:

> [H]e is at the interface of the exclusivist and inclusivist position. His Christology is exclusivist, saving faith is in Christ; but his exclusivism is not myopic. His openness to others and the pursuit of truth, his view that God would judge by the light that people had received, all move toward the inclusivist position. To place him simply in this latter category would be an injustice to his doctrine of regeneration and saving faith. Therefore, I suggest he is at the interface of the two.[84]

Mellor's deft juxtaposition of general broadmindedness with pneumatological soteriology indicates one of the reasons Pentecostals may find Wesley's way of addressing pluralism attractive as an option for themselves.

Based on original research, my post-September 11 study of Wesley's attitude toward Islam also illustrates Wesley's overall theology of religions.[85] I found that Wesley frequently compared Muslim and other religions' life and thought with Christians. Wesley was usually honest and humble in these comparisons, noting both negative and positive characteristics. He would however, use other religions as a polemical weapon to spur Christians to action. His comments show that he went to some extent to analyze Islam in order to understand it accurately, even reading the Koran and biographies of Mohammed and studies of Islamic history and culture. Later in life, Wesley carefully articulated more what earlier chapters of the present study identified as an inclusive theological-soteriological framework of faith.[86]

John Wesley always continued to insist on the uniqueness and necessity of the scriptural revelation of God in Christ and Christ's redemptive work. Yet he also argued that God's just and merciful providence excludes no one but encompasses even the unevangelized and devout of non-Christian religions. He posited differing degrees of faith appropriate to Heathen, Muslims, and Jews as well as Christians. According to Wesley, God reveals himself through general revelation and through human conscience to those who do not have or have not authentically heard his special revelation. Finally, God will judge everyone only according to their faithfulness to walk in the light they have.[87]

Wesley based his inclusive theology of religions on his study of the Scriptures, patristic writers, and through interaction with mentors and peers. The story of the Magi from the East (Matt 2:1-2) and the testimony of Psalm 19 were important for him regarding God's revelatory reach beyond Israel or Judaism. The Acts accounts of generous encounters between Peter and the Roman centurion Cornelius and Paul and the Athenians seem especially significant for Wesley.[88] He also frequently quotes Psalm 145:9 and John 1:9 in support of God's universal benevolence and self-disclosure. He thought Romans 1:19-21 and 2:12-16 provide a firm exegetical basis for Christian inclusivism. His interpretation of Galatians 4:1-6 distinguished between the faith of a "servant" and of a "son" in substantiation of his conviction on differing degrees of faith. Wesley also resonated with important Church Fathers such as Justin Martyr and Clement of Alexandria as well as more contemporary thinkers such as James Arminius and John Fletcher with inclusive theologies.[89] As part of his inclusivist outlook, Wesley always insisted on the importance of evangelism and witness among other religions, though he felt a holy life more important than only words.[90]

I conclude that Wesley demonstrates a theology of religions characterized by balance, understanding, honesty and humility, strong foundations in scripture and theology, reliance on the righteousness of divine providence, a broad and deep view of the nature of God and of salvation, and the continuing importance of Christian evangelism and witness in holy words and deeds.[91] For Wesley, divine providence regarding the unevangelized or other religions centers in his concern for the just character of God. Above all, Wesley maintained that God is fair and just to everyone.[92]

John Wesley was no religious pluralist. Although John Cobb gives a fair evaluation of Wesley's inclusive theology of religions, he honestly admits that he breaks sharply with Wesley when he pushes into pluralism.[93] Runyon is much closer to Wesley when he affirms tolerance toward other religions based on the limits of religious language, though with communicative sufficiency, and, significantly, the activity of the Holy Spirit through prevenient grace. Above all, he affirms that Wesley's bases his combination of openness to others and staunch Christian conviction on divine love.[94]

Well within the Wesleyan tradition, Kenneth Collins notes that Christians defining "spirituality" today need enough breadth and inclusiveness to recognize "the spiritualities of Jews, Muslims, Buddhists, agnostics and others" and enough specificity to "show the distinct place that Christian insight, experience, and teaching play in this larger arena.".[95] Yet later he adds that Christian spirituality "in contradistinction to other kinds, is not simply the attempt to encounter an amorphous personal God, but represents, more specifically, the revelation of God *in Jesus Christ* through the Holy Spirit."[96] Here Wesley's spirit shines forth in the admittedly difficult, delicate, but dynamic both/and affirmation of Christ's uniqueness and necessity and Christian openness to others. The best in Wesleyan tradition follows suit.[97] Pentecostals will do well to endeavor to rise to that serious challenge.

Specific Construction[98]

Classical Pentecostal "Exclusivism"

One of the oft repeated errors regarding Pentecostalism (frequently even by Pentecostals!) is an assumption that the movement is monolithic.[99] It is not, and its theology of religions reflects this diversity as well.[100] As generally noted in the previous chapter, but more specifically here as used in the context of the discipline of the theology of religions, "exclusivism" reflects a closed attitude, positing that a conscious personal response to the preached gospel is not only normative but also necessary for salvation. Typically, it argues that there is no salvation outside the Church or apart from the Church's proclamation of the gospel. On the other end of the spectrum, "pluralism" essentially equates all religions while denying superiority to any. Typically, it focuses at the more general level of God or "ultimate reality" rather than on the particularity of Christ (or Buddha or Mohammed, etc.). The more moderating position, "inclusivism," is a christocentric and pneumatic openness regarding the present state and eternal fate of the unevangelized or adherents of other religions. It affirms salvation ultimately only of and by Christ, even as it allows for the possibility that the unevangelized or adherents of other faiths may experience salvation according to the mysterious grace and mercy of God. Admittedly, a great deal of ambiguity and overlap exists among these broad categories. However, each has a fundamentally different view of religious others.[101]

Usually Pentecostals are assumed to be exclusivists, and indeed there is a track record to that effect.[102] At one level, Pentecostal exclusivism connects to its understanding of the Great Commission. The call to go into the world and proclaim the gospel to everyone has led them to view religious others narrowly, that is, primarily as objects of evangelism. Hence, Pentecostals have asserted that the Spirit's saving work is limited to the Church, and it is precisely as members of the Church allow themselves to be used by the Spirit to witness to their non-Christian neighbors, even those of other religions, that salvation is also made available to the world.[103] Insofar as Pentecostals think evangelism mandate and inclusivist openness to the possibility of the salvation of the unevangelized (not to mention pluralism) are incompatible, their ardent evangelistic orientation requires, they often assume, that they must be exclusivists.[104]

Another way to understand Pentecostal exclusivism is to note their historical connections with Fundamentalism and conservative Evangelicalism. Historic Pentecostal closed-mindedness may be a remnant of their landing on the fundamentalist side of the fundamentalist-liberal (or modernist) divide during the first quarter of the twentieth century, an excessive literalist approach to biblical hermeneutics, and an overall suspicion toward ecumenism in general.[105] Since the early Pentecostals were shunned on both the left and the right —by liberals because of Pentecostalism's uncultured and unsophisticated spirituality, and by fundamentalists because of their charismatic enthusiasm and experientialism[106]—Pentecostals have imbibed a sectarian mentality, almost as if for reasons of self-preservation. This rejection has produced a long history of ecumenical isolationism vis-à-vis the other churches as well as a theological exclusivism vis-à-vis other religions. Moreover, since Pentecostals have not given serious thought to developing a formal theology of religions of their own until very recently, they have historically not felt the need to go beyond the exclusivism they shared with many Evangelicals (and all Fundamentalists) regarding the religions.

Of course, there is also the gloomy possibility that Pentecostals are just exclusivists by nature, and without further evidence, deciding is difficult. Fortunately, as the following suggests, there is further evidence for investigation.

Pentecostal-Charismatic "Inclusivism"

Formative Influences.[107] Several non-Pentecostal influences on Pentecostalism have been evident, including the general Christian tradition, both Catholic and Protestant, and Evangelical and Wesleyan movements.[108] Two individual major theologians who continue to influence Classical Pentecostals heavily are Jürgen Moltmann and Clark Pinnock. Both are creative and innovative thinkers and consequently difficult to categorize specifically. Yet they have both associated and collaborated with Pentecostals extensively. Their strong sense of pneumatology brings them into conversation with Pentecostals. This conversation spills over into theology of religions in various ways.

Moltmann's pneumatologically focal text, *The Church in the Power of the Spirit,* insists that "Because of its foundation in Christ and its existence for the future of the kingdom of God, the church is what it truly is and what it can do, in the *presence and power of the Holy Spirit.*[109] It also informs readers that Moltmann has learned to appreciate "the charismatic experiences" of some of the churches.[110] Significantly, Moltmann explains that this pneumatological treatise is indicative of his theological arrival "at Pentecost and the sending of the Spirit," after having started at Easter and travelled by way of Good Friday.[111] Finally, Moltmann remarks that "Both perspectives would be incomplete if 'the sending of the Spirit', its messianic history and the charismatic power of its church were not added."[112] Notably, in this intentionally pneumatological text Moltmann chooses to address extensively hopeful relationships of the Church with Israel and with world religions.[113] Not surprisingly, Currie succinctly summarizes Moltmann's theological development as climactic movement toward Pentecost.[114]

Moltmann's entire agenda is a radically robust theology of hope in which he systematically rethinks theology in terms of divine promise and eschatological future.[115] He vows to assess "the breadth of the horizon of hope opened up through Christ for Christianity".[116] Not surprisingly, therefore, Moltmann insists eschatological hope is not merely for Christians, but "if it is to be the eschatology of the all-embracing kingdom, it must also be unfolded as the eschatology of Israel, of the religions, of human social systems and of nature."[117] As for the religions, Christianity's dialogical relationship with them must flow out of the depths of its own unique nature, specifically its "abiding origins in Israel, it permanent orientation to Israel's hope,"[118] and its "resulting special vocation to prepare the way of the coming kingdom in history".[119] The new increasing interdependent and globally shifting world situation brings indigenous Christianity into dialogue, encounter, and cooperation with indigenous religions in a new and living way not propelled by power majorities.[120] In addition to the Church's missionary goal to evangelize and convert, another goal of qualitatively enhancing life for others also exists and is involved.[121] Moltmann notes that "Qualitative mission takes place in dialogue."[122]

In qualitative missionary dialogue with other religions Christianity[123] will need to set aside prejudices such as the absolutism of the Church,[124] the absolutism of faith,[125] and the relativism of the Enlightenment.[126] Moltmann recommends considering the natural and supernatural model of Christianity and the religions as "the supernatural truth of natural truths" enabling Christianity to affirm its own supernatural truth while being open to the natural truth of others and to integrate their natural goodness and truth according to its own supernatural "yardstick of the absolute self-manifestation of God."[127] Christianity can accordingly become "the critical catalyst" in the world of religions by its mere presence and performance.[128] Moltmann insists that Christianity must proceed to the point of acquiring and articulating its own profile in the context of dialogue with others and that such dialogue is a sign of hope for all.[129] Accordingly, genuine dialogue will be open to mutual benefits.[130]

Interestingly for pneumatology-minded Pentecostals, Moltmann suggests, which he argues is contra syncretism, "the charismatic quickening of different religious gifts, powers, and potentialities for the kingdom of God and the liberation of men."[131] He does not, however, have in mind "a religious mixture" but a "charismatic activation of cultural and religious forces in the interests of the messianic future" which "looks forward."[132] He argues that cultures and religions can be "charismatically absorbed and changed in the power of the Spirit" and that though they will not be "ecclesiastical" or "Christianized" in the process, they will be given "a messianic direction towards the kingdom."[133]

Richard Bauckham's extensive study of Jürgen Moltmann's thought includes references to his views regarding world religions. Particularly important for

Bauckham is Moltmann's ecclesiology.[134] He points out that for Moltmann, the "church does not exist in, of or for itself, but only in relationship and can only be understood in its relationships", including its "open and critical relationship with other realities, its partners in history, notably Israel, the other world religions, and the secular order" [135]. Israel, however, enjoys a special partnership with Christianity in this schema, though all religions, and indeed, all the world, are moving toward the eschatological and messianic Kingdom of Jesus Christ.[136] Moltmann supposes that these dialogue partners will never become the Church, that the Church represents a complementary part of a whole, but Bauckham challenges him on this a bit, agreeing with Moltmann's openness but arguing that real reciprocity may include these others coming to faith in Jesus as the Messiah. Bauckham here seems to be guarding against limitations on the Church's mission of calling all people to Christ.[137]

Bauckham notes that Moltmann's openness regarding other religions is also evident in his pneumatology.[138] For Pentecostals this aspect is important. Bauckham says, "Moltmann achieves a strong continuity between creation and redemption, and between the creative and salvific activities of the Spirit".[139] Bauckham quotes Moltmann's appreciation for signs of the Spirit outside the Church and for the Spirit's work beyond the borders of the Church in his claim that the Spirit is greater than the Church and has purposes beyond it. Moltmann expressly affirms the Spirit's salvific purposes beyond the Church, and chides the Church not to be jealous of the Spirit's extra-ecclesial activities.[140] Accordingly, and along the line of his views of experiencing God, Moltmann's carefully qualified appreciation for the tradition of mysticism has perhaps drawn more heavily on Jewish mystics than on Christian.[141] Indeed, Moltmann does stress the commonly shared experience of eschatological hope not only of Jewish and Christian but also of Muslim religions.[142]

In 1994, a premier Pentecostal theological journal, *The Journal of Pentecostal Theology*, dedicated several articles of a single issue to Moltmann's pneumatology. Several major Pentecostal scholars dialogued with Moltmann and he responded.[143] Later, Macchia offered a further response.[144] Later still, Andrew Lord offered a helpful analysis of the overall dialogue from the perspective of mission theology with a suggestion for a way forward.[145] Energy and insight characterized the entire discussion. Participants expressed mutual appreciation and agreement, as well as some strong criticism. This study can only be interested in intersections with theology of religions. That in itself is significant and substantial.

According to Lord's summary analysis, Moltmann and Pentecostals agreed on a mutual desire for a holistic and experiential pneumatology.[146] Their disagreement arose in relating the particular to the universal and the immanent to the transcendent.[147] Plainly put, Pentecostals stress the mission of the Spirit in the Church and Moltmann emphasizes the Spirit's mission beyond the Church in all of creation.[148] As a way forward, Lord suggests developing a pneumatology capable of embracing "*polarity* between the particular (the church) and the universal (the creation)." A reciprocal back and forth movement from the particular to the universal (Moltmann) and the universal to the particular (Pentecostals) thus occurs by the Holy Spirit. Pneumatologically grounded Christian mission therefore protects the uniqueness of the Church without restricting the reach of the Spirit.[149] For Pentecostal theology of religions, this suggestion would entail recognizing the Spirit's presence and influence among the religions without sacrificing the Spirit's participatory role in the Church's missionary identity and activity.[150] The implications could be immensely positive for positioning toward inclusivism.

A prolific thinker and writer, Clark Pinnock, himself a Charismatic Baptist, has worked closely with Pentecostals scholars and thus built a relationship of mutual respect.[151] He is clearly inclusivist in his theology of religions.[152] While continuing to affirm unequivocally the incarnation and revelation of God in the person of Jesus Christ, he refuses to restrict the Spirit's reach to those who have specifically heard the gospel. In fact, it has been precisely his commitment to biblical authority and a high christology that has led Pinnock to develop his pneumatology. The result has been an openly and optimistically inclusivist stance wherein he seeks to avoid the twin errors of overemphasizing either universality or particularity to the exclusion of the other. For Pinnock, the Spirit (though not entirely or only) represents universality and the Son (though not entirely or only) represents particularity.[153] This is not an either/or but a both/and proposition. Building upon John Wesley's concept of "prevenient grace" (the grace that goes before), Pinnock posits the Spirit's presence in the religions bringing God's revelation into contact with some who will receive and thus perhaps be saved.[154] He does not see non-Christian religions as vehicles of salvation, yet he resists restricting God the Spirit to the Church. One may discern this prevenient process in action through the presence of the Spirit's fruit. Pinnock, therefore, refers in hope to the unevangelized or adherents of other religions as "pre-Christian" rather than "non-Christian." [155]

Some leading Evangelicals more or less strongly disagree with Pinnock on his inclusive and pneumatological theology of religions. He has, however, continued to defend his views on biblical and theological grounds with consistence and persistence.[156] Other leading Evangelicals express agreement with his inclusive views.[157] Moreover, at least some Pentecostals are surprisingly open to Pinnock. For instance, leading Pentecostal theologian of religions Amos Yong affirms and even extends Pinnock's approach.[158] Barry Callen, himself a Wesleyan, helps explain Pentecostal attraction to Pinnock. He recounts Pinnock's own intellectual and spiritual journey into ever deepening appreciation of the Holy Spirit and his increasing identification with a wing of Evangelicals—Anabaptist, Wesleyan, and Pentecostal—who share pneumatological emphases.[159] The fact that Pinnock, personally and theologically, is open to pneumatological experience and understanding helps prepare Pentecostals to consider seriously his inclusive theology of religions. However, arguably none of this association would be sufficient unless Classical Pentecostalism found within itself resources for more openness and optimism than that with which it is usually accredited. Those resources are identifiable in the early and authentic Pentecostal tradition.

Original Wells.[160] No doubt, Moltmann and Pinnock have heavily influenced some Pentecostals in the direction of inclusivism.[161] Yet at least an embryonic inclusive Pentecostal theology of religions goes back farther than them. Even in historic, Classical Pentecostalism "strands of openness" to those of other religions crop up sporadically in the midst of a history and environment of exclusivity.[162] Recently attention has been drawn to the fact that early and original elements of Pentecostalism had significant inclusivist strains.[163] Such a stance may be gleaned from the theology of none other than Charles Fox Parham, an important early founder, leader, and teacher in the movement. Parham advocated an eschatological inclusivism of uncompromising loyalty to Christ coupled with compassionate openness to devout adherents of other religions.[164] For Parham commitment to the absolute uniqueness and necessity of Jesus Christ as Lord and Savior complements openness to a possibility of divine reality and redemption in extra-Christian religions consummated in the eschaton by Christ.

Contemporary Pentecostals can also respond to the challenges of religious pluralism through an appropriation of the optimistic and hopeful theology of Bishop J. H. King, another important and early Pentecostal pioneer leader and thinker.[165] Central and crucial for King was the universal significance of Christ, a refined doctrine of universal atonement, the reality and efficacy of general revelation, a qualified acceptance of religious experience over rigid doctrinal propositionalism, and, though somewhat less directly, a dynamic and progressive view of the process of salvation. King also accepted that "the religion of Christ"—the religion centered in the person of Christ himself rather than in institutional Christianity—predates and exists apart from ecclesial Christianity, that is, among other world religions, though Christianity may be in a special sense truly called "the only true religion." When put together to address the questions of religious pluralism, Bishop King's theology invites a more inclusive stance toward the religions than the rhetoric of Classical Pentecostalism suggests.

In fact, as noted above, arguably, a generally and genuinely inclusive theology of religions flows quite naturally out of the Wesleyan-Arminian heritage of the Holiness-Pentecostal revival.[166] The time appears ripe for Pentecostals to explore a "balanced Pentecostal approach to Christian theology of religions."[167] Such an inclusive Pentecostal theology of religions, especially of the kind articulated in dialogue with major streams of the early Pentecostal tradition, is a "back to the future" approach that simultaneously looks backward and forward and stresses both continuity and creativity.

Development toward a Pentecostal Theology of Religions[168]

Pentecostal theology of religions appears to be developing in uniquely pneumatological directions. One recognized Pentecostal theologian who has led the way on the issue of theology of religions is Veli-Matti Kärkkäinen.[169] If theology of religions "attempts to account theologically for the meaning and value of other religions,"[170] then a distinctively Christian theology of religions, Kärkkäinen suggests, must be trinitarian. Very briefly, Kärkkäinen's trinitarian theology of religions suggests that trinitarian theology serves as a critique of a so-called "normative" pluralism (which usually collapses the differences between religions). Also, he maintains that the Triune God of the Bible is unique, and that a high christology plays a critical role in the doctrine of the Trinity. For him, the Church in the power of the Holy Spirit anticipates the Kingdom of God, always pointing beyond itself to the eschaton, or the coming of the Kingdom and unity of all people under one God. Finally, he argues that the doctrine of the Trinity indicates the communal nature of God capable of relating in unity and difference; and that trinitarian communion can include critical relationship with religious others in tolerance. Essentially, Kärkkäinen is suggesting that a full-orbed trinitarian theology emphasizes the role of the Spirit not only in the trinitarian life of God but also in the presence of relationship between God and the Church and in the relationship between the Church and the world.

Obviously pneumatologically robust, Kärkkäinen is nonetheless faithfully christocentric and ecclesiological.[171] The Spirit who reaches out beyond the Church into the Kingdom and into the world is always the Spirit of Christ who abides in unique relation with his Church. No wedge is driven between the Spirit and Christ, or between the Spirit and the Church. Thus other religions are not salvific but discerning appreciation for the presence of the Triune God in their midst is possible. This approach opens the way wide for relational engagement, and includes a responsibility for genuinely appreciative and cautiously critical interreligious dialogue and encounter. For Kärkkäinen, a truly trinitarian theology of religions enables interreligious dialogue as a mutually respectful process of learning and sharing.[172]

If Kärkkäinen has reflected theologically on the religions as a Pentecostal, Amos Yong has attempted to develop a distinctively Pentecostal theology of religions.[173] He advises fellow Pentecostals to develop a theology of religions because of their international roots and global presence, because of their need to attend to urgent missiological issues such as syncretism, the relations between gospel and culture, and the balance between proclamation and social justice, and because of the importance of this topic for further delineating Pentecostal identity.[174] Yet the Pentecostal experience produces its own "pneumatological imagination", a way of thinking and theologizing informed by the Pentecostal/Charismatic experience of and orientation toward the Holy Spirit, which suggests the possibility of the Spirit's presence and influence in the world in general and in the world's religions more particularly. Further, such a Pentecostal theology is also sensitive to the fact that there are many "spirits" in the world, much less in the world of the religions, which require Christian discernment. The criteria for discerning the Holy Spirit from other spirits, then, includes the fruits of the Spirit, ethical conduct, and the signs of the coming kingdom. In such a Pentecostal theological framework, then, Yong also emphasizes that, "the pneumatological imagination derived from the outpouring of the Spirit" enables a relatively impartial, sympathetic, yet critical engagement with the religions.[175]

For Kärkkäinen and Yong, then, it is important that a Pentecostal theology of religions should help Pentecostal Christians engage the religions through discernment rather than through any *a priori* views about the religions. This means that people of other faiths need to be heard first on their own terms, even while (Pentecostal) Christians would also be invited or even required to testify in their own tongues. The key here is to be able to comprehend other religions according to their own self-understanding, without prejudging or defining them according to our own Christian (or Pentecostal) theological categories (for example, in exclusivist, inclusivist, or pluralist terms). Such a Pentecostal approach thus sustains and motivates the interreligious encounter, and does so as part of the Christian mission. Subsequently, Yong has also begun to emphasize the theme of biblical hospitality as a model for interreligious encounter and dialogue.[176] In sum, he offers a biblical and theological study of positive results when the hospitable beliefs and practices of Jesus and the post-Pentecost Church are applied to Christian relations with persons of non-Christian faiths today, essentially arguing contemporary practice needs to catch up with the biblical teaching of extending hospitality beyond every boundary of faith, nation, and ethnicity.[177] Implications for dialogue may be immense.

Assessing Pentecostal Theologies of Religions

This section will expound shortly on these insights toward a Pentecostal and pneumatological theology of religions.[178] Before doing so, however, some assessment is in order. To begin, it should be clearly stated, as Kärkkäinen has already pointed out and as the previous chapter of this study already argued that pluralism is not an option for Pentecostals.[179] At the same time, a narrow exclusivism, that is, a view that Christ and the Spirit are restricted entirely to the Church or its members, sits uncomfortably with a distinctively Pentecostal theology of religions that is definitively pneumatic in nature. However, a more open inclusivism could fit with it, and it is noteworthy that those working most directly and pointedly in the area of Pentecostal theology of religions seem to be inclining in generally inclusivist directions. As of yet, no major theological voice from within the movement itself is sounding an alarm (even while recognized Pentecostal theologians like Frank Macchia are turning in what might be called inclusivist directions).[180] Though that may happen at some point, likely the burden of proof rests with those seeking to limit or restrict the Spirit rather than otherwise.

However, it is interesting to ask why Pentecostal scholars and theologians who are publishing on the religions have not resorted to the established categories of exclusivism, inclusivism, etc. Perhaps there are more exclusivists present than one is aware of, but if they are not explicitly using (or defending) the exclusivist model in their writings, they would be identifiable as exclusivistic only with difficulty.[181] Hence, concluding that inclusivism has won or will win the day is premature.

Of course, inclusivism itself is not without its challenges. One of the major hurdles that inclusivists need to confront is that their theological paradigm remains wedded to the soteriological question about the salvation of the unevangelized or of those in other religions. Inclusivism, in other words, was developed more for Christian self-understanding than for answering the questions related to theology of religions. Hence, inclusivism is inappropriate when applied in a dialogue with people of other faiths since that would entail Christians either granting salvation to people of other faiths who are not seeking such salvation (i.e., union with God in Christ), or Christians labeling people of other faiths according to categories foreign to those religious traditions. In the contemporary pluralistic world, the challenge is to understand religious others on their own terms even while remaining committed to one's own religious vision, including that of bearing witness to Christ in the power of the Spirit.

The theologies of religions of Kärkkäinen and Yong are in search of ways to resolve this inclusivist dilemma. Both emphasize a robust trinitarian pneumatology (even if Kärkkäinen stresses the trinitarian a bit more and Yong the pneumatological) precisely in order to open up theological space to appreciate the particularities of the religions and their differences from Christian faith. While Kärkkäinen's emphasis is on how the real trinitarian differences may correlate with real differences between the religions, Yong's "pneumatological imagination" is designed to both recognize and yet bridge the vast chasm separating Christian faith from other religions. In this sense, both recognize the shortcomings of the dominant categories of exclusivism, inclusivism, and pluralism and explore the questions such as if, and how, we might advance beyond this paradigm.[182] Yet their efforts, along with those of Moltmann, Pinnock, and others, are also indications that Pentecostal theology of religions is an exciting but complex undertaking. Pentecostals appear ready to take their appropriate place in the global community amidst the interreligious encounter.

Distinctive Theology

Common Ground and Early Identity

Easily observed from the above is that Pentecostals share much common ground with other Christians regarding contemporary approaches to Christian theology of religions. The experience of the general or historic Christian traditions, Catholic and Protestant, the context of Evangelicalism, and specific particulars of the Wesleyan way all weld well with many Pentecostal insights and concerns.[183] The christological, ecclesial, pneumatological, and soteriological concerns raised by Moltmann and Pinnock move even closer to Pentecostal mores. However, connectivity to the broader Christian tradition remains concretely in place. Pentecostalism's desire and need to formulate and articulate its own distinctive approach to theology of religions, and interreligious encounter and dialogue, does not diminish the fact that connectivity to broader Christianity consistently continues. For example, a name which frequently appears among Pentecostals as of seminal significance in discussions of Christian theology of religions is that of the ever popular British apologist C. S. Lewis.[184] Lewis is in effect an ecumenical figure with far-reaching influence beyond his own Anglican affiliation. Lewis's theology of religions suggests why Pentecostals taking steps in an inclusivist direction would appreciate its significance.[185]

However, a concern to root contemporary Pentecostal theology of religions in Pentecostalism's early identity is significant. Two points stand out in particular. It is significant for defensive purposes and for directional purposes. In the defensive sense, Pentecostalism's history of exclusivity has been mentioned above. Pentecostal exclusivists tend to suspect inclusivists of compromising for the sake of currently popular political or theological correctness. Some even think inclusivism is nothing other than incipient or incremental pluralism. Discovering early, original resources in historic, Classical Pentecostalism for more openness toward theology of religions is often extremely helpful in demonstrating otherwise and in persuading critics to become comrades.

In the directional sense, harking back to early Pentecostal views on other faiths and their relations to Christ and Christianity helps establish a sense of which way contemporary Pentecostal theology of religions might best proceed. Without fear of contradiction, the theologies of religions of Parham or King meet the criteria laid out in the last chapter. They are faithful to an uncompromised Christology, an undiminished view of the inspiration and authority of Scripture, an undistorted soteriology, and a non-minimal ecclesiology. They can thus help Pentecostals today avoid the pitfalls of pluralism. However, they are also open and optimistic about the universality of God's love and the reach of Christ's lordship. They can thus help Pentecostals avoid the extremes of exclusivism.

A delicate and intricate balancing act is essential for developing a Pentecostal theology of religions today that is both accurate and acceptable. Biblical and theological accuracy are first, but without acceptance by Pentecostals in the ranks and files of the movement, no approach will help equip it to meet the needs of the day. In illustration of these points, perhaps a recent review by a Pentecostal of missionary-pastor-theologian Lesslie Newbigin's theology of religions is telling. Some Pentecostals may be surprised at Newbigin's inclusivist speculations about the unevangelized and adherents of other religions. They need not be. Researching resources among the earliest Pentecostals clearly suggests similar attitudes among early members of the movement. He then quotes Newbigin's self-description may apply to many:

> The position which I have outlined is exclusive in the sense that it affirms the unique truth of the revelation in Jesus Christ, but it is not exclusivist in the sense of denying the possibility of the salvation of the non-Christian. It is inclusivist in the sense that it refuses to limit the saving grace of God to the members of the Christian Church, but it rejects the inclusivism which regards the non-Christian religions as vehicles of salvation. It is pluralist in the sense of acknowledging the work of God in the lives of all human beings, but it rejects a pluralism which denies the uniqueness and decisiveness of what God has done in Jesus Christ.[186]

Possibly one of the most beautifully balanced descriptions of Christian theology of religions ever, it perhaps display the delicate, intricate balance necessary for some Pentecostals to understand and endorse.[187]

Yet so far, with occasional amendments, many Evangelicals and Wesleyans as well as other Catholics and Protestants may share this general view. Pentecostals do have some truly unique experiences and understandings that are applicable. The following section exemplifies a more intentionally distinctively Pentecostal appropriation of biblical and theological categories for Christian theology of religions.

Intentionally Distinctively Pentecostal[188]

One of the main problems that plague traditional theologies of religions is how to honor and respect the particularities of other faiths even while remaining committed to one's own (in this case, Pentecostal Christianity). This is parallel to the perennial philosophical challenge of the relationship between the one and the many. Historically, responses have either privileged the one, which risks rejecting the many, or emphasized the many, which lapses into anarchy or relativism.[189] Does a Pentecostal and pneumatological perspective shed light on this ancient debate?

The Day of Pentecost narrative in Acts 2 provides some perspective on this issue. Two observations can be made.[190] First, it should be noted that the one outpouring of the Spirit did not cancel out but rather enabled an eruption of a diversity of tongues. On the one hand, there is a cacophony of tongues, yet on the other hand, there is a harmony of testimonies, each witnessing in their own way to God's deeds of power. Correlatively, there is both mass confusion but yet also an astonishment born of understanding.[191] In these ways, Pentecost signifies, perhaps, a unique resolution of the one and the many: the many (tongues) retain their particularities even as they participate in the one (Spirit's outpouring).[192] Whereas before there were just the many tongues, now the many tongues are brought together, not so that they might cancel or drown one another out, but so that precisely out of the plurality of utterances strangers might be brought together and the goodness of God might be declared.

This leads, second, to the observation that the many tongues of Pentecost did indeed signify the many cultures of the ancient Mediterranean world. Whereas the cultural and religious domains of human life are neither identical nor synonymous, one could argue that they are also not completely distinct. Rather, languages are related to cultures and both are related to religious traditions, even if each is a distinguishable aspect of human life. Given this interrelationship, however, might one might suggest the many tongues of Pentecost not only represent many cultures but also, at least potentially, many religious traditions? If so, then the outpouring of the Spirit points not only to the redemption of the many languages, but also to the redemption of many cultures and perhaps of many religious traditions.[193]

What one means by redemption, however, should be qualified.[194] First, the claim about the redemption of other faiths is an eschatological one: "In the last days it will be, God declares, that I will pour out my Spirit upon all flesh" (Acts 2:17a). If the eschatological gift of the Spirit means, in part, that the outpouring of the Spirit has occurred, is occurring, and will continue to occur, then the redemption of any thing, the religions included, may have past, present, and, most importantly, future aspects to it. In that sense, then, every person, including those in other faiths, is a candidate for the future reception of the Spirit (if not already having been touched by the Spirit whose winds blow where they may), and such reception may depend in part on their interactions with us (as Christians). How one approaches or responds to people of other faiths may determine "if and when" the gift of the Spirit will be given to them. And, given the fact that there are varying degrees of ignorance and knowledge about Christ, one would underscore God's redemptive work in the lives of individuals as a dynamic process depending not on others' certification of their salvation, but on the gracious gift of God in Christ and the Holy Spirit. So then, in anticipating the possibility of the redemption of the religions, it is not being said either that Luke means every person since the Day of Pentecost has received the Spirit or that all people of other faiths are already saved. Second, in speaking about the redemption of cultures and of religious traditions, it is by no means suggested that all cultures or religious traditions as wholes are now conduits of the saving grace of God. Cultures and religions, like languages, are not monolithic, and aspects of each of them are antithetical to the purposes of God (hence their fallenness). At the same time, neither are languages, cultures, and religions static, so that whatever in them might be hostile to the purposes of God today might not be so tomorrow. The Day of Pentecost attests to God's gracious and incomprehensible freedom to redeem – take up and use – the diversity of languages for his purposes. Similarly, it is suggested, God has the freedom to do this redemptive work with the various cultures and religions of the world.[195]

But, further, any unqualified optimism must also be avoided, as critics of inclusivism have warned. Hence, discussion of the redemption of the religions, even if understood in eschatological perspective, must provide guidelines for discerning engagement with them on this side of the eschaton. If this position is to avoid both a universalistic soteriology in which all people are finally saved (which Pentecostals repudiate), and a blanket endorsement of the religions as already redeemed of God (which Pentecostals reject), then what is the proper posture with which Pentecostals should approach people of other faiths? For this task, one must be discerning not only of the many tongues (beliefs or doctrines) of other religious traditions, but also of their many practices. Let a Pentecostal and pneumatological approach to discerning the religions, then, that avoids the pitfalls identified above in the traditional approaches, be outlined.

To begin, a Pentecostal and pneumatological theology of religions underwrites an a posteriori approach to interreligious engagement. Just as in a congregational context, "Let two or three prophets speak, and let the others weigh what is said." (1 Cor. 14:29), so also in the interfaith encounter: one must look and listen carefully before rendering judgment. The goal is to allow the tongues (testimonies) of other religious people to be heard first on their own "insider's" terms (just as Pentecostals clamor to be heard on their terms). Any theology *of religions*, even a pneumatological one, must be deeply informed by the empirical reality of the religions, rather than be an a priori projection of the Christian imagination.[196]

Second, a Pentecostal and pneumatological theology of religions engages in critical analysis (discernment) of the religious phenomenon or teaching under scrutiny. Here we might bring to bear a multitude of disciplinary perspectives, being cautious about not imposing a reductionist interpretation on what we are attempting to discern. Also here, an attempt is made to compare and contrast what Christians are looking at or listening to with their Christian convictions (beliefs and practices).[197] Such analysis is not always straightforward. At one level, they might be attempting to compare very disparate realities, and if so, any conclusions will have missed the point.[198] Part of the task involves application of what might be called a "hermeneutics of charity" that attempts to empathize with the other faith perspective as much as possible from their point of view. Always at work, however, will be the Christian (and Pentecostal) "hermeneutics of suspicion" (regarding the other faith) that is vigilant about the urgency of the gospel.

At some point in the discerning process, they might have to "come to a decision." So long as they remember that any such judgments are always provisional, subject to later confirmation (or not), they recognize that as historically situated beings, life requires that they discern the Holy Spirit's presence and activity to the best of their ability. Decision is followed by action. The hermeneutical circle requires, however, if they are to be honest, that they then reassess the process of discernment to see if they have missed the mark.

Conclusion/Summary

The preceding endeavors as concisely and yet completely as possible to give an indication of the current state of Pentecostal theology of religions. It suggests that certain elements of the general Christian tradition, the Evangelical and Wesleyan movements, and key theologians are playing an important role in Pentecostal self-understanding and development. Furthermore, Pentecostal theology itself is rapidly advancing in theology of religions in constructive and distinctive directions. An inclusive Pentecostal theology of religions seems to be forming, one that endeavors to be true to its roots in creative ways adequate for its present and its future.

No attempt has been made thus far to refute either pluralism or exclusivism in favor of inclusivism. However, the rather pragmatic supposition has been suggested that neither pluralism nor exclusivism comfortably fit with Pentecostal mores or values properly understood or sufficiently face contemporary societal pluralistic realities. Later, some attempt will be made at further defining and defending this supposition. For the present, increasingly clear is that Pentecostal spirituality and theology contains rich reserves for utilization in theology of religions. This would seem to portend positive implications for contemporary Pentecostals hoping to deal effectively with religious pluralism. Avoided are the isolationism of exclusivism and relativism of pluralism while optimism for engaging encounter seems implied. What remains is to see how all of this active energy translates in actual interreligious encounter and dialogue. Therefore, the next chapter will look at interreligious encounter and dialogue in an attempt to understand and articulate it according to a Pentecostal perspective.

Notes

1. The following does not intend to be an exhaustive overview of Christian theology of religions. It only attempts to establish the basic tonal context for an emerging Pentecostal theology of religions. For an excellent overview of the entire field see V.M. Kärkkäinen, *An Introduction to The Theology of Religions: Biblical, Historical, & Contemporary Perspectives* (Downer's Grove: InterVarsity Press, 2003).

2. E.g., see the official denominational website of the Church of God (Cleveland, TN USA) at http://www.churchofgod.org/about/church_is.cfm. The term "Foundational" is apparently a way of expressing commitment to doctrinal tenets of Fundamentalism while distancing itself from its unpopular political reputation. The term "Organized" indicates commitment to centralized ecclesial government in contrast to a significant group of "Independent", or autonomous, Pentecostals within the broader Pentecostal movement. Other terms seem self-explanatory.

3. E.g., C.W. Conn, *Like a Mighty Army: A History of the Church of God: Definitive Edition* (Cleveland: Pathway, 1996), 14, 15, 22, 35, 336-37, 501.

4. E. .L. Blumhoffer, *Restoring the Faith: The Assemblies of God, Pentecostalism, and American Culture* (Champaign, IL: University of Chicago Press, 1993), 134, 243.

5. Cf. H.V. Synan, "International Pentecostal Holiness Church," *NIDPCM*, 798-801.

6. A. Anderson, *An Introduction to Global Pentecostalism: Global Charismatic Christianity* (Cambridge: Cambridge University Press, 2004), 1-15.

7. Anderson, *Introduction*, 183.

8. Anderson, *Introduction*, 286.

9. The immeasurably important influence of the African American church on Pentecostalism further contributes to its diversity. Holiness and Evangelical streams also converge in that context. E.g., see W.C. Turner, Jr., *The United Holy Church of America: A Study in Black Holiness-Pentecostalism* (New Jersey: Gorgias, 2006) and L.F. Morgan, "The Flame Still Burns," *Charisma* (November 2007), 42-48, 50, 52, 54, 56, and 58.

10. M.A. Noll, *Turning Points: Decisive Moments in the History of Christianity* (Grand Rapids: Baker Academic, 1997), 28-29, 41.

11. Noll, *Turning*, 78-80.

12. Noll, *Turning*, 165-66.

13. L. Guy, Introducing Early Christianity: A Topical Survey of Its Life, Beliefs & Practices (Downer's Grove: InterVarsity Press, 2004), 13-16, 22.

14. Guy, *Introducing*, 40-41.

15. Guy, *Introducing,* 194-95.

16. Noll, *Turning*, 76. Cf. K.A. Burton, *The Blessing of Africa* (Downer's Grove: InterVarsity Press, 2007).

17. Amazingly, the popular mind at least often now considers Islam as indigenous to Africa and Christianity as an interloper or latecomer. See P. Jenkins, *The Next Christendom: The Coming of Global Christianity,* revised and expanded edition (New York: Oxford, 2007), 19-20.

18. Noll, *Turning*, 120.

19. Noll, *Turning*, 139-42.

20. Jenkins, *Next,* 192-94.

21. Jenkins, *Next,* 192-96. Jenkins also suggests that complex relations between the Abrahamic faiths, Judaism, Christianity, and Islam, will be increasingly important for global diplomacy and security, 212-14, as well as Christian relations with Hinduism and Buddhism, 214-17.

22. M.E. Marty, *Pilgrims in Their Own Land: 500 Years of Religion in America* (New York: Penguin, 1984), 12, 18-19, 429-30.

23. J.L. González thinks *Summa Contra Gentiles* one of Aquinas' most important and enduring works, *A History of Christian Thought: From Augustine to the Eve of the Reformation* (Nashville: Abingdon, 1971, 1988), 261. R.E. Olson, *The Story of Christian Theology: Twenty Centuries of Tradition & Reform* (Downer's Grove: InterVarsity, 1999), agrees, 334. R.G. Clouse, "Francis of Assisi," *Eerdmans' Handbook to the History of Christianity* (Grand Rapids: Eerdmans, 1977, 1988), demonstrates that Francis' sense of mission to other religious cultures was not peripheral but central to his life, even evoking trips to far countries and attempts to evangelize the Sultan of Egypt, 264-65.

24. Noll, *Turning,* 100-01.

25. Noll, *Turning,* 277.

26. Noll, *Turning,* 287-91. P. Jenkins argues in favor of flexibility for understanding global Christianity: "Companions for Life: A Supple Faith," Christian Vision Project, *Books & Culture* 13:2 (March/April 2007), 9-18.

27. Noll, *Turning,* 215-16.

28. D. Aikman, *Jesus in Beijing: How Christianity is Transforming China and Changing the Global Balance of Power* (Washington, DC: Regenery, 2003), discusses some consistent complexities confronting Christianity in China.

29. Noll, *Turning,* 216-19. D.J. Hesselgrave, in *Paradigms in Conflict: 10 Key Questions in Christian Missions Today* (Grand Rapids: Kregel, 2005), helpfully explains how important underlying assumptions are for missilogical praxis.

30. Adaptability continues to be characteristic of contemporary Pentecostalism as well. See S.S. O'Neal, *Bridges to People: Communicating Jesus to People and Growing Missional Churches in a Multi-Ethnic World* (USA: Xulon Press, 2007).

31. Noll, *Turning,* 287-89. Cf. O.L. Fisher, *The Role of the Spirit in the World and Life: How God is Immanent in His Creation* (USA: Xulon Press, 2004), though elements are theologically problematic.

32. Noll, *Turning,* 288. Worth noting is that this process among Pentecostals all seems rather occasional and not at all intentional. Part of the argument of the present work is that Pentecostals need intentionally to address the issue of other religions and their relations with them. Yet these incidents are extremely important as guiding precedents.

33. K. Warrington, *Pentecostal Theology: A Theology of Encounter* (New York: T & T Clark, 2008), 40.

34. Warrington, *Encounter,* 40-44. Warrington notes that this is not a move toward universalism or a weakening of Christianity, but rather an enlargement of understanding regarding the lordship of Christ (44).

35. This section is in dialogue with the work of Sir Norman Anderson.

36. Kärkkäinen, *Theology of Religions,* observes that "Undoubtedly, the person who up until the early 1990s made the largest impact on the evangelical movement in terms of a more inclusive theology of religions" was Anderson, 261. Elsewhere, Kärkkäinen compares or groups Anderson with C.S. Lewis in this regard. See his "Evangelical Theology and the Religions," *The Cambridge Companion to Evangelical Theology,* ed. T. Larsen and D.J. Treier (Cambridge: Cambridge University Press, 2007), 199-212 (199; cf. 204).

37. N. Anderson, *Christianity and World Religions: The Challenge of Pluralism* (Downer's Grove, IL: InterVarsity Press, 1970, rev. ed., 1984). S. Neill's *Christian Faith and Other Faiths* (Downer's Grove: InterVarsity Press, 1984) has also been foundational. Evangelicals generally following in Anderson and Neill's footsteps include, G.R. McDermott, *Can Evangelicals Learn from World Religions: Jesus, Revelation, & Reli-*

gious Traditions (Downer's Grove: InterVarsity Press, 2000) and *God's Rivals: Why Has God Allowed Different Religions? Insights from the Bible and the Early Church* (Downer's Grove: IVP Academic, 2007), T.C. Tennent, *Christianity at the Religious Roundtable: Evangelicalism in Conversation with Hinduism, Buddhism, and Islam* (Grand Rapids: Baker Academic, 2002), and J.G. Stackhouse, Jr., Ed., *No Other Gods Before Me? Evangelicals and the Challenge of World Religions* (Grand Rapids: Baker Academic, 2001). Stackhouse dedicated his book to Sir Norman Anderson.

38. Anderson, *Christianity*, 12.

39. Including that of W.E. Hocking, A. Toynbee, Ramakrishna, Gandhi, or D.H. Lawrence, cf. Anderson, 16-20. However, G. McFarlane, "Atonement, Creation, and Trinity, 192-207, gen. eds. D. Tidball, D. Hilborn, & J. Thacker, *The Atonement Debate: Papers from the London Symposium on the Theology of the Atonement* (Grand Rapids, MI: Zondervan, 2008), argues for a broader theology of the atonement that takes into account its indebtedness to and interrelatedness with the doctrine of creation and the nature of the Triune God.

40. Similarly, J. Rodman Williams, *Renewal Theology: Systematic Theology from a Charismatic Perspective*, three volumes in one (Grand Rapids: Zondervan, 1996), who has inclusivist inclinations, insists emphatically on the essentiality of Christ, 3:474-76.

41. Anderson, *Christianity*, 30-34 (31).

42. Anderson, *Christianity*, 32. Cf. 145-55.

43. Similarly, T. George, "Evangelical Theology in North American Contexts," *The Cambridge Companion to Evangelical Theology*, ed. T. Larsen and D.J. Treier (Cambridge: Cambridge University Press, 2007), 275-92, suggests that well known Evangelical theologian M. Erickson's robustly Christological contributions on theology of religions and soteriological inclusivism also have been more constructive than critical, 289. E.g., see Erickson, *How Shall They Be Saved? The Destiny of Those Who Do Not Hear of Jesus* (Grand Rapids: Baker, 1996).

44. Anderson, *Christianity*, 34-35.

45. Anderson, *Christianity*, 35-36.

46. Anderson, *Christianity*, 36-37. In fact, Anderson often draws heavily on L. Newbigin's *A Faith for this One World* (London, 1961), *The Finality of Christ* (London, 1969), and *The Open Secret* (Grand Rapids, 1978). Cf. Anderson, 18.

47. Anderson, *Christianity*, 37-45. As will be seen further below, how to account for the religious experiences of others is a crucial question for theology of religions.

48. Cf. Anderson, *Christianity*, 46-8, 50-1. Such strong critiques remind that Evangelicalism sometimes confessedly causes 'negative vibes" in some, but even P.F. Knitter, *Introducing Theologies of Religions* (New York: Orbis, 2002, 2004), certainly no Evangelical, admits that it is impossible to do justice to contemporary Christianity or its theologies of religions without considering Evangelicals, 19, addressing Pentecostals as part of this faith family, 21. Yet he argues that for such diverse figures as K. Barth to historic Fundamentalists and contemporary Evangelicals, theology of religions is not about Christianity at all, but really all about Jesus Christ, 26 (cf. 28).

49. Cf. Anderson, *Christianity*, 69.

50. Anderson, *Christianity*, 108-09.

51. Anderson, *Christianity*, 110. Here is the crux of the controversy of inclusivists with pluralists on the one hand and with exclusivists on the other hand. Inclusive amounts to a *via media* between the other two.

52. Interestingly, Y. Congar, *I Believe in the Holy Spirit (IBHS)* 3 vols. trans. David Smith (New York: Seabury, 1983), admits that in the early OT documents "there are parallels and similarities in other religions" (e.g., shamanism) regarding the "external

effects" of the Spirit, but notes that the OT distinctively attributes to God what others ascribe to the forces of nature (1:5).

53. Anderson, *Christianity*, 114-18, 129. Interestingly, R.H. Gause, a prominent Pentecostal biblical scholar and theologian (Church of God, Cleveland, TN), elucidates an alternative to fundamentalist dispensationalism through a careful comparison-contrast of dispensational theology and a theology of progressive revelation. Gause explains that progressive revelation does not divide up biblical history as dispensationalism. It does not hermeneutically distinguish between the Church, Israel, and the Kingdom of God. The nature of God, the history of salvation, and the character of the people of God are progressively revealed. Earlier events anticipate and predict later events. The inspiration of the Holy Spirit gives Scripture a progressive and even prophetic or predictive quality. In stark contrast to the hermeneutical compartmentalizing of dispensationalism, progressive revelation affirms a more unified approach to biblical interpretation and understanding. For Gause, considerations of the unchangeableness and unity of God and God's Word consistently lead to this conclusion. See his *Revelation: God's Stamp of Sovereignty on History* (Cleveland: Pathway, 1983), 18-21. Cf. to C. Hodge, *Systematic Theology, vol. 1* (Peabody: Hendrickson, 2003), 446.

54. Anderson, *Christianity*, 137.

55. Congar warns that the Word should never be considered an obstacle to the Breath of the Spirit because "We do not, after all, know where the Breath comes from or where it is going!" Yet whatever the Spirit reveals ultimately comes from and leads to Christ. See *The Word and the Spirit* (*WS*), trans. David Smith (San Francisco: Harper & Row, 1986), 71.

56. Anderson, *Christianity*, 138.

57. Anderson, *Christianity*, 142-43; original italics. Ironically, inclusivists manage to displease everyone here. Pluralists deny the uniqueness of the Savior, exclusivists the universality of his salvation. Inclusivists affirm both. E.g., note that T.R. Philips, "Christianity and Religions," *EDT*, 231-34, complains and attempts to change this typology and terminology, 231, because of prejudicial use against the favored exclusivist position, but then caustically criticizes inclusivism prejudicially through stereotypical analysis, 233. Indeed, he attacks inclusivism more aggressively than he does pluralism, apparently satisfied with raising questions rather than refuting its claims, 234.

58. Anderson, *Christianity*, 143-45.

59. This consistent insistence is contrary to the exclusivist contention that inclusivism diminishes the importance of Christian evangelism and mission. Cf. Philips, "Christianity and Religions," without proof or support, claims that inclusivism "undermines the urgency of missions", 233.

60. Anderson, *Christianity*, 145-55.

61. Anderson, *Christianity*, 148, 159-60. Cf. B. Witherington III, *The Problem with Evangelical Theology: Testing the Exegetical Foundations of Calvinism, Dispensationalism, and Wesleyanism* (Waco, TX: Baylor University Press, 2005), who warns against the recent resurgence of religious fundamentalism in all three of the great Abrahamic faiths, 249.

62. Anderson, *Christianity*, 160-61.

63. Anderson, *Christianity*, 162-69.

64. Anderson, *Christianity*, 169-75. Note: Sir Norman is also an advocate of interreligious dialogue but the next chapter analyzes that aspect of his work.

65. Cf. R. Chia, *Hope for the World: A Christian Vision of the Last Things*, Christian Doctrine in Global Perspective, series editor, David Smith, consulting editor, John Stott (Downer's Grove: InterVarsity Press, 2005).

66. Chia, *Hope,* 41, 95, 97,
67. J. Nkansah-Obrempong, "The Contemporary Theological Situation in Africa: An Overview", *ERT* 31:2 (April 2007), 140-50.
68. Nkansah-Obrempong, "Africa," 148-50. The same may be said for global Christianity.
69. R. Zacharias, *Jesus Among Other Gods: The Absolute Claims of the Christian Message* (Nashville: W Publishing/Thomas Nelson, 2000).
70. R.P. Richard, *The Population of Heaven: A Biblical Response to the Inclusivist Position on Who will be Saved* (Chicago: Moody, 1994).
71. K. Daugherty, "*Missio Dei:* The Trinity and Christian Missions," *ER T* 31:2 (April 2007), 151-68.
72. H. Netland, *Encountering Religious Pluralism: The Challenge to Christian Faith & Mission* (Downer's Grove, ILL: InterVarsity, 2001). Kärkkäinen, *Theology of Religions,* 332, presents Netland as exemplifying "a middle position among evangelicals".
73. Netland, *Encountering,* 281-83.
74. G.A. Boyd & P.R. Eddy, "The Destiny of the Unevangelized Debate," *Across the Spectrum: Understanding Issues in Evangelical Theology* (Grand Rapids: Baker Academic, 2002), 178-92. Cf. W.V. Crockett and J.G. Sigountos, eds., *Through No Fault of Their Own? The Fate of Those Who Have Never Heard* (Grand Rapid: Baker, 1991), M.J. Erickson, *How Shall They Be Saved? The Destiny of Those Who Do Not Hear of Jesus* (Grand Rapids: Baker, 1996), and R.H. Nash, *Is Jesus the Only Savior?* (Grand Rapids: Zondervan, 1994). See also S.N Gundry, D.L. Okholm, and T.R. Phillips, eds., *Four Views on Salvation in a Pluralistic World* (Grand Rapids: Zondervan, 1995), C.H. Pinnock, *A Wideness in God's Mercy: The Finality of Jesus Christ in a World of Religions* (Grand Rapids: Zondervan, 1992), and J. Sanders, *No Other Name: An Investigation into the Destiny of the Unevangelized* (Grand Rapids: Eerdmans, 1992) and G. Facre, R.H. Nash, and J. Sanders, *What About Those Who Have Never Heard: Three Views on the Destiny of the Unevangelized* (Downer's Grove: InterVarsity, 1995).
75. Notable exceptions to the prevalent Evangelical soteriological fixation are T. Tennent and G. McDermott. The next chapter will consider their work more closely.
76. Amazingly, Evangelicalism includes leaders and thinkers as diverse as high Calvinist Jonathan Edwards and Anglican Arminian John Wesley Cf. V. Synan, "Evangelicalism," *NIDPCM,* 613-16.
77. This section is in dialogue with the work of John Wesley and his successors.
78. Noll, *Turning,* 221-28.
79. Noll, *Turning,* 298-302.
80. Noll, *Turning,* 239-40.
81. L.W. Wood, *The Meaning of Pentecost in Early Methodism: Rediscovering John Fletcher as John Wesley's Vindicator and Designated Successor* (Lanham: Scarecrow, 2002). On Wesley's theology of religions specifically, see Kärkkäinen, *Theology of Religions,* 87-89, 132, 149.
82. Cf. R.H. Gause, *Living in the Spirit: The Way of Salvation* (Cleveland: Pathway, 1980) and S.J. Land, *Pentecostal Spirituality: A Passion for the Kingdom* JPTSup 1 (Sheffield: Sheffield Academic Press, 1993). Cf. G. McFarlane, *Why Do You Believe What You Believe About the Holy Spirit?* (Theological Foundations), (Eugene, OR: Wipf & Stock, 2009), for an accessible unpacking of biblical teaching and doctrinal development on the Holy Spirit, and an explanation of how certain presuppositions may distort understanding and expectation of the Spirit.
83. For T.C. Oden in *The Living God: Systematic Theology: Volume One* (Prince: Peabody, MA. 2001) Thomas Aquinas and John Wesley are representative of "the best

Christian teaching" which is not "contemptuous of other religions" but rather "views each history of religious struggle as a statement of the presence of the Holy Spirit in all of human history" (374).

84. G.H. Mellor, "Evangelism and Religious Pluralism in the Wesleyan Tradition," *Theology and Evangelism in the Wesleyan Heritage,* ed. James C. Logan (Nashville: Kingswood Books, 1994), 109-26 (119-20).

85. T.L. Richie, "Mr. Wesley and Mohammed: A Contemporary Inquiry Concerning Islam," *ATJ* 58:2 (Fall 2003), 79-99. Many Christian books today on the subject of the religions are really addressing pluralism, universalism, and/or syncretism (e. g., M. Green's *"But Don't All Religions Lead to God?" Navigating the Multi-Faith Maze* [Baker: Grand Rapids, 2002]; R. Zacharias' *Jesus Among Other Gods: The Absolute Claims of the Christian Message* [Thomas Nelson: Nashville, 2000]; J.H. Berthrong's *The Divine Deli: Religious Identity in the North American Cultural Mosaic* [Orbis: NY, 1999]). None of these categories correctly applies to Wesley's thought on the unevangelized or non-Christian religions.

86. See *CWJW* (The Wesleyan Heritage Collection; Ages Software, Inc. Rio, WI: 2002), 7:67, 58; 6:340-41, 45; 7:216, 377. Cf. Richie, "Wesley and Mohammed," 80-85. R.L. Maddox in "Wesley and the Question of Truth or Salvation in Other Religions," *WTJ* 27 (1992), 9-29, discusses the progression and maturation of Wesley's thought on religions through his "early," "middle," and "late" periods.

87. Richie, "Wesley and Mohammed," 83-85. Many of Wesley's comments on the religions are incidentally scattered throughout his vast corpus. Occasionally, however, he approaches the topic more systematically. E.g., see his "On Divine Providence," *CWJW*, 6:335-47 (esp. 340-42), or "On Faith," 7:214-21 (216-17, 220), and "On Charity," 7:56-67 (58, 67).

88. Cf. *Notes on the New Testament: Matthew-Romans* by John Wesley (The Wesleyan Heritage Collection; Ages Software, Inc. Rio, WI: 2002), 390 and 417.

89. Richie, "Wesley and Mohammed," 86-90. For an interesting study along this line, see N.D. Anderson, *A Definitive Study of Evidence Concerning John Wesley's Appropriation of the Thought of Clement of Alexandria* (Lampeter, Ceredigion, Wales: Edwin Mellen, 2004).

90. Richie, "Wesley and Mohammed," 90-91.

91. Richie, "Wesley and Mohammed," 91-93.

92. T. Richie, "God's Fairness to People of All Faiths: A Respectful Proposal to Pentecostals for Discussion Regarding World Religions," *Pneuma* 28:1 (2006), 105-19 (109-113). Inclusive aspects of Wesley's thought have been discussed by, among others, Maddox in "Wesley and Other Religions," 9-29. Also, see C.H. Pinnock, *Flame of Love: A Theology of the Holy Spirit* (InterVarsity Press: Downer's Grove, IL. 1994), 179, 199, 203, 239, 251, and, M. Lodahl, *The Story of God: Wesleyan Theology and Biblical Narrative* (Beacon Hill: Kansas City; 1994), 227-33. Cf. Boyd and Eddy, *Across the Spectrum*, 178-192.

93. J.B. Cobb, Jr., *Grace & Responsibility: A Wesleyan Theology for Today* (Nashville: Abingdon, 1995), 145-53.

94. T. Runyon, *The New Creation: John Wesley's Theology Today* (Nashville: Abingdon, 1998), 215-21.

95. K.J. Collins, ed. *Exploring Christian Spirituality: An Ecumenical Reader* (Grand Rapids: Baker, 2000), 10.

96. Collins, *Exploring,* 13. Original italics.

97. Cf. E.B. Chappell, *Studies in the Life of John Wesley* (Salem, OH: Schmul, 1991 [1911]), 104, 170-76, H.B. McGonigle, *Sufficient Saving Grace: John Wesley's Evan-*

gelical Arminianism (Waynesboro, GA: Paternoster, 2001), 76, 266-67, 318-30, and J.L. Walls, *The Problem of Pluralism: Recovering United Methodist Identity* (Wilmore, KY: Good News, 1986), 24-27 and 29-50.

98. Some parts of this section are indebted to A. Yong and T Richie, "Bearing Witness in a Religiously Pluralistic World: Pentecostal Missiology, the Religions, and Interreligious Encounter," *Studying Global Pentecostalism: Theories and Methods*, eds. A. Anderson, M. Bergunder, A. Droogers & C. van der Laan (Berkeley, CA: University of California Press, 2010).

99. Cf. Kärkkäinen, *Theology of Religions*, 139.

100. Cf. Kärkkäinen, *Theology of Religions*, 140.

101. For the classic presentation of the categories of exclusivism, inclusivism, and pluralism in theology of religions see A. Race, *Christians and Religious Pluralism: Patterns in the Theology of Religions* (Maryknoll: Orbis, 1983).

102. A. Yong, *Discerning the Spirit(s): A Pentecostal Charismatic Contribution to Christian Theology of Religions* (Sheffield: Sheffield Academic, 2000), 185.

103. Cf. Kärkkäinen, *Theology of Religions*, 140-42.

104. Yong, *Discerning*, 184, 186.

105. Yong, *Discerning*, 185-87.

106. Cf. H.V. Synan, "Evangelicalism," *NIDPCM*, 613-16.

107. This section will be in dialogue with the work of Jürgen Moltmann and Clark Pinnock.

108. A fascinating study in this regard is D.W. Dayton, *Theological Roots of Pentecostalism*, Foreword by M.E. Marty (Grand Rapids: Zondervan, 1987). Dayton highlights the Wesleyan-Methodist-Holiness Movement trajectory, itself having diverse currents.

109. J. Moltmann, *The Church in the Power of the Spirit: A Contribution to Messianic Ecclesiology* (London: SCM Press, 1977), xiv. Italics are original.

110. Moltmann, *Church,* xv.

111. Moltmann, *Church,* xvi.

112. Moltmann, *Church,* xvii.

113. Moltmann, *Church,* 133-63.

114. D.A. Currie, "Moltmann, Jürgen," *EDT,* 784. Specifically, he describes a tri-fold theological approach in which "the crucifixion and resurrection form the core dialectic" of God's "promised future" and "impetus for Christian involvement in overcoming suffering in the meantime" occurs "through the power of the Spirit."

115. See S.M. Smith, "Hope, Theology of," *EDT,* 577-79 for a short summary. Moltmann's own more exhaustive and seminal work on the topic is *Theology of Hope: On the Ground and the Implications of a Christian Eschatology,* trans. J.W. Leitch (London: SCM, 1967). R.A. Neal, *Theology as Hope: On the Ground and Implications of Jürgen Moltmann's Doctrine of Hope,* Princeton Theological Monograph Series (Eugene, OR: Wipf & Stock, 2008), provides a study of Moltmann's enormous output as an ongoing development of his paradigmatic thought on hope.

116. Moltmann, *Church,* 133.

117. Moltmann, *Church,* 135. Cf. Neal, *Theology as Hope*, 201. Currie, "Moltmann," *EDT,* 784, expresses questions over Moltmann's integration of Christian eschatology and social ideology, claiming some see it as religious Marxism and that therefore some Christians do not trust its Marxist root and some Marxists do not trust its Christian heart. Cf. D.D. Webster, "Liberation Theology, *EDT,* 686-88 (esp. 688).

118. Cf. Neal, *Theology as Hope,* 69.

119. Moltmann, *Church,* 150. For Moltmann, the appellation of the Spirit as Lord testifies of Pentecost as Yahweh's liberating Exodus deliverance in anticipation of the

Kingdom and its "determinative" presence in the present, *The Spirit of Life: A Universal Affirmation,* trans. Margaret Kohl (Minneapolis, MN: First Fortress, 1991, 2001), 271. Cf. 239, where Moltmann actually denominates "the kingdom of the Spirit".

120. Moltmann, *Church,* 151-52.

121. Moltmann, *Church,* 152.

122. Moltmann, *Church,* 152. For Moltmann, mission and pneumatology are inseparable, as evidenced in subsequent claims that Christ's sense of identity and mission were affirmed through his experience of the Spirit, *Spirit of Life,* 60-61, and that, furthermore, for "the people who experience themselves in the presence of the Spirit", a twofold movement occurs of gathering as church and sending out in mission, 234.

123. Congar, *IBHS,* contended that "The time of the Church is essentially a time of mission, bearing witness and kerygma" (1:58) yet agreed that the Church's dialogue with the world and its cultures, including other religions, benefits both and presupposes the Spirit's presence in both, 2:219.

124. Moltmann, *Church,* 153-54.

125. Moltmann, *Church,* 154-55.

126. Moltmann, *Church,* 155-57.

127. Moltmann, *Church,* 157-58.

128. Moltmann, *Church,* 158-59. Although Moltmann admits equivocal elements in the world religions that present special challenges, *Spirit of Life,* xiii.

129. Moltmann, *Church,* 159-63.

130. On mutual benefits of dialogue, see D.R. Smock, ed., *Interfaith Dialogue and Peacebuilding* (Washington, DC: United States Institute for Peace, 2002), J. Liechty, "Migration in Northern Ireland: A Strategy for Living in Peace When Truth Claims Clash," 89-102 (92) and D.R. Smock, "Conclusion," 127-32, (131). Cf. Moltmann, *Church,* 159, 161.

131. Moltmann, *Church,* 162-63. Interestingly, Moltmann argues that Christians must experience charismatic gifts of personal awakenings and ecclesial testimonies in order to be enabled to experience charismatic gifting for political and social relevance and service, *Spirit of Life,* 186. Accordingly, he insists "the charismatic movement must not become a non-political religion, let alone a de-politicized one" (186).

132. Moltmann, *Church,* 163.

133. Moltmann, *Church,* 163.

134. Cf. Neal, *Theology as Hope,* 69.

135. R. Bauckham, *The Theology of Jürgen Moltmann* (Edinburgh: T & T Clark, 1996), 13-14; cf. 126.

136. Bauckham, *Moltmann,* 131.

137. Bauckham, *Moltmann,* 149-50.

138. Cf. Neal, *Theology as Hope,* 174.

139. Bauckham, *Moltmann,* 18. In "A British Appraisal" of Moltmann's *Spirit of Life,* M.W.G. Stibbe, observes that Moltmann seeks to cast off narrower restrictions of the Spirit to the Church in order to expand the Spirit's living presence more broadly into all of creation, *JPT* 4 (1994), 5-16 (8). Although grateful for the holistic and ecumenical emphases of Moltmann's pneumatology, 8-12, Stibbe has questions about such issues as possible blurring of immanence and transcendence, 12, or extreme monism, 13, etc. Accordingly, he thinks the greatest weakness of Moltmann's pneumatology may be the lack of a purposeful paradigm for distinguishing between Spirit and spirits, the divine and the demonic, 15-16. However, Moltmann, "A Response to My Pentecostal Dialogue Partners," JPT 4 (1994), 59-70, attempts to answer these and other criticisms by explaining

his context, 61, arguing his points biblically and theologically, 62, 65, and clarifying his statements, 67.

140. Bauckham, *Moltmann,* 125. Cf. Moltmann, *Church,* 64-65.

141. Bauckham, *Moltmann,* 221, 227.

142. Cf. J. Moltmann, "Hope", *NHCT,* 239-41 (240).

143. *JPT* 4 (1994): M.W.G. Stibbe, "A British Appraisal," 5-16, P. Kuzmic, "A Croatian War-Time Reading," 17-24, F.D. Macchia, "A North American Response," 25-33, S. Chan, "An Asian Response," 35-40, J. Sepúlveda , "The Perspective of Chilean Pentecostalism," 41-49, J.J. Lapoorta, "An African Response," 51-58, and J. Moltmann, "A Response to My Pentecostal Dialogue Partners," 59-70.

144. F.D. Macchia, "The Spirit and Life: A Further Response to Jürgen Moltmann," *JPT* 5 (October 1994), 121-27.

145. A. Lord, "The Pentecostal-Moltmann Dialogue: Implications for Mission," *JPT* 11:2 (2003), 271-87.

146. Another interesting conversation would be Pentecostals with the Catholic pneumatologist, Y. Congar, which A. Yong, *The Spirit Poured Out on All Flesh: Pentecostalism and the Possibility of Global Theology* (Grand Rapids: Baker, 2005), has briefly initiated in the context of pneumatological ecclesiology, 133, 134-51, but not on mission. Yong himself does, however, connect pneumatology, ecclesiology, and missiology, 83, 123-24, 175-76, and 265-66. Also, Congar interacts significantly with the Charismatic Renewal. E.g., see *IBHS,* 2:149-72.

147. Lord, "Dialogue," 274-81.

148. Lord, "Dialogue," 281.

149. Lord, "Dialogue," 284.

150. The next chapter more fully discusses Christian evangelistic mission and theology of religions in a context of interreligious encounter and dialogue.

151. E.g., C.H. Pinnock, "The Work of the Holy Spirit in Hermeneutics," *JPT* 2 (April 1993), 3-23 and F.D. Macchia, "Tradition and the Novum of the Spirit: A Review of Clark Pinnock's *Flame of Love,*" *JPT* 13 (1998), 31-48. See C.H. Pinnock, "The Church in the Power of the Holy Spirit: The Promise of a Pentecostal Ecclesiology," *JPT* 14:2 (April 2006), 147-65. Responses include F.D. Macchia, "Pinnock's Pneumatology: A Pentecostal Appreciation," *JPT* 14:2 (April 2006), 167-73, T.L. Cross, "A Response to Clark Pinnock's 'Church in the Power of the Holy Spirit," *JPT* 14:2 (April 2006), 175-82, and R.H. Gause, "A Pentecostal Response to Pinnock's Proposal," *JPT* 14:2 (April 2006), 183-88.

152. E.g., Pinnock, *Wideness.*

153. Pinnock, *Flame,* 185-214.

154. Prevenient grace represents "the first dawning of grace in the soul", before the bright light of conversion shines, and actually empowers human beings to respond to or resist God's redemptive provision. Conscience, therefore, is present in all humans as God's gracious gift, and is an instrument of the Holy Spirit. See C.W. Williams' *John Wesley's Theology Today: A Study of the Wesleyan Tradition in the Light of Current Theological Dialogue* (Nashville: Abingdon, 1960, 1990), 39-46, esp. 40-44 (40).

155. For further discussion of Pinnock's charismatic and inclusivist theology of religions, see A. Yong, "Whither Theological Inclusivism? The Development and Critique of an Evangelical Theology of Religions," *EQ* 71:4 (October 1999), 327-48.

156. E.g., M.J. Erickson, *The Evangelical Left: Encountering Postconservative EvangelicalTheology* (Grand Rapids: Baker, 1997), 112-30, and T. Gray & C. Sinkinson, eds., *Reconstructing Theology: A Critical Assessment of the Theology of Clark Pinnock* (Waynesboro: Paternoster, 2000).

157. E.g., H.H. Knight III, *A Future for Truth: Evangelical Theology in a Postmodern World* (Nashville: Abingdon, 1997), 193-94, 251-52. Cf. S.J. Grenz, *Renewing the Center: Evangelical Theology in a Post-Theological Era* (Grand Rapids: Baker, 2000), 249-86 (cf. 257, 258, 260, 267, 279).

158. See Yong, "Whither Theological Inclusivism?" 327-48.

159. B.L. Callen, *Clark H. Pinnock: Journey Toward Renewal* (Nappanee: Evangel, 2000), e.g., 77-81, 176-78.

160. This section draws on the work of C.F. Parham and J.H. King.

161. E.g., see Yong, *Discerning,* on Moltmann, 69-70 and 148 fn. 70, and on Pinnock, 200-03.

162. See Yong, *Discerning*, 187-97.

163. See D. Jacobsen, *Thinking in the Spirit: Theologies of the Early Pentecostal Movement* (Bloomington & Indianapolis: Indiana University Press, 2003), 130-32, 150-56, 177-79, and 192-93, and W.J. Hollenweger, 'From Azusa Street to the Toronto Phenomenon: Historical Roots of the Pentecostal Movement', *Pentecostal Movements as an Ecumenical Challenge,* eds. J. Moltmann and K.J. Kuschel, *Concilium* 1996/3 (Maryknoll, NY: Orbis, 1996), 3-14. Cf. T. Richie, "'The Unity of the Spirit': Are Pentecostals Inherently Ecumenists and Inclusivists?" *JEPTA* 26 (2006), 21-35.

164. C.F. Parham, *The Sermons of Charles F. Parham* (NY: Garland, 1985 pr). This is a collection of earlier and separate publications by Parham previously published as *A Voice Crying in the Wilderness* (1902) and *The Everlasting Gospel* (1919). E.g., see *A Voice,* 85, 103-08, 121-23, 134-38, and *Everlasting,* 92-95. Cf. T. Richie, "Eschatological Inclusivism: Exploring Early Pentecostal Theology of Religions in Charles Fox Parham," *JEPTA* 27:2 (2007), 138-52.

165. E.g., see Bishop J.H. King, *Yet Speaketh* (Franklin Springs, GA: Publishing House of the Pentecostal Holiness Church, 1949), 21-31 and 43-61, and *From Passover to Pentecost* (Franklin Springs, GA: Advocate, 1911, 1976 [fourth edition]), 5-8, 14-16, 33, 39-40, 101-04, and 109-11. Cf. T. Richie, "Azusa-era Optimism: Bishop J. H. King's Pentecostal Theology of Religions as a Possible Paradigm for Today," *JPT* 14:2 (April 2006), 247-60. T. Moon cautions to keep this aspect of King's thought in mind. Whatever else it was, King's theology of religions was not a rosy-eyed optimism denying dark and demonic elements often found in the religions. See his J.H. King's Theology of Religions: 'Magnanimous Optmism?' *JPT* 16:1 (2007), 112-32. Cf. Richie, "A Moderate Move or Missing the Point? A Response to Tony Moon's 'J.H. King's Theology of Religions: "Magnanimous Optimism?"' *JPT* 16:2 (April 2008), 118-25.

166. See Yong, *Spirit Poured Out*, ch. 6. Nevertheless, this is not meant to exclude inclusivists from other traditions. E.g., some of the leading inclusivists are post-Vatican II style Catholics. Congar helpfully offered a clear "Christological criterion" for "the authenticity of a pneumatology", defining it as "fundamentally to look for the way in which the actions and fruits that are attributed to the Holy Spirit are of a piece with or at least in accordance with the work of the incarnate Word, Jesus Christ the Lord" (*IBHS,* 2:210; cf. 2:211). Therefore, "We simply do not know the frontiers of the Spirit's work in this world, nor the ways in which he acts", although "We can be sure that they are related to Christ" (*WS,* 126). For him, "the Spirit is the one who in secret gathers up and binds together everyone who is trying to stammer the words 'Our Father'" (127).

167. T. Richie, "Neither Naïve nor Narrow: A Balanced Approach to Christian Theology of Religions," *CPCR* 15 (Feb. 2006) http://www.pctii.org/cyberj/cyber15.html].

168. This section is in dialogue with the work of Veli-Matti Kärkkäinen and Amos Yong.

169. For an explication of how Kärkkäinen's Pentecostal identity informs his work as a theologian in general and as a theologian of religions in particular, see Yong, "Whither Evangelical Theology? The Work of Veli-Matti Kärkkäinen as a Case Study of Contemporary Trajectories," *ERT* 30:1 (2006): 60-85.

170. See especially V.M. Kärkkäinen, *Trinity and Religious Pluralism: The Doctrine of the Trinity in Christian Theology of Religions* (Aldershot, UK, and Burlington, VT: Ashgate, 2004), 2; cf. also his *Toward a Pneumatological Theology: Pentecostal and Ecumenical Perspectives on Ecclesiology, Soteriology, and Theology of Mission*, ed. A. Yong (Lanham: University Press of America, 2002), ch. 14.

171. E.g., V.M. Kärkkäinen, "Toward a Pneumatological Theology of Religions: A Pentecostal-Charismatic Inquiry," *IRM* 91: 361 (2002): 187-98, and "How to Speak of the Spirit among Religions: Trinitarian 'Rules' for a Pneumatological Theology of Religions," *IBMR* 30:3 (2006): 121-27.

172. Interestingly, F.D. Macchia, *Baptized in the Spirit: A Global Pentecostal Theology* (Grand Rapids: Zondervan, 2006), suggests Kärkkäinen, along with several other Pentecostal theologians, though effective, are contributing to a trend away from distinctively Pentecostal theology through explicitly ecumenical efforts, although he commends ecumenism itself, 24-26. Not surprisingly, Macchia's own theology of religions highlights Spirit baptism, 178-90. M.L. Tan-Chow, *Pentecostal Theology for the Twenty-First Century: Engaging with Multi-Faith Singapore* (Surrey, UK: Ashgate, 2007), in a non-Western Pentecostal approach, agrees that Pentecostalism can transcend traditional exclusivism by drawing on its own resources of spirituality and theology, 22-23.

173. See Yong, *Discerning*.

174. However, Congar, who did not doubt that God is active in the Pentecostal and Charismatic movements, *IBHS*, 2:145, warned, in the interests of ecumenism, "that those who belong to the Renewal should recognize that they have no monopoly on the Spirit and its activities do not form a Church for them" (2:209).

175. Yong, *Spirit Poured Out*, 254.

176. A. Yong, *Hospitality & the Other: Pentecost, Christian Practices, and the Neighbor* (Maryknoll, New York: Orbis Books, 2008).

177. Yong, *Hospitality*, 131-39.

178. When stressing the pneumatological aspect of theology of religions, important to remember is that this is always in relation to the Christological aspect. As Congar insists: "The essential thing is to respect the two missions, of the Word and of the Spirit, on the pattern of the succession which derives from the procession from the Trinity" (*IBHS*, 1:25). However, always "Christ and the Spirit both carry out the same work of salvation" (1:50). Thus, inarguably the "relationships between the Paraclete and Christ are also extremely close in the economy of salvation" (1:56). One might say the Christ and the Spirit, and therefore Christology and pneumatology, are distinct but not divided.

179. See Kärkkäinen, "A Response to Tony Richie's 'Azusa-era Optimism: Bishop J. H. King's Pentecostal Theology of Religions as a Possible Paradigm for Today'," *JPT* 15:2 (April 2007): 263-68.

180. See Macchia, *Baptized*, 178-90.

181. For example, it appears that the exclusivist position is defended in this essay— R.L. Gallagher, "The Holy Spirit in the World: In Non-Christians, in Creation, and Other Religions," *AJPS* 9:1 (2006): 17-33—although the author does not put it in those terms.

182. As suggested in A. Yong, "Can We Get 'Beyond the Paradigm' in Christian Theology of Religions? A Response to Terry Muck," Interpretation 61:1 (January 2007): 28-32. Note that Kärkkäinen himself organized his *An Introduction to The Theology of Religions* using a different set of categories than exclusivism, inclusivism, and pluralism.

For further discussion of the unresolved difficulties for each of these approaches, see part 1 of A. Yong, "The Spirit, Christian Practices, and the Religions: Theology of Religions in Pentecostal and Pneumatological Perspective," Asbury Journal 62:2 (2007): 5-31.

183. E.g., note that Yong, *Spirit Poured Out*, suggests Pentecostals might have more in common with Congar's dynamic and charismatic ecclesiology than ordinarily might be suspected due to its Roman Catholic background, 147-48 and 150. On the inclusive Church and other religions see Congar, *IBHS*, 2:219-24.

184. E.g., Kärkkäinen, *Theology of Religions*, 148-49, and Yong, *Beyond*, 105. Pinnock particularly expresses indebtedness to Lewis. See his *Flame*, 105, 151, 175, 204-05, and Callen's *Journey*, esp. 23-24 and 169-70, etc.

185. In his classic apologetic, *Mere Christianity* (New York: Collier, 1960), Lewis argued that "If you are a Christian you do not have to believe that all the other religions are simply wrong through and through. If you are an atheist you do have to believe that the main point in all the religions of the whole world is simply one huge mistake. If you are a Christian, you are free to think that all these religions, even the queerest ones, contain at least some hint of truth. When I was an atheist I had to try to persuade myself that most of the human race have always been wrong about the question that mattered to them most; when I became a Christian I was able to take a more liberal view. But, of course, being a Christian does mean thinking that where Christianity differs from other religions, Christianity is right and they are wrong. As in arithmetic—there is only one right answer to a sum, and all other answers are wrong: but some of the wrong answers are much nearer to being right than others (29). See L. Summer, "Non-Christian Religions," *The C. S. Lewis Readers' Encyclopedia*, eds. J.D. Schultz and J.G. West Jr. (Grand Rapids: Zondervan, 1998), 294-95. Cf. T. Richie, "Hints from Heaven: Can C. S. Lewis Help Evangelicals Hear God in Other Religions?" *ERT* 32:1 (January 2008), 38-55.

186. L. Newbigin. *The Gospel in a Pluralist Society* (London: SPCK, 1989), 182-83. Not surprisingly, Yong, *Spirit Poured Out*, points out that Newbigin's missionary ecclesiology is robustly pneumatological, 155. Cf. L. Newbigin, *The Household of God: Lectures on the Nature of the Church* (London: SCM, 1953). Further, H.D. Hunter, "We are the Church: A New Congregationalism—a Pentecostal Perspective," *Pentecostal Movements as an Ecumenical Challenge*, ed. J. Moltmann and K-J. Kuschel (London: SCM; Maryknoll, NY: Orbis, 1996) builds on Newbigin's ecumenical ecclesiology, 17-21 (18).

187. Cf. T. Richie, "Effectively Engaging Pluralism and Postmodernism in a So-Called Post-Christian Culture: A Review Essay of Lesslie Newbigin's *The Gospel in a Pluralist Society*," *PR* (Fall 2007), 27-39.

188. Although a joint project with mutual input and agreement, this section addresses insights uniquely from A. Yong in Yong and Richie, "Bearing Witness in a Religiously Pluralistic World".

189. See F.C. Copleston, *Religion and the One: Philosophies East and West* (New York: Crossroad, 1982).

190. Cf. A. Yong, "'As the Spirit Gives Utterance...': Pentecost, Intra-Christian Ecumenism, and the Wider Oekumene," IRM 92:366 (July 2003): 299-314; "The Spirit Bears Witness: Pneumatology, Truth, and the Religions," SJT 57:1 (2004): 14-38; and *Spirit Poured Out*, ch. 4.

191. On these points, this writing will follow the brilliant reading of the Acts 2 narrative provided by M. Welker, *God the Spirit*, trans. J.F. Hoffmeyer (Minneapolis: Fortress, 1994), ch. 5.

192. Cf. J. Jacques-Suurmond, *Word and Spirit at Play: Towards a Charismatic Theology*, trans. John Bowden (Grand Rapids: Eerdmans, 1995), 201.

193. Glossolalia has become an increasing complex topic among Pentecostal theologians. E.g., F.D. Macchia, "Theology, Pentecostal," *NIDPCM,* 1120-41, sees speaking in tongues as an unifying force for ecumenism, 1132, and as theophanic sacrament, 1133; C.S. Keener, "Why Does Luke Use Tongues as a Sign of the Spirit's Empowerment?" *JPT* 15:2 (April 2007), 177-84, argues Luke intentionally uses the sign of speaking in tongues to emphasize baptism in the Spirit as power to testify for Christ cross-culturally; S.J. Land, "The Nature and Evidence of Spiritual Fullness," ed. R. White, *Endued with Power: The Holy Spirit in the Church* (1995), 55-82, associates tongues with a life of prayerful service to God in powerful witness of redemptive reality, 69-78, and describes the practice as participation in the distinctive eschatological language of the Kingdom of God through which the Christian community testifies to the advent of the last days with demonstration and power, 69-72; T. Richie, "Transposition and Tongues: Pentecostalizing an Important Insight of C. S. Lewis," *JPT* 13:1 (October 2004), 117-37, describes tongues as part of the divine-human interface that occurs through the operation of the Holy Spirit in the experience of believers through the principle of "transposition." Additional is the discussion of initial evidence as in G.B. McGee, ed., *Initial Evidence: Historical and Biblical Perspectives on the Pentecostal Doctrine of Spirit Baptism* (Peabody, MA: Hendrickson, 1191). Cf. W.W. and R. Menzies, *Spirit and Power: Foundations of Pentecostal Experience* (Grand Rapids: Zondervan, 2000).

194. On these points, see the brilliant reading of the Acts 2 narrative provided by Welker, *God the Spirit*, ch. 5.

195. Cf. Jacques-Suurmond, *Play*, 201. Cf. Congar, *IBHS,* 2:219 and *WS,* 71. Yet important to remember is that while the Spirit's "freedom" to work when and where the Spirit will, "really exists," always "it is the freedom of the living and glorified Lord Jesus together with his Spirit" (*WS,* 61).

196. Cf. K. Cracknell, *In Good and Generous Faith: Christian Responses to Religious Pluralism* (Peterborough, UK: Epworth, 2005), 97-100, 102-05.

197. Yong describes the task of comparative theology in a religiously plural world, *Beyond*, chap. 7.

198. The difficulties associated with obtaining adequate comparative categories across religious lines are discussed extensively throughout R.C. Neville, ed., *The Comparative Religious Ideas Project*, 3 vols. (Albany: SUNY Press, 2001).

Chapter 3

Interreligious Dialogue through a Pentecostal Lens

Introduction

Preceding chapters have briefly overviewed and analyzed the contemporary global context of religious pluralism and the current state of Pentecostal theology of religions in response. Implications of the study to this point include urgency for addressing religious pluralism, both as a concrete fact and as a conceptual philosophy. Furthermore, while Pentecostals have made a strong start toward this eventual end, more direct and practical progress needs to occur in the area of actual interreligious encounter, dialogue, and cooperation.

This chapter will survey the subjects of interreligious encounter and dialogue through what is currently underway in the field. It will first look at the rise of the ecumenical movement and Pentecostal responses to it. Then it will look at the beginnings and developments of specific Pentecostal ideas on interreligious encounter and dialogue. Next, it will survey a sampling of approaches reflecting the environment out of which Pentecostals and others may address the field. Finally, it will briefly analyze relevant aspects of the above from a Pentecostal standpoint with a view toward establishing the potential significance of the testimonial paradigm for interreligious encounter and dialogue explored in subsequent chapters. Throughout, the study in this chapter makes an effort to understand and articulate the significance and nature of interreligious encounter and dialogue in order to further inform and develop Pentecostal theology of religions and dialogue praxis.

Ecumenical Background

General Terminology, History, and Ideology

With the rise of the modern ecumenical movement, words like "dialogue" and "ecumenism" or "ecumenical" have become technical terms with quite specific connotations and applications.[1] Actually, the determinative terms "ecumenism" and "ecumenical" derive from the NT Greek *oikoumene*, usually used during the days of the Roman Empire to signify the whole inhabited world.[2] In recent times however, these terms have come to signify a movement dedicated to renewing the unity of the Church, and eventually affirming the unity of all humankind. Common fellowship, service, and witness are prevalent themes of this ecumenical movement. NT passages such as John 17:20-23 are hallmarks for the movement.[3]

"Dialogue" is a crucial method of the movement for promoting ecumenical cooperation and growth.[4] Essentially, it usually involves mutual conversation between differing faith groups for purposes of seeking common ground and gaining understanding about God's ways and wisdom in others. The ecumenical movement, though focusing on Christian unity, has always recognized the importance of Christian relations with other living faiths. However, in recent decades the significance of interfaith relations has increasingly attracted more attention.[5] This interfaith aspect and its application in dialogue is a central concern of the present work.

The World Council of Churches, an international confederacy of Protestant churches founded in 1948 and headquartered in Geneva, Switzerland, has long been a leading proponent of ecumenism, and therefore, of ecumenical dialogue, including, especially since the 1960s, interfaith dialogue.[6] The most important WCC document on interreligious dialogue bases the practice of dialogue on 'our common humanity' and 'increasing contemporary human inter-relatedness.'[7] WCC operates on several general assumptions.

- God is omnipresent. The Christian is free to enter into dialogue since God is with both partners of the dialogue.

- The liberating gospel is the basic contribution to the dialogue.

- The Spirit is blowing everywhere, without limits; therefore, the dialogue may lead to unexpected results.

- Each partner should anticipate a greater understanding of his or her own as well as of the other's faith.[8]

Institutionally Pentecostals have primarily been skeptical and suspicious of the WCC, mostly out of concerns over alleged liberal compromises, but several important individuals have braved the opposition for the sake of unity. Future relations are still unsure but interest seems to be increasing.[9] Beginning in the early 1990s, WCC "Consultations with Pentecostals," eventually evolving into the "WCC-Pentecostal Joint Consultative Group," now in its second round, also suggests possible developing appreciation and respect.[10]

Since Vatican II, an important Roman Catholic council convened by Pope John XXIII (1962) and closed by Pope Paul VI (1965), Catholicism has also been a vital force in ecumenism.[11] More recently, in 1991, the document on "Dialogue and Proclamation" sought to find a balance between dialogue and proclamation. Theologically it affirms interreligious dialogue on the basis of shared humanity through creation in God's image, with a calling to a common destiny in the fullness of life in God, and in the Holy Spirit's presence in other religious traditions. Yet its approval of dialogue signals no disavowal of evangelistic proclamation. Roman Catholics persistently maintain that the risen Christ has mandated proclamation.[12]

Classical Pentecostals inherited typically suspicious attitudes toward Catholicism from the Protestant Reformers. However, the Catholic Charismatic Renewal, along with other factors, has resulted in some interesting adjustments to that attitude. Ongoing dialogue between Catholics and Pentecostals has therefore become an intriguing reality.[13] Evangelicals have not traditionally been involved in ecumenism—at least not as partners with WCC or Roman Catholicism. Recently however, more Evangelicals are apparently developing ecumenical interests, including ecumenical dialogue.[14]

The NT usage of *oikoumene* includes the geographical sense but usually without cultural connotations (e.g., Matt 24:14; Acts 17:31).[15] It therefore signifies the entire inhabited world. Those within the ecumenical movement today tend to stress ecumenism as implying "unity" and "universality".[16] A concern of some, especially of more theologically conservative Evangelicals, has been that in order to maintain amiable associations between those of vastly divergent theologies, ecumenists intentionally downplay the importance of theology.[17] Yet ecumenical appreciation has strong roots in the ancient history and tradition of the Church. The Eastern Church, for instance, speaks of "ecumenical" councils and synods, and the Roman Church calls its councils "ecumenical". Even Evangelicals refer to the Apostles', Nicene, and Athanasian creeds as "ecumenical".[18]

Pentecostal Capitulation and Recovery[19]

Pentecostal ecumenist and historical theologian Cecil Robeck insists that important early Pentecostal leaders shared a unifying ecumenical vision.[20] However, he speaks of a subsequent "sordid history" in which that initial vision characteristically "optimistic and outward looking" then "slowly began to decay, turning in upon itself, becoming increasingly defensive, pessimistic, compromising, and protectionistic."[21] Robeck adds that "it was and is a depressing history" involving "specific personalities, power struggles, misunderstandings, and above a large measure of fear and disinformation."[22]

Nevertheless, Robeck concludes that Pentecostals are inherently ecumenical, that is they prize genuine Christian unity, but that they have their own version and vision of it.[23] Moreover, Pentecostalism's multicultural nature is an important element of its approach to Christian diversity and unity.[24] However, any approach to ecumenism must take into account Pentecostalism's inherent and entrenched evangelistic identity and impulse.[25] Significantly, Robeck thinks the Pentecostal tradition is "now more globally informed, less individualistic, more realistic, less triumphalistic, more willing to listen, less willing to talk."[26] Yet he urges Pentecostals to be more willing to engage in dialogue, to move past parochialism, to grapple with the meaning of globalization, and to make a stringent process of self-examination a priority.[27] He admits that his counsel will require transformative understanding and creative action, but is convinced that "the potential for Pentecostals to contribute substantially to greater Christian Unity is enormous."[28]

As Allan Anderson reports, contrary to the pattern of North American Classical Pentecostals a few Latin American Pentecostal churches early on became formal members of WCC, and therefore, to some extent at least, of its ecumenical agenda.[29] Subsequently however, their ecumenical involvement became a controversial issue.[30] Similarly, most of the European Pentecostal churches are isolationist with some being more ecumenical.[31] Admittedly, at times opposition from others to speaking in tongues hindered Pentecostal instincts toward and involvement in ecumenicity.[32] South African David du Plessis (1905-87) became such a global representative of Pentecost in ecumenical circles he acquired the distinctive title of "Mr. Pentecost".[33] Yet his role as a Pentecostal ambassador-at-large was fraught with controversy from within the Pentecostal movement's administrative leadership.[34] By its very nature, the Charismatic wing of "Pentecostalism" has often been more ecumenical, thus influencing Catholics and Protestants in unprecedented measures.[35]

Yet Pentecostalism per se has not typically exercised its ecumenical potential. However, changes in attitudes toward other Christians and other religions are occurring through a new generation of Pentecostals, in large part due to increasing education and contact with the academy. Anderson credits Swiss historian and analyst of Pentecostalism Walter Hollenweger with initiating and generating much of this "seismic change." Hollenweger undoubtedly has helped make the broader Christian world and the Pentecostals be more aware of and informed about one another.[36]

Quite significantly, Anderson observes that, "strong ecumenical convictions abounded in the early years" among Pentecostals, both in North America and in Europe. However, external rejection and internal division robbed the movement of its rich ecumenical potential.[37] Pentecostals do often recognize their need to unite with each other, and the rise of the Charismatic movement in the mid-twentieth century raised some ecumenical issues for them, as did increasing attention and affirmation from ecumenical leaders such as Bishop Newbigin. Yet by-and-large they viewed individuals, such as du Plessis and Donald Gee (and more recently, Mel Robeck), who attempted to lead them into ecumenical involvement with mistrust and suspicion.[38] Hollenweger hopes that Pentecostals are completing a cycle in which they return to their dialogical roots. The ecumenical examples of Latin American Pentecostals in Brazil and Chile suggest he could be correct.[39]

Further hopeful signs of increasing ecumenical openness among even Classical Pentecostals include dialogues in recent decades between Pentecostals and Catholics and Pentecostals and the WCC.[40] Pentecostals are also increasingly involving themselves in interracial and cross-cultural dialogue, sometimes with almost miraculous results.[41] Fortunately, people like Mel Robeck determinedly continue to hold out the ecumenical challenge in effective fashion.[42] Anderson suggests that whether one adopts a broad/experiential definition of Pentecostalism or a narrow/doctrinal definition has immense implications for the future of Pentecostal ecumenism.[43] The former recognizes as Pentecostal those who distinctively experience the Spirit's fullness and spiritual gifts even in the midst of doctrinal differences. The latter insists only those accepting traditional teaching on subsequence and initial evidence are genuinely or legitimately called Pentecostal. Obviously, an experiential definition of Pentecostalism opens up a way for more appreciative interaction among its practitioners, and perhaps even with others.

Recognizing and Retrieving Pneumatological Ecumenism and Inclusivism[44]

Similarly to Allan Anderson (and others) but perhaps in stronger terms, I have insisted early Pentecostals originally were committed to ecumenical and inclusivist values. I have argued that inherent within Pentecostalism by virtue of the innate unifying agency of the Holy Spirit is an impulse toward ecumenism and inclusivism in relation to religious others which has often been neglected through over identification with anti-Pentecostal ideologies.[45] I cite arguments and examples from the NT, historical precedents in early classical Pentecostalism, and contemporary practice of missions by the global Pentecostal movement to support this thesis.[46] I call upon contemporary Pentecostals to help bring healing to the brokenness of the Body of Christ and to exorcise demonic assumptions and tensions regarding non-Christian religions through the power of Pentecost.[47] Yet I insist relationship with religious others be placed within the context of an uncompromising loyalty to the Lordship of Jesus Christ. I do not seek doctrinal or organizational assimilation.[48] Nonetheless, I think Pentecostals should enthusiastically embrace ecumenism and inclusivism in meeting today's challenges of religious diversity and plurality with an uncompromising, all-encompassing stance faithful to Christ and his Spirit through the apostolic injunction of "the unity of the Spirit".[49]

My involvement in ecumenical dialogue and interfaith activities has led me to note widely varied responses to such work among fellow Pentecostals.

> On the academic level I have encountered interest driven by understanding that this is an important and inevitable endeavor. At issue here seems more the way to do it well rather than whether it ought to be done at all. On the grassroots congregational level, I have generally encountered enthusiasm driven by experiences of actual inter-religious relations among family, friends, or in the work force. Issues here seem to be relational almost as much as theoretical. On the grassroots ministerial level, I have occasionally encountered anxiety driven by inferences about an ever-increasing encroachment of ideological pluralism. Here doctrinal rather than practical issues come to the fore. At the administrative level, I have often encountered intimidation driven by insecurity regarding possible political fallout. The predominant issue here may be about power more than about progress.[50]

In my opinion, "These responses seem broadly representative of some of the basic concerns for many Pentecostals today."[51] My main concern is that "an inherent impulse of the Holy Spirit embracing unity in diversity not be neglected" by Pentecostals "to the tragic detriment of our movement and possible forfeiture of our vision." In other words, I fear quenching the Spirit and the consequences (cf. 1 Th 5.19).[52]

Pentecostal Beginnings
In Theological-Pneumatological Approaches[53]

Amos Yong and Veli-Matti Kärkkäinen are two leading Pentecostals working in theology of religions. While they have usually focused on theological issues regarding relations among the religions such as the role of pneumatology and of trinitarian thought, they have also begun to think about actual encounter and dialogue between Christians and non-Christians. Yong is a pioneer in Pentecostal theology of religions. He champions a pneumatological approach accenting the universality of the Holy Spirit among all peoples while affirming orthodoxy on Christology and soteriology. Yong suggests a Pentecostal-Charismatic theology of religions should "free human beings for participation in the interreligious dialogue." The goal of dialogue is not to establish agreement or ignore differences, but rather to serve the righteousness, peace, and truth characteristic of the Kingdom of God. Dialogue can provide "the kind of self-criticism that leads to the mutual and, ultimately, eschatological transformation of religious traditions, including the Christian faith."[54]

Yong argues that Christian theology of religions cannot be adequately developed in isolation from religious others but requires conversation with others.[55] To critics of interreligious dialogue he replies that not all are called to formal interreligious dialogue, though all are called as witnesses; that bearing witness can take the form of dialogical relationship; and, that Christianity is "impoverished and debilitated" if it avoids directly asking the questions interreligious dialogue requires.[56] Yong's work reflects a sophisticated theology of openness to interaction with religious others that labors to be loyal to its own inner Pentecostal ethos.

Kärkkäinen is another Pentecostal author who addresses theology of religions. For Kärkkäinen all knowledge of God has "universal intention and is to be shared by all".[57] In Christian dialogue with other religions the central tenets of the Christian faith are to be presented to religious others "in the spirit of a confident, yet humble witness",[58] that is, without arrogance with humility and respect. Nonetheless, dialogical purpose is not only information but also persuasion—though always—and this is especially significant—"in ways that honor the Other and give him or her the right to make up his or her own mind."[59] Interreligious dialogue is not a neutral experience or process. The followers of all faiths have convictions about ultimate questions that should be shared. A reciprocal shaping should also be expected, unless true dialogue degenerates into only "two or more monologues." Interreligious dialogue, Christian missions, and cooperative social concerns are not incompatible.[60]

Kärkkäinen staunchly suggests an acknowledgement and critical assessment of the Spirit's presence in other religions "ties the church to dialogue with the Other" because wherever God's presence is found "it bears some relation to the church." Thus, discovery and discernment through dialogue of the Spirit's gifts in the religions are demanded.[61] Kärkkäinen's work reflects a more subtly Pentecostal approach to interreligious engagement than that of Yong, and is perhaps more intentionally ecumenical, but is nonetheless sustained by the same commitment to major guiding principles of the movement's belief and practice.

In a Pragmatic-Pneumatological Approach[62]

My hands-on involvement in interreligious encounter and dialogue has led me to make some very pragmatic observations and applications about Pentecostal involvement. I believe that while Pentecostals may at first glance appear to adherents of other faiths to be unlikely participants for interreligious dialogue, they really ought to be, and some actually are, more like hopeful partners.[63] Admittedly, Pentecostals have tended to be pessimistic toward other religions, viewing them more as targets of evangelism than they do anything else. Yet I argue this pessimism is a betrayal of original and authentic Pentecostalism.[64] I am sure that Pentecostalism's involvement with interfaith encounters is in the best interests of the Pentecostal faith itself, the broader Christian family of faith, and all people of faith everywhere—and even the people of the world who may claim no particular religious faith.[65] One of the most significant, if not the most significant, efforts for justice and peace in our world today begins with religions talking and working together toward those noble ends. The volatile global situation of interreligious tensions suggests no less. I concede, however, that many Pentecostals do not agree. One of the main reasons has to do with perceived violations of evangelistic fervor. I disavow "aggressive" evangelism as implying coercion, but affirm "energetic" and "enthusiastic" evangelism as sufficiently conveying Pentecostals evangelistic values. Accordingly, for me dynamic evangelism and dialogue are not at odds.[66] In fact, authentic evangelism should include ethical and social concerns as well as conversional ones. In short, "robust-but-not rude Pentecostal evangelism is not inimical to sincere Pentecostal participation in ecumenical and interreligious dialogue."[67]

I think Pentecostals really have much to gain and to give in interreligious dialogue and partnership.[68] As for what they can gain, first, Pentecostals can increase their effectiveness through cooperative social efforts. Second, Pentecostals will be challenged to stretch themselves, to deepen and develop spiritually and theologically, through engagement with those who confront us with competing or even contradictory worldviews. Third, frankly interfaith fields are fertile ground for sowing seeds of witness regarding their Christian faith. Fourthly, their exposure to devout, well-trained representatives of other faiths enables them to understand what religions other than their own offer their adherents.[69]

As for what Pentecostals can give, first, all they expect to receive they expect to reciprocate. Religious others will conceivably gain from partnership with them in cooperative social efforts, will be stretched and challenged by engagement with them, will share their beliefs and practices with them, and will perhaps begin to perceive why so many people around the world choose to be Pentecostal Christians. Second, their unique pneumatological approach to the Christian faith and life has much to offer. A robust pneumatology recognizing the Spirit's universal presence and influence and Christ's unique significance is a potent explanation for non-Christian religious reality and Christian identity from a Christian perspective.[70] Third, the sheer size of their movement, arguably suggests it taps into an enormous religious energy field that seems to be transforming today's religious world; conceivably, it may be contagious.[71]

Finally, I have urged Pentecostals to employ "five significant values" in interaction with religious others. *Charity* witnesses to religious others by letting the light of Christ's love shine through words and deeds, not just generally but specifically toward those of other faiths (Lu 10:25-37). *Hospitality* in personal or social interaction treats them as neighbors-in-need rather than as religious rivals or eternal enemies, becoming a multifaceted means of God's grace (1 Pet 4:9-10). *Availability* indicates that without pressuring or pushing Pentecostals place themselves at their disposal when they eventually inquire about Pentecostal belief (1 Pet 3:15). *Certainty* stands strong for faith convictions, being upfront about what one really believes (1 Co 14:8). *Humility* works hard at not coming across arrogantly as if one has the final word on all divine truth; one can confess one can only "know in part" (1 Co 13:9). I suggest that, "Practicing these five values can witness to the truth and power of faith in Jesus Christ to those of other faiths."[72]

A Premier Paradigm[73]

A Non-Colonial Model

Walter J. Hollenweger is the premier historian and analyst of Pentecostalism, and an exceptionally prolific author.[74] Lynne Price's excellent study of Hollenweger, *Theology Out of Place,* includes important theology of religions and interfaith dialogue applications.[75] In a chapter on his pneumatology, Price summarizes Hollenweger's prolific writing to introduce his overall thought. Price notes that Hollenweger uses the Acts 10 account of Peter and Cornelius, which for him is as much about the conversion of Peter as it is about the conversion of Cornelius. He accordingly declares that the gospel is objective, that it stands over against both evangelist and evangelized so that both may together learn of Christ, otherwise an evangelist is only a propagandist after all.[76] Hollenweger admits all Christians should share their experience of Christ with others but the question is how and how to do so without internal contradiction of the message. For Hollenweger it must be "dialogical and situational" (Peter and Cornelius are paradigmatic). A "colonial approach, assuming the form of Christianity presented by the evangelist is the only form, should be avoided."[77]

The Worldwide Reach of the Spirit

Price further points out that, according to Hollenweger, OT understanding of the Spirit and experience of the Spirit in non-Western churches indicate the Spirit is at work in the world as well as within the Church. He deplores the weakness of Pentecostal-Charismatic pneumatology due to following the Western Roman Catholic and Protestant version of the *filioque*, thereby limiting the Spirit to Christ. For Hollenweger the Sprit-led syncretism of the OT and indigenous non-white churches of the Third World today suggest the Spirit's presence in all cultures and religions.[78] Hollenweger has even called for a "theologically responsible syncretism."[79] Even science (e.g., physics) with its principle of the interchangeability of energy and matter suggests the presence of Spirit in all creation as the vital force of all life, that is, as the Spirit of Life. Accordingly, spiritual discernment looks for the manifestation of the Spirit wherever the Spirit is working "for the common good" (1 Co 12:7), even among other religions and traditions, and Christian evangelism and mission cooperates with those doing the same.[80]

Price summarizes Hollenweger's argument that Western pneumatology is weak, including Pentecostal and Charismatic varieties, because it is not based on an adequate doctrine of creation allowing and inviting the Spirit's presence and influence to be active everywhere. Hollenweger directly challenges Pentecostals to develop a more robust and well rounded pneumatology.[81] That healing gifts and forces are released in Christians and non-Christians alike illustrates the Spirit's presence in them all.[82] The same is true of Hollenweger's investigations into parapsychology, spirit possession, and exorcism—though here he often sounds quite Jungian as he refuses to differentiate sharply between good and evil, God and the Devil, and even suggests Satan may be the shadow side of God.[83]

A Pneumatology of Dignity and Liberty

For Hollenweger non-Christian religions are a very practical issue requiring Christian response. Indeed, he argues that Christians cooperating and listening not only to each other but to those of other religions is essential for confronting global issues of survival and progress.[84] Building on a foundation of the Quaker doctrine of the "inner light" as a cooperative principle within the body of Christ he extends the investigation into other religions. He advocates interreligious dialogue and suggests the religious enterprise is open-ended (quoting Lu 6:21). Again, in his dialogue with science Hollenweger re-visits his discussion of Spirit and body/energy and matter as fertile soil for theological growth. In his discussion of the Spirit and the Church Hollenweger argues that by virtue of divine creation all people have Spirit-given charisms, and that the Spirit is at work in the world as well as in the Church.[85] In his discussion of the Trinity God the Father is transcendent over his creation, the Spirit is immanent in creation, and Jesus Christ is the one in whom God decisively reveals himself. Hollenweger awards a dignity and liberty to the Holy Spirit not often found in Western theologies, and he affirms a variety of Spirit traditions in the biblical tradition. Hollenweger is especially concerned "that pneumatology should not be reduced to Christology and the recognition of the Spirit outside the churches and outside the influence of the Christian gospel".[86]

Hollenweger refers to the syncretistic influence of black slave religion, drawing from its pre-Christian African past, on North American Pentecostalism, to Korean Shamanism re-emerging as Korean Pentecostalism and elements of American Indian culture surfacing in Latin American Pentecostalism to support his emphasis on the Spirit and creation.[87] Price notes that,

> The realities of the variety of Christian experience, practice and understanding, plus the interaction of Christianity with pre-Christian and non-Christian cultures,

present, for Hollenweger, impelling reasons for consideration of the Spirit in a broader field of vision.[88]

For Hollenweger history testifies to the blowing of the Spirit outside of the Church.[89] He ever insists that pneumatology is not a static truth or doctrine "but a continuous experience-dialogue-reflection-action process".[90]

Deepening Pentecostal Development[91]

The Spirit of Hospitality

Signs exist that Pentecostals are trying to take their understanding of interreligious encounter and dialogue to higher horizons. In a joint publication, Yong and I advance a more carefully developed view of Pentecostals missions and interfaith practices appropriating a particularly Pentecostal and pneumatological model of hospitality.[92] We suggest that a Pentecostal-pneumatological perspective sheds new light on the perennial question of the one and the many in ways that allows us to affirm the diversity of tongues, cultures, and religions without being uncritical in our affirmation. We propose that holding together conviction about Christian faith amidst the many religions invites a posture of engagement and discernment. Next, we expand on this by arguing that a pneumatological approach that begins with the many tongues of Pentecost opens up to the many practices of the empowering Spirit. More precisely, we argue that the Spirit of encounter is also the Spirit of hospitality, and that a pneumatological theology of hospitality nourishes many practices through which Christians can and need to bear witness to the gospel in a pluralistic world. We present this line of thought first by looking at the life of Jesus, and then that of the early church. As Pentecostal theologians, we turn to the two volumes of Luke and Acts.[93]

Jesus Christ as Paradigmatic Host and Exemplary Guest

For Yong and me, Jesus himself can be understood both as the paradigmatic host of God's hospitality, and as the exemplary recipient of hospitality.[94] From his conception in Mary's womb (by the Holy Spirit) to his birth in a manger through to his burial (in a tomb of Joseph of Arimathea), Jesus was dependent on the welcome and hospitality of others.[95] As "the Son of Man has nowhere to lay his head" (Lk 9:58), he relied on the goodwill of many, staying in their homes and receiving whatever they served. But it is in his role as guest that Jesus also announces and enacts the hospitality of God. Empowered by the Spirit, he heals the sick, casts out demons, and declares the arrival of the reign of God in the midst of the downtrodden, the oppressed, and the marginalized.[96] While he is the "journeying prophet" who eats at the tables of others, he also proclaims and brings to pass the eschatological banquet of God for all who are willing to receive it. So sometimes Jesus breaks the rules of hospitality, upsets the social conventions of meal fellowship (e.g., Jesus does not wash before dinner), and even goes so far as to rebuke his hosts.[97] Luke thus shows that it is Jesus who is the broker of God's authority, and it is on this basis that Jesus establishes the inclusive hospitality of the kingdom to the marginalized of his day (women, children, and the "disabled").[98]

Biblical Hospitality Paradigms

Yong and I note that this more inclusive vision of divine hospitality is most clearly seen in the parable of the Good Samaritan (10:25-37).[99] It is the Samaritan, the religious "other" of the first century Jewish world, who fulfills the law, loves his neighbor, and embodies divine hospitality.[100] What are the implications of this parable for contemporary interreligious relationships? Might those who are "others" to us Christians not only be instruments through whom God's revelation comes afresh, but also perhaps be able to fulfill the requirements for inheriting eternal life (10:25) precisely through the hospitality that they show to us, their neighbors?[101]

In Acts, Yong and I continue, the hospitality of God manifested in Jesus the anointed one (the Christ) is now extended through the early church by the power of the same Holy Spirit.[102] As with Jesus, his followers are also anointed by the Spirit to be guests and hosts, in either case representing the hospitality of God. St. Paul, for example, is also both a recipient and conduit of God's hospitality.[103] He was the beneficiary of divine hospitality through those who led him by the hand, Judas (on Straight Street), Ananias, other believers who helped him escape from conspiring enemies, and Barnabas. Then during his missionary journeys, he is a guest of Lydia, a new convert, and has his wounds treated by the Philippian jailer. Paul the traveling missionary is also a guest of Jason of Thessalonica, Prisca and Aquilla and Titius Justus at Corinth, Philip the evangelist (and his daughters) at Caesarea, Mnason in Jerusalem, and unnamed disciples at Troas, Tyre, Ptolemais, and Sidon, etc. Along the way, Paul is escorted by Bereans, protected by Roman centurions, and entertained by Felix the governor. During the storm threatening the voyage to Rome, Paul hosts the breaking of bread. After the shipwreck, Paul is guest of the Maltese islanders (*barbaroi*, according to the original Greek of Acts 28:2) in general and of Publius the chief official in particular, and then later of some brothers on Puteoli. Acts closes with Paul as host, welcoming all who were open to receiving the hospitality of God. Throughout, Paul is the paradigmatic guest and host representing the practices of the earliest Christians who took the gospel to the ends of the earth by the power of the Holy Spirit.[104]

Empowered Practices of the Spirit

The Spirit's empowerment to bear witness to the gospel takes the form of many different practices in the lives of Jesus and the early Christians, each related to being guests and hosts in various times and places.[105] Yong and I suggest that these many practices of the Spirit are related to the diversity of tongues spoken on the Day of Pentecost.[106] Even as the many tongues of the Spirit announce the redemptive hospitality of God, so also the many works of the Spirit enact God's salvation through many hospitable practices.[107] As believers interact with and receive the hospitality, kindness, and gifts of strangers of all sorts, even Samaritans, public or governmental officials, and "barbarians," a diversity of practices ensues. In short, many tongues require many hospitable practices because of the church's mission in a pluralistic world.[108]

Retrieving and Re-appropriating the Spirit's Practices

How do these many practices redeem the traditional theologies of exclusivism, inclusivism, and pluralism? Yong and I suggest that a Lukan, Pentecostal, and pneumatological theology of hospitality allows us to retrieve and reappropriate the wide range of practices implicit in these models without having to endorse the full scope of their theological assertions. From the pluralist perspective, for example, an emphasis on social justice is prevalent in Jesus' concerns for the poor and the marginalized, and in the Spirit's producing a new community, the church, in which the traditional barriers of class, gender, and ethnicity no longer hold; but pluralism's "all-roads-lead-to-God" idea can be rejected.[109] The inclusivist insistence on recognizing possibility of divine revelation and activity among the unevangelized is likewise preserved, especially given the Pentecostal conviction regarding the miraculous gift of the Spirit that enables understanding amidst the cacophony of many tongues; at the same time, inclusivism's crypto-imperialistic stance can be recognized and guarded against.[110] And finally, the exclusivist commitment to the proclamation of the gospel is upheld since authentic hospitality is redemptive, and this includes declaration of the gospel in the proper time and place; but exclusivism's triumphalism and arrogance can be rejected.[111] In short, the practices of the models are redeemed without their theological and attitudinal liabilities.

Hence, Yong and I argue, a pneumatological theology of hospitality[112] empowers a much wider range of interreligious practices more conducive to meeting the demands of our time. This is in part because Christians often find themselves as guest or as hosts, sometimes (as in the lives of Jesus and Paul) simultaneously. In these various circumstances, there are many socio-cultural protocols that will inform Christian practices. Sometimes, Christians will defer to their hosts, embodying epistemic humility, and in the process be enriched by their interactions with people of other faiths. In other cases, Christians are hosts, with the responsibility to care for their guests of other faiths, and to do so at the many levels at which such care can be given (the physical, the material, the intellectual, the spiritual, etc.). In all cases, however, the conventions of hospitality will resist imperialistic approaches or better-than-thou attitudes, even as such conventions mediate honest dialogue and mutual interaction.[113]

Interreligious Hospitality and Christian Transformation and Salvation

Perhaps most importantly, as Yong and I affirm, a Pentecostal-pneumatological approach to theology of religions opens up to the kinds of Christian practices through which Christians themselves are transformed and even saved.[114] A parallel parable to the Good Samaritan is that of the Sheep and the Goats (Matt. 25:31-46), and in this case, the salvation of the Sheep was mediated by their ministering to Jesus through their encounter with the poor, the naked, the hungry, and those in prison.[115] Of course, many people of faith, both

Christian and non-Christian, are poor, hungry, and marginalized. Will we who have experienced the redemptive hospitality of God in turn show hospitality to such people? And if so, the Spirit has surely empowered us to bear witness to the gospel in these encounters. But at the same time, such hospitable interactions become the means of the Spirit to lavish on us the ongoing salvific hospitality of God.[116] In these cases, rather than "looking down" on those in other faiths because "we" have something "they" do not, Christians are in a position similar to that of the Jewish man by the wayside in the parable of the Good Samaritan. Thus, Christians are thankful to the God of Jesus Christ for revealing himself to them and saving them by the power of the Holy Spirit in and through the lives of their many neighbors in a pluralistic world.[117]

Interrelatedness and Interdependency of Disciplines and Practices

What Yong and I have suggested is that Pentecostal missiology, theology of religions, and interreligious encounter and dialogue are or ought to be interrelated and interdependent.[118] These important disciplines should not be developed or practiced in isolation. Further, we have suggested that fresh and vigorous Pentecostal-pneumatological insights while building upon longstanding classical commitments yield exciting possibilities for their theological development and practical implementation.[119] Continuity and creativity here may be integrated and applied profitably.[120] While existing conceptual categories – such as exclusivism, pluralism, and inclusivism – are relatively helpful, the conversation needs to be able to move past those boundaries to explore potentially fertile regions beyond.[121] For Yong and me, the challenge for today is for Pentecostal scholars, missionaries, theologians, dialogue participants, and others to move forward into the future under the power of the anointing of the Holy Spirit.

Relating Pentecost, Christian Beliefs, and Practices

Individually, Amos Yong takes this hospitality theme even farther. Yong relates issues of hospitality to current contexts of global terrorism and religion-related violence,[122] to "performing theology" or the connections between Christian theology and beliefs and practices, including theology of religions.[123] He further develops "performing hospitality" in connection with a pneumatological theology of interreligious engagement, and shows how the "welcoming Spirit" brings together a theology of hospitality and interreligious practices issuing in the practice of interreligious dialogue.[124] Yong's own summary of his theology of dialogue practice can hardly be improved upon, and is worth quoting in full.

> We have so far in this chapter sketched a vision of ecclesial practices vis-à-vis those in other faiths understood as participation in the *missio Dei* and extended this to consider the church's social witness understood as shaped by and participating in the eschatological hospitality of God. Our goal has been to explore how the many tongues of the Spirit open up to many hospitable practices. In this final section, I want to bring the discussion to a close by elaborating on the many practices at the more personal level of the interreligious encounter in these times between the cross/Pentecost and the eschaton. We will do so by formulating a the-

ology of the love of neighbor understood as the religious other, suggesting a theology of friendship appropriate to our globalized situation, and sketching a theology of interreligious dialogue understood as the heart of Christian practice in a religiously plural world. This discussion presumes the fundamental conviction that Christian identity is expressed in Christian mission, but that Christian mission is inclusive of rather than an alternative to the work of social justice and interreligious dialogue. But the focus now prescinds from that of ecclesial and social practices to the more pointed personal question: What should we do as Christians "in this between" time of our postmodern and pluralistic situation as we celebrate the redemptive hospitality of God revealed in Christ and yet await the eschatological hospitality of God to be ushered in finally by the Spirit?[125]

Contemporary Environment
Heart and Spirit of another Religion[126]

Comparing and contrasting developments in Pentecostal approaches to interreligious encounter and dialogue with major impulses within the broader Christian movement is informative. Bishop Stephen Neill earlier did for interreligious encounter and dialogue what Sir Norman Anderson (see previous chapter) did later for theology of religions: showed how to do it well from the perspective of a committed, uncompromising evangelical Christianity. His *Christian Faith and Other Faiths* has become a classic resource in the field.[127] Netland describes Neill, in a context with Max Warren, Kenneth Cragg, and Lesslie Newbigin, as "a man of amazing gifts" who is "difficult to categorize".[128] For examples, Neill embraces apparently paradoxical positions, being committed both to ecumenism and orthodoxy, evangelism and dialogue, and a high Christology and respect for non-Christian religions.[129] Notably, Yoder affirms Neill's elaboration of the marks of the Church, uncompromisingly emphasizing vital Christian mission, calling Neill's remarks "the *notae missionis*".[130] Of course, those, such as for example, Heba Raouf Ezzat, a Muslim political scientist, who wish to enter a "post-conversion mentality" for interfaith relations,[131] would not endorse Neill's understanding precisely because he does not downplay or replace the importance of conversion even though he does affirm and accentuate the importance of dialogue and understanding.[132]

Neill believes that, so much as is possible, interreligious dialogue requires participants to enter into the "heart and spirit of another religion" though always "without disloyalty to one's own".[133] Idealistic unrealistic objective detachment is not necessary. Experience shows that those most committed to their own religion can often display the greatest sympathy and discrimination toward another—so long as a certain patient willingness to "suspend judgment" is at least temporarily in place. Those who have "the deepest and most confident faith" are often best equipped to interact with religious others.[134] Christians should also endeavor to meet others at their best, not at their weakest, and to do so with humility.[135] Neill insists, "Self-assertion is always a sign of lack of inner confidence."[136] Therefore, the Christian does not need to fear opening up to other faiths. The Christians can joyously celebrate "unexpected treasures" discovered in dialogue as indicators of Christ's richness and wideness.[137]

In the bulk of the book Neill demonstrates his approach by taking his Christian discussion to the Jews, Muslims, Hindus, Buddhists, primitive or indigenous religions, and, somewhat surprisingly, even to Marxists and existentialists.[138] In each case, he attempts to appraise others as if from the inside. Often he consults their religious writers, letting them speak for themselves, though he also uses Christian students of these movements. He asks the hard questions, admits Christian and non-Christian mistakes and misunderstandings and accredits great accomplishments too.[139] Obvious appreciation for stunning beauty and symmetry in other religions occasionally shows. Yet Neill ultimately defends a Christian view, but very significantly, frequently a more informed view that bears transforming marks of the dialogue. He refuses to compromise or minimize Christian faith but is eager to enhance it, enlarge it, in whatever ways possible.[140]

Neill is interested in no mere academic talks.[141] Dialogue for him involves an element of engagement, including the wide range of human emotions arising from religious competitiveness carried out in friendship and respect.[142] The life and death struggle for truth must occur and may be intense. Accordingly, claims to universality need not be avoided, but for genuine dialogue to occur a "spirit of narrow and bitter aggressiveness" must give way to "sincerity and integrity" on both sides.[143] In all of this encounter and dialogue, the constant goal is to authentically represent and present Jesus Christ.[144]

In an effort to meet in dialogue the best of other religions with the best of the Christian religion, Christians must be sensitive to their own presuppositions and traditions—often no mean feat.[145] Furthermore, Christians who ask hard questions expecting honest answers must prepare for the same in return. Neill says, "Dialogue becomes dialogue only when question is met with question."[146] Mutual interrogation may result in mutual transformation. He is fully prepared for that eventuality. However, from the Christian side of the dialogue table, Neill lists seven "basic convictions" that are nonnegotiable if one is to remain recognizably Christian.

1. There is only one God and Creator, from whom all things take their origin.
2. This God is a self-revealing God, and he himself is active in the knowledge that we have of him.
3. In Jesus the full meaning of the life of man, and of the purpose of God for the universe, has been made known. In him the alienated world has been reconciled to God.
4. In Jesus Christians see the way in which they ought to live; his life is the norm to which they are unconditionally bound.
5. The Cross of Jesus shows that to follow his way will certainly result in suffering; this is neither to be resented nor to be evaded.
6. The Christian faith may learn much from other faiths; but is universal in its claims; in the end Christ must be acknowledged as Lord of all.
7. The death of the body is not the end. Christ has revealed the eternal dimension as the true home of man's spirit.[147]

These cardinal points may be debated but not ceded.

Finally, Neill insists Christians approach interreligious encounter and dialogue with congeniality and humility. In that spirit, Christians may in turn ask their interfaith friends whether they have taken Christian history seriously, or "ever really looked at Jesus Christ and tried to see him as he is?" Lastly, Christians ask both themselves and others how Christ's life has affected their own lives. In other words, "What manner of men ought ye to be?"[148]

Learning without Turning[149]

Sir Norman Anderson's evangelical and inclusive theology of religions includes an approach to interreligious encounter and dialogue.[150] He believes Christians may indeed learn much about virtue or even truth from adherents of other religions through contact and dialogue. However, real syncretism is simply not possible. The Christian must say, "Dialogue, yes; syncretism, no." Christianity, in a certain sense, will see every other system as somehow false or at least imperfect.[151] Dialogue is not a mix and match process.

Yet Anderson asserts that dialogue is an essential element of Christian proclamation (using the example of Paul in Athens).[152] He advises against argumentation in favor of more respectful genuine encounter and mutual exchange that may lead to mutual transformation as well as information. He does not support an idea of total objectivity (on either side of the table), which he regards as phony or artificial.[153] Sir Norman advocates an irenic attitude. In the example of Peter and Cornelius both benefited by the dialogue (cf. Acts 10).[154] In fact, good dialogue may prepare the way for evangelism, or be a part of it.[155] True, dialogue involves an element of risk but is worth it when carried out with confidence in the lordship of Christ and the power of the Holy Spirit.[156] A distinction must be made between "empirical Christianity" (what we have made of the faith) and the gospel (what it is in its essence), and an openness to change accepted regarding the former but not the latter. Ultimately, this kind of dialogue is more about personal relation than religion.[157] Anderson finally says,

> the clear-cut line that some would draw between dialogue and evangelism is itself misleading; for the Christian participant must of necessity speak of Christ and what he means to him—and he may, at any moment, find that the dialogue has undergone a metamorphosis, and that he is pointing his friend to the One who alone can meet man's deepest needs.[158]

The God of love has willingly become "vulnerable" in a sense through creation and redemption. Christians should labor in love to participate in that vulnerability and witness and reflect that love whether in proclamation, argument, dialogue, or fellowship.[159]

Evangelicals Following in Inclusive Footsteps

Plundering the Egyptians.[160] Gerald McDermott and Timothy Tennent are two Evangelicals who are following in the footsteps of Norman Anderson and Stephen Neill.[161] Both McDermott and Tennent boldly press beyond the boundaries of common Evangelical soteriological fixation to discuss actual interreligious encounter and dialogue. In an earlier work, McDermott argues for recognizing limited divine revelation in other religions.[162] He builds his views on biblical precedents along with classic, historic Christian theology.[163] Accordingly, he suggests Christians can learn from other religions through dialogue and interaction. In fact, he demonstrates historically that Christians have "plundered the Egyptians" since their earliest days.[164] For contemporary possibilities, McDermott gives examples of Christian exchanges with Buddhism, Daoism, Confucianism, and Islamism.[165] Against all objections, he insists Christians can without compromise benefit from discerning dialogical interaction with other religions.[166]

McDermott's more recent work pushes even farther past many of his peers by asking what are the religions and why are they there. He draws on biblical and patristic resources in his search for answers to those questions. As for why, McDermott concludes that God permits other religions out of perpetual love for all of humanity. God's gracious commitment to human freedom uses other religions to prepare people for Christ, to teach them morally and spiritually, in spite of distortions, by progressive stages, about the truth that is Jesus Christ.[167] As for what, McDermott concludes that the religions may be the result of activity by divine powers, created by God and therefore once good, but now fallen. These divine powers distort the truth for their own purposes in the religions but because of the seeds of truth scattered throughout them by the Logos some good still remains. Accordingly, the religions are a mixed bag of truth and error. They are not, however, salvific. Yet indirectly they do point to the truth of Christ.[168]

McDermott's point is that the religions are not just natural, but they have a supernatural component involving real cosmic entities and powers. He also stresses that co-religionists are not enemies of Christians but rather any battle is with spiritual beings behind the scenes. Persuasion and loving witness are therefore better than hostile argument. Commonalities between Christians on non-Christians are often evident. As Christians begin to think differently about other believers, they may also think differently about Christ, although always consistently with biblical revelation. The Spirit may also use other religions to purify the Church. That is, they may challenge Christian levels of commitment and consecration. However, it is essential to remember that salvation is not available through the religions but only through Jesus Christ. Yet these insights enlarge one's view of God beyond the realm of any one religion or even all of the religions.[169]

Engaged Exclusivism.[170] Tennent describes his own position as that of an "engaged exclusivist". He finds pluralism wrong and inclusivism wanting. However, his version of exclusivism, that is "engaged exclusivism", is much less restrictive than is typically the case for that category.[171] If anything, Tennent's views demonstrate that the traditional categories are not airtight compartments, but often have significant overlap. Nevertheless, and most important for the attention of this study, Tennent staunchly defends and advocates interreligious dialogue.[172] In fact, he disavows "a one-way defense of historic Christianity" in favor of "a vigorous two-way exchange of ideas."[173] This position in itself is a distinct departure from traditional Evangelical exclusivism, though

Tennent himself mentions a few other notable exceptions. One notes that engaged exclusivism shares much in common with inclusivism at least in this regard for dialogue.[174] Indeed, with the entry of engaged exclusivism it may be fairly said that all three of the theology of religions soteriological schemas—exclusivism, pluralism, and inclusivism—now participate in interreligious dialogue. The differences would seem to be more over how and why than if.

More to the point, Tennent employs four "ground rules" for the dialogues he portrays between Christianity and Hinduism, Buddhism, and Islam that inform this investigation. First, "all differences of opinion or perspectives should be shared honestly without being pejorative." Second, "no one is permitted to exploit abuses in a religion that are at odds with widely accepted beliefs and practices." Third, "the questions, responses, clarifications, and rejoinders must all pertain to the central theme being discussed." Finally, and quoting from the Koran, he insists there should be "no compulsion in religion" (cf. Surah 2:256).[175] Most of all, Tennent seeks to preserve a balance between theology and missiology "by challenging twenty-first century evangelicals to engage in interreligious dialogue as committed Christian witnesses."[176]

Tennent's basic premise is that "genuine dialogue can occur in a way that is faithful to historic Christianity and yet is willing to listen and respond to the honest objections of those who remain unconvinced."[177] Along the way, he says a firm "no" to religious pluralism.[178] He also argues that dialogue is or can be on the one hand a form of persuasive witness and on the other hand a way to stimulate Christian self-understanding. He firmly believes a present encounter between postmodernism and the gospel makes for an opportune time for engaging religious others.[179] Therefore, it is safe to say that a wide range of otherwise divergent Christian traditions and theologies, WCC, Roman Catholic, mainline Protestant, and even Evangelical, all agree that interreligious dialogue is an important and necessary process in the contemporary context of global religious pluralism.[180] Pentecostalism also needs forthrightly to face the issue of intentional interfaith interaction.

Loving Witness through Truly Dialoguing.[181] Calvin Shenk is an American Mennonite teacher and scholar of religions who has lived and traveled extensively in Africa, Asia, and the Middle East. He has had intensive interaction with other religions and their adherents academically and personally. His work is somewhat distinctive in the manner in which it carefully relates and connects comparative religions, sociology of religion, theology of religions, and interreligious dialogue through a consistently strong biblical foundation and christological center.[182] Shenk stresses the Church's mission of witness to Christ.[183] However, he expansively defines "forms of witness" to include not only church, presence, service, and evangelism, but also dialogue.[184]

Before proceeding directly to analysis of Shenk's thought, setting its context in contemporary Mennonite theology of religions may prove helpful. Valuable assistance for this task is found in the work of a leading Mennonite theologian, Thomas Finger.[185] Finger argues that values of "religious normativity" and "cultural normativity" shape Mennonite understanding in that these Anabaptist heirs of the Radical Reformation tend to critique cultural norms in view of their religious faith.[186] Finger outlines four general Anabaptist affirmations that shape Mennonite belief and practice.[187] First, Jesus Christ, his teachings, example and way of life, provide the ultimate norm for all human living. Second, peacemaking, sharing with others, and pursuit and practice of justice are at the heart of Mennonite normativity. Third, the way of life in Jesus generally appeals more to the oppressed, marginalized, and poor than to others. Fourth, the greatest opposition to this normative way of Christ comes from perverted forms of Christianity rather than from non-Christian religions.[188]

The fourth general affirmation opens the way for Finger to enumerate and elucidate specific affirmations regarding Anabaptist and Mennonite theology of religions. To begin with, he suggests Mennonites, who affirm ultimate truth in Christ, should nevertheless be open to learning from other religions.[189] For him, Christ is the norm for divine revelation but not God's sole revelation, and following Christ loving example allows and invites appreciation for and interaction with religious others.[190] Next, he stresses that Mennonites should chiefly seek to emphasize and embody the story of Jesus, with a dialogue of interpersonal involvement, and that this involves specific or particular relationships of witness and respect rather than general discourses on the universal meaning of history.[191] The following suggests Shenk is well aligned with this general Anabaptist and Mennonite tradition as outlined by Finger but also informed by unique experiences and insights.

Shenk suggests that, "Witness assumes that conversations must occur between Christians and adherents of other religions, that there should be dialogue between the Christian story and other stories." He adds, "We can be committed to Christ and the gospel and still be open to and accepting of the other." In fact, for him "Holding to our confession can make us more sensitive to others rather than less sensitive." In a word, "Because Christian faith has a dialogical nature, dialogue should not preclude witness but enhance witness."[192]

Shenk notes that dialogue may be formal or informal, involving everything from people of faith living in close proximity to intentional cooperation to planned conversations.[193] Dialogue is needed to overcome isolation and hostility, and involves content and relationship. Often relationship determines how content is heard.[194] Ideally, dialogue contributes to mutual understanding. It requires genuine communication rather than a single-minded monologue, which includes really listening to another's self-definition and engaging in mutual questioning. Dialogue can help Christians attain better self-understanding of their beliefs and practices, possibly including some unsuspected presuppositions. Interreligious dialogue should affirm commonalities but explore real differences too. At their points of difference may be a place where the most productive dialogue occurs. Importantly, dialogue often demands processing over time with further discussion among Christians regarding interreligious encounters.[195]

Dialogue and witness, according to Shenk, are neither identical nor in opposition. Dialogue does not diminish the need for witness but can actually "invite, extend, and deepen witness." However, though it is compatible with witness, dialogue is not "explicitly evangelistic or only pre-evangelism." Yet it often opens up avenues of authentic witness.[196] Productive dialogue requires commitment and discernment about one's own faith and a journey of discovery regarding truth. Yet dialogue does not compromise or lead to syncretism. One should not approach dialogue as a clandestine effort to convert, but neither should one rule out the possibility of conversion. Christians should engage in dialogue with conviction balanced by openness. Ultimately, dialogue is an exercise in trusting God. God can and does work in ways that surpass human understanding. The dialectic tension between witness and dialogue is an example.[197]

However, for Shenk interreligious dialogue is much more than a calm conversation among scholars. It is personal. It involves personal faith. For Christians, at the center of faith is not simply a list of teachings about Jesus but Jesus himself. Therefore, Jesus should always be central to any truly Christian dialogue. Though some consider the subject of Jesus a "barrier" to dialogue, approached properly he is really more of a "bridge" in dialogue. Ultimately, Christian dialogue desires not to commend to others Christianity or Christians, but to commend Christ (2 Co 4:5).[198]

For Shenk dialogue is a form of witness. Moreover, for him relationship among participants is primary, though interreligious witness also requires critique and judgment.[199] Attitude in dialogue and witness is all-important. Specifically, Christians should approach religious others with understanding, respect, humility, tolerance, and even vulnerability.[200] Overall, Shenk typifies an approach suggesting firmly devout Christian belief reaching out in loving witness of Christ through genuine interreligious dialogue. Perhaps most importantly for Pentecostals, Shenk demonstrates that evangelism and dialogue are not either/or propositions. Both may be forms of witness for specifically appropriate interreligious encounters.[201]

Representative Views from Other Faith Cultures

Christian Distinctiveness through Honest Dialogue[202]

Listening only to Western voices seriously and significantly impoverishes Christian theology of religions and interreligious dialogue. An example of a non-Western approach to Christian theology of religions highlighting elements of interreligious encounter and dialogue forthrightly confronting existing interreligious tensions is Sri Lankan theologian Vinoth Ramachandra's work.[203] Kärkkäinen observes that Ramachandra's careful interaction with his Asian context, in which dealing with religious pluralism is a major element, enriches his theology significantly.[204] Notably, Netland often quotes Ramachandra as positive examples of or in support of his own anti-pluralist arguments.[205] However, although affirming his evangelical orientation, Kärkkäinen also admits that Ramachandra gives more credence to the value of non-Christian religions than some other evangelical theologians.[206] Nevertheless, Ramachandra is clearly concerned to rehabilitate Christian mission in terms of its continuing validity as an essential task of the Church.[207]

Ramachandra points out that although religion is often center stage in global cultural conflict, it is also a source of moral order. Though tensions exist between faith communities, the question needs asked, what are the sources of these tensions?²⁰⁸ The real reasons behind religions' conflictive relations need assessed and addressed. For example, Ramachandra argues that Islam and the West are not incompatible rivals with unbridgeable differences.²⁰⁹ Rather, some use an appeal to religion to justify economical and political strategies.²¹⁰ Furthermore, Ramachandra debunks the prevalent myth of Hindu tolerance by a look at its pervasive history of violence.²¹¹ According to him, Hindu inclusivism is really something of an illusion, implying a hidden imperialism that minimizes real differences and undermines real dialogue.²¹² Significantly, Christian missionaries have often helped affect positive, permanent changes in Hindu society and spirituality as part of the "renouncer" tradition, that is, as ascetics who effectively challenge the status quo.²¹³

Ramachandra thinks India's struggle to deal with cultural and religious pluralism may be something of a window into the future of other, older democracies, suggesting secularization or privatization of religious traditions approaches will fail.²¹⁴ The God of universal history worked through particular history, through some (Israel) for all (the world).²¹⁵ Particularity is rejected by ancient Indian and post-Enlightenment Western worldviews that demand universal abstractions, but should be understood in context of biblical teaching of election, God's choosing of some for the sake of all.²¹⁶

Ramachandra thinks it significant for interaction with religious others to assert that Jesus ministered among the marginalized, challenging the status quo whether religious or otherwise.²¹⁷ Significantly, Jesus' self-understanding testifies to his sense of unique identity and destiny. Comparison of Jesus Christ with truly great religious founders and leaders, as well as a host of imposters, undergirds a sense of his authentic uniqueness.²¹⁸ Jesus' resurrection testifies to his deity.²¹⁹ He underscores that not only the uniqueness but the "*unique nature of the uniqueness*" of Jesus Christ is significant.²²⁰

Ramachandra insists that though the cross scandalizes all other religions, and even the Christian religion, because even the best of humanity's endeavors are stained with sinfulness, disciples of Christ can and should learn from other stories of divine-human encounter.²²¹ But this learning is always and only from the perspective of the story of Jesus Christ, the story which informs, explains, and edits all stories regarding relations between God and humankind.²²² He notes Muslims have traditionally had difficulty dealing with diversity and pluralism but Sufi mystics and some contemporary Muslims influenced by Sufis and/or Western pluralism have opened up more.²²³ Furthermore, in Hinduism, "particularity, difference and critique are swallowed up in a suffocating universalism".²²⁴ Buddhists often employ the idea of "skillful means", the claim that each religion is appropriate to the condition of its devotees.²²⁵

Ramachandra argues that the problem of particularity should not be confused with the ultimate status of those who have not heard the gospel. Conceivably, Christ may still logically benefit them.²²⁶ Importantly, Peter and Cornelius are examples of "double conversion", a mutually transforming evangelistic and dialogical event.²²⁷ Christian cross-cultural missions have often combined "indigenous" (particularities of a culture) and "pilgrim" (on the way as part of the universal family of God) principles.²²⁸ Bible translation by missionaries is an example of Christian appreciation and appropriate of diverse cultures while Hindus insist on Sanskrit and Muslims on Arabic for their sacred texts (considering them untranslatable!), arguably an example of exclusivism.[229] Conversely, Christians come from many cultures and languages but share continuity with the OT and NT and loyalty to Christ.[230] Ramachandra reasons that the Genesis account of patriarchal devotion to El represents God's own humble and gracious accommodation to their ancestral religion in order to move them beyond those limitations to faith in Yahweh. This accommodation would be a precedent that might suggest both that Jesus Christ has been doing the same in many different cultures and religious contexts and that Christian proclamation is accordingly more important not less.[231]

Ramachandra concludes that Christian distinctiveness shows best in dialogue with others, and that authentic evangelism includes discovery as well as witness.[232] Many Christians have and do suffer for their faith but Christianity must also confess its sins against others.[233] Christianity and Christian ideas have also been a boon to civilization and even to other religions and its own critics.[234] He is convinced that what the world needs from Christians and Christianity today, is not compromise or condescension but for them to remain truly Christian and for the Church to be truly Church.[235]

Borrowing for Mutual Benefit[236]

Charles Jones, a comparative religions scholar in Asian religions, argues for striking balance between "openness and integrity" regarding theology of religions that can transcend conservative/liberal issues.[237] He notes that Christian missions have not usually been successful among the literate of non-Christian religions.[238] This failure seems to suggest a need for fresh approaches. Jones therefore argues strongly for balancing dialogue and mission.[239]

Jones lists four ways of doing dialogue: theological and philosophical dialogue, contemplative-monastic-spiritual dialogue, social welfare concerns and activism, and cultural and artistic dialogue.[240] He warns against overdoing a concern for common ground and failing to make impact upon home traditions.[241] In addition to traditional (and problematic) ways of doing mission, he mentions the Buddhist model and the "leavening" model. The Buddha sent his disciples out among the populace with instructions to be responsive to questions as a form of proclamation. Jones thinks this invitation and response method may therefore serve Christians well in an Asian environment. "Leavening" is more a matter of Christians living and serving among religious others and passing on their values, not altogether in conversion, but perhaps even through transplantation into other religious traditions.[242]

Jones argues stringently against mutually exclusive understandings of dialogue and mission, saying, "What we ultimately need, then, is not an argument for choosing dialogue over evangelism or vice versa, but a model for relating the two that takes into account their mutual interdependence."[243] Drawing on Confucius and Jesus and interreligious history, Jones suggests a model of "mutual transformation" with participants trusting God to guide the process.[244] Jones' dialogue model is an excellent example of a Christian dialogue approach tailor-made to a particular culture and religious tradition. Practical benefits of establishing shared points of contact seem obvious. However, I have discovered in practice that sometimes religious others may find it offensive when another religion "borrows" their beliefs and practices for use "against" them in conversion and evangelism.[245] As always, discernment and sensitivity are in order in the delicate and difficult process of interreligious dialogue.

A Brief Critique

Ecumenical Necessities

This section does not offer a point-by-point assessment of the preceding. Rather, it responsively articulates a few major motifs that seem to arise out of it. The preceding clearly indicates that concerns over interreligious encounter and dialogue are not limited to any one Christian tradition. Major bodies of Catholics and Protestants, and to a lesser extent even Evangelicals and some Charismatics, and others are already heavily involved. Accordingly, Pentecostals might be truer to their original and ecumenical heritage by taking the lead on interreligious dialogue.[246] Without being triumphalistic, Pentecostals are already in the lead in a sense on the level of interreligious encounter through their massive missions programs. The need is perhaps not so much for more encounters as for more informed and intentional encounters.

Discernment is an important concept. Discernment is necessary not only regarding relations with non-Christian religions, but also regarding cooperation with other Christian groups in interreligious encounter.[247] It is not necessary and probably not possible anyway, for Pentecostals to work with only those who are entirely like themselves, or even almost or mostly like themselves. Perhaps it is not even desirable. Entering the practice of dialogue with other faiths should include improved relations with other Christians too. Cooperation without compromise should be their mantra. Pentecostals can and should always endeavor to allow their own distinctive beliefs and values to show, even to shine, wherever they are present. Indeed, a light shines the brightest when the night is the darkest. Pentecostals need to have enough faith to go into what they at least may consider dark places and let their lights shine for Jesus by the power of the Holy Spirit. Moreover, Pentecostals may be pleasantly surprised to discover other lights shining alongside theirs.

Balancing Boundaries and Openness

The importance of boundaries stands out. Almost every representative of interreligious dialogue in this chapter has more or less emphasized that Christians involved in interreligious dialogue know the foundations of their faith with unshakable conviction while seeking divine truth beyond their own borders. Several gave lists of what cannot be negotiated even though it can be, and should be, discussed. The second chapter of this study listed some nonnegotiable issues for Pentecostals. It insisted that a Pentecostal theology of religions adequate for the contemporary task of interreligious coexistence must be faithful to its own inherent values. Faithfulness for Pentecostal theology of religions includes attention to an uncompromised Christology, an undiminished view of the inspiration and authority of Scripture, an undistorted soteriology, and a non-minimal ecclesiology.

Furthermore, for Pentecostals, these values come together in a distinctive pneumatological framework. Pentecostal participation in interreligious dialogue must respect and reflect these vital values. Notably, these vital Pentecostal values exhibit much overlap with some of the lists complied earlier in the present chapter. However, in addition to the distinctively pneumatological framework, Pentecostal interpretation and application of their values will also contribute significantly to their appropriate exercise.

Along with commitment to clear boundaries, a dialectical attitude of openness seems assumed as well. None of the vital values mentioned require close-mindedness or narrow-mindedness. In fact, vaunted Pentecostal appreciation for the Spirit's ongoing speaking and revealing seem to point in precisely the opposite direction. Of all movements, Pentecostalism ought to be most open to fresh insights and inspiration from the Spirit's moving and self-manifesting in surprising ways. Accordingly, so long as biblical truth is unthreatened and Christ's person is unvarnished, Pentecostals ought to approach interreligious dialogue with an excited expectation that they may learn something new and notable in the experience.

Unique Needs and Nuances

Pneumatological Missiology. Each tradition brings to the table a set of unique needs and offers contributions consistent with those needs. Catholics and magisterial Protestants have historical, theological, and ethical concerns that surface and re-surface throughout their declarations and practices of interreligious dialogue. Evangelicals have a consistent commitment to their understanding of *kerygma* or the basic biblical gospel of Christ that influences and flavors their at times admittedly tentative steps toward interreligious dialogue.[248] Pentecostals have unique missiological and pneumatological concerns and can make unique missilogical and pneumatological contributions. Unique missiology and pneumatology arise naturally, perhaps even inevitably and irretrievably, out of Pentecostal history, identity, spirituality, and theology. It cannot be that Pentecostal theology of religions and the practice of interreligious dialogue are unaffected.

Pentecostals have the reputation of being the most aggressive and active missionaries and evangelists in the world—ever.[249] Pentecostals from earliest times to the present have understood their evangelistic fervor and effectiveness to be directly derivative from their Pentecostal experience of Spirit baptism. Acts 1:8 is a favorite text in this regard: "But you will receive power when the Holy Spirit comes on you; and you will be my witnesses in Jerusalem, and in all Judea and Samaria, and to the ends of the earth" (NIV). Now it is finally becoming evident that the Church's biblically-based, Christ-centered, and Spirit-empowered mission is broad enough to embrace such wide-ranging activities as evangelism, social activism, and interreligious dialogue.[250] What if the same Spirit-inspired enthusiasm and energy that have propelled Pentecostalism around the globe as witnesses to the world of Christ's saving, healing, and delivering grace, now extends to social activism and interreligious dialogue? Might not similarly phenomenal results occur? Moreover, this delightful projection assumes there will be no diminishment of evangelical fervor either.

Missiological Pneumatology. Of course, Pentecostal pneumatology is the other unique nuance that cries out for consideration. Pentecostals decry the tragic diminishment of the Holy Spirit that results in an anemic and impotent Christianity vis-à-vis the bold and powerful Church of the New Testament.[251] And Pentecostal theology of religions is indeed fervently building on pneumatological foundations.[252] Further, it may be fairly assumed that the structure stretching skyward off that foundation will continue to be Spirit sensitive.[253] The role and work of the Holy Spirit is and ought to be a primary feature of Pentecostal theology of religions and of its applied practice in interreligious dialogue.

Yet already it is becoming evident, for examples, in Kärkkäinen and Yong, that a prime focus on the Holy Spirit need not necessitate a blind focus on the Holy Spirit. Pentecostals are increasingly calling forth Trinitarian and Incarnational themes for stability in the liberty of pneumatology. Here deciding whether Hollenweger is pushing pneumatology to a dangerous extreme or is a prophetic voice is at times difficult.[254] Probably, he is a bit of both—as extremism and prophethood often, though not always, go together. His efforts to extend Pentecostal understanding of and appreciation for the Holy Spirit beyond charismatic gifts into the wide world are certainly commendable. Moreover, recognizing the Spirit's reach beyond the Church is essential for Pentecostal theology of religions and interreligious dialogue.

However, there is true danger in indiscriminately regarding all of life as the direct, undiminished work of the Spirit.[255] This hazard is especially horrendous if one fails to distinguish at all between creative and redemptive ministries of the Holy Spirit. Not merely universality but the error of universalism lies in that direction. Furthermore, when everything becomes sacred, then nothing continues sacred. Pentecostals do well to expand and extend their understanding of the Holy Spirit's presence and influence. Yet clear distinction should always remain between the ministries of the Spirit in the Church and in the world. Although the entire created order may be a sacrament signifying divine presence, Christ is uniquely reincarnate in the Body of Christ, the Church, through the Spirit of Christ. From hence comes the unique nature of the Pentecostal missiological pneumatology.

The above-mentioned caveat does not contend for constraining pneumatological soteriology or divine disclosure to the Church. It still recognizes the possibility of salvation and of divine truth beyond ecclesial and sectarian borders. Rather, it notes the necessity of pneumatological moorings. How might Pentecostals best maintain moorings without minimizing the Spirit's unrestrained self-manifestation? Unless the Spirit's presence and influence in the world is naturalized into a kind of universal attributive possession of the *Imago Dei,* or into a kind of "supernatural existential" (see Chapter 2), the Spirit's distinctive presence in the Christian must be ever affirmed. It simply must be maintained that the Spirit is present in Christians in a manner that the Spirit is not present in non-Christians (John 14:17). In addition, accompanying this affirmation must be an equally adamant affirmation that the Holy Spirit is in some sense present in humanity and in some devout adherents of other religions (Num 16:22; 27:16).

The suggestion is that Pentecostals can perhaps best maintain this delicate and intricate pneumatological nuance through the classic Wesleyan concept of prevenient grace (see Chapters 2 and 3).[256] The grace of the Spirit that "precedes" or "goes before" actual conversionary salvation, wooing and working according to God's providential purposes, allows affirmation of the Spirit's real (and potentially salvific) presence and influence in religious others without destroying the distinction between the Spirit's regenerating and sanctifying work in those with explicit faith in Jesus Christ. Moreover, prevenient grace presumes that the Spirit's "pre-conversion" wooing and working nonetheless inclines toward and climaxes in Jesus Christ and Christian conversion at some point in time and in some, perhaps mysterious, manner. Thus, Pentecostals resist possible extremes of unbounded pneumatology without restricting rich possibilities of a balanced pneumatology.

Pentecostal pneumatology informed by Wesleyan prevenient grace results in a distinctive approach to interreligious dialogue.[257] For one thing, it assumes that religious others may have some measure of the Spirit's grace to which appeal is not wasted. Yet again, it understands that the Spirit's grace may work on both sides of the table to bring about mutual benefit. For another thing, however, it does not assume that the outcome is a foregone conclusion. Everyone is not already "saved" in spite of his or her present spiritual state. Therefore, the Church's dual missions of evangelism and of dialogue are not mutually exclusive but are different aspects of the Spirit's gifts.[258]

Searching for a Model with Familiarity and Specificity

Though generally pragmatic paradigms abound, familiar and specific models for interreligious dialogue are rare, especially for a Pentecostal dialogue model. Yong, with hospitality, is helpful. The hospitality model admirably presents and develops an attitudinal, conceptual, and practical framework for interfaith relations with firm biblical and theological foundations. Kärkkäinen's intra-trinitarian participatory conversation is also a rich resource with classic, historic associations. I attempt to help remind Pentecostals of their early ecumenical and inclusive heritage.

However, my focus on early founders in the Pentecostal movement flounders at the point of dialogue because they did not directly address interreligious dialogue in their day. It is simply not in their field of vision. It did not in fact exist in their day, as it is understood today. Neither does hospitality or Trinity, though certainly sound biblically and theologically, necessarily resonate with Pentecostals in any particularly distinctive fashion, especially regarding non-Christian religious relations. For many, hospitality may be just the way one is supposed to treat people in general. Likewise, the Trinity is a subject of intra-Christian discourse for advanced theologians.[259] Further, these are themes easily and often encountered in the broader Christian movement. For example, hospitality is quite common in WCC circles as a model for dialogue, and this work has already noted its use by Martin Marty.[260] For another example, prominent Catholic theologian Gavin D'Costa employs Trinitarian theology of religions.[261]

This study does not suppose that a Pentecostal model should have no continuity with or similarity to models in other traditions. Yet Pentecostals need an already recognizable symbol capable of immediate application and utilization in interreligious dialogue. What they need for an adequate dialogue model is a "familiar face", a "player" out of their own lineup. One hopes no one will misunderstand the use of a military metaphor. Saul's armor will not work for Pentecostals; they need their own well-worn smooth stones and sling (cf. 1 Sa 17:38-40). Put differently, what Pentecostals desperately need is a specific strategy for dialogue distinctively true to their own tradition that works well today. But this combination of familiarity and specificity is precisely what they do not yet possess.

Other Christian traditions assume, perhaps accurately, but not adequately, at least for Pentecostals, that unity is in and of itself sufficient for motivation and a conversational model is sufficient for implementation. This present work has argued that Pentecostals, because of their unifying experience of the Holy Spirit, have an inherent impulse toward unity. Yet even if correct, that impulse to unity has not proved sufficient to motivate Pentecostals against a stern tide of opposition into the open arms of ecumenism even with other Christians much less with non-Christian religions. Further, though it may do well for others, the idea of a friendly little conversation is not sufficient for Pentecostals as a model for interreligious dialogue. Pentecostals need more. Pentecostals are not much for chit-chat. They are more for strong, stirring speech. How do Pentecostals implement that into interreligious dialogue?

Nothing in the present or previous chapters clearly suggests the specific model Pentecostals need for authentic engagement in interreligious dialogue. What this study does suggest to this point is much more in the line with an idea that there indeed is a dire need for such a model. Accordingly, this work dedicates itself to the task of identifying and developing a model for Pentecostal interreligious dialogue with appropriate familiarity and specificity. A model for Pentecostal interreligious dialogue must meet certain criteria. For one thing, of course, it must be adequate and effective in the practice of dialogue. For another thing, it must arise naturally out of an authentic and already-existent Pentecostal belief and practice. Finally, it must be capable of application and development according to the current state of Pentecostal theology of religions. For reasons to be made clear later, I offer the category of Pentecostal testimony as a possibility for meeting the need for a Pentecostal model of interreligious dialogue in accordance with these stated criteria.

Conclusion/Summary

The present chapter has attempted a succinct survey of the field of interfaith dialogue as it relates to Pentecostalism. It builds on the preceding chapters that suggest that a cultural context of religious pluralism and the current state of Pentecostal theology of religions require Pentecostal engagement in interreligious encounter and dialogue. Pentecostal theology of religions and thought and practice of interreligious dialogue are at an early and exciting stage of formation and development. Pentecostals are beginning to marshal rich resources of their pneumatic experience and teaching for application in dialogue with religious others. However, increasingly clear is that Pentecostalism needs a model for dialogue with familiarity and specificity from within the movement. The bare suggestion has been presented that the category of testimony will serve well. Before advancing to a direct treatment that correlates testimony and dialogue, this study will pause in the next chapter to overview the nature of Pentecostal testimony in preparation for that process. However, the study is now beginning to move into the phase of constructive concerns. The subsequent chapter will then explore the category of Pentecostal testimony for use as a distinctively and specifically Pentecostal model for interreligious dialogue. It will also offer possible applications of testimony for Pentecostal engagement in interreligious dialogue.

Notes

1. M. Kinnamon, "Ecumenism," *NHCT*, eds. D.W. Musser & J.L. Price (Nashville: Abingdon, 1992), 142-45.

2. Kinnamon, "Ecumenism," 143.

3. Kinnamon, "Ecumenism," 143-44. "Ecumenism" in the sense of an impulse toward Christian reconciliation and unity in the face of division is traceable in the NT and throughout Christian history, J. Gros, E. McManus, and A. Riggs, *Introduction to Ecumenism* (Mahwah, NJ: Paulist, 1998), and has been a "glorious and tragic" process, 9-10 (10). Further, Catholic ecumenism tends to focus on principles of religious liberty, spiritual ecumenism, and collaboration in mission, 74.

4. However, the search for a common expression of apostolic faith can also be a crucial element of dialogue, A. Maffeis and L.F. Fuchs, *Ecumenical Dialogue* (Collegeville, Minnesota: Unitas, 2005), 65. Cf. Kinnamon, "Ecumenism," 144.

5. Kinnamon, "Ecumenism,"145.

6. See *Guidelines on Dialogue with Men of Living Faiths and Ideologies* (Geneva: World Council of Churches Publications, 1979).

7. Cf. V.M. Kärkkäinen, *An Introduction to The Theology of Religions: Biblical, Historical, & Contemporary Perspectives* (Downer's Grove: InterVarsity Press, 2003), 155-58.

8. Kärkkäinen, *Theology of Religions*, 158. Quoted from H. Ott, "The Horizons of Understanding and Interpretative Possibilities," ed., S.J. Samartha, *Faith in the Midst of Faiths: Reflections on Dialogue in the Community* (Geneva: World Council of Churches, 1977), 85-86.

9. C.M. Robeck, Jr. and J.L. Sandidge, "World Council of Churches," *NDPCM*, 1213-17.

10. For more information, see Pentecostal-Charismatic Theological Inquiry International at http://www.pctii.org/wcc/index.html.

11. Kinnamon, "Ecumenism," 143-44. See R.B. Sheard, *Interreligious Dialogue in the Catholic Church Since Vatican II: An Historical and Theological Study* Toronto Studies in Theology vol. 31 (Lewiston/Queenston: Edwin Mellen Press, 1987). Also see *Growth in Agreement III: International Dialogue, Texts, and Agreed Statements, 1998-2005*, eds. Jeffrey Gros, Lorelei F. Fuchs, and Thomas F. Best (Geneva: WCC, 2007).

12. Kärkkäinen, *Theology of Religions*, 121-22. See "Dialogue and Proclamation," (December 26, 2007) at: http://www.vatican.va/roman_curia/pontifical_councils/interelg/documents/rc_pc_interel g_doc_19051991_dialogue.

13. Cf. T.P. Thigpen, "Catholic Charismatic Renewal," *NDPCM*, 460-67 and C.M. Robeck, Jr. and J.L. Sandidge, "Dialogue, Roman Catholic and Classical Pentecostal," *NDPCM*, 576-82.

14. J.H. Gerstner, "Ecumenical," *BDT*, eds. E.F. Harrison, G.W. Bromiley, and C.F.H. Henry (Grand Rapids: Baker, 1960, 1987), 176-77.

15. See "*he oikoumene*," *TDNT*, eds. G. Kittel and G. Friedrich, trans. and abridged by G.W. Bromiley, (Grand Rapids: Eerdmans, 1985, 1990), 679.

16. Cf. R.A. Koivisto, *One Lord, One Faith: A Theology for Cross-Denominational Renewal* (Wheaton: Bridgepoint/Victor, 1993), 79-82, 332.

17. Koivisto, *One*, 84. E.g., A.G. Reddie, *Black Theology in Transatlantic Dialogue* (New York: Palgrave MacMillan, 2006), suggests an inordinate concern among white evangelicals for an ultimate primacy of doctrinal purity negatively influenced black Christians, including Pentecostals, away from involvement in interfaith dialogue, 69-70.

18. Gerstner, 176-77. Cf. Koivisto, *One*, 188-90.

19. This section is in dialogue with the work of Cecil Robeck and Allan Anderson.

20. C.M. Robeck, Jr. "Taking Stock of Pentecostalism: The Personal Reflections of a Retiring Editor," *Pneuma* 15:1 (Spring 1993), 35-60 (esp. 37).

21. Robeck, "Taking Stock," 37.

22. Robeck, "Taking Stock," 37. Cf. also Gros, et al, *Introduction*, for an account of Pentecostalism's checkered ecumenical history, 214-33.

23. Robeck, "Taking Stock," 39-45. E.g., Pentecostals, unlike Roman Catholics, do not approach ecumenical unity from a creedal perspective, Gros, et al, *Introduction*, 207.

24. Robeck, "Taking Stock," 45-51.

25. E.g., see J.R. Williams, *Renewal Theology: Systematic Theology from a Charismatic Perspective* (*RT*), three volumes in one (Grand Rapids: Zondervan, 1996), 3:133-36, and L.D. Hart, *Truth Aflame: Theology for the Church in Renewal* (Grand Rapids: Zondervan, 1999, 2005), 23, 26, and 491. Cf. Robeck, "Taking Stock," 51-58.

26. Robeck, "Taking Stock," 39. Non-Pentecostal ecumenical observers and participants also seem concerned for Pentecostals finding a place at the dialogue table, Maffeis and Fuchs, *Ecumenical Dialogue*, 15, 44.

27. Robeck, "Taking Stock," 58-60. A central place for ecumenism for the future seems vital for Gros, et al, *Introduction*, 234-35.

28. Robeck, "Taking Stock," 60.

29. A. Anderson, *An Introduction to Global Pentecostalism: Global Charismatic Christianity* (Cambridge: Cambridge University Press, 2004), 67-68.

30. Anderson, *Introduction*, 73, 75.

31. Anderson, *Introduction*, 98.

32. Anderson, *Introduction*, 98-99.

33. R.P. Spittler, "Du Plessis, David Johannes," *NIDPCM*, 589-93 (592).

34. The sacrificial service and ecumenical influence of David du Plessis is inestimable. See C.M. Robeck, Jr., "David du Plessis and the Challenge of Dialogue," *Pneuma* 9 (Spring 1987), 1-4, and Spittler, "Du Plessis," *NDPCM*, 589-93. Cf. Anderson, *Introduction*, 146-47. British administrator, pastor, teacher, and writer Donald Gee was another early and influential Pentecostal ecumenist on the international scene. See D.D. Bundy, "Gee, Donald," *NDPCM*, 662-63.

35. Anderson, *Introduction*, 152.

36. Anderson, *Introduction*, 245.

37. Anderson, *Introduction*, 249-50.

38. Gadfly C.M. Robeck, Jr. is a driving force in promoting Pentecostal ecumenism today. Out of many possible examples, consider his "Pentecostals and the Apostolic Faith: Implications for Ecumenism," *Pneuma* 9 (Spring 1987), 61-84, and "When Being a 'Martyr' is not Enough: Catholics and Pentecostals," *Pneuma* 21 (1999), 3-10. However, Robeck's work focuses on intra-Christian rather than interreligious relations. Cf. R.P. Spittler, "Robeck, Cecil Melvin, Jr.," *NDPCM*, 1023-24. Cf. Anderson, *Introduction*, 250-52.

39. Anderson, *Introduction*, 252-53. Cf. W.J. Hollenweger, "Charisma and Oikemene: The Pentecostal Contribution to the Church Universal," *One in Christ* 7 (1971), 332-33.

40. Anderson, *Introduction*, 253-55.

41. E.g. the spontaneous dissolution of the racially segregated Pentecostal Fellowship of North America, founded in 1948, at its 1994 meeting in Memphis, TN, and its reformulation as the interracial Pentecostal Charismatic Churches of North America is commonly denominated "the Memphis Miracle". See E.L. Blumhofer and C.R. Armstrong, "Assemblies of God," *NIDPCM*, 333-40 (339-40), and W. E. Warner, "Pentecostal Fellowship of North America," *NIDPCM*, 968-69.

42. Anderson, *Introduction*, 255-56.

43. Anderson, *Introduction*, 256-58.

44. This section draws on some of my own earlier work.

45. T. Richie, "The Unity of the Spirit: Are Pentecostals Inherently Ecumenists and Inclusivists?" *JEPTA* 26:1 (2006), 21-35 (esp. 21-23). In the interest of providing a thorough account of contemporary context, I am required occasionally and apologetically to overview some of my own previous work in the following sections. As I have been an active participant in Pentecostal interreligious dialogue, the survey would be unacceptably incomplete without some inclusion of my work. This will in no wise substitute for the original work of the subsequent research.

46. In fact, possibly Pentecostal identity has often been obscured or altered by its unfortunate, unequal association with ideologically anti-Pentecostal groups.Cf. W.J. Hollenweger's, 'Biblically Justified Abuse: A Review of Stephen Parson's *Ungodly Fear: Fundamentalist Christianity and the Abuse of Power*,' *JPT* 10.2 (2002), 129-35. Cf. Richie, "Unity," 23-29.

47. Richie, "Unity," 29-34.

48. Richie, "Unity," 34-35.

49. Indeed, the biblical symbol of *koinonia* reveals rich pneumatological-ecumenical implications that many Pentecostals may find amicable. See Gros, et al, *Introduction*, 60-62, 73. Richie, "Unity," 35.

50. Richie, "Unity," 34. Nevertheless, authentic Pentecostal community requires a broadening vision. See M. Wenk, *Community Forming Power: The Socio-Ethical Role of the Spirit in Luke-Acts* (Sheffield, Eng: Sheffield Academic, 2000), e.g., 44-49, 309-17.

51. Richie, "Unity," 34. Early on, however, Pentecostals leaders and thinkers such as Richard Spurling, Jr. and D. Wesley Myland stressed love and unity in the Spirit much more than later Pentecostals. Cf. D. Jacobsen, *Thinking in the Spirit: Theologies of the Early Pentecostal Movement* (Bloomington & Indianapolis: Indiana University Press, 2003), 150-56 and 130-32.

52. Cf. W. Hollenweger, 'From Azusa Street to the Toronto Phenomenon: Historical Roots of the Pentecostal Movement,' *Pentecostal Movements as an Ecumenical Chal-*

lenge, eds. J. Moltmann and Karl-Josef Kuschel, *Concilium* 1996/3 (Maryknoll, NY: Orbis, 1996), 3-14 (9). Richie, "Unity," 34.

53. This section is in dialogue with the work of Amos Yong and Veli-Matti Kärkkäinen.

54. A. Yong, *Discerning the Spirit(s): A Pentecostal-Charismatic Theology of Religions*, *JPT* Supplement Series 20 (Sheffield, England: Sheffield Academic Press, 2000), 313.

55. A. Yong, *Beyond the Impasse: Toward a Pneumatological Theology of Religions* (Grand Rapids: Baker Academic, 2003), 19-20. Yong has been criticized, sometimes harshly, for diminishment of Christology in favor of pneumatology. E.g., see J.R.A. Merrick, "The Spirit of Truth as Agent in False Religions? A Critique of Amos Yong's Pneumatological Theology of Religions with Reference to Current Trends," TJ 29:1 (Spring 2008), 107-25. However, others argue that critics have sometimes misunderstood Yong and responded unfairly. Cf. T. Richie, "The Spirit of Truth as Guide into All Truth: A Response to James R.A. Merrick, 'The Spirit of Truth as Agent in False Religions? A Critique of Amos Yong's Pneumatological Theology of Religions with Reference to Current Trends,' *CPCR* (Jan 2010).

56. A. Yong, *The Spirit Poured Out on All Flesh: Pentecostalism and the Possibility of Global Theology* (Grand Rapids: Baker Academic, 2005), 256-57.

57. V.M. Kärkkäinen, *Trinity and Religious Pluralism: The Doctrine of the Trinity in Christian Theology of Religions* (Burlington, VT: Ashgate, 2004), 180.

58. Kärkkäinen, *Trinity,* 180. Indeed, perhaps a humble mindset ought to characterize all dialogue efforts. M. Gopin, "The Use of the Word and Its Limits: A Critical Evaluation of Religious Dialogue as Peacemaking," 33-46, ed. D.R. Smock, *Interfaith Dialogue and Peacebuilding* (Washington, DC: United States Institute for Peace, 2002), argues that "We must pursue dialogue as reconciliation, but with great humility and elasticity, readying and willing to combine it with or supplant it with other modes of reconciliation, especially in terms of deed, symbol, and emotional reconciliation" (35). Cf. 43.

59. Kärkkäinen, *Trinity,* 181.

60. Kärkkäinen, *Trinity,* 181. Cf. Kate McCarthy, *Interfaith Encounters in America* (Piscataway, NJ: Rutgers University Press, 2007), in an interesting chapter titled "Strange Bedfellows: Mulitfaith Activism in American Politics," 45-83. McCarthy suggests "an important move is being made to stake out a space for religion in which multiple religious voices might weigh in on matters of public concern" (83). For her, the vast diversity of the American religious population, including Evangelicals and Pentecostals, makes this development extremely significant, 6.

61. V.M. Kärkkäinen, "The Uniqueness of Christ and the Trinitarian Faith", in *Christ the One and Only: A Global Affirmation of the Uniqueness of Jesus Christ,* ed. S.W. Chung (Grand Rapids: Baker Academic, 2005), 111-35 (128).

62. This section draws on some of my own earlier work.

63. T. Richie, "A Pentecostal in Sheep's Clothing: an Unlikely Participant but Hopeful Partner in Interreligious Dialogue," *CD* 48 (December 2006), 9-15. This view assumes, "the church does not exist in, of or for itself, but only in relationship and can only be understood in its relationships." See R. Bauckham, *The Theology of Jürgen Moltmann* (Edinburgh: T & T Clark, 1996), 13.

64. Richie, "Sheep's Clothing," 9.
65. Richie, ""Sheep's Clothing," 10.
66. Richie, "Sheep's Clothing," 10.
67. Richie, "Sheep's Clothing,"11-12 (12).

68. In her assessment of my work, J.I. Smith, *Muslims, Christians, and the Challenge of Interfaith Dialogue* (Oxford/New York: Oxford University Press, 2007), describes my stance on evangelism and dialogue as "Always trying to keep a middle position" and perhaps portending future directions among Evangelicals, 107-09 (108). Smith warns against a covert or secret evangelistic agenda in dialogue, 50 and 73, but suggests evangelism may well include respectful conversations with other religions, 66, though some sharply distinguish between biblical evangelism and dialogue for appearances of theological unity even while advocating dialogue as an instrument for breaking down stereotypes of religious others, 109.

69. Richie, "Sheep's Clothing," 13-14.

70. Of course, pneumatology and Christology are always interrelated. See Y. Congar, *The Word and the Spirit*, (*WS*) trans. David Smith (San Francisco: Harper & Row, 1986), "If I were to draw but one conclusion from the whole of my work on the Holy Spirit, I would express it in these words: no Christology without pneumatology and no pneumatology without Christology" (1).

71. Richie, "Sheep's Clothing," 14.

72. Richie, "Sheep's Clothing," 14. Cf. T. Richie, "Being Faithfully Pentecostal in a World of Pluralistic Faiths", *COGE* (August 2006), 6-7 (7). For further development of my ideas on interreligious encounter and dialogue see my "Much More than a Man among Men: The Supreme Significance of Jesus Christ," *COGE* (December 2007), 6-7 and "A Threefold Cord: Weaving Together Pentecostal Ecumenism, Ethics, and Evangelism in Conversion," *CD* 50 (January 2008), 47-54. Cf. also his "Healing Fire from Heaven: A Wesleyan-Pentecostal Approach to Interfaith Forgiveness and Reconciliation", *WTJ* 42:2 (Fall 2007), 136-54. However, T.G. Moon, has argued that I, while not altogether incorrect about some level of inclusive values and positive directions for dialogue, overstate my case. For him, there is a much more moderate mindset in Pentecostal leaders such as J.H. King. E.g., see "J.H. King's Theology of Religions: 'Magnanimous Optimism?' *JPT* 16:1 (2007), 112-32. Cf. Richie, "A Moderate Move or Missing the Point? A Response to Tony Moon's 'J.H. King's Theology of Religions: "Magnanimous Optimism?"' *JPT* 16:2 (April 2008), 118-25. Yet V.M. Kärkkäinen, "A Response to Tony Richie's 'Azusa-era Optimism: Bishop J. H. King's Pentecostal Theology of Religions as a Possible Paradigm Today," *JPT* 15:2 (April 2007), 263-68, though pressing me to clarify and develop, has appreciatively affirmed my essential approach. Cf. Richie, "A Reply to Veli-Matti Kärkkäinen's 'Response to Tony Richie's Paper on "Azusa Era Optimism: Bishop J.H. King's Pentecostal Theology of Religions as a Possible Paradigm for Today,"' *JPT* 15:1 (April 2007), 269-75. Furthermore, J. Moltmann, "Preface," viii-xii, ed. V.M. Kärkkäinen, *The Spirit in the World: Emerging Pentecostal Theologies in Global Contexts* (Grand Rapids: Eerdmans, 2009), has suggested my work on King's Pentecostal theology of religions points to a theological solution to "the problem of particular faith and universal grace" and that it presents "a good approach for interfaith dialogue" (xi).

73. This section is in dialogue with Walter J. Hollenweger.

74. D.D. Bundy, "Hollenweger, Walter Jacob," *NDPCM,* 729. Hollenweger's now classic work *The Pentecostals,* Peabody, Hendrickson, 1988, first published in English by SCM Press Ltd., London, 1972. V.M. Kärkkäinen, *Pneumatology: The Holy Spirit in Ecumenical, International, and Contextual Perspective* (Grand Rapids: Baker, 2202), says this volume and its sequel, *Pentecostalism: Origins and Developments Worldwide* (Peabody, MA: Hendrickson, 1997), are "the most prominent presentation of the history and theologies of worldwide Pentecostalism", (87, fn. 103).

75. L. Price, *Theology Out of Place: A Theological Biography of Walter J. Hollenweger* (*Journal of Pentecostal Theology Supplement Series*, (Sheffield, Eng: Sheffield Academic Press, 2002). See also W.J. Hollenweger, "Evangelism: A Non-Colonial Model," *JPT* 7 (1995), 107-28. Cf. T. Richie, "Revamping Pentecostal Evangelism: Appropriating Walter J. Hollenweger's Radical Proposal", *IRM* 96:382-83 (July-October 2007), 343-54.

76. Smith, *Challenge,* points out that fears of propaganda go both ways for religions, e.g., both Christians and Muslims resent propaganda (perceived or real) from the other, 10, 124. See Price, *Out of Place,* 113-14.

77. Price, *Out of Place,* 114-15. See Hollenweger, "Critical Issues for Pentecostals," A. Anderson and W.J. Hollenweger, editors, *Pentecostals after a Century: Global Perspectives on a Movement in Transition, Journal of Pentecostal Theology* Supplement Series 15, Sheffield, Sheffield Academic Press, 1999), 176-91 (esp. 178, 183-88, and 190-91). Evangelical scholar Sir Norman Anderson, in *Christianity and World Religions: The Challenge of Pluralism* (Downer's Grove, InterVarsity Press, 1984), similarly uses the example of Peter and Cornelius, observing that both benefited by the dialogue; that good dialogue may prepare the way for evangelism, or be a part of it; and, that true, dialogue involves an element of risk but is worth it when carried out with confidence in the lordship of Christ and the power of the Holy Spirit, 188-91.

78. Price, *Out of Place,* 128-31. Interestingly, Hollenweger insists Pentecostalism originated in African American spirituality. See W.J. Hollenweger, "Black Roots of Pentecostalism," *Pentecostals after a Century,* 33-44 (esp. 33, 36). Significantly, Hollenweger considers African American W.J. Seymour the movement's real founder, 41-43. Cf. Hollenweger, "From Azusa Street to the Toronto Phenomenon: Historical Roots of the Pentecostal Movement," *Concilium* 3 (1996), 3-14, where Hollenweger stresses Catholic and Wesleyan spirituality in Pentecostalism.

79. Hollenweger, *Origins and Developments,* 132-41.

80. Price, *Out of Place,* 131-32.

81. Hollenweger, *Creator Spiritus:* The Challenge of Pentecostal Experience to Pentecostal Theology," *Theology* 81 (1978), 32-40. Cf. Price, *Out of Place,* 132-33. Also see Hollenweger, "All Creatures Great and Small: Towards a Pneumatology of Life," eds., David Martin and Peter Mullen, *Strange Gifts? A Guide to Charismatic Renewal* (Oxford: Basil Blackwell, 1984), 41-53. He continues to press Pentecostals in "Priorities in Pentecostal Research: Historiography, Missiology, Hermeneutics and Pneumatology," *Experiences of the Spirit: Conference on Pentecostal and Charismatic Research in Europe at Utrecht University 1989,* ed., J.A.B. Jongeneel (Frankfurt: Peter Lang, 1991), 7-22.

82. Price, *Out of Place,* 134-36.

83. Hollenweger suggests, in *Geist und Materie. III. Interkulturelle Theolgies* (Munich: Kaiser Verlag, 1988), "The lines between God and the devil cannot be so sharply drawn", 115. See Price, 136-38. Cf. W.B. Clift, *Jung and Christianity: The Challenge of Reconciliation* (New York: Crossroad, 1996), 129-39. Yong discusses the retrieval of the category of the demonic and Hollenweger's contribution, *Discerning,* 128, fn. 40. Pentecostalism's confrontation with evil powers of a particular culture may be responsible for some of its global appeal, Hollenweger, *The Pentecostals,* 300.

84. Hollenweger, *Origins and Developments,* 292.

85. Price, *Out of Place,* 139-41. Cf. Yong, *Discerning,* 175.

86. Price, *Out of Place,* 141-43. Pneumatology in contexts of mission and witness is particularly important in the Evangelical/Wesleyan/Pentecostal tradition. E.g., see J.C. Logan, "The Evangelical Imperative: A Wesleyan Perspective," 15-34, *Theology and*

Evangelism in the Wesleyan Heritage, ed. J.C. Logan (Nashville: Kingswood Books, 1994), 20.

87. Hollenweger, *Origins and Developments,* argues that Pentecostalism is at a critical moment in its journey, 399, and suggests it is essential that attention be given to its varied roots, 334-55. According to Yong, *Discerning,* Hollenweger's work suggests "a truly pluralistic Pentecostalism needs to be recognized, one that is in tune with the international movement of the Spirit and that is able to meet the needs of diverse cultures, societies, and places" (208). Yong complains that Pentecostalism has too long ignored the repeated pleas of Hollenweger to give attention to developing systematic cultural and theological understanding, 26-27. He does, however, admit that some Pentecostals are following up on aspects of Hollenweger's advice in several important areas, 171, fn. 30. Indeed, Yong's own work is an intentional attempt to do so, 18-19, fn. 2.

88. Price, *Out of Place,* 144.

89. Price, *Out of Place,* 144-46; cf. 150. Cf. J.T. Snell, "Beyond the Individual and Into the World: A Call to Participate in the Larger Purposes of the Spirit on the Basis of Pentecostal Theology," *Pneuma* 14:1 (Spring 1992), 43-57. Although Snell is essentially interested in involving Pentecostals in social action, his approach implies that the Spirit's purpose and work extend beyond the household of faith, or the Church, to include the larger world or cosmos based on Christ's atonement in application of an already existing implicit Pentecostal theology. Notably, he argues insistently that all creation and all humans are ultimately objects of God's mercy, 48-51. Cf. G. McFarlane, "Atonement, Creation, and Trinity," 192-207, gen. eds. D. Tidball, D. Hilborn, & J. Thacker, *The Atonement Debate: Papers from the London Symposium on the Theology of the Atonement* (Grand Rapids, MI: Zondervan, 2008).

90. Cf. Price, *Out of Place,* 151. Interestingly, Hollenweger, *Origins and Developments,* suggests Pentecostals should develop a theology of ancestors, 77, 266-67, and 383. However, worth remembering is that Hollenweger tends to define Pentecostalism itself quite broadly. See Hollenweger, "After Twenty Years of Research on Pentecostalism," *IRM* 75 (January 1986), 6.

91. This section draws on the work of Amos Yong, Tony Richie.

92. A. Yong and T. Richie, "Bearing Witness in a Religiously Pluralistic World: Pentecostal Missiology, the Religions, and Interreligious Encounter," *Studying Global Pentecostalism: Theories and Methods,* eds. A. Anderson, M. Bergunder, A. Droogers & C. van der Laan (GloPent, forthcoming 2010).

93. Cf. the following with A. Yong's "Guests, Hosts, and the Holy Ghost: Pneumatological Theology and Christian Practices in a World of Many Faiths," in D. Jensen, ed., *Lord and Giver of Life: A Constructive Pneumatology* (Louisville: Westminster John Knox Press, 2008), part I, and Yong, *Hospitality and the Other: Pentecost, Christian Practices, and the Neighbor* (Maryknoll: Orbis, 2008), esp. chaps. 2 and 4.

94. Cf. Yong, "Guests, Hosts, and the Holy Ghost," part I, and Yong, *Hospitality,* esp. chaps. 2 and 4.

95. See B.P. Prusak, "Hospitality Extended or Denied: *Koinonia* Incarnate from Jesus to Augustine," *The Church as Communion,* ed., J.H. Provost; Permanent Seminar Studies 1 (Washington, D. C.: Canon Law Society of America, 1984), 89-126. Cf. Yong, *Hospitality,* 101.

96. Yong, *Hospitality,* 101-102. A particular concern for marginalized peoples, e.g., the poor, has always characterized Pentecostalism. E.g. see T.W. Jennings, Jr., "Good News to the Poor in the Wesleyan Heritage," 139-56, Logan, *Theology and Evangelism,* 140-41. However, W. Ma suggests Pentecostalism is more a religion *of* the poor than *for* the poor, "'When the Poor are Fired Up': The Role of Pneumatology in Pentecos-

tal/Charismatic Mission," 40-52, Kärkkäinen, *Spirit in the World,* 41-42, which does not diminish concern for the poor but directs its specific construction.

97. Yong, *Hospitality,* 101.

98. Yong, *Hospitality,* 102-03. Cf. B. Byrne, *The Hospitality of God: A Reading of Luke's Gospel* (Collegeville, MN: Liturgical Press, 2000).

99. Cf. B. von Elderen, "Another Look at the Parable of the Good Samaritan," *Saved by Hope: Essays in Honor of Richard C. Oudersluys,* ed. J.I. Cook (Grand Rapids: Eerdmans, 1978), 109-19, and L.W. Mazamisa, *Beatific Comradeship: An Exegetical-Hermeneutical Study on Lk 10:25-37* (Kampen, Neth.: J.H. Kok, 1987), esp. 164-72.

100. Yong, *Hospitality,* 103.

101. Yong probes these questions at greater length in *Spirit Poured Out,* 241-44.

102. Yong, *Hospitality,* 103-05. Cf. Prusak, "Hospitality Extended or Denied," 89-126.

103. Cf. E.M. McGuire, "Hospitality in Luke-Acts" (M.A. thesis, Abilene Christian College, 1966), D.B. Gowler, *Host, Guest, Enemy, and Friend: Portrait of the Pharisees in Luke and Acts,* Emory Studies in Early Christianity 2 (New York: Peter Lang, 1991), A.E. Arterbury, *Entertaining Angels: Early Christian Hospitality in Its Mediterranean Setting,* New Testament Monographs 8 (Sheffield: Sheffield Phoenix, 2005), chap. 5. See Yong, *Hospitality,* 104.

104. Yong, *Hospitality,* 104. See D.P. Moessner, *Lord of the Banquet: The Literary and Theological Significance of the Lukan Travel Narrative* (Minneapolis: Fortress: 1989), and J.P. Heil, *The Meal Scenes in Luke-Acts: An Audience-centered Approach,* SBL Monograph Series 52 (Atlanta: Scholars Press, 1999).

105. Building creatively on the basis of traditional Pentecostal emphasis on Spirit empowerment for witness is not uncommon in Yong. E.g., see *Spirit Poured Out,* 83, 123-24, 175-76, and 265-66.

106. See Yong, *Hospitality,* 62, 112, 118, and 126.

107. This theme of hospital practices as Christian mission has roots in various motifs of Scripture. See J. Navone, "Divine and Human Hospitality," *New Blackfriars* 85 (2004), 329-40, A.E. Arterbury and W.H. Bellinger, Jr., "'Returning' to the Hospitality of the Lord: A Reconsideration of Psalm 23, 5-6," *Biblica* 86:3 (2005), 387-95, and K. Koyama, "'Extend Hospitality to Strangers': A Missiology of *Theologia Crucis*," *Currents in Theology and Mission* 20:3 (1993), 165-76.

108. Yong, *Hospitality,* 129-30. Elsewhere Yong argues that there is a hermeneutical spiral of beliefs informing practices and practices shaping beliefs. See *Spirit-Word-Community: Theological Hermeneutics in Trinitarian Perspective* (Burlington, VT, and Aldershot, UK: Ashgate, 2002), 10-11.

109. Yong, *Hospitality,* 65-67, 84-98 (esp. 97-98). Admittedly, America has its own unique brand of cultural and religious pluralism. Cf. P.W. Williams, *America's Religions: From Their Origins to the Twenty-First Century* (Urbana, ILL, and Chicago: University of Illinois Press, 2002), W.S. Green, "Diversity and Tolerance: Religion and American Pluralism," *The Religion Factor: An Introduction to How Religion Matters* eds., W.S. Green and J. Nuesner (Louisville, KY: Westminster John Knox, 1996), and B.A. McGraw and J.R. Formicola, eds., *Taking Religious Pluralism Seriously: Spiritual Politics on America's Sacred Ground* (Waco, TX: Baylor University Press, 2005).

110. Yong, *Hospitality,* 97-98. For Christians, the relationship of the religions and their adherents can be incredibly complex. Karkkainen, *Theology of Religions,* suggests ecclesiocentric (centrality of the Church), Christocentric (centrality of Christ), theocentric (centrality of God), but P.F. Knitter, *Introducing Theology of Religions* (Maryknoll, New York: Orbis, 2002), suggests four models: replacement (only one true religion), fulfill-

ment (one fulfills many), mutuality (many true religions in dialogue), and acceptance (many true religions—so be it). Cf. S.M. Ogden, *Is There Only One True Religion or Are There Many?* (Dallas: Southern Methodist University Press, 1992) and P. Schmidt-Leukel, "Exclusivism, Inclusivism, Pluralism: The Tripolar Typology—Clarified and Reaffirmed," *The Myth of Religious Superiority: Multifaith Explorations of Religious Pluralism*, ed., P.F. Knitter (Maryknoll, New York: Orbis, 2005), 13-27. Note that each model is developed around a different theme, e.g., salvation or central concern or question of truth. According, ambiguity and overlap may be inevitable.

111. Yong, *Hospitality*, 97-98. There are subtle but substantive differences between claiming Christ is truly savior, as in C. Braaten, *No Other Gospel: Christianity among the World's Religions* (Minneapolis, MN: Fortress, 1992), and claiming Christ is not the only Savior, as in P.F. Knitter, *The Uniqueness of Jesus: A Dialogue with Paul Knitter*, ed. L. Swindler and P. Mojzes (Maryknoll, New York: Orbis, 1997). Cf. G. Moran, *Uniqueness: Problems or Paradox in Jesus and Christian Traditions* (Maryknoll, New York: Orbis, 1992).

112. Literature on the theology of hospitality is growing quickly. E.g., see L. Richard, *Living the Hospitality of God* (New York: Paulist, 2000) and A. Sutherland, *I Was a Stranger: A Christian Theology of Hospitality* (Nashville: Abingdon, 2006). However, a Christian theology of hospitality does not attempt to deny, diminish, or destroy the verity and value of the distinctive and genuine otherness of guests and hosts. E.g., C.D. Pohl, *Making Room: Recovering Hospitality as a Christian Tradition* (Grand Rapids: Eerdmans, 1999), a Wesleyan writer, suggests that boundaries are necessary for physical and psychological safety, 140. Nevertheless, at the margins of life vibrantly practicing hospitality is paramount, Pohl, chap. 6. Indeed, L. Bretherton, *Hospitality as Holiness: Christian Witness amid Moral Diversity* (Burlington, VT, and Aldershot, UK: Ashgate, 2006), regards hospitality as a moral imperative and responsibility. H. Boersma, *Violence, Hospitality, and the Cross: Reappropriating the Atonement Tradition* (Grand Rapids: Baker Academic, 2004), insists hospitality viably confronts evil, 35. However, Boersma, "Irenaeus, Derrida and Hospitality: On the Eschatological Overcoming of Violence," *Modern Theology* 19:2 (2003), 163-80, also insists that human hospitality ought to be grounded on God's eschatological hospitality precisely because God's eschatological hospitality is more capable of dealing with evil and establishing trust and hope, 168-69.

113. Cf. Yong, *Hospitality,* 34-36, 150-56. Thus, Yong appropriately advances interreligious dialogue as authentic Christian practice, 156-60.

114. Cf. R.F. Harding with R.E. Harding, "Hospitality, Haints, and Healing: A Southern African American Meaning of Religion," *Deeper Shades of Purple: Womanism in Religion and Society*, ed. S.M. Floyd-Thomas (New York: New York University Press, 2006), 98-114 (esp. 101-02). Cf. Yong, *Hospitality,* 122-26.

115. Yong, *Hospitality,* 152. Cf. W.D. Davies and D.C. Allison Jr., *A Critical and Exegetical Commentary on the Gospel According to Matthew* (Edinburgh: T & T Clark, 1997), 418-29, H. Boers, *Theology Out of the Ghetto: A New Testament Exegetical Study Concerning Religious Exclusivism* (Leiden: Brill, 1971), chap. 3, and G. Gay, "The Judgment on the Gentiles in Matthew's Theology," *Scripture, Tradition, and Interpretation: Essays Presented to Everett F. Harrison by His Students and Colleagues in Honor of His Seventy-fifth Birthday,* ed. W.W. Gasque and W.S. LaSor (Grand Rapids: Eerdmans, 1978), 199-215.

116. Yong, *Hospitality,* 155-56.

117. Of course, the dangerous tendency is to forget one's alien status, one's former/future need of hospitality, and then fail to offer hospitality to others, including religious others. See Yong, *Hospitality,* 110-11.

118. Essentially, this amounts to a call for an enlargement (not diminishment) of the traditional understanding of Christian mission or *missio Dei*. Cf. D.J. Bosch, *Transforming Mission: Paradigm Shifts in Theology of Mission* (Maryknoll, New York: Orbis, 1991), 389-93, and C.F. Cardoza-Orlandi, *Mission: An Essential Guide* (Nashville: Abingdon, 2002), chap. 2. Cf. also Richie, "A Threefold Cord," 47-54, and Yong, *Hospitality*, 130-39.

119. Yong, *Hospitality*, 99.

120. Richie, "Azusa-era Optimism: Bishop J. H. King's Pentecostal Theology of Religions as a Possible Paradigm for Today," *JPT* 14:2 (April 2006), 247-60 (esp. 258).

121. Richie, "Azusa-era Optimism," 258-60. Cf. Richie, "Neither Naïve nor Narrow: A Balanced Pentecostal Approach to Christian Theology of Religions," *CJPCR* 15 (February 2006), http://www.pctii.org/cyberj/cyber15.html.

122. Yong, *Hospitality*, 140-43. Similarly, M. Soerens and J. Hwang, *Welcoming the Stranger: Justice, Compassion, and Truth in the Immigration Debate* (Downer's Grove, IL: InterVarsity, 2009), relate hospitality to economic and political issues of immigration. See 83, 139, and 173.

123. Yong, *Hospitality*, 38, 65, 99.

124. Yong, *Hospitality*, 99-160. The idea that believers need to prepare themselves through an inviting attitude of openness and responsiveness to the Holy Spirit's coming upon them is not new in Pentecostal circles. See e.g., Wesley Campbell, *Welcoming a Visitation of the Holy Spirit* (Lake Mary, FL: Charisma House, 1996). Indeed, that visitations of the Spirit empower movement toward others in mission and works of mercy is also affirmed, Campbell, 190. However, that the Spirit might empower and equip recipients of the Spirit themselves to be more receptive to others is a more novel nuance, although arguably an obviously appropriate extension or application. Cf. Soerens and Hwang, *Welcoming the Stranger*, 134.

125. Yong, *Hospitality*, 150.

126. This section is in dialogue with the work of Bishop Stephen Neill.

127. Stephen Neill, *Christianity and Other Faiths: Christian Dialogue with Other Religions*, second edition (New York: Oxford University Press, 1961, 1970). Neill also wrote important monographs such as *Colonialism and Christian Missions* (New York: McGraw-Hill, 1966) and *A History of Christian Missions*, rev. ed. (Hammondsworth, UK: Penguin, 1986).

128. H. Netland, *Encountering Religious Pluralism: The Challenge to Christian Faith & Mission* (Downer's Grove, ILL: InterVarsity, 2001), 47.

129. Netland, *Encountering*, 47. However, Netland himself, when climactically closing his own book, appeals to Niell's summary of the Christian approach to the interfaith context, saying, "we can do no better" than to quote Niell, 347-48.

130. J.H. Yoder, "The Church in the World: Theological Interpretation," *The Concept of the Believer's Church*, ed. James Leo Garret (Scottdale, PA: Herald, 1969), 250-83. Cf. Neill, *The Unfinished Task* (London: Lutterworth, 1957), 19-20.

131. H.R. Ezzat, "Dialogue with Passion," *Changing the Present, Dreaming the Future: A Critical Moment in Interreligious Dialogue*, ed. H. Ucko (Geneva: World Council of Churches, 2006), 22-27. An example of the complexity of the topic of interreligious conversion, might be R. Niebuhr's argument in *Pious and Secular America* (New York: Charles Scribner's Sons, 1958), that, although perhaps not necessarily denying the value of conversion in general or even of interreligious conversion to Christianity, Christian missionary activity toward Jews is wrong because "the two faiths are sufficiently alike for the Jew to find God more easily in terms of his own religious heritage than by subjecting himself to the hazards of guilt feeling involved in conversion", 108.

132. Dialogue participants often admit that interreligious conversion is a sometimes painful always difficult topic nevertheless demanding attention. See Ucko, "Group Reports," *Changing, Dreaming,* 74-84 (esp. 81-82). Andrew Wingate studies the topic of interreligious conversion from a contextualizing perspective in *The Church and Conversion: A Study of Recent Conversions to and from Christianity in the Tamil Area of South India* (Kashmere Gate, Delhi: ISPCK, 1997), see esp. 277-79 and 288-96.

133. Neill, *Christianity,* 4-5. Of course, approaches to the tasks and tools of dialogue greatly vary. Cf. e.g., Ucko, *Changing, Dreaming*: Rev. Valson Thampu, "Models of Interreligious Dialogue," 36-41, Rabbi Naamah Kelman, "The Holy Work of Dialogue," 42-45, and Dr Parichart Suwanbubbha, "Moving Together through Action and Dialogue," 46-53.

134. Neill, *Christianity,* 18.

135. E.g., J. Wesley frequently compared Muslim and other religions' life and thought with Christians, and, though occasionally polemical, was usually honest and humble in these comparisons, noting both negative and positive characteristics. See *CWJW* (The Wesleyan Heritage Collection; Ages Software, Inc. Rio, WI: 2002), 7:67, 58; 6:340-41, 45; 7:216, 377. Cf. also with R. Niebuhr's instructions that interreligious interaction requires great commitment to humility and charity, *The Children of Light and The Children of Darkness: A Vindication of Democracy and A Critique of Its Traditional Defense* (New York: Charles Scribner's Sons, 1944, 1960), 126-38.

136. Neill, *Christianity,* 19.

137. Neill, *Christianity,* 18-19. Cf. 207.

138. Neill, *Christianity,* 20, 40, 70, 99, 125, 153, 178.

139. Evangelical elder statesman J.R. Stott praises Neill's commitment to integrity in dialogue, "Dialogue, Encounter, Even Confrontation," D.A. Pittman, R.L.F. Habito, and T. Muck, eds., *Ministry and Theology in Global Perspective: Contemporary Challenges for the Church* (Grand Rapids: Eerdmans, 1996), 408-414 (413).

140. Neill, *Christianity,* 205-32.

141. P.F. Knitter, *One Earth, Many Religions: Multifaith Dialogue and Global Responsibility* (Maryknoll, New York: Orbis, 1995), talks about the essential place of "liberative practice" and "practical philosophy" in interfaith dialogue (82). For him, it is "by practice and feeling" that dialoguers actually get to know each other, 179. Thus, practical suggestions about actual implementation are essential ingredients, 136. Cf. R.K. Mays, *Interfaith Dialogue at the Grass Roots* (Philadelphia: Ecumenical Press, 2009).

142. Neill, *Christianity,* 29.

143. Neill, *Christianity,* 29. Knitter also argues for integrity in examining different truth claims in a dialogical relationship, *One Earth,* 33-34.

144. Struggles against Christocentric theology often end up being Christocentric in some sense anyway in order to remain identifiably "Christian." See Henrique Pinto, *Focault, Christianity, and Interfaith Dialogue* (London: Rutledge, 2003), 26-28. See Neill, *Christianity,* 69, 124.

145. Neill, *Christianity,* 207-34.

146. Neill, *Christianity,* 224-31 (224). Cf. Knitter's, *One Earth,* 175, 181, stress on wrestling with questions together.

147. Neill, *Christianity,* 231-32. Pluralists approach these nonnegotiable issues differently. E.g., Knitter argues that his pluralistic theology does not deny the divinity of Christ but only redefines it so that Christ is simply no longer thought of as the only or solely divine savior. Yet he still attempts to argue for some diluted, diminished sense of the uniqueness of Christ and of Christianity. See *One Earth,* 34-35. However, severe problems with such pluralistic theology have not been satisfactorily answered, S. Ogden,

"Problems in the Case for a Pluralistic Theology of Religions," *Journal of Religion* 68 (1988), 483-508.

148. Neill, *Christianity,* 232-34.

149. This section is in dialogue with the work of Sir Norman Anderson.

150. Netland, *Encountering,* applauds Anderson against Hick, 176 (cf. 341 fn. 70). Cf. Anderson, *The Mystery of the Incarnation* (London: Hodder & Stoughton, 1978).

151. Anderson, *Christianity,* 139-40.

152. Just how much Anderson has influenced American Evangelical theology of religions and approaches to interreligious dialogue is evident in the work of highly respected theologian S.J. Grenz, *Renewing the Center: Evangelical Theology in a Post-Theological Era* (Grand Rapids: Baker, 2000), 249-86 (261).

153. Anderson, *Christianity,* 184-88.

154. Anderson, *Christianity,* 187-88.

155. Anderson, *Christianity,* 189. Interestingly, Grenz, *Renewing,* says, that "we must engage in the task of evangelism until the end of the age" while avoiding "making the reality of judgment the sole motivation for our proclamation" (285). Speculating on "the final outcome of eschatological judgment" for religious others is simply not "our prerogative" for what may well be "a day of surprises" (285-86). The task of evangelism may be multilayered, "sometimes to bear the truth into realms of darkness, sometimes to bring to light truth that is already hidden, and sometimes to bring to explicit confession of Christ the implicit covenant with God already present in our hearers" (286).

156. Anderson, *Christianity,* 190-91. Grenz, *Renewing,* insists the Spirit's voice in Scripture is the primary authority for Christians and the Church, 209, but suggests that, according to Scripture itself, the Spirit's voice may also be heard in culture, 210-11(including religious culture).

157. Anderson, *Christianity,* 191-92.

158. Anderson, *Christianity,* 192.

159. D. Tracy, *Dialogue with the Religious Other: The Inter-Religious Dialogue* (Grand Rapids: Eerdmans, 1990), suggests "the transformative praxis of inter-religious dialogue" requires that a partner become "not a projected but a genuine other" (95). According to Tracy, dialoguers must be "willing to put everything at risk" while nonetheless entering into dialogue from the perspective of their own faith (95). For him, this may involve analyzing previous Christian theological answers in the experience of dialogue, 97. He suggests that in some cases at least, "Christian theology will not be the same when that finally occurs" (120). See Anderson, *Christianity,* 192.

160. This section is in dialogue with Gerald McDermott's work.

161. From another perspective, D.K. Swearer's *Dialogue: The Key to Understanding Other Religions* (Philadelphia: Westminster, 1977) is part of the *Biblical Perspectives on Current Issues* series, H.C. Kee, Gen. Ed. Pluralistic in content and in tone, it describes the three usual categories of exclusivism, inclusivism, and pluralism under the headings of discontinuous, fulfillment, and cooperative before adding a fourth preferred by the author: dialogue. Dialogue for Swearer does not mean the theological interchange of scholars, however; that would only be comparative religion. It is the actual spiritual engagement on the personal level of people of differing religious traditions.

162. G.R. McDermott, *Can Evangelicals Learn from World Religions? Jesus, Revelation, & Religious Traditions* (Downer's Grove: InterVarsity Press, 2000), 45-72.

163. Tracy, *Dialogue with the Other,* suggests Christian theology can learn much from Jewish thought through the centuries, especially on "the need for radically new interpretations after radically disruptive events" (120).

164. McDermott, *Learn?* 73-132.

165. McDermott, *Learn?* 133-206.
166. McDermott, *Learn?* 207-19.
167. G.R. McDermott, *God's Rivals: Why Has God Allowed Different Religions? Insights from the Bible and the Early Church* (Downer's Grove: IVP Academic, 2007), 159-62.
168. Thus Tracy, *Dialogue with the Other,* suggests "belief in general revelation and the universal salvific will of God disclosed with finality in Jesus Christ" have been central to theological inclusivism (96). See McDermott, *God's Rivals,* 162-64.
169. McDermott, *God's Rivals,* 164-68. D. Tracy, *Dialogue with the Religious Other: The Inter-Religious Dialogue* (Grand Rapids: Eerdmans, 1990), though often obtuse and usually pedantic, provides some excellent insights on approaching the dialogical process by an experienced and expert leader in the field. Tracy argues that much of religious history, spirituality, theology, Christian and otherwise, has been affected immensely by a mystical-prophetic dichotomy. He suggests that interreligious dialogue can proceed most productively only if the great religious traditions, Christianity included, recover a balance of the mystical and the prophetic—primarily in terms of individual experience and social action—both in their own traditions and in their relations with other traditions.
170. This section is in dialogue with Timothy Tennent's work.
171. T.C. Tennent, *Christianity at the Religious Roundtable: Evangelicalism in Conversation with Hinduism, Buddhism, and Islam* (Grand Rapids: Baker Academic, 2002), 22-27.
172. Somewhat similarly, D.A. McGavran, "Contemporary Evangelical Theology of Mission," ed. Pittman, et al, *Ministry and Theology in Global Perspective,* 247-53, argues that biblical faith and practice are compatible with interreligious dialogue, and invites Christians to use dialogical method and properly engage in dialogue so long as "he or she holds firmly to the truth of the Bible …", 251-52 (252).
173. Tennent, *Roundtable,* 27.
174. Cf. D.J. Hesselgrave, "Evangelicals and Interreligious Dialogue," Pittman, et al, *Ministry and Theology in Global Perspective,* 425-28, who argues that the question for contemporary Evangelicals is not whether to engage in dialogue but in what kinds of dialogue in which to engage, 425. Accordingly, interreligious dialogue that answers questions and objections of unbelievers, proclaims the good news of Christ, and invites repentance and faith, but does not compromise the gospel or countermand the Great Commission, is fully acceptable, 425-26. Practically speaking, Hesselgrave recommends dialogue on the nature of interreligious dialogue; that promotes freedom of worship and witness; that is concerned with meeting human need; that is designed to break down barriers of distrust and hatred; and, that has as its objective mutually comprehending conflicting truth claims, 426-27. Hesselgrave concisely challenges ecumenists to consider dangers of compromise in past approaches to dialogue, and Evangelicals to reconsider attitudes of disinterest and nonparticipation, 427.
175. Tennent, *Roundtable,* 31-32.
176. Tennent, *Roundtable,* 33. On interfaith dialogue as participation in and reflection of Christian witness, note Yong, *Spirit Poured Out,* 256-57, and Anderson, *Christianity,* 192. Tracy, *Dialogue with the Other,* observes that some of the complexity is traceable to diversity in Christianity's original authoritative texts, 114.
177. Tennent, *Roundtable,* 239.
178. As C.H. Pinnock, *Flame of Love: A Theology of the Holy Spirit* (Downer's Grove, IL: InterVarsity Press, 1996), exemplifies, inclusivists tend to hold in almost equal tension resistance to universalism and restrictivism, 190-92, and acceptance of universality and particularity, 192-96, a framework not conducive to pluralism.

179. Tennent, *Roundtable,* 239-43.
180. Significantly, Stott, "Dialogue," who insists Evangelicals be willing where necessary to encounter and even confront other faiths, nevertheless argues for an important place for dialogue, 411. Specifically, he argues that "true dialogue" is "a mark" of authenticity, humility, integrity, and sensitivity, 412-14.
181. This section is in dialogue with the work of Calvin Shenk.
182. C.E. Shenk, *Who Do You Say That I Am? Christians Encounter Other Religions* (Scottsdale, PA: Herald, 1997). Shenk cautiously considers a "wider hope" (inclusivist) soteriology to be consistent with biblical revelation but stresses the importance of witness over speculation, 228-44 (esp. 243-44). In *When Kingdoms Clash: The Christian and Ideologies* (Hazen, AR: Herald, 1988), Shenk argues that much of the tension in the world derives from competing systems of thought but he focuses on economic, political, and racial rather than interfaith issues. Shenk also has a Forward in Gordon D. Nickel, *Peaceable Witness Among Muslims* (Hazen, AR: Herald, 1999), which draws on Anabaptist peacemaking heritage in developing a peaceable method of communicating the gospel among Muslims. Shenk has also written denominational studies such as *Understanding Islam: A Christian Reflection on the Faith of our Muslim Neighbors* (Mennonite Mission Network, 2002) and *A Relevant Anabaptist Theology for the Nineteen Nineties* (Council of Int'l Ministries, 1990).
183. Shenk, *Who?* 174-91.
184. Shenk, *Who?* Cf. 192-208 with 209-27.
185. Specifically, T. Finger, "A Mennonite Theology for Interfaith Relations," *Grounds for Understanding: Ecumenical Resources for Responses to Religious Pluralism,* ed. S.. Heim (Grand Rapids: Eerdmans, 1998), 69-92. Kärkkäinen points out, *Theology of Religions,* that Finger's work is representative of the Mennonite movement as it was first prepared as an official voice in 1994, 136, fn. 4. However, as Rock points out, "Resources in the Reformed Tradition," Heim, *Grounds for Understanding,* assuming to speak for all of any particular tradition is untenable, 47.
186. W.R. Estep, *The Anabaptist Story: An Introduction to Sixteenth Century Anabaptism* (Grand Rapids: Eerdmans, 1975, 1996), calls the birth of Anabaptism "the most revolutionary act of the Reformation", noting the overriding emphasis on "the New Testament pattern" for the Church and "the absolute necessity of personal commitment to Christ" (14). See Finger, "Mennonite," 71-72.
187. Finger, "Mennonite," 73-77. A.E. McGrath, *Historical Theology: An Introduction to the History of Christian Thought* (Oxford, UK, Malden, MA: Blackwell, 1998), lists "a number of common concerns" for Anabaptists/Radical Reformers, including, "a general distrust of external authority; the rejection of infant baptism in favor of the baptism of adult believers; the common ownership of property; and an emphasis on pacifism and non-resistance" (162).
188. Finger, "Mennonite," 73-77.
189. Finger, "Mennonite," 77. Guarding against false religions, however, was a common concern in early Anabaptism; yet this mostly seemed to apply to perversions of pure Christian witness, Estep, *Anabaptism,* 158 and 256. Compassionate concern for the souls of adherents of other religions, e.g., Jews and Muslims, was clear, 298-99. Nevertheless, early Anabaptists stridently defended freedom of religion and uncoerced faith, including the rights of non-Christian religions, 263, sometimes in dramatic contrast to earlier attitudes and aggression, 96, a tradition that, though not unchallenged, remains unchanged, 306.
190. Finger, "Mennonite," 78.

191. Finger, "Mennonite," 80. In Finger's thorough treatment of Anabaptist theology, *A Contemporary Anabaptist Theology: Biblical, Historical, Constructive* (Downer's Grove, IL: InterVarsity, 20004), he wrestles in depth with issues of evangelism and dialogue, universality and particularity, and the ideology of pluralism. E.g., see 256-57, 266, 271, 304-05, and 314, for strong inclusivist heritage.

192. Shenk, *Who?* 209.

193. Shenk, *Who?* 210-11.

194. Although Finger, *Anabaptist Theology,* supports a tradition of dialogue, 303, 309, he also critiques pluralist approaches to dialogue, 278-82, especially for built in biases. See Shenk, *Who?* 211-12.

195. Shenk, *Who?* 213-19.

196. For Finger, *Anabaptist Theology,* evangelism still remains an important dimension of Christian mission but compatible with dialogue, 257-88. A similar view surfaces in Y. Congar, *I Believe in the Holy Spirit* 3 vols. trans. David Smith (New York: Seabury, 1983), who argued that "The time of the Church is essentially a time of mission, bearing witness and kerygma" (1:58), but agreed that the Church's dialogue with the world and its cultures, including dialogue with other religions, benefits both and presupposes the Spirit's presence in both, 2:219. See Shenk, *Who?* 219-20.

197. Shenk, *Who?* 220-25.

198. Finger makes clear that for Anabaptists [similar to Pentecostals] the centrality of Christ is as much or more about practical obedience as doctrinal development, *Anabaptist Theology,* 364, 376. Interestingly, he sometimes connects Pentecostal and Quaker traditions, 110 and 156. See M.S. Clark, "Pentecostalism's Anabaptist Roots: Hermeneutical Implications," *The Spirit and Spirituality: Essays in Honor of Russell P. Spittler,* ed. W. Ma and R.P. Menzies (New York: T & T Clark, 2004). Cf. D.A. Shank and J.H. Yoder, "Biblicism and the Church," 67-101 (67), and P. Peachy, "Epistolary: An Exchange by Letter," 145-57 (156), ed.V. Vogt, *The Roots of Concern: Writings on Anabaptist Renewal, 1952-57* (Eugene, OR: Wipf & Stock, 2009). R.E. Olson, in *The Story of Christian Theology: Twenty Centuries of Tradition & Reform* (Downer's Grove, IL: InterVarsity Press, 1992), groups Anabaptists and Pentecostals together as non-creedal and free church movements, 159. Grenz, *Renewing,* however, although broadly including Anabaptists as evangelicals, excludes them from a more specific Evangelicalism because of historical and theological trajectories, 16. See Shenk, *Who?* 225-27.

199. Shenk, *Who?* 247-53.

200. Shenk, *Who?* 253-64.

201. In the interest of transparency, I have served as Chairperson for the Church of God/Mennonite Church (USA) dialogue for several years, and note that many Mennonites do confess (or express) struggles with appropriately balancing values of dialogue and evangelism, personal and social responsibilities, and so on. However, Church of God/Pentecostal participants in this dialogue have also confessed (or expressed) similar struggles, though perhaps with different emphases.

202. This section enters into dialogue with the work of Vinoth Ramachandra.

203. E.g., V. Ramachandra, *Faiths in Conflict: Christian Integrity in a Multicultural World* (Downer's Grove, IL: InterVarsity Press, 1999). Nevertheless, in *The Recovery of Mission: Beyond the Pluralist Paradigm* (Carlisle, UK: Paternoster, 1996), Ramachandra attempts to rehabilitate Christian mission in terms of its continuing validity as an essential task of the Church. Furthermore, commitment to Christian mission spurs him to examine relations between modern idolatry and Christian mission in *Gods That Fail: Modern Idolatry and Christian Mission* (Downer's Grove, IL: InterVarsity, 1996).

204. Kärkkäinen, *Theology of Religions,* 333. Indeed, much of Ramachandra's work is a response to the religious pluralism of the likes of, e.g., S.J. Samartha, *One Christ, Many Religions: Toward a Revised Christology* (Maryknoll, New York: Orbis, 1991). Cf. Ramachandra, *Faiths in Conflict,* 18-20, 96. Ramachandra also reacts against the pluralistic pneumatology of R. Panikkar, *The Unknown Christ of Hinduism,* rev. ed. (London: Darton, Longman & Todd, 1981) (e.g. 57), in *Recovery of Mission,* 91-95.

205. E.g., Netland, *Encountering,* 31, 32n, 215-16, 285n, 336n, 341-42.

206. Kärkkäinen, *Theology of Religions,* 319. Yet T. Keller, *The Reason for God: Belief in an Age of Skepticism* (New York: Penguin, 2008), notes that Ramachandra defends the utterly unique nature of Christian soteriology in contrast to other religions, 223-24. T.L. Tiessen, *Who Can Be Saved? Reassessing Salvation in Christ and World Religions* (Downer's Grove, IL: InterVarsity, 2004), thinks that Ramachandra "From an evangelical standpoint," "nicely describes the combination of the particularity of Christ's saving work and the variety of revelation and faith experiences" (182).

207. E.g., Ramachandra, *Recovery.* Furthermore, commitment to Christian mission spurs him to examine relations between modern idolatry and Christian mission in *Gods That Fail.* C.J.H. Wright, *The Mission of God: Unlocking the Bible's Grand Narrative* (Downer's Grove, IL: InterVarsity, 2006), commends Ramachandra's reading of biblical mission in the Book of Jonah, 461, fn 7, also asserting that Ramachandra presses for analysis of modernity's assumptions, 166. P. Hiebert, *Transforming Worldviews: An Anthropological Understanding of How People Change* (Grand Rapids: Baker, 2008), relies heavily on Ramachandra assessment of modernity and its implications for religious belief and practice, 143, 148, and 150. For him, Ramachandra sets the discussion in the context of the biblical story and Christian mission, 234 and 300.

208. Ramachandra, *Recovery,* 10-11.

209. Notably, W.A. Dryness, H.A.G. Blocher and W.A. Dryness, "Anthropology, Theological," *GDT,* 42-52, suggests Ramachandra is an important participant in an Asian Christian conversation with the West and its assumptions about Buddha and Buddhism, the person and work of Christ, and human self and sense of personhood, 51. M. Lee, "Asian American Theologies," *GDT,* 70-77, presents Ramachandra as an example of "Asian evangelical theologians attempting to be more open and aggressive in engaging Asian culture and religious heritage with the gospel" (76). See Ramachandra, *Recovery,* 37-39.

210. Ramachandra, *Recovery,* 13-46. Cf. Hiebert's, *Transforming Worldviews,* appeal to Ramachandra's critical perspective on nationalism, 178-89. Cf. D.J. Treier, *Introducing Theological Interpretation of Scripture: Recovering a Christian Practice* (Grand Rapids: Baker, 2008), 159.

211. As Tiessen, *Who Can Be Saved?* observes, Ramachandra is prone to expose false perceptions, often amounting to misguided myths, of religions by both the East and the West, 461. See Ramachandra, *Recovery,* 69-72.

212. Ramachandra, *Recovery,* 72-75. Cf. Tennent, *Roundtable,* 26-27. Interestingly, J. Rock, "Resources in the Reformed Tradition for Responding to Religious Plurality," *Grounds for Understanding: Ecumenical Resources for Responses to Religious Pluralism,* ed. S. Heim (Grand Rapids: Eerdmans, 1998), 46-58, argues that "the continuing affirmation of religious pluralism rests on a basis which is *christological* and *conversational* [original italics]", 48, thus developing simultaneously both the community's commitment and its willingness to honestly engage as essential elements in interreligious dialogue.

213. Ramachandra, *Recovery,* 75-81. Cf. Tennent, *Roundtable,* 53-54.

214. Ramachandra, *Recovery,* 81-85.

215. Interestingly, Catholic scholar G. Lohfink presents Israel as paradigmatic for Jesus' ministry goal of establishing an historical eschatological community. See *Jesus and Community* (Philadelphia/New York: Fortress/Paulist, 1982/1984).
216. Ramachandra, *Recovery*, 95-97. Significantly, D.P. Hollinger, *Choosing the Good: Christian Ethics in a Complex World* (Grand Rapids: Baker, 2002), quotes Ramachandra in support of his argument for a soteriology affirming the goodness of material creation stretching beyond the traditionally "spiritual" realm, 70.
217. Ramachandra, *Recovery*, 99-103.
218. Ramachandra, *Recovery*, 103-11.
219. Ramachandra, *Recovery*, 111-15.
220. Ramachandra, *Recovery*, 115 (original italics). Accordingly, H. Netland, "The East Comes West: Or Why Jesus Instead of Buddha?" ed. P. Copan and W.L. Craig, *Passionate Conviction: Contemporary Discourses on Christian Apologetics* (Nashville, TN: B & H, 2007), approvingly quotes Ramachandra's insistence that the unique divinity of Christ is the dividing line with pluralists, an unbridgeable offense, 164. However, S. Escobar, *The New Global Mission: Gospel from Everywhere to Everyone* (Downer's Grove, IL: InterVarsity, 2003), reminds that Ramachandra also challenges established presuppositions about Christ, 101 and 111.
221. Of course, Christ's atonement tends to be at the heart of Pentecostal theology, including Pentecostal theology of religions. E.g., see Bishop J. H. King, *From Passover to Pentecost* (Franklin Springs, GA: Advocate, 1911, 1976 [4th ed.]), 5-8, 14-16, 39-40, 101-104, and 109, and *Christ-God's Love Gift: Selected Writings of J.H. King: Vol. I* (Franklin Springs, GA: Advocate Press, 1969), 110-11.
222. Ramachandra, *Recovery*, 117.
223. Ramachandra, *Recovery*, 119-20. Tiessen, *Who Can Be Saved?*, quotes approvingly Ramachandra's argument that the Church is a particular community among other particular communities but with a universal mission—an argument arising from Israel's history as well, 344.
224. Ramachandra, *Recovery*, 121.
225. Ramachandra, *Recovery*, 121. Tiessen, *Who Can Be Saved?*, reminds that Ramachandra traces religious relativism as far back as second century Gnosticism rather than identifying it as an entirely modern phenomenon, 305.
226. Ramachandra, *Recovery*, 130-31.
227. Ramachandra, *Recovery*, 135.
228. Ramachandra, *Recovery*, 135-37.
229. Ramachandra, *Recovery*, 137-38.
230. K.R. Ross and D.A. Kerr, in their "Conclusion" to the book they edited, *Edinburgh 2010: Mission Then and Now* (Pasadena, CA: William Carey International University Press, 2009), recount Ramachandra's recommendation of a pneumatological approach to theology of religions so long as there is "both a firm identification of the Spirit with Jesus Christ, and an open-ended faithfulness to Jesus that allows for deeper insights that the Spirit affords" (311). Thus, Christian witness can be both responsible and responsive, 311. Indeed, such a balance well represents the thrust of the present work as well. Cf. Ramachandra, "A World of Religions and a Gospel of Transformation," 139-54, in Ross and Kerr, *Edinburgh 2010*. See Ramachandra, *Recovery*, 138-39.
231. Cf. Tiessen's, *Who Can Be Saved,?* discussion of Ramachandra's assertion of "the uniqueness of Jesus as divine" while also arguing that "this does not cancel out all other stories of the divine-human encounter" because of God's grace (418-19). See Ramachandra, *Recovery*, 139-40.

232. Ramachandra, *Recovery*, 167. Escobar, *New Global*, suggests Ramachandra "not only takes us well beyond the pluralist paradigm but also develops a well-argued evangelistic and missionary proposal for our time" (180).

233. Ramachandra, *Recovery*, 167-68.

234. Cf. P.G. Hiebert's, "The Missionary as Mediator of Global Theologizing," 288-308, ed. C. Ott and H. Netland, *Globalizing Theology: Belief and Practice in an Era of World Christianity* (Grand Rapids: Baker, 2006), affirmation of Ramachandra's efforts to engage "sociocultural contexts" (298). See Ramachandra, *Recovery*, 168-69.

235. Ramachandra, *Recovery*, 170-71. M.T. Thangaraj's *Relating to People of Other Religions: What Every Christian Needs to Know* (Nashville: Abingdon, 1997) is also an interesting little book ending up with an affirmation of tolerance and openness (he calls it "gentleness and reverence") to mutual dialogue as essential.

236. This section dialogues with the work of Charles Jones.

237. C.B. Jones, *The View from Mars Hill: Christianity in the Landscape of World Religions* (Cambridge, MA: Cowley, 2005), 17, 19.

238. Jones, *View*, 84-85.

239. Jones, *View*, 167-92. See H.D. Hunter and P.D. Hocken, eds. *All Together in One Place: Theological Papers from the Brighton Conference on World Evangelization* (JPTSup 4, Sheffield, Eng: Sheffield Academic Press, 1993). Therein C.H. Pinnock, in "Evangelism and Other Living Faiths: An Evangelical Charismatic Perspective", 208-14, and A.O. Gbuji, "Evangelization and Other Living Faiths: A Roman Catholic Perspective", 215-18, both argue for the compatibility of evangelism and interfaith dialogue in Pentecostal/Charismatic theology of religions.

240. Jones, *View*, 168-75. P.C. Phan, *Christianity with an Asian Face: Asian American Theology in the Making* (Maryknoll, New York: Orbis, 2003), suggests the Asian church's threefold mission includes human development, interreligious dialogue, and inculturation, 185. Cf. 188.

241. S.J.M. Barnes, *Theology and the Dialogue of Religions* (Cambridge, UK Cambridge University Press, 2002), argues that dialogue is complex in all it forms and "begs questions about how identities are established" (23). However, for Barnes, dialogue is not some problem solving task; it is "about forming the community of faith with those Christlike virtues and qualities which listen and respond to the Spirit, which enable a facing of the other with critical respect" (239). See Jones, *View*, 175-77.

242. Jones, *View*, 177-81.

243. Jones, *View*, 182-91 (187).

244. Jones, *View*, 190-92. Cf. J.H. Berthrong, *The Divine Deli: Religious Identity in the North American Cultural Mosaic* (Mary Knoll, Orbis: 1999) and James L. Fredericks, *Buddhists and Christians: Through Comparative Theology to Solidarity* (Mary Knoll: Orbis, 2004).

245. E.g., see my discussion with Rabbi Haim Dov Beliak during Jews on First teleconference panel regarding evangelistic efforts by Messianic Jews, "Southern Baptists Rely on Deception in Efforts to Convert Jews: Messianic Congregations Offer Reassuring Jewish Symbols," at http://www.jewsonfirst.org/07c/baptist_messianic.html on June 25, 2007.

246. C.M. Robeck, Jr., and J.L. Sandidge, "Dialogue, Catholic and Pentecostal," *NIDPCM*, 574-82, state that although the early hope that Pentecostalism would contribute to bringing the church together was disappointed, recently the movement has become involved in "vital dialogue", 574. However, the dialogue process is difficult both for Pentecostal and their partners, and overcoming stereotypes and proceeding with great patience are needed, 580-81; but mutual spiritual growth is occurring, 581. Cf. F.D. Mac-

chia, "Dialogue, Reformed-Pentecostal," *NIDPCM,* 575-76. The previous refers to dialogue between Pentecostals and other Christians. Dialogue between Pentecostals also sometimes occurs, G. Traettino, "Italy," *NIDPCM,* 133-41, (esp. 138-39).

247. Discernment is a key concept for Amos Yong's thought. In a short article, Yong, "Discernment, Discerning the Spirits," *GDT,* 232-35, summarily points out that discernment has various facets, including New Testament references, historical paradigms, and contemporary theological developments and applications, 232. Furthermore, he notes that modern Pentecostalism has "retrieved and revised" the category of discernment, 234. Among those features with applicability to theology of religions included is the discernment of the Holy Spirit in general and in identifying the pagan or demonic in other religions, 234. Yong argues for a holistic theology of discernment that is phenomenological, ecclesiological, sociological, and multidisciplinary, 234-35. In a fuller treatment Yong, among other things, attempts to establish "provisional, pneumatological guidelines" by which "to distinguish the presence, activity and absence of the Holy Spirit in the world of religions", *Discerning,* 137-48 (137). Yong wrestles with affirming a fundamentally Christological and scriptural set (1 John 4:1-3 is key) of criteria while being fair to other religions' "own internal criteria", 137-40 (141). He eventually concludes other faiths' religious symbols, practices and doctrines "can be accessed as modalities" in discernment of "divine blessedness" or "demonic condemnation and destruction" (312). He nonetheless intends all evaluation to be provisional and to occur both pneumatologically and christologically, 314-15. Finally, he affirms and emphasizes human fallibility and the necessity of categories of the Holy Spirit and of the demonic, 321-22. In *Beyond the Imappse,* Yong insists on the importance of discerning the Spirit and religions, 94-96, and critiques others for shortcomings in this area, 125-28. He labors to establish the biblical basis of discernment, 140-49, but also affirms discernment in "the hermeneutics of life", 149-60, and especially relates the hermeneutics of life and the religions, 164-67. In *Spirit Poured Out* Yong suggests discerning the Spirit(s) in the religions involves discerning the "various background factors" brought to interfaith encounter, 253, paying close attention to "the multifarious phenomena" of the religions, 245, and that this "multileveled inquiry" is "best measured by its fruits", 255. Returning to the question of criteria for discernment in the phenomenology of religions, Yong offers five suggestions presented as a series of questions (here summarized): (1) Are the fruits of the Spirit being manifest? (2) Are the works of the kingdom as manifest in the life of Jesus visible? (3) Is salvation in its various dimensions observable? (4) Is conversion in the various human domains occurring? (5) Is holiness in its various senses discernible, however dimly? (256). However, he also argues for the charismatic dimension of discernment, though in a considerably broadened form, 295-96 (cf. 301).

248. All of these groups are exploring how their own unique identities interface with attempts at dialogue endeavors. E.g., see M.A. Noll, "The History of an Encounter: Roman Catholics and Protestant Evangelicals," *Evangelicals & Catholics Together: Toward a Common Mission,* ed. Charles Colson and Richard John Neuhaus (Dallas: Word, 1995), 81-114, and K.J. Collins, "Introduction: The Many Dialogue Partners of American Evangelicalism," *The Evangelical Moment: The Promise of an American Religion* (Grand Rapids: Baker Academic, 2005), 11-17. Cf. Stott, "Dialogue, Encounter, Even Confrontation," 408-414, and D.J. Hesselgrave, "Evangelicals and Interreligious Dialogue," 425-28.

249. See G.L. McClung, Jr., "Evangelism," *NIDPCM,* 617-20 (esp. 617, 620). Collins, *Evangelical Moment,* notes that in addition to emphases on charismata and pneumatology, divine healing and eschatology, Pentecostals stress "the cruciality of redemption" in an emphatically evangelical manner, 33. He observes that Pentecostals

stress personal conversion, and the new birth or regeneration in particular, 52-57 (esp. 54). Of course, Pentecostals are uniquely known "in terms of their celebration of the freedom of the Spirit", 67. Yet Collins is sure that Evangelicals, specifically including Wesleyans and Pentecostals, have much to learn from other traditions, 208. Notably, Collins has criticized M. Noll, *The Scandal of the Evangelical Mind* (Grand Rapids: Eerdmans, 1994), for his failure to accurately or adequately comprehend or represent Wesleyans and Pentecostals, 78-79, specifically in his minimization of the quality of their theological contributions.

250. See D.E. Miller and T. Yamamori, *Global Pentecostalism: The New Face of Christian Social Engagement* (Los Angeles: University of California Press, 2007), 1-3. Indeed, C.B. Johns, "The Adolescence of Pentecostalism: In Search of a Legitimate Sectarian Identity," *Pneuma* 17:1 (1995), 3-17, asserts that Pentecostalism "was birthed out of the hungering cries of simple people who desired to see the glory of God", 13-14. In that context, B.L. Callen, *Discerning the Divine: God in Christian Theology* (Louisville, KY: Westminster John Knox, 2004), adds, "The divine heart is one of compassionate love, and the Spirit's power is exercised on behalf of all whom God loves", 147. Cf. Richie, "Pentecostal Spirituality Politically Applied," *Pax Pneuma* 5:1 (Spring 2009), 28-33, who argues that social justice, peace, and tolerance are values meshing remarkably well with Pentecostalism's tradition of world evangelism and individual discipleship or spiritual formation, 32. For him, a Pentecostal politick applied from Pentecostal spirituality appears to be characterized by a strong pneumatic element and an egalitarian and liberating impulse, 32. Cf. 29-30.

251. Callen, *Discerning the Divine*, argues that beginning with Augustine there was a tendency to depersonalize the Holy Spirit leading to diminishment, 100. Down through the centuries, including in John Wesley's day, though he resisted it rigorously, and subsequently, "the church has often been ambiguous or even antagonistic toward the contemporary work of the Holy Spirit" because of fear of "chaos" through "subjectivity" and "lack of order" (101). Callen credits the ecumenical movement with helping to turn around the disparaging trend, which picked up considerably with "the dramatic spread of Pentecostalism" and was further advanced through Pope John Paul II's "special devotion to the Holy Spirit" (101). Accordingly, Callen succinctly says, "The tide has turned in the Spirit's favor" (101). Callen sees "a worldwide surge of interest in the Holy Spirit" precipitated by the rapid growth of Pentecostalism as a sign that a past sense of God's remoteness is "no longer tolerable" (106). Cf. J. Macquarrie, *Thinking about God* (New York: Harper & Row, 1975), 131. However, C.H. Pinnock, "The Holy Spirit in the Theology of Donald G. Bloesch," *Evangelical Theology in Transition: Theologians in Dialogue with Donald Bloesch* (Downer's Grove, IL: InterVarsity, 1999), 119-35, repeatedly criticizes leading evangelical theologian D. Bloesch for continuing to minimize the role of the Holy Spirit in Christian theology and spirituality, e.g., 124, 126, 128, 133.

252. E.g., Pinnock, *Flame of Love*, chap. 6, or A. Yong, *Beyond the Impasse*. Cf. Kärkkäinen, *Theology of Religions*, 272-73 and 277-81.

253. Indeed, even apart from Pentecostals a pneumatological trend in the field of theology of religions seems assured as many leading thinkers have been turning in that direction. E.g., see Kärkkäinen, *Trinity,* 50-52, 56, 62-63, 76, 86, 101. In fact, Merrick, "False Religions," complains caustically about too much attention to pneumatology in theology of religions, 108, 123. Nevertheless, Karkkainen's observation that most Pentecostals limit the working of the Spirit "to the church and its proclamation of the gospel, although they acknowledge the work of the Holy Spirit in the world, convicting people of sin", *Theology Religions,* 141, is probably still applicable.

254. Perhaps helpful is Congar's explanation that there are several different forms of prophetism, including that which is unique to the Church and its ministry, that which is distinctively charismatic, and that which may even be non-religious, *WS,* 67-71.

255. E.g., as Congar notes, none should ever lose sight of the Spirit's association with Christ. After all, "the Holy Spirit is active in the cosmos and is the *Spiritus Creator* only because he is one with the Word and with 'God'" (*WS,* 131). S. Chan, *Pentecostal Theology and the Christian Tradition* (Sheffield, Eng: Sheffield Academic, 2000, 2003), wisely cautions against possible pitfalls in a too casual approach to the *Creator Spiritus* concept, 111-16, not arguing against it altogether but advising that "its usage must be carefully circumscribed" (114).

256. Cf. T.C. Oden, *John Wesley's Scriptural Christianity: A Plain Exposition of His Teaching on Christian Doctrine* (Grand Rapids: Zondervan, 1994), 243-52. Oden argues that divine knowledge stemming from prevenient grace "does not necessarily include specific awareness of the Christian gospel, though it may also be formed by the history of revelation." He underscores that Wesley understood prevenient grace as involving a supernatural gift of God in terms of pneumatology, 252. For a fuller and richer study of pneumatological grace, though not focusing on prevenient grace, see L. Wood, *Pentecostal Grace* (Grand Rapids: Zondervan, 1984).

257. S. Solivan suggests Pentecostals recognize the prevenient workings of the Holy Spirit in every human being as well as the diverse and pluralistic character of the Spirit's manifestations across religious boundaries, making a commitment cautiously to "examine the diverse ways the Spirit is at work among other people of faith". See "Interreligious Dialogue: An Hispanic American Pentecostal Perspective", S. Mark Heim (ed.), *Grounds for Understanding: Ecumenical Responses to Religious Pluralism* (Grand Rapids: Eerdmans, 1998), 37-45 (43). J. Bowers observes that, "Wesleyan-Pentecostals rarely if ever used Wesley's term 'prevenient grace', but shared with him the belief that salvation began with the work of God's grace in the sinner." See his "A Wesleyan-Pentecostal Approach to Christian Formation", *JPT* 6 (1995), 55-86 (64, fn. 32). Conversion, therefore, though a definite experience, is also a dynamic process beginning before and continuing after justification/regeneration.

258. G. H. Mellor, "Evangelism and Religious Pluralism in the Wesleyan Tradition," *Theology and Evangelism in the Wesleyan Heritage,* ed. James C. Logan (Nashville: Kingswood Books, 1994), 109-26, urges authentic dialogue in association with evangelistic mission (120-26).

259. Thus R. Parry, *Worshiping Trinity: Coming Back to the Heart of Worship* (Cornwall, UK: Paternoster, 2005), speaks of "the terrifying Trinity", 3. Cf. tone of Duffield and Van Cleave, *Foundations,* 86-87.

260. M.E. Marty, *When Faiths Collide,* (Malden: Blackwell, 2005), 1, 66, 128-42.

261. G. D'Costa, *The Meeting of Religions and the Trinity* (Maryknoll, New York: Orbis, 2000). In fact, D'Costa and John Hick have carried on a conversation arising out of D'Costa's trinitarian critique charging Hick's pluralism leads to denial of otherness and difference. See D'Costa, "Christian Theology and Other Religions: An Evaluation of John Hick and Paul Knitter," *Studia Missionalia* 42 (1993), 161-78, and Hick, "The Possibility of Religious Pluralism: A Reply to Gavin D'Costa," *Religious Studies* 33 (1997), 161-66.

PART TWO:
FRAMING THE STRUCTURE

Chapter 4

The Paradigmatic Story of Pentecostal Testimony

Introduction

The preceding chapters have studied contemporary society's increasingly pluralistic trends, and then, conversely, the preparedness of the current state of Pentecostal theology of religions and Pentecostal mores to address the present situation. The diagnoses arising from this analysis are that the situation is critical, that Pentecostalism possesses reservoirs of resources for addressing it but that these are not being sufficiently plumbed or at a satisfactory rate for matching the need of the hour. Accordingly, the time for taking bold steps has arrived. At this point, therefore, the study will turn from description to prescription (or, according to the mapping analogy, from preparation to construction).

The general thesis for this project is that Pentecostal pneumatology provides space and support for a distinctive and productive approach to theology of religions. Its special focus is on Pentecostal pneumatology as experienced and expressed in the practice of personal testimony providing space and support as well as substantive direction for understanding and engaging in contemporary interreligious encounter and dialogue. Accordingly, exploring ways of authentically and profitably exploiting Pentecostal testimony for that purpose will be an important step in this process. This task will be taken up in the next chapter. Examining just what is meant by "Pentecostal testimony" will be the task of this chapter. The present chapter aims to supply the structure for the contents of the next. First, it will identify what is distinctive about Pentecostal testimony, and second, consider its multifaceted context.[1]

The Tapestry of Human Testimony

Universal but Varied

Apparently, testimony is universally prevalent among humans but present in varied ways, occurring in juridical, religious, or social contexts.[2] Plüss explains that sometimes "testimony is expressed as a sign of something that exists" but more often "in terms of a claim that something happened," and that it is "given by a person or a group of people in dialogue with others."[3] Testimony quite closely relates to witness, though the former focuses on the issue of truth and the latter on factuality of an occurrence.[4] Theologically, testimony is important because it relates to "the understanding of one's faith", and why or how a particular experience or event is significant.[5] Notably, testimony requires interpretation, evaluation, and judgment as well as weighing against the character of the one who testifies; it is, therefore, significant both individually and socially.[6] Important to understand are some of the layers of meaning and levels of methodology regarding both religious and nonreligious functions of testimony activity.

Paul Ricoeur, with a more philosophical approach based in part on his conception of the narrative identity and ontology of the human self,[7] links testimony with attestation as exemplifying not "I believe-that" but "I believe-in"; or, in other words, it is "a kind of belief" but not that of modernistic rationalism—although assuredly no less important because of it.[8] Accordingly, suspicion and trust are unavoidable elements in assessing credibility and reliability of testimony.[9] Thus, "tests of sincerity" "are not verifications but trials that finally end in acts of trust" in spite of "intermediary episodes of suspicion."[10] An avowal may or may not be accepted, but when it is, it takes on something of the character of "a shared confession".[11] Of course, mutual testimony is necessary as well.[12] For Ricoeur, "Testimony is therefore the mode of truth" of an "auto-exhibition of the Self, the inverse of the certainty of the ego", and, again, not so far removed from personal attestation.[13]

Personal History

In one sense, one can understand testimony as expressive of personal history. For example, when Jewish poet and literary artist David Rosenberg began his introduction to a collection essays and stories arising out of and about the Holocaust, he explained that it contained "many surprising approaches to personal history".[14] Yet he immediately comments on "how crucial it is to pass on what one has seen" and to make private experiences public, and asserts that the "immediacy of testimony must be kept alive."[15] For him, testimony is above all personal but also critical and connected to literal events.[16] It may also involve redefining private myths to discover deep meaning.[17] For another example, when historian and former Nation of Islam activist Vibert White published his analysis of that group, he combined his account of personal experiences with extensive journal notes and historical analysis in addition to interviews and insights from other insiders.[18] Yet it was White's own "insider status," including a process of ideological and theological indoctrination and a crisis of recantation, which made his book testimony as well as history.[19]

Diverse Fields

Furthermore, shades of meaning in testimony surface depending on the field of endeavor involved. In literary genre, testimony may refer to a particular cultural approach to literature.[20] For a journalist, testimony is often associated with informants and witnesses regarding stories reported.[21] In a courtroom, eyewitness testimony can be decisive for judge and jury even in the face of possible fallibilities.[22] For oral historians, oral testimony can be an essential instrument for recording and communicating information and attitudes, especially where capturing and conveying human experience is involved.[23]

Religious Testimony

Of course, religious testimony is also a specific and distinctive category of its own. James found recorded testimonies helpful instruments for understanding the psychology of religious experience.[24] Although, as Proudfoot notes, most of James' examples came from the Christian tradition, he viewed them as having parallels in other religious traditions.[25] Proudfoot himself argues that religious language is "not only the expressive, receptive medium ... It also plays a very active and formative role in religious experience."[26] Interestingly, Maslow concluded that people in various cultures, religions, and of various castes or classes who had "transcendent experiences" tended to describe these in "the same general way," though language and content is necessarily different, and that "ineffable experience" found "the best verbal phrasing" "not good enough" and seemed restrained and even restricted by the limits of language.[27] Accordingly, speech descriptive of religious experience, that is, testimony, necessarily tends more toward use of "poetical and metaphorical language" as it is "more efficacious in communicating certain aspects of the ineffable" than analytical or logical language.[28] Thus, religious testimony may be very emotional and moving, potentially even stirring up similar experiences within listeners.[29] However, a serious and insurmountable obstacle to communication occurs when a listener is "a literal, non-peaker [i.e., not sharing in the experience described]" to the extent that "rhapsodic, isomorphic communication will not work."[30]

Christian Testimony

Plüss suggests Christian testimony arises rather directly out of the biblical tradition of the community of faith's encounter with God in God's self-revelation so that God "is experienced and remembered as the one who is present and changes the destiny of humankind."[31] Accordingly, testimony should be related to its biblical roots and context, but still include the need for interpretation and awareness of both its religious and social significance.[32] Similarly, New Testament theologian Richard Bauckham argues that one may best understand the biblical gospels as eyewitness testimonies.[33] Plüss summarily suggests that the theological significance of testimonies inheres, first, in that it relates one's perception of God, second, in that it points away from self to God, third, in that testimony avoids deceptiveness through a process of careful evaluation.[34] Furthermore, and importantly, testimony "engenders action", that is, "What begins with a religious perception leads to praise and ultimately to ethical commitment."[35] Perhaps it is not surprising, then, when Long insists that talking together about belief may even be fundamental to building the character of personal and corporate faith.[36]

In a somewhat different approach to the topic, Alan Jacobs distinguishes between general testimony, as in "a" or "the" testimony, and the more personal "my" testimony.[37] Testimony is a genre of speech involving open attestation or public acknowledgement and profession; but, especially in Fundamentalist or Evangelical circles, it has fashionably come to include specific details about pivotal changes in life's direction presented in quite dramatic terms.[38] Jacobs expresses concern over those who may not feel like they "have a testimony" because the drama of sin and salvation has not been emphatically experienced in their lives—at least, not according to the popular schemas.[39] In any case, testimony's purpose is to "represent in verbal form a life."[40] When this life movement narrates faith in the decisiveness of Christ it is Christian testimony.[41] Testimony uniquely commits the testifier "to making a full account of her life's direction" in its inherent wholeness.[42] It makes connections between the events and experience of life and forms meaningful stories out of the perceived reasons for those connections.[43] That is, Christian testimony maintains an inner logic and integrity to the overall narrative of a human life in the faith of Christ.[44] Moreover, the biblical narrative context has determinative hermeneutical significance.[45] The value of verbal testimony, however, is inadequate without accompanying behavioral or moral testimony.[46]

So then, testimony is universally prevalent among humans but present in varied ways, and occurs in juridical, religious, or social contexts.[47] Yet for all the diversity of testimony there seems to be a commonality in testimony of giving an account of experiences or occurrences with which one has some more or less direct contact.[48] Christian testimony interprets and proclaims the narrative integrity of a life in Christ.[49] Therefore, based on the preceding, generally one may assume that historically testimony usually involves accounts of personal experiences or insights, actual in occurrence but interpreted and applied holistically for different purposes and functions and with varying degrees of reasonable authority and credibility.[50] Now this study will move on to the specificity of Pentecostal testimony.

The Distinctiveness of Pentecostal Testimony

Definition

Functional-Practical.[51] Pentecostals do not primarily define testimony etymologically. Of course, they are not unaware of *mártyros* and *martyréo* and their cognates signifying various dimensions of testimony and witness.[52] Neither are they unaware of the historical development of these terms from ancient legal and non-religious statements of fact, to biblical usage, to Christian witness of Christ and the gospel even to the point of death.[53] However, Pentecostals tend to understand testimony more functionally. For example, in a chapter on "The Doctrine of Divine Healing" Classical Pentecostal scholars Duffield and Van Cleave advise those who experience physical healing to, among other things, "Keep Testifying of What God Has Done." They elaborate thusly:

> Keep telling others of God's gracious goodness to you. This must be done with a real sense of humility, and no thought that receiving healing from the Lord makes you better than others. Some have lost miraculous healings because they failed to testify of the deliverance God has wrought for them.[54]

Here testimony is an important functional part of retaining a profound spiritual and physical experience.[55] Pentecostals tend to understand testimony more in terms of what it does or helps to do than through cognitive terminological nuances.

A similar outlook is evident in Classical Pentecostal New Testament scholar and theologian French Arrington's *Encountering the Holy Spirit*. In a work that he himself describes as primarily "a practical guide", he insists that a full understanding of the Holy Spirit's work is not attainable by scholarly study alone but necessarily entails "listening and learning from the experiences of individuals in our Christian community, and experiencing a relationship with the Holy Spirit in our own lives."[56] Accordingly, after his scriptural study he includes a large selection of personal stories and testimonies of Pentecostal experience.[57] For Arrington, testimonies of spiritual experiences help "illuminate, clarify and verify" God's work. They pass on the faith to future generations, inviting others to join in a walk on sacred ground. Testimonies help hearers see the Pentecostal faith more clearly. Like a building with stained glass windows, only by standing inside as the sunlight streams through can one behold the real beauty. Testimonies allow hearers an inside look.[58] Furthermore, testimonies are reminders that God still works in human lives and in the world today. His grace and power have not ceased to bless and touch.[59] Whenever a Pentecostal testifies to their being saved, sanctified, and filled with the Holy Spirit, or to their being healed and delivered, or to an amazing or possibly miraculous answer to prayer or divine intervention of some kind, the always implicit, and sometimes quite explicit, message is God still does these things today. Moreover, implicitly at least, "Because God has done it for me, that means he will do it for you too."[60] That is how Pentecostal testimony functions in actual practice.

Transformational.[61] For Pentecostal educator and scholar Cheryl Bridges Johns testimony occupies an important place in a paradigm of Pentecostal catechesis for spiritual formation.[62] As it brings together the realities of daily life with the ongoing story of the community of faith, it helps to "decode reality", that is, to re-interpret life in the light of faith. Furthermore, testimony encourages a liberated and open corporate liturgy that is mutually empowering. Life experiences, curses as well as blessings, are addressed publicly to the glory of God in the context of the Christian story. Testimonies and the personal experiences they recount all stand under the final authority of inspired Scripture. Submitting a testimony allows and invites corporate discernment and judgment in the interpretative process. Moreover, in effect testimony can and often does serve as a practical training procedure for eventual ministers as they test their voice under the anointing of the Holy Spirit.[63] Testimony does not appear to be a peripheral aspect of Pentecostal spirituality and theology. Rather, it is an essential element in the incubation, cultivation, and maturation of Pentecostal disciples.[64]

For Cheryl Johns, testimony is part of a complex of transforming "movements" arising out of the Pentecostal context of various forms of Spirit energized worship, for example as in group Bible study. These movements, aiming at intentional spiritual formation, include first the sharing of testimony, then searching the Scriptures, yielding to the Spirit, and, finally, responding to the resultant call upon one's life.[65] The sharing of testimony challenges both an individual and the group to know themselves and one another through "the giving of a personal account of the ongoing confrontation of the uncertainties of life in Christ."[66] Testifying, which of course takes place in the present, involves memory, reflection, and interpretation. In a wonderfully concise and insightful statement, Johns observes that, "Testimony is a selective act in which specific events of the past are brought to bear on specific aspects of the present in an effort to give meaning to the present."[67] Furthermore, in testimony one publicly offer's oneself for ministry to the body of Christ and for the giving of glory to God. Testimony also involves a sense of the future, as participants live in present and anticipatory engagement with the coming reign of God in dialogue with the Scriptures. Teachers or leaders in such a setting are more partners with "the Paraclete-Teacher" than anything else as the Spirit leads and moves according to the Spirit's sovereign will. Again, "the central issue" is always total participation or involvement by all. Everyone ought to "have the opportunity to reflect upon their present in light of their past and with anticipation of their future."[68] Pentecostal testimony, therefore, can be a powerful life-changing and enhancing force for believing participants, both speakers and listeners.

Liturgical.[69] Pentecostal Old Testament scholar Jerome Boone takes a similar track. Johns and Boone share an emphasis in Christian spiritual formation, but Boone focuses more on testimony in corporate worship settings.[70] In spite of an appreciation for ecumenical unity, Boone is nonetheless concerned over the assimilation of Pentecostal distinctiveness through increasing contact with conventional Christianity. He argues that a distinctive sense of Pentecostal community and worship is essential for the retention and perpetuation of authentic Pentecostal values in the movement.[71] For him, the worship service, with its emphasis on encountering God, is at the heart of Pentecostal spirituality.[72] In corporate worship, the transforming power of the manifest presence of God is often experienced in a special manner.[73] Set in a context of an overall articulation of the Pentecostal narrative worldview, he identifies testimony, along with congregational singing, prayer, and the sermon/altar service, as key elements for facilitating divine encounter and the subsequent transformative formation necessary for Pentecostal faith and vitality.[74]

Drawing on Johns in defining testimony, he argues additionally that "testimony is an important ritual" in Pentecostal worship.[75] Significantly, he has already described Pentecostal ritual in terms of freedom and spontaneity of the Spirit as mediated but direct encounter with God's powerful transformational presence. Ritual in this sense constructs and transforms reality.[76] Moreover, testimony is set in the context of a community of faith engaged in dialogue including both contradiction and confirmation as Spirit-led communication and change occur.[77] Pentecostal testimonies express the stories of God's people in ways that transform the spiritual reality of worshipers as an important element in encountering God's Spirit and power in and through worship.

Foundational Orientation

A Deeply Rooted Oral Tradition.[78] A distinctive Pentecostal practice of testimony arises naturally enough out of its unique spirituality and theology. Swiss theologian and scholar of Pentecostalism and intercultural theology Walter J. Hollenweger is a prominent analyst and historian of the Pentecostal movement.[79] His prolific writings, including his magnum opus *The Pentecostals*,[80] have made him a major authority on the movement's history, spirituality, and theology. Hollenweger traces Pentecostalism's oral and narrative distinctiveness to an "amazing capacity to incorporate oral and narrative structures from the American slave religion" so influential and formative in its origins.[81] More specifically, he identifies five features rooted in black spirituality influencing Pentecostalism:

—orality of liturgy;
—narrativity of theology and witness;
—maximum participation at the levels of reflection, prayer, decision-making and therefore a form of community that is reconciliatory;
—inclusion of dreams and visions into personal and public forms of worship; they function as a kind of icon for the individual and the community;
—an understanding of the body/mind relationship that is informed by experiences of correspondence between body and mind; the most striking application of this insight is the ministry of healing by prayer.[82]

Hollenweger, who considers the first ten years of the movement its vibrant heart rather than its undeveloped infancy, still finds "a fair amount of the original elements" of early Pentecostalism present in the contemporary movement. However, he worries whether "speech, narrative and communication" will be overwhelmed by "status, education, money and juridical power."[83] The premium of testimony would surely diminish if that were the case. Somewhat surprisingly, therefore, Hollenweger, in a friendly review of bestselling author and Harvard theologian Harvey Cox's masterpiece on Pentecostalism, *Fire from Heaven*, suggests that the famous theologian, first taken with testimony then takes it up and adapts Pentecostalism's penchant for testimony.[84] Rather than Pentecostal narrative and oral qualities diminishing, this observation would seem to suggest that they might actually be overspreading into other Christian traditions in unexpected avenues.

Notably, however, Pentecostal theologian Frank Macchia offers a careful critique of Hollenweger's almost exclusive emphasis on the oral and narrative nature of Pentecostalism. For Macchia, the narrative nature of Pentecostal theology includes more dialectic with rational approaches to systematic theology than often recognized.[85] A Pentecostal dialectic between narrative and cognitive theology is evident, Macchia suggests, in the development of the doctrine of Spirit baptism and glossolalia. Nevertheless, Macchia is not refuting or rejecting an oral or narrative understanding of Pentecostal spirituality and theology so much as he is integrating and qualifying it. Accordingly, without any inconsistency Macchia begins his Pentecostal systematic theology with a person testimony of his experience in the Spirit.[86] Similarly, John Poirier criticizes specific approaches to "narrative theology" that he sees as confusing epistemology and alethiology, or categories of knowledge and truth, resulting in contradictions to Pentecostal commitments. Nevertheless, he clearly confirms the narrative nature of Pentecostalism as exemplified in Hollenweger and with its missiological applications.[87]

The above indicates that a proper understanding of Pentecostal testimony, along with Pentecostal approaches to preaching, praying, singing, and so on, underscores that it is not merely a notable feature of its unique worship. Testimony taps into the original authentic ethos of the movement. Pentecostalism is an oral and narrative movement calling everyone to tell their story in the light of Christ's story in the boldness and power of the outpoured Spirit as an en-fleshed or incarnate witness of God's continuing dynamic relationship with his people and the world. In reality, Pentecostal testimony becomes a dynamic example of Incarnational Christianity.

A Highly Prized Practice.[88] Pentecostal historical theologian Mel Robeck's intriguing account of the catalyst-like Azusa street mission and revival, racially mixed and spiritually charged as it was, to which contemporary Pentecostals owe so much, if not always in direct origin at least in original influence, reveals a high priority on the value of testimony.[89] Even decades later, Robeck found testimonials of what when on at Azusa Street to be "compelling and vibrant" accounts of divine encounters with God.[90] In fact, after some hesitancy and uncertainty, hearing the testimony of Mrs. Lucy Farrow to her Spirit baptism experience, with speaking in tongues, was decisive for William J. Seymour, who later became the founder and leader of the Azusa revival.[91] From the beginning, testimonies were not only an important part of the revival but served as primary impetus for it as well.[92] Early on, the literature of the revival began highlighting testimonies of what God was doing.[93] Pastor Seymour successfully created a climate in which the value of freedom of speech for all the saints was high, but admittedly this could sometimes lead to trouble with those inclined to instability taking advantage of it.[94]

Robeck reports that worship through testimony, continued to be "a remarkable feature" of the unique services at the Azusa Street mission throughout its heyday. Some considered the testimonies to be "the highlight of the meetings" and claimed it was "impossible not to be touched" by them. Indeed, one is inclined to agree even when reading a cynical journalist's report included by Robeck.[95] Nevertheless, prayer seemed to be the real "centerpiece" of the revival, with testimonies, songs, sermons, and spiritual gifts flowing out of fervent prayer.[96] Yet Robeck's research shows that testimonies were such a prominent part of the proceedings that they are too numerous to recount without tedium. However, they all commonly "speak of a personal quest for a divine encounter that put them in direct touch with the God they worshipped."[97] Pentecostal missionaries associated with Azusa Street soon realized that testifying to what they had experienced was an effective way of spreading the Pentecostal experience in other lands as well.[98] Back at Azusa Street during the latter days of the revival's high point, the mission used the presence (or absence?) of "burning testimonies" to gauge the continuing fervor of the revival.[99]

Inspired Speech.[100] Obviously, testimony imbibes and exhibits the oral and narrative nature of Pentecostal spirituality, and is an opportunity to express them through congregational participatory liberty. Consequently, Pentecostal testimony is one significant aspect of the overall oral and narrative nature of the movement. Not surprisingly, Hollenweger includes a lengthy account of a Pentecostal worship service with 'a testimony meeting'. In it 'a large number of the more faithful testify to their personal experience and joy in religion, some mutteringly, some loudly, fervidly,' but with almost all saying 'they are proud to speak for Christ, and not ashamed to speak out for their master in church.'[101] Of the Pentecostal penchant for inspired speech, Hollenweger says,

> An astonishing degree of communication, never achieved in other churches, takes place in these services. In Pentecostal worship—which only a casual observer could describe as unstructured and unliturgical—everyone can express himself with the means of speech at his disposal. The criterion is not conceptual clarity, but communicability.[102]

Although at its lowest and worst, testimony can sometimes become inane rambling or distracting diatribe, at its highest and best, it can and often does become truly inspir*ed* and inspir*ing* speech from the Spirit. Here pastoral wisdom and oversight are required to help testifiers and their listeners experience the best the tradition has to offer.

Experience and Praxis in Oral-Narrative/Liturgy.[103] Cheryl Johns speaks of "an experiential, praxis-oriented Pentecostal hermeneutic" as "a way of theologizing which may be defined as oral-narrative." Oral-narrative allows the Christian story, life experiences, and theology to all come together in "the life of the community of faith." Significantly, communication is primary and information is kept and transmitted through stories and testimonies.[104] Not unnaturally, oral theology allows much room for "justice, peace, dialogue and authentic self-giving love". Pentecostal narrative beliefs are conducive to a true participation in the story of salvation that is empowering, liberating, transforming.[105] In a sense, "the voice of the people is, therefore, empowered by the Holy Spirit to become the speech of God."[106] Practices such as testimony overflow in all kinds of uplifting ways.

Johns argues that an oral-narrative invites and invigorates an oral liturgy. Pentecostal worship, though not without intention or structure, displays great fluidity and variety. What really matters the most is "the full participation of every member." Such worship is active and can be revolutionary. As might be expected, Johns stresses that Pentecostal worship "becomes *the place* for dialogue for all people of all backgrounds, ethnic and economic levels."[107] Barriers between people are broken down. Equal appreciation goes to the wisdom of the words of the oppressed and poor with those from other strata of society.

The Context of Pentecostal Testimony

Autobiographical Context[108]

Pentecostal understanding of testimony is quite distinct from that of Christian confessional traditions seeing testimony in terms of shared statements of theological convictions or dogmatic formulations.[109] Pentecostal testimony does not arise out of but indeed in some ways appears to be a counterpart to creedal ecclesiology in the sense that Pentecostals do not define themselves primarily in terms of creeds or other statements of faith.[110] Pentecostal historical theologian Kimberly Ervin Alexander appropriately points out that the Church of God (Cleveland, TN USA), one of the oldest and largest Classical Pentecostal denominations, "did not develop or publish a formal statement of faith" until 1948. She identifies its "early anti-creedal stance" as the basis of this reticence. However, as Alexander also observes, the lack of a formal creed did not signal the lack of informally shared understandings of theology and practice.[111] Nevertheless, as the Church of God traces it origins to 1886, this means the denomination was some 62 years old before formalizing its doctrine. Even then, it did so in very brief, simple terms continuing as its major standard of doctrine to the present.[112]

Contrary to formal creedal or dogmatic theological confessions, which tend to be exercises in corporate intellectualism, for Pentecostals "a word of testimony" tends to have a high autobiographical element, as John Christopher Thomas notes.[113] Center stage is what God is doing in one's own life. Inferences of and for faith by listeners drawn from an individual's public praise for God's active intervention in one's daily life is an implied expectation.[114] Pentecostal testimony, therefore, is sharply distinguished from formal creeds or confessions.[115] More often than not, they recount experiences or stages in an individual's spiritual journey.[116] Sometimes in popular parlance Pentecostals accent this distinction by use of the additional adjective "personal" to make the phrase "personal testimony" but more often than not they do not bother, settling for 'a word of testimony'.[117] A good rule of thumb is to assume that testimony means *personal* unless otherwise explained. One will often hear remarks comparable to, "He/she gave his/her testimony" or even "They gave their testimonies." These do not signify intellectual or theological formulations.[118] They are autobiographical and doxological stories of God's activity as experienced in human lives here and now.[119]

Biblical Context[120]

The category of testimony is exceedingly important in Scripture. Closely aligned with the legal sense of testimony (Hebrew *ya'ad*, Greek *marturein*) in a court of law, it "broadly influences the thought patterns, truth claims, and theology of nearly all of Scripture." Biblically, "sound testimony" includes historically certifiable and reliable content. In the Old Testament, testimony has to do mainly with God's self-revelation to Israel, and in the New Testament, with the additional revelation of Jesus Christ to the world. The former focuses on the theme of the divine law court and the proclamation God as Lord and Savior. The latter looks at the identity of Jesus and his testimony about God, the role of the Gospel as the Church's decisive evidence, the witness of the Spirit as divine testimony, and the role of Jesus as the Word of God.[121] Interestingly for this discussion of Pentecostal testimony, biblically "the tangible evidence of the Spirit's presence" which is "displayed both in Jesus' life and in the experience of the church" serves to verify forensically the authenticity and historicity of the testimony (John 15:26; 1 John 5:6-12). The Spirit's witness as divine testimony includes inward assurance (Rom 8:16; 1 John 3:24) and outward signs and wonders (Heb 2:3-4).[122]

Combining or conflating testimony and witness occurs in some examples of biblical theology studies.[123] A distracting tendency, it is nevertheless understandable given the interconnectedness of these concepts. Usually, the emphasis tends to fall on evangelistic proclamation of one kind or another. Yet for present purposes, distinguishing important unique elements of testimony as used by Pentecostals is essential. Pentecostals traditionally use "witness" specifically of evangelism, especially personal evangelism, but also even corporate evangelism.[124] However, among Pentecostals "testimony" is almost universally a technical term often signifying the telling of one's personal narrative or spiritual story as it participates in or illustrates the story of Christ and his gospel.[125] Though testimony in this sense is also witness, undoubtedly it is a distinct kind of witness not entirely or even predominately evangelistic.[126]

A sort of "reciprocal reshaping" of history and experience, similar to that which often occurs in the Psalms, is, according to Pentecostal biblical scholar Scott Ellington, an identifiable feature in Pentecostal testimony.[127] What has happened and is remembered from the past informs the needs of the present and results in experiences of fresh encounters with God that may result in some reinterpretation of the past. In Pentecostal testimony, the deeds of God are told in faith that these deeds will be repeated in different contexts as the need arises.[128] In this way, Pentecostal testimony is not only a retelling of the history of the biblical story but also its recapitulation or reenactment in actual human experience for the glory of God and blessing of God's people.[129] Pentecostal testimony, therefore, involves an ongoing dynamic between human experience, the biblical story, and God. In Pentecostal testimonies, this reciprocation creates and undergirds an exciting and open-ended but nonetheless well-grounded account of divine activity in Christ today.[130] The biblical text is not merely an ancient document, not even an ancient sacred document, but a paradigm for God's ongoing active involvement with his people.[131] For Pentecostals, testimonies are concrete assurances, even, carefully qualified, convincing evidences, at least for eyes of faith, of one of their most foundational convictions: that "Jesus Christ is the same yesterday and today and forever" (Heb 13:8 NIV).[132]

Pentecostal Johannine scholar Chris Thomas notes that a failure to appreciate the narrative nature of the context of complex biblical statements, such as those on the Paraclete in the Fourth Gospel, has led to misunderstanding of their meaning.[133] Again, Thomas's observation indicates further the Pentecostal sensitivity to story for understanding not only the biblical text itself but also how the text applies to and interacts with one's own story.[134] When Pentecostals offer testimonial interpretations of their life experiences, they are in a sense simply extending their approach to biblical hermeneutics to embrace their own story from a framework of faith. The complexities of life can be best confronted by setting them in the context of one's own life story and interpreting them according to the story of Christ, which for the Pentecostal, also includes the story of the Spirit.[135]

Theological Context[136]

As stated, for Pentecostals "a word of testimony" tends to have a high autobiographical element.[137] One's personal experience of God and God's intervention in life is in the forefront. However, one ought not to interpret this autobiographical accent as indicative of theological vacuity. Classical Pentecostal theologian William MacDonald suggests that Pentecostal theology is a particular type of theology, theology with "the character of a 'witness' experience."[138] That is, it is a kind of "witness event".[139] This kind of theology is much more "oral-aural" than "optic-literary" in its mode of transmission.[140] Therefore, MacDonald explains, it is especially well suited for preaching, testifying, and one-on one-contact. Emphasis is on the integrity of the witness in communicating truth. A witness testifies of what God has done for him or her, and is willing to do for anyone. The integrity and purity of the witness's character is support for the verity of their testimony.[141] Missing the theological content of Pentecostal testimony because of its mode of communication would be a categorical mistake.

Therefore, Pentecostal testimony holds more theological content than commonly recognized. Arguably, the practice of Pentecostal testimony is fraught with theological significance. Latin American Pentecostal theologian Juan Sepúlveda asserts that because of its experiential nature, which transcends conceptual categories, Chilean Pentecostal theology is founded upon testimonies.[142] Foundational for Pentecostal theology is an experience that is both personal and communal, and that this theology "is developed through testimony" as "God is shown to be real through testimony, not through a doctrine."[143] In fact, he argues that, "The only theology that can give an account of this experience is a *narrative* theology whose central expression is testimony."[144] This theologically identifiable feature is particularly evident in Pentecostal groups less influenced by foreign missionaries. The "Pentecostal experience" includes not only forgiveness/justification, transformation/sanctification, but also, through Spirit baptism, strength to live under adverse social and cultural conditions and to share testimony with others. Chilean Pentecostals bear testimony by the power of the Holy Spirit to their new life in the midst of this world order and system. The role eschatological hope plays in Chilean Pentecostals is further borne out by their preaching and testimonies, but even these sources include a strong emphasis on salvation here and now. Accordingly, Pentecostal testimony in Chile builds on the past for a present experience of a gloriously envisioned future. Whiling waiting expectantly for Christ to come again, these Pentecostals see themselves as bearing testimony to God's present work of the Spirit in their lives.[145]

More specifically, Sepúlveda suggests that Latin America Pentecostal testimony uniquely communicates in the language of the people, rather then in specialized clerical terminology, and is thus popularly attractive.[146] Furthermore, typically testimonies communicate great intensity and warmth.[147] Furthermore, Pentecostal testimony, rather than focusing on doctrines of an "other-worldly salvation", focuses on "the opportunity of a salvation here and now."[148] For Sepúlveda, the Church is a priestly community, and Pentecostal testimony, focusing on "the simple proclamation" of one's own conversion and experience, has priestly significance within that particular community.[149] Additionally, such testimony has important missiological aspects, that is, evangelistic effectiveness.[150] However, the potential for abuse of testimony by mass media evangelism, which may reduce testimony to anecdotal illustrations or nullify its personal richness, concerns Sepúlveda.[151] Yet he is convinced that "The key to Pentecostal evangelism is the personalized proclamation of a testimony of a changed life."[152]

The Classical Pentecostal tradition of testimony may be the congregational precursor and counterpart of contemporary advanced academic theological discussions regarding dynamic interchanges between biblical hermeneutics, theological agendas, and corporate and personal autobiography and spiritual journey. Pentecostal theologian Kenneth Archer argues that the Pentecostal tradition historically utilizes a meaning-producing hermeneutic arising out of Scripture, especially its narrative portions, as it intersects with the story of the journey of the movement and its adherents in formulating the traditional Pentecostal worldview.[153] Utilizing the analogy of a spider's web, Archer suggests his readers think of Jesus in the center with "five stabilizing theological strands identified as the full or fivefold gospel" (Jesus as savior, sanctifier, Spirit baptizer, healer, and soon coming king) serving as "central narrative convictions of the community." For him, "Woven into this web are testimonies, experiences, and scriptural passages" serving to 'strengthen the whole web, which is the story." The unique result is "a living theological tradition—Pentecostalism."[154]

Archer's argument accords well with Pentecostal attitudes toward experiencing Scripture as truth. Less informed, or more biased, as the case may be, critics charge Pentecostals and Charismatics with placing personal experience above Scripture.[155] Quite to the contrary, Pentecostal theologian Steve Land posits a dynamic, interdependent relation between Scripture and personal experience. As another Pentecostal theologian, Amos Yong, says, "truth is what emerges from our experience of the biblical story".[156] Baptist Charismatic Clark Pinnock ably argues his case for the illuminating work of the Holy Spirit in biblical hermeneutics, a stance that recognizes a greater role for experience.[157] Of course, clearly experiencing and testifying to experiencing closely interconnect for Pentecostals. Accordingly, it is appropriate to view Pentecostal testimony in the context of its scriptural underpinnings as well as its practical emphasis on contemporary spiritual life and experience. It is also appropriate to identify testimony as an important part of a dynamic interplay between history, story, and testimony in the process of locating truth in the way believers experience God interacting with people as the ultimate test for appropriate biblical hermeneutics.[158]

However, Asian Pentecostal theologian Simon Chan issues a warning regarding the narrative nature of Pentecostalism and the need for theological development and transmission.[159] He is concerned with "Pentecostal traditioning", or with how Pentecostals pass on their faith to future generations.[160] While recognizing the strength of Pentecostal narrative, the success of testimonies in spreading the faith and experience of Pentecost, and even their socially transforming potential, he still warns about what he perceives as its weakness. Narrative, Chan points out, lacks the ability to explain itself. For that, and for maturity, critical self-reflection is necessary. Restrictive and reductionist qualities of some major Pentecostal distinctive teachings, for example, Spirit baptism itself, tend to suggest a need for deeper critical self-reflection.[161] Yet Asian American Pentecostal theologian Amos Yong understands as crucial for traditioning "the category of testimony" because through testimony "the message of the gospel is empowered by the Spirit through words and deeds".[162]

For Chan, the oral nature of Pentecostalism presents a problem for "traditioning". He fully concurs that "oral traditioning" has vitality, and recognizes this as "the peculiar strength of the practice of giving 'testimonies' in Pentecostal churches." Pentecostals encounter truth in a simple, direct way. However, he argues that in a changing culture, what one might call modern/late modern or postmodern culture, with its technology and changing epistemology, a more reflective approach is needed "to ensure that the Pentecostal reality is bequeathed to the next generation basically intact."[163] Nevertheless, Chan has also noted that narrative theology has much appeal for the church in Asia as it taps into that culture's "penchant for storytelling" In fact, storytelling and testimony apparently occupy an especially important place in the Chinese church.[164] Hence, like Macchia, Chan does not refute or reject an oral or narrative understanding of Pentecostal spirituality and theology so much as he integrates and qualifies it.[165] Significantly, Harvey Cox "testifies" he learned that "it is a serious mistake to equate Pentecostals with fundamentalists" by listening to Pentecostal testimonies and ecstatic speech and watching accompanying body movements.[166] Therefore, Pentecostal theology is not the rigid and rationalist theology of fundamentalists but a more free-flowing theology of liberated speech and energized action.[167] However, the wise words of Chan and Macchia are nonetheless needed for balance and poise helping avoid abuses and extremes.

Pastoral Context[168]

Charles W. Conn, the official historian of the Church of God (Cleveland, TN), one of the oldest and largest Classical Pentecostal denominations, notes that from the earliest days of their participation in the revival, personal testimonies were an important part of meaningful congregational worship services and contributed to the revival's momentum. In these testimonies, people "shared with others their spiritual experience, thereby comforting and edifying one another."[169] However, more recently Robert McCall has studied the phenomenon of Pentecostal testimony in the congregational or pastoral context in the Church of God in depth.[170]

McCall is concerned that the rich tradition of storytelling and testimony is being lost in the contemporary Pentecostal movement, and proposes practical steps for reversing that unfortunate phenomenon through intentional congregational training. While storytelling in American pulpits was common in the nineteenth century, and may have served as the crucible out of which Pentecostal testimony arose, he thinks Pentecostalism's "lively stories and inspiring personal testimonies" were "most distinctive".[171] In an overview of the overall Pentecostal movement, McCall concludes that storytelling and testimony are "normative modes of communication for the Pentecostal community worldwide", but that these are in dire danger of being lost because of a tendency toward decline resulting from upward social mobility among today's Pentecostals.[172] In describing his own denomination, McCall finds that Church of God members have always been a people with "stories and testimonies, willing to share them." In fact, he attributes much of the amazing expansion and energy of the Church of God throughout the world to "the witness and spiritual power of simple people willing to share their stories and testimonies with all who would listen."[173]

Significantly, in presenting his case for the imperative reclamation of storytelling and testimony, McCall proposes three arguments. Pentecostals should reclaim stories and testimonies to

> 1) help us deal with our own insecurities, inconsistencies, and uncertainties through shared testimonies and stories in a secure environment where fellow believers are willing to listen with interest and respond with understanding, care and mutual support; 2) help outsiders better understand what is truly significant within our community of faith; and 3) more importantly, to reach hungry souls with the living water and solid bread of the Gospel in the story of Jesus told in the power of the Holy Spirit and testified to from personal experience.[174]

Interestingly, McCall's study of contemporary society suggests that the electronic media is for many people filling in the vacuum left by declining attention to narrative in Pentecostal Christianity. Unfortunately, the substitute is often less than conducive for sound spiritual health.[175] For McCall, this electronic trend is even more reason for Pentecostals to reclaim their rightful heritage.[176] Boldly, he believes that Pentecostal storytelling and testimony used with "a prophetic voice" can challenge and change the status quo within his own denomination, broader Pentecostalism, and the Christian Church as a whole.[177] Apparently, Pentecostal testimony is in the unique position of standing on established tradition while being poised for non-traditional applications.

Doxological Context[178]

A frequent feature of Pentecostal worship is the "testimony service." Either as a service all its own or as part of a larger context of worship including other elements, a series of individual Pentecostals will "give their testimony." Usually testimonies are more or less spontaneous, at times Spirit-inspired and Spirit-anointed storytelling, though often directed or at least led to some extent by a pastor or worship leader, and can be on occasion highly demonstrative or expressive. Pentecostal testimonies are highly personalized and often highly dramatized versions of the biblical pattern of worship as responsive "representation" or "recital" of God's saving acts.[179] This connection is especially cogent if "God's saving acts" include not only conversion/new birth but also a host of attendant divine blessings (e.g., healing and deliverance, Spirit baptism, answered prayer or special strength and encouragement, etc). In other words, Pentecostal testimonies are soteriologically based doxological narratives of historical occurrences viewed through the lens of faith. Plainly put, people tell stories of what they believe God has graciously done in their lives for the express purpose of giving glory to God in the presence of their hearers. The assumption, even expectation, is that those who hear in faith will then join in praising the Lord for his mighty acts of love and power.[180] The emphasis is not at all on creedal confession. Obviously, however, these testimonies do serve to affirm and encourage faith in God's actual intervention in the daily lives of believers, sometimes in miraculous manners.[181]

In a fascinating foray into Pentecostal doxological experience and praxis, African American Church historian David Daniels suggests that even the very sound of distinctively Pentecostal testimony, along with that of prayer, preaching, singing, music-making, and silence, arose out of a deeply embedded sound of primal cries, speech, music, and ambient sounds generating an alternative (to traditional orality-literary) way of knowing.[182] Accordingly, Pentecostal testimony, along with other kinds of Pentecostal sound, may be termed liberated and liberating worship. Devotees are set free from "the hierarchy of the senses that privileged sight, and the hierarchy of the races" to worship with unprecedented egalitarian abandonment.[183]

Pneumatological Context[184]

Myung Soo Park believes Pentecostal spirituality may be properly understood through studying Pentecostal testimony.[185] For Park, testimonies are a way of accessing "the spiritual experiences of ordinary believers."[186] He notes that testimony time is a highlight in Pentecostal worship services, probably because of the emphasis on personal spiritual experience and because testimony is narrative, a preferred form of Pentecostal expression.[187] Although conservatism and progressivism both object, Evangelical theology is beginning to understand the proper place of testimony in spirituality and theology. Spiritual experience does not replace but rather confirms the Bible.[188] It is not exalted above the Bible but rather reflects its truth in contemporary life. Along with certain contemporary thinkers, Park cites John Wesley as an amicable precedent for affirming the validity of testimony in theological research and understanding.[189] The nature of spiritual experience is such that it may often be best understood through testimonies.[190]

Through analysis of testimonies of the people of Yoido Full Gospel Church, Park finds that they exhibit a Pentecostal spirituality that has as a starting point a divinely given ability finally to cope with life at its worst, that is, during times of desperation, and practice fervently a faithful life of intense prayer and fasting, and spiritual warfare.[191] He also found that the testimonies signify that the turning point for many members was their reception of Spirit baptism and spiritual gifts, including speaking in tongues, healing, and others.[192] Furthermore, the

Spirit-filled life resulted in a new heart or inner life and new action, powerful work of good deeds and social service, and a miraculously enhanced ability to cope with the problems of life, whether spiritual apathy, physical illness, or financial difficulty.[193] In all of this process, that the experience of the Holy Spirit infuses it all with a supernatural energy and quality is quite evident, although inward morality and stability are perhaps more important than often acknowledged.[194]

As a participant-observer in innumerable Pentecostal testimonial services, I can bear witness that a strong sense of the Holy Spirit's anointing and inspiration is not unusual. The connection Park makes between research and testimony understands testimony as an appropriate expression of spiritual experience. I would agree, and add that partly that is true because Pentecostal testimony itself not only tells of spiritual experience but also at times actually taps into spiritual experience in the telling. A testifier may reflect in advance about what he or she plans to say, may begin to speak in measured and articulate tones, but often a change of intensity and volume will occur as the speaker continues. Although, testifiers usually stand at their place in the pew, it is not unusual for them to begin to pace and gesture as they proceed. More than anything, the change signifies to Pentecostal initiates a moving from human-inspired intentionality to Spirit-inspired spontaneity. While this change is doubtless partly attributable to human enthusiasm and excitement, many claim to feel the Spirit's presence in a powerful way during the experience. Listeners often agree that it was "of the Lord," that is, inspired and anointed by the Holy Spirit, because they also felt the "witness of the Spirit."[195] Accordingly, Pentecostals view testimony through a pneumatological frame of reference.

The above sounds very similar in many ways to the Pentecostal understanding of Spirit-inspired speaking in preaching. Pentecostals often speak of "the Spirit's anointing" in this instance.[196] Drawing on a longstanding Christian tradition of interpreting the biblical terminology of anointing with oil as indicative of the work of the Holy Spirit, Pentecostals describe experiencing exceptional liberty and power during preaching as the Spirit's anointing. Although not on a par with canonical scripture or presented as any kind of infallible authority, such preaching is inspired speech. Anointed preaching is very highly valued by Pentecostals. Though further study is needful, possibly testimonials at times function as opportunities for lay versions of anointed preaching.[197] A testimony may even serve as an entry point for preaching, or as a part of the preaching service. Many preachers do in fact begin their ministries by testifying before attempting formal preaching. Nevertheless, many anointed lay people testify without ever dreaming of becoming preachers. The phenomenon of Spirit-inspired and anointed testifying fits well with the Pentecostal understanding that the Spirit-filled congregation is a prophetic community. Some Pentecostals even speak of the "prophethood of believers" in tones comparable to Protestantism's "priesthood of believers."[198] For our purposes, it is enough to understand that in certain circumstances, that is, when the Spirit so leads and moves, in Pentecostal worship services testimony can function as Spirit-inspired speech.

Historical Context[199]

When Australian Pentecostal Shane Clifton undertook to look at the ecclesiological history of a Classical Pentecostalism denomination, the Assemblies of God, in Australia, he recognized that typical theological methods were inadequate. Accordingly, he decided to employ the category of Pentecostal testimony in a unique approach.[200] He asserts that there is no better way to know Pentecostals than by listening to their testimonies. According to Clifton, Pentecostals engage more in symbolic narrative recollection than in actual narrative recollection. In other words, they "remember selectively," using history to serve a purpose or send a message.[201] Partly this historical selectivity is the more or less natural consequence of Pentecostalism's restorationist impulse. Restorationism tends to take on an ahistorical character. Symbolic narrative recollection does not mean the events did not occur historically. Rather, un-dramatic events are often lost or missed while the accent frequently falls on events that are more dramatic, especially to the extent that they tell the desired story. This characteristic increases the complexity of studying testimony as history.[202] One does not achieve critical or systematic results. Pentecostal self-understanding is a prominent consideration.

However, these are common features of all oral history and do not usually render interpretation impossible.[203] Yet historical discernment and judgment are required. For Clifton, it is noteworthy that a narrative structure to ecclesiology (and so on) is well suited to Pentecostal self-understanding. Pentecostals have not defined themselves institutionally or doctrinally but narratively. Clifton agrees with Scott Ellington that in "emerging pentecostal theology" it is evident that "pentecostalism is an orally based, narratively expressed tradition". This narrative orientation signifies "that testimonies of what God has done in the life of the individual believer and the local community of faith" forms "an integral part of pentecostal worship and faith."[204]

Sociological Context[205]

A sociological investigation of testimony in Catholic Pentecostal prayer groups suggests that it represents "a central commitment mechanism". Although glossolalia serves as a symbol of commitment to a movement that may separate one from the surrounding society, public testimony to that fact is the act that signifies "abandonment and involvement".[206] Testimony may be the moment when irreversible bridge burning occurs. Though focusing on Catholic Pentecostals rather than Classical Pentecostals, or those who more specifically identify with Pentecostal denominations arising out of the modern Pentecostal movement, this observation is no doubt relevant for Classical Pentecostals as well.

In a similar vein, though as a historical analyst, Wacker suggests Pentecostal testimony can be an important part of strengthening identity formation.[207] First, testimonies strengthen one's personal identity in the narrating of "God's wondrous handiwork" in their individual lives, and second, testimony strengthens collective identity by "sealing the link between the individual and the group."[208] Third, and for Wacker most important, they clothe "individual lives with timeless significance."[209] Whatever place one might hold in society, their personal existence and experiences are significant in light of the narrative of their place and purpose in the larger plan of God.[210]

Significantly, in my congregational and pastoral experience in Pentecostalism, initiates into Spirit baptism are always instinctively urged to testify publicly of their experience as soon as possible, preferably immediately.[211] Notably, those who seem reluctant or timid in their testimony are usually not confident in their experience. Conversely, those who boldly testify of their Pentecostal experience rarely recant or retract subsequently.[212]

Summary/Conclusion

At the least, the preceding paragraphs of this chapter generally suggest that Pentecostal testimony is part of a distinctive overall oral and narrative tradition that is far reaching in its power. Energy and vitality are its obvious characteristics. Moreover, testimony presupposes an ability to communicate through inspired (and inspiring) speech that is supra rational. It is not dogmatic. It is emotive. It is engaging. It can easily address a wide audience. These and other qualities qualify testimony as a possible medium for encounter and dialogue beyond the confines of Pentecostal congregations.[213] The Classical Pentecostal tradition of testimony can be a rich and rewarding experience for worshipers, both speakers and hearers. I have come to think that it is also a basis and impetus for sharing with religious others what God has done in one's life. Yet the transposition of testimony from the worshiping community to the dialogue table is not a facile move. It requires caution out of respect for original worshipers on the one hand, and compassion for eventual conversation partners on the other hand. In the next chapter, this study will turn to discussing how Pentecostal testimony and interreligious dialogue can come together for meeting the pressing needs of the day in a global society increasingly characterized by conflictive interreligious encounter.

Notes

1. Although, as stated, this study focuses on Pentecostal testimony, it is appropriate to acknowledge that testimony and narrative theology are also prized and practiced by other groups, e.g., Evangelicalism, and that some are beginning to see these as a means of "bridging the gap" between different faith cultures. See W.A. Dryness, *Invitation to Cross-Cultural Theology: Case Studies in Vernacular Theology* (Grand Rapids, MI: Zondervan, 1992).

2. J.D. Plüss, "Testimony," *GDT,* 877-79 (877). An intriguing discussion involves resemblances of folktale and testimony. See V. Propp, *Morphology of the Folktale* (2nd ed., Austin, TX: University of Texas Press, 1968).

3. Plüss, "Testimony," 877.

4. R. Otto, *The Idea of the Holy,* trans. John Harvey, (New York: Oxford University Press, 1958), speaks of "the testimony of genuine religious experience" (214) and suggests testimony would have been crucial in transmitting the experience of Christ's resurrection, 222, (cf. 226). See Plüss, "Testimony," 877.

5. Plüss, "Testimony," 877.
6. Plüss, "Testimony," 877.
7. P. Ricoeur, *Oneself as Another,* trans. Kathleen Blamey (Chicago, IL: University of Chicago Press, 1992, 1994), 1-26 (cf. 140-59).
8. Ricoeur, *Oneself as Another,* 21. Ricoeur considers the modern foundationalist notion of absolute knowledge impossible, P. Ricoeur, "Hermeneutics of Testimony," *Essays on Biblical Interpretation,* ed. L. S. Mudge (Philadelphia, PA: Fortress, 1974, 1980), 119-54 (152). L.W. Wood, *Theology as History and Hermeneutics: A Post-Critical Conversation with Contemporary Theology* (Lexington, KY: Emeth, 2005), observes that Ricoeur rejects modernistic dualism in favor of a view affirming "human life as part of the world" in which "it senses a unity between its inner and external world (134). Rationalistic dualism is therefore "simply inadequate for understanding the apostolic testimony" (134). Therefore, Wood says, Ricoeur "proposes a post-critical view of truth, combining both the poetic, imaginative depths of reality and an empirical experience of the real world" (134). Thus, he is able to affirm contemporary faith through a post-critical construct, 130.
9. Wood, *Theology as History and Hermeneutics,* explains that for Ricoeur "the language of faith" is similar to "the concept of truth given by the testimony of a witness in a courtroom" (136). See Ricoeur, "Hermeneutics of Testimony," 124. Of course, Wood adds, this "Testifying truth is largely a matter of interpretation, and interpretation is judged in terms of what the witness observed" (136). Significantly, a witness empirically experiences (sees/hears), understands (interprets), and reports (testifies), whether for legal purposes or of faith experiences, 136-37. Ultimately, the reliability and trustworthiness of the witness's testimony are critical for validation (contra "verification"), Ricoeur, "Hermeneutics of Testimony," 121, 123-25. See Ricoeur, *Oneself as Another,* 22.
10. Ricoeur, *Oneself as Another,* 72.
11. Ricoeur, *Oneself as Another,* 72. Notably, Wood, *Theology as History and Hermeneutics,* suggests, Ricoeur argues that the Bible focuses on testimony, 138, and that its words are "signs and testimonies of God's gracious actions toward humanity" which "appeal to our imagination" and open us up to the possibilities of divine manifestation and truth (139). I.e., the text of Scripture is "original, poetic language as a testimony to the revelation of God and a summons to faith" (143). Cf. Ricoeur, "Hermeneutics of Testimony," 119-54 (101). Thus, the contemporary reader may experience (and testify to) the original revelation of the text, 145.
12. Ricoeur, *Oneself as Another,* 322.
13. Ricoeur, *Oneself as Another,* 340. Ricoeur develops "a philosophy of testimony" in contrast to modernistic epistemological categories as a means of demonstrating the validity of faith in Christ today, Wood, *Theology as History and Hermeneutics,* 225. However, arguably, his insights have implications for the broader practices of Christian preaching and testimony as well, 228 (cf. 231and 235-38). For an in depth overview of Ricoeur, see D.F. Ford, "Paul Ricoeur: A Biblical Philosopher on Jesus," ed. P.K. Koser, *Jesus and Philosophy: New Essays* (New York: Cambridge University Press, 2009), 169-98. For an intensive study by Ricoeur himself on the topic of testimony, see "Emmanuel Levinas: Thinker of Testimony," 108-28, P. Ricoeur and M.I. Wallace, *Figuring the Sacred* (Minneapolis, MN: Augsburg, 1995).
14. D. Rosenberg, "Introduction: In a Forgotten Mirror," ed., D. Rosenberg, *Testimony: Contemporary Writers Make the Holocaust Personal* (New York: Time/Random House, 1989), xiii. However, compare to L. Gilmore, *The Limits of Autobiography: Trauma and Testimony* (New York: Cornell University Press, 2001), especially the category of "bastard testimony" (45-70).
15. Rosenberg, "Introduction," xiii.

16. Rosenberg, "Introduction," xiii-xiv.
17. Rosenberg, "Introduction," xxii.
18. V.L. White, Jr., *Inside the Nation of Islam: A Historical and Personal Testimony by a Black Muslim* (Gainesville, FL: University of Florida Press, 2001), xiii-xv.
19. White, Jr., *Inside,* see esp. chap. 4.
20. Cf. *The Oxford Book of the American South: Testimony, Memory, and Fiction,* ed., E.L. Ayers and B.C. Mittendorf (New York/Oxford: Oxford University Press, 1997).
21. D. Rabinowitz, *No Crueler Tyrannies: Accusation, False Witness, and Other Terrors of Our Times* (New York: Free Press, 2003).
22. E. Loftus and K. Ketcham, *Witness for the Defense: The Accused, The Eyewitness, and the Expert Who Puts Memory on Trial* (New York: St Martin's, 1991). M.A. Hagen, *Whores of the Court: The Fraud of Psychiatric Testimony and the Rape of American Justice* (New York: HarperCollins, 1997), stingingly challenges the entire psychiatric industry of expert testimony in legal trials, stressing the poor track record of the practice. From another angle, J.F. Meyer, *Inaccuracies in Children's Testimony* (New York/London: The Haworth Press, 1997), argues that expectation, imagination, stress, and suggestibility, coupled with prompting and inclination to obey adult authority, can seriously distort the testimony of children in abuse cases.
23. R.J. Grele, ed., *Envelopes of Sound: Six Practitioners Discuss the Method, Theory and Practice of Oral History and Oral Testimony* (Chicago: Precedent, 1975). Grele affirms oral testimony and oral tradition for its "human direction and spontaneity" and suggests it "offers extraordinary insights into the lives and struggles of ordinary people" (2). However, he argues that, at least in terms of the historical interview, linguistic analysis, personal interaction, and cultural milieu are influencing factors requiring close observation, 8. Cf. Grele, "Movement Without Aim: Methodological and Theoretical Problems in Oral History," *Envelopes of Sound,* 126-43. Cf. D.A. Ritchie, *Doing Oral History: Using Interviews to Uncover the Past and Preserve it for the Future* (New York: Oxford University Press, 2003), esp. on the contemporary importance of oral history, 19-29, the role of memory, 30-40, and the public sphere, 41-46 (cf. theme of "community history", 223-29).
24. W. James, *The Varieties of Religious Experience* (New York: Triumph, 1902, 1991). E.g., 128, 157-60, 170, 176, 184.
25. W. Proudfoot, *Religious Experience* (Berkley, CA: University of California, 1985), 184. Cf. James, *Varieties,* 383.
26. Proudfoot, *Religious Experience,* 23. Hay, "Experience, Religious," *NWDCS,* 295-97, affirms the importance of religious experience in the Judeo-Christian tradition, although he finds the terminology problematic, 295, and outlines several approaches to religious experience, many reductionist and relativistic, 296-97, but notes that religious experience may reasonably signify the reality of "direct encounter with and recognition of God" (297).
27. A.H. Maslow, *Religions, Values, and Peak Experiences* (New York: Viking, 1964, 1970, 1973), 72.
28. Maslow, *Peak Experiences,* 84-85. Maslow's chapter heading describes this language as "Rhapsodic, Isomorphic Communications", 84. Somewhat similarly, M. Kelsey, *Discernment: A Study in Ecstasy and Evil* (New York: Paulist, 1978), argues for the language of myth and imagery, 86-105 (esp. 86, 90-97).
29. Maslow, *Peak Experiences,* 85.
30. Maslow, *Peak Experiences,* 86. Interestingly, Maslow concluded those he had thought of as "non-peakers" were really "weak peakers" and only needed to be made aware of the potential for profound experience already latent within them, 86-87. He

nevertheless warns against artificial (or superficial?) communications that may arise from this realization, something he himself encountered firsthand, 90.

31. Plüss, "Testimony," 877-78 (877). As Plüss himself affirms the universality and variety of testimony, 877, this apparently describes the distinctiveness of Christian testimony but does not deny its relatedness to other forms of human testimony, such as, e.g., that described in the preceding.

32. Plüss, "Testimony," 877-79. Cf. E.L. Cleary and J. Sepúlveda, "Chilean Pentecostalism: Coming of Age," ed., E.L. Cleary and H. Stewart, *Power, Politics, and Pentecostals in Latin America* (Boulder, Colorado: Westview, 1996), 97-122 (107). See also A.S. Walsh, *Latino Pentecostal Identity* (New York: Columbia University Press, 2003), esp. 75-76, 101.

33. R. Bauckham, *Jesus and the Eyewitnesses: The Gospels as Eyewitness Testimony* (Grand Rapids: Eerdmans, 2006), 1-11. B. Freeman, *The Triune God in Experience (The Testimony of Church History)* (Spokane, WA: Ministry, 1992), presents Christian history as essentially ongoing ecclesial testimony to the experience of God.

34. Plüss, "Testimony," 879.

35. Plüss, "Testimony," 879.

36. T.G. Long, *Testimony: Talking Ourselves into Being Christian,* Practice of Faith Series (San Francisco: Jossey-Bass, 2004), esp. 3-20. A.C. Florence, *Preaching as Testimony* (Louisville, KY: John Knox Westminster, 2007), suggests the best homiletic tradition draws heavily on testimony, xiii, xvii-xxx.

37. A. Jacobs, *Looking Before and After: Testimony and the Christian Life* (Grand Rapids: Eerdmans, 2008), 19.

38. Jacobs, *Looking,* 22-24. E.g., in John Newton's "Amazing Grace" the lost/found and blind/see contrast may be paradigmatic for such testimonies, 22-24. A.W. Tozer, *The Best of Tozer: Book One* (Camp Hill, PA: Wingspread, 2007; repr. Baker, 1978), warned Evangelicals and Pentecostals against giving a "stock testimony", 201. For him, the centrality of Jesus in attaining victory in the struggles and trials of life is essential, A.W. Tozer, *The Best of Tozer: Book Two* (Camp Hill, PA: Wingspread, 2007; repr. Baker, 1980, 1995), 274-75.

39. Jacobs, *Looking,* 13-15 and 39. Cf. 52.

40. Jacobs, *Looking,* 24.

41. However, M.J. Cartledge, *Encountering the Spirit: The Charismatic Tradition,* Traditions of Christian Spirituality (New York: Orbis, 2007), notes the central significance of testimony among Charismatics and Pentecostals, 83. See Jacobs, *Looking,* 25.

42. Jacobs, *Looking,* 24, 25. Similarly, D.S. Whitney, *Spiritual Disciplines for the Christian Life* (Colorado Springs, CO: NavPress, 1991), links testimony with vital spirituality expressed in disciplined living. Cf. 81, 102, 111, and, though negatively, 236.

43. Jacobs, *Looking,* 27-29.

44. For Cartledge, *Encountering the Spirit,* testimony, like speaking in tongues, prophecy, preaching, messages of wisdom and knowledge, etc., etc., is inspired speech, 32, 58, 69, and 119. Notably, Pentecostals consider such inspired speech completely consistent with the inspiration and authority of Scripture and the illumination of the Holy Spirit, existing quite comfortably alongside each other, 47 and 78. Personal experience of the Holy Spirit can thus serve as an enduring basis for possible testimony, 77. Of course, the assessment of the faith community is always essential, 124-25. Cf. Jacobs, *Looking,* 27.

45. Jacobs, *Looking,* 35. Cf. Mark J. Cartledge, *Testimony: Its Importance, Place, and Potential* (Cambridge: Grove, 2002).

46. Jacobs, *Looking,* 36-38. For differences and similarities in the Pentecostal tradition of testimony and its Pietist heritage, see D.D. Bundy, "European Pietist Roots of Pentecostalism," *NIDPCM,* 610-13, and C. Bunners, "Paul Gerhardt (1607-1676)," ed., C. Linberg, *The Pietist Theologians: An Introduction to Theology in the Seventeenth and Eightennth Centuries* (Malden, Massachusetts: Wiley-Blackwell, 2004), 68-83. Cf. M. Matthias, "August Hermanne Franke (1663-1727)," Linberg, *The Pietist Theologians,* 100-14, and D.W. Brown, *Understanding Pietism* (Nappanee, IN: Evangel, 1996), 25, 46, 48-51, 72-73, 78 and 96.

47. Plüss, "Testimony," *GDT,* 877.

48. Plüss, "Testimony," *GDT,* 877.

49. Jacobs, *Looking,* 35-38.

50. Cf. R. Kennedy, *A History of Reasonableness: Testimony and Authority in the Art of Thinking* (Rochester Studies in Philosophy) (Rochester, New York: University of Rochester, 2004).

51. The following section is in dialogue with the work of Guy P. Duffield and N. M. Van Cleave; French L. Arrington.

52. E.g., J.B. Shelton, "Matthew," *FLBC,* 119-253 (esp. 176, 185). Additionally, Shelton argues that the writer of the Gospel of Matthew wrote as not only an eyewitness to events and a compiler of written records, but in personal testimony of belief, and that affects the nature of his witness, which the Early Church nonetheless recognized as authentic, 120.

53. Cf. *TDNT,* eds. G. Kittle and G. Friedrich, trans. G.W. Bromiley, abridged in one volume by G.W. Bromiley (Grand Rapids: Eerdmans, 1985, 1990), 564-70.

54. G.P. Duffield and N.M. Van Cleave, *Foundations of Pentecostal Theology* (Los Angeles: L.I.F.E. Bible College, 1983, 1987), 402.

55. This example indicates Pentecostalism's general tendency to insist on follow up after definitive experiences. Thus an observer, Kelsey, *Discernment,* says, "One of the facts which convinces me of the reality of the Pentecostal religion is its emphasis on the very experience of testing and trial which follows the initial experience of tongues" (104). Cf. D. Martin, *Tongues of Fire: The Explosion of Protestantism in Latin America* (Cambridge, Massachusetts: Wiley-Blackwell, 1993), on importance of "open testimony" in permanently overcoming demonic domination, 167.

56. F.L. Arrington, *Encountering the Holy Spirit: Paths of Christian Growth and Service* (Cleveland: Pathway, 2003), 20-21.

57. Cf. D. Martin, *Pentecostalism: The World Their Parish* (Cambridge, Massachusetts: Wiley-Blackwell, 2008), 134-35, 137-38. See Arrington, *Encountering,* 421-66.

58. Arrington, *Encountering,* 423. Cf. with Simon Chan's critique below.

59. Cf. Arrington, *Encountering,* 463.

60. Arrington, *Encountering,* 463.

61. This section dialogues with the work of Cheryl Bridges Johns.

62. Interestingly, Martin, *Tongues of Fire,* argues that speaking in tongues and testimonies to divine blessings are "signals of transformation", or signs of God's transformative activity, and arise out of the pattern of the biblical Pentecost in Acts 2, 163. Cf. also with Martin, *Pentecostalism,* 14.

63. C.B. Johns, *Pentecostal Formation: A Pedagogy among the Oppressed* JPTSup 2 (Sheffield, England: Sheffield Academic Press, 1993, 1998), 126-27.

64. P. Pettite, ed., *Foundations of Spiritual Formation: A Community Approach to Becoming Like Christ* (Grand Rapids: Kregel, 2008), highlights Evangelical approaches to spiritual formation in contexts of community but without direct reference to Pentecostalism. M.R. Mulholland, *Invitation to a Journey: A Roadmap for Spiritual Formation*

(Downer's Grove, IL: InterVarsity, 1993), emphasizes relational and social aspects of personal spiritual formation from a Wesleyan perspective, but also without reference to Pentecostals. However, S. Chan, *Spiritual Theology: A Systematic Study of the Christian Life* (Downer's Grove: IVP, 1998), addresses spiritual formation from a specifically Pentecostal and Charismatic perspective, although also identifying with a global contextualism and with evangelical themes, 15, 24-39. Not surprisingly, Chan stresses a dynamic interplay of the Holy Spirit, Scripture, and Church through testimony in communal and personal spiritual formation. Cf. 81-88, 109, 111, 194, 209, and 232. Cf. Johns, *Pentecostal Formation*, 130-31.

65. Johns, *Pentecostal Formation*, 130-38.

66. Johns, *Pentecostal Formation*, 131. Note especially testimonies of Asian Christians in difficult contexts in Chan, *Spiritual Theology*, 26 and 245.

67. Johns, *Pentecostal Formation*, 132.

68. Johns, *Pentecostal Formation*, 131-33 (133).

69. This section is in dialogue Jerome Boone.

70. R.J. Boone, "Community and Worship: Key Components of Pentecostal Christian Formation," *JPT* 8 (1996), 129-42.

71. Boone, "Community," 138-39.

72. Notably, Y. Congar, *The Word and the Spirit* (*WS*), trans. David Smith (San Francisco: Harper & Row, 1986), seeks to balance an inner, individual, and outer, ecclesial, testimony of the Spirit, and thus overcome the dangers of individualism by looking for the Spirit's witness "not only in the believing individual, but also in the believing community" (32). Therefore, the Spirit gives life to everything, including to all the tradition and liturgy, 35.

73. Boone, "Community," 139-40.

74. Boone, 141-42. R.M. Griffith, "Network of Praying Women," E.L. Blumhoffer, R.P. Spittler, G.A. Wacker, *Pentecostal Currents in American Protestantism* (Champaign, IL:University of Illinois, 1999), informs that in contemporary Women's Aglow meetings, prayer and testimony work as "important narrative practices for participants", 139. Additionally, Aglow testimonies, structured around the move from sin and suffering to redemption and healing through prayer, have been an effective evangelism tool, 139. Cf. A. Adams, "*Bricando el Charco*/Jumping the Puddle: A Case Study of Pentecostalism's Journey from Puerto Rico to New York to Allentown, Pennsylvania," Cleary, *Power*, 163-78 (173).

75. Boone, "Community," 142.

76. S.J. Land says testimonies "develop in the hearers the virtues, expectancy, attitudes, and experiences of those testifying", *Pentecostal Spirituality: A Passion for the Kingdom* JPTSup 1 (Sheffield: Sheffield Academic Press, 1993), 80. See Boone, "Community,"138-39.

77. Boone, "Community,"134-35.

78. This section is in dialogue with the work of Walter J. Hollenweger, Frank D. Macchia, and John C. Poirier.

79. D.D. Bundy, "Hollenweger, Walter Jacob," *NIDPCM* (Grand Rapids, Zondervan, 2002), 729.

80. W.J. Hollenweger, *The Pentecostals*, Peabody, Hendrickson, 1988, first published in English by SCM Press Ltd., London, 1972.

81. Hollenweger, *Pentecostals*, xxviii.

82. W.J. Hollenweger, "After Twenty Years of Research on Pentecostalism," *IRM* (January 1986), 3-12 (6).

83. W.J. Hollenweger, "Pentecostals and Charismatics," in *The Study of Spirituality*, eds. C. Jones, G. Wainwright, and E. Yarnold, SJ (New York: Oxford University Press, 1986), 549-54 (549, 552).

84. W.J. Hollenweger, *"Fire from Heaven:* A Testimony by Harvey Cox," *Pneuma* 20:2 (1998), 197-204. Cf. H. Cox, *Fire from Heaven: The Rise of Pentecostal Spirituality and the Reshaping of Religion in the Twenty-First Century* (New York: Addison-Wesley, 1995). Cox does indeed positively note the significance of testimony for Pentecostals. E.g., see Cox, 15, 71, 128-34, and 199.

85. F.D. Macchia, *Baptized in the Spirit: A Global Pentecostal Theology* (Grand Rapids: Zondervan, 2006), 49-51. However, cf. Martin, *Tongues of Fire,* 165.

86. Macchia, *Baptized,* 51-7. Cf. 11-14. Moreover, as Clark Pinnock notes, methodologically Macchia looks "to a narrative theology of Spirit baptism drawn from the book of Acts and placed in relation to other voices in the canon." See Pinnock, "A Review of Frank D. Macchia's *Baptized in the Spirit: A Global Theology,"* *JPT* 16:2 (April 2008), 1-4 (2).

87. J.C. Poirier, "Narrative Theology and Pentecostal Commitments," *JPT* 16:2 (April 2008), 69-85 (72, fn: 8). Specifically, Poirier has problems with a particular version of formal philosophical narrative theology associated with H. W. Frei's *The Eclipse of Biblical Narrative: A Study in Eighteenth and Nineteenth Century Hermeneutics* (New Haven: Yale Press, 1974). See Poirier, 70-72.

88. This section dialogues with William J. Seymour and Cecil M. Robeck.

89. C.M. Robeck, *The Azusa Street Mission & Revival: The Birth of the Global Pentecostal Movement* (Nashville: Nelson, 2006). As the title suggests, many consider the Azusa Street work to be the birthplace of the modern Pentecostal movement, though there were spontaneous, sporadic outpourings of the Holy Spirit elsewhere more or less simultaneously. Cf. S.M. Burgess, "The Pentecostal Tradition," *CHB* 58:17:2 (1998), 40-41, and G. Strachen, *The Pentecostal Theology of Edward Erving* (Peabody: Hendrickson, 1973, 1988).

90. Robeck, *Azusa Street,* 2-4. Cf. 14, 16.

91. Robeck, *Azusa Street,* 46.

92. Robeck, *Azusa Street,* 68-69. Although perhaps in part due to the general lack of education among early Pentecostals, that alone does not fully explain the almost irresistible attraction of testimony. More likely, testimony represents an exciting intersection of multiple values including inspired speech, lay ministry, narrative theology, and contemporary experience.

93. Robeck, *Azusa Street,* 106.

94. Robeck, *Azusa Street,* 115, 135.

95. Robeck, *Azusa Street,* 154-58 (154). This continues to be a frequent feature of contemporary Pentecostalism, though perhaps exhibited with more restraint than may have been common in the early days.

96. M.M. Poloma, "Divine Healing, Religious Revivals, and Contemporary Pentecostalism: A North American Perspective," *The Spirit in the World: Emerging Pentecostal Theologies in Global Contexts,* ed. Veli-Matti Kärkkäinen (Grand Rapids: Eerdmans, 2009), 21-39, argues the central importance of prayer in revivalism, specifically in Pentecostalism, 32-33. See Robeck, *Azusa Street,* 139.

97. Robeck, *Azusa Street,* 186.

98. Indeed, R.F. Culpepper, *The Great Commission: The Solution...* (Cleveland, TN: Pathway Press, 2009), suggests personal testimony continues to be key for evangelistic endeavors in the Church of God (Cleveland, TN), 86-88. See Robeck, *Azusa Street,* 252-53.

99. Robeck, *Azusa Street,* 281.

100. This section dialogues with Walter Hollenweger.

101. Hollenweger, *Pentecostals,* pp. 54-56 (55). Hollenweger lifts the service account from L. Pope, *Millhands and Preachers* (New Haven: Yale University Press, 1942, 1958), 130.

102. Hollenweger, *Pentecostals,* 466. Small wonder that Y. Congar, *I Believe in the Holy Spirit* 3 vols. trans. David Smith (New York: Seabury, 1983), insists the Holy Spirit makes life in Christ real, personal, and inward, 2:100.

103. This section is in dialogue with the work of Cheryl Johns.

104. Johns, *Pentecostal Formation,* 87.

105. Walsh, *Latino Pentecostal Identity,* lists "orality, music, intercessory prayer, testimony, informality, and relaxing of class signifiers" as elements of Pentecostalism's inviting "transcendent value" that is "an offering of a ritual life to groups who do not feel welcome in other surroundings" (112).

106. Johns, *Pentecostal Formation,* 81.

107. Johns, *Pentecostal Formation,* 89-90. Italics are original.

108. This section draws on the work of Kimberly Ervin Alexander and John Christopher Thomas.

109. E.g., M.L. Cook, "Confessional Theology," *NHCT* eds. D.W. Musser and J.L. Price (Nashville: Abingdon, 1992), 96-98 and L.J. Biallas, "Dogmatic Theology," *NHCT,* 127-30.

110. *NHCT,* J.H. Leith, "Ecclesiology," 135-38 (136). Cf. R.E. Webber, *Ancient-Future Worship: Proclaiming and Enacting God's Narrative* (Grand Rapids: Baker, 2008), who thinks of creeds as "sound-bite testimonies", 49.

111. K.E. Alexander, *Pentecostal Healing: Models in Theology and Practice* JSup Series (DEO, 2006), 103.

112. See http://www.churchofgod.org/about/declaration_of_faith.cfm. Interestingly, Pentecostals sometimes refer to the doctrine of initial evidence as their "distinctive testimony", G.B. McGee, "Initial Evidence, *NIDPCM,* 784-91, (788-89).

113. Otto, *Holy,* traces this autobiographical character in the Apostle Paul's frequent testimony of his conversion experience, 37. Cf. J.C. Thomas, "The Charismatic Structure of Acts," *JPT* 13:1 (October 2004), 19-30 (26). Interestingly, A. Thomas (no relation), author of two personal memoirs and nationwide lecturer on writing memoirs, suggests that personal identity for humans is essentially internalized in story form and may be best expressed in the same genre. In other words, to some extent testimony may be intrinsic to human identity. See A. Thomas, "Everyone Has a Story to Tell," *AARP* (July/August 2008), 30-34. Cf. A. Thomas, *Thinking About Memoir* (AARP Books/Sterling, 2008).

114. Or as Arrington, *Encountering,* says, testimonies "remind us of how the Holy Spirit still works in our lives and in the world today" (463). Delton Alford, "Music, Pentecostal and Charismatic," *NIDPCM,* 911-20, notes that the revivalist worship roots of the Pentecostal tradition emphasized a "heartfelt, sincere, and enthusiastic approach" that was "joyful in spirit and consisted primarily of congregational expressions of praise and testimony" (912).

115. However, G. Wacker, *Heaven Below: Early Pentecostals and American Culture* (London, Eng: Harvard University Press, 2001), warns that, at least in their surviving written forms, autobiographical Pentecostal testimonies can be highly stylized, indicating a strict threefold pattern of problem, solution, and benefits; nevertheless he opines that oral forms must have been more spontaneous, 58-59.

116. As evidence of the intricacy of autobiography and story, note that analytical psychologist C. G. Jung hypothesized that behind psychosis and its aberrations is a story.

Jung said, "Therapy only really begins after the investigation of that whole story." See Jung, *Memories, Dreams, Reflections,* ed. A. Jaffé, trans. R. and C. Winston (New York: Pantheon, 1963), 117, 124.

117. See Cox, *Fire,* 199. Cf. Thomas, "Charismatic Structure," 26. Cf. V. Synan, *Voices of Pentecost: Testimonies of Lives Touched by the Holy Spirit* (Ann Arbor, Michigan: Servant Books, 2003), 78, and 57, and R. Owens, "The Azusa Street Revival: The Pentecostal Movement Begins in America," ed., V. Synan, *The Century of the Holy Spirit: 100 Years of Pentecostal and Charismatic Renewal* (Nashville, TN: Nelson, 2001), 39-68 (57).

118. Martin, *Pentecostalism,* wonders if there are "other forms of encounter through testimony, gesture, song, and healing which do not lie under the guillotine of progress but are intrinsic to the human condition" (176).

119. J. Moltmann, no Pentecostal himself yet often in dialogue with Pentecostals, flatly states that, "Because this is my personal experience of God, I hold fast to it and am not open for reasoned criticism." See Moltmann, *A Broad Place: An Autobiography,* trans. M. Kohl (Minneapolis: Fortress, 2008), 192-96 (195). He was speaking of his Trinitarian theology of the cross in the context of his own indescribable suffering in World War II. It is as if he knows autobiographically and experientially the passion of Christ so deeply and profoundly that ultimately all he can do is testify of it.

120. This section is in dialogue with the work of Scott A. Ellington and John Christopher Thomas.

121. See H. D. Buckwalter, "Testimony," *BTDB,* ed. Walter A. Elwell (Grand Rapids: Baker, 1996), 765-69 (766).

122. Cf. Culpepper, *Great Commission,* 38, 86. See Buckwalter, "Testimony," *BTDB,* 768.

123. E.g., F.L. Fisher, "Witness, Testimony," *BDT,* eds. E.F. Harrison, G.W. Bromiley, C.F.H. Henry (Grand Rapids: Baker, 1960, 1987), 555-56.

124. Cf. P.A. Pomerville, "The Pentecostals and Growth," ed., L.G. McClung, Jr., *Azusa Street and Beyond: Pentecostal Missions and Church Growth* (South Plainfield, NJ: Logos, 1986), 151-55 (esp. 152-54). Cf. McClung, "Introduction: Spontaneous Strategy of the Spirit: Pentecostal Missionary Practices," *Azusa Street and Beyond,* 71-81 (esp. 74-75). Interestingly, general Christian usage of the terms "evangelism" and "witness," and the practices they signify, may be undergoing transitional development. Cf. B. Stone, *Evangelism after Christendom: The Theology and Practice of Christian Witness* (Grand Rapids: Brazos, 2007). See also *The Changing Face of World Missions: Engaging Contemporary Issues and Trends,* ed., M. Pocock, G. Van Rheenen, D. McConnell (Grand Rapids: Baker Acacemic, 2005).

125. The term can be and occasionally is used in other ways but this is atypical. E.g., see J. Gros, F. S. C., "A Pilgrimage in the Spirit: Pentecostal Testimony in the Faith and Order Movement," *Pneuma* 25:1 (2003), 29-53. Here Gros is using "testimony" in a much more academic way than is customary in congregational usage.

126. As Cox, *Fire,* observes, more than anything Pentecostal testimony witnesses to an experience of God that is "so total it shatters the cognitive packaging", 71, and makes any kind of classification difficult, 199.

127. E.g., S.A. Ellington, "The Reciprocal Reshaping of History and Experience in the Psalms: Interactions with Pentecostal Testimony," *JPT* 16:1 (2007), 18-31. Thus, the testimonial character of Scripture informs both history and hermeneutics and these in turn clarify the nature of Pentecostal testimony, 30-31.

128. Ellington, "Reciprocal Reshaping," 18-21. Ellington insists, "Testimony bears witness to the power of memory to transform the present and cast a new vision of the

future" (30). May Ling Tan-Chow, *Pentecostal Theology for the Twenty-First Century* (Burlington, VT: Ashgate, 2007), describes Pentecostal testimonies as worship through remembering as Pentecostals engage "the core memory of the Christian faith" (144). Thus, testimonies involve "re-presentation of their salvation history" and is not in "discursive but in celebrative and transformative" mode in a manner that provokes commitment and "enhances the vitality of faith because it keeps memory alive and truth real" (144). For Pentecostals, biblical and contemporary reality is thus fused, 144. Tan-Chow says that, "In this way, testimonies shape Pentecostal identity, theology, and practices" (144).

129. Ellington, "Reciprocal Reshaping, 24-27.

130. Accordingly, Ellington, "Reciprocal Reshaping," argues, "Testimony in the Psalms is an act of traditioning in which Israel's story is brought into the present, experienced anew, and projected into the future. And it is in Pentecostal testimonies ... that we see the closest approximation of the Psalm's understanding of 'history'. Recalling the biblical stories is never divorced from the concerns of the present and it is the God exemplified in those stories rather than a detached historical reconstruction that is paramount" (28).

131. W.G. Rollins's research into famed analytical psychologist C. G. Jung's psychological interpretation of scripture suggests a dynamic hermeneutic for facilitation of divine encounter and experience. See Rollins, *Jung and the Bible* (Atlanta: John Knox Press, 1983).

132. Thus, Ellington, "Reciprocal Reshaping," suggests Pentecostal testimony's unique juncture of past and present, memory and experience links the question "Did it happen?" with "Does it happen?" (30). Cf. Tan-Chow, *Pentecostal Theology*, 129.

133. J.C. Thomas, *The Spirit of the New Testament* (Netherlands: Deo, 2005), 157-74 (158). Increasingly apparent is the importance of biographical narrative for contextual understanding of the didactic sayings of Scripture. Cf. R.A. Burridge, *Imitating Jesus: An Inclusive Approach to New Testament Ethics* (Grand Rapids: Eerdmans, 2007), 25-31, 86-87, 228-29, and 377.

134. Cf. Thomas, "Charismatic Structure," 26.

135. Thomas, *Spirit of NT*, argues for a "confessional" approach to Pentecostal scholarship functioning as "a testimony from the margins to a world desperately seeking meaning and comfort" (13).

136. This section has several dialogue partners, including William MacDonald, Juan Sepúlveda, Kenneth J. Archer, Steven J. Land, Amos Yong, Clark Pinnock, and Simon Chan.

137. Thomas, "Charismatic Structure," 26.

138. W.G. MacDonald, "Pentecostal Theology: A Classical Viewpoint," *Perspectives on the New Pentecostalism*, ed. Russell P. Spittler (Grand Rapids: Baker, 1976), 58-75 (61-62).

139. MacDonald, "Pentecostal Theology," 61.

140. MacDonald, "Pentecostal Theology," 61. However, D. Jacobsen, *Thinking in the Spirit: Theologies of the Early Pentecostal Movement* (Bloomington, IN: Indiana University Press, 2003), argues somewhat differently. He asserts that although Pentecostals certainly have uniquely utilized testimony in their theology, the difference from other Christian traditions may be more one of degree than kind, and when attempting to be more systematic or thorough even Pentecostals will use argumentation for explanatory purposes and testimony for transformative purposes, 7-8. However, he is quick to admit that even in such comparatively systematic treatises testimony will not usually be entirely absent, 8.

141. MacDonald, "Pentecostal Theology," 62. MacDonald argues that Pentecostal theology is "experience-certified," 62, through the distinctive experiences of Spirit baptism and speaking in tongues, 65, and the gifts of the Spirit, 66, but is still facing several important "frontiers" in developing their theology further, 68.

142. J. Sepúlveda, "Characteristics of Indigenous Pentecostalism: Chile," *In the Power of the Spirit,* eds. Dennis A. Smith and B. F. Guiterrez, http://www.religion-online.org/showchapter.asp?title=374&C=9 (downloaded November 7, 2007). Cf. Cleary and Stewart, *Power, Politics, and Pentecostals in Latin America:* E.L. Cleary, "Introduction: Pentecostals, Prominence, and Politics," 1-24 (6, 16), C.L. Mariz and M.D.C. Machado, "Pentecostalism and Women in Brazil," 41-54 (48), and Cleary and Sepúlveda, "Chilean Pentecostalism," 100.

143. J. Sepúlveda, "Reflections on the Pentecostal Contribution to the Mission of the Church in Latin America," *JPT* 1 (1992), 93-108 (101).

144. Sepúlveda, "Reflections," 101. Italics are original.

145. Cf. Sepúlveda, "Characteristics," http://www.religion-online.org/showchapter.asp?title=374&C=9.

146. Sepúlveda, "Reflections," 98. P. Alexander, *Peace to War: Shifting Allegiances in the Assemblies of God* (Telford, PA: Cascadia, 2009), similarly suggests North American Pentecostals initially embraced more involvement from the people, especially women and laity, but slowly shifted to more exclusive positions through their sectarian development (or abandonment), 303. Significantly, a tradition Alexander suspects has been seriously compromised but hopes may be in the process of recovery is the Pentecostal "peace testimony", 340-42.

147. Thus, Alexander, *Peace to War,* somewhat sarcastically relates the ironic misuse of Pentecostal testimony for political agendas, 240, 267, and 273. See Sepúlveda, "Reflections," 100.

148. Sepúlveda, "Reflections," 102.

149. Sepúlveda, "Reflections," 103.

150. Sepúlveda, "Reflections," 104.

151. Martin, *Pentecostalism,* suggests personal testimony, not mass media, is the more effective means of transmission for the Evangelical and Pentecostal message, 99, 163. See Sepúlveda, "Reflections," 105.

152. Sepúlveda, "Reflections," 108.

153. K.J. Archer, "Pentecostal Story: the Hermeneutical Filter for Producing Meaning," *JPT* 26:1 (2004), 36-59.

154. Archer, "Pentecostal Story," 59. Of course, Pentecostalism's unique theological contributions do not necessarily preclude its drawing upon other traditions as well. E.g., K. Kim, *The Holy Spirit in the World: A Global Conversation* (Maryknoll, NY: Orbis, 2007), points out that Pentecostal/Charismatic pneumatology can be compatible with contributions of liberation theology, *Holy Spirit in the World,* 168.

155. E.g., J.F. MacArthur, Jr., *Charismatic Chaos* (Grand Rapids: Zondervan, 1992), 25-53. Cf. V. Synan, "Charismatic Renewal Enters the Mainline Churches," Synan, *Century of the Holy Spirit,* 149-76 (175), and Synan, "The 'Charismatics': Renewal in Major Protestant Denominations," 177-208 (205).

156. A. Yong, ""Tongues of Fire" in the Pentecostal Imagination: The Truth of Glossolalia in Light of R.C. Neville's Theory of Religious Symbolism", *JPT* 12 (1998), 39-65 (64). Cf. Land, *Pentecostal Spirituality,* 74-75.

157. C.H. Pinnock, "The Work of the Holy Spirit in Hermeneutics," *JPT* 2 (1993), 3-23.

158. S.A. Ellington, "History, Story, and Testimony: Locating Truth in a Pentecostal Hermeneutic," *Pneuma* 23:2 (2001), 245-63 (261-63).

159. E.g., S. Chan, *Pentecostal Theology and the Christian Spiritual Life* JPTS 21(Sheffield, UK: Sheffield Academic, 2000, 2003).

160. Chan, *Pentecostal Theology*, 7-16. There seems little doubt that testimony, in various forms at least, will continue to play a prominent role in the future of Pentecostals. Even the most cutting-edge Pentecostal theology emerging today still draws creatively on the tradition of testimony. E.g., see *Spirit in the World*, ed. Kärkkäinen: M.M. Poloma, "Divine Healing, Religious Revivals, and Contemporary Pentecostalism: A North American Perspective," 21-39 (24, 32); W. Ma, "'When the Poor are Fired Up': The Role of Pneumatology in Pentecostal Charismatic Mission," 40-52 (42-43, 46-47, 48, 51); K.D. Yun, "Pentecostalism from Below: *Minjung* Liberation and Asian Pentecostal Theology," 89-114 (92); O.U. Kalu, "*Sankofa:* Pentecostalism and African Cultural Heritage," 135-54 (149-50); V.M. Kärkkäinen, "Pentecostal Pneumatology of Religions: The Contribution of Pentecostalism to Our Understanding of the Work of God's Spirit in the World," 155-80 (159, 167); O. Onyinah, "Deliverance as a Way of Confronting Witchcraft in Contemporary Africa: Ghana as a Case Study," 181-202 (189, 192, 194, 200); A. Yong, "From Azusa Street to the Bo Tree and Back: Strange Babblings and Interreligious Interpretations in the Pentecostal Encounter with Buddhism," 203-226 (205, 211, 217, 218); and T. Richie, "Azusa-Era Optimism: Bishop J.H. King's Pentecostal Theology of Religions as a Possible Paradigm for Today," 227-43 (229, 232).

161. Chan, *Pentecostal Theology*, 20-21.

162. A. Yong, *The Spirit Poured Out on All Flesh: Pentecostalism and the Possibility of Global Theology* (Grand Rapids: Baker 2005), 146-47. Cf. 161-62.

163. Chan, *Pentecostal Theology*, 23-24.

164. S. Chan, *Spiritual Theology: A Systematic Study of the Christian Life* (Downer's Grove: IVP, 1998), 38, 245.

165. Macchia, *Baptized*, 49-57.

166. Cox, *Fire*, 15.

167. Cf. Johns, *Pentecostal Formation*, 126-27. Thus, K. Warrington suggests Pentecostals may have a good deal of fluidity regarding beliefs and doctrines but a commitment to encountering God's presence and power is consistently characteristic, *Pentecostal Theology: A Theology of Encounter* (New York: T & T Clark, 2008), 17-27.

168. This section draws on Charles W. Conn and Robert Duncan McCall.

169. C.W. Conn, *Like a Mighty Army: A History of the Church of God: Definitive Edition* (Cleveland: Pathway, 1996), 23-24.

170. R.D. McCall, "Storytelling and Testimony: Reclaiming a Pentecostal Distinctive," unpublished Doctor of Ministry Dissertation, Columbia Theological Seminary, 1998.

171. McCall, "Storytelling and Testimony," 1-35. McCall's work includes many examples of these uplifting testimonies.

172. McCall, "Storytelling and Testimony," 36-59 (58). The continuing testimonial emphasis on practical, including physical and financial, needs and corresponding blessings globally suggests a trend away from these kinds of testimonies, if there is one, would be more Western or even North American than worldwide. Cf. Ma, "When the Poor are Fired Up," 43, 46.

173. McCall, "Storytelling and Testimony," 60-94 (93). Indeed, McCall proposes a category of "prophetic-theologian" for those bringing about transformation and praxis using storytelling and testimony as "effective prophetic vehicles", 94.

174. McCall, "Storytelling and Testimony," 52.

175. According to Kim, *Holy Spirit in the World*, Pentecostal testimonies may provide key insights into the movement's spiritualities, 115, theologies, 122, and experiences of the divine, 163. However, testimonies, as with other practices, are always expected to be directed by Scripture, 39, 99, centered in Christ, 167, 169, and rooted in the Holy Spirit, 27, 39, and in prayer, v, vii, 91, and 134.

176. McCall, "Storytelling and Testimony," 95-104 (104).

177. McCall, "Storytelling and Testimony," 142.

178. The following section involves dialogue with Cheryl Bridges Johns, Jerome Boone, and David Douglas Daniels III.

179. See R.E. Webber, ed., *The Complete Library of Christian Worship: Volume 1, The Biblical Foundations of Christian Worship*, (Nashville: StarSong, 1993), 81-91. While one could conceivably study Pentecostal testimony's doxological feature under the biblical section, it is of such distinctive and emphatic significance that it is better to place it in its own category.

180. Cf. with Johns and Boone above on testimony as praise and worship.

181. Cf. Arrington, *Encountering*, 463, and Ellington, "Reciprocal Reshaping," 30.

182. D.D. Daniels III, "'Gotta Moan Sometime': A Sonic Exploration of Earwitnesses to Early Pentecostal Sound in North America," *Pneuma* 30:1 (2008), 5-32. Cf. Martin, *Tongues of Fire*, 178.

183. Daniels, "'Gotta Moan Sometime," *Pneuma*, 5.

184. Myung Soo Park, David Cho, Ray H. Hughes, Sr., and Roger Stronstad are dialogue partners for this section.

185. M.S. Park, "Korean Pentecostal Spirituality as Manifested in the Testimonies of Believers of the Yoido Full Gospel Church," *AJPS* 7:1 (2004), 35-56. Cf. also M.S. Park, "David Yonggi Cho and International Pentecostal/Charismatic Movements," *JPT* 12:1 (2003), 107-28.

186. Park, "Testimonies of Believers," 35.

187. Park, "Testimonies of Believers," 36.

188. However, even some from within the Pentecostal movement have criticized a tendency sometimes to fall back on "personal testimony rather than on solid biblical exposition." See Wacker, *Heaven Below*, 120. Nevertheless, many held that 'an ounce of testimony' could be more valuable than 'a pound of doctrinal teaching', although arguing also that 'the weight and value of testimony' comes out of its 'Scripturalness, simplicity, depth, brevity, and intensity' (85). J.S. Conn, *Growing Up Pentecostal* (Xulon Press, 2006), relates humorously how as a youngster in church hearing dramatic testimonies of sinners-turned-preachers he initially decided to backslide in order to acquire a proper testimony but eventually settled on forgoing the testimony and preaching the Bible instead, 179. However, he also admits that testimonies and sermons had a way of reinforcing each other, 163.

189. Park, "Testimonies of Believers," 36-37. L.T. Holdcroft, *The Holy Spirit: A Pentecostal Interpretation* (Sumas, WA: CeeTec, 1999), notes somewhat incredulously that the majority of Pentecostals seem to have adopted Keswick theology but Wesleyan practices—including the testimony meeting, 133.

190. Cf. Maslow, *Peak Experiences*, 84-85, and Kelsey, *Discernment*, 86, 90-97).

191. Park, "Testimonies of Believers," 38-41. Park's work on Cho and Yoido Full Gospel Church in the context of testimony has been widely recognized by some contemporary Pentecostal scholars. E.g., see Ma, "'When the Poor are Fired Up'," 47; P. Alexander, *Signs & Wonders: Why Pentecostalism is the World's Fastest Growing Faith* (San Francisco: Jossey-Bass, 2009), 101, 161; and, Yong, *Spirit Poured Out*, 51.

192. Park, "Testimonies of Believers," 42-46.

193. Park, "Testimonies of Believers," 46-52. Of course, struggling with these issues is something of a universal experience and may help account for the widespread appeal of Pentecostalism as a solution.

194. Park, "Testimonies of Believers," 52-56.

195. Cf. C.M. Robeck, *The Azusa Street Mission & Revival: The Birth of the Global Pentecostal Movement* (Nashville, TN: Nelson, 2006), 2-4, 154-56. Robeck describes Pentecostal testimony as involving an electrifying atmosphere about it, 156.

196. See R.H. Hughes, *Pentecostal Preaching* (Cleveland: Pathway, 1981). Billy Graham, *The Holy Spirit: Activating God's Power in Your Life* (Nashville, TN: Thomas Nelson, 1978, 1988), speaks of an anointing for special tasks, including, among others, preaching, 123, 124. Cf. 210.

197. E.g., popular Pentecostal preacher, entrepreneur, media personality, and motivational speaker T.D. Jakes, *Release Your Anointing: Tapping the Power of the Holy Spirit in You* (Shippensburg, PA: Destiny Image, 2008), specifically identifies testimony as an area "in which the Holy Ghost wants to speak" (136; cf. 138, 219, and 244). For Jakes, the anointing brings power and wisdom, and defeats Satan, 40. Indeed, popularly the Holy Spirit anointing may be perceived as extending into the totality of a Spirit-filled believer's life, F. Pickett, *Walking in the Anointing of the Holy Spirit: Book II* (Lake Mary, FL: Charisma House, 2004). The anointing may be an important goal of one's practice of devotional disciplines, L. Keefauver, *Receiving the Anointing of the Spirit* (Lake Mary, FL: Strang Communications, 1997). One can easily multiply the resources on this popular topic with texts such as D.E. Schroeder, *Walking in Your Anointing: Knowing that You are Filled with the Spirit* (Bloomington, IN: AuthorHouse, 2007). K. Miller's *Surrender to the Spirit: The Limitless Possibilities of Yielding to the Spirit* (Shippensburg, PA: Destiny Image, 2006), has a telling chapter on "The Treasure of the Anointing," 41-50. Another Pentecostal media personality, B. Hinn, *The Anointing* (Nashville, TN: Thomas Nelson, 1992, 1997), prizes testimonies of God's working, e.g., in healings, 37, but chides those who focus on anointed testimony of personal experiences to the point Christ may no longer be central, 128-29.

198. E.g., see R. Stronstad, *The Charismatic Theology of St. Luke* (Peabody: Hendrickson, 1984), 56, and F.L. Arrington, *The Acts of the Apostles: Introduction, Translation, and Commentary* (Peabody: Hendrickson, 1988), 28.

199. This section dialogues with the work of Shane Clifton and Scott Ellington.

200. S. Clifton, lecture to PhD students on "Experience in Australian Pentecostalism Pragmatic Ecclesiology: What have Australian Pentecostals gained and lost in the search for a contemporary church?" at Macquarie University. The manuscript is available at http://www.anchist.mq.edu.au/CTE/Documents/Shane%20Clifton%20on%20experience.doc.

201. Cf. with U. Sommer's adoption of the expression "testimony to faith" in describing the interrelatedness of the historical-theological dynamic of the passion narratives of the Gospels in *WUNT* 2:58 (Tubingen: J. C. Mohr, 1993) as discussed by Carroll and Green in *The Death of Jesus in Early Christianity*, J.T. Carroll and J.B. Green et al (Peabody: Hendrickson, 1995), 7. Testimony does not devalue history but neither is the telling of history devoid of aims.

202. Thus Otto, *Holy*, refers to "the full light of history and the fullest testimony of history" regarding the early Christians' conviction that miraculous charismata were present among them, 208. His comments seem to have particular bearing on similar Pentecostal testimonies.

203. Cf. Grele, "Movement Without Aim," 126-43, and Ritchie, *Doing Oral History*, 19-29.

204. See S.A. Ellington, "The Costly Loss of Testimony," *JPT* 16 (2000), 48-59.
205. This section dialogues with Meredith B. McGuire and Grant Wacker.
206. See M.B. McGuire, "Testimony as a Commitment Mechanism in Catholic Pentecostal Prayer Groups," *JSSR* 16:2 (June 1977), 165-68. Interestingly, J.F. White, *Roman Catholic Worship: Trent to Today* (Collegeville, Minnesota: Liturgical Press, 2003), recounts the rise of the Catholic Pentecostal/Charismatic movement and its (eventually) welcome reception, including the continuing importance of prayer meetings (as described by McGuire), 135. Cf. E.D. O'Connor, *The Pentecostal Movement in the Catholic Church* (Notre Dame: Ave Maria Press, 1971). See also K. McDonnell, *Charismatic Renewal and the Churches* (New York: Seabury Press, 1976).
207. See Wacker, *Heaven Below*, 68-69. Perhaps many Pentecostals would be unsurprised to hear sociologists J.A. Holstein and J.F. Gubrium, *The Self We Live By: Narrative Identity in a Postmodern World* (Oxford/New York: Oxford University Press, 2000), argue the interrelatedness of self identity and human narrativity. Psychologists D.P. McAdams, R. Josselson, and A. Lieblich, eds., *Identity and Story: Creating Self in Narrative* (American Psychological Association, 2006), argue that people living in modern societies give meaning to their lives by constructing and internalizing self-defining stories. Irrespective of how Pentecostals might argue about the details of narrative construction and identity formation, some connection between one's story/testimony and one's self-identity/understanding seems clear enough.
208. Wacker, *Heaven Below*, 68-69.
209. Wacker, *Heaven Below*, 69.
210. Wacker, *Heaven Below*, 69.
211. See Ellington, "Costly Loss," 49. This tendency helps account for the pattern of constant testimony in Pentecostal gatherings. See Synan, *Century of the Holy Spirit*: P.A. Deiros and E.A. Wilson, "Hispanic Pentecostalism in the Americas," 293-324 (307, 323), D.E. Harrell, Jr., "Healers and Televangelists after World War II," 325-48 (341), Synan, "Streams of Renewal at the End of the Century," 349-80 (368).
212. Ellington, "Costly Loss," explains that the loss of lament and testimony in the Pentecostal community tends to open up doors for illegitimate expressions of fear and anger in the life of faith as well as for confusion and failure, 58-59. Cf. S.A. Brown and P.D. Miller, eds., *Lament: Reclaiming Practices in Pulpit, Pew, and Public Square* (Louisville, KY: Westminster John Knox, 2005). Interestingly, in this volume B.K. Blount, "Breaking Point: A Sermon," 145-54, thinks the biblical treatment of testimony is sometimes ironic in that the same testimony can be a source of both suffering and victory, 151 (on Rev. 12:11). See also A. Weems, *Psalms of Lament* (Louisville, KY: Westminster John Knox, 1995).
213. Specific interfaith applications of testimony await the next chapter. However, note here for an example how Moltmann belatedly discovered that listening to the stories/testimonies of Holocaust survivors greatly enhanced the Jewish-Christian dialogue process in which he and post-war German theologians engaged. See Moltmann, *A Broad Place*, 276.

Chapter 5

Testimony as a Resource for Interreligious Dialogue

Introduction

Previous chapters have endeavored to set forth the context out of which the present one arises and to which it applies. First, the reality and philosophy of religious pluralism calls for immediate, urgent treatment by all the major world faiths, including Christianity. Pentecostalism of course, should approach this problem and opportunity in a manner consistent with its authentic identity. Second, the current state of Pentecostal theology of religions indicates Pentecostalism itself is rapidly advancing a theology of religions in constructive and distinctive directions. An inclusive Pentecostal theology of religions seems to be forming, one that endeavors to be true to its roots in creative ways adequate for its present and its future. Third, though Pentecostals are beginning to marshal rich resources of their pneumatic experience and teaching for application in dialogue with religious others, increasingly clear is that Pentecostalism needs a model for dialogue with familiarity and specificity from within the movement. The suggestion is that the category of testimony will serve well.

The immediately preceding chapter suggests great energy and vitality are characteristic of Pentecostal testimony. Accordingly, it may be an exceedingly energetic and rich resource for appropriation in interreligious encounter and dialogue. The present chapter specifically explores the tradition of testimony as a resource for interreligious dialogue. It will approach this task by mining the major implications of the last chapter on testimony for application at the dialogue table.[1] It will address practical as well as theological issues. Therefore, the present chapter is intended as the most constructive and creative endeavor of this overall study, and is of critical and pivotal significance. According to the carpentry mapping model it would represent the interior of the house.

Basis for Dialogue[2]

Inherent Applications

A Key to Continuing and Increasing Energy and Vitality. Pentecostals tend to define testimony in a functional mode. For example, testifying can be an important means of receiving and retaining one's own experience of divine blessing, say of divine healing.[3] A thought is present that failure to testify of what God has or is doing could result in diminishment or loss of the benefit. Testimony in this sense is not entirely or only for the other but is needful for oneself. Implicit in this theology of testimony is an affirmation of the power of inspired speech in the process of constructing reality.[4] Biblically, the creative power of speech is a divine characteristic to some extent graciously shared with those of receptive, prayerful faith (cf. Gen 1:3, 6, 9, 14, 20, 24, 26, 29; Mk 11:20-25).[5] Practically, testimony, therefore, may be a means of receiving and then subsequently retaining a promise of divinely blessed reality.[6]

Pentecostal engagement in interreligious dialogue through testimony suggests a process in which Pentecostals themselves are the first to benefit. Conversely, failure to do so is to their detriment. Pentecostals believe God raised them up to bear witness, to evangelize, and to testify, and that ceasing to do so will undermine their original identity.[7] Though Pentecostals have not typically applied this understanding to interreligious dialogue, there is no cogent reason for excluding it. Accordingly, as Pentecostals testify before religious others, they themselves are also blessed.[8] First, testimony before religious others helps Pentecostals retain their original energy and vitality. Far from compromise or condescension, testimonial engagement with religious others can be an important part of being faithful to their original ethos.[9] Second, testimony before religious others helps Pentecostals receive ever deepening enrichments of spiritual energy and vitality. Sharing one's innermost, intimate experiences of the Spirit of Christ before those of other faiths can actually elevate one's levels of intensity and maturity.[10]

If Pentecostals want to avoid the dreary road to dry institutionalism that so often can come over time to the many charismatic groups,[11] perhaps one way to do so is to take the telling of their testimonies beyond the stain glass windows and safe walls of their church buildings before communities of no faith or of other faiths. Such a process seems guaranteed to move them (or anyone else) beyond casual or complacent commitment. Pentecostals believe they have experienced and do experience the presence and power of God's Holy Spirit in a special way.[12] However, if they do not tell others about their experience of Christ's Spirit, if they do not testify of it, if they become introverted or isolated, then, according to their own standards, they could lose it. The movement of Pentecost out into the world, including into the world of religions, through its testimony of God's graciousness, is essential to its own survival and sustenance.

A Door to Deepening Understanding. The nature of Pentecostalism's distinctive spirituality and theology is such that one cannot adequately explain or understand it in purely propositional terms.[13] For Pentecostals to enter interreligious encounter and dialogue as if it is a only or mostly a doctrinal discussion among competing conceptual systems would not only be inappropriate, it would be tragic.[14] Pentecostals more appropriately and effectively access and articulate their experiences of the Holy Spirit through stories and testimonies. Pentecostalism is not about creeds and confessions. It is about divine encounter.[15] This statement need not negate the necessity of solid biblical teaching and theological development. In fact, if anything, in a way they are even more essential for the role they do play in providing balances and boundaries of the acceptable parameters of belief and practice. However, it does reveal the inadequacy of cognitive categories alone to communicate Pentecostalism's inner ethos.[16]

Pentecostal interreligious dialogue participants, therefore, should not attempt to press themselves into the mold of "mainline" Christianity in its typical approach of cognitive conversation.[17] They should come to the dialogue table prepared to tell stories, to give testimonies that for them communicate and illustrate their own inner identity. As their partners begin to understand them authentically, then there will be room for discursive discussion as relationships progress. Ideally, it may even lead to others sharing their stories in return. Accordingly, Pentecostals could then authentically understand their partners as well. In a resulting reciprocal movement mutual understanding and appreciation can occur.

None of this is due to any inherent rational weakness in Pentecostalism. For example, it is simply not the case today that Pentecostals lack the sophistication required for discursive discussion. Rather, the nature of Pentecostalism surpasses and transcends cognitive categories. Pentecostalism is not sub-rational but supra rational.[18] Though testimonial narrative may to an extent lack the precision theologians and others properly appreciate, it nonetheless opens up the heart of Pentecostal faith and life in an especially insightful way.[19] In some ways, it is more profound, more powerful. It is almost like the difference between prose and poetry. Poetry is so much more than sentence structure and syntax. Testimonies are like Pentecostal poetry.[20] They are a Pentecostal way of telling what is really inside them.[21] Accordingly, they can help others to do something that is critically important to the dialogue process: gain an insider's view of another faith. If interreligious dialogue appropriately has as one of its primary goals an enhanced reciprocity of understanding then storytelling and testimony around the table is essential for effective Pentecostal participation.[22]

A Chance to Share and a Challenge to Change. For Pentecostals, approaching interreligious dialogue through testimony suggests a goal of mutual moral and spiritual formation and transformation.[23] Arguably, people of faith—all faiths—are in a process of development helped along through interaction with others involved in the same, or at least in some ways, a similar, endeavor. Ideally, they are not present only for information or entertainment. Of course, nothing is wrong with either. However, change may not be limited to the intellectual or bound by the political. It ought to be moral and spiritual as well else it is not true to the ultimate nature of religious faith.[24]

For Pentecostals, interreligious testimony is still a telling in faith of how the Christian story as told in Scripture gets lived out in contemporary lives by the power of the Spirit.[25] Religious others may be then expected and invited to respond according to their own perceptions. Here testimony contributes to dialogue as it involves genuine exchange between participants.[26] Of course, discernment and judgment are necessary in evaluating testimonies offered around the dialogue table.[27] From the Pentecostal perspective, Scripture and the anointing of the Holy Spirit give reliable and worthy guidance. The contextual environment of the historical or traditional community of faith and the input of rational thought are also helpful aids.[28] Presumably, the rich traditions of religious others will also provide them with tradition specific standards by which to hear and evaluate testimonies. Comparing and contrasting not only the respective testimonies, but the standards of evaluation may be at times one of the most informative and interesting aspects of some dialogues.[29]

Of primary importance is participation.[30] Everyone should be encouraged to share and/or interact with those who do share.[31] One of the differences between testimony and other forms of public sharing, such as, for examples, academic lecturing or presenting position papers, which admittedly have their proper places too, is its superior ability through story to draw everyone in as interested and respected participants and partners. Everyone loves a good story. Pentecostals are good storytellers too. If a story were not good enough, they would probably assume that somehow someone is missing the most exciting point of what God is doing in a real human life. Pentecostal interreligious testimony, therefore, may arguably involve a greater number of participants at deeper levels of emotional interaction than approaches show casing the cerebral.[32]

Exceedingly important is not to overly anticipate *how* lives change through interreligious dialogue. That is, many different types of development and enrichment, entirely consistent with each respective faith, may occur that do not qualify as conversion in a technical sense.[33] Here is one of the thorniest themes in interreligious dialogue. Is the goal of dialogue conversion?[34] Well, perhaps yes and no.[35] In a general sense, all change may be "conversion" to a degree. Conversion is not necessarily changing one's religious affiliation so much as it is positive transformation in one's relation to God, to the world, and to others.[36] Undeniably, Pentecostals still do believe strongly in crisis conversion experiences of repentance and regeneration.[37] However, increasingly Pentecostals are discovering that conversion may involve both process and crisis more so than exclusively one or the other.[38] Especially in interreligious dialogue, one should not presuppose too much about what to expect. One must leave such things up to God. Allow the Holy Spirit to work according to the will of the Lord. Furthermore, a significant advantage of Pentecostal testimony is its assumption that spiritual formation and transformation ought to occur all around.[39] That is, both speakers and hearers reciprocate in the spiritual reality recounted. Pentecostal interreligious testimony does not mean that Pentecostals arrive at the dialogue table looking for an excuse to "preach" to a "captive" audience for purposes of gaining converts. Everyone has a chance to share and a challenge to change.

The Way of Worship. Pentecostal testimony is a distinctive act of ritual worship.[40] As such, it is addressed primarily to God and is expressed primarily for God. True to Pentecostal worship experience and understanding, testimony focuses on the realized presence of God as it facilitates a dramatized divine-human encounter through sharing together in the Spirit what God is doing in and among his people through faith in Christ.⁴¹ Speakers are rehearsing God's words and deeds as a public act of personal praise.⁴² True, listeners are invited to judge what is heard that they might potentially join in giving praise. Yet as already stated above that is always a matter of discerning decision.⁴³ Ideally, all can gladly give glory to God together for God's mighty acts among the people. Intriguingly, this mutual giving glory to God may at times involve Pentecostals in praising God for God's work in and among religious others as well.⁴⁴

Therefore, one of the primary advantages of Pentecostals engaging in interreligious dialogue through utilizing testimony is that they may see themselves as giving glory to God in the presence of religious others.⁴⁵ Why should Pentecostals engage in interreligious dialogue? Because it is true to an all-important part of their tradition, the joyous privilege of giving glory to God in Spirit-inspired and Spirit-energized worship (John 4:21-24). Questions of conversion and issues of doctrinal debate aside, interreligious dialogue is an opportunity for Pentecostals to praise and worship God. Pentecostals tend to note that praise and worship are exciting essentials of their experience of the Holy Spirit baptism and spiritual gifts.⁴⁶ In fact, some Pentecostals insist that it is not coincidental that the Pentecostal manifestations of the Spirit they prize so highly repeatedly occur in contexts of corporate blessing, praise, prayer, and worship.⁴⁷ Accordingly, it does not seem incredible that Pentecostals should engage in interreligious dialogue in testimony as a manifestation of God's words and deeds in expectation that the sovereign Holy Spirit might move in the process (1 Co 12:7, 11).

Of course, the suggestion is not being made that Pentecostals can or should try to transform the dialogue table into a Pentecostal worship platform. That would not be appropriately respectful of their dialogue partners.⁴⁸ Neither would it be seriously submissive to the scriptural injunction that "everything should be done in a fitting and orderly way" (1 Co 14:40 NIV). Rather, the insight here shared is simply that Pentecostals can approach interreligious dialogue through testimony as an act of worship. They are not present primarily to convert or to convince. They are present to give glory to God. The expectation may also be present in their minds that in ways determined only by the divine will that the Holy Spirit may work in that process to bringing glory to the Lord in the presence of others. Regardless however, of others' evaluation, Pentecostals themselves may enter dialogue in adoration of their Lord and Savior.

Notable Features

Cross Cultural Connections. The Pentecostal distinctive of testimony arises naturally enough out its unique spirituality and theology which has been in turn heavily influenced and informed by non-Western forms of religious faith cultures. For an important instance, the heritage of African American slave religion in Pentecostal Christianity has contributed greatly to the narrativity-orality nature of the movement, including its ongoing emphasis on testimony. Pentecostal testimony reaches back to the East even as it reaches out to the West. It bridges both hemispheres.⁴⁹ This fact potentially enables Pentecostalism to transcend the usual lamentable limitations of a rationalist approach to Christian faith and conversation overly reliant on Western conceptual categories with its Eurocentric/Enlightenment history.

In actual practice, the Eastern-Western conceptual divide often hinders interreligious dialogue dramatically.[50] Other religions, not so bound by Western philosophy as is what may be termed incautiously "conventional" Christendom, simply do not find themselves talking about the same things in the same ways as their Christian partners. Either that or they find themselves unfairly pressured, intentionally or not, to adopt and adapt categories foreign to their native faith in order to converse "intelligently". Moreover, Christians also struggle with understanding and being understood within the scope of their traditional cognitive and communicative patterns.[51] At times like these, interreligious dialogue can seem a delightful dream frustratingly confronted with almost insurmountable obstacles.

However, Pentecostal testimony admirably transcends the Eastern and Western communication hurdle between the world religions. Again, it bridges both hemispheres.[52] In addition, oral narrative is a rich resource for interreligious dialogue precisely because it is capable of carrying the most sublime of ideas in a mode that is accessible and even enjoyable: story.[53] The history of humanity confirms this intuitive reality. It is not for nothing that the Hebrew and Christian Scriptures are predominately in narrative form. Along with the enduring and insightful power of myth in all societies, this confirms the ability of story to say what cannot be otherwise so well said. Testimony therefore assists Easterners and Westerners, non-Christians and Christians, in overcoming one of the chief challenges to communicating with one another.[54]

None of the above, however, construes that there is no place for cognitive conceptualization in interreligious conversation. Rather, it balances out the unfortunate fact that discursive ideas overly dominate so much of such conversation by adding to and thus enriching the process with a greater flexibility and variety. It is not either desirable or possible always or indefinitely to avoid what various religious experiences and ideas may mean in rational discourse among people of differing faiths. Yet neither is it the case that interreligious dialogue, or for that matter, any human conversation, is a purely propositional enterprise. Testimony allows for at least a measure of more openness in describing and expressing the innermost meaning of ultimately indescribable and inexpressible religious faith.[55]

Triadic Complex of Prayer, Testimony, and Dialogue. As important as testimony is in traditional Pentecostal belief and practice it does not stand alone, but is part of a balanced complex of blending components. These include prayer, preaching, singing, and spiritual gifts, especially speaking in tongues and divine healing. All are obviously oracular. These components may inform the practice of testimony in interreligious dialogue in several ways, though somewhat indirectly.[56] Again, one does not suggest that the dialogue table is an appropriate place for an outburst of speaking in tongues or Pentecostal preaching. However, these distinctively Pentecostal practices may form a matrix out of which Pentecostals approach dialogue. For instance, through advance preparation in prayer one avoids the temptation to approach interreligious dialogue as either debate between competing ideological worldviews or as only interfaith friendship building.[57]

Prayer is primary.[58] Prayer reminds ones one that interreligious dialogue is a spiritual encounter and not just an intellectual event or emotional experience. Prayer invites and expects divine participation and empowerment in the dialogue process. Moreover, for Pentecostals prayer often includes "praying in the Spirit" or praying in tongues, a particularly intense and intimate form of prayer.[59] Arguably, when one prays extensively and intensely in a spiritual mode prior to engaging in dialogue, the process will potentially take on energy perhaps not otherwise present. In a sense, atmosphere is everything. Pentecostal prayer sets the tone for Pentecostal testimony. Prayer and testimony are therefore inseparable.[60] This symbiotic state is especially significant for the task of interreligious dialogue. That means that prayer, testimony, and dialogue are inseparable.[61]

Participatory Liberty and Experiential Praxis. The Pentecostal oracular reputation arises rightly enough out of their conviction that the Holy Spirit supernaturally inspires speech in those full of God's Spirit (Acts 2:1-4).[62] Becoming better known are ecumenical aspects of their pneumatological narrativity and orality.[63] In actual practice, highly valuing Spirit-inspired speech results in a commitment to a perhaps unparalleled level of participatory liberty.[64] Testimony is a prime example of this tendency.[65] Although pastors and other preachers hold a special place in pulpit ministry, others enjoy a high level of input as well.[66] The anointing of the Holy Spirit is not limited to the bishopric, or to patriarchal or economic class. Laity, women, the poor, those not formally educated, and even the outright illiterate are often heard to share a "word of testimony."[67] At its best, the tradition of Pentecostal testimony transcends race well as class.[68]

For interreligious dialogue, a broad base of participation can be significant. Everyone can be involved. Interreligious dialogue ought not to be only about or between "the experts".[69] True enough, interreligious dialogue can be delicate business at points possibly requiring special experience or training.[70] However, until interreligious dialogue brushes past the academicians and pushes beyond the politicians into the grassroots give and take of congregational faith and life it will never have the impact it needs in order to facilitate interfaith relations. The tradition of Pentecostal testimony as a model for interreligious dialogue challenges one to find constructive and creative avenues for including the so-called common constituents of the faiths in interfaith conversations. Congregations need to meet and to talk.[71] The Pentecostal testimonial service itself may serve as something of a general paradigm for this process. A designated time of informal mutual sharing by lay people in a discerning but uncritical atmosphere may do more to help those of other faiths become really acquainted and comfortable with each another than all the formal dissertations and presentations ever made. True to Pentecostal style, trust in the Holy Spirit's gracious guidance serves well at this point of contact.

Shape of the Dialogue[72]

Telling the Right Testimony

Autobiographical Orientation. For all this study has said about storytelling and testimony, Pentecostal testimony is much more than merely good, or even great, storytelling. It is telling "his-story", the story of Christ, again. Yet it is even more than that. It is telling one's own life story caught up in the story of Christ, conveying its truth and power afresh and anew.[73] Utilizing Pentecostal testimony in interreligious dialogue is not just telling stories with a moral point to make or a spiritual perspective to pass on to others. The kind of story told is of considerable importance. The selection of testimonies for telling before an interfaith audience is therefore an especially significant process requiring careful standards of assessment.[74] For Pentecostals, however, the guidelines are clear. For one thing, an autobiographical orientation is essential.

The temptation to tell well-crafted generalized, and therefore potentially anemic, homilies should be resisted at all costs. The power of Pentecostal testimony resides in demonstrating that the ongoing consistency of Heb 13:8, "Jesus Christ is the same yesterday and today and forever" (NIV), applies in contemporary human lives.[75] That demonstration is most convincingly accomplished through what has happened directly to the teller. That is what a Pentecostal testimony involves. In interfaith dialogue testimony, therefore, Pentecostals should share out of their own experience. Unapologetically, though sensitively of course, Pentecostals can speak before religious others about what they believe God has done and is doing in their own lives through Christ by the power of the Holy Spirit. Anything else is less than true Pentecostal testimony.[76]

The vulnerability of faith is evident in such a testimonial-dialogical process. Faith shows in a speaker's assurance that one's own life can potentially speak to others about ultimate reality.[77] Vulnerability is present in an acknowledgement that perhaps not all hearers will equally affirm its validity for themselves. Yet a testifier voluntarily places him/herself in the position of presenting what has happened to them in the context of their own faith. The testifier is, or ought to be, completely convinced in their heart and mind that their personal narrative exemplifies the ways of the Lord in their particular existential context. Moreover, he/she also believes that where others' existential reality intersects with theirs similar though distinctive results may be reasonably expected from a God whose self-revelation unquestionably suggests congruity, dependability, and reliability. Nevertheless, a testifier does not seek so much to persuade as to present. Admittedly, rejection of one's own story, even if only of its specific applicability to or for another, can be painful and might move some to a defensive posture. One should avoid that unacceptable outcome assiduously. A testifier ought always to leave the results of their words to the working of the Lord in the hearts of hearers according to the guidance of their own conscience.[78] More than adequate compensation is those times of overcoming barriers to understanding between those of other faiths as a testimony "rings true" in the hearts of its hearers.[79]

Biblical and Theological Foundations. Pentecostal testimony involves an ongoing dynamic between human experience, the biblical story, and God.[80] In Pentecostal testimonies, this reciprocation creates and undergirds an exciting and open-ended but nonetheless well-grounded account of divine activity in Christ today.[81] Accordingly Pentecostal testimony, interfaith or otherwise, is not simply telling one's life story or sharing interesting snippets from it. It is specifically descriptive of how biblical narrative and autobiographical narrative intersect and inform one another. This interrelatedness implies a certain selectivity and style in the telling. For the purpose of interreligious dialogue, one selects and shares testimonies based on how they correlate and integrate what becomes an almost seamless biblical-autobiographical narrative.[82]

One of the most fundamental of values of the Pentecostal faith is quite quotably couched in Malachi 3:6: "I the LORD do not change" (NIV).[83] Pentecostals popularly take this to mean that the God of the Bible speaks and acts today in complete consistency with the divine words and deeds in the Bible.[84] Testimonies endeavor to lift up this philosophy in irrepressible fashion. For example, true to the Exodus history of ancient Israel, a strong emphasis on divine dependability for deliverance is prominent in Pentecostalism.[85] Therefore, Pentecostal testimonies abound with stories of how believers went through almost unbearable battles but through perseverant faith were inevitably and usually dramatically rescued by the power of God from an apparently doomed situation and ushered into enjoyment of almost indescribable blessings and promises.[86] To be true to the inner ethos of Pentecostalism, interreligious testimony ought to highlight this aspect of their identity and self-understanding. Interfaith testimonies should tell of how Christian faith from a Pentecostal perspective encounters and addresses the vagaries and vicissitudes of life today as God works deliverance.

Sometimes one's story includes dramatic tales of drug and alcohol addiction, sexual immorality, or even penal incarceration. Otherwise, it may include the unfortunately always prevalent but less dramatic dehumanization of spirit and soul endured by human beings living in a modern materialistic maze that often subtly afflicts, binds, and drains them of the divinely destined reality of their full, real self. Either way, Pentecostals interpret God's gracious intervention in terms of divine deliverance commensurate with the biblical experience of Israel paradigmatically displayed in the Exodus event and repeatedly displayed throughout the Hebrew Scriptures, and ultimately, climaxed and consummated in Christ.[87] Significantly, Pentecostal testimonies stress not only deliverance from the afflictive and negative but also enjoyment of the abundant bounty of grace, or entrance into "the land of promise". They may tell not only of spiritual but also of physical, emotional, and financial blessings and provisions. They are convinced that Christ came in order that "they may have life, and have it to the full" (John 10:10 NIV). Sharing sensitively but unreservedly these stories of deliverance and abundance is altogether appropriate for interfaith dialogue designed to glorify God and allow others an insider's view of one's own faith journey.[88]

Listeners may notice a note of triumphalism in Pentecostal testimonies, even in an interfaith context. Correctly considered, Pentecostal triumphalism is not the issue sometimes suggested.[89] Pentecostals very much recognize and even emphasize the reality of the trials and tribulations of everyday existence in this life "below."[90] In fact, they decidedly stress themes such as spiritual warfare, or doing battle against debilitating and destructive forces believed to originate in the demonic realm. But for Pentecostals, the glory of Heaven comes down into the gravel of this world and elevates it into the grace of victorious faith. One might say they move from "Hell on earth" to "Heaven below".[91] In interfaith testimonies, Pentecostals will likely find it necessary to note these nuances clearly for religious others.

For Pentecostals, a testimonial dialogue approach means the story of Christ and of Christ's Spirit is central and crucial to the telling. The virgin birth, sinless life, sacrificial death, bodily resurrection, and ascension into glory of Christ apply redemptively to human life today.[92] Furthermore, the outpouring of the Holy Spirit at Pentecost energizes and infuses the story of human redemption and witness with divine power. However, a particular theological locus, known as "the full gospel", emphatically informs Pentecostal spirituality and theology.[93] As noted previously, the specifics of the full gospel are its firm faith claim that Jesus is savior, sanctifier, Spirit baptizer, healer, and soon coming king. It is appropriate, therefore, that Pentecostal testimonies delivered at interfaith dialogue tables delineate these dynamics. These loci provide a rubric out of which to arrange Pentecostal testimonies for presentation to religious others. It is not desirable, feasible, or probably even possible to tell everything about one's faith-life testimony.[94] Yet for clarity and concision, how the full gospel impacts one's individual life is essential for religious others even to begin to understand who Pentecostals are and what they are all about as Pentecostal Christians.

An important note is worth pointing out. As Pentecostals, more or less like others but pressingly so still, sit at the dialogue table with religious others they have a multifaceted task before them.[95] First, they generally represent all people of faith. Second, they specifically represent the Christian faith. Thirdly, they precisely represent Pentecostal faith. Presumably, everyone at the table shares the first task. Depending on whether it is a bi-lateral or multi-lateral dialogue, there may be Christians of various traditions present. In either case, Pentecostals can only contribute effectively as for their final tier of representation by telling who they really are in and of themselves in distinction from others. Especially for non-Christians, understanding inner distinctions between Christian groups can be challenging in itself. Pentecostals will discover it practical to aid their interfaith friends through honestly and humbly sharing testimonies arranged around their full gospel framework. Doctrinal definitions or ecclesial descriptions will not be adequate. Testimonies of full gospel belief and practice alone will suffice.[96]

Otherwise, as experience shows, the relation can easily degenerate into a misunderstanding that Pentecostals are just more extreme elements of the broadly Christian group. These miscomprehensions have led to Pentecostals being wrongly but widely identified almost exclusively with fundamentalists and even more fanatical fringes of the Christian religion. Pentecostals owe it to others and to themselves to clear up such misinformation and misidentification. The facts are that Pentecostal belief in the dynamism of the Spirit makes them much more amenable to fresh insights and experiences than the stereotypical portrait often painted. But it is difficult to capture Pentecostal dynamism in purely propositional terms.[97] It stands out most clearly in their full gospel narrative.[98] Full gospel testimony uniquely combines and encompasses Pentecostal self-understanding and personal experience; therefore, it is an excellent avenue for bypassing or surpassing the ideological stereotyping of Pentecostal devotees and for helping others authentically to know who they really are in their innermost ethos.

Telling the Testimony Right

Pastoral and Prophetic Application. Arising out of the congregational context of typically marginalized people groups, Pentecostal testimonies characteristically include dual emphases on pastoral and prophetic concerns.[99] Pentecostal testimony addresses issues revolving around the care of souls, family life, and practical day-to-day survival, even physical and emotional healing and battles with temptation. It also addresses critical concerns of the uneducated, of the poor, of women, and of the otherwise needy or disenfranchised and powerless.[100] Accordingly, the use of testimony in interfaith dialogue cannot miss or dismiss these concerns either. Interfaith dialogue cannot afford to sidestep the difficult issues of the life of faith in the contemporary world. Pentecostal testimonies in interfaith settings should forthrightly address practical though at times difficult or unpleasant realities of daily existence.[101] Conceivably, adherents of other religions will get to know Pentecostals better personally by this means than by all of the dogmatic formulations ever devised.

Pentecostal testimonies can help elevate awareness and understanding regarding life in this world as a person of faith. On the one hand, they can incorporate tales of congregational and pastoral life into their testimonies. Unfortunately, interreligious dialogue can often be quite cerebral and theoretical. Pentecostals can enhance the process by telling of how their faith works in the "trenches" of daily life. How is it that the Pentecostal experience informs and empowers believers as they face daily financial challenges? How does it affect spiritual, mental, emotional, and physical health and wellbeing? How does it influence personal familial and social relationships? What is it like to be a Pentecostal believer as far as one's devotional life and discipleship are concerned? How does a Pentecostal typically deal with the trials and tribulations of living in a less than perfect world order? Pentecostals have a characteristically comprehensive soteriology embracing a worldview that their acceptance of Christ and experience of the Holy Spirit directly touches and transforms all of life.[102] Their insights on the outworking of that multidimensional soteriology can be informative for others.[103]

On the other hand, Pentecostals can incorporate into their interfaith testimonies prophetic and pragmatic concerns.[104] Pentecostalism abounds with biographies of people who were poor or displaced but whose gifts of the Spirit began to be recognized and utilized. They frequently accomplished something fantastically memorable for the Kingdom of God. There are Black pastors who spearheaded international and interracial revival.[105] There are women who became leaders of denominations made up mostly of men.[106] There are untaught preachers who founded great universities.[107] There are farmhands who became global ecumenical representatives. Countless lives of Pentecostal believers reaffirm and reenact these success stories on local levels.[108] Sharing these kinds of testimonies in the presence of religious others, can conceivably be an instructive challenge for recapitulating a persistent pattern of personal and social liberation, elevation, and vocation.

A Single-Minded Motivation. Already observed above is the importance of approaching interreligious testimony as a verbal act of praise and worship.[109] It bears brief repetition here for Pentecostals bordering on the brink of embracing interreligious dialogue as an authentic Christian ministry gift of the Holy Spirit. Pentecostal testimony is liturgy or doxology.[110] That is, it is an offering of praise and worship to God. That alone is or ought to be sufficient to motivate Pentecostal participation. In the interreligious setting, Pentecostals through testimony avail themselves of an opportunity to give glory to God in the presence of those with whom they may have no other opportunity to do so. Becoming entangled in issues of potential compromise or the problem of conversion is simply a distracting detour. Though these are important concerns in their places, paramount is the priority of giving glorious praise to God in the tenor of Psalm 96:3: "Declare his glory among the nations, his marvelous deeds among all peoples" (NIV). Through testifying of God's "marvelous deeds", Pentecostals can and should declare God's glory among the nations and all peoples even, and perhaps especially, those of other world religions.[111]

Pneumatic Inspiration. Pentecostal testimony is not merely a telling but a showing.[112] Because of what Pentecostals believe is an experience of the Spirit's anointing upon speakers, Pentecostal testimony not only states spiritual insights but also demonstrates spiritual energy.[113] An advantage in using testimony in interreligious dialogue is its ability to transcend common communication. Not only the words said but also the way they are said becomes important. Often a transcendently joyful countenance and peaceful spirit are discernible. A vital spiritual energy is evident. Pentecostals believe this energy is present because they testify under inspiration of the Spirit.[114] Although it is difficult to define or describe, Pentecostal testimony accesses spiritual experience as much as it expresses it. For interreligious dialogue, such testimony suggests a way of helping others outside the Pentecostal tradition experience something of its heart and soul, a measure of its spiritual appeal and potency. When Pentecostal testifiers are inspired and anointed of the Holy Spirit, they become personal instruments or vessels of the Spirit's presence and power to those who are willing to be alike inspired and anointed to hear.

Arguably, what Pentecostals bring to the interreligious world is their conviction that at its deepest, starkest level real religion is about a personal encounter with the presence of God.[115] Therefore, for Pentecostals engaging in interreligious dialogue perhaps the chief challenge will be to seek humbly thus to be anointed of the Spirit of God and of Christ that they may become personal instruments or vessels of the Spirit's presence and power. Testifying before religious others ought to be executed in the agency of the Holy Spirit. Natural technique is inadequate. A sense of supernatural, spiritual presence is alone sufficient.[116] Listeners ought to be able personally to experience an encounter with the Holy Spirit through one's testimony.[117] The only realistic way for that to occur is if the testifier draws directly and deeply out of his/her own experience of the Holy Spirit in the telling. In a sense, this is Incarnational ministry in motion. The speaker bears the uncreated Spirit in his/her own fleshly, human life and words into the presence of others in the midst of this created world order. They then, like with Christ and like with Pentecost, may choose or refuse. But the actual experiential encounter must occur. So then, above everything else, Pentecostal dialogue participants will want to make the presence of God real around the dialogue table.[118]

Participant Qualification. The historical factuality of interfaith testifying should be carefully guarded. Fact and faith should be rooted in the same soil. Listeners should have every reasonable assurance that the events recounted occurred as described. Historical integrity in giving testimony accounts is essential. However, Pentecostal testimony is not simply a history lesson.[119] While it does not do less than tell the bare facts, it does much more as well. It views the facts through the lens of faith. Faith adds meaning to the facts. Pentecostal testimony appropriately describes what took place and what it means from the perspective of faith.[120]

Moreover, there is a difference between exaggeration and dramatization. The former makes more of the facts than is legitimately justified. The latter makes all of the facts that can be legitimately justified. Verity and faith are united. The determinative factor is truth in faith.[121] In other words, testimony is about the truth of faith and the faith of truth or, faith-truth, truth expressed in faith. What Pentecostal interfaith testimony should actually aim at accomplishing is to help others see what and why Pentecostals believe about God's intervening activity in their stories. There should never be any disillusionment about the dynamic of faith. Pentecostal testimony is not a descriptive statement with an invitation to draw a conclusion. That misses a vital middle step. It is a true story about what happened according to the conclusion drawn by faith with an invitation for hearers to believe also.[122]

Pentecostals, without behaving brashly, thus can nevertheless boldly tell their spiritual biographies.[123] Pentecostal testifiers should therefore be completely committed to the faith-truth of their testimonies and to the community of faith out of which they arise. Pentecostals should never be anything less than Pentecostal in their relations with religious others. Succumbing to any temptation to tone down their convictions will be untrue to their own identity and unfair to the integrity of their dialogue partners. Public testimonies exhibit their willingness to stand openly and unapologetically, though hopefully inoffensively, in explicit identification with the Pentecostal worldview.[124] At the dialogue table there often seems to be an unspoken pressure to affirm common ground. While identifying and appreciating commonalities is in itself a laudable endeavor to a certain extent, it is in identifying and appreciating "uncommonalities" where dialoguers may make the greatest progress. Accordingly, Pentecostals should be willing to talk about that which is most different about their own faith.[125]

Openly expressing one's faith through testifying is for Pentecostals a self-consecration to commitment.[126] Interfaith dialogue employing testimony therefore expresses strongly held and dearly loved commitments on the part of the speakers. Only those Pentecostals who can and do hold the distinctive commitments of the movement most staunchly and stoutly ought to be involved in interfaith dialogue testimony. Furthermore, when one bears public testimony of these personal commitments one ought to expect the sense of commitment in the diverse (and perhaps, at least occasionally, adverse) environment of the present interreligious context, to become, if anything stronger than ever.[127]

Making of the Dialogue

Thinking Ahead about the Event

With the outline of analysis already laid above, what remains is for a few practical steps of actually doing interreligious dialogue through testimony. This section arises out of my experience in interreligious dialogue in application of the principles of testimony this study is exploring. Though it focuses on the practical side, it flows out of the theological schema outlined thus far.[128]

Understandably, various dialogues have vastly differing dynamics.[129] Depending on whom the participants are, and what the particular context may be, many different issues may surface as of special significance. An effective dialoguer will anticipate in advance as much as possible the situation that he/she reasonably expects to occur. Questions about location and situation need no address here. These factors are usually in the hands of event organizers. However, for the purposes of Pentecostal testimony a few factors need consideration. First, who will be the participants? Knowing something about one's partners, at least in general, can be helpful, and it may affect testimony selectivity and delivery. It is not inappropriate to tailor one's testimony to a specific audience in order to address timely themes in a relevant fashion. Of course, "tailoring" in this context applies to selectivity and structure. In other words, to some extent the audience affects which testimony one tells and how one tells it.

Second, Pentecostal testimony tends to be more easily given in less formal or more devotional settings.[130] The extent to which one can influence such factors varies, but asking for an informal and devotional atmosphere can sometimes be a simple request. In some cases, the issue will be no more than making others aware that one intends to use testimony as a format for interfaith dialogue. Third, Pentecostal dialogue participants need to be adaptable and flexible. Fortunately, flexibility is one of the primary features of testimony. It may be that a certain approach to or order of discussion is arranged that does not allow for a specific protracted testimony. In such cases, the would-be testifier will need carefully to integrate several (if possible) shorter testimonies into the table discussion at helpful points. Caution against monopolizing the time of others needs to be considered, but still much profit can come from brief testimonies at a seasonable session.[131]

A Sample Story for Testimony[132]

The following is an actual testimony delivered by me several times in different interfaith dialogue contexts.[133] It intends to give in concrete form a suggestive guideline, in the sense of a sample, for implementation of the principles lifted up in the present study.[134]

> In the early 1960s when I was a small boy, under 2 years of age, I became quite seriously ill. This condition lasted for months. I lost my appetite, and when I did try to eat, I could not keep food on my stomach. I became pale and listless, as well as weak and emaciated, eventually even losing the ability to walk. During her husband's absence on an extended preaching tour, or a series of out of state revival or evangelistic tent meetings, my mother and I were staying with her mother in the southeastern Appalachian mountains of Perry county Kentucky. Although without insurance coverage or financial provision, she sought medical attention for me. As she could not drive an automobile, Mom's brother took us to a physician in Hazard, the nearest city, which was about 30 miles distant across hazardous mountain roads deep in coalmining country. Medical tests indicated severe problems with my blood. The doctor suggested I had leukemia. He also attested its probable terminal nature. He prescribed blood building and digestion aiding medicines, and sent us home. Neither proved effective, however. My condition steadily worsened. Anxious to the point of panic, my mother attempted to contact my father. I had not seemed seriously ill at his departure. At the time, there were no telephones in that remote region, so she had to rely on the slow process of writing a letter and waiting for a reply.
>
> Meanwhile, my father, a full time evangelist, or itinerant preacher, continued conducting revival services, protracted meetings designed to invite attendees to Christ and to promote divine healing and deliverance from demons, Spirit baptism, speaking in tongues, and other related charismatic phenomena. Not having yet received his wife's letter about the boy's condition, after preaching one night in Scott county Indiana, after just closing another meeting in Chicago, Illinois, he had a visionary experience. While in his room, he saw himself walking over and laying hands on his obviously seriously sick son, and saw his son rise up off a sick bed healed and whole. He immediately had prayer for his son's health and life. That very night the young minister wrote his wife a letter explaining what had occurred that evening. He mailed it early next day. He still had not yet received her letter. In fact, the letters passed each other in the mail. When he received her letter, he learned for the first time the specifics of their son's condition. When she received his letter, she learned for the first time of the miraculous revelation and provision that her husband felt God had made for their son.
>
> Even before my young mother received her husband's letter, an exciting and incredible development occurred. She had placed me on a homemade pallet, a pile of quilts, in a corner of the kitchen the better to watch me while she and my grandmother worked about the house. As stated, I had been unable to eat, walk, or even sit up very well. Suddenly, I sat up, and began asking for food. They fed me, and were again amazed that I did not become nauseous. In a little while, I began moving about and playing normally. I had been so unused to walking that I had to learn to walk again but took to it quickly. Then Mom received Dad's letter.

She immediately took me back to the doctor. Tests confirmed that I was perfectly well. Perplexed, the doctor said he did not know what to make of it. When she affirmed her belief that it was a miracle of healing, he acknowledged the same. From that time to the present, I have never had any further problems with my blood. Family and friends continually give glory and praise to God for this miraculous healing.[135]

A few years ago (around 2002-2003), I, now also a minister, in a time of meditation and prayer, experienced what I believe was a revelation from the Spirit regarding that early and dramatic healing. I had noticed that throughout my life I had not always experienced instant and complete healing of every illness. I used (and use) medical means when necessary. I felt the Holy Spirit revealed to me that this particular and admittedly dramatic healing was for a special purpose. My father and mother always, and still, insist that it was so that my life as a minister and preacher would not be prevented. In addition, I myself feel that the Spirit revealed to me that just as I experienced healing in my body, so God wills to heal the Body of Christ of its divisions, and to heal relations between Christians and those of other religions. Accordingly, my healing fits with and promotes the deeper purposes of God. Namely, for me pastoral, ecumenical, and interfaith ministry arises out of this experience of divine healing. I have since dedicated myself to pursuing those purposes.[136]

A brief analysis of the preceding testimony suggests that is in alignment with the principles outlined in this chapter. It is autobiographical, doxological, is consistent with Pentecostal interpretations of the Bible and of theology, communicates Christ in the full gospel, and it conveys the energy and anointing of the Holy Spirit, including spiritual gifts, and so on.[137] It even shows the historical personal and social context shared by many Pentecostals. In spite of the preeminence of a few urban centers, such as Azusa Street Mission in Los Angeles, a rural geographical setting and culture has been a prominent feature of Pentecostalism in the United States. Deep poverty, often leading to great familial personal sacrifices for the purposes of "spreading the word," is a common occurrence among adherents, including, and in some ways especially, among the clergy (or "ministry").[138] Furthermore, the reliance on the miraculous for which Pentecostals are so noted reveals itself as a pragmatic part of existence for those daily struggling against odds for which they plainly have no natural resources available for assistance. Their belief that they can and do receive miraculous intervention in the insurmountable obstacles of life is not theoretical; it is a matter of survival.[139] These observations represent significant features of Pentecostal faith best known through personal testimony.[140] Perhaps some of these would rarely manifest themselves at all in any other way. Arguably, some will be unknown altogether unless heard from those who have lived them.[141]

Finally, and for the performance of interreligious dialogue very important, this testimony has a clear purpose.[142] In this case, it explains to hearers that this particular Pentecostal's personal testimony has actually brought me to the dialogue table.[143] It reveals my innermost motive and self-understanding regarding my involvement in contemporary interreligious dialogue. It shows others where I am "coming from".[144] It invites others to join me if they will on a mission of mutual healing. Plainly put, I believe my miraculous healing as a child points to

God's providential calling and equipping for my ministry to others in proclaiming and bringing healing in ecumenical and interfaith contexts. This testimony can (and has and does) provide much for people to talk about at the dialogue table regarding Pentecostal involvement. For the present purpose, it shows one way Pentecostal might inform others about themselves and engage them in dialogue as well.

Hearing the Hearers

Ideally, one's interfaith dialogue partners can and will feel free to speak openly about some of their responses to one's testimony.[145] At times, this responsive interaction may occur more privately, on a more personal level. A surprising amount of interfaith work can occur during breaks in which participants frequently pair off to talk.[146] Dialoguers should avoid the natural urge to gravitate toward those of their own faith, and to attempt, so much as is possible, to converse with those of other faiths during these times.

In any case and at all times, the testifier needs to listen very carefully to their input. It will be essential in ascertaining whether or to what extent one's message is rightly understood, or that its intended faith-truth point is communicated well. Yet the listening is not only to make sure that one is him/herself being authentically heard; one should also make sure one is hearing the other authentically. Here the need for real listening to occur is paramount.[147] Testifying is not only about speaking. Good testifiers also listen to others' testimonies. One's own testimony may inspire someone, even a person of another faith, to share a testimony from his or her own story. Likely, when a person of another faith links a Pentecostal testimony with an experience in their faith journey and begins to liken them to one another, they together launch a level of dialogue that is deeper than any comparison or contrast of distinctive dogmas could have done.

Talking It Over Together

Again, ideally, there will be time and opportunity for discussing in the give and take of genuine dialogue what the faith-truth of one's testimony involves. At this point, everyone may know and grow together. At times even intentionally inviting this process may be appropriate and helpful as one comes to a closing of his or her testimonial sharing. Important to understand regarding this section versus the previous one, is that the emphasis in the former is on listening while here emphasis on discussion is resumed. At the risk of sounding as if one is advocating dialogue about dialogue, nevertheless talking together again about what has been said can be productive.[148] Like a transoceanic flight, in which reaching the desired destination, or in this case, the agreed upon goal, can require constant course corrections depending on conditions encountered, testimonies, like other kinds of conversation, often involve back and forth feedback for communicative clarity to occur.

Essential is that one communicate his or her real feelings and thoughts with religious others in dialogue.[149] Being real, that is, acting and speaking with authenticity in the sense of congruity with one's experience and perception of reality, is required for effective dialogue. The two-way communication of interreligious dialogue is not only about real listening, but also about real speaking.[150] Although testimony begins as a kind of one-way speech, one should approach it in a manner that invites and enables two-speech. In the communicative/dialogical encounter between religious others, expressing one's true feelings and thoughts is therefore essential for understanding and advancement to occur. In addition to aiding communication, that is also imperative for establishing a sense of trust on an emotional level.[151] Moreover, an environment of truth and trust, and they go together, is essential for maximal effectiveness in interreligious dialogue. Needless to say, emotional trust based on communicative truth does not negate the pragmatic wisdom of diplomacy and tactfulness. Insensitivity under the guise of honesty is inexcusable in volatile conversations. One's partner or partners need to know that one is both honest and humble.[152]

Thinking after the Audience

After the event has ended, one needs to reflect and, if necessary, revise one's understanding of what transpired through the giving and receiving of interfaith testimony.[153] It may be that future deliveries of the same or similar testimonies are informed and enhanced thereby. In one of the first encounters I had with interfaith testimony at the dialogue table, an African American Muslim woman gave her testimony in a dialogue at Hyde Park in Chicago.[154] She spoke of her upbringing in the South in a Christian home. She spoke of her rejection of Christianity due to racial conflicts with what she perceived as "a white man's religion". She spoke of a journey that for her accented recovering her racial heritage and identity through Islam. She touchingly shared her difficult but still intimate relationship with her parents (especially her father), who continue to be committed Christians. I found myself very moved by her "word of testimony." Afterward, I joined heartily in the group discussion around the relationship of race and religion that arose out of her testimony. Only upon later rumination, did I realize that, in addition to the power of her story itself, the power of her use of testimony deeply touched me. Then I was not surprised, given shared sentiments among African Americans and Pentecostals in the South, to discover this connection.[155]

On another occasion, I was invited to share with a Reformed Jewish group at a large synagogue in New York City (White Plains).[156] We had two meetings, one in the evening Shabbat service, then another in Shabbat School on the next morning. In the first, I chose to share my testimony of deliverance out of a life of drug and alcohol abuse, petty crime and jail time, and even agnosticism into a life of faith, joy, and peace through faith in Christ. Though I accented the inclusive nature of my faith, at times, the discussion afterwards was difficult and tense. However, overall it moved forward. The next morning in the follow up meeting, I preached and taught from the Hebrew and Christian Bible regarding Pentecostal Christianity. I sensed, and was assured by the supportive and receptive rabbi and congregation, an amazing energy and liberty. They extended the meeting in duration, and finally closing it only when another service began. The relationship between this Pentecostal (and my wife) and those precious Jewish people continues to be warm. In subsequent reflection, I concluded that even though difficult because of its inclusion of the controversial issue of conversion, the opening time of testimony prepared the way for deeper work together that might not have occurred at all otherwise. I also learned that I had not broached the subject of conversion in my testimony in the wisest way. I learned from that experience that not only the subject but also its presentation should be carefully crafted according to specific contexts. Furthermore, I learned that even when interfaith conversations take on a tense tone it does not mean the prevention of progress. Sometimes working together through difficult topics or with strong personalities can open up new vistas of trust. These and other comparable lessons have been invaluable in the continuing practice of dialogue.

Conclusion/Summary

The present chapter has explored the tradition of Pentecostal testimony as a resource for interreligious dialogue. It mined the major implications of the last chapter on testimony for application at the dialogue table, assuming as well the descriptive and theological work of the previous chapters. It has presented Pentecostal testimony as a feasible and viable resource for interreligious encounter and dialogue. The broad contours of this study suggest that testimony authentically connects Pentecostal tradition with the goals of contemporary interreligious dialogue. It thus embraces an environment of constructive continuity and creative connectivity promising great potential for progress in the current crisis of relations among the world religions. The next chapter will attempt to anticipate and answer possible objections to Pentecostal involvement in interreligious dialogue, including dialogical utilization of its tradition of testimony. Thus, this study will begin to move from the overtly constructive to the intentionally introspective.

Notes

1. Noting further the direct and indirect connections between the last chapter's overall study of testimony and its interpretive application in the present chapter may be helpful. The first two parts of this chapter directly arise out of a sequential and thematic development of the previous one. The third or last part of the present chapter is a practical application of its own previous two parts and, therefore, though less directly, draws on the previous chapter as well. This interlocking unfolding is important to remember in explicating the research process herein adopted.

2. M.L. Tan-Chow, *Pentecostal Theology for the Twenty-First Century* (Burlington, VT: Ashgate, 2007), insightfully discusses testimony in the context of "Interfaith Dialogue and the Issue of Truth," 162-64. For her, there are many levels of interfaith engagement but dialogue is not an optional one; rather, it is essential to mission, 162. Dialogue with religious others is "intrinsic to the nature of the triune God" and finds "justification in the incarnation and the movement of the Spirit" (162). The issue of truth between the religions is essential to face in dogmatic fashion, 162. Interfaith dialogue attempts to overcome "distortions of communication" that turn into separations and militate against peace, 162-63. Therefore, dialogue is not only verbal exchange but "a living encounter in thought and life that entails focused listening, generosity of heart and mind,

and mutuality and friendship" (163). One thus indwells the narratives of the other, 163. Accordingly, listening to the testimonies of religious others requires friendship, allowing the other's particularity and uniqueness to be revealed so that mutual understanding based on openness can be achieved, 163. However, C. Mayrargue, "The Expansion of Pentecostalism in Benin: Individual Rationales and Transnational Dynamics," 274-92, ed., A. Corten and R.R. Marshall-Fratani, *Between Babel and Pentecost: Transnational Pentecostalism in Africa and Latin America* (Bloomington, IN: Indiana University Press, 2001), argues that some forms of Pentecostalism can emphasize opposition and rupture with other religions, and even with other Christians, and that in that context testimony can serve as a strong symbolic act undergirding an antagonistic attitude, 286. Testimony thus dramatically conceived may be described in terms of "a relationship of force" regarding proselytism of other faiths, P.J. Laurent, "Transnationalisation and Local Transformations: The Example of the Church of the Assemblies of God in Burkina Faso," 256-73, Corten, *Babel,* 263. However, H. Cox, *Fire from Heaven: The Rise of Pentecostal Spirituality and the Reshaping of Religion in the Twenty-First Century* (New York: Addison-Wesley, 1995), recounts a strident public exchange between Pentecostals and Muslims in England that he described as "interfaith dialogue in the raw", 189, but still carefully guarded against "out-of-bounds behavior, 190.

3. G.P. Duffield and N.M. Van Cleave, *Foundations of Pentecostal Theology* (Los Angeles: L.I.F.E. Bible College, 1983, 1987), 402. Cf. A. Corten, "Transnationalised Religious Needs and Political Delegitimisation in Latin America," 106-23, Corten, *Babel,* 114.

4. Pentecostals tend to believe that anything done through merely natural ability is inadequate; therefore, prayer, song, testimony, or sermon must be done through spiritual agency and is a distinctively spiritual act and spiritual event, D. Jacobsen, *Thinking in the Spirit: Theologies of the Early Pentecostal Movement* (Bloomington, IN: Indiana University Press, 2003),122.

5. Cf. I.H. Marshall, *New Testament Theology: Many Witnesses, One Gospel* (Downer's Grove, IL: InterVarsity Press, 2004), 59 and 62-63.

6. F.L. Arrington, *Encountering the Holy Spirit: Paths of Christian Growth and Service* (Cleveland: Pathway, 2003), 20-21.

7. Interestingly, though in a different context, former General Overseer/Presiding Bishop of the Church of God (Cleveland, TN USA) makes a similar observation. See J.E. Cossey, "The State of the Church 2008: An Interview with G. Dennis McQuire," *COGE* (January 2008), 24-26 (24).

8. Fascinatingly, testimonies from those in other faiths converted to Christ by some miraculous occurrence do occur. E.g., see C.M. Robeck, Jr., "Junk, Thomas," *NIDPCM,* 814.

9. R.D. McCall, "Storytelling and Testimony: Reclaiming a Pentecostal Distinctive," unpublished Doctor of Ministry Dissertation, Columbia Theological Seminary, 1998, 36-59 (58).

10. McCall, "Storytelling and Testimony," 60-94 (93). Arguably, Pentecostalism uniquely testifies to a definite, personal spiritual experience. Cf. L.G. McClung, "Introduction: Truth on Fire: Pentecostals and an Urgent Missiology," ed., Grant L. McClung, Jr., *Azusa Street and Beyond: 100 Years of Commentary on the Global Pentecostal, Charismatic Movement* (Alachua, FL: Bridge-Logos, 2006), 77-88 (81).

11. Cf. Max Weber's sociology of religion on the transformation and routinization of charisma through institutionalization. See R. Bendix, *Max Weber: An Intellectual Portrait* (New York: Doubleday, 1960, 1962), 303-05, 327-28.

12. W. César, "From Babel to Pentecost: A Social-Historical- Theological Study of the Growth of Pentecostalism," 22-40, Corten, *Babel,* note that testimonies present this pneumatic encounter as an "indescribable experience", 31. R.P. Spittler, "Spirituality, Pentecostal," *NIDPCM,* 1096-1102, explains that Pentecostals are "Christians who value the Bible highly, take their commitment with the utmost seriousness, prizing the spontaneity of life in the Spirit and conveying all of this through oral testimony and 'sharing'" (1102).

13. C.M. Robeck, Jr., "Azusa Street Revival," *NIDPCM,* 344-50, stresses the spontaneity of early Pentecostal worship, describing a free flowing context of singing (with or without music), testimony, prayer, altar call, and preaching, 346. G. Wacker, *Heaven Below: Early Pentecostals and American Culture* (London, Eng: Harvard University Press, 2001), suggests many early services were a spontaneous and repetitive cycle of songs, testimonies, and choruses that lacked sermons entirely, 113. Yet Wacker admits that eventually "a loose pattern" including "singing, testimonies, prayer, sermon, and call to come forward to receive salvation, healing, and baptism" began to form, 107-08.

14. As R.J. Stephens, "Assessing the Roots of Pentecostalism: A Historiographic Essay," at American Religious Experience, http://are.as.wvu.edu/pentroot.htm (n. d.; site last modified October 2007). See also his *The Fire Spreads: Holiness and Pentecostalism in the American South* (Boston: Harvard University Press, 2007), has pointed out, downplaying the importance of doctrinal and theological issues in Pentecostalism is a mistake. However, Kärkkäinen, *Pneumatology,* also appears correct in contending that such categories are not what are most important. What is "important to note is that Pentecostalism emphasizes lived charismatic spirituality rather than discursive theology" (94). Significantly, Pentecostal publications often combine and intertwine doctrinal discussions and personal testimonies. See D.D. Bundy, "United Methodist Charismatics," *NIDPCM,* 1158-60 (1160). This integrative tendency appears even in scholarly studies, P.D. Hocken, "Montague, George T.," *NIDPCM,* 903. Furthermore, F.D. Macchia, "Theology, Pentecostal," *NIDPCM,* 1120-41, suggests Pentecostals have always "favored testimonies, choruses, and prayers over intellectual or critical reflection as the means by which to interpret the gospel, 1120. However, this does not mean Pentecostal theology is non-academic, but only that it has its own unique approach, 1120. Macchia says Pentecostal life "largely feeds theological reflection in the form of testimonies", 1122. He argues from early Pentecostal sermons and testimony as a way of understanding Pentecostal doctrine, 1131, and suggests Pentecostals have been misunderstood, even by close kin such as Charismatics, because of failure to mine their distinctive literature and testimonies, 1124. In fact, he suggests Pentecostal experience and testimonies are in a sense prior to theological constructs, though the former are also informed by the latter, 1123. Macchia even faults early Pentecostal's own attempts at systematic theology for failing to include their distinctive emphasis on experience and testimony, 23. Cf. F.L. Ware, "Spiritual Egalitarianism, Ecclesial Egalitarianism, and the Status of Women in Ordain Ministry," ed. E. Alexander and A. Yong, *Philip's Daughters: Women in Pentecostal-Charismatic Leadership,* Princeton Monograph Series (Eugene, OR: Pickwick, 2008), 215-34 (230, fn. 30).

15. C.J. Sanders, *Saints in Exile: The Holiness-Pentecostal Experience in African American Religion and Culture* (Religion in America) (New York: Oxford University Press, 1999), observes that "The critical aspect of testimony, as opposed to preaching, is its subjectivity; testimony conveys one's story of divine encounter in strictly personal terms" (84).

16. In many ways, Pentecostal identity runs counter to primary assumptions of modernism and rationalism, pointedly stressing the miraculous and paranormal, Kärkkäinen,

Pneumatology, 92-93, and therefore purely cognitive categories would be sorely insufficient.

17. I tend to use the term "mainline" as a concession to its popularity but with serious reservations as to its applicability. As Hollis Gause rightly notes, this terminology tends to marginalize Pentecostals and Charismatics especially, and even Evangelicals in general. He appropriately asks, "What is meant by mainline? Mainline from what origin and toward what destiny?" He insightfully adds, "If origin is the gift of Christ on the day of Pentecost (Acts 2) and destiny is the return of Christ (the Parousia), then Pentecostals would see themselves in this movement of God." Of course, the term perhaps arose to note numerical preponderance, but then that is no longer correct either. See Gause, "A Pentecostal Response to Clark Pinnock's Proposal," *JPT* 14:2 (April 2006), 183-88 (187).

18. K. Warrington, *Pentecostal Theology: A Theology of Encounter* (New York: T & T Clark, 2008), 130. Cf. V. Synan, "Evangelicalism," *NIDPCM*, 613-16.

19. Herein lays a controversial issue between mystical and theological interfaith conversations. See Cox, *Fire*, 208.

20. See J. Sepúlveda, "Reflections on the Pentecostal Contribution to the Mission of the Church in Latin America," *JPT* 1 (1992), 93-108 (98). Cf. Maslow, *Religions, Values, and Peak Experiences*, 84-85. See also M. Kelsey, *Discernment: A Study in Ecstasy and Evil* (New York: Paulist, 1978), 86-105 (esp. 86, 90-97).

21. Arrington, *Encountering*, 20-21.

22. Arrington, *Encountering*, 243.

23. A. Yong, *Beyond the Impasse: Toward a Pneumatological Theology of Religions* (Grand Rapids: Baker, 2003), suggests "in-depth engagement with religious others" involves and invites "genuine dialogues that produce authentic transformation in both parties" (182).

24. C.B. Johns, *Pentecostal Formation: A Pedagogy among the Oppressed* JPTSup 2 (Sheffield, England: Sheffield Academic Press, 1993, 1998), 130-31. A.E. McGrath, *The Future of Christianity*, Blackwell Manifesto (Malden, Massachusetts: Wiley-Blackwell, 2002), suggests one of the main reasons Pentecostalism's growth has been outstripping mainline Protestantism has been "because it stresses a direct, immediate experience of God, and avoids the rather dry and cerebral forms of Christianity which many find unattractive and unintelligible" (108).

25. Johns, *Pentecostal Formation*, 126-27. Interestingly, K.J. Archer, *A Pentecostal Hermeneutic: Spirit, Scripture, Community* (Cleveland, TN: CPT, 2009), argues that Pentecostal understanding of the Bible is open to public scrutiny even by non-Christians, 259, and exhorts the global Pentecostal community to come together "to share their testimonies and to discern a proper way of living as an authentic countercultural community whose life and power come from the Spirit" (260). Similarly, Sanders, *Saints in Exile*, describes the community of faith coming to an assurance of divine guidance through sharing testimonies, 24.

26. A somewhat rare but certainly outstanding example of official Pentecostal engagement in interreligious dialogue (i.e., Pentecostal-Hindu), and in which integrative testimonies play a pivotal role, is the Apostolic Christian Assembly (India). See R.E. Hedlund, "Apostolic Christian Assembly (India)," *NICPCM*, 322.

27. E.g., early Pentecostal eventually adapted their teaching on xenoalia (preaching in tongues or missionary tongues) because no one could produce "reliable testimony" verifying the practice, McGee, "Initial Evidence," 786. That they would be willing thus to adapt an important early doctrine speaks of the importance they attached to testimony and also to judging its reliability. Cf., however, A. Anderson, *Spreading Fires: The Missionary Nature of Early Pentecostalism* (New York: Orbis, 2007), 59-60, 61, 63. R.A.N.

Kydd, "Healing in the Christian Church," *NIDPCM*, 698-711, points out that in the historical healing ministry of the Church, even when "testimonies about healing were strong", a need to examine inadequately verfiable accounts existed; nevertheless, "some claims were impressive" (707). Cf. with the significance of 'a true testimony', in R.E. Hedlund, "Indigenous Churches," *NIDPCM*, 779-84 (782). A. W. Tozer, *The Best of Tozer: Book One* (Camp Hill, PA: Wingspread, 2007; repr. Baker, 1978), in a discussion on "How to Try the Spirits," particularly warns against allowing psychological or colorful elements in testimonies to sway against the clear testimony of Scripture, 189.

28. Cf. D.A.D. Thorsen, *The Wesleyan Quadrilateral: Scripture, Tradition, Reason, & Experience as a Model of Evangelical Theology* (Grand Rapids: Zondervan, 1990). Wacker, *Heaven Below,* warns that evaluating testimonies can be tricky business, perhaps saying as much or more about observers than the observed, 60.

29. J. Moltmann, *The Church in the Power of the Spirit: A Contribution to Messianic Ecclesiology* (London: SCM Press, 1977), 159, 161. For O. Kalu, *African Pentecostalism: An Introduction* (Oxford/New York: Oxford University Press, 2008), biographical testimonies serve as validation for the beliefs and practices of a religious community, 268, and thus Pentecostals draw directly from Scripture in generating an interface of faith and life, 269. Cf. 184. W. James, *The Varieties of Religious Experience* (New York: Triumph, 1902, 1991), expresses his aim "to keep the testimony of religious experience clearly within its proper bounds" (396).

30. Johns, *Pentecostal Formation*, 131-33 (133). Cf. V. Synan, ed., *The Century of the Holy Spirit: 100 Years of Pentecostal and Charismatic Renewal* (Nashville, TN: Nelson, 2001): P. Hocken, "The Catholic Charismatic Renewal," 209-32 (214, 219), and S.C. Hyatt, "Spirit-Filled Women," 233-64 (236).

31. K.J. Archer, *Pentecostal Hermeneutics: Spirit, Scripture, and Community* (Cleveland, TN: CPT, 2009), says that "Pentecostalism encourages high levels of community participation", adding that "testimonies or narratives of faith" are an important part of that process as an experience of the Holy Spirit, 256.

32. Johns, *Pentecostal Formation*, 81, 87. Cf. S.A. Ellington, "The Reciprocal Reshaping of History and Experience in the Psalms: Interactions with Pentecostal Testimony," *JPT* 16:1 (2007), 18-31 (24-27). Important to remember is the Pentecostal claim that their testimonial responsibilities include non-Christians, L.T. Holdcroft, *The Holy Spirit: A Pentecostal Interpretation* (Sumas, WA: CeeTec, 1999), 202.

33. E.g., Tan-Chow, *Pentecostal Theology*, suggests that interreligious dialogue and testimony require "a conversion of the mind and speech" as the Spirit leads into deeper truth and its communication (163). However, she also insists that either "imposition" or "repression" of truth is unacceptable, 163.

34. H.R. Ezzat, "Dialogue with Passion," *Changing the Present, Dreaming the Future: A Critical Moment in Interreligious Dialogue,* ed. Hans Ucko (Geneva: World Council of Churches, 2006), 22-27. Cf. R. Niebuhr, *Pious and Secular America* (New York: Charles Scribner's Sons, 1958), 108.

35. S Neill, *Christianity and Other Faiths: Christian Dialogue with Other Religions,* second edition (New York: Oxford University Press, 1961, 1970), asserts that in encounter and dialogue, the constant goal is to authentically represent and present Jesus Christ, 69, 124. Arguably, to convert or not to convert is simply in the hand and mind of God.

36. J. Oswalt warns, "We should not impose Christian patterns of conversion" on eschatological relations of the nations with the God of Israel although "it is to God, and because of God, that the nations are said to come". See *The New International Commentary on the Old Testament: The Book of Isaiah: Chapters 40-66* (Grand Rapids: Eerdmans, 1998), 546. Israel's privileged responsibility was not merely to make Jews out of

Gentiles but to reflect the Lord's glory that they might be drawn to it even more directly. Similarly, Christians involved in interfaith dialogue are not merely out to make converts to Christianity but to reflect and radiate the glory of the Lord for all to see it and to desire it for itself.

37. Yet F.D. Macchia, "Finitum Capax Infiniti: A Pentecostal Distinctive?" *Pneuma* 29:2 (2007), 185-87, argues against "absolutizing these [conversionary experiences of justification/regeneration, sanctification, and Spirit baptism] as rigid stages" (185). For him, Pentecostal redemptive experience allows and invites more of a view of life in the Spirit with "a beginning, a development, and an eschatological fulfillment (Eph 3:14-19)", 187. Nevertheless, as D.J. Wilson, "Church Membership," *NIDPCM,* 529-30, observes, "All Pentecostal churches require testimony of a conversion experience for admission to membership" (529). Note that conversion and testimony are closely linked in this case. Evangelism and testimony are also frequently linked, J-P. Bastian, "Pentecostalism, Market Logic and Religious Transnationalisation in Costa Rica,"163-82, Corten, *Babel,* 175.

38. At an interreligious dialogue in Lariano, Italy 12-16 May 2006, conducted by the Inter-Religious Relations Dialogue of the WCC and the Pontifical Council on Interreligious Dialogue of the Vatican, I presented "Pentecostal Theologies of Conversion: Assessing the Reality and Exploring Interreligious Applications." He compared and contrasted the "traditional" view, characterizing conversion as an express act, with the "dynamic" view, recognizing some flexibility and fluidity, and with the "developmental" view, emphasizing possibilities of pre-Christian experiences and processes on a continuum toward Christian conversion. For me these views are not mutually exclusive but do entail careful integration.

39. Pentecostal testimonies themselves tend to relate transformative encounters with the immanent presence of God occurring in miraculous contexts, Robeck, "Azusa Street Revival," 349. Wacker, *Heaven Below,* warns against sentimentalizing these testimonies (as if testifiers became always worry free ever after), 63, while recognizing their amazing life altering reality, 64. Cf. David Martin, *Tongues of Fire: The Explosion of Protestantism in Latin America* (Cambridge, Massachusetts: Wiley-Blackwell, 1993), 163.

40. Macchia, "Theology," explains that Pentecostal testimonies are "given to the glory of God in worship" (1122). Interestingly, even a favorite form of music in worship services for years among Pentecostals was the gospel hymn, a song of testimony. See D. Alford, "Music, Pentecostal and Charismatic," *NIDPCM,* 911-20 (915). Gospels songs are thought to offer "a vehicle for testimony and prophecy" to believers and unbelievers, 914. Sanders, *Saints in Exile,* explained the intimate connection of music with prayer, preaching, and testimony in Black Pentecostalism, 83-85, and also testimonies' prominence in and as worship, 51, 53. Cf. with the ritual and social context of Pentecostal conversion testimonies, L. Hubron, "Pentecostalism and Transnationalisation in the Caribbean," 124-41, Corten, *Babel,* 128.

41. Some Pentecostals believe their "distinctive testimony" is to the experience of this divine energy, D. Gee, "Spiritual Gifts and World Evangelization," McClung, *Azusa Street and Beyond,* 113. Cf. 109.

42. Cf. C.M. Robeck, "Pike, John Martin," *NIDPCM,* 988-89 (988). Of course, testimonies also serve as "a means to attract others or encourage the faithful", W.E. Warner, "Periodicals," *NIDPCM,* 974-82 (975).

43. Archer, *Pentecostal Hermeneutics,* provides personal testimonies an important place in discernment of spirits and validation of meaning, 256.

44. Of course, this will require what Amos Yong, *Beyond the Impasse,* calls "empathetic listening", 178. Cf. D.J. Hesselgrave, "Evangelicals and Interreligious Dialogue,"

Pittman, et al, *Ministry and Theology in Global Perspective*, 425-28, who considers promoting freedom of worship and witness an important task of dialogue, 426-27. See Johns, *Pentecostal Formation*, 130-38, and R.J. Boone, "Community and Worship: Key Components of Pentecostal Christian Formation," *JPT* 8 (1996), 129-42 (esp. 138-40).

45. Boone, "Community," 142. Cf. S.J. Land, *Pentecostal Spirituality: A Passion for the Kingdom* JPTSup 1 (Sheffield: Sheffield Academic Press, 1993), 80.

46. E.g., F.L. Arrington, "The Acts of the Apostles," *FLBCNT*, eds. F.L. Arrington & R. Stronstad (Grand Rapids: Zondervan, 1999), 543, 588-89, and 637. Of course, others also realize, though differently, the role of the Holy Spirit in the life of prayer and praise. See Of course, others also realize, though differently, the role of the Holy Spirit in the life of prayer and praise. See Y. Congar, *I Believe in the Holy Spirit* (*IBHS*) 3 vols. trans. David Smith (New York: Seabury, 1983), 2:113-14. Cf. 2:209-10.

47. See R. H. Gause, *Living in the Spirit: The Way of Salvation* (Cleveland: Pathway, 1980), 79-84.

48. Respect is an important element of the "humanization" of which Archer, *Pentecostal Hermeneutics*, speaks about in the practice of testimony (28).

49. See P. Jenkins, *The Next Christendom: The Coming of Global Christianity* (Oxford, UK/New York, NY: Oxford University Press, 2007), 8-9. McGrath, *Future of Christianity*, argues that Pentecostalism's effectiveness arises in part out of its ability to use "a language and form of communication which enables it to bridge cultural gaps", specifically stories, songs, and testimonies, 108-09 (108).

50. E.g., Moltmann admits frustrating failure in a Buddhist-Christian dialogue at the World Mission Assembly in Bangkok (29 December 1972-9 January 1973) arising primarily out of cross-cultural miscommunication or misunderstanding. See J. Moltmann, *A Broad Place: An Autobiography*, trans. Margaret Kohl (Minneapolis: Fortress, 2008), 170. Cf. the awkwardness of Korean Christians struggling with syncretism in the presence of a Western Christian, 179-80.

51. Increasingly even conservative Evangelicals are realizing that gospel truth involves much more than bare propositional reality. See J. Danaher, "Our Journey into the Truth, Beauty, and Holiness of the Gospel," *ERT* 32:1 (January 2008), 56-64.

52. Anderson, *Spreading Fires*, notes that Pentecostal missionaries frequently employed testimonies in public services; however, sometimes these were described by other, more established, mission personnel in terms of propaganda, 226. See *The Changing Face of World Missions: Engaging Contemporary Issues and Trends*, M. Pocock, G. Van Rheenen, D. McConnell (Grand Rapids: Baker Academic, 2005), 131-59 (note 145). Jenkins, *Next Christendom*, 8-9. Nevertheless, some early Pentecostal missionaries did attempt to use testimonies as a way of proselytizing other Christians, though not so much non-Christians. See G.B. McGee, "Missions, Overseas (N. American Pentecostal)," *NIDPCM*, 885-901 (889). However, V.M. Kärkkäinen, "Missiology, Pentecostal and Charismatic," *NIDPCM*, 877-85, notes that some have suggested personal testimonies, along with numerous other important factors, have played an important part in Pentecostal missions strategy and success, 877.

53. Including testimony, César, "From Babel to Pentecost," Corten and Marshall-Fratani, *Babel,* say of transnational Pentecostalism, "The spoken word is the motor which drives this new spirituality, and oral performance is the most important aspect of the religious service" (28). However, Tozer, *Best I,* explained that speaking long and loud is not the badge of spirituality: "Now a vigorous testimony, frequent prayers and loud praise may be entirely consistent with spirituality, but it is important that we understand that they do not in themselves constitute it or prove that it is present" (113).

54. See *Changing Face*, Pocock, et al, 343-45.

55. Tan-Chow, *Pentecostal Theology,* suggests effectively listening to the testimonies of religious others requires friendship, respects the other's particularity and uniqueness, and results in mutual understanding based on authentic openness, 163. Cf. Congar, *IBHS,* 2:219.

56. Cf. F.D. Macchia, *Baptized in the Spirit: A Global Pentecostal Theology* (Grand Rapids: Zondervan, 2006), 49-51. Cf. J.C. Poirier, "Narrative Theology and Pentecostal Commitments," *JPT* 16:2 (April 2008), 69-85 (70-72).

57. Cf. Tan-Chow, *Pentecostal Theology,* 90.

58. W.J. Hollenweger, "After Twenty Years of Research on Pentecostalism," *IRM* (January 1986), 3-12, relates and integrates, among others, elements of Pentecostal orality and prayer that depict a mindset of this kind (6).

59. For a brief overview of such Pentecostals practices see R.P. Spittler, "The Pentecostal View," *Christian Spirituality; Five Views of Sanctification,* ed. Donald L. Alexander (Downer's Grove: InterVarsity Press, 1988), 133-54 (147-49).

60. Early Pentecostal chronicler F. Bartleman, *Azusa Street* (originally *Another Wave Rolls In)* (New Kensington, PA: Whitaker, 1982), recounts how the Spirited intermingling of prayer, testimony, and praise produced "an atmosphere that something wonderful and imminent was about to happen" and "an assurance that the supernatural exists, and that in a very real sense" (21).

61. Not surprisingly, prayer and testimony often occur interchangeably or almost simultaneously. See, e.g., C.M. Robeck, *The Azusa Street Mission & Revival: The Birth of the Global Pentecostal Movement* (Nashville: Nelson, 2006), 66-69, 92-95, 136-44.

62. Some Pentecostal scholars even speak of "the prophethood of believers" in this regard. E.g., see R. Stronstad, *The Charismatic Theology of St. Luke* (Peabody: Hendrickson, 1984), 56, and F.L. Arrington, *The Acts of the Apostles: Introduction, Translation, and Commentary* (Peabody: Hendrickson, 1988), 28.

63. Because of its interlocking themes of speech expressing "unity-in-diversity", A. Yong calls Acts 2:1-12 "*an Ecumenical Prototype*" (subheading) in *The Spirit Poured Out on All Flesh: Pentecostalism and the Possibility of Global Theology* (Grand Rapids: Baker, 2005), 171-72. Cf. Martin, *Tongues of Fire,* 178, and also with D. Martin, *Pentecostalism: The World Their Parish* (Cambridge, Massachusetts: Wiley-Blackwell, 2008), 14.

64. Commitment to belief in Spirit-empowered ministry arising out of an experience of Spirit baptism often communicates into highly egalitarian forms of ministry practice. See E. Alexander, "Introduction," Alexander and Yong, *Philip's Daughters,* 3-4.

65. H.L. Turner, "Pentecostal Currents in SBC: Divine Intervention, Prophetic Preachers, and Charismatic Worship", ed., E.L. Blumhoffer, R.P. Spittler, G.A. Wacker, *Pentecostal Currents in American Protestantism* (Champaign, IL:University of Illinois, 1999), 209-28, notes a classification of Pentecostal testimony as a form of "prophetic activity" alongside "other spiritual gifts" (215). J.E. Powers, "Pentecostalism 101: Your Daughters Shall Prophesy," Alexander and Yong, *Philip's Daughters,* 133-51, agrees in that early Pentecostals saw as "prophetic ministry ... all forms of Spirit-empowered ministry of the Word" and that these included "preaching, teaching, testimony, supernaturally-inspired messages, words of exhortation, and encouragement"—all qualifying "as prophetic ministry" (144).

66. E.g., Robeck, *Azusa Street,* 2-4, 68-69, 143.

67. E.g., see J.R. Zeigler, "Full Gospel Business Men's Fellowship," *NIDPCM,* 653-54 (653). See also Sanders, *Saints in Exile,* 84. Testimonies abound also of those in a severe situation of hardship experiencing some kind of economic miracle, A. Pedro and

P. Semán, "Brazilian Pentecostalism Crosses National Borders," 181-95, Corten, *Babel,* 192.

68. See P. Freston, "The Transnationalisation of Brazilian Pentecostalism: The Universal Church of the Kingdom of God," 196-215, Corten, *Babel,* 210-11. A central theme of Robeck's *Azusa Street* is the race issue among Christian brothers and sisters experiencing Pentecost in the early days of the movement. E.g., see 12-16, 217-20, and 317-19. See Anderson, *Spreading Fires,* 175-76. Today it continues to be of import for many Pentecostals around the world. See J.W. Hayford with G. Howse and M. Posey, *Race and Reconsiliation: Healing the Wounds, Winning the Harvest* Spirit-Filled Life Kingdom Dynamics Study Guides (Nashville, TN: Nelson, 1996). Cf. D.E. Miller and T. Yamamori, *Global Pentecostalism: The New Face of Christian Social Engagement* (Berkley, CA: University of California, 2007), 55, 75.

69. Notably, M.L. Fitzgerald and J. Borelli, *Interfaith Dialogue: A Catholic View* (New York: Orbis, 2006) argue for more interfaith interaction at the parish level with intentional lay involvement. For them, restricting interfaith dialogue to professional hierarchical "Churchocrats" is an error. See esp. Part I, Chap. 4 and Chap. 5.

70. Cf. with the principles laid out for Pentecostal participation in interreligious dialogue by Samuel Solivan, "Interreligious Dialogue: An Hispanic-American Pentecostal Perspective," ed., S.M. Heim, *Ground for Understanding: Ecumenical Responses to Religious Pluralism* (Grand Rapids: Eerdmans, 1998), 37-45.

71. S.M. Heim, *Salvations: Truth and Difference in Religion* (Maryknoll, NY: Orbis, 1995, 1999), suggests that "the most obvious issues in dialogue are whom we shall choose to talk with (and who will choose to talk with us) and what we will talk about" (100). Significantly, he includes among the types of appropriate dialogue a "popular dialogue" mode, 100.

72. Tan-Chow, *Pentecostal Theology,* argues that "Pentecostalism, with its strong pneumatology and eschatology and its inherent ecumenical thrust" can be an agent of dialogue and peace in a world of religious plurality, xv-xvi (xvi). A central concern of her work is the contention that Pentecostalism "may contribute positively to human flourishing in the context of religious plurality and to construct a sustainable theology to negotiate the fundamentally complex issue of the religious other" (xvi).

73. In fact, Christian testimony arises out of and is rooted in the story of Christ and his gospel. See J.-D. Plüss, "Testimony," *GDT,* 877-79 (877). R.F. Culpepper, *The Great Commission: The Solution...* (Cleveland, TN: Pathway Press, 2009), firmly fixes the practice of personal testimony among Pentecostals in the overarching story of Jesus, 86-88..

74. This is in keeping with the Pentecostal habit of selecting and presenting testimonies in a highly stylized pattern, apparently with explicit purposes in mind. See Wacker, *Heaven Below,* 58-59.

75. Thus, Ellington, "Reciprocal Reshaping," makes a critical claim when he contends that in Pentecostal testimony the question addressed is not only "Did it happen?" but "Does it happen?" (30).

76. Arrington, *Encountering,* asserts that Pentecostal testimony is a listening and learning process of what the Holy Spirit has done in individual lives, 20-21. Cf. Moltmann, *A Broad Place,* 192-96 (195).

77. Pentecostals thus tend to think of testimonial content as on some level demonstrating the reality of God. See J. Sepúlveda, "Reflections on the Pentecostal Contribution to the Mission of the Church in Latin America," *JPT* 1 (1992), 93-108 (101).

78. Plüss, "Testimony," 877.

79. Johns, *Pentecostal Formation*, suggests Pentecostal stories and testimonies are conducive to a true participation in the story of salvation. It is as if "the voice of the people is, therefore, empowered by the Holy Spirit to become the speech of God" (81). James, *Varieties*, faced straightforwardly the question of whether "we ought to consider the testimony true", which he had found "unanimous" regarding "a common nucleus" of experience among the religions, and answered in the affirmative, 383-88 (383). He concluded that the testimony of the religions, "*is literally and objectively true, so far as it goes*", 388 (original italics), and that "God is the natural appellation, for us Christians at least, for the supreme reality"—in short, "God is real" because God "produces real effects" (389). Arguably, although inadequate for creedal formulations by the various faiths, James's position may present profound possibilities for interfaith dialogue concerning diverse testimonies of experiencing the divine.

80. Ellington, "Reciprocal Reshaping, 18-31. Thus, the testimonial character of Scripture informs both history and hermeneutics and these in turn clarify the nature of Pentecostal experience and the testimony thereof, 30-31. Cf. Plüss, "Testimony," 877-78.

81. Ellington, "Reciprocal Reshaping," argues that through Scripture "Israel's story is brought into the present, experienced anew, and projected into the future." Furthermore, it is in Pentecostal testimonies that "we see the closest approximation" of this experiential process. Accordingly, the biblical stories are "never divorced from the concerns of the present" (28). See Arrington, *Encountering the Holy Spirit*, 463 and 487-88.

82. See J.C. Thomas, "The Charismatic Structure of Acts," *JPT* 13:1 (October 2004), 19-30 (26). Cf. A. Thomas, "Everyone Has a Story to Tell," *AARP* (July/August 2008), 30-34, and *Thinking About Memoir* (AARP Books/Sterling, 2008).

83. Early Christians, such as Hilary of Potiers and Novation, interpreted this text to indicate there is no place for improvement or progress in the nature and being of the Divine, *ACCS Old Testament XIV, The Twelve Prophets*, gen. ed. T.C. Oden, ed. A. Ferreiro, 303. Using Malachi 3:6, Origen defended the Incarnation against charges of change in the Divine Being by the pagan Celsius by appealing to "the condescension of God to human affairs" by which he became incarnate "but did not need to undergo transformation", ibid., 303-04 (304). More recently, A. Clarke, *Clarke's Commentary: Malachi*, Wesleyan Heritage Collection (Rio, WI: Ages Software, 2002)) explains that Malachi 3:6 indicates that the changing dispensations of God's covenant in Christ do not undermined the unchangeableness of God's character or commitment to Israel, 12. On this text, Jameson, Faussett, and Brown (*Jamieson, Fausset, and Brown Commentary*, Electronic Database, 1997, 2003, Biblesoft, Inc) suggest it offers assurances that God's unchanging faithfulness to God's covenant is not affected by changing events or times or by Israel's inability to understand God's actions. Contemporary scholarship on Hebrews 13:8 (e.g., D.A. Hagner, *NIBC: Hebrews*, New Testament, ed. W.W. Gasque (Peabody, MA: Hendrickson, 1983, 1990; 238-41, 35) similarly applies the idea of eternal divine constancy and permanency, as well as of faithfulness in the midst of life's vicissitudes, to Jesus Christ, building on texts such as Psalm 102:27 and Isaiah 48:12 (cf. also Heb 1:12), a point affirmed by Pentecostal scholarship (e.g. J.W. Adams, *Hebrews, FLBC*, 1295-1399 (1391-92).

84. On a popular level, Pentecostals consistently connect Malachi 3:6 and Hebrews 13:8, frequently contending commitment to the doctrine of God's immutable character as exemplified in Christ indicates that God continues to act miraculously and wondrously in believers' lives today. E.g., see Duffield, *Foundations*, 69-70 (esp. 69), 377-79, and 405-08 (esp. 406).

85. Cf. E. Murphy, *The Handbook for Spiritual Warfare*, revised and updated (Nashville, TN: Nelson, 1992, 1996, 2003), 9, 233-37.

86. R.P. Spittler, "Glossolalia," *NIDPCM,* 670-76, points out that "psychological analysis and personal testimony converge to suggest occasional coincidence of personal or social stress and the use of glossolalia" (674-75). Perhaps the joy and peace often accompanying glossolalia are part of its appeal. In the context of this chapter, the convergence of science and testimony is noteworthy.

87. An intriguing account by an early Classical Pentecostal of how the Exodus event serves paradigmatically for belief and practice is J.H. King, *From Passover to Pentecost* (Franklin Springs, GA: Advocate, 1911, 1976, 4 ed.).

88. Cf. Boone, "Community," 142, and Land, *Pentecostal Spirituality,* 80.

89. Cf. T. Richie, "Is Pentecostalism Just Another American Success Story? A Response to Jürgen Moltmann on the Place of Optimism in the Pentecostal Tradition," *Refleks* 5:2 (2006), 77-93.

90. Jamaican Pentecostals, e.g., testify to rejecting religious systems that do not account for the problems they face in everyday life, Hurbon, "Caribbean," Corten, *Babel,* 129. In some contexts, one may observe in testimonies "the chain" of "spiritual healing, physical healing, financial healing", 114-15 (115), identifying and prioritizing redemptive provision for human needs.

91. See Wacker, *Heaven Below.*

92. Thus T.L. Cross, "A Proposal to Break the Ice: What Can Pentecostal Theology Offer Evangelical Theology?" *JPT* 10:2 (2002), 44-73, points out that Pentecostal pneumatology is not a replacement for Christology but a framework for in which Pentecostalism testifies of the redemption in Christ through the power of the Spirit, 71. Cf. M. Habets, "Spirit Christology: Seeing in Stereo," *JPT* 11:2 (2003), 199-234.

93. Synan, *Century of the Holy Spirit*: V. Synan, "The Pentecostal Century: An Overview," 1-14 (9), and Synan, "The Holiness-Pentecostal Churches," 97-124 (121).

94. Popular pastor and biblical and devotional author H. Blackaby speaks of the "defining moments" in every person's life in *Chosen to be God's Prophet: Lessons from the Life of Samuel* (Nashville: Nelson, 2003), 3-16 (3-4). Perhaps these defining moments supply the best material for a testimony designed to help people of different faiths understand one another.

95. Partly this is the case because both Christians and their dialogue partners bring their general and specific convictions to the discussion table. Cf. Heim, *Salvations,* 227-29. Furthermore, authentic dialogue characterized by "cautious optimism" will require "engagement on all fronts", as Yong, *Beyond the Impasse,* 110, notes of C. Pinnock, "Toward an Evangelical Theology of Religions," *JETS* 33:3 (1990), 359-68 (366). Yong himself insists that dialogue is complex, often involving not only "interreligious dialogue" but "intra-religious dialogue" (187).

96. Notably, Yong, *Beyond the Impasse,* argues that "dialogue in the most comprehensive sense" includes "testimonials, arguments, and even apologetics" (55).

97. Cf. V. Synan, "Evangelicalism," *NIDPCM,* 613-16, and Kärkkäinen, *Pneumatology,* 94.

98. Macchia, "Theology," suggests Pentecostal theology is rooted in a person, not a proposition (1140).

99. These emphases are exemplified, e.g., in the popular testimony-centered ministry of Pentecostal Dave Roevers and in the practice of testimony in Pentecostal services. See Spittler, "The Pentecostal View," 145, 147. Cf. V. Synan, *Voices of Pentecost: Testimonies of Lives Touched by the Holy Spirit* (Ann Arbor, Michigan: Servant Books, 2003), esp. 12-13. These testimonies might also include a range of experiences regarding conversion, sanctification, Spirit baptism and spiritual gifts, healings, deliverances, miracles, and so on. Cf. 26, 80, 83, 95, 96, 101, 103, 114, etc. Cf. also Corten, "Latin America,"

Corten, *Babel,* 106. Archer, *Pentecostal Hermeneutics,* suggests testimonies represent in part openness to others involving the "humanization" of those often overlooked or undervalued (28). Arguably, that openness and humanization could and should include religious others.

100. C.B. Johns, *Pentecostal Formation,* studies how Pentecostalism often works for social liberation and transformation in settings of disenfranchisement. Cf. R.M. Anderson, *Vision of the Disinherited: the Making of American Pentecostalism* (New York: Oxford University, 1979) and M. Crews, *The Church of God: A Social History* (Knoxville: University of Tennessee Press, 1990). Tan-Chow, *Pentecostal Theology,* describes dialogue between the religions advancing cooperative efforts in society as "collaboration", 164.

101. A. Anderson, "Global Pentecostalism in the New Millennium," A. Anderson and W.J. Hollenweger, eds., *Pentecostals after a Century: Global Perspectives on a Movement in Transition,* JSup 15 (Sheffield, Eng: Sheffield Academic Press, 1999), 209-23, stresses Pentecostal social involvement. He suggests "the essence of the pentecostal gospel" is a pragmatic gospel that meets practical needs, and spirituality with liberationist overtones and a high priority on evangelism (210, 214-18).

102. Cf. Yong, *Spirit Poured Out,* 91-98. Testimonies can serve to affirm the moral and spiritual liberation and transformation of converts, Kalu, *African Pentecostalism,* 260. Sometimes, however, triumphalism can occur, Kalu, 209. Nevertheless, in African religious culture, Pentecostal testimonies have served effectively to assist converts transitioning from the oppressive power of evil or false spirits and to provide a platform in public worship for rituals of "degradation and bridge burning" (183). On testimonies about evil spirits, see R. Marshall-Fratani, "Mediating the Global and Local in Nigerian Pentecostalism," 80-105, Corten, *Babel,* 99-100. Sanders, *Saints in Exile,* speaks of the Christian testimony of Black Pentecostals in the United States "finding public manifestation in an ascetic lifestyle and high moral standards" (Preface).

103. Accordingly, Pentecostals especially value "firsthand testimonies" from a wide variety of participants. See Synan, *Voices of Pentecost,* 11-12. Cf. 116, 126, 134, 146, 160, and 167. Cf. Synan, *The Century of the Holy Spirit:* R. Owens, "The Azusa Street Revival: The Pentecostal Movement Begins in America," 39-68 (49), and Robeck, "Azusa Street Revival," 347. A testimony may even be defined explicitly as "a firsthand authentication of a fact", Holdcroft, *The Holy Spirit,* 111. Dramatic testimonies were sometimes published for purposes of expounding and spreading Pentecostal belief and experience, *Voices,* 38, 120-21. Cf. Synan, "Pentecostal Roots," Synan, *Century of the Holy Spirit,* 15-38 (27-28). However, A.W. Tozer, a popular devotional writer among Evangelicals and Pentecostals, in *Best I,* warned that the "concerted testimony" of the saints of the ages should have weight for contemporary Christians, 191 (cf. 17).

104. Famous Pentecostal evangelist and healer Smith Wigglesworth liked testimony services of people highlighting these kinds of experiences. See Synan, *Voices,* 166. Cf. also 58. Wacker, *Heaven Below,* somewhat oddly suggests he eventually accepted the hypothesis of Pentecostal pragmatism in spite of the evidence of their testimonies about themselves, 13.

105. Not surprisingly, some leading black theologians, such as, e.g., J. Cone, identify "primary sources for doing black theology" in "sermons, songs, testimonies, and slave narratives" along with emphasis on "the Christ-event as the exaltation-liberation event", L. Lovett, "Black Theology," *NIDPCM,* 428-32 (430). Cf. C.T. Gilkes, "'You've Got a Right to the Tree of Life': The Biblical Foundations of an Empowered Attitude Among Black Women in the Sanctified Church," Alexander and Yong, *Philip's Daughters,* 152-69 (156, 160), and Sanders, *Saints in Exile,* ix.

106. Hyatt, "Spirit-Filled Women," 245. See also R.M. Griffith and D. Robuck, "Women, Role of," *NIDPCM,* 1203-09 (1206).

107. Perhaps such incredible journeys are possible partly because Pentecostals are so committed to the idea that everyone's testimony may have value, C.M. Robeck, Jr. and J.L. Sandidge, "Dialogue, Catholic and Pentecostal," *NIDPCM,* 575-82 (581). Indeed, early Pentecostalism periodicals notably published news and testimonies "from around the world and attributed equal value to all", D.D. Bundy, "Bibliography and Histiography," *NIDPCM,* 405-417 (406).

108. A. Hollingsworth, in "Spirit and Voice: Toward a Feminist Pentecostal Pneumatology," *Pneuma* 29:2 (2007), 189-213, ably argues that the Spirit gives voice to diverse groups of the oppressed or marginalized, in this case, namely women. As an example, she expressly says, "Public testimony is also a powerful way in which Pentecostal Latinas find and express their voices" (203). Not surprisingly, and significantly, she also says, "the polyvocality of Spirit has implications for ecumenical and interreligious dialogue" (208).

109. Interestingly, Pentecostals see gospels songs as offering "a vehicle for testimony and prophecy" to both believers and unbelievers, Alford, "Music," 914. Testimonies themselves may serve for diverse audiences as well.

110. A blurb on the back cover of Synan, *Century of the Holy Spirit,* sums up the general thrust of Pentecostal testimony as it aims to uplift God's activity in praise: "This is a powerful testimony of the hand of God". Cf. Owen, "Azusa Street Revival," 55-56. Testimonies are often explicitly associated with praise, 57.

111. This assertion does not deny that Pentecostal testimony has traditionally carried within itself a strong presupposition regarding evangelistic urgency arising out of the "overriding ethos of Pentecostalism", G.B. McGee, "To the Regions Beyond: The Global Expansion of Pentecostalism," Synan, *Century of the Holy Spirit,* 69-96 (71). It merely notes that the doxological element can also be properly appropriated for interreligious dialogue and that in such a context the emphasis would naturally be adjusted. Cf. Owens, "Azusa Street Revival," who closely associates testimonies with contexts of praise, 57.

112. E.g., one hears that "the burning, convicting power of Pentecostal testimony filled the room" so that through "the Pentecostal fire" burning in the heart of a testifier conviction gripped "spiritually cold" hearts, Synan, *Voices of Pentecost,* 78. Cf. Owens, "Azusa Street Revival," 58, and, McGee, "To the Regions Beyond," 92. However, in spite of what may be called an almost compelling power in some Pentecostal testimonies, they are not always "warmly received", G.B. McGee, "Moss, Virginia E.," *NIDPCM,* 909. In fact, some were reportedly persecuted severely for their testimony, E.B. Robinson, "Johnson, Bernard, Jr.," *NIDPCM,* 812-13 (812). Not uncommon was expulsion for testifying to the Pentecostal experience, P.D. Hocken, "House Church Movement," *NIDPCM,* 773-74 (773).

113. Frequently accompanying prayer and testimony services are "manifestations of ecstatic energy", Owens, "Azusa Street Revival," 41. Cf. 48, 60. Often, timid persons are thus transformed into dynamic ministers in the practice of testifying. Cf. W.E. Warner, "Montgomery, Carrie Judd," *NIDPCM,* 904-06 (905). These accompaniments are not atypical for Pentecostals, some of whom have testified of various physical manifestations and even sensations of fiery burnings as they experienced the Holy Spirit's presence, C.E. Jones, "Holiness Movement," *NIDPCM,* 726-28 (727). Sometimes during testimonies jerking body movements occur and hats fly off, as worshipers speak in tongues, Wacker, *Heaven Below,* 101. Mayrargue, "Benin," Corten, *Babel,* suppose that testimonies are how Pentecostalism "displays its power and its efficacy" (287). A trance-like state and

glossolalia are not uncommon accompaniments of testimonies in certain contexts, Hurbon, "Caribbean," Corten, *Babel,* 128.

114. Some even believe that God specifically directs who should testify and when they should do it. Cf. J.R. Zeigler, "Shakarian, Demos," *NIDPCM,* 1058.

115. Cox calls this "primal spirituality" in *Fire from Heaven* (e.g., 81-82, 132). W. DeArtega in *Quenching the Spirit: Examining Centuries of Opposition to the Moving of the Holy Spirit* (Lake Mary, FL: Creation House, 1992) says this is what the Christian religious world has fought for centuries to keep quiet. Cf. Sanders, *Saints in Exile,* where Black Pentecostals are described as testifying to the primary reality of the Holy Spirit in their lives, 136.

116. As Spittler, "Spirituality," explains, this is typical of Pentecostals' own testimonials of encounters of "deepened personal experience with the Lord" (1100). Further, Pentecostal testimonies themselves often relate occasions when the Holy Spirit "fell" on believers in an amazing or miraculous manner, J.R. Williams, "Baptism in the Holy Spirit," *NIDPCM,* 354-63 (356). Interestingly, long before the modern Pentecostal movement began, the radical reformer T. Müntzer argued that spiritual gifts are signs or testimonies of God's presence and power, S.M. Burgess, "Holy Spirit, Doctrine of Reformation Traditions," *NIDPCM,* 763-69 (768).

117. E.g., R. Marie Griffith, "A Network of Praying Women: Women's Aglow Fellowship and Mainline American Protestantism," Blumhoffer, et al, *Pentecostal Currents,* 131-51, informs prayer and testimony in Aglow meetings "are meant to have a transformative effect on both the storyteller and her listeners" (140).

118. Interestingly, distinguished psychologist C.R. Rogers bases much of his innovative (at the time) approach to therapy on the premise that one of the foundations of all healthy human relationships is the willingness to be real with others. See his *On Becoming a Person* (Boston: Houghton Mifflin, 1961), e.g., 34-35, 37-38.

119. For Pentecostals, healings, miracles, and spiritual manifestations, as well as conversions and other dramatic experiences, are primarily witnesses and testimonies to "the power of God", G.L. McClung, Jr., "Introduction: Spontaneous Strategy of the Spirit," ed. McClung, *Azusa Street and Beyond,* 146. Testimonies in Pentecostal worship imply a "re-experiencing" of the biblical text and include an assumption that they "provide evidence" that God is working miraculously in the present in the lives of the members of the believing community as it interprets God's actions in faith, Archer, *Pentecostal Hermeneutics,* 168. Accordingly, Pentecostals often find parallels between stories they encounter in Scripture and their own stories, 166. This pervasive pattern initiates a hermeneutical dialectic in which Scripture and personal testimony are mutually informative, 163. Archer uses the terminology of "echo", 163, and that is quite appropriate as the testimonies bear just such a symbiotic relation with the Scriptures (cf. 161).

120. Testimony can be a surprisingly complex concept. For early Pentecostal pioneer and preacher F. Bartleman, *Azusa Street,* the prominence of songs, prayers, and testimonies, along with some diminishment of sermonizing, indicated clerical, ecclesiastical, and hierarchical monopolizing had been overturned, 57, 94-95. Pentecostal historian, S.M. Burgess, "Reformation," observes that Luther and Calvin primarily used testimony of an inner witness of the Spirit to conversion reality or scriptural truth, 763-65. Pentecostals affirm this aspect of the testimony of the Spirit, suggesting it is an aid to developing enduring faith, Holdcroft, *The Holy Spirit,* 63. Pentecostal testimony terminology, however, shares more in common with the popular conception of testimony as a public event. Cf. Rosenberg, "Introduction: In a Forgotten Mirror," ed., D. Rosenberg, *Testimony: Contemporary Writers Make the Holocaust Personal* (New York: Time/Random House, 1989), xiii, and, Johns, *Pentecostal Formation,* 130-31. Some Pentecostals argue theo-

logically that the Holy Spirit produces "an internal sense of confidence toward God" and "an external manifestation of testimony toward the world", Jacobsen, *Thinking in the Spirit* (95). Amazingly, early Pentecostals may have devoted as much as a third of their worship services "to public testimonies about their spiritual journeys", Wacker, *Heaven Below* (58). Robeck and Sandidge, "Dialogue, Catholic and Pentecostal," note that while Pentecostals often approach theology from "a personal witness or pastoral dimension", and that therefore "Testimony, oral theology, song, and narrative approaches are essential" to them, Catholics are more comfortable with precise theological formulations and less so with private or personal aspects of Pentecostal testimonies (580). Both Catholics and Pentecostals, however, may be dedicated to building "a united Christian testimony" before a watching world (577). For Pentecostals and Charismatics, "Renewal in the Spirit is everywhere marked by a focus on Jesus Christ. Testimonies constantly refer to an encounter with Jesus, a deeper yielding to Jesus, and a fuller acceptance of Jesus as Lord." See P.D. Hocken, "Charismatic Movement," *NIDPCM,* 477-519 (514). Additionally, Wacker, *Heaven Below,* suggests that, especially early on in the movement, frequent worship including testimonies tended to strengthen the bonds between believers in the face of painful events in their lives, 111.

121. Tan-Chow, *Pentecostal Theology,* argues that interreligious dialogue and testimony requires "Negotiating truth with religious others" in honesty and humility, 163. Cf. also Tan-Chow regarding the interfaith event of the testimony of the narrative of the biblical Book of Jonah, 141.

122. Interestingly, Ware, "Spiritual Egalitarianism," Alexander and Yong, *Philip's Daughters,* 230, details that A. von Harnack, *The History of Dogma, Volume I* (New York: Dover, 1961), stressed the centrality for Christianity of experiential encounter with God or Christ, and the essential importance of giving testimony , which Harnack defined as "self-reporting, witness, or narrative", in response. Harnack considered such testimony essential for "the propagation of the faith", and claimed it holds forth "the possibility for other persons to encounter God" (16, 72).

123. Pentecostals humbly believe "their personal faith stories" bear "normative implications for others", Wacker, *Heaven Below,* (58).

124. Proto-Pentecostal Phoebe Palmer even identified the willingness to publically testify of one's experience in the Holy Spirit as an essential stage of the process of sanctification. See S.C. Stanley, "Wesleyan/Holiness and Pentecostal Women Preachers: Pentecost as the Pattern for Primitivism," Alexander and Yong, *Philip's Daughters,* 19-37 (23; cf. Powers, "Pentecost 101," 137). Cf. H.E. Raser, *Phoebe Palmer: Her Life and Thought* (Lewiston, NY: Mellen, 1987), 247-48, and C.E. White, *The Beauty of Holiness: Phoebe Palmer as Theologian, Revivalist, Feminist, and Humanatarian* (Grand Rapids: Asbury/Zondervan, 1986), 123.

125. A. Kireopoulos, a Greek Orthodox theologian and the NCC Senior Program Director for Faith & Order and Interfaith Relations, in his "Reflection on Pope Benedict XVI's Encyclical Letter, *Spe Salvi*" (November 30, 2007), appropriately observes that, "Oftentimes, Christians are the first in interfaith dialogue to be reticent in affirming their respective truth claims. Ultimately, this is not helpful, because it prevents an honest dialogue on theological differences. More to the point, however, is how such truth claims are expressed in dialogue with others. One of the greatest challenges today for Christians engaged in interfaith dialogue is discussing their own theological beliefs, or to give "an accounting for the hope that is in [them]" (1 Peter 3:15, NRSV), in a way that is neither triumphalistic nor dismissive of others' beliefs."
See http://www.ncccusa.org/news/071217spesalvi.html.

126. Spittler, "Spirituality," explains that Pentecostals "take their commitment with the utmost seriousness" and convey it "through oral testimony and 'sharing'" (1102).

127. F.W. Jordan, "At Arms Length: The First Presbyterian Church, Pittsburg, and Kathryn Kuhlman," ed. Blumhoffer, et al, *Pentecostal Currents,* 188-208, reports an impromptu 'testimony meeting' that occurred on a plane during a transatlantic flight that completely changed the perception of non-Pentecostal Christians toward a favorable view, helping establish personal friendships, 193.

128. As the stated purpose of this research project involves exploring and exploiting the pneumatological nature of Pentecostal testimony in developing a paradigm for contemporary interreligious encounter and dialogue, it is deemed appropriate to draw on actual experience in interfaith conversations, and to offer suggestions for improvement. Nevertheless, the intellectual interpretation has been done for the practical application.

129. Cf. Moltmann, *A Broad Place,* 170, 179-80, and Hesselgrave, "Evangelicals and Interreligious Dialogue," Pittman, et al, *Ministry and Theology,* 425-28. See Solivan, "Interreligious Dialogue," Heim, *Ground for Understanding,* 37-45.

130. See D.J. Austin-Broos, "Jamaican Pentecostalism: Transnational Relations and the Nation-State," 142-62, Corten, *Babel,* 142, and E.D. Apprill, "The New Pentecostal Networks of Brazzaville," 293-308, Corten, *Babel,* 305-06.

131. Careful planning of this kind is often, though not always, an important element of interreligious dialogue, Calvin E. Shenk, *Who Do You Say That I Am? Christians Encounter Other Religions* (Scottsdale, PA: Herald, 1997), 210-11.

132. Important to note is that I am here following a well established pattern among Pentecostals of modeling through testimony the applicability and integrity of argumentation. E.g., see Archer, *Pentecostal Hermeneutics,* 37-38. In fact, for Pentecostals the "Proof of one's call" lies in "the person's testimony to such a call and in the perceived fruit of a Spirit-empowered ministry" rather than in some more formal process of ecclesiastical selection or promotion, Alexander, "Introduction," Alexander and Yong, *Philip's Daughters,* 3-4. Indeed, often a first prompt reaction to hearing that the Lord is doing something in one's life, including a call to ministry of whatever kind, is an urgent exhortation to stand and tell the church. See D.G. Roebuck, "'Cause he's My Chief Employer': Hearing Women's Voices in a Classical Pentecostal Denomination," Alexander and Yong, *Philip's Daughters,* 38-60 (48).

133. Since I was very young, and since multiple persons are involved in the incident, my parents supplied many of the details of this testimony. Although for purposes of academic objectivity, this testimony, couched here in formal language, appears in actual delivery in a more personal form that helps establish the human connection so essential to its effectiveness.

134. Pentecostal men and women who eventually enter various forms ministry have often done so out of their own testimonial encounter and public responses to it, and, furthermore, the direction of their ministry has often been influenced by it. Carrie Judd Montgomery's testimony of healing helped her overcome personal and social obstacles to launch a successful healing ministry, Warner, "Montgomery," 905. C.H. Mason, Church of God in Christ founder and leader, began as a lay minister giving his testimony, I.C. Clemmons, "Mason, Charles Harrison," *NIDPCM,* 865-67 (865). Cf. *NIDPCM:* S. Strang, "Gimenez, John," 668; C.M. Robeck, Jr., "Farrow, Lucy F.," 632-33 (633); G.B. McGee, "Ball, Henry Cleopas," 354. Similarly, outstanding ecumenist David J. du Plessis began his ecumenical encounters through sharing his testimony with non-Pentecostals, E.L. Blumhoffer and C.R. Armstrong, "Assemblies of God," 333-40 (336).

135. Testimonies of miraculous healings abound in Pentecostalism, offering proof of God's power and reinforcing the faithful, Hurbon, "Caribbean," Corten, *Babel,* 134.

Sometimes these testimonies feature failures by medical procedure or prayers of other religions followed by successful healing prayer by Pentecostals, 134.

136. This ministerial directive toward ecumenical and interfaith dialogue out of a testimonial mode of being appears to comply with the explanation of Archer, *Pentecostal Hermeneutics,* that the Spirit provides direction concerning "a particular practice or concern through experience, visions, gifts, and testimonies to a new understanding" that is "rooted in Scripture" but "yet will move beyond it" (251). Thus the faith community provides the context for the Spirit's manifestation to occur and for the Spirit's voice to be heard; personal testimonies, charismatic gifts, preaching, teaching, witnessing, serving the poor, and praying provide opportunities for the Spirit's manifestation (248-49).

137. Of course, not every testimony need include every concern. Furthermore, this testimony is consistent with the high view of Scripture held by Pentecostals, and with their acceptance of its testimonial character and nature. See Archer, *Pentecostal Hermeneutics,* "The Bible is understood to be an authoritative and trustworthy testimony about the living God produced by humans that were inspired by the Holy Spirit" (251). Sanders, *Saints in Exile,* describes the testimonies of Black Pentecostals as part of "a united witness to the efficacy of the Bible in the life of the believer" (139).

138. As noted by Archer, *Pentecostal Hermeneutics,* also 24. Yet from around the world testimonies frequently have a theme of God's provision for those called to such labors. See M Bergunder, *The South Indian Pentecostal Movement in the Twentieth Century,* Studies in the History of Christian Missions (Grand Rapids: Eerdman, 2008), 195.

139. See Corten, "Latin America," Corten, *Babel,* 106. When introducing the subject of the miraculous, one might expect an undercurrent of incredulity, even outright challenge. At least two considerations make it worth the risk. First, that is who Pentecostals are; they believe in the contemporary validity of miracles. They cannot be real without expressing this belief. Better to discuss it than deny it or diminish it. Second, even beyond Pentecostalism, some highly intelligent and even brilliant people believe in miracles also, and give some cogent arguments for their belief. One thinks of C.S. Lewis, *Miracles* (London: G. Bless, 1947; HarperCollins ed., 2001). Document cases of dramatic healings, e.g., are common in Pentecostal literature. See Anderson, *Spreading Fires,* 178-79. One ought not to dismiss the category simply due to its controversial nature. Pentecostals tend to point back to the testimony of miracles in Scripture, Holdcroft, *The Holy Spirit,* 73. Sometimes speaking in tongues may even be referred to as a kind of "testimony of the wonders of God", 94.

140. The testimony of miracles can have something of a confirmatory or validating aspect for Pentecostals. See Archer, *Pentecostal Hermeneutics,* 154.

141. See Holdcroft, *The Holy Spirit,* 111, and *Voices of Pentecost,* 38, 120-21.

142. Pentecostalism arises out of a tradition of conviction that Spirit baptism is an empowerment for ministry subsequent to regeneration for the express purpose of enhanced testimony and witness, Anderson, *Spreading Fires,* 24.

143. This is in clear contradiction to stereotypical assumptions that Pentecostalism is innately adverse to dialogue. Further, the testimonies of other Pentecostals involved in ecumenical work mark the same message. E.g., see "Du Plessis, David Johannes," *NIDPCM,* 589-92, and "Gee, Donald," *NIDPCM,* 662-63. Conversely, it was misinformed fear of destroyed testimony that caused many Pentecostals to avoid ecumenical interation for years, C.M. Robeck and J.L. Sandidge, "World Council of Churches," *NIDPCM,* 1213-17 (1214). Strangely enough, Fundamentalists distanced themselves from Pentecostals out of concern that the latter were "an injury" to the "sane testimony" of the former, H.V. Synan, "Fundamentalism," *NIDPCM,* 655-58 (657).

144. At times, some Pentecostals tell of what might be described as a divine compulsion to testify for the glory of God, Gilkes, "'You've Got a Right,'"Alexander and Yong, *Philip's Daughters,* 161.

145. Wacker, *Heaven Below,* notes that "Like countless Christians before them, early pentecostals assumed that their personal faith stories bore normative implications for others" (58).

146. In fact, though the present study focuses on formal interfaith conversations, the principles of testimony outlined herein are also adaptively applicable to informal conversations between family, friends, and fellow workers of different faiths in certain social settings. Cf. Shenk, *Who?* 210-11.

147. According to Rogers, "an ability and minimal willingness on the part of each to receive communication from the other", that is, reciprocal listening, is an important component of "A General Law of Interpersonal Relationships". See *On Becoming a Person,* 344-45.

148. Tan-Chow, *Pentecostal Theology,* lists six "Guidelines for an Ethic of Negotiation" in interreligious dialogue: the need to confront honestly current and local culture; facing up to the history of Scripture and formative events in Church history; necessity of self-critique in the light of Scripture; absolute cruciality of a deep, rich and robust conception of the Holy Spirit; the remembering crucial to the lived ethic of negotiation; and, negotiation as an act of love and celebration, 164-66.

149. Cf. Kireopoulos, "Reflection on Pope Benedict XVI's Encyclical Letter." See http://www.ncccusa.org/news/071217spesalvi.html.

150. Shenk, *Who?* 213-19.

151. See Rogers, *On Becoming a Person,* 315-18, 318-23. Cf. 323-25 also. If one wonders at the appropriateness of psychotherapy for interreligious dialogue processes, one may note that the healing of persons and their relations is very much what both are about.

152. See Neill, 69, 124. Cf. 224-31. Cf. also A. Yong, *Hospitality and the Other: Pentecost, Christian Practices, and the Neighbor* (Maryknoll: Orbis, 2008), 34-36, 150-56; T.C. Tennent, *Christianity at the Religious Roundtable: Evangelicalism in Conversation with Hinduism, Buddhism, and Islam* (Grand Rapids: Baker Academic, 2002), 31-32, 239; V.M. Kärkkäinen, *Trinity and Religious Pluralism: The Doctrine of the Trinity in Christian Theology of Religions* (Burlington, VT: Ashgate, 2004), 180-81; and Tan-Chow, *Pentecostal Theology,* 164-66.

153. Archer, *Pentecostal Hermeneutics,* insists that, even within the Pentecostal community, "The sharing of testimonies always involves and requires discernment" (225). Active participation through discussion, testimonies, and charismatic gifts are elements essential for a Pentecostal hermeneutical strategy, 225. Archer addresses this topic from within the Pentecostal faith community explicitly, 224, but this study assumes some general, broader applications to interfaith conversation. Of course, for the Pentecostal Christian, in whatever conversational context, "the working of the Holy Spirit and the testimony of Scripture" is always utmost, 198. Pentecostal theology is more than experiential testimony, but it does emphatically affirm that biblical exposition and theological articulation ought to apply demonstratively to everyday life, Archer, 193, fn. 88.

154. For a fascinating account of Christian-Muslim dialogue at a theological level still retaining a personal element and even friendly environment, see B.D. Kateregga and D.W. Shenk, *A Muslim and A Christian in Dialogue* (Scottsdale, PA: Herald, 1997). F.E. Accad, *Building Bridges: Christianity and Islam* (Colorado, Springs, Colorado: NavPress, 1997), mentions the importance of tactful testimony in Muslim-Christian dialogue, 24. Cf. 35.

155. Primacy of place for "doing black theology" often goes to "sermons, songs, testimonies, and slave narratives", Lovett, "Black Theology" (430). Sanders, *Saints in Exile*, explains "the underlying ethical and theological context of sanctified [Black Pentecostal] worship is the corporate testimony of being 'saved, sanctified, and filled with the Holy Ghost'" (70).

156. After years of apparently intense and intimate dialogue participation, M.C. Boys, *Jewish-Christian Dialogue: One Woman's Experience* (New York: Paulist, 1997), focuses on stories of dialogue encounter and maintains the importance of interreligious testimony, 23, 44, 49-50. In fact, she freely confesses that in times of deep dialogue she falls back primarily on her testimony of faith—which has been informed and formed in her dialogues with religious others, 75. H. Heinz, "Presentation of the Discussion Group Jews and Christians," 1-16, Hanspeter Heinz and Michael A. Signer, *Coming Together for the Sake of God: Contributions to Jewish-Christian Dialogue from Post-Holocaust Germany* (Collegeville, Minnesota: Michael Glazier, 2007), says, "Christians and Jews have the right to listen to each other's testimony of faith, and to reflect on it before God, even if they are unable to approve of it"—even while expressing hope it is not "a hidden attempt at conversion" (6). Moreover, this group maintains the importance of personal testimony and of witness in dialogue, 9, 12, and of some shared testimony, 18, 30, as well as, of course, unique testimony, 37. Critical is for both Jewish and Christian dialogue partners to learn "the ability and the readiness to listen to the word of the other as a testimony about their relationship with God" (19). Together, Jews and Christians may help fulfill the biblical mandate for a minimum of "two witnesses" to truth, 158 (cf. Deut 19:15; Matt 18:16; 2 Co 13:1; 1 Ti 5:19).

PART THREE: PASSING INSPECTION

Chapter 6

Representative Objections to Pentecostal Involvement

Introduction

The section now being begun corresponds roughly to that phase of a building project in which the inspector makes sure it is "up to code." Therefore, the purpose of this chapter is an attempt to anticipate some of the more obvious objections that may be raised against the hypothesis of this project. This chapter will therefore first record some of the more prominent objections and then respectfully respond to each. It does not attempt an exhaustive analysis of criticisms or their extensive refutation. Rather, it endeavors to demonstrate that there are plausible responses to possible objections. Accordingly, the suggestion that Pentecostals, undergirded by a developing inclusivist theology of religions rooted in the soil of their distinctive pneumatology, employ the category of testimony for engagement in interreligious encounter and dialogue, should be judged on the basis of its own merit (or lack thereof) rather than on assumptions or presuppositions excluding it in an inappropriate *a priori* fashion. The approach taken here is to look first at possible objections based on biblical interpretation, and then at those regarding suspected betrayal of the Pentecostal tradition or a stealthy minimization of Christian ecclesial mission. It also addresses questions of competing interreligious truth claims from the perspective of a concern for relativization of religious truth and whether interfaith conflict is practically resolvable and the role that dialogue may play therein.[1]

Runs Counter to Scripture

A Critical Concern[2]

Amos Yong notes that reaction among conservative Evangelicals to inclusivist arguments "has been sizable." The critical arguments against inclusivism include charges that it "fails exegetically" and that "the authority of scripture has been compromised."[3] Indeed, for many the real issue among Evangelicals regarding exclusivism and inclusivism (pluralism not counting for much for this group) is "which approach is more faithful to Scripture." The challenge for inclusivists is "to pass muster biblically".[4] (Yong therefore sets up a quite rigorous context by which to test the biblical, historical, and theological foundations of an inclusive theology of religions against "the empirical reality of the historical religions.")[5] That much the more serious, therefore, is the almost ubiquitous charge that only exclusivism is biblically sane and sound. For instance, Ramesh Richard argues adamantly that "the inclusivist position" is incorrect from the biblical perspective.[6] For example, he argues that John 14:6 allows no room for soteriological inclusivism, mostly by insisting on the essentiality of epistemological content through what he calls the "explicitness of the faith-in-Christ principle".[7] Yet in this critically important text describing Jesus as the Way (*hodos*), the Truth (*alethia*), and the Life (*zoe*), Richard does not deal with its context or address its implications. However, Morris observes that Jesus speaks of the way to God in continuity with such OT statements as "Teach me your way, O Lord; lead me in a straight path" (Ps 27:11) and that in Acts "the Way" is sometimes used of Christianity (9:2; 19:9, 23; 24:14, 22).[8] Arrington suggests Christ's followers may have come to be known in Acts as "the Way" stemming from OT expressions of "the way of God" or "the way of righteousness" or even that "it may have come from Jesus calling himself 'the way' (John 14:6)".[9] Of course, undoubtedly, as Morris says, "Jesus is asserting in strong terms the uniqueness and the sufficiency of his work for men". Yet the truth Jesus speaks of refers as much to his own "utter dependability" as to "the saving truth of the gospel". In fact, the emphasis seems to be on the "complete reliability of Jesus in all that He does or is" rather than on dogma.[10] In other words, this text is not primarily about propositional epistemology as much as experiential and relational knowledge.

Obviously, simplistically interpreting John 14:6 to refute inclusivism is problematic.[11] Yet just thus Richard argues that inclusivists compromise "a specific Christocentric salvation" and the epistemological character of faith. Furthermore, he thinks inclusivists are inconsistent in their application of divine universality. He opines that biblical salvation makes epistemology conditional for salvation. He accordingly concludes that inevitably the unevangelized are divinely damned.[12] Of course, not all exclusivists claim the biblical evidence goes so far.[13]

Specifically Pentecostal grievances include concerns that anything other than traditional exclusivist approaches to other religions is contrary to Scripture (quoting Acts 4:12 and John 3:18[14]), replaces the obligation for world evangelism (again, quoting Matt 18:28; Mk 16:15)[15] with interreligious dialogue, and that those who fail to fulfill the Great Commission are compromising Christ's Lordship.[16] These are not lightweight lance thrusts for Pentecostals. As Arrington observes, "Convinced that the Scriptures are God's Word, Pentecostals uphold the authority of the precious written Word and accept it as completely trustworthy for faith and conduct."[17] However, Arrington also instructs that Pentecostal interpretation of Scripture, along with utilization of recognized historical and grammatical principles, is pneumatic and experiential as well.[18] This does not mean, "Anything goes!" It does mean Pentecostal biblical interpretation transcends piling up bare "proof texts". Rather, it opens itself up to the Holy Spirit's illuminating of the human heart with divine truth. In other words, not the letter alone but the S/spirit in the letter is where the life of truth resides for Pentecostals (cf. 2 Co 3:6).[19] This observation suggests caution is advisable for Pentecostals (or anyone else) plumbing the depths of Holy Scripture in search of support for personal positions (of whichever view). One should beware of prematurely supposing that the Evangelical or Pentecostal who simply cites the greatest number of texts for his/her viewpoint is actually ahead on exegesis. In actuality, approaching Christian theology of religions and interreligious dialogue from a biblical perspective may yield some surprising results.[20]

Speaking from its Christological perspective, Pannenberg suggests citing texts such as Acts 4:12 in a soteriologically exclusivist sense actually conceals the greater point of its truth and power.[21] Yet even Erickson approaches Acts 4:12 more as a statement on the anthropological extent of salvation than on its Christological source.[22] More carefully, famed NT scholar F.F. Bruce insists Acts 4:12 indicates salvation is "inextricably bound up" with the name of Jesus and persistent refusal will "bring destruction", but intriguingly adds, "The founders of the great world-religions are not to be disparaged by followers of the Christian way. But of none of them can it be said that there is no saving health in anyone else; to one alone belongs the title: the Savior of the world".[23] Pentecostal NT scholar French Arrington approvingly references Bruce's contention that "salvation" in this text includes both physical and spiritual healing, adding that it indicates "Jesus was made indispensable by God" and that "the message of the gospel excludes every other way of salvation and demands trust in Jesus and obedience to him".[24] Certainly, probably all Evangelicals and Pentecostals as well as many other Christians, would likely agree with the gist of these statements. The difficulty lies in determining whether or to what extent an exclusive Christology implies or requires an exclusive soteriology; or, to be more precise, if and how an exclusive soteriology is tied to epistemology. An ancient ambiguity, it shows up in Augustine also. Augustine clearly contended that Acts 4:12 indicates there is no other savior than Jesus and no other salvation save through faith in Jesus, but then immediately expanded the nature of that faith so as to include not only pre-Incarnation Israelites but even those before and beyond that nation. Perhaps Pentecostals may be particularly pleased that Augustine specifically argued that the redemptive God's grace in Christ was broadly applied through the mysterious working of the Holy Spirit (referencing John 3:8), that is, a strong pneumatological motif surfaces in Augustine's theology of religions even in connection with its central Christological focus.[25] Thus, Acts 4:12 may be interpreted as expressing Christological and soteriological exclusivity with allowances for unique nuances of universality. Arguably, it could be supportive of rather than oppositional to inclusivism. Apparently, espousing or defending epistemological exclusivity from Acts 4:12 goes beyond the clear teaching of that text.

Thus, Yong shows that, in spite of harsh rhetoric, Pentecostals have at times exhibited surprising openness to religious others.[26] He also argues that traditional Pentecostal antipathy toward religious others arises more out of Pentecostalism's involvement in the fundamentalist-modernist debate and their consequent anti-intellectualism than from anything else (such as, e.g., biblical exegesis). Additionally, he mentions their overly literalist biblical hermeneutic and ardent evangelism emphasis as contributing factors to interfaith antipathy.[27] Arguably, a complex conceptual context colors even objections purporting to be on biblical grounds.[28] Accordingly, Yong argues that Pentecostals and Charismatics need and desire to develop a theology of religions, including dedication to dialogue, for three reasons: because it flows freely out of their ecumenical roots and global presence, because it is true to their emphasis on missions, and because it furthers their continuing quest for theological identity and truth.[29] With these possibilities in mind, the present study will proceed to offer a biblical basis for the congruency of an inclusivist approach to interreligious encounter and dialogue.

A Biblical Definition of Religion[30]

Given the preceding section, the question remains germane: Is an inclusivist theology of religions and its consequent engagement in interreligious dialogue, biblically based? The answer depends, in part, on where one starts. If one starts with Scripture itself, then the answer is likely affirmative. Noted Anglican biblical theologian Alan Richardson insisted that current debate on religion (and religions) begin with a biblical definition of religion. For him there is clear distinction between non-biblical and biblical understandings of religion. Non-biblical definitions tend to see religion as occurring at humanity's initiative but a biblical definition insists that, "God rather than man is the primary agent in all religious activity." He accordingly adds that, "From the biblical point of view human religious activity in all its forms, pagan as well as Christian, is man's response to something which God does."[31] Richardson avers that the Christian definition of religion "as the human response to the divine initiative" is true not only of biblically based religions but of all the religions of the world. This means that, "God is the origin as well as the goal of the quest" of the religions. Richardson thinks St Paul's sermon to the Athenians in Acts 17 suggests the "divine quest for man finds its response in every religion of the world."[32] Nevertheless, he avoids pluralism, explaining that not all religions are equally true and that religion often perverts from its pure spiritual essence. The perversion of religion is how he understands such stringent NT passages as Roman 1:21-23.[33] Yet before the Word of God ever became incarnate in Christ, it was already present in the world.[34]

Richardson cites the examples of the religious traditions of India, Greece, or North Africa, as well as Europe, in support of the idea that seeds of gospel truth were present before its full flowering. He also calls on the Fourth Gospel and St. Augustine for canonical and classical confirmation. For him, the sum is that the Christian gospel "at the same time corroborates, corrects, and transcends the conjectures and gropings of the searchers after truth of all the nations." Richardson is not reticent to take to task an "older generation of missionaries" for theological and strategic wrong-headedness in "excoriating all the religious ideas and practices of the non-Christian world". He blames their error on a failure to identify and distinguish religion from the perversion of religion.[35] Richardson's reflections also relate to this study's focus on dialogue. Note the following.

> The dialogue between Christians and men of other religions, so urgently needed today in the face of the rising challenge of secularism, must be conducted out of the knowledge of each religion at its best, since parodies of religion merely supply its enemies with ammunition, and the scoring of debating points leads no one into the way of truth. ... [M]en of all religions are involved in a common predicament and would do well to face it together.[36]

Richardson tellingly concludes: "Christians who believe that God is not far from each one of us, should expect to discover in every religious aspiration traces of that word without whom nothing was made that has been made."[37]

Richardson's work as a biblical theologian suggests that far from being counter to Scripture an inclusivist approach to interreligious dialogue builds on a balanced interpretation of Scripture itself. Differing views on Scripture are found among various biblical scholars and theologians; but to identify an approach as "unbiblical" that has strong support from recognized and respected biblical researchers appears to be overly biased. True, an end to debate is not achieved. However, a casual assumption that intentional interreligious encounter and dialogue, such as presented in this study, is contrary to the Bible, cannot stand up under careful scrutiny.

An Abrahamic Precedent[38]

The scope of this present study does not permit an exhaustive analysis of interreligious relations in the entirety of Scripture or even in its various parts. However, demonstrating that Scripture is not necessarily exclusivistic is plausible, and is the proposed task of this section. It thus employs a few brief examples of biblical exegesis. It will examine two biblical passages, Genesis 20 and Genesis 21:22-34[39] to see whether they offer a supportive impetus for an inclusive and dialogical approach to interreligious dialogue such as extended in this project, including its emphasis on testimony. The rationale behind the specific selection of these passages lies in their potential role as a precedent for Abrahamic faiths regarding interreligious relations. If a good case may be made for an affirmative evaluation of these passages regarding this project's purpose, then the argument may be put forth that it suggests objections on biblical grounds appears ill founded.

There appears to be a tantalizing tradition of comparative openness to encountering religious others even within canonical scripture itself. This is not a particularly innovative observation on its own. Even some of the early Church Fathers acknowledged as much.[40] Genesis 20 is an excellent example. The well-known story of Abraham's sojourn in Gerar narrates his encounter with Abimelech, evidently a forerunner of the infamous Philistine kings.[41] The patriarch Abraham deceived Abimelech regarding his wife Sarah. Thinking she was unmarried, and according to the customs of the time, Abimelech took her into his royal harem. Yet God providentially warned Abimelech in a dream of impending judgment for his sin. He, however, understandably claimed innocence in the matter, and God graciously accepted his claim, explaining that his warning was redemptive rather than retributive in nature (1-7). Origen points out that Abimelech acted very differently from Pharaoh in a similar situation (Gen 12), even describing Abimelech as pure of heart and virtuous by comparison. In fact, he argues that God vindicates Abimelech because he is a representative of "the studious and wise men of the world". For Origen, he is a philosophical, pious, ethical, and moral man. The only reserve is in waiting for the coming of Christ as the promised redeemer. The healing of his harem, which God had struck with barrenness, seems to suggest to Origen soteriological implications.[42]

Of course, Abimelech confronts Abraham. Abraham admits he indulged in at least partial deception, and explains his motivation as fear due to an assumption that the people of that place were impious and immoral. Abimelech generously bestows material prosperity on Abraham, also allowing him liberty in the land, and Abraham prays an intercessory prayer for Abimelech and his household, which had been stricken with infertility (thus amounting to a sentence of death by degrees). God then heals them (8-18). Chrysostom argues that God used Abraham's encounter with Abimelech as a teaching tool to bring the man (and his nation) into a more complete knowledge of God and God's ways. God also wanted to teach Abimelech about the greatness of Abraham and his confidence in God.[43] Origen continues to insist that Abimelech was a virtuous philosopher but that it was "not yet time for the grace of God to pass over from the former people to the Gentiles." Origen insists that the coming of Christ is necessary for "complete and perfect virtue to pass over to the church of the Gentiles." Here he presents Abimelech and his wives and their children as a prophetic allegory of the Gentile Church.[44] Notably, Origen appears to be attempting to pair two superficially polar ideas: some Gentiles' genuine piety before Christ and their genuine redemptive need of Christ. Attributing to (at least some) Gentiles before Christ an incomplete but authentic measure of God's grace and virtue only fully realized in Christ with his historical incarnation and passion resolves any apparent disparity.[45]

Leaping forward several centuries in scholarship strengthens the conception that the Abraham-Abimelech narrative reinforces a rather benevolent bent toward the Philistines—perhaps as representatives of other religious others as well. Sailhammer notes that chapters 20 and 21 of Genesis both focus on the relationship between Abraham and the nations and his role in blessing them according to 12:3. Sailhammer identifies Abimelech as a "righteous Gentile". He even favorably contrasts him with Lot (Gen 19), who, though in the Abrahamic family sadly exemplifies "the mixed multitude", while Abimelech, who is not part of the family, is "the righteous sojourner (Gen 20).[46] Sailhammer thinks that more than anything else the narrative is actually about "the fate of the Philistines". Moreover, it shows that Abraham (and others?) had misjudged them religion wise.[47] The recurring refrain is that Abimelech and his people are righteous or innocent of blame in the entire affair. Indeed, God testifies to that fact. Sailhammer compares this incident to the story of Book of Jonah, with Abimelech and the Philistines resembling the reverent sailors and Abraham the reluctant prophet. (Thus, neither event represents isolated incidents. Perhaps they are more of a subtle but persistent pattern.) Abraham had apparently misjudged the Philistines because he had not made an actual assessment of them, but was misled by his prejudices. Even in forgiveness and reconciliation, Abimelech is the model of moral maturity. Nevertheless, Abraham's intercessory prayer is critical for a positive conclusion to this account. Though Sailhammer does not mention it, wondering if there is a redemptive implication about salvation through the seed of Abraham is natural enough. At the least, this obviously inclusive account still suggests that healing/forgiveness does come to the world (including the world religions?), through the mediation and intercession of the people of the God of Abraham.[48] That supposition is strengthened even more so by something he does mention—that Abimelech's people were doomed to death through barrenness without the restorative relationship made possible by the prayer of Abraham.[49] The soteriological inferences of Origin's speculations about the healing of Abimelech's house here resurface, and lend some weight to implicit inclusivism (though obviously not to pluralism).

OT scholar and commentator John Hartley notes that "interchange of action (vv. 2, 8, 14, 17-18) and dialogue (vv. 3-7, 9-13, 15-16)" characterize the unfolding drama between Abraham and Abimelech. Notably, "Dialogue occurs before and after the meeting." Like Origen and others, Hartley also favorably compares Abimelech's handling of the harem crisis to that of Pharaoh in Genesis 12. He agrees Abimelech acted "much more honorably" in the matter.[50] Apparently somewhat in Abraham's defense, he also observes that ancient monarchs "had the reputation of expanding their harems" at others' expense. Yet, significantly, he sees God's speaking directly to a Gentile king as "demonstrating that though he was working primarily through Abraham, God was not silent to the rest of humanity." God also honored Abimelech "for his efforts to promote a high standard in his realm."[51] The portrait painted in the interactions and dialogue between Abraham and Abimelech demonstrates that God acts justly with "foreign rulers in their dealings with his people." The reciprocal process of confession and compensation humbles (and empowers) both parties.[52]

Interestingly, Hartley points out that the entire situation arose out of Abraham's fear and proceeded along as Abimelech and his counselors began to fear.[53] Thus, fear is an essential issue. One might add that Abraham's "fear" of personal injury specifically revolved around the question of whether the "fear of God" was present among the Philistines while Abimelech's fear actually arose out of the fear of God's judgment (cf. 11 and 8).[54] In fact, the fear of God was present in this place among this people. John Wesley's comments on this passage bear quoting.

> There are many places and persons that have more of the fearof God in them than we think they have; perhaps they are not called by our name, they do not wear our badges, they do not tie themselves to that which we have an opinion of; and therefore we conclude they have not the fear of God in their hearts![55]

Furthermore, Rabbi Telushkin observes that this is the first time "the Bible associates lack of belief in God with lack of morality."[56] Telushkin also informs that for many in the Jewish tradition fear of God liberates from oppression and motivates ethical treatment of the vulnerable.[57] These elements of liberty, morality, and vulnerability are easily apparent in the interactions of Abraham and Abimelech. A fascinating interface between human fear of danger and fear of the divine surely seems obvious.[58] No wonder Hartley says Abraham acted inappropriately, Abimelech acted justly, and Abraham's misjudgment of Abimelech and his people caused the misunderstanding.[59] Nevertheless, Hartley is quick to note that Abimelech, by taking Sarah into his harem without proper protocol, including investigation of her marital status and official permission from her "brother," was not without partial blame.[60] Yet he did act to "restore the honor of Abraham and Sarah as well as his own" and for this God removed "the curse of infertility" which had come upon the Philistines consequent of the incident.[61]

Hartley also adds important insights from the follow up account of a further encounter between Abraham and Abimelech in Genesis 21:22-34.[62] In this case, Abraham and Abimelech enter into a mutually beneficial covenant of protection and prosperity. Importantly, Hartley points out the word translated "kindness," as shown by Abimelech to Abraham, is *hesed*.[63] This word can convey a broad range of related ideas such as goodness, kindness, love (including steadfast love, unfailing love, and even the archaic lovingkindness), mercy, and so on. Most significantly, many have argued that, though it occasionally occurs in human interpersonal relations, in several contexts it is indicative of special covenant loyalty between God and his people.[64] *Hesed* may be as important for the vocabulary of OT faith as say, grace, is for the vocabulary of NT faith. Accordingly, there may be implicit indication that Abraham and Abimelech are joining not only with each other but also with God in covenant relationship. Of course, the narrative context clearly indicates their covenant is ratified in shared acknowledgement of divine presence (22-23).

The narrative-oral-testimonial nature of Genesis 20 and 21:22-34 dovetails nicely with the present study. First, one might note up front that the divine-human encounter occurs in the context of God-given dreaming, prophethood, actual conversational communication, and healing by prayer. These activities suggest strongly pneumatological accents for Pentecostals arising out of their understanding of such biblical texts as Acts 2:14-21 (especially vv. 17-18) and 1 Corinthians 12:8-10.[65] Further significant is the unfolding of the narrative itself. The theological and thematic praxis developed thereon also clearly conjoin nicely. Particularly noteworthy is that the author/narrator infuses the text with an ideological point of view theologically pregnant with inclusivist and dialogical possibilities. The plot itself climaxes with the prayerful healing of non-Abrahamic peoples and the establishment of covenant relations on divine premises. The characterization of the chief Gentile involved is that of a pious and righteous person before God and in his dealing with other humans. The setting of the entire narrative is firmly within the patriarchal tradition establishing them as pilgrims in a foreign land learning to relate well to people of other faiths. Implicit within the thrifty commentary in the narrative is an explication of the role of the God who relates to diverse religious persons or parties. Arguably, readers in the Abrahamic tradition can hardly conclude otherwise than that the encounters between Abraham and Abimelech set a precedent for understanding and dealing with religious others that transcends rigid exclusivist paradigms.[66]

Based on this short survey of Abraham's encounters with Abimelech in Genesis 20 and 21:22-34, several observations relevant to the present study are apparent. First, assumptions that all religions outside the direct Abrahamic line of salvation history are rejected outright as intrinsically evil would be inaccurate. At least some religious others are described in much higher tones. Obviously, this is not a blanket assessment. The OT from the patriarchs onward indisputably decries and denounces in no uncertain terms the examples of idolatry and immorality that were all too prevalent (e.g., Ex 23:23; Num 33:52,53; Deut 20:16,17).[67] The Book of Judges presents the Philistines themselves in strongly uncomplimentary terms.[68] Abraham himself obviously, and ultimately with divine approval, properly judged as impious and immoral the people of Sodom (Gen 14 and 18).[69] However, neither should these harsh but honest assessments be unilaterally applied to all non-Abrahamic (or, later, non-Israelite) religious faith. And exceptions can be important precedents.[70]

Second, in the Bible, interreligious relations were at least sometimes characterized by dramatic and dynamic openness, interchange, and dialogue, even including prayer and testimony.[71] At this point, given the testimonial orientation of the present study, it may be appropriate to note that Abraham shared a personal testimony with the other in explaining his perspective on their predicament (20:11-13). Therefore, a testimony approach to interreligious dialogue appears biblically based for those of the Abrahamic faiths. Again, there are ample instances of religious war and interfaith conflict in the OT (as in the rest of religious history, whether Christian or otherwise). However, there is also a steady strain of suggestive interreligious encounter in contexts of mutual openness and respect.[72] Given the increasing acceptance of the theological currency of biblical narrative as essential in the witnessing tradition of Scripture, that a contemporary theology of interreligious encounter and dialogue utilizing testimony is quite evidently congruent with the Abrahamic encounters with Abimelech could be quite significant.[73]

Finally, arguably, the example explored herein of Abraham and Abimelech indicates a biblical precedent for (at least) the Abrahamic faiths. Those who are the spiritual children of Abraham (Gal 3:7; 4:28-31)[74] ought to emulate his example. If Abraham learned not to misjudge religious others, if he learned to engage in interaction, dialogue, and prayer with and for religious others, if he saw God healing religious others even through his own testimony, then so ought his heirs. If Abraham did all this without losing anything of his special witness (Gen 12:3), in fact, in vital fulfillment of that very witness to the nations and the world, then so ought his heirs. Accordingly, though no contrary suggestion is made concerning non-Abrahamic religions, at the very least the Abrahamic religions, that is, Judaism, Christianity, and Islam have a right and a responsibility to engage in open encounter with religious others and in interreligious dialogue.[75] To the extent that they are verily faithful to the Abrahamic tradition as presented in the Bible, these religions have the ability and the responsibility thus to proceed.

Betrays the Pentecostal Tradition

Deeply Practicing Real Religion[76]

As noted above some Classical Pentecostals are concerned lest an increasingly popular inclusivist orientation betray the bedrock values of their tradition. Yet Chapter 2 of this work argues that a moral and spiritual obligation rests with all faith groups, including Pentecostals, for mitigation of current conflict arising out of indiscreet and, therefore, indiscriminate interreligious encounters. A Yale theologian from a Croatian Evangelical Pentecostal background, Miroslav Volf demonstrates decisively that the Christian religion, when "deeply practiced," does not foster violence. He examines the intricacies of forgiveness and justice to arrive at a view in which forgiveness and reconciliation embrace the other.[77] He bases his Christian theology of forgiveness, reconciliation, and justice squarely on the model of God's action in the cross of Christ.[78] The major thrust of Volf's essay is that the Christian religion, when "practiced deeply," does not foster violence, but rather promotes a realistic experience of justice and peace in the present age as it moves toward an idealistic realization in the eschaton. Only a shallow exercise of Christian religion stripping Christianity of its transcendent values and made subservient to some political or economic ideology, is a weapon of war. Therefore, in a society ripped apart by religious violence, Volf calls for more not less religion as the antidote to inter-religious acrimony.[79]

Though it has indeed been an instrument of atrocities, even a casual observer familiar with the values of the faith can see that in such cases Christianity has betrayed its own bedrock foundations and would have been better served by a deeper practice of its own faith. The same may be said for Pentecostalism. Pentecostals, because of a robust pneumatology, ought to recognize the presence and influence of the Holy Spirit throughout all realms of reality, and then apply their deepest and best to being part of the solution for religion-related problems of global conflict and violence. Pentecostals through cooperative interfaith endeavors can help counter the influence of violence perpetrated in the name of religion and contribute to fostering justice and peace. Importantly, doing so is true to the actual, original Pentecostal tradition. Veli-Matti Kärkkäinen argues, along with other Pentecostal scholars such as Walter Hollenweger and Cecil Robeck, that Pentecostalism began as a movement that was open to religious others, later became sidetracked into exclusivism, but is today beginning to be restored to its original more visionary faith.[80] Apparently, though the fact has often been forgotten, Pentecostalism has an inherent ecumenism and inclusivism that is particularly applicable for today's religious environment. Arguably, ecumenical and inclusive awareness is not a faddish development of the times, which have only drawn attention forcefully to preexisting dilemmas of religious unity, diversity, and plurality, but is intrinsic to Pentecostalism to the extent the movement is faithful to its own innermost identity and impulse.

Drawing Fresh Water from Old Wells[81]

Unfortunately, Pentecostal identity has often been obscured or altered by its unfortunate, unequal association with ideologically anti-Pentecostal groups.[82]

Restoration of authentic Pentecostal identity tends to ecumenism and inclusivism. Pentecostalism is a multifarious movement and variety helps shape its identity.[83] The current global condition of contemporary Pentecostalism adds even greater "variety and heterogeneity" to the movement.[84] Such diversity and variety easily lends itself to ecumenism and inclusivism. Accordingly, rather than a departure from or betrayal of authentic Pentecostal tradition these values arise readily out of its own ethos and identity. An "ecumenical root" may be seen in early Pentecostal leaders throughout the world, including Jonathan Paul in Germany, Alexander Boddy in England, and Louis Dallière in France.[85] Contemporary Pentecostals can be comfortable that ecumenical and inclusivist implications of pneumatology being drawn out today are indeed amicable to their original spiritual and theological heritage.

Efforts to force Pentecostalism into an ideological mold void of ecumenical interaction appear contrary to the original and intrinsic nature of Pentecostalism. Again, Kärkkäinen notes that, "from the beginning Pentecostalism has been characterized by variety," even suggesting a need to speak in the plural, of "Pentecostalisms," rather than of Pentecostalism as a single phenomenon.[86] Authentic Pentecostalism embraces and expresses a variety and diversity rightly described as ecumenical and inclusive. This is not surprising given Pentecostalism's varied roots including formative influences from the Wesleyan-Holiness movements, Catholic spirituality and mysticism, and an African American enthusiastic, corporeal worship style.[87] And a gregarious early Pentecostalism grew some inclusive trunks and branches out of these roots. Douglas Jacobsen points out that Bishop J. H. King, an important pioneer among Classical Pentecostals, articulated an optimistic, inclusivist theology of religions.[88] Other early Pentecostals such as Charles Parham and G. T. Haywood also advocated rather open attitudes toward adherents of other religions.[89] Kärkkäinen laments that Pentecostals succumbed to alien ideologies on theology of religions and ignored their own heritage, and calls for contemporaries to correct the deficit.[90]

Rather than betraying the Pentecostal tradition through engagement in interreligious dialogue, the same appears to be more in tune with a returning to an underlying element of an original and authentic ethos of early Pentecostalism. To the extent that any movement, religious or otherwise, ought to consider its founding vision fundamental to its ongoing identity and activity, Pentecostalism ought to be unashamedly involved in interreligious encounter and dialogue. Not compromise but continuity is occurring.

Minimizes Christian Mission

Enlarging, not Limiting, Mission[91]

An appropriate concern for Pentecostals is that an inclusive theology of religions replaces the obligation for world evangelism (quoting Matt 18:28; Mk 16:15)[92] with an alternate emphasis on interreligious dialogue, and that those who fail to fulfill the Great Commission are compromising Christ's Lordship.[93] However, is this necessarily the case? When facing objections about the nature of the Church's "missionary mandate" and its relation to issues of conversion, dialogue, and truth, reexamining this superficial assumption is helpful. For instance, OT biblical scholar from a Wesleyan perspective, John Oswalt, says of the inclusivist teaching of Isaiah the prophet,

> It is often debated whether Israel had a missionary mandate. If "missionary mandate" means a commission to make converts, then there is room for debate. But if it means the obligation to declare to the world the truth of what had been revealed to them, there is no room for debate whatsoever. If Israel's God is the only God, and if even the Cyruses of the earth serve him, then he is the God of every person under the sun.[94]

Yet Oswalt says Isaiah 57:15 ("For this is what the high and lofty One says — he who lives forever, whose name is holy: "I live in a high and holy place, but also with him who is contrite and lowly in spirit, to revive the spirit of the lowly and to revive the heart of the contrite." NIV) is "one of the finest one-sentence summaries of biblical theology in the Bible." It emphasizes the "utter transcendence of God." In other words, "God is not part of this world or its processes. He created it as something other than himself, and he stands over against it, both to judge it and to save it." For Oswalt, "This is the truth that separates biblically based religions (Judaism, Christianity, Islam) from all others."[95] In an explanatory footnote, Oswalt further says, "Christianity is differentiated from the other two by its insistence that salvation is by divine grace alone, mediated to us through the death and resurrection of Jesus Christ."[96] First Oswalt affirms inclusivism and then evangelism. Apparently, for him they are not mutually exclusive.

Indeed, one may view evangelism and inclusivism as two sides of the same commitment.[97] Evangelism is committed to proclaiming the good news of God in Christ to all that they may respond, hopefully, in faith. Inclusivism is committed to articulating and acting upon the principle that God is not limited to humanity's efforts. However, though the practice of dialogue, in part, arises out of recognition that God has been at work already and will continue to be so, it does not conclude that God's call to humanity to enter together into that work as co-laborers has been suspended. Pinnock puts it well:

> Isn't it wiser to engage in mission with hope, trusting the God who has been at work beforehand. Hope can be an encouragement rather than an impediment to evangelism. It fosters good relationships and encourages points of contact. God does not send us into mission knowing the final destiny of every soul. It is not our job to judge the world or identity the elect. Jesus did not do so, and he warned that there would be surprises for those who tried. He said the first would be last and the last first.[98]

Evangelizing Authentically[99]

Throughout this study, attention has been directed to its Wesleyan-Pentecostal orientation. John Wesley was very much concerned with winning the world to and for the Lord Jesus Christ. He bemoaned bitterly the fact that so much of the world population of his day was Heathen, Jewish, or Muslim and that Christian missions had made so little global progress.[100] He laid the blame for that sad fact squarely at the door of Christians themselves. He opined that the hypocrisy and immorality of so many Christians hinders Muslims from authentically hearing the Gospel. When that "grand stumbling-block" is "happily removed out of the way," then Jews, Muslims, and Heathen will "look upon them with other eyes, and begin to give attention to their words."[101] High hopes may be entertained that when sincere adherents of other religions meet Christians whose lives genuinely radiate the vitality and power of the Holy Spirit in words and in works they will respond by honoring the Son as they do the Father (cf. John 5:23).[102] Consequently, a Christianity that recommends itself to Jews, Muslims, and Heathens will necessarily consist of people who truly "have 'the mind which was in Christ,' and who 'walk as he also walked', whose inmost soul is renewed after the image of God; and who are outwardly holy, as He who hath called them is holy".[103] Obviously, for Wesley issues relative to life in the Holy Spirit and to holiness are dominant considerations for any disciple of Christ interested in evangelizing members of other religions.

Wesley's approach to the evangelism of adherents of other religions seems to arise out of a number of convictions. First, he is convinced of the inestimable advantage to absolutely everyone for receiving Jesus Christ in personal faith and obedience. Second, he is convinced anyone sincerely walking in the light he or she has will recognize and respond positively to the fuller or more complete light of God in Christ when it is authentically presented. Third, he is convinced that the greatest witness to the world of the truth in Christ is a life transformed by the power of the Holy Spirit from the guilt and bondage of sin to a life of holiness and freedom.

The kind of situation that Wesley envisioned in which adherents of other religions are brought into close contact with authentic Christians undoubtedly necessitates a profound level of personal relation. Passing out tracts or mass media preaching will not suffice. Ongoing and close up scrutiny of heart and life, of a Christian's character and conduct, is required. Informally, and to some extent, unintentionally, such interreligious interpersonal interaction could occur as family, friends, or fellow workers of different faiths are exposed to each other's company (and character) long term. Yet formally, and intentionally, this kind of interreligious interpersonal interaction could occur through the framework of substantive, sustained interfaith dialogue partnerships. Accordingly, Wesleyan-Pentecostal historic evangelistic identity is compatible with an inclusive and dialogical approach to interfaith relations. In fact, it may demand it.[104]

Trades Absolutes for Relativism

Truth as Provisional Eschatology[105]

Veteran missionary to India Leslie Newbigin insisted, "The question of truth must be faced." He further exhorted that in addition to "telling of the story," Christians also must "embody the truth of the story."[106] In Evangelical and Pentecostal circles, the cry often goes forth that interreligious dialogue implicitly assumes some sort of relativistic theory of religious truth. In other words, at least practically speaking, it tends to deny absolute truth. This section will briefly address that concern. Its eventual assertion is that intentional interreligious encounter both boldly faces the question of truth and embodies truth in Christian belief and practice. The thought of Wolfhart Pannenberg, a leading Continental European systematic theologian, has enjoyed ongoing attention from Pentecostals on a number of topics, but especially regarding pneumatology.[107] In relation to his theology of religions, he argues for an understanding of world religions as competing for universal truth.[108] Pannenberg therefore provides Pentecostals with a helpful conversation partner regarding the nature of truth and interreligious dialogue.

For Pannenberg "all depends on the question of truth" and "everything depends on the reality of God". He fears a tendency to avoid confronting the truth question by thinking of the biblical narrative as "story" or "myth". For him the question of truth is not only a theological question but also a question of reality in all of life. Truth may be experienced or perceived differently, but a unity of all experience is essential. Consequently, he regards a coherence of all experience as the "final criterion of truth". Pannenberg says that, "Whatever is true must finally be consistent with all other truth, so that truth is only one, but all-embracing, closely related to the concept of the one God."[109]

Pannenberg distinguishes between "the level of reflection" and "the realm of experiential immediacy." Christian theology is concerned with the truth question at the level of reflection, the level where truth claims are to be judged or examined and confirmed. For him, theology is not only "to investigate the origin and the original content of truth claims" in Christianity, but also "to determine the truth which is contained in that tradition." The unchanging truth of the historical tradition must be repeatedly reformulated in each generation though the content of truth remains the same. Therefore, the theological task regarding truth is both systematic and critical. For Pannenberg a systematic and comprehensive presentation of teaching is "itself a test of truth" because "coherence belongs to the nature of truth."[110]

A distinctive trait of Pannenberg's theory of truth is its eschatological and therefore provisional character.[111] He insists: "It is only in the event of final salvation that the reality of God will be definitively established."[112] Until that time, Christian doctrine does not have "a prior guarantee of truth" so that "the question of truth should be regarded as open." Pannenberg sees this position as a contemporary application of the Pauline perspective on the present state of the imperfection of knowledge (cf. 1 Co 13:9).[113] For him this involves exciting exploration of the truth of God including interaction with secular disciplines, but he warns against ever assuming we have "the truth at our disposal."[114] Yet Pannenberg adamantly maintains a distinction between "indifference" to truth claims and "tolerance" of competing truth claims, as exist in, for example, relations between Christianity with other world religions. While he is willing to include religious others in the benefits of Christ in some way, he is not willing to exclude the necessity of Christ from the availability of those benefits. Tolerance is required because we are "aware of the provisional form of the human predicament" in that we "do not yet see the final truth in ultimate clarity." But Christians cannot surrender Christian truth claims without ceasing to be Christian. Rather, Christians must show reasons for their truth claims, specifically about Christ as the Son of God and Savior of fallen, sinful humanity.[115] Ultimately, for Pannenberg in the eschaton, that is, in the future of God, God will declare final truth. In the meanwhile, the sonship of Jesus Christ reflected in the reality of his resurrection from the dead provides Christians with a basis for their belief that the eternal truth of God has been manifested in the personal history of Jesus Christ.[116]

Grenz and Olson add that Pannenberg's connection of "the basic religious phenomenon" of human nature with the experience of God found in the religions opens the way for viewing "the rivalry of the religions as the location of the revelation of truth."[117] For Pannenberg the history of religions, including their ongoing interaction, is actually a theater of truth. But "[t]he religious orientation that best illumines the experience of all reality will in the end prevail and thereby demonstrate its truth value." In the interim prior to the eschaton Jesus is the "prolepsis" or "historical preview" of God's self-disclosure or truth "which ultimately lies at the end of history."[118] Significantly, though truth in its final form will emerge only in the eschaton, Grentz and Olson claim that for Pannenberg "people of faith can obtain a greater degree of certainty than is often admitted."[119]

A serious problem that Pentecostals have with Pannenberg's basic schema is its tendency to deemphasize the role of the Holy Spirit in human responsiveness to historical revelation. He seems later on, however, to attempt an adjustment to this unfortunate propensity.[120] Nevertheless, perceptive Pentecostals still have questions regarding Pannenberg's pneumatology, including taking issue with how it affects his approach to truth. Pentecostal theologian Veli-Matti Kärkkäinen ably articulates some of the more salient concerns.[121] Though Kärkkäinen deals with several issues in Pannenberg's pneumatology, the main concern here is with his critique of its applications to the task of truth determination. Pannenberg claims that the eschatological verification of provisional truth occurs in human hearts presently by the operation of the Holy Spirit, but insists that the Spirit "adds" nothing to the truth.[122] Kärkkäinen thinks Pannenberg wants to be able to argue that anyone can see the historical revelation of God quite apart from any special illuminating agency, and that he wishes to avoid any subjectivist arguments for truth verification. But he still strangely posits some sort of vague "convicting ministry of the Spirit and truth" which he just does not clearly explicate. Kärkkäinen finally concludes in frustration that Pannenberg "is a bit confusing" on this particular point due to his failure to provide clear analysis of his ideas.[123] Kärkkäinen also notes that Pannenberg seems incognizant of developments in pneumatology arising out of the Pentecostal-Charismatic movement. If correct, this deficit surely hinders dialogue between Pentecostals and Pannenberg.[124]

The eschatological dimension of Pannenberg's program is appealing to Pentecostals.[125] As Land has shown, Pentecostalism may be understood as "an eschastological intensification" of "restorationist, perfectionist, premillennialist motifs" in nineteenth-century holiness and revialist movements.[126] Furthermore, he insists of the earliest Pentecostals that, "A passion for the kingdom of God was the unifying center of the movement", adding of contemporary participants, that "Even in their divisiveness the Pentecostals still share this passion."[127] More directly, Macchia approvingly references Pannenberg in his own eschatological and pneumatological arguments. Pannenberg is cited supportively in Macchia's "now-not yet" eschatology bringing together present-future dimensions of Christ's ministry through the liberating power of the Holy Spirit and in his teaching that Christ's identity as the one who bestows the Spirit flows out of his historical resurrection from the dead toward eschatological realization.[128]

As Kärkkäinen points out, Pannenberg's strong view of comprehensive truth is nevertheless clearly compatible with the sustained practice of interreligious dialogue.[129] Pannenberg enters dialogue with a commitment to truth as a unified and coherent whole, and to the superiority of the Christian view of God. Yet, although he sees Christ as "a final revelation of God," he is not exclusive.[130] Obviously, he is not pluralistic either. Thus, Pannenberg's approach carries great potential for interreligious dialogue. Significantly, authentic dialogue does not try to "soften the differences" between the religions or "blur the importance" of their common search for truth. With Pannenberg's acceptance of an eschatological establishment of the question of truth, the penultimate dialogical process becomes extremely important. The religions and their truth claims are provisional, and await divine approbation or adjustment in an essential attitude of honesty and humility. Therefore, Pannenberg's view affirms the unique revelation of God in Christ but avoids being restrictive.[131]

Wolfhart Pannenberg serves as an excellent example for Pentecostals that a strong view of Christian truth and engagement in interreligious dialogue are compatible and constructive. That is, commitment to interreligious dialogue does not entail diminishment of commitment to absolute truth. Quite the contrary is actually the case. Consenting to the common religious quest for truth, the Christian dialoguer nonetheless approaches the task of interfaith conversation with honest but humble confidence in the ultimate confirmation of the truth of the crucified and risen Christ. Therefore, proceeding in the power of the Spirit of Truth, Pentecostals may testify before religious others of God's grace and glory in Christ (John 15:26-27).[132]

Truth as Dialogical Activity[133]

Wesleyan theologian Laurence Wood demonstrates in *Theology as History and Hermeneutics,* the question of religious truth, or for that matter, any truth, has increasingly become a thorny theological theme. Myriad pre-modern, modern, and postmodern philosophical issues are enmeshed. Some of the greatest thinkers, religious and non-religious, and past and present, are engaged as well. However, there seems to be a growing consensus that reevaluating and redefining post-Enlightenment, rationalistic understandings of truth are necessary.[134] Congruent with the present work, Wood notes that what he calls "post-critical evangelicalism", a significant stream within currently developing evangelicalism after its previously overly rationalistic era, suggests that, "Not doctrinaire truth and rational criteria, but testifying truth and historical narrative represent the essential format of the Bible." Additionally Wood argues that, "theology is being faithful to itself, not when it accommodates to the spirit of the times, but when it responsibly connects to the present age." Accordingly, "theology is dialogical because there is a dialectical relationship between faith and culture."[135] The present study therefore understands that truth is indeed a dialogical activity nevertheless surrendering nothing of its stance on the strength of truth vis-à-vis the relativism it perceives to be rampant in religious pluralism.

In large part, then, how one views the place of truth in interreligious dialogue probably depends on one's overall philosophy of truth. This section does not attempt to delineate a comprehensive view of truth.[136] What it does attempt to do is to demonstrate that a respectful, strong view of the nature of Christian truth is not necessarily opposed to a process of dialogue and interaction with other religions. It recruits the aid of a Christian apologist, Jerry Gill, in developing and defending the idea that dialogue and truth are not only compatible but also companionable. Gill's basic posture is that religious faith can and should engage dialogically with the world around it. He explains that, "the only apologetic approach both to the nature of Christian belief and to the pluralistic character of our times is one which is open enough to acknowledge the limitations of religious knowledge and faith as well as to affirm their reasonableness." Accordingly, he advocates "a dialogical posture ... that *listens* as well shares."[137] For him, dialogical posture is a matter of "dialogical interaction between our God-given capacity to think and the revelatory activity of God in nature, history, and community."[138] The bulk of book then engages dialogically with natural science and the central issue of reductionism, social science and the issue of relativism, the humanities and humanism, and, world religions and pluralism.

Gill's chapter on dialogue with world religions essentially affirms the ultimate and universal truth of Christ while accepting that there is truth elsewhere as well, and that dialogue is an important process of reciprocal growth.[139] He says, "In short, others may grow closer to the truth as a result of our dialogue—*and* I, too, may grow closer to it in the same way." He adds, "As a Christian, my responsibility is not to convince others that I am right, but simply to share and to serve."[140] Significantly, he later explains that his overall philosophy of truth is essentially a "postcritical perspective" advocating "the essentially *relational* character of religious knowledge" (as opposed to purely propositional).[141] Therefore, knowing God is not simply a cognitive grappling with or grasping of an eternal abstract idea but an experienced reality with personal and multidimensional awareness and activity.[142] Gill therefore recommends dialogical engagement of Christian faith with the world, including but not only world religions. However, the proper attitude for doing so is twofold. Christians engaged in dialogue, for the present purposes, specifically in interreligious dialogue, should exhibit an attitude of "confidence" and "humility."[143] Christians can and should be confident in their confession of their own faith, even while being humbly willing to listen to others.[144]

The preceding suggests that not only is truth compatible with dialogue but dialogue is its close companion too. Out of conversation with others, whether religious or otherwise, fresh insights for the truth of faith may be spoken and heard that might not be known just so in any other way. This does not mean that divine revelation in the Scriptures is incomplete. It does not mean that historic

Christian doctrine is incorrect. What it does suggest is that the Holy Spirit may use human encounter and conversation to instruct the people of God. That is an idea completely consistent with biblical and Pentecostal faith and values (cf. Acts 8:26-40).[145] Accordingly, interreligious dialogue, properly approached, does not compromise, minimize, or relativize the absolute nature of divine truth. Therefore, Pentecostals can and should engage in interfaith conversation without fear of faultiness.

Faces Irresolvable Situation

Understanding Religion-Related Violence[146]

Sometimes a sense of helplessness and even hopelessness overshadows efforts to reconcile rival religions or bring about global peace through religious resources. Critics doubt if any amount of interreligious dialogue or political negotiation will be effective for any permanent settlement. Consequently, it often seems as if it is all no more than a waste of time and energy. It is a good idea, driven by admirable sentiments, but not feasible, not practical, just not workable. Therefore, interreligious dialogue is regrettably but realistically untenable.[147] One often hears in Pentecostal circles this cynicism regarding the Middle East, including relations between Jews and Muslims.[148] Especially since September 11, 2001 and the terrorist attack by radical Islamists on the World Trade Center in the United States and the subsequent declaration of America's War on Terror, the same sentiment often extends to Muslim-Christian relations as well.[149]

Catholic theologian Hans Küng, one of the foremost advocates of interreligious dialogue today, addresses forthrightly the problem of religious violence and a path toward global peace that resources the religions.[150] A brief summary of some of his main conclusions appears in his essay "Global Ethics and Education".[151] Küng's study is set in the context of educating the young regarding a global ethic. Küng begins with the rise of graphic violence in modern media, particularly in videos, and with the reality of the "orientation jungle", or loss of viable foundations for navigating life, in much of contemporary society. These contribute to an almost unchecked and certainly unprecedented escalation of violence in global society, which in turn demonstrates a dire need for a global ethic capable of restoring order.[152] Küng admits that to many, both religious and non-religious, the religions appear incapable of peace. In fact, they may be inherently aggressive and can contribute to violence.[153] However, Küng concludes, in conversation with the discipline of psychology, that not only the religions but also humanity as a whole is inherently aggressive as a built-in survival strategy. A certain aggression is essential for survival. The problem is not aggression, which is necessary for self-assertion, but resorting to violence as an inappropriate expression of aggression. Accordingly, Küng does not advocate attempting the destruction of aggression but for reconstruction in positive directions.[154] The religions, whose constituents are after all human beings, naturally "possess a certain element of aggression." Especially when threatened, both "religious persons and religions as such also exhibit aggressive behavior." Sometimes this aggression becomes inordinate and contributes to harmfulness and violence. Yet, as Küng shows with concrete examples, religious persons and religions are also often in the forefront of peacemaking.[155]

Developing a Global Ethic for Peace

As Hans Küng sees it, the challenge before contemporary society, both religious and non-religious, is developing and adopting a global ethic capable of guiding the world away from violence toward peace.[156] The ecumenical movement, in its broad sense of interaction and cooperation among the world's religions, can be of major assistance in that process. As an example of a right step in interreligious ethics, he cites the September 1993 Parliament of the World's Religions declaration on "Toward a Global Ethic".[157] This declaration affirms basic agreement of humane treatment for all people. Küng discusses it in the context of "The Golden Rule," found in some form or fashion in the traditions of most of the religions, and expressed positively as "that which you would have others do to you, do also to others." For him, this Golden Rule can serve as the norm for human ethical behavior in all spheres of life. He elaborates on it through "four comprehensive, ancient imperatives of humane behavior found in most of the world's religions". He suggests applying these for commitment to a culture of nonviolence and reverence for all life, of solidarity and to a just economic order, of tolerance and a life of truthfulness, and of equality and partnership of man and woman.[158]

Küng feels that education, beginning with children, concerning ethics, especially a global ethic, will help lead the world toward an attainable and sustainable peace.[159] He has four ascending observations motivating and molding implementation of the global ethic. First, he insists, "Humankind will not survive without world peace." Second, "There will be no world peace without world justice." Third, "There will be no world justice without truth and humane behavior." Fourth, "There will be no true humanity without coexistence in partnership."[160] Pedagogy that is thoughtful and ethical can help establish this global ethic. Küng closes with a description of the kind of religion than can help bring peace to a war-torn world: "religiosity with a foundation, but without fundamentalism; religiosity with religious identity, but without exclusivity; religiosity with certainty of truth, but without fanaticism."[161]

For the purposes of the present discussion, Hans Küng here helps in a twofold manner. First, he demonstrates that interreligious dialogue, as a component in peacemaking is not a rosy-eyed, "pie in the sky" endeavor ignoring the hard realities of life on the ground. Second, he also demonstrates that the world religions can contribute significantly and effectively to the peacemaking process through cooperative efforts among people of faith. A pessimist attitude will certainly be self-defeatist. Passivity will bring about a self-fulfilling prophecy. However, some energetic and enduring effort to utilize the resources of the religions through interfaith dialogue and cooperation can bring about real change. It will not be easy or instantaneous, but one has grounds for optimism.

Conclusion/Summary

The purpose of this chapter has not been the giving of an exhaustive apology for this project's approach to interreligious encounter and dialogue. That requires more space and time than are available at this point. However, it has endeavored to demonstrate that the approach presented herein can offer defensible and reasonable support for itself against a selection of possible objections that may be anticipated. The aim has been to exhibit congruence with the pattern of biblical and theological faith consciously prevalent in Pentecostalism. In other words, it is a valid point of view regarding a Pentecostal approach to current crises precipitated by radical religious pluralism, on the one hand, and on the other hand, extremist-fundamentalist religion related violence. Now a turn will be made in the next chapter to consider a vision for the future of Pentecostal interfaith involvement. The idea of determining whether our interreligious dialogue edifice is legitimately inhabitable continues to guide the process

Notes

1. These objections are not selected arbitrarily. They represent the kind of concerns I have encountered from other Pentecostals when discussing the dialogical process. Indeed, this apologetical chapter primarily intends to address Pentecostal rather than non-Pentecostal critics, though there is obvious overlap at times.

2. This section draws on the work of Amos Yong.

3. A. Yong, *Discerning the Spirit(s): A Pentecostal-Charismatic Contribution to Christian Theology of Religions* JSup 20 (Sheffield: Sheffield Academic, 2000), 55.

4. A. Yong, *Beyond the Impasse: Toward a Pneumatological Theology of Religions* (Grand Rapids: Baker, 2003), 106.

5. Yong, *Beyond the Impasse*, 107.

6. R.P. Richard, *The Population of Heaven: A Biblical Response to the Inclusivist Position on Who Will be Saved* (Chicago: Moody, 1994).

7. Richard, *Population,* 66-67 (67).

8. L. Morris, *NICNT: The Gospel According to John,* (Grand Rapids, MI: Eerdmans, 1971, 1987), John, 640.

9. Arrington, "Acts," *FLBCNT,* 578.

10. Morris, *John,* 641.

11. Michaels, *John,* does assert that Jesus' answer, in the context of Thomas's question about "How can we know the way?" (v. 5), indicates that "What is necessary is simply to know Jesus in personal faith and to trust him as the only one who can lead the searching disciple to the Father" (258-59). However, Michaels denies that Jesus is outlining a way to heaven, which apocalyptic Judaism sought, or "a formula for escaping this world and attaining salvation", which Gnosticism and Hellenistic mystery religions sought (258). Rather, John 14:6 puts "simultaneous stress on Jesus as the Way and on the Father as the Destination" (259). Akers, "John," in fact, argues from v. 7 that central to the conversation was that Jesus' own disciples still did not really know him and therefore could not really know the Father either, 84. Morris suggests that though they have known Jesus "in a sense" they "did not know Him in His full significance"—which would mean for them to know the Father as well, 642. Morris thinks this text represents an advance through Christ over the hitherto limited knowledge of God characteristic of the OT, so that henceforth they would "really know God" through what Christ had done, resulting in

"a revolution both in religious experience and in theological understanding" (642). Accordingly, one might suggest that knowing here has complex rather than simplistic implicative overtones. At the least, several shades of "knowing" appear in the text and its context. D.M. Smith, "John," 1044-76, *Harper's Bible Commentary,* gen. ed. J.L. Mays (San Francisco, CA: Harper & Row, 1988), even suggests Jesus' purpose actually may be to reassure his disciples during the dilemma of their present state of inevitable ignorance, as indicated by their persistent and puzzled questioning, by anticipating a coming time of more complete knowledge (vv. 8-11), 1067-68. Yet, again, there is no doubt that "Jesus uses this", as Aker says, to "emphasize the uniqueness of his redeeming work. Only through him can one get to God" (84). Therefore, that "Jesus is both life, and the source of life" (Morris, 641) is indisputable and unquestionable for biblical faith. Yet, this brief survey suggests Richard is wrong to suppose all-too-blithely and briefly that John 14:6 cannot be properly interpreted inclusively; more likely, epistemological and soteriological exclusivism is challenged to go beyond bare superficial exposition. Amazingly, exclusivists like Richard insist John 14:6 obviously requires complete epistemological awareness for status as Jesus' disciples while the text itself actually exposes the incomplete epistemological awareness of Jesus' own disciples! And as if that is not sufficiently startling, their incomplete epistemological awareness had to do precisely with Jesus' own identity and relation to the Father! Finally, a more epistemologically modest interpretation of John 14:6 is consistent with the overall theology of the Fourth Gospel, as I.H. Marshal, *New Testament Theology: Many Witnesses, One Gospel* (Downer's Grove, IL: InterVarsity Press, 2004), observes: "Although this Gospel makes more of the way in which the whole life of Jesus reveals God and knowledge of the truth brings freedom ... *far more is said about faith than about knowledge as the way to eternal life. Knowledge of God is the content of eternal life rather than the way to it*" (526; italics added).

12. Richard, *Population,* 145-49.

13. E.g., C. Sinkinson, "In Defense of the Faith: Clark Pinnock and the World Religions," *Reconstructing Theology: A Critical Assessment of the Theology of Clark Pinnock,* eds. T. Gray & C. Sinkinson (Waynesboro, GA: Paternoster, 2000), 155-83, concludes that based on "the cognitive criteria of Scripture" "there is simply nothing we can say about those who have never heard." However, he does think one can make judgments on the religions as institutions, 183.

14. Morris, *John,* suggests John 3:16-21 is a reflection of the Evangelist rather than the direct words of Jesus, 228. Accordingly, John wishes to convey the breadth of God's love as for the whole world and the centrality of Christ as God's saving gift, 229, against a backdrop of eternal life vis-à-vis perishing or judgment, 229-31. Morris asserts that John "attributes the salvation in question ultimately to the Father" (232). Faith in Christ is essential for salvation and persistent unbelief brings inevitable condemnation, 232-33. Yet the divide between faith and unbelief or salvation and condemnation occurs as part of a process of responding either to the light (faith/salvation) or to darkness (unbelief/condemnation), 233. Although Morris acknowledges that those who choose darkness/reject Christ are those who already make a practice of persistent wrongdoing and those who choose light/accept Christ are those who already do that which is true, 234-35, he suggests the tendency to respond in an admittedly predisposed manner is perhaps best explained through the theme of election, 235. However, as Morris thinks John explicitly rejects "a rigid and hopeless determinism" because it "deprives [people] of any power of choice", insisting "John is concerned with meaningful moral choice, not blind fate", 234, then some prior divine influence and activity freely inclining toward the light of Christ and of salvation seems implied. If so, then arguably this passage on the necessity of faith in Christ for salvation could carry with it an assumption of voluntary implicit faith re-

sponding positively to the light. Indeed, J.R. Michaels, *NIBC: John* (1984, 1989), says this passage indicates that "Coming to Jesus proves God has *already* [original italics] been at work in one's life" (59), and that faith in Christ expresses that reality, 60. Like Morris, Michaels also turns to "a strong doctrine of election" to explain this predisposition to salvation, but explains that "From a human perspective the new birth is a conversion, but from God's perspective 'conversion' simply brings out in the open the true nature of those whom God has chosen" (60). Further, he adds that "What matters in history is whether a person decides to remain in darkness or to come to the light that has dawned in Jesus Christ" (60). Smith, "John," *Harper's*, suggests John's explanation of why some avoid the light while others come to it "could mean that Jesus as light only confirms a preference for light or darkness, depending on people's previous disposition and conduct" (1051). Accordingly, "Faith in Jesus would then be morally predetermined" (1052), though Smith reminds that John's context included "alienation of communities (church and synagogue)" (1052). Apparently, the complexity of responsiveness to Christ in faith exhibited in John 3:18-21 leaves ample room for pre-explicit response inclination to faith, or, i.e., implicit faith—which would not necessarily rule out inclusive epistemological considerations discussed above (Fn 8). In any case, at the least, appeals to texts such as Acts 4:12 and John 3:18 to support traditional exclusivism or refute inclusivism appear superficial upon close inspection.

15. Although Matt 18:28-35 actually focuses on appropriate interpersonal responses to divine forgiveness, R.H. Mounce, *NIBC: Matthew* (1985, 1991), 178. The emphasis on miraculous signs in the longer ending of Mark 16:9-20, L.W. Hurtado, *NIBC: Mark* (1983, 1989), 287, may make it more attractive to some Pentecostals, but it supplies no reason to assume that evangelism and dialogue are incompatible. W.J. Brown, in his *Pneuma* 31:2 (2009), 291-92, review of P.N. Thomas, *Strong Religion, Zealous Media: Christian Fundamentalism and Communication in India* (New Delhi/London/Thousand Oaks, CA: Sage, 2008), welcomes "a covenantal approach to reconciliation among differing religious groups" and suggests "Pentecostals and evangelical Christians should strongly promote mutual respect and understanding with those of other faiths" (292), even as he ardently defends enthusiastic Christian evangelism, 291. Of course, Pentecostals are aware of the controversy concerning vv. 9-20, but can be somewhat suspicious that a section including miraculous signs might be rejected early on by skeptics discomfited by the charismatic. See NT scholar J.C. Thomas's review of D.A. Black, ed. *Perspectives on the Ending of Mark* (Nashville, TN: Broadman & Holman, 2008), in *Pneuma* 31:2 (2009), 322.

16. Yong, *Discerning,* 184. Fn 1 on the same page expresses Assemblies of God concerns not only with *inter*religious dialogue but also with even *intra*-religious Christian ecumenism. However, popular leaders within Pentecostal and Charismatic movements, e.g., Peter Wagner and Cindy Jacobs, are increasingly declaring that the Great Commission is much more than evangelism. Wagner, in his Forward to Jacobs, *The Reformation Manifesto: Your Part in God's Plan to Change the Nations Today* (Bloomington, Minnesota: Bethany House, 2008), confesses that many, including himself, "have for too long harbored a truncated view of the kingdom of God", explaining further that they "began by over-identifying the church with the kingdom" and proceeded to limit their mission to saving souls without improving society (10). He specifically names the Great Commission, confessing again, that he "used to think making disciples meant getting people saved and multiplying churches" but that he has come to see a broader vision, in agreement with Jacobs, that includes "sustained social transformation" (10). While neither Wagner nor Jacobs is specifically speaking of ecumenical or interreligious dialogue, their broadening of the thrust of the Great Commission for social action arguably applies in

these areas as well. (Although Jacobs herself may not agree with that application, 91 and 177-78.) Of course, such arguments are not either/or regarding personal evangelism and social action, but both/and attempts to minister effectively today, 23-24.

17. F.L. Arrington, *Christian Doctrine: A Pentecostal Perspective*, Volume I (Cleveland: Pathway, 1992), 25.

18. Arrington, *Doctrine I*, 82-83, 76-78.

19. Cf. G.D. Fee, *God's Empowering Presence: The Holy Spirit in the Letters of Paul* (Peabody, MA: Hendrickson, 1994, 2005), 304-07, for discussion in context of contrasts between the Mosaic Law and the New Covenant in Christ by the Spirit. See also J.M. Scott, *NIBC: 2 Corinthians* (1988), 70-72, and J. Hernando, "2 Corinthians," 915-62, *FLBCNT*, 933-34.

20. E.g., V.M. Kärkkäinen, *An Introduction to The Theology of Religions: Biblical, Historical, & Contemporary Perspectives* (Downer's Grove: InterVarsity Press, 2003), J.R. Edwards, *Is Jesus the Only Savior?* (Grand Rapids: Eerdmans, 2005), and F.A. Spina, *The Faith of the Outsider: Exclusion and Inclusion in the Biblical Story* (Grand Rapids: Eerdmans, 2005) argue for broader biblical support for less exclusivistic approaches. J. Orr's *Biblical Faith and Natural Theology* (New York: Oxford, 1993) is still interesting too.

21. See W. Pannenberg, *An Introduction to Systematic Theology* (Grand Rapids: Eerdmans, 1991), 53-55.

22. M.J. Erickson, *The Evangelical Left: Encountering Postconservative Evangelical Theology* (Grand Rapids: Baker, 1997), 139.

23. Bruce, *NICNT: Book of Acts* (1988), 93-94 (94).

24. F.L. Arrington, *The Acts of the Apostles: Introduction, Translation, and Commentary* (Peabody, MA: Hendrickson, 1988), 47.

25. Augustine, *ACCS: NT V: Acts*, ed. F. Martin, 49. Likewise, Bede, *ACCS: NT V: Acts*, ed. F. Martin, also adamantly argued from Acts 4:12 that there is no other savior than Jesus and no other salvation save through faith in Jesus, but insisted that "although the sacramental signs differed by reason of the times" "the same faith" and "the same dispensation of Christ" "learned from the apostles" is always everywhere present because "there is no redemption of human captivity [to sinfulness] except in the blood of him who gave himself as a redemption for all" (49).

26. Yong, *Discerning*, 185, 187.

27. Yong, *Discerning*, 185-86. Although Pentecostals are "Biblicists," they can be creative in the hermeneutical application of their commitment to biblical inspiration and authority, M.A. Rubenstein, "Taiwan," *NIDPCM*, 259-64 (262-63).

28. Although Pentecostal commitment to doing biblical theology is unquestionable, that they have been at times influenced awkwardly by foreign (i.e., non-Pentecostal, particularly fundamentalist) hermeneutical paradigms ultimately making some interpretative conclusions questionable is also the case, F.D. Macchia, "Theology, Pentecostal," *NIDPCM*, 1120-41 (1121-23).

29. Yong, *Discerning*, 206, 206-19.

30. This section draws on the work of Alan Richardson.

31. A. Richardson, *Religion in Contemporary Debate* (London: SCM, 1966), 30-33 (30, 32). The myriad, almost maze-like, difficulties in defining religion, especially when loosed from biblical moorings, are briefly illustrated in A.K. Rule, "Religion, Religious," *BDT*, eds. E.F. Harrison, G.W. Bromiley, and C.F.H. Henry (Grand Rapids: Baker, 1960, 1987), 441-42. Cf. also J.B. Wiggins, "Religion," *NHCT*, eds. D.W. Musser & J.L. Price (Nashville: Abingdon, 1992), 397-402, and J.H. Stek, "Religion," *BTDB*, ed. W.A. Elwell (Grand Rapids: Baker, 1996), 665-67.

32. Richardson, *Religion*, 33-34. M. Milligan, "Religious Life," *NWDCS*, 537-38, speaks of "religious life" as arising out of "human longing for the Absolute," and describes Christian religious life as "a distinctive life which is both simple and complex" (537). Religious life may be developed as a work of the Spirit but involves diversity of gifts in active service with an ecclesial orientation and prophetic thrust, 537. The culture in which religious life is formed influences it as well, 538. She thinks the "challenges to religious life of a postmodern, globalized and violent world are enormous" (538). "Faith and fidelity to the Spirit", "openness to the other and otherness", as well as continuing "contemplative discernment and love for God and humanity" will be essential for the future of religious life (538).

33. Thus, J.R. Edwards, *NIBC: Romans* (Peabody, Massachusetts: Hendrickson, 1992), says "The root sin in verses 18-23, and the reason for God's wrath, is the sin of *idolatry*" (53). Original are italics. Cf. 46-48. See also, V. Johnson, "Romans," 693-797, *FLBCNT*, 709. Although stressing the significance of Judaism, Christianity, and Islam having common commitment to monotheism, 1:84, J.R. Williams, *Renewal Theology: Systematic Theology from a Charismatic Perspective* (*RT*), three volumes in one (Grand Rapids: Zondervan, 1996), suggests that, tragically, idolatry appears to be "the prevailing condition" of humankind (1:246) and "the source of human perversion" (1:253).

34. Richardson, *Religion,* 34-35.

35. Richardson, *Religion*, 35-36.

36. Richardson, *Religion*, 36.

37. Richardson, *Religion*, 36. Significantly, Richardson most dramatically contrasts religion with secularism. In fact, he presents religion as the "abolition" of the secular. See 30-48. This contrast underscores the obvious fact that all religions, no matter how diverse, have something in common with each other over against secularism. Religion is by definition opposed to some hypothetical "sphere where God is not present or active". Cf. Richardson, *Religion*, 40-42 (36).

38. This section draws on the exegetical and expository work of Origen, Chrysostom, John H. Sailhammer, John Hartley, John Wesley, and Rabbi Joseph Telushkin.

39. Interestingly, J.S. Kselman, "Genesis," 85-128, *Harper's,* connects the stories of Abraham, Sarah, and Abimelech in Genesis 20 and of Abraham, Sarah, Hagar, and Ishmael in 21:1-20. Genesis 20 "reveals an openness to non-Israelites" as "Abimelech the righteous Gentile" "displays a proper fear of God and receives a divine communication," but "Abraham underestimated the extent of God's influence and power" (99). Similarly, "the theme of the righteous Gentile" recurs in Hagar, "who like Abimelech the God-fearer is given a message from God and whose child is saved by divine intervention" (99). Perhaps even more intriguingly, Kselman discovers "echoes of the Exodus story" in Hagar and Ishmael's expulsion into the wilderness and subsequent divine deliverance, and in Ishmael's divine deliverance from imminent death an anticipation of Isaac's deliverance in Genesis 22:1-24, 99. C.T. Fritsch, *The Layman's Bible Commentary: Genesis*, ed. B.H. Kelly, et al (Richmond, VA: John Knox Press, 1959, 1963), suggests the narrative of Hagar and Ishmael's expulsion exemplifies "Divine care and mercy for those who are outside the special Covenant relation", presenting something of "a parallel to 'holy history,' blessed by God but not a part of the Covenant seed" (72). Indeed, J. Ellicott, *Ellicott's Bible Commentary in One Volume,* D. Bowdle, editor (Grand Rapids: Zondervan, 1971, 1980), discerns in the change of the divine name from its covenant form "Jehovah" to the more general "Elohim" a sign of a more general salvation, saying "it is Elohim, and not Jehovah, the covenant God of the chosen race, who saves her" (50). However, of Abimelech Ellicott, although admitting that even Elohim agrees with his assertion of integrity, insists, the "words mean no more than that he was not consciously

violating any of his own rules of morality" (48). Ellicott explains that "The inner light is but a faint and inconstant glimmering, but Christ is the true light; for only in him does the law of nature become a clear rule for human guidance (John 1:9; Rom 2:14, 15; Matt 6:23)" (48-49). Ellicott's observation seems more an attempt to place the matter of righteous Gentiles in proper Christian perspective rather than to deny their existence or importance. Overall, perhaps the significance of Genesis 20 and 21:22-34 for biblical theology of religions is further strengthened when duly noting the Abimelech-Hagar/Ishmael-Abimelech pattern of righteous Gentiles.

40. C.H. Pinnock in *A Wideness in God's Mercy: The Finality of Jesus Christ in a World of Religions* (Grand Rapids: Zondervan, 1992), 35, and J. Sanders in *No Other Name: An Investigation into the Destiny of the Unevangelized* (Grand Rapids: Eerdmans, 1992), 267-80, name numerous fathers, including Clement of Rome, Justin Martyr, Irenaeus, and Clement of Alexandria, who espoused inclusivism, as it has come to be called, in some form. G.R. McDermott defines an inclusivist as one who says "Jesus is ontologically but not epistemologically necessary for salvation" and lists Clement of Alexandria, Justin Martyr, and Irenaeus, along with the more recent representatives John Wesley, C.S. Lewis, Pinnock, Sanders, J N.D. Anderson, and M. Erickson, *Can Evangelicals Learn From World Religions? Jesus, Revelation & Religious Traditions* (Downers' Grove, IL: IVP, 2000, 40-41). Even Augustine argues in *City of God* that some individuals outside the race of Israel belonged to the fellowship of the heavenly city through divine revelation that was ultimately from Christ as the one Mediator between God and man, XVIII. 47, *Nicene PostNicene Fathers* 1 (Peabody, MA: Hendrickson, 1999 ed. 2:389-90). T.C. Oden, *The Living God: Systematic Theology: Volume One* (Peabody, MA: Prince, 2001), identifies John Wesley's inclusivism as part of "a central ecumenical stream" that includes Irenaeus, Gregory Nazianzen, John Chrysostom, Ambrose, and Augustine, 6.

41. See ABIMELECH, *NIBD* ((Nashville: Thomas Nelson, 1986). Cf. *The InterVarsity Bible Background Commentary: Old Testament*, ed. J.H. Walton, V.H. Matthews, M.W. Chavalas (Downer's Grove, IL: InterVarsity Press, 2000), 52, and *The Oxford Bible Commentary*, eds. J. Barton, J. Muddiman (Oxford, UK: Oxford University Press, 2001), 22, 27, 53-55.

42. *ACCS: OT II: Genesis 12-50*, ed., M. Sheridan, 85. Chrysostom repeatedly draws moralizing lessons from the story of Abraham, Sarah, and Abimelech, particularly in regards to the Gentile learning more fully the ways of God from the man of faith, 85, 87. Similarly, Chrysostom, while emphasizing the amazing resourcefulness of God's providential design, also recognizes a pagan Pharaoh's ability to discern divine revelation in Joseph's interpretation of his dream, 268, although Kselman, *Harper's,* only says Pharaoh was "Impressed by his sagacity" (119). Ellicott, *Ellicott's,* however, acknowledges that Pharaoh recognized Elohim's truth in Joseph's words, and further that Joseph was gifted by Elohim for service, 77. Of Joseph's encounter with Pharaoh and the surrounding circumstances and subsequent developments, Fritsch, *Genesis,* stresses that it is "theologically significant that these events in the life and history of Egypt are determined by the eternal purpose of God, and come to pass according to his holy will" (109). He adds that "God's holy purpose is at long last fulfilled in the life of Joseph for the salvation of his people" (109). A kind of dual emphasis on God's simultaneous broader and narrower purposes seems implicit.

43. *ACCS: OT II*, 87-88.

44. *ACCS: OT II*, 88-89. Origin's Alexandrian school was particularly partial to the use of allegory. Cf. J.L. Gonzalez, *A History of Christian Thought: From the Beginnings to the Council of Chalcedon* (Nashville: Abingdon, 1970, 1978), 186-227.

45. Clement of Alexandria (c. 150-216 AD), Origin's mentor and teacher, may have influenced him in this inclusive kindness toward non-Israelite thought. See Gonzalez, *Beginnings*, 204. An important metaphor in Clement is the bee and its process of gathering for honey. These portray a process of gathering truth from many sources and making it one substance. Thus all genuine truth, whether scattered among the Hebrews or the Greeks, is ultimately the one truth of Christ. See Clement, *ANF*, 2: *Exhortation to the Heathen*, chap. 1; *The Instructor*; and, 3:12, and *Miscellanies*, 1:1. R.E. Olson, *The Story of Christian Theology* (Downer's Grove, IL: InterVarsity Press, 1999), asserts that "More than any other Christian writer, Clement of Alexandria valued the integration of Christian faith with the best learning of the day." Olson says the "motto" of Clement was "all truth is God's truth wherever it may be found" (86-87).

46. J.H. Sailhammer, *The Pentateuch as Narrative: A Biblical-Theological Commentary* (Grand Rapids: Zondervan, 1992), 174. Cf. Josephus' terse account in *The Antiquities of the Jews*, *The Works of Josephus: New Updated Edition*, Complete and Unabridged, trans. W. Whiston (Peabody, Massachusetts: Hendrickson, 1987), 41-42.

47. Sailhammer, *Pentateuch*, 175.

48. Abraham's intercessory prayer for those of another nation and religion implicitly anticipates the calling and commissioning of Israel as "a kingdom of priests". Cf. commentary on Ex 19:6: "As the priest is a mediator between God and man, so Israel is called to be the vehicle of the knowledge and salvation of God to the nations of the earth" (*WBC*, Electronic Database. Copyright © 1962 by Moody Press). Moreover, it is completely consistent with God's original calling of Abraham. Cf. commentary on Gen 12:2-4: "He and his descendants would constitute a channel by which God would bless all the peoples of the world" (*WBC*). Peter sees the NT Church as the eventual recipient of these promises and prerogatives (1 Pe 2:9). Peter seems to suppose that obedience to the calling as "a royal priesthood" primarily involves doxological declarations regarding the experience of God's redemptive work—in other words, testimony. Pentecostal educator and administrator B.E. Lyons considers this "kingdom of priests" as equivalent to the Protestant doctrine of the "priesthood of all believers" and to include laity as well as clergy but does not address its interfaith implications. See his *Kingdom of Priests* (Cleveland: Pathway, 1977).

49. Sailhammer, *Pentateuch*, 175-76. Sailhammer also notes, however, that the interactions of Abraham and Abimelech, especially Abraham's long-term residence in the land of the Philistines, may say something about the incompleteness of Abraham's experience as one who continues in "exile". See 176-77.

50. J.E. Hartley, *NIBC: Genesis* (2000), 192.

51. Hartley, *Genesis*, 193.

52. Kselman, *Harper's* accents the interconnectedness of several Genesis stories dealing with Abram/Abraham and Egypt/Egyptians. After noting the irony of Abram's role in endangering the promise and resulting enrichment, 94-95, Kselman observes that in Abram's initial encounter with Pharaoh (chap. 12) he "experiences in advance" what his descendants "would later undergo": descent into Egypt because of famine, involvement with Pharaoh, enrichment, plagues, and release, and also that deception of Pharaoh occurs in both accounts, 95. This same "anticipation of the Exodus", Kselman contends, occurs also in the Hagar stories (chaps. 16, 21), as well as a similar contrast between human plans and Yahweh's plans in the Joseph story (45:5-8; 50:20) and in later wisdom literature (Prov 16:9; 19:21), 95. Fritsch, *Genesis*, thinks it significant that in Abram's encounter with Pharaoh "God's power is described as extending beyond the borders of Canaan into Egypt itself" (55). Even at this early point it seems, the Genesis text ex-

presses God's universality—a point consistent with God's status as Creator of all (cf. Gen 1-2). See Hartley, *Genesis,* 194.

53. Hartley, *Genesis,* 194. Although seeing this episode as a "model" for Israel's relation with the Philistines, Hartley also wisely warns that it is "important not to prejudge the use of the term Philistines as an anachronism". Cf. 196 and 204.

54. Notably, in their next recorded encounter (21:22-34), Abimelech appears afraid that Abraham's obvious power with God may result in his own diminishment in the land wherein they both dwelled. One may speculate that this was an implicit recognition and acceptance of Abraham's eventual inheritance of the land (assuming that he had heard of God's promise, which seems highly likely), and an attempt to prepare and safeguard himself for that development. If so, Abimelech's disposition during this encounter sounds quite similar to that which John Wesley attributes to Abraham himself upon departing from his country and kin to pursue God's promise. That is, it is "implicit faith" based not on knowledge of specific securities but on a general trust in God. Wesley said, "[H]e must follow God with an implicit faith, and take God's word for it in the general, though he had no particular securities given him". See *WNOT: Genesis-Ruth* (Ages Software, Inc. Rio, WI: 2002), 70.

55. Wesley, *Genesis-Ruth,* 102.

56. Rabbi Joseph Telushkin, *Biblical Literacy* (New York: William Morrow, 1997), 26. However, not atheism but idolatry seems to be the issue.

57. Telushkin, *Biblical Literacy,* 415-16. In fact, most dangerous is a tyrant, even a religious tyrant, who has no fear of God, 416-17.

58. In v.11, the Hebrew root word for fear (*yir'ah*) signifies reverence in the dreadful presence of the divine. In v. 8, "afraid" (*yare'*) is a primitive root meaning to fear, and morally, to revere. See *Strong's* (Copyright © 1994, 2003 Biblesoft, Inc. and International Bible Translators, Inc.)

59. Hartley, *Genesis,* 195.

60. Hartley, *Genesis,* 195-96.

61. Hartley, *Genesis,* 196. In biblical terms, removal of the curse is a redemptive act for entry into enjoyment of the blessing (cf. Gal 3:10-14). However, at this point, i.e., with Abimelech and his kingdom, the thrust appears more on the taking away of the negative (curse of death/infertility) than on enjoyment of the positive (covenant blessing/status). However, in 21:22-34, Abimelech and Phicol, though at first unapologetically concerned with avoiding mistreatment (curse/negative), also seem to have some understanding of and desire for "kindness" (blessing/positive) as covenant partners with Abraham and, indirectly perhaps, through Abraham, with Abraham's God. Yet since Abimelech only asked for a continuing return of the kindness he had already shown Abraham, a question remains as to how much he expected to experience in relation to Abraham's God. Given the orientation toward material prosperity of these accounts, and the patriarchal period in general, the possibility that these elements represent tokens of the then current understanding of divine blessings is plausible too. Speculatively, one might extrapolate from the exchanges that they provide some basis for an understanding of devout non-Abrahamic believers in God as avoiding damnable judgment (curse) and enjoying a measure of divine benefits (blessing) but not necessarily in the fullness of which Abrahamic believers themselves participated.

62. Although Kselman, *Harper's,* sees this section as mostly a pact settling a dispute over water rights, 99, and Fritsch, *Genesis,* as merely an explanation of the naming of Beersheeba, 73.

63. Hartley, *Genesis,* 202-03.

64. Cf. "*Hesed,*" *TWOT* (Copyright (c) 1980 by The Moody Bible Institute of Chicago).

65. Also, cf. 1 Corinthians 12:3, John 15:26-27, Acts 1:8, 2:4, interesting texts demonstrating the connectivity of pneumatology and orality that undergirds the Pentecostal testimony serving as a paradigm for this work. A. Richardson declares that, "Above all else, the Holy Spirit is the Spirit of testimony; his chief function is to bear witness to Christ (John 15.26; 16.13-15) or alternatively to the truth (☐☐☐☐☐☐), for Christ is truth (John 16.6)." See his *An Introduction to the Theology of the New Testament* (New York: Harper & Brothers, 1958), 112. Y. Congar, *The Word and the Spirit*, (*WS*) trans. David Smith (San Francisco: Harper & Row, 1986), asserts that there is a "unity of function" of witness coming from the Father, concerning Jesus, given by the Spirit, and continuing in the Church (30).

66. Cf. G.R. Osborne, *The Hermeneutical Spiral: A Comprehensive Introduction to Biblical Interpretation* (Downer's Grove: InterVarsity Press, 1991), 153-64.

67. Thus, C. Wright, *NIBC: Deuteronomy* (1996, 2003), comments on 4:15-20 of that book "that idolatry not only corrupts God's redemptive achievement for God's people" but "perverts and turns upside-down the whole created order" (51). Later, he explains the prominent place of prohibition against idolatry in the Decalogue based on similar reasoning, 72-73, admitting that this truth "easily grates on the modern person because of the infectious pluralism that disapproves such exclusivity" (72). Yet he consistently insists that "biblically, idolatry is the fundamental human sin" and that "Apostasy and idolatry are the classic root sins of Israel in the OT, because they are the essential marks of the human condition" (73). Accordingly, one might argue that radical religious pluralism may be an insipient (re)introduction of a resilient idolatry that has plagued human relations with the Divine for millennia. Rather than a tolerant step forward, it would instead represent a gigantic leap backward.

68. Although, as C.A. Brown, in J. Harris, C. Brown, and M. Moore, *NIBC: Joshua, Judges, Ruth* (2000), points out, an ancient Israelite tradition somewhat ambiguously regarded the Philistines and other nations or surrounding peoples as providentially provided by Yahweh to test and to train them, 159-60.

69. Cf. Fritsch, *Genesis,* 57-59 and 67-68. However, Fritsch emphasizes that Abraham was compassionately concerned for the people of Sodom and also passionately convinced of "the ultimate justice and goodness of God" toward all people (68). Ellicott, *Ellicott's,* suggests "the primary object" of Genesis 18 was "making known the perfect justice of God's dealings with men," and that it "further showed that the Gentile world was both subject to Jehovah's dominion, and that there was mercy for it as well as for the covenant people" (46). Interestingly, Ellicott finds this story of Sodom comparable to that of the later lesson of the Book of Jonah, 46.

70. E.g., Spina, *Faith of the Outsider*, argues that "female outsiders" in the genealogy of Jesus in Matthew supply examples with continuing import, 138, and that Nineveh's exceptional response to Jonah's preaching became "a model for how to respond to the Israelite prophets" (112).

71. An informative and interesting resource regarding just how prayer or meditation by those of one faith may appear to those of another is *Christians Talk about Buddhist Mediation, Buddhists Talk about Christian Prayer,* eds. R.M. Gross and T.C. Muck (New York: Continuum, 2003).

72. E.g., Gen 14:18-20; Num 16:22; 27: 16; the Book of Job, Ps 145:9, 13, 17; the Book of Jonah; Isa 44:28; 45:1, 13; etc. The OT pattern can be seen replicated in NT passages such as Matt 15:21-28; John 4:1-42; Acts 10; 17:22-31; Rom 2:12-16; etc. E.g., traditionally commentators struggle with Pharaoh's claim against Josiah that he was ad-

vancing at God's command but it is not inconsistent with this stream of inclusive possibilities. See 2 Chron 35:21-22, *Barnes' Notes*, Electronic Database Copyright © 1997, 2003), and 2 Chron 35:20-27, *Keil and Delitzsch Commentary on the Old Testament* (New Updated Edition, Electronic Database. Copyright © 1996).

73. See J. Goldingay, *Models for Scripture* (Grand Rapids: Eerdmans, 1994), 25-28, 58-60.

74. L.A. Jervis, *NIBC: Galatians* (1999), observes that in affirming the Abrahamic sonship of Gentile Christians Paul draws on inheritance tradition and develops it in terms of grace, 95. Furthermore, Paul, through "interpretative boldness" (125) consistent with his gospel convictions compares and contrasts fleshly and spiritual birth to affirm the freedom of those who are Abraham's descendants by faith, 125-26. Paul is, however, specifically discussing covenant faith in Christ rather than the more general monotheism shared by Jews, Christians, and Muslims.

75. The Koran says that Abraham was neither Jew nor Christian but a true believer in God (Surah 2:136-40). The point is of course technically correct as speaking of Jews, Christians, or Muslims during Abraham's day would be incredibly anachronistic. However, none of this appears aimed at denying the commonality of the Abrahamic faiths. In fact, the same statement is made about Jesus and others. Furthermore, many modern day Muslims openly prefer to stress commonalities with Christians. See "A Common Word between Us and You" (an open letter from more than one hundred thirty-eight Muslim leaders to Christian churches and leaders (October 13, 2007) http://www.acommonword.com/. H. Küng, *Islam: Past, Present, and Future*, trans. J. Bowden (Oxford: Oneworld, 2008), understands that Jews, Christians, and Muslims see Abraham as their "common ancestor", 45. However, rather than a unifying factor, the seeds of subsequent discord were sown in the relationships of Abraham with his two sons, Ishmael and Isaac, 46. Nevertheless, the biblical narrative may leave more room for rapport than is sometimes assumed, 46-49. Küng points out that Abraham is a very important figure in the Qu'ran, 49-51, and suggests Abraham may still be a rich resource for binding the three Abrahamic religions, Judaism, Christianity, and Islam, together for fruitful dialogue, 51-54.

76. This section will dialogue with the work of Miroslav Volf.

77. N.T. Wright, *Surprised by Hope: Rethinking Heaven, the Resurrection, and the Mission of the Church* (New York: HarperCollins, 2008), agrees with Volf's observation that exclusion prepares the way for embrace, 179. See M. Volf, *Exclusion and Embrace: A Theological Exploration of Identity, Otherness, and Reconciliation* (Nashville: Abingdon, 1994).

78. M. Volf, "Forgiveness, Reconciliation, and Justice: A Christian Contribution to a More Peaceful Social Environment," *Forgiveness and Reconciliation*, eds. R. Helmick, S. J., and R.L. Petersen (Radnor, PA: Templeton Foundation, 2001), 27-49. Cf. T. Richie, "Healing Fire from Heaven: A Wesleyan-Pentecostal Approach to Interfaith Forgiveness and Reconciliation", *WTJ* 42:2 (Fall 2007), 136-54.

79. Regarding Volf and the role of religion in culture and society, see L. Kishkovsky, "Response to Miroslav Volf," *IBMR* 20:1 (Jan 1996), 31-36.

80. V.M. Kärkkäinen, ed. A. Yong, *Toward a Pneumatological Theology: Pentecostal and Ecumenical Perspectives on Ecclesiology, Soteriology, and Theology of Mission* (Lanham, Maryland: University Press of America, 2002), 39-40. Williams, *RT*, suggests one of the effects of the coming of the Spirit is a deepening of fellowship among various believers, accompanied by a heightened sense of community and unity, 2:314-29. He even states that "this renewal in the Spirit" may be "the most profound ecumenical development of twentieth century" (2:318). He affirms "the growing ecumenical concern" and

argues "its solution is to be found only in and through the renewal of Holy Spirit" (2:318-19). Participation in the Charismatic Renewal is paramount, and perhaps prerequisite: "As people, as churches, and as individuals are profoundly renewed by the Holy Spirit, the whole situation is transformed from a search after unity to its realization" (2:319). Yet, Williams warns against "a party spirit" (2:319). For him, "the overarching fact is that through the renewal of the Spirit there is a new and profound gift of unity that alone can bring into fulfillment the genuine oneness of the body of Christ. When this is realized afresh and is acted on accordingly, the prayer of the Lord will find its ultimate fulfillment" (2:319). Williams is firmly convinced that "through the gift of the Holy Spirit the love of God is truly shed abroad in the hearts of all," and that "there is then a deep creation of fellowship, sharing, and unity with one another" and therefore "Through such God-given love we become the koinonia of the Holy Spirit" (2:319; cf. fn. 36). Cf. Williams' excellent extended discussion of the ecumenical movement, *RT,* 3:43-48.

81. This section dialogues with Walter Hollenweger, Veli-Matti Kärkkäinen, Douglas Jacobsen, and Tony Richie.

82. E.g., W.J. Hollenweger's, "Biblically Justified Abuse: A Review of Stephen Parson's *Ungodly Fear: Fundamentalist Christianity and the Abuse of Power*," *JPT* 10:2 (2002), 129-35.

83. S.J. Land, Pentecostal Spirituality: A Passion for the Kingdom (Sheffield, England: Sheffield Academic Press, 1997), 47.

84. Kärkkäinen, *Theology of Religions,* 139.

85. W.J. Hollenweger, 'From Azusa Street to the Toronto Phenomenon: Historical Roots of the Pentecostal Movement', *Pentecostal Movements as an Ecumenical Challenge,* eds. J. Moltmann and K.J. Kuschel, *Concilium* 1996/3 (Maryknoll, NY: Orbis, 1996), 3-14 (9). Cf. *NIDPCM:* D.D. Bundy, "Boddy, Alexander Alfred," 436-37; P.D. Hocken, Dalliere, Louis, 569-70, D.D. Bundy, "Paul, Jonathan Anton Alexander," 958.

86. V.M. Kärkkäinen, *An Introduction to Ecclesiology: Ecumenical, Historical & Global Perspectives* (Downer's Grove, IL: InterVarsity Press, 2002), 69-70.

87. V.M. Kärkkäinen, *Pneumatology: The Holy Spirit in Ecumenical, International, and Contextual Perspective* (Grand Rapids, MI: Baker, 2002), 88.

88. D. Jacobsen, *Thinking in the Spirit: Theologies of the Early Pentecostal Movement* (Bloomington & Indianapolis: Indiana University Press, 2003), 177-79, 192-93. See Bishop J.H. King, *Yet Speaketh* (Franklin Springs, GA: Publishing House of the Pentecostal Holiness Church, 1949), *From Passover to Pentecost* (Franklin Springs, GA: Advocate, 1911, 1976 [fourth edition]), and *Christ-God's Love Gift: Selected Writings of J.H. King: Vol. I* (Franklin Springs, GA: Advocate Press, 1969). Cf. T. Richie, "Azusa-era Optimism: Bishop J. H. King's Pentecostal Theology of Religions as a Possible Paradigm for Today," *JPT* 14:2 (April 2006), 247-60.

89. Jacobsen, *Thinking in the Spirit,* 41, 212, and 230-32. See C.F. Parham, *The Sermons of Charles F. Parham* (NY: Garland, 1985 pr), a collection of early publications including *A Voice Crying in the Wilderness* (1902), 137-38, and *The Everlasting Gospel* (c. 1919) (50-51). Cf. T. Richie, "Eschatological Inclusivism: Exploring Early Pentecostal Theology of Religions in Charles Fox Parham," *JEPTA* 27:2 (2007), 138-52.

90. See Kärkkäinen, *Pneumatological Theology,* pp. 220-31, 238-39.

91. This section interacts with the thought of John N. Oswalt and Clark Pinnock.

92. Cf. Mounce, *Matthew,* 178, and Hurtado, *Mark,* 287. However, as R.H. Fuller, *Harper's:* "Matthew," 951-82, explains, the classic "Great Commission" text, Matthew 28:16-20, probably comparable to Moses' farewell speech (Deut 33), emphasizes discipleship, teaching, and Christ's abiding presence, 981, rather than explicit evangelism (although certainly implicit). Fuller says: "That Jesus is constantly present with his

church, working through its teaching mission, is a fitting conclusion and an effective summary of the Gospel" (981). Mounce, *Matthew,* notes that "the teaching is here set forth as ethical rather than doctrinal" (268). Cf. Ellicott, *Ellicott's,* 756. J.B. Shelton, *FLBCNT,* "Matthew," 119-253, notes that the grammar, especially the repetition of πας in vv. 18-20, pointedly signifies the universality of Christ and of the Church's commission, 252. Again, cf. Ellicott, *Ellicott's,* 756. In any case, there appears no inherent contradiction between the Great Commission and interreligious dialogue. One might even reasonably argue that dialogue necessarily would be included in any informed effort to teach Christ to the nations with any kind of authentic universality as in obedience to the assertion of the Great Commission.

93. Yong, *Discerning,* 184. Popularly, many Pentecostals see themselves as existing denominationally or organizationally for the express purpose of fulfilling the "Great Commission". See *COGE,* 99:9 (September 2009): J.E. Cossey, "The Holy Spirit and the Great Commission," 3, and C.E. Fischer, "The Theology of the Great Commission," 8-9. However, this evangelistic emphasis is usually considered compatible with social ministries, G. Moxley, "Commissioned to Care," 12-13.

94. J.N. Oswalt, *The Book of Isaiah: Chapters 40-66: The New International Commentary on the Old Testament* (Grand Rapids: Eerdmans, 1998), 283. For more on the missionary implications of the prophetic message, Oswalt refers readers to his essay on, "The Mission of Israel to the Nations," *Through No Fault of Their Own,* ed. W.V. Crockett and J. Sigountos (Grand Rapids: Baker, 1991), 85-95. See Oswalt, *Isaiah,* 284 (fn. 88).

95. Oswalt, *Isaiah,* 487.

96. Oswalt, *Isaiah,* 487, fn. 67. Cf. G.R. Sumner, *The First & the Last: The Claim of Jesus Christ and the Claims of Other Religions* (Grand Rapids: Eerdmans, 2004), who argues for the "final primacy" of Christ, i.e., that all religions narratives and truth claims be finally related to Christ, and yet energetically affirms both evangelism and dialogue. In fact, he says, "final primacy is friendly to dialogue, even though it redefines dialogue even as it promotes it", 210. His redefinition of dialogue is modest. The point is, though, that strong ideas about Christ, salvation and truth and openness to religious others, as well evangelism and dialogue, often can and in fact do co-exist without contradiction.

97. An approach embracing evangelism and inclusivism appears compatible with the biblical text of the Great Commission itself. See Fuller, *Harper's,* 981, Mounce, *Matthew,* 268, and Shelton, "Matthew," 252.

98. C.H. Pinnock, *Flame of Love: A Theology of the Holy Spirit* (Downer's Grove: InterVarsity Press, 1996), 213.

99. This section draws on the ideas of John Wesley.

100. *CWJW* (The Wesleyan Heritage Collection; Ages Software, Inc. Rio, WI: 2002), 6:298-99. Cf. 7:303-04; 9:169; and 9:180. Cf. T.L. Richie, "Mr. Wesley and Mohammed: A Contemporary Inquiry Concerning Islam," *ATJ* 58:2 (Fall 2003), 79-99.

101. *CWJW,* 6:305-06. Cf. 9:34; 10:190.

102. Mounce, *Matthew,* suggests that response to Jesus and to the Father are inextricably bound together, adding that the intent to honor the Son is "universal in scope" but warning that "a negative note" of confrontation and rejection can and does occur too, 92. Morris, *John,* suggests the stress of 5:23 on "the unity of the Father and the Son" asserts "the inherent dignity of the Son and his intimate relationship with the Father", implying the Son's deity too, warning against the seriousness of dishonoring the Son, 315.

103. *CWJW,* 8:521 and 9:180.

104. A further thought brought out by G. Van Rheenen, in "Changing Motivations for Missions: From "Fear of Hell" to "the Glory of God," *The Changing Face of World Mis-*

sions: Engaging Contemporary Issues and Trends, eds. M. Pocock, G. Van Rheenen, D. McConnell (Grand Rapids: Baker, 2005),161-81, addresses motivation for missions. An inclusive and dialogical approach to missions is free to focus on publicly glorifying God in the presence of the other rather than merely frightening anyone into conversion. In the process, missions are redirected rather than diminished.

105. This section dialogues with the work of Leslie Newbigin and Wolfhart Pannenberg.

106. L. Newbigin, *The Gospel in a Pluralist Society* (London: SPCK, 1989), 182-83.

107. E.g., V.M. Kärkkäinen, "The Working of the Spirit of God in Creation and in the People of God: The Pneumatology of Wolfhart Pannenberg," *Pneuma* 26:1 (2004), 17-35, *The Work of the Spirit: Pneumatology and Pentecostalism*, ed. M. Welker (Grand Rapids: Eerdmans, 2006), 27-46, and F.D. Macchia, *Baptized in the Spirit: A Global Pentecostal Theology* (Grand Rapids: Zondervan, 2006), 109-11, 121-25.

108. Kärkkäinen, *Theology of Religions*, 235-44. Cf. T Richie, "Approaching the Problem of Religious Truth in a Pluralistic World: A Pentecostal-Charismatic Contribution," *JES* 43:3 (Summer 2008), 351-69.

109. W. Pannenberg, *An Introduction to Systematic Theology* (Grand Rapids: Eerdmans, 1991, 1992), 4-6.

110. Pannenberg, *Introduction*, 6-8.

111. Cf. S.J. Grenz and R.E. Olson, *20th Century Christian Theology: God & the World in a Transitional Age* (Downer's Grove, IL: InterVarsity Press, 1992), 189-90.

112. Pannenberg, *Introduction,* 12.

113. Pannenberg, *Introduction,* 16, 16. M.L. Soards, *NIBC: 1 Corinthians* (1999), suggests that 13:8-10 be understood in light of Paul's abiding teaching on the passing of the present age of imperfection into eschatological perfection, 274. Cf. A. Palma, "1 Corinthians," 799-913, *FLBCNT,* who makes the double-edged point that imperfection will pass eschatologically into perfection but that this present imperfect and partial age still requires spiritual gifts, including prophesying, tongues, knowledge, and revelations, 879. When Christ comes, then "we will be like him (1 John 3:2) and will transcend the need for partial, imperfect, and temporary insights and revelations" (879).

114. Pannenberg, *Introduction,* 18, 19. R. Niebuhr, *The Children of Light and The Children of Darkness: A Vindication of Democracy and A Critique of Its Traditional Defense* (New York: Charles Scribner's Sons, 1944, 1960), argues that interreligious toleration requires "that religious convictions be sincerely and devoutly held while yet the sinful and finite corruptions of these convictions be humbly acknowledged; and the actual fruits of other faiths be generously estimated", 137.

115. Pannenberg, *Introduction,* 54-55.

116. Pannenberg, *Introduction,* 55-69.

117. Interestingly, R.E. Webber, *The Divine Embrace: Recovering the Passionate Spiritual Life* (Grand Rapids: Baker, 2006), agrees that experience is key to Pentecostal spirituality, 87, and affirms religious experience in non-Christian religions, but takes issue with those who would separate spiritual experience from the founding and guiding stories of the religions in question, 171. Furthermore, he warns experientially oriented Evangelicals and Pentecostals against centering too much on the subjective self, 89, and glorifying ignorance or demeaning intellectual endeavors, 190. Webber strongly affirms the centrality and essentiality of story for Christian spirituality and theology, portraying it in the light of the advent of postmodernism, 16-17. Comparably, Philip Sheldrake, "Postmodernity," *NWDCS,* 498-500, suggests "the restoration of dialogue between spirituality and theology owes something to the theories of postmodernism" (500). Notably, some Pentecostals seem to be attempting to address the postmodern perspective. E.g., see

S.S. O'Neal, "Sharing the Gospel in a Postmodern World," *COGE,* 99:9 (September 2009), 14-15. As might be expected, for Pentecostals this diverse context sometimes comes together in expression through testimonial forms. E.g., see R. Bailey, "Telling Your Faith Story," *COGE,* 99:9 (September 2009), 20.

118. Grenz, *20th Century Theology,* 191-92.
119. Grenz, *20th Century Theology,* 198.
120. Grenz, *20th Century Theology,* 197.
121. Kärkkäinen, "Working of the Spirit," 17-35.
122. Congar, *WS,* insists that, as the Spirit of Truth, the Holy Spirit is always relative to Christ, "the way, the truth, and the life" (John 14:6), who is the fullness of the Word of God; although truth is ultimately eschatological it is experienced presently by the Spirit, 42-46.
123. Kärkkäinen, "Working of the Spirit," 18-19.
124. Kärkkäinen, "Working of the Spirit," 34-35.
125. As J. Moltmann rightly reflects in his Foreword to P. Althouse, *The Spirit of the Last Days: Pentecostal Eschatology in Conversation with Jürgen Moltmann* (London/New York: T & T Clark International, 2003), "Pentecostal movements are eschatological movements. In the expectation of the imminent coming of Christ the energies of the Holy Spirit are experienced, which according to Heb. 6.5 are 'the powers of a future world'" (vi).
126. Land, "Passion for the Kingdom," 19.
127. Land, "Passion for the Kingdom," 41.
128. Macchia, *Baptized,* 97, 111.
129. Interestingly, A.J. Köstenberger, "'What is Truth?' Pilate's Question in Its Johannine and Larger Biblical Context," 19-52, R.A. Mohler, J.P. Moreland, *Whatever Happened to Truth?* (Wheaton, IL: Crossway, 2005), notes that the Johannine "dialogue" between Jesus and Pilate in John 18:37-38 ironically hinged on a misunderstanding of the nature of truth, 46. Cf. A.G. Padgett and P.R. Keifert, eds. *But Is It All True? The Bible and the Question of Truth* (Grand Rapids, MI: Eerdmans, 2006).
130. Kärkkäinen, *Theology of Religions,* 243.
131. Kärkkäinen, *Theology of Religions,* 243-44.
132. Pentecostals are prone to stress the testifying activity of the Holy Spirit to Jesus through believers in the context of the Church's mission. See B. Aker, "John," 1-118, *FLBCNT,* 91-92. Notably, Morris, *John,* also strongly stresses both the Christological centrality of the Spirit's testimony (or witness) and the apostolic and subsequent ecclesial participation in the same, 683-84.
133. This section dialogues with writings of Laurence W. Wood and Jerry H. Gill.
134. L.W. Wood, *Theology as History and Hermeneutics: A Post-Critical Conversation with Contemporary Theology* (Lexington, KY: Emeth, 2005).
135. Wood, *History and Hermeneutics,* ix.
136. For more in depth studies on the nature of truth see M.J. Erickson, "Postmodernity and Theology", in *Christian Theology* (Grand Rapids: Baker, 1998, 2nd ed.), 158-74, S.J. Grenz, *Renewing the Center: Evangelical Theology in a Post-Theological Era* (Grand Rapids: Baker, 2000), H.H. Knight III, *A Future for Truth: Evangelical Theology in a Postmodern World* (Nashville: Abingdon, 1997), and H. Netland, *Encountering Religious Pluralism: The Challenge to Christian Faith & Mission* (Downer's Grove, IL: InterVarsity Press, 2001), 181-211, and R.E. Webber, *Ancient-Future Faith: Rethinking Evangelicalism for a Postmodern World* (Grand Rapids: Baker, 1999). For specifically Pentecostal or Charismatic treatments see, J.D. Johns, "Pentecostalism and the Postmodern Worldview," *JPT* 7 (1995), 73-96; Pinnock, "Spirit & Truth", in *Flame of Love,* 215-

45, and A. Yong, "Foundational Pneumatology and Theology of Religions", in *Beyond the Impasse*, 57-81.

137. J.H. Gill, *Faith in Dialogue: A Christian Apologetic* (Waco: Word, 1985), 12. Italics are original. Gill's view of truth depends heavily on the philosophy of Michael Polanyi. See Polanyi, *Personal Knowledge,* (Chicago: University of Chicago, 1958).

138. Gill, *Faith in Dialogue,* 13.

139. E.T. Charry, "Walking in the Truth: On Knowing God," 144-69, *But Is It All True?,* describes modern epistemology as "under investigation" by a postmodern postcritical approach "reconnecting knower with knowledge and truth with goodness, so that the knowledge of God may again be epistemologically possible" 146-47 (147). For Charry, a postcritical approach may be a helpful resource for correcting the disjunctive problems of modern epistemology, 147, being able to retain modernity's "insistence on evidence for knowledge" but still "recognize wider parameters for it" (148). See Gill, *Faith in Dialogue,* 94-105.

140. See Gill, *Faith in Dialogue,* 105.

141. See Gill, *Faith in Dialogue,* 112-37 (136). Italics are original.

142. D. Hay, "Experience, Religious," *NWDCS,* 295-97, outlines several approaches to religious experience, many reductionist and relativistic, 297, but notes that contemporary philosophers such as W. Alston, *Perceiving God: the Epistemology of Religious Experience* (Ithaca, NY: Cornell University Press, 1991), maintain that "religious experience is a matter of direct encounter with and recognition of God" (297), a position with possible affirmative experiential alethiological and epistemological ramifications.

143. Gill, *Faith in Dialogue,* 139-56.

144. Significantly, the French Christian philosopher Ricoeur has argued that the language of faith approaches the concept of truth similarly to the testimony of a witness in a courtroom. For him, authentic testimony includes interpretation by a witness as to what he/she has observed. Even the Bible itself should be appreciated as testimony to God's actions. See P. Ricoeur, *Essays in Biblical Interpretation,* ed. with introduction by Lewis S. Mudge (Philadelphia: Fortress, 1980), 121, 124-25. While legal testimony and religious testimony are not identical, the basic point is valid. The present project, with its emphasis on integration of interreligious dialogue and Pentecostal testimony, affirms a view of truth that confidently testifies to the truth of the Christian faith even while non-condescendingly conversing with interfaith partners.

145. As Arrington, "The Acts of the Apostles," 535-692 *FLBCNT,* says of Philip the Evangelist (Acts 8:26-40), "He has been a Spirit-inspired witness in the city of Samaria, performing prophetic signs of power; now the Lord directs him to bear witness to a single individual" (577).

146. This section and the following one draw on Hans Küng.

147. E.g., comparatively optimist assessments of progress towards peace in the Middle East between Israelis and Palestinians, or Jews and Arabs, are often disappointing in practice and inevitably followed by assessments emphasizing ongoing complexities and problems. Cf. G. Frankel *Beyond the Promised Land: Jews and Arabs on a Hard Road to a New Israel* (New York: Simon & Schuster, 1994), with C. Chapman, *Whose Promised Land? The Continuing Crisis over Israel and Palestine* (Grand Rapids: Baker, 2002).

148. An infamous example is J. Hagee, *Jerusalem Countdown* (West Jefferson, NC: Cliffside, 2006, 2007).

149. For a political science discussion of the role of religion in violence, see S.P. Huntingdon, *The Clash of Civilizations and the Remaking of World Order* (New York: Touchstone, 1996). For a religious discussion of religious violence, see C. Kimball, *When Religion Becomes Evil* (New York: HarperSanFrancisco, 2002).

150. C.C. Simut, *A Critical Study of Hans Küng's Ecclesiology*, (New York: Palgrave MacMillan, 2008), stresses that for Küng the Church is a serving community that, though it should never pursue political power, should always be active socially, pursuing its spiritual goals without violence, 108. However, Simut criticizes Hans Küng severely for replacing Christian theology primarily concerned with salvation from sin through Jesus Christ with political theology primarily interested in "a stable political and social order" or, in other words, "a new order that is governed by peace and harmony" (137). Simut does not denounce the pursuit of peace but he does pronounce Küng as "hopelessly idealistic" for attempting to achieve world peace without first dealing forthrightly with the problem of human sin (137). I agree that the Church should be active socially, including promoting peace, but also assumes (and/or hopes) that Pentecostals (and most others) attempting to contribute to the cause of peace through interreligious dialogue (as well as other means) will not neglect to address the vicious role of sin in promoting violence or the need for personal salvation from the power of sin and its temporal and eternal penalties. Cf. R. Niebuhr, *The Nature and Destiny of Man: A Christian Interpretation, I and II* (Louisville, KY: Westminster John Knox, 1996), who exemplifies a socially involved Christianity deeply mindful of the destructive force of sin in the world (e.g., *Nature I,* xxv, xxvi).

151. In H. Küng, "Global Ethics and Education," *The Future of Theology: Essays in Honor of Jürgen Moltmann*, eds. M. Volf, C. Krieg, T. Kucharz (Grand Rapids: Eerdmans, 1996), 267-83. Simut, *Critical Study,* calls Küng's conviction that the world can achieve a global ethic, "the peak of idealism" based on his modernist following of the world toward a temporal, worldly goal rather than an eternal, heavenly goal more in line with traditional Catholic Christian theology, 138 (however, cf. 111 and 123). For him, Küng is replacing the eschatological hope of traditional Christianity with "a sort of historical hope ... characterized by global peace based on a global ethic" (139). Even though Simut overdoes it when he calls Küng's proposal for a global ethic of peace "a sort of hippie theology", 140, some element of merit may reside in his concerns. Nevertheless, I, in tune with the Pentecostal tradition, might argue that this worldly/earthly/temporal and other worldly/heavenly/eternal concerns need not be mutually exclusive. Cf. with the Pentecostal "full gospel" message" in Kärkkäinen, *Pneumatology* (92-93). Certainly, Pentecostals would likely approve and perhaps applaud Küng's inseparable connection between the Holy Spirit and peace, Simut, *Critical Study,* 4.

152. Küng, "Global Ethics," 267-70.
153. Küng, "Global Ethics," 271-72.
154. Küng, "Global Ethics," 272-75.
155. Küng, "Global Ethics," 276-77 (276).

156. Thus Niebuhr, in *The Children*, discussing the dread of nuclear war, said: "If we escape disaster it will only be by the slow growth of mutual trust and tissues of community over the awful chasm of the present international tension", x. P. Alexander, *Signs & Wonders: Why Pentecostalism is the World's Fastest Growing Faith* (San Francisco: Jossey-Bass, 2009), connects Pentecostal/Charismatic spirituality with social energy and strength to work for peace, 148. For him tongues-speech is "a protest and worship language that is socially empowering, especially for the downtrodden and oppressed" (56).

157. Cf. H. Küng and K.-J. Kuschel, eds., *A Global Ethic: The Declaration of the World's Religions* (New York: Continuum, 1993).

158. Küng, "Global Ethics," 277-78.

159. Many Pentecostals and Charismatics would likely agree with Williams, *RT,* that universal peace will only be eschatologically realized, 3:501. Cf. J.N. Oswalt, *The Book of Isaiah: Chapters 1-39: The New International Commentary on the Old Testament*

(Grand Rapids: Eerdmans, 1998), who argues that "the idea of peace as a result of the mutual agreement of nations is not a biblical one. The biblical (and Isaianic) idea is of a peace which results from mutual submission to an overwhelming Sovereign (e.g., 9:3-6 [Eng 4-7]; 63:1-6; Rev 19:11-16)" and will only occur eschatologically (288). However, that does not necessarily equal lack of responsible concern for penultimate peace (cf. Rom 14:19 and Heb 12:14).

160. Küng, "Global Ethics," 278-80.

161. Küng, "Global Ethics," 278-80. Interestingly, if one takes seriously R. Niebuhr's observations about the innate societal tendencies toward immorality, usually arising out of sinful self-interest, engaging in interreligious dialogue in pursuit of peace would not mean naively negotiating from a position of weakness but from a bastion of strength. See *Moral Man and Immoral Society* (New York: Charles Scribner's Sons, 1932, 1960).

Chapter 7

Future Pentecostal Engagement with Non-Christian Religions

Introduction

An idea of determining, to some extent, whether this program is feasible still directs this chapter. Therefore, there is still something of an introspective attitude in this chapter as in the last, though less overt perhaps. An assumption is that for successful utilization of Pentecostal testimony in interreligious dialogue the socio-political context of the conversation will have to be conducive. In other words, this research now outlines in anticipatory fashion specific demographical and political contexts for its constructive application

Previous chapters of this study lay out an ambitious and optimistic program of interreligious encounter and dialogue by Classical Pentecostals utilizing their tradition of testimony. Given the pioneering nature of this work, it seems well advised to attempt some (optimistic) envisioning of future developments through the anticipated application of its insights. The eschatological and teleological nature of human identity and existence and of much of religious identity and existence as well, particularly of Pentecostal identity and existence, make this section not only possible but also plausible.[1] Nevertheless, due to the boundaries of human prescience, the more speculative nature of this section ought honestly and humbly to be acknowledged. However, as even this section is not random but rooted in the scholarly research, the aim is for circumspect speculation rather than sensational sophistry. The approach here taken is of offering suggestive observations first for Pentecostals themselves, then for other Christians, for non-Christian religions, for the world, that is, for societal culture in its overtly nonreligious mode, and finally even in relation to God. However, a prior step will be to consider the context of interreligious conversation in the world today as a basis for future developments.

Contextual Trends of Interfaith Conversation

Clear but Complex Religious Roots[2]

Recently, an impressive array of interreligious scholars, led by Rabbi Jacob Neusner, presented the notion that Western civilization is inextricably interwoven with the histories and philosophies of the great religious traditions of the Abrahamic faiths; but also, that various economic, ideological, nationalistic, and political influences and factors either essentially or practically non-religious are heavily involved. Therefore, the complex cultural condition is one in which religion, either in general or in particular, and Western society is neither entirely separate nor synonymous.[3] All of these diverse factors figure into the future of the dialogical task. Accordingly, anticipating some of the future developments in interreligious dialogue involves some familiarity with interdisciplinary trends. In other words, one must not only know as well as possible one's own religious tradition and that of one's dialogue partners, but also something of the history of their interactions and of the contemporary economic and political context of their ensuing interaction.

In addition, essential for understanding the religious nature of Western society, which seems to be itself essential for progress in interreligious dialogue, is how the above observation affects relations among the three major religions most prominent in the West: Judaism, Christianity, and Islam. For example, Jon D. Levenson addresses interreligious dialogue as an important feature of recent relations between Judaism and Christianity.[4] Moreover, some of his observations are of value for understanding interreligious dialogue beyond specific sectarian boundaries. He notes that interreligious dialogue has "its own inner tensions." For him, the "most important of these concerns the very goal of the enterprise." He warns against adopting "a model of conflict resolution or diplomatic negotiation" as a basis for interfaith conversation.[5] While affirming commonalities among religions, dialogue must also "deal responsibly with the fact of diversity in religion." Else, it "quickly turns into a monologue" losing its energy and efficiency. In other words, it is "self-defeating". Levenson commends a twofold model. First, it seeks good relations between the religions, requiring them to confront and destroy misunderstanding and prejudice. Second, it insists on the importance of "the theological core" of each tradition, and invites them to reckon with its full import "even when it not only contradicts but also critiques one's own".[6]

Bruce Chilton has a provocative paragraph that highlights the need for dialogue participants seriously to consider history.

> Although both Fundamentalism and the reaction against Fundamentalism by liberal theology have shied away from history, history has not retreated from them. The basic facts of the Holocaust, emerging out of Christianity's post-Enlightenment crisis, and of militant Islam, a direct consequence of Christian policies of war and oppression, have rooted thought afresh in historical contingency. Dialogue with Judaism has proceeded vigorously, and the inclusion of Islam within comparative theology has clearly been signaled.[7]

Awareness of such history and complexity helps debunk stereotypes that can hinder true dialogue. For example, Th. Emil Homerin quotes the historical and theological argument of Ali S. Asani for a pluralist tradition within Islam that, among other things, supports and promotes dialogue.[8] Asani notes leaders in the African-American and South African Muslim community who have called for dialogue and for the faiths to go beyond dialogue to work together against all forms of injustice.[9]

However, herein lays a possible pitfall for interreligious dialogue, at least from a Pentecostal perspective: the danger of derailing dialogue due to partial subordination or even total usurpation of the religious aspect for some overt or covert social agenda highlighting economics or politics.[10] Though many contemporary Pentecostals are of course concerned about and committed to social ethics and their practical application, probably few would be prone to promote an interfaith version of the so-called "social gospel."[11] Accordingly, the future of Pentecostal involvement in interfaith conversation will require special effort to make sure the focus is on the religious. As already stated above, relating with other areas will be necessary but the prime objective will have to be the religious goals of interreligious dialogue. Even the prospect of world peace would not motivate people to compromise their faith for that effect. Their faith, or rather the object of their faith, God, is their ultimate value, and everything else is penultimate at best. Yet none should assume that social agendas or even the secular, in a certain sense, and the religious inevitably or inherently oppose each other. Rather, as Pentecostals are often pleased to point out, the ministries of Jesus and of the Holy Spirit in the Church incorporate an anointing for multidimensional aspects of life (cf. Lu 4:16-21).[12] Yet sustaining focus is essential for any endeavor, and for inter*religious* dialogue, the focus ought to be religious.

Fortunately, theology and politics need not necessarily be at variance regarding interfaith conversation. Well known for his "political theology," Jürgen Moltmann mentions that "Whereas once politics deregulated the economy, today politics are regulated by the economy, for this has become trans-national, whereas politics are still persistently national." Accordingly, he says, "Theology 'with its face turned toward the world' must therefore also become an economic and ecological theology if it wishes to take on the forces of our time."[13] Yet Moltmann warns that the "reduction of politics to economics" combined with the "undervaluation of culture and religion" results in irrelevance.[14] Therefore, Pentecostals, as well as others desiring to influence existentially the present age, not only may but also perhaps must address a plethora of issues. However, they can and should do so always from the perspective of their own theological moorings. This perspective would doubtless include attention to the religious boundaries of the discussion while not excluding areas of economic and political interfaith interface.

The American Experiment[15]

Not a Christian Nation but a Religious Republic.[16] Historian Jon Meacham eloquently declares that, "The great good news about America—the American gospel, if you will—is that religion shapes the life of the nation without strangling it."[17] His main point is that from early times until the present the United States government has labored to balance faith and freedom through adopting a kind of generic public religion that allows individuals to choose and practice the specific religion their conscience dictates. Early Americans, many of them fleeing from the carnage of European religious wars still all too fresh in their memories, nevertheless chose not freedom *from* but freedom *of* religion. Led by the likes of George Washington, Thomas Jefferson, John Adams, Benjamin Franklin, James Madison, and others, they chose retaining religion in principle without maintaining any religion in particular.[18] Accordingly, even though often avowing the predominantly Christian, or later sometimes, Judeo-

Christian, heritage of the majority of Americans, the American system of government carefully built itself on the platform of a pragmatic pluralism.[19] This frank confession of the reality of religious diversity often implicit and occasionally quite explicit throughout history of American government points the way to a promising future for interfaith dialogue.

Of course, an argument could be made that, as the preponderant religious faith and values of early Americans were indeed undeniably of a Christian background, that the "pluralism" the founding fathers envisioned and espoused was mostly a matter of multiple Christian sects co-existing harmoniously. Perhaps it mostly was so. However, Meacham demonstrates that it certainly was not entirely so. For example, he records George Washington reassuring the Muslim nation of Tripoli that 'the government of the United States is not in any sense founded on the Christian religion'.[20] Elsewhere Washington declares that the 'bosom of America' is open to 'the oppressed and persecuted of all nations and religions' whether they be 'Mohometans, Jews, Christians of any sect,' or even 'atheists.'[21] John Adams went so far as to attribute the rise of the respective religions of the Hebrews, Christians, and Muslims to 'the Providence of the first Cause, the Universal Cause'.[22] Thomas Jefferson explained that his pioneer bill for religious liberty was expressly 'meant to comprehend, within the mantle of its protection, the Jew, the Gentile, the Christian and the Mahometan, the Hindoo, and the infidel of every denomination.'[23] Furthermore, the 'formal political equality' afforded Jews have been long present as a priceless part of the heritage of the United States.[24] Meacham concludes that "the Founders lived in and consciously bequeathed a culture shaped and sustained by public religion, one that was not Christian or Jewish or Muslim or Buddhist but was simply transcendent, with reverence for the 'Creator' and for 'Nature's God.'"[25] Evidently, the religious diversity envisioned by the founders of America's system of government included both Christian and non-Christian religions.

Although exclusivist religious fundamentalists may look upon it unfavorably, there appears to be almost overwhelming historical evidence suggesting the political and religious climate of the United States of America is and apparently always has been highly flavored with an incontrovertible pluralist and secularist element.[26] As above, this fact could and should foster interfaith dialogue in the present century of American involvement in the global conflicts often arising out of interreligious misunderstanding. Authentic interfaith conversation may best serve, and conserve, the future of faith in America. Fortunately, the plural and secular background of the historical and political development of the United States effectively opens a door inviting interfaith involvement on a high level.

A Religious Republic but Still a Christian Country.[27] Yet there is more, much more, to the history, and continuing story, of faith in America than recounting the official government line on religion or the religions. The context of American religion may be better understood through the American people themselves.[28] In spite of, or perhaps because of, all of the religious diversity and plurality indicative of the official government stance on religion, the people of America have been and are fervently fascinated with Jesus when it comes to religious faith. Scholar of American intellectual and cultural history, including an emphasis on religion, Richard Fox explains that, "Whether Jesus is the eternal Son of God or only a great first century Palestinian Jewish wise man, there is no doubt about his prominence as an American cultural figure over the last four centuries."[29] Fox argues gently but insistently that there are indeed many (sometimes conflicting) cultural interpretations and applications of the life and teachings of Jesus, some of them uniquely American, in the nation. Yet nevertheless, Christ is "the single most important American cultural hero and religious figure."[30] He notes that, "Jesus continues to help a huge population of Americans make sense of their deepest hopes, fears, cravings, and transgressions." Moreover, he adds that, "In all likelihood Jesus is permanently layered into the American cultural soil."[31] He admits that some American Christians will see their faith in Jesus in an exclusive way but thinks the ability of Christian faith to reflect on itself will help control those tendencies.[32]

Fox describes American Pentecostalism as part of a subcultural tradition that has significantly contributed to the deepening of the "overall national infatuation with Jesus".[33] Its eclectic nature is particularly prominent, for example, in Latino syncretism of Catholicism and Protestantism in various forms of Pentecostalism.[34] He also distinguishes between Fundamentalists and Pentecostals but notes that they both sharply diverge from the modernist liberal version of religious faith so controversial in American culture. Their differences fade regarding their high views of the person of Christ.[35] Indeed Fox suggests Pentecostals, rooted in the Holiness and revivalist traditions, may be the "most vibrant force" in contesting and countering the liberal anti-supernaturalism wing of Christianity. Pentecostalism has brought an energy and assurance to American Christianity that had been greatly diminished.[36] However, their stance toward politics remains ambiguous though focused to some extent on personal morality issues such as combating abortion and homosexuality.[37]

Fox comes across as a still respectful but not quite reverent Roman Catholic. In conclusion, he suggests Christianity has "staying power in America" for several reasons. First, it provides "respectable conformity, relief from anxiety, or a promise of eternal happiness." Somewhat paradoxically, Christianity also provides Americans with an "alternative to conformity, or a correction to their complacency." Yet most of all Fox thinks most Americans simply admire the real life examples of Christians just living and telling the love of Jesus.[38] The idea that America is a pluralist and secular nation, though apparently accurate, at least officially, does not explain the total religious make up of America. The religious reality also includes the eclectically but predominantly Christian constituency of the American people.[39] Accordingly, future trajectories of interreligious dialogue in the American context or in collaboration with it should appropriately acknowledge the predominantly Christian presence and influence.

Pentecostals should not be dismissive toward the intentionally plural and secular quality of America's public religion. It flows together with their belief in the values of religious liberty. However, it should never be used, or rather misused, as in the case of some contemporary movements of political correctness that seem designed and dedicated to stifling all religion in general and Christianity in particular, to suggest America is in any way an anti-religious or anti-

Christian nation. Extreme secularism misses the point as much or more than extreme sectarianism.[40] Though some (but not all) of the Founding Fathers were unconventional, even unorthodox, in their Christianity, they nonetheless expressed their highest admiration for Jesus Christ, his moral example and teachings, and for Christianity, as they understood it. Yet they ardently wished for and tirelessly worked for a political state free from the domineering tyranny of any specific religious faith.[41] Therefore, interfaith dialogue in the spirit of the American experience would recognize and respect the reality of religious pluralism but be unapologetic and unashamed of its specifically Christian heritage.[42]

This understanding will be utterly essential for Pentecostal Christians committed to engaging in interreligious dialogue without compromising their Christian convictions. Most Pentecostals probably view America as an essentially Christian nation but have significant and negative caveats about its faithfulness to that faith. Understanding that America may be best thought of as a nation with a dual religious identity, politically plural but popularly Christian, could help Pentecostals approach interreligious dialogue without being aggressive toward its pluralistic makeup or defensive of its Christian heritage. So long as pluralists or secularists do not attack Christianity as an enemy of liberty, or so long as fundamentalists do not attempt to officially impose Christianity on others, interfaith conversation can proceed in positive directions.[43] Therefore, American Pentecostals intending to engage in interreligious dialogue will find ingeniously juxtaposing competing or conflicting paradigms of "theo-political" national identities necessary.[44]

Global Condition

Global Christianity.[45] Philip Jenkins' high profile study of developments in Christianity outside of the Western hemisphere informs the global context of interreligious dialogue as well. He asserts that "one of the most transforming moments in the history of religion worldwide" is currently occurring as "the center of gravity in the Christian world" shifts south, that is, toward Africa and Latin America.[46] In fact, while the West (especially Europe) becomes increasingly secular Christianity is growing rapidly in these global areas.[47] Jenkins notes that these developments have "countless implications for theology and for religious practice." For one thing, the nature of Christianity itself is changing through synthesis with the thought of other cultures. In a word, Christianity is becoming much more diverse. Moreover, it is becoming much more "Pentecostal" or "Charismatic" as these groups lead the Church in global growth.[48] Contrary to what may have been the expectations of some, Christianity is not dying, but it is diversifying. Yet notably, the "dominant theological tone of emerging world Christianity" is what Jenkins describes as "traditionalist, orthodox, and supernatural." Again, this description fits much better with Pentecostal Christianity than with so-called mainstream, liberal Protestantism.[49]

In the South, Jenkins predicts the possibility of "a new Christendom," that is, of new national alliances formed around the commonality of Christianity. If so, this development may portend increasing conflict between "Christian" and "Muslim" nations, especially when they are neighboring nations. Of course, diplomats and other political leaders will need to be very informed about religions as well as common economic and political concerns if they are to avoid the horrors of religious wars.[50] Historically, when nations with national religions expanded rapidly, "interfaith relations were transformed swiftly, and horribly."[51] Therefore, in the future, it will become increasingly important for policymakers to understand relations between and among the three major Abrahamic religions: Judaism, Christianity, and Islam. In fact, Jenkins says "the politics of the coming decades" will likely "revolve around interreligious conflict," especially that between Christianity and Islam.[52]

If, as appears likely, Jenkins is correct, then given the above, interreligious dialogue will become even more vital in the future, and not only for religious people but for the rest of the world as well. For a time, the religions, or even religion itself, may be made out to be the culprit for global conflict; but over time, it will become evident that not eradicating religion but rather improving interreligious relations is the track to take. Moreover, special attention will be advisable for relations between Christianity and Islam or, more importantly, between Christians and Muslims. Furthermore, whether positively or negatively, that is, whether in support or in opposition, the increasingly important place of Pentecostalism in the grand scheme of things among Christians, and therefore among others as well, suggests Pentecostals will likely play a major part in future developments among various faiths. Their role may be either unconsciously reactionary or intentionally visionary. The former will foster unintended but nonetheless just as hurtful strife, but the latter will help pave a pathway to peace. As the present work often argues and always assumes, the latter is preferable. Pentecostals could and should play a powerful and positive role in the future of interfaith relations. To date, the patently obvious is that interreligious dialogue is a first, great step in the right direction. This work attempts to lift up the paradigm of testimony as an authentically Pentecostal way of entering the engagement of religious others through dialogue.

Global Pentecostalism: Ecumenical and Interfaith Implications of Pentecostalism's Diversity, Commonality, and Spirituality.[53] Allan Anderson, himself a practicing Pentecostal primarily placed in the United Kingdom and South Africa, is an authoritative analyst of global Pentecostalism.[54] He argues that, "from its beginning, Pentecostalism has consisted of a variety of local movements with particular contextual responses to imported forms of Christianity."[55] For him, the exponentially burgeoning Pentecostal movement may be best understood in terms of great diversity in the midst of strong commonalities. Of key concern are spiritualities affirming spiritual experience and gifts rather than theologies affirming subsequence or initial evidence (see Introduction of present work). Although Anderson acknowledges the unique contributive role of Pentecostalism in the United States to the worldwide movement, he is particularly concerned to contend for contributions of what he calls the Majority World (believers living in the non-Western/non-European or North American nations) to the ongoing development of Pentecostalism. He argues that the Pentecostal and Charismatic movements "have indeed become globalized in every sense of the word" and asserts that, "this has enormous ecumenical implications, and adherents are often on the cutting edge of encounter with people of other faiths."[56] Pentecostals have had a checkered past when it comes to ecumenism, but early on exhibited ecumenical tendencies. Furthermore, Pentecostals outside the West seem to have "far fewer 'hang ups' when it comes to ecumenism" than their counterparts.[57] A pattern of increasing ecumenical dialogue between Pentecostals and Roman Catholics, and Pentecostals and the WCC, is discernible.[58] Yet Pentecostals struggle with understanding their ecumenical and multicultural identity—partly because of the outside influence of Fundamentalism.[59]

According to Anderson Pentecostalism has had, and evidently will continue to have, an immense impact upon world Christianity. Global Pentecostalism effectively endeavors to bring renewal to the Church, initiate interfaith encounter and dialogue, and build indigenous churches creatively but uncompromisingly adapted to their cultural, social, and spiritual contexts. Of special significance for the present study, Pentecostals tend to engage those of other faiths on a very practical level through personal and missional interaction on the global scene rather than through academic speculation, and because of their (perhaps unconscious) "absorption" of their cultural and religious contexts surprisingly share in common a great deal with their neighbors of other faiths.[60] Thus opens up a way for "a constructive Pentecostal theology of religions" exploring the Spirit's presence among other religions. Often a mutually challenging and enriching exchange occurs as Pentecostalism and pre-Christian religions encounter each other in the field.[61] Anderson warns that an inordinate fear of syncretism, that is, of an inappropriate influence of religions upon each other, forgets that humans are authentically able to know only in epistemologically enabling cultural contexts.[62] In other words, believers comprehend or understand the gospel in terms of their own philosophical and religious cultural underpinnings. Therefore, some exchange of ideas between religions can be beneficial if it aids in contextualizing the gospel without compromising it. For Anderson, then, interfaith dialogue and ecumenical cooperation and social action are important components for the future of vital Pentecostal faith.[63]

Global Pentecostalism: Ecumenical and Interfaith Implications of Spreading Progressive Pentecostalism.[64] Non-Pentecostals Donald Miller and Tetsunao Yamamori, both of the University of California, have created a new term for what they see as a special brand of Pentecostals: Progressive Pentecostalism. The term describes members of the movement who continue to affirm the apocalyptic return of Jesus but also are concerned about social issues and compassionate service in the present.[65] Testing churches according to criteria of fast-growing, location in the developing world, having active social programs, and being indigenous, self-supporting congregations, they were initially shocked to discover 85% of their sampling meeting the standard to be Pentecostal. Now they unabashedly propose the startling thesis that Progressive Pentecostalism is emerging as one of the most important global social movements rooted in religion.[66]

Significant for the present study, Miller and Yamamori opine that Pentecostalism's phenomenal growth is in itself something of a response to prevalent religious pluralism and rampant skepticism, as well as pervasive secularism.[67]

Although Miller and Yamamori consider worship to be the "engine" that drives the dynamic of Pentecostalism, and though emphases on healing and neighborly love are extremely important, also contributing to its gargantuan growth patterns is an amazingly effectiveness in recognizing and utilizing resources in pre/non-Christian religious cultures without compromising their strong Christian convictions.[68] Furthermore, in efforts to defend and promote children's rights (and other egalitarian causes), Progressive Pentecostals have shown themselves willing to form cooperative partnerships with groups of other faiths. In fact, they have developed a holistic philosophy of ministry that reaches out to those of other religious faiths, such as for example, Buddhists in China, without any preconditions regarding conversion. They have accordingly been able to express and enact love unconditionally in religiously plural settings.[69] Yet Miller and Yamamori honestly opine that a critical question facing Pentecostals is whether "they can creatively incorporate ideas from other religious traditions ... without losing the fire that drives their compassion."[70]

Miller and Yamamori admit that the Pentecostal movement is "more like a wild shrub than a tree with symmetrical branches."[71] Thus, it tends to grow and develop in unpredictable (and unprecedented) ways. Yet its future development, especially among Progressive Pentecostals, will likely continue to deepen a balanced approach to evangelism and social action and, inspired by the Holy Spirit and the life of Jesus, a holistic address to the spiritual, physical, and social needs of people in their communities.[72] Miller and Yamamori try very hard to integrate honestly the sociological and theological issues called for by such diversely driven developments.[73] Along the way, they debunk many of the reductive and stereotypical myths more or less mistakenly associated with Pentecostals.[74] Moreover, they admit that, "Pentecostalism has multiple expressions" and that "Pentecostalism is not a uniform phenomenon."[75] Therefore, not all Pentecostals are "progressive." Not all engage in social action or ecumenical and interreligious dialogue and cooperation. Yet the future of Progressive Pentecostalism appears bright nonetheless. Arguably, increasing engagement of surrounding society, including religious others, with its balancing of evangelism and social action, vividly reflect "the maturation of the Pentecostal movement."[76] Accordingly, one might reasonably expect ecumenical and interreligious dialogue and cooperation to become increasingly important though without decreasing enthusiasm for world evangelism or ecstatic worship.

In sum, the theological and political components of national (i.e., American) and international contemporary societal contexts suggest an increasing awareness of the urgent need for the practice of interreligious dialogue, and furthermore, of Pentecostal involvement in that process. The future of interfaith conversation, therefore, is likely to include an eclectic variety of pragmatic and thematic elements beyond doctrinal discussions. It is also likely to include ever-increasing Pentecostal participation, and to be dramatically impacted thereby. Part of that contribution may very well be the intentional incorporation of the Pentecostal tradition of testimony into the practice of dialogue. In the universal and yet unique narratives of human life common desires and needs are most deeply shared.

Projected Trajectories for Pentecostal Interfaith Conversation[77]

Ever Expanding Pentecostal Energy and Engagement[78]

One factor likely to affect immensely the future of interreligious encounter and dialogue is the apparent expansion of Pentecostal engagement. If true to form, that is if Pentecostals approach this field with characteristic energy and enthusiasm, they may make major contributions to its ongoing development and practice. As already noted, there are evidentiary indications that among certain groups of Pentecostals involvement in the wider arena of societal concerns is increasing. Also noted, this has sometimes touched on areas of interreligious encounter, cooperation, and dialogue. Given current global conditions, one may only expect that trend to increase.[79]

A stirring question would be whether these Pentecostal groups and their proponents will be successfully able to invite the broader movement to embrace their cause. This question is especially applicable for the North American context where Pentecostals today tend to be more monolithic and less innovative than elsewhere.[80] Evangelical activist Jerry Redman supplies an example for an argument that they not only will but also are already doing so. Redman, an ordained minister in the Church of God (Cleveland, TN), a Classical Pentecostal organization, leads a missional community called "The Crossroads Community" in Chattanooga, Tennessee. It exists to deliver the gospel through social action/social justice initiatives. He argues that the time has come for Evangelicals to expand their horizons building on solid biblical and theological foundations for involved social action. He stridently challenges them to catch up with the rest of the world in their humanitarian concerns. The plight of the poverty-stricken, those without availability of clean drinking water, climate change, peace and justice, AIDS, and so on are legitimate concerns calling for Evangelical attention and action.[81]

Significantly, Redman specifically includes the positive impact of conservative Christian social action on interfaith understanding with non-Christian religions.[82] He also argues that Evangelicals and other Christians should be willing to dialogue and partner with other groups with whom they may not agree on important points in order to cooperate in accomplishing shared social goals.[83] Furthermore, for him this proposed partnership is essential for influencing popular culture in positive directions.[84]

Exceptionally interesting, Faith News Network, an official online news agency of the Church of God (Cleveland, TN), as stated, a leading Classical Pentecostal organization, carried Redman's article. Recently, other such articles have also begun to appear more frequently in this venue. These kinds of articles on this kind of site surely suggest expanding Pentecostal interest in wide-ranging ethical and social issues. Here the Church of God, of Wesleyan heritage and orientation, appears to be moving consistently in keeping with that broad tradition.[85] There is no reason to suppose interreligious dialogue will not become an increasing concern as well. Quite to the contrary, Chapter Three of the present work demonstrates Pentecostals are indeed entering this conversation, and that they are bringing their own unique ideas and experiences to the discussion table. More will be addressed to issuances from these new avenues later; but for the present, it is enough to note that future interfaith conversations will have to take into account Pentecostal input.[86]

Furthermore, rather than isolated activity, the move of Evangelicals and Pentecostals into social activism appears to have more of a groundswell of support. For example, popular preacher and writer Fleming Rutledge is an ordained Episcopal priest identified as "evangelical" but ministering among mainline denominations as well. She specifically challenges Evangelicals and Pentecostals that their "gospel is too small" when they limit it to only individual redemptive experience just as much so as when liberals limit it to social action only. Rutledge recognizes that at heart this is a theological and spiritual issue with individual and institutional dimensions. She insightfully suggests Evangelical-Pentecostal belief in the delivering and liberating power of the gospel of Christ is broad enough and bold enough to encompass both individual and institutional evil. She suggests there is a supernatural component to both individual addiction, for example, and institutional oppression for profit, for example, that the power of God in the gospel of Christ directly addresses. Accordingly, she suggests there needs to be a widening of the vision of the gospel's applicability and energy, and a moving beyond sympathy for the needy to action in their behalf. Fleming eloquently argues that God may in fact be "disturbing the peace," or causing discontent and unrest, among his people as a part of God's own move to motivate change in the present world order.[87]

Again, as with Redman above with the Church of God publication, that Rutledge's cutting-edge article appeared in the widely read and highly respected conservative, Evangelical organ *Christianity Today* is probably indicative of a major movement among grassroots Evangelicals becoming more actively involved in a societal sense. That it specifically targets Pentecostals is telling also. It is probably indicative of a desire to recruit the energy and vitality of the massive Pentecostal movement and of some discernment that perhaps many Pentecostals are open to such a turn. Rutledge identifies "racial injustice, poverty, pollution, inferior education, sex trafficking, inadequate health care, prison recidivism, political corruption, and yes, terrorism" as items demanding attention. She does not include interreligious relations in the list. Arguably, however, once Evangelicals and Pentecostals become more attentive to these undeniably lamentable problems, taking only a small step leads to becoming more aware of the laudability of attentiveness to the individual and societal importance of interreligious dialogue as well.[88]

Help and Hope for the World through World Religions[89]

Jon Meacham asks an all-important question also underlying the aim of the present work. "Can religion be a force for unity, not division, in the nation and in the world?" He answers in the affirmative and immediately adds that, "For many, reverence for one's own tradition is not incompatible with respect for the traditions of others."[90] Another analyst of the current political and religious scene, Jim Wallis, argues for a moral rather than a military solution to terrorism, and calls for the religions to lead the way.[91] These views affirm the content and intent of the present work. It would only add that an important component of the religions' ability to help today's global society and bring hope to the world is a courageous commitment to and engagement in interreligious dialogue, and that Pentecostals should commit to helping in this laudable endeavor.

In the foreseeable future, both formal and informal interfaith conversations likely will only increase both in frequency and in intensity. As Marty and Moore opine, attempting to get "rid of religion" will just not work. Even if it did, results would be yet worse.[92] Quite to the contrary, religion at its best will become a societal resource for overcoming religion at its worst. There will likely always be those who blame religion (and God) for all their problems. These will wrathfully recommend rejecting all religion—and thus all the religions—altogether.[93] However, increasingly evident is that intelligent and educated people continue to accept the possibility of God and the validity of religion as an authentic expression of faith in God.[94] Though ecumenical, and even interfaith, dialogue is not new, the contemporary demand and need for it will increase its practical relevance and therefore its practicable occurrence. Interreligious encounter and dialogue will probably become less and less of an academic exercise for the intellectually inquisitive and more and more of a pressing practical process essential for planetary survival. Although perhaps only the overly idealistic would suggest that interreligious dialogue alone will suffice to solve conflictive encounters of competing religions and cultures involved in their clashes, perhaps only the overly naïve would deny its proper place as an all-important component of the solution to these situations admittedly including other complex economic and political factors. Harmonious human relations by those sharing the same planet will increasingly demand interfaith conversation.

None of the above should be construed in such a manner as to sidestep the difficulties that will inherently and inevitably be involved in conversations between those of vastly differing worldviews. Cardinal Jean-Louis Tauran, president of the Vatican's Pontifical Council for Interreligious Dialogue, has said religions should be prepared to ask difficult questions, such as on religious freedom, freedom of conscience, conversion, extremism, and so on. Facing these issues of faith is essential because it is unrealistic to live as if there was only one global faith. He insists interreligious dialogue is not a betrayal of the mission of Christ, not a new method of winning members to Christianity, nor an effort to control the spread of other religions. Rather, dialogue is a bridge-building exercise, dealing with the promotion of harmony and tolerance among religions.[95] Accordingly, one may reasonably expect the future of interfaith conversation to include straight talk about tough questions. Yet its goal is not adversarial but irenic. Moreover, one may expect that the "harmony and tolerance among religions" exemplified in interreligious dialogue might also spill over into the larger society of which they are a part at least to the extent that religion influences its fundamental shape—which may be monumental.

The Role of the Church in Reaching Out to the Religions

Emerging Pentecostal Ecclesiologies and Ecumenical Implications.[96] To a greater or lesser degree, liberals have long advocated religious pluralism.[97] What is new is that conservative Evangelical and Pentecostal Christians are becoming involved in the conversation, that is, other than in periodically issuing denunciatory diatribes. However, they do not advocate pluralism. This study advances that some of them are adopting an inclusivist attitude. One area becoming critical in this process is ecclesiology. Many Pentecostal theologians agree that Pentecostalism, due to an early lack of emphasis, has not developed an articulate ecclesiology. However, Dale Coulter persuasively demonstrates that there are important strands of early Pentecostalism, specifically, the Church of God (Cleveland, TN), that contribute significantly to Pentecostal understanding on the nature of the Church.[98] Interestingly, Coulter finds significant ecclesiological resources for Pentecostal engagement in ecumenical exchanges, namely similarities with Catholic and Orthodox ecclesiologies and strong pneumatic and charismatic elements within Pentecostalism.[99] This exciting recovery of early Pentecostal ecclesiology may presage potentially fecund developments for dialogue.

Another Pentecostal theologian, Simon Chan of Singapore, also argues for the pneumatological nature of a proper Pentecostal ecclesiology. He especially argues for the unity of pneumatology and ecclesiology.[100] For him, this includes the transmission and development of doctrine in the Church by the power of the Holy Spirit without which there is no vital future for the Church. Again, this has immense ecumenical and even catholic implications compatible with the instincts of early Pentecostalism.[101] Yet again, Australian Pentecostal Shane Clifton argues for a "concrete ecclesiology" incorporating both divine and human, that is, theological and sociological, insights accounting for the ecclesial narratives of the Spirit in the rich diversity of the Pentecostal movement.[102] Through his heuristic definition, Clifton is countering what he sees as unsatisfactory idealistic ecclesiologies incapable of analyzing the complex reality of indigenous Pentecostalism particularly as ecclesial change occurs.[103] Obviously, ecumenical diversity and opportunity arise out of Pentecostal ecclesiology/ecclesiologies.

Pentecostals have conversed extensively with Evangelical theologian Clark Pinnock on Pentecostal ecclesiology as well. Several articles in a single issue of the *Journal of Pentecostal Theology* were devoted to this discussion.[104] Pinnock proposes a provocative and optimistic pneumatic Pentecostal ecclesiology accenting the identity of the Church as the Spirit-anointed herald of God's Kingdom, a relational and social trinitarian reflection, a church oriented to mission, a fellowship of the Spirit, and with a continuing charismatic structure that yet has an institutional dimension.[105] Pentecostal theologians such as Frank Macchia, Terry Cross, and Hollis Gause generally received his remarks well. Macchia wants to stress an even fuller relation of the Spirit to justification and to develop further the charismatic structure of the Church.[106] Cross wishes to explore the nature of the Church from a Trinitarian Pentecostal perspective as a people of God's presence and power.[107] Gause, like Coulter but distinctively, reminds that there were early Pentecostal ecclesiologies that have been insufficiently acknowledged because they were not couched in academic constructs.[108] However, all were appreciatively responsive to Pinnock's proposal.

One strand of thought clearly consistent throughout the differing approaches to ecclesiology emerging among Pentecostals is its pneumatological orientation. In addition, arising out of almost any pneumatological ecclesiology are explicit ecumenical implications. While this in itself is notable and commendable, it points beyond itself to the possibility of implicit interreligious implications. Once Pentecostals, affirming that the Spirit is of key significance for the character of the Church, also acknowledge the Spirit in the wider world, implications for understanding and dialoguing with world religions reasonably occur as well. Future interfaith conversations involving Pentecostals therefore may well invite even further ecclesiological advancement and development along this line.

A Pneumatological and Ecumenical Ecclesiological Assist from Moltmann.[109] As Chapter 3 of the present work observes, Pentecostals have tended to engage Jürgen Moltmann in conversation on complex theological issues. Ecclesiology may yield yet another such exchange, especially in light of theology of religions and interreligious dialogue. Moltmann scholar Richard Bauckham offers assistance here. Bauckham's extensive study of the thought of Moltmann includes references to the thinker's views regarding world religions. Particularly important is Moltmann's ecclesiology. For Moltmann, the "church does not exist in, of or for itself, but only in relationship and can only be understood in its relationships", including its "open and critical relationship with other realities, its partners in history, notably Israel, the other world religions, and the secular order".[110] Israel, however, enjoys a special partnership with Christianity in this schema—though all religions, and indeed, all the world, are moving toward the eschatological and messianic Kingdom of Jesus Christ.[111] Moltmann supposes that these dialogue partners will never become the Church, that the Church represents a complementary part of a whole, but Bauckham challenges him on this a bit, agreeing with Moltmann's openness but arguing that real reciprocity may include these others coming to faith in Jesus as the Messiah. Bauckham here seems to be guarding against limitations on the Church's mission of calling all people to Christ.[112]

Moltmann's openness regarding other religions is also evident in his pneumatology. Bauckham says, "Moltmann achieves a strong continuity between creation and redemption, and between the creative and salvific activities of the Spirit".[113] Indeed, Moltmann does show his appreciation for signs of the Spirit outside the Church and for the Spirit's work beyond the borders of the Church in his claim that the Spirit is greater than the Church and has purposes beyond it.[114] Moltmann expressly affirms the Spirit's salvific purposes beyond the Church, and chides the Church not to be jealous of the Spirit's extra-ecclesial activities.[115] Unsurprisingly, Moltmann sees his perennial theme of hope present not only in Christianity but also in other Abrahamic religions.[116]

Moltmann's pneumatology, among other things, challenges Pentecostals not only to think of the Church pneumatologically, as they already tend to do, but also to see the Church as an expression of the Spirit's larger ministry to the wider world, which they have not always done. Yet, unless they essentially equate Church and Spirit, which Pentecostals adamantly avoid, the Spirit is greater than and cannot be confined to the Church. Therefore, Moltmann's pneumatology may be a potentially rich resource for Pentecostals moving into ecumenical avenues and interreligious directions.

A Pneumatological and Ecumenical Ecclesiological Assist from Irenaeus[117]

Patristic apologist Irenaeus of Lyons is of great interest regarding contemporary developments in Pentecostal ecclesiology.[118] For one thing, one of the most widely known theological statements about the Spirit and the Church comes from his work. In Chapter 24 of his *Against Heresies* Irenaeus recapitulates some of the various arguments adduced against Gnostic heretics. Preeminent were the doctrinal consistency of the true Church and the evident vitality of the Holy Spirit in that Church. On the Spirit he succinctly said, "For where the Church is, there is the Spirit of God; and where the Spirit of God is, there is the Church, and every kind of grace; but the Spirit is truth."[119] Obviously, this resonates well with Pentecostals today. Patristic scholar J. N. D. Kelly notes that for Irenaeus the Church is "the unique sphere of the Spirit," that the Spirit "has been especially entrusted" to the Church, and that thus only through the Church is communion with Christ attainable.[120] Extremely important to remember, however, is that Irenaeus writes in a polemical mode against heretics. As shall be suggested below, his pneumatological ecclesiology is not necessarily to be interpreted in an exclusive sense beyond that specific context, but is capable of inclusive applications. (Indeed, Pentecostal theologian Frank Macchia argues that though the Church is the unique "locus" of the Spirit this does not eliminate the Spirit from the rest of the world, even from world religions.)[121] In any case, it seems clear that Irenaeus means to make the Church dependent on the Spirit, not the Spirit dependent on the Church.

Another patristic scholar, Mary Ann Donovan, comments on Irenaeus' teaching on "the Church as the place of the Spirit" also. For her, this means that the "Church is defined by the Spirit". Yet she very insightfully notes that this understanding complements (rather than contradicts or undercuts) Irenaeus' emphatic imagery of the Church as "a bank or repository of the apostolic tradition" of doctrinal truth.[122] Donovan decides that Irenaeus intuitively holds together institutional and charismatic ecclesiologies. She thinks this implies that Irenaeus held to a view of "the *living* nature of truth, equated with the living Spirit of God." Accordingly, "Truth so understood is sovereignly free," and the Church, gathered by Christ, yet "finds her place as docile to that Spirit."[123] Truth and Spirit, then, are compatible and complementary ecclesiological images. Significantly, relating the Church to Spirit and Truth does not result in a rigid, exclusive ecclesiology, but in a dynamic, inclusive ecclesiology that nonetheless champions truth over against relativistic compromise without caving into rationalistic reductionism. The unchanging truth of the apostolic tradition grants the Church solid and trustworthy boundaries for belief and practice. The dynamic verity of the Spirit graces the Church with innovative openings for its belief and practice. Such boundaries and openings may hold up both the uniqueness of the Church and the universality of the Spirit.

Regardless of the particular track taken, the pneumatological contributions characteristic of Pentecostal ecclesiology appear to lend themselves readily to inclusive applications for ecumenical and interreligious encounter, dialogue, and cooperation. An important element of the future of Pentecostalism will likely include developing and relating its ecclesiology and pneumatology to ecumenical and interreligious fields of endeavor. Probably these advancements and developments will also affect Christology and soteriology but without significant alteration of traditional commitments. Accordingly, the future of Pentecostal interfaith conversation will likely look much the same doctrinally or theologically as historic Pentecostalism but will include enhanced and nuanced applications thereof. Yet predictably, enhanced and nuanced applications of historic Pentecostal doctrine and theology will yield richly surprising results for the continuing and deepening dynamic of the maturing movement.

Overcoming Obstacles in the Pentecostal Tradition

Pentecostals, Peace, and Spiritual Warfare.[124] The present study has repeatedly proffered that world peace, though by no means the only, nonetheless is a major motivator for advocates of interreligious dialogue (e.g., Chapter 1). Unfortunately, when Pentecostals think of peace, as in the fruit of the Spirit, they usually relate it to "having" peace rather than "making" peace. In other words, they refer to a sense of inner peace rather than working to make peace among others in the world around them.[125] Of course, the former is not incorrect but it is incomplete. Complicating matters more, Pentecostals do have a long and legitimate tradition of spiritual warfare against wickedness and its whole range of manifestations.[126] However, spiritual warfare, or struggling against the spiritual forces of evil, should not be confused with natural or physical warfare. Unfortunately, sometimes the uninitiated radically misconstrue the rhetoric of spiritual warfare just so.[127]

Yet Pentecostals do have a strain within their tradition from its early origins of not only peacemaking but also even of pacifism. Moreover, some contemporary Pentecostals are calling for a restoration of pacifism to Pentecostalism.[128] Whether or not a majority or a significant minority of Pentecostals turn to (or return to) absolute pacifism, there is undoubtedly ample room for Pentecostals to be actively involved in peacemaking efforts. In the context of the contemporary global condition, peacemaking necessarily includes attention to interreligious relations and, therefore, to interreligious dialogue. Even ecumenical relations, that is, relations among and between Christians, must improve if peace is a worthwhile pursuit. The undeniable difficulty that many Christians have with living in harmony with each other appropriately compares to the conflictive familial relations observed in sibling rivalry.[129] Such rifts are often not serious in themselves but when sustained until deep-seated and long-lasting suspicion sets in they become so. Therefore, arguably Pentecostals may need to confront and overcome their own hesitance and reluctance to relate redemptively to religious others in order to progress toward peace in accordance with Christ's beatific pronouncement (Matt 5:9).[130]

Reality of Pentecostal Diversity and Adversity.[131] Even in the last few decades, attitudes among Evangelicals, including Pentecostals, appear to have been in a process of development regarding ecumenical dialogue. For instance, Mark Ellingsen has argued that the relationship among Evangelicals between Pentecostal and non-Pentecostal wings of the movement is considerably complex. Most Evangelicals consider Pentecostals to be part of the Evangelical movement, and probably most Pentecostals consider themselves Evangelical. Yet there is much mutual disagreement and at times outright suspicion all around. Even so, Ellingsen says, this sort of delicate integration of diversity, even at times adversity, with real underlying unity, makes for an interesting model of ecumenical dialogue. It might extend to other Christians, that is, Christians outside the overtly Evangelical camp.[132] However, for the purposes of the present study, significant is that Pentecostals themselves appear to be in a process of increasingly engaging others, for example, Roman Catholics, and for another example, Lutherans, in direct bilateral dialogue.[133] Although these examples involve intra Christian encounter and dialogue, the trend toward dialogue may extend even farther—that is, in the direction of interreligious dialogue. In fact, Ellingsen claims that to some extent conservative Evangelicals, including Pentecostals, have already been actively engaging in an ongoing interfaith dialogue with Judaism.[134]

Such trends signal future possibilities for interfaith conversation involving Evangelicals and Pentecostals with those of other faiths. Yet the very real reservations of some wings of Pentecostalism about reaching out to religious others for relational engagement and development ought not to be ignored. As the divisive history of Pentecostalism demonstrates, sometimes the more or less healthy diversity of the movement can explode into outright adversity. Nevertheless, in tandem with the overall tenor of the rest of this present study, one expects Pentecostals will find ecumenical and interfaith isolationism increasingly untenable. Therefore, in spite of realistically expected opposition, one may reasonably expect many Pentecostals to participate in such dialogues more and more as the future unfolds. In fact, in the current global context continuing future Evangelical and Pentecostal viability may depend in large part on their ability to relate well to religious others.

Promise and Peril of Pentecostal Eschatology: Saddled with a Strangling Eschatology.[135] Pentecostal eschatology has often provided the spirituality and theology of the movement with an energetic evangelism and missional momentum that would doubtless have been unavailable (or unimaginable) otherwise.[136] Yet even obviously fair-minded observers such as Miller and Yamamori admit that, "Pentecostalism is saddled with an eschatology" so focused on the imminent return of Christ that it "militates against long-term social and economic struggle."[137] In other words, certain prominent forms of traditional Pentecostal eschatology disengage Pentecostals from present society more so than they engage them with it. Anderson explains that, "the narrow premillennial dispensationalism" dominating North American Pentecostalism particularly during much of the twentieth century "resulted in elaborate and often fanciful interpretations of both future and current events in popular apocalyptic literature." Furthermore, "US Pentecostal theology and political attitudes were profoundly affected by its eschatology". This all in spite of the fact that dispensationalism, which espouses cessationism, or the theory that spiritual gifts ceased with the first century church, is intrinsically at odds with Pentecostal spirituality and theology.[138] While endowing Pentecostals with energy for evangelism through its intense sense of imminence and urgency, dispensationalist eschatology did not allow them time for present social concerns.[139] This, of course, would include ecumenical and interreligious dialogue.

Hollis Gause, a prominent Pentecostal theologian in the Church of God (Cleveland, TN), elucidates an alternative to fundamentalist dispensationalism through a careful comparison-contrast of dispensational theology and a theology of progressive revelation. Gause explains that progressive revelation does not divide up biblical history as dispensationalism. It does not hermeneutically distinguish between the Church, Israel, and the kingdom of God. The nature of God, the history of salvation, and the character of the people of God are progressively revealed. Earlier events anticipate and predict later events. The inspiration of the Holy Spirit gives Scripture a progressive and even prophetic or predictive quality. In stark contrast to the hermeneutical compartmentalizing of dispensationalism, progressive revelation affirms a more unified approach to biblical interpretation and understanding.[140] Gause concludes that "the view of progressive and unified revelation of the history of salvation offers the better interpretation of Scripture."[141] For Gause, considerations of the unchangeableness and unity of God and God's Word consistently lead to this conclusion.[142] Interestingly, Gause does not sacrifice Pentecostalism's staunch emphasis on premillennial eschatology through espousal of progressive revelation.[143]

Promise and Peril of Pentecostal Eschatology: Embracing an Expansive Eschatology.[144] However, the "already-not yet" (or sometimes, "now-not yet") eschatology increasingly prominent among contemporary Pentecostal scholars retains an emphasis on the apocalyptic and imminent return of Christ while seeing the present age as an authentic arena of the Spirit's activity both individually and socially.[145] The present life of faith is a joyful foretaste of an eternal feast that will be fully experienced only in the eschaton with Christ.[146] The present experience of the Spirit is the "down payment" on eternal benefits (Eph 1:13-14).[147] Yet a serious struggle is underway in the present age as the forces of good and evil cohabitate and clash. Nonetheless, Pentecostals are confident not only that final and full victory will be granted but also that it has already been guaranteed through the cross-resurrection-ascension-Pentecost grace of God in Christ and in the Spirit. Pentecostals, therefore, can anticipate the imminent return of Christ even while they participate in the incomplete world of the present. Thus, they are eschatologically catapulted into concerns that conjoin both the present and the future in fresh and vitalizing ways. This means that social action, and ecumenical and interreligious dialogue, may be increasingly lauded as legitimate areas for Pentecostal attention.

However, Pentecostals will have to face the effects of their eschatology on their present activity. Hanging on to outdated and worn out schemas that never did really fit will not work. In reality, it never did. Welcome reassurance may arise from knowledge of the fact that some important early Pentecostals advocated an inclusive theology of religions, and participated in at least limited interreligious dialogue, largely based on their more expansive eschatological vision.[148] Today's Pentecostals can "go and do likewise" (Lk 10:37b).[149] The future of Pentecostals in ecumenical and interfaith conversation and cooperation and other forms of social activity may well depend largely on their progress on this point.[150] This study argues that a now-not yet eschatology allows or enables Pentecostals to retain their essential emphasis on the apocalyptic and imminent second coming of Christ without sacrificing practical interests until that spectacular happening. Present business is therefore not neglected because of future hope nor is future hope abandoned for present business (cf. Lk 19:13).[151]

British NT exegete Andrew Lincoln has persuasively posited that a now-not yet eschatology arising from the Pauline corpus retains but refines the biblical apocalyptic literature already established in his day.[152] Notably, tensions between the immanent and the transcendent, the present and the future, and earth and heaven are not dismissed but rather are dialectically maintained in Christ who encompasses all these in his own person. Ultimately, even this dialectical tension will be fully resolved at Christ's *parousia* as all are brought together in Christ.[153] Until Christ's *parousia* the Holy Spirit "constitutes the vital bond" between the various people and dimensions of heaven and earth.[154] In other words, the Holy Spirit creates and confirms the unifying link of otherwise disparate dimensions.[155]

Promise and Peril of Pentecostal Eschatology: Releasing the Eschatological Spirit into the Present.[156] Especially appealing for Pentecostals is the prominent role of the Spirit in the now-not yet paradigm. Pentecostal exegete and Pauline scholar Gordon Fee refers to the Spirit as "eschatological fulfillment" precisely because the Spirit fills and fulfills both the present and the future.[157] For Fee, Paul's already-not yet end-time perspective is firmly established biblically, and suggests that "empowered by the Spirit, we now live the life of the future in the present age, the life that characterizes God himself."[158] Here is an eschatology almost tailor made for Pentecostals. Likewise, Pentecostal theologian Peter Althouse elucidates a hopeful eschatology eschewing dispensational rigidity and exchanging it for a pneumatological dynamism quite capable of embracing present political and social engagement.[159] Additionally, Macchia intrinsically connects pneumatology and eschatology with contemporary activity in suggesting that the soteriological goal of history is the indwelling of all things by the Spirit and that this calls believers in the present age to bear the image of the divine Spirit in anticipation and signification (cf. 1 Co 15:20-28; Heb 6:5).[160] Again, Andrew Lord argues for an eschatological ecclesial mission understanding that the Spirit brings a foretaste of the Kingdom into the present age through gradual growth and dramatic in-breaking of the future. This enlarges mission beyond evangelism to include social action and ecumenical dialogue without abandoning evangelism.[161]

The choice for Pentecostals therefore, is not between present and future or this-worldly and otherworldly concerns: but, rather between an ill-fitting eschatology (dispensationalism) resulting in a narrowing of their natural vision, and a well-suited eschatology (now-not yet/pneumatological) enabling an expanding of their horizons. As more and more Pentecostals adopt similar eschatological schemas, Pentecostal involvement in the issues of the present, including ecumenical and interreligious dialogue, in all probability will increase exponentially, though without necessarily decreasing attachment to the passionate hope of Christ's coming that spurs on so much of Pentecostal spirituality.[162]

Anticipating Effects of Future Pentecostal Involvement[163]

Anticipating Effects on Pentecostals. Up to this point the present chapter has focused on some general trends and particular trajectories liable to influence future Pentecostal involvement in interfaith conversations. Now it will look at more specific suggestions regarding the approach outlined in this work, that is, of utilizing the Classical Pentecostal tradition of testimony as a resource for interreligious dialogue. At this point, the study will draw more heavily on pastoral experience in situations involving testimony, though all the while cognizant of the more academic underpinnings of testimony in Chapters 5 and 6.[164] Furthermore, it employs a process of extrapolation and application, that is, it takes observable features of Pentecostal testimony in congregational settings and speculates how these may play out in dialogue settings.

Pentecostals frequently speak of a strong sense of inner compulsion regarding their responsibility to testify publicly.[165] This is referred to as the "leading of the Lord" and can result in severe contrition if ignored. Intense mental and emotional anguish, even to the point of loss of appetite and sleeplessness, are often descriptive accompaniments of what is colloquially termed "disobeying the Lord." Pentecostals have been known to come to a worship service expressly intent on completely and immediately correcting such a condition publicly. When they have done so, that is, when they have yielded to the inner urge to testify, which by this time includes confessional reporting on repentance of earlier unwillingness, they often speak of a reassuring sense of peace finally enveloping them. Important to remember is that this is not merely an emotional moment for them. Pentecostals believe in and speak of being in God's "perfect will" (cf. Rom 12:2),[166] and this process is one of discernment and correction with spiritual connotations as they respond to the "convicting" (i.e., convincing) work of the Holy Spirit (John 16:5-11).[167]

By a process of extrapolation and application, from the congregational context to that of the dialogue table, one may suggest that Pentecostals finally giving in to the goading of the Spirit to enter into ecumenical and interreligious testimonial dialogue will experience just such a sense of approbation. Pentecostals who refuse to share what they believe God has done in their lives with others could be expected to experience the contrary disapprobation. In other words, one effect on Pentecostals of engaging religious others through testimony may be that longed for and invaluable sense of being in God's perfect will, while refusal could result in the spiritual unpleasantness accompanying a sense of disobedience to the divine. Pentecostals often assume that when in the latter state, a state of parental-like discipline known as chastisement (cf. Heb 12:4-13),[168] that many of God's best blessings are "blocked" or hindered from entering one's life.[169] The case may well be that Pentecostals, according to their own biblically pragmatic typology, can only experience the abundant blessings so central to their belief system as they testify to others, including religious others. As they do so, they may well expect God to bless them in the process and in many other surprising and unpredictable ways (cf. Eph 1:3).[170]

Anticipating Effects on Other Christians. When non-Pentecostal Christians hear Pentecostals testify, they often have one of two, or sometimes a mixture of the two, responses: inspiration or incredulity. As Pentecostal testimonial style tends toward the dramatic, people are often either inspired by reports that God is doing marvelous, even miraculous, works among their contemporaries, or else they find such reports almost beyond rational belief. More often than not, probably some of both are present in the hearts of such hearers. Yet those who are able to look beyond the (sometimes) admittedly exaggerated claims of (some) testifiers, may still discover authentic evidence of divine providence at work in wondrous ways among those of such devout faith. Practically legendary among Pentecostals are stories of skeptics who could not be convinced by the strongest arguments but were finally persuaded to faith by the sights and sounds of a Pentecostal worship service, including, of course, testimonies along with various manifestations of the Spirit.

Again employing extrapolation from the congregational setting and application to the dialogue table, one may opine that ecumenical audiences exposed to Pentecostal testimony might similarly be inspired, even if sometimes they find some parts a bit incredible. In fact, Pentecostals are not at all unaware that for some their reports sound incredible, and often emphasize the importance of hearing in faith.[171] They, however, like to compare this tendency to incidents in the biblical tradition in which reports and results were mixed but those who believed prevailed (e.g. Num 13; Josh 2).[172] Nevertheless, putting all that aside for the moment, perhaps many ecumenical Christians will be so pleased to find Pentecostals at the table that they will realize something extraordinary is indeed underway. Accordingly, Pentecostal testimony can potentially be a vehicle for opening up fresh avenues of understanding within the Christian family of faith. Pentecostals believe the often contagious energy and enthusiasm associated with their movement are themselves inspired by the Holy Spirit. They do not, therefore, unreasonably expect others with open minds and hearts to be inspired as well.[173]

Anticipating Effects on People of Other Religions. If Pentecostals themselves experience spiritual approbation in testimony, and if other Christians experience inspiration, then perhaps fair to say is that those of non-Christian religions may experience a sense of intrigue amounting to attraction and, hopefully, eventuating in appreciation.[174] Attraction is not meant here in the sense of conversion, though that is not excluded out of hand, but in the sense of being drawn closer to discover more. Often people of other religions, whether Jews, Christians, Muslims, Hindus, Buddhists, or Indigenous, only know of each other bare doctrinal facts or stereotypical behavior that comes through secondhand sources.[175] Testimony is by nature more personal and relational, less incriminating or intimidating, than discursively determined communication.[176] People are set free through telling their stories to get to know each other for who they really are in their inmost identity.[177]

Moreover, people of different faiths are, given human nature, incurably curious about each other. Yet a safe faith environment for developing relationships is an almost overwhelmingly difficult achievement. Testimonial dialogue helps a long way toward initiating and nurturing a safe faith environment.[178] Accordingly, the attraction associated with Pentecostal testimony in interreligious contexts can conceivably grow into mutual appreciation as well. This happens in Pentecostal worship services with testimony.[179] Those that seem different or just unfamiliar become first known and then loved as they tell testimonies revealing who they are and what they are about in the context of their faith life. That is similar to what transpired between Abraham and Abimelech (Gen 20; 21:22-34).[180] Not unreasonably, therefore, Pentecostal participation in testimonial dialogue with adherents of other religions may be expected to enhance attraction and appreciation between the different faiths involved.[181]

Anticipating Effects on People of the World. By "the world" is meant those who do not regulate their lives by commitment to any of the great religious traditions.[182] They are secular, though they may or may not be atheists, or they may even consider themselves vaguely "spiritual," but they do not formally associate with or support a particular religion. Some but not all are antagonistic toward religion. Many are simply among the undecided or uncommitted.[183] Here this study addresses cultural and global society in its not essentially religious mode of existence. Occasionally cynics and skeptics who were not even Christians much less Pentecostals have attended Pentecostal worship services seeking an opportunity to offer scorn or suggest scandal regarding Pentecostals.[184] As Chapter 4 of the present work covers in more detail, testimony has often been at the forefront of such encounters.[185] Yet though more than a fair share of cynicism, skepticism, and even scorn and scandal, have indeed attended such happenings, such observers have also sometimes confessed to being surprisingly impressed with the proceedings. Essentially, they see a reality and sense a sincerity that they were not prepared in advance to encounter.[186] Those who do not actually convert nevertheless sometimes go away convinced. They begin to express a certain admiration for those who are willing to surrender their lives so freely to the fullness of the Spirit. They may not, indeed usually do not, agree with all that the Pentecostals believe and do, but they still express, perhaps grudgingly, perhaps generously, affirmation of a spiritual reality that transcends disagreement. True to their penchant for interpreting everything biblically, Pentecostals tend to describe such encounters and their consequences in terms of those who are "almost persuaded" (cf. Acts 26:28 KJV).[187] For Pentecostals, they serve as proof of the power of the good news to surpass all barriers. The hope is that such "seeds" will eventually take root and grow in unregenerate hearts before "it's too late."[188]

Such cautious admiration and qualified affirmation may also result through Pentecostal interreligious testimony before an unbelieving world. While it is unlikely that non-religious people will actually attend interreligious dialogue sessions, involving Pentecostals or not, news travels fast and far in a day of massive media coverage. Moreover, reports will spread informally too. As the world hears of Pentecostal involvement in interreligious dialogue and perhaps of some of the testimonials as well, they may also be inclined to inch toward at least a grudging admiration and affirmation. The perhaps well-deserved reputation of Pentecostals as some of the most aggressive and conservative of Christians[189] can in turn contribute to the attention and reaction of non-participatory observers to their overtures toward honest and humble openness. Hopefully, they may perceive it all as a uniquely demonstrative example of true Christian identity and unity (cf. John 13:35; 17:20-23).[190] Accordingly, the world's admiration and affirmation of Pentecostal Christians and the Spirit of Christ can result from Pentecostal participation in interfaith conversation.[191]

Anticipating Effects on God[192] Pentecostals have testimonial services primarily for one reason: to glorify God. Relating to listeners what God has done or is doing in one's life is a public act of divine adoration. The major motivation is doxological. Glory is given to God as the one who is able to save, heal, and deliver, to guide and lead his people through the ups and downs of life, and to bless and keep them in a world of evil and trouble. Pentecostals consider themselves to be called and chosen to publicly declare the praises of God to all who will hear (cf. 1 Pe 1:9).[193] The heartthrob of their identity is to worship God "in spirit and in truth" (John 4:24).[194] Testimonies are an important part of giving glory to God, that is, of holy adoration.[195] As Pentecostals reach out in witness of God's goodness and greatness, they allow their light to shine brightly for the glory of God the Father through illuminative deeds and words (Matt 5:16).[196]

Pentecostal involvement in interreligious testimony will call attention to the goodness and greatness of God. It will glorify God through both the content of the testimony, which relates God's actions, and through the act of testifying, which reveals God's character. The nature of the incomparable God who has compassionate concern for all humanity will be highlighted and lifted up for all to know.[197] Potentially, one of the grandest outcomes of Pentecostal entry into interreligious testimony is that the altogether wrong perception some have of God as narrow or mean will be debunked and replaced with a more biblical model of a God who cares for all and communicates with all. In fact, in Christ God speaks a word of love and life to the whole world (cf. John 1:1, 14, 18; 3:16).[198] Moreover, when people hear of and see God's wondrous works they instinctively express praise (Matt 15:31; Acts 4:21).[199] Perhaps a decisive and determinative point for Pentecostals to be encouraged toward engaging others through testimony is the plain hope of bringing glory to God in the process.

Conclusion

This chapter has attempted some envisioning of future developments through the anticipated application of insights suggested in this presentation of Classical Pentecostal involvement in interreligious dialogue through its tradition of testimony. Though rooted in the research of the overall work, as well as in further investigation into the nature of religion and religious dialogue in the present chapter, this section has at times indulged in a mite more speculative approach than previous sections for the purpose of postulating futuristic developments. More than a way forward it is perhaps somewhat of a hypothetical or prognosticative "what if"—though hopefully not overly facile. Primarily it has offered suggestive observations first for Pentecostals themselves, then for other Christians, for non-Christian religions, and finally for the world, and even in relation to God. However, an important prior step was to consider the context of interreligious conversation in the world today as a basis for future developments. Therein it concentrated on the increasingly complex qualities of religion as it coexists and overlaps with other disciplines of corporate human life such as economics and politics as well as national and international attitudes and ideologies. Always the accent has been on better understanding Pentecostalism and its place in relation to interreligious dialogue. Throughout, the suggestion seems clearly justified that Pentecostal involvement in interreligious dialogue, in general and in testimonial mode, will indeed contribute significantly to the status of interreligious relations and global harmony and stability along with distinctively fulfilling Pentecostalism's own authentic spiritual and theological destiny. In a preliminary perspective, that is, in an outlook admittedly dependent on the eventual evaluation of others, the judgment is made that the present work passes inspection and makes code in its attempt to erect, not a flawless but a feasible, edifice for interfaith interaction. Now remains only for the next chapter to summarily conclude and draw to a succinct close the overall study.

Notes

1. E.g., psychologist A. Adler suggested what might be by interdisciplinary transposition identified theologically as an eschatological orientation to reality. According to Adler, humans quite early form ideational patterns of interpreting reality according to expectations of future events or experiences, a process he labeled "fictional finalism" because the construct may more or less correspond to actual reality. Mental health or illness may be largely influenced by the viability of one's future orientation. K. Boa, *Augustine to Freud: What Theologians & Psychologist Can Teach Us About Human Nature* (Nashville: Broadman, 2004), 128-29, 152-53, 162. Cf. H. Vaihinger, "Fictionalism and Finalism," 76-100, eds. H. Ansbacher and R.R. Ansbacher, *The Individual Pschology of Alfred Adler* (New York: Harper & Rox, 1956). A. Adler, *Understanding Human Nature: The Psychology of Personality* (Center City, Montana: Hazeldon, 1998 repr), sets infant and later human development in the context of a survival struggle for power, 18, 23.

2. To an extent, this section relies on the work of Rabbi Jacob Neusner, Jon D. Levenson, Bruce Chilton, Th. Emil Homerin, and Ali S. Asani.

3. *Religious Foundations of Western Civilization: Judaism, Christianity, and Islam*, ed. J. Neusner (Nashville: Abingdon, 2006), ix-xvi. Of course, this complexity is not limited to the West. E.g., O.R. Rahimiyan, Ben-Gurion University, has shown that Iranian Jews prospered under the Pahlavi dynasty, especially under the reign of Mohammed Raza Shah, 1941-79, until resentment arose over their economic affluence as a class. Then later, after the revolution against the Shah, when Jews became concerned over anti-Semitism, the Ayatollah Khomeini, the senior Shi'a cleric and future Supreme Leader of the country, reassured them that he and his government made a distinction between Jews as a religious and ethnic group and Zionists as political opponents. See her "Modern History of Iranian Jews: Iranian Jewry under the Islamic Republic of Iran," http://www.myjewishlearning.com (April 1, 2008).

4. J.D. Levenson, "Judaism, Christianity, and Islam in Their Contemporary Encounters: Judaism Addresses Christianity," *Religious Foundations*, 581-608 (582-83, 606). Some might even speak of the "trialogue" of the Abrahamic faiths. E.g., I.R. Al-Fārūqī, *Trialogue of the Abrahamic Faiths: Papers Presented to the Islamic Studies Group of the American Academy of Religions* (Herndon, VA: International Insttitute of Islamic Thought, 1991).

5. Levenson, "Judaism Addresses Christianity," 582.

6. Levenson, "Judaism Addresses Christianity,"" 583.

7. B. Chilton, "Judaism, Christianity, and Islam in Their Contemporary Encounters: Christianity Meets Other Religions," *Religious Foundations*, 609-19 (616).

8. Th. E. Homerin, "Judaism, Christianity, and Islam in Their Contemporary Encounters: Islam and Pluralism," *Religious Foundations*, 621-37 (624-36). See A.S. Asani, "So That You May Know One Another," *Annals*, AAPSS 58 (July 2003), 40-51.

9. Homerin, "Islam and Pluralism," 623.

10. Which is precisely what C.C. Simut, *A Critical Study of Hans Küng's Ecclesiology* (New York: Palgrave MacMillan, 2008), accuses Küng of doing because of his emphasis on pursing world peace, 137. However, W. Pannenberg, *Ethics*, trans. K. Crim (Philadelphia: Westminster, 1981), argues for interconnecting "The Peace of God and World Peace," 151-74. For him, the pursuit of world peace is not identical to the peace of Christ but does develop authentically out of encounter with Christ's cross and resurrection, not as the full realization of God's Kingdom in the provisional and temporal, but as a viable eschatological foretaste or foreshadowing of it nonetheless, 154-55, 166. Furthermore, he contends that a contribution to the cause of world peace arising out of Christian faith and truth includes cooperative partnership with non-Christians and embraces appreciation for societal diversity and plurality, 170, 173-74.

11. See C.M. Robeck, Jr., "Pentecostals and Social Ethics," *Pneuma* 9 (Fall 1987), 103-07. Cf. also M.D. Palmer, "Ethics in the Classical Pentecostal Tradition," *NIDPCM*, eds. Stanley M. Burgess and Eduard M. Van Der Maas (Grand Rapids, Zondervan, 2002), 605-10 (605-07).

12. F.L. Arrington, "Luke," 375-534, *FLBCNT*, says this text "announces the pattern of Jesus' total ministry of preaching and teaching, healing and deliverance", 512, but does not note that it includes much more as well. However, *The Full Life Study Bible*, gen. ed. D.C. Stamps, assoc. ed. J.W. Adams (Grand Rapids, MI: Zondervan, 1992) on which Arrington also served on the editorial committee, affirming that "Jesus gives the purpose of his Spirit-anointed ministry", adds that "All those who are filled with the Spirit are called to share Jesus' ministry in these ways", specifying that this includes to those who are in "a condition of bondage to evil, brokenheartedness, spiritual blindness and physical distress" (1526). Accordingly, multidimensional aspects of redemption manifest themselves.

13. J. Moltmann, *A Broad Place: An Autobiography*, trans. Margaret Kohl (Minneapolis: Fortress, 2008), (Minneapolis: Fortress, 2008), 157-58. See J.E. Spero and J.A. Hart, *The Politics of International Economic Relations* (Boston, MA: Wadsworth, 2003), 427-40, which traces the evolution of international economic governance, the challenges it poses for global governance, and the continuing characteristics of a new system system of governance.

14. Moltmann, *A Broad Place*, 294.

15. My American orientation, coupled with the prominent role of American Pentecostals in global Pentecostalism and with the role of American churches in general in interreligious dialogue, seems to justify some specific attention to the religious identity of the United States. Notably, in terms almost equal parts charming and alarming, Moltmann says, "The American experiment of all humanity has not failed yet, but it has not as yet succeeded either." See his *A Broad Place*, 132.

16. This section draws on the work of Jon Meacham.

17. J. Meacham, *American Gospel: God, the Founding Fathers, and the Making of a Nation* (New York: Random House, 2006), 5. Cf. I. Kramnik and R.L. Moore, *The Godless Constitution: A Moral Defense of the Secular State* (New York: W. W. Norton & Co, 2005) and F. Lambert, *The Founding Fathers and the Place of Religion in America* (Princeton: Princeton University Press, 2003).

18. On the crucial concept of freedom of religion in the Founding Fathers, see Meacham, *American Gospel,* 90, 98, 214, 230, and 246. For later interpretations or applications, cf. 110 and 129. Meacham opines that "the Founding Fathers left us with a tradition in which we could talk and think about God and politics without descending into discord and division" (16). G. Wills, *Under God: Religion and American Politics* (New York: Simon & Schuster, 1990), suggests religion has often been a progressive force in American politics, and that the Church, ironically, has been made stronger by the separation of Church and State.

19. Meacham, *American Gospel*, 3-35. This would be along the lines of what Chapter 1 of this work described as recognition of the reality of pluralism in the sense of multiple religious faiths actually co-existing in human society. Nevertheless, even according to Meacham there were and are those who argue that America was founded on a more sectarian style of religious government as a specifically Christian nation, 144 and 215-19. E.g., T. LaHaye, *The Faith of Our Founding Fathers: A Comprehensive Study of America's Christian Foundations* (Green Forest, AR: Master, 1995). Wills, *Under God,* suggests the cyclical and sectarian nature of Protestantism diffuses its political influence while Catholicism and Judaism are influential all out of proportion to their numbers because of their abiding continuity, 305.

20. See "Treaty of Peace and Friendship Between the United States and the Bay and Subjects of Tripoli of Barbary," in Meacham, *American Gospel*, Appendix A, "In Their Own Words: Selected Documents on Religion in America," 262.

21. For original quote, see J. Hutson, ed., *The Founders on Religion: A Book of Quotations* (Princeton: Princeton University Press, 2005), 120-21. Cf. George Washington's letter "To Tinch Tilghman," 555-56, George Washington and John H. Rhodehamel, *George Washington: Writings* (New York: Library of America, 1997). Cf. "Washington's Letter to the Hebrew Congregation at Newport," (18 August, 1790), Meacham, *American Gospel*, Appendix A, "In Their Own Words: Selected Documents on Religion in America," 260-62. Meacham maintains that Washington's Christian piety was mostly legend but admits that he did make frequent appeals to providence and promoted "the value of religion as a force for moral conduct" (252). However, cf. Washington's personal use of

Christian language, Washington and Rhodehamel, *Washington: Writings,* 108, 279. See Meacham, *American Gospel,* 19, 245-46.

22. Meacham, *American Gospel,* 178. Original quote is in Hutson, ed., *Founders on Religion,* 127. However, T. Beal, *Religion in America: A Very Short Introduction* (New York: Oxford University Press, 2008), argues that religious diversity was perhaps an unexpected and, for some, unintended result of differing understandings of freedom of religion, 70-74.

23. Meacham, *American Gospel,* 11. See Thomas Jefferson, *Writings* (New York: Library of America, 1984)*,* 346. Later, Eisenhower insisted that the religious liberties enjoyed by American churches extends to Islamic mosques and centers too, 179-81. See *The New York Times,* June 29, 1957. Nevertheless, former Vice President for Governmental Affairs of NAE, Richard Cizik, "A History of Public Policy Resolutions of the National Association of Evangelicals," 35-63, eds., Ronald J. Sider and Diane Knippers, *Toward an Evangelical Public Policy: Political Strategies for the Health of the Nation* (Grand Rapids: Baker, 2005), relates that the minutes of the 1954 annual convention of the NAE include commendation of Eisenhower because "the nation" was "being blessed by his Christian testimony" (43).

24. Meacham, *American Gospel,* 107-09.

25. Meacham, *American Gospel,* 233. Cf. D.L. Eck, *A New Religious America: How A "Christian Country" Has Become the World's Most Religiously Diverse Nation* (New York: HarperCollins, 2001).

26. American theologian and political and social analyst and theorist Reinhold Niebuhr, in *The Children of Light and The Children of Darkness: A Vindication of Democracy and A Critique of Its Traditional Defense* (New York: Charles Scribner's Sons, 1944, 1960), described original American secularism as "standing somewhere between" the French, i.e., a secular state as an expression of a secular culture, and the English, i.e. religious freedom achieved within a Christian culture. The "original pattern" in America was "a secular state, favored by sectarian (highly diversified) Christianity." However, increasing modern secularization trends (as of his writing) have been toward a "partially secularized community, favoring religious freedom" though dismissive of the significance of the role of religion in public life (129). As seen in the present chapter of this study, secularist philosophies dismissive of religion have fallen on hard times in recent decades.

27. This section draws on the work of Richard W. Fox.

28. American understanding of Jesus may arguably have more to do with the cultural identity of the people than the official policies of the government. See S.J. Nichols, *Jesus Made in America: A Cultural History from the Puritans to the Passion of Christ* (Downer's Grove, IL: IVP Academic, 2008) and S. Prothero, *American Jesus: How the Son of God Became a National Icon* (New York: Farrar, Straus, and Giroux, 2004). Cf. Wills, *Under God,* 22-23.

29. R.W. Fox, *Jesus in America: Personal Savior, Cultural Hero, National Obsession* (New York: HarperSanFrancisco, 2005), 11. P. Jenkins, *The Next Christendom: The Coming of Global Christianity,* revised and expanded edition (New York: Oxford, 2007), argues that "America remains today substantially what it has always been, a Christian country." However, he immediately makes clear that this does not translate into "partisan or intolerant" views of "some extremists" regarding government-controlled religion. He believes that "religion flourishes best when it is kept farthest away from any form of government intervention, even the best-intentioned." He only means to affirm that while "the United States is home to a remarkable number of religious denominations, overwhelmingly, these are traditions within the broader stream of Christianity." Though im-

migration has brought into the USA people of other non-Christians faiths, it has also brought in many Christians. Percentage wise Christianity is still by far the most common religion. See 122-24 (122). See also William Charles Inboden, *Religion and American Foreign Policy, 1945-60: The Soul of Containment* (Cambridge: Cambridge University Press, 2008), and Wolfhart Pannenberg, "Christian Empire and Civil Religion," *Human Nature, Election, and History* (Philadelphia: Westminster, 1977), 62-82.

30. Fox, *Jesus in America*, 1-27 (26).

31. Fox, *Jesus in America*, 24. E.g., Wills, *Under God,* notes that many Americans say they are more likely to vote for a politician who confesses Christ as Savior, 387.

32. Fox, *Jesus in America*, 24-25.

33. Fox, *Jesus in America*, 14.

34. Wills, *Under God,* also indicates that the stringent ethics of Holiness-Pentecostal Christians has heavily impacted many Americans, 43. Additionally, Pentecostals have been primarily responsible for the popular and political impact of national media figures such as Pat Robertson, 168, 171, as well as having had some of the most direct impact on people in poverty, 391. See Fox, *Jesus in America*, 14-15.

35. Fox, *Jesus in America*, 331-33.

36. Fox, *Jesus in America*, 336-42 (336).

37. Fox, *Jesus in America*, 387. An intriguing discussion is to what extent the original ideas of the founders of American democracy have been or are being either realized or compromised. See R. Niebuhr, *The Irony of American History: With a New Introduction by Andrew J. Bacevich* (Chicago: University of Chicago Press, 1952, 2008). Cf. R.H. Weibe, *Self-Rule: A Cultural History of American Democracy* (Chicago, IL: University of Chicago, 1995), 64, 220.

38. Fox, *Jesus in America*, 405-12 (405-06).

39. Niebuhr argues that the resources of the Christian faith are an oft unrecognized but rich reservoir for the tasks of democracy and global community. See *The Children*, 186-90.

40. E.g., as is in the case of Madalyn Murray O'Hair. See Meacham, *American Gospel*, 232-37 (235-36). Wills, *Under God,* notes that the secularity of Michael Dukakis and the religiosity of both Pat Robertson and Jesse Jackson made the 1988 American presidential election a bold study in contrasts, 62. Accordingly, Dukakis appeared even more noticeably secular than might have otherwise been the case while Robertson and Jackson demonstrated the wide range of extreme religious ideologies, 62.

41. Meacham, *American Gospel*, 8-10. Abraham Lincoln is an interesting example of a president's evolving attitude toward religion. Early on in his career, he might have been somewhat skeptical about God's existence, but began more and more to appeal to the same "Divine Being" as helped Washington, before finally being quite specifically Christian in his ideas and habits. See B.P. Thomas, *Abraham Lincoln* (New York: Barnes & Noble, 1952, 1994), 239, 304, 478, and 497.

42. Notably, Jenkins says that, "despite all its critics, American Christianity is very much alive and well." See *Next Christendom*, 248. The controversy over America's religious identity apparently stems in part from the failure to distinguish between the religious identity of the government and that of the citizenship. The former is religious but not Christian, and the latter Christian in its religion. Add to this that many government leaders are individually Christian but politically committed to the public religion, that some are thoroughly secular, and that a few belong to other faiths, and that each of these may have an agenda for their own version of the American religious vision, and perhaps one sees how the complexity erupts into controversy.

43. M.E. Marty with J. Moore, in *Politics, Religion, and the Common Good: Advancing a Distinctively American Conversation About Religion's Role in Our Shared Life* (San Francisco: Jossey-Bass, 2000), assert that Americans "remain confused about the ways religion relates to government and the way politics gets webbed with religion." This is due in part to complexities in the nation's founding, and in part to evolving attitudes even among its leaders. See 1-3 (1). Yet there is really no doubt that religion always has had a large public role in the United States (14-15). Furthermore, Martin and Moore argue that involvement of religious people in political conversation is a positive activity, including ecumenical and interfaith movements as part of undertaking that process (157-66, 111-17). Cf. P. Brian Campbell SJ, "Blessed and Broken: How Religion Infuses and Confuses American Presidential Politics," *Thinking Faith: The Online Journal of the British Jesuits,* 22 April 2008, http://www.thinkingfaith.org/articles/20080422_1.htm.

44. Note that "theo-political" can signify religion related government without necessarily suggesting religion run government, or theocracy. Most Americans intuit that when religion controls and dominates government, some dire consequences can occur, especially if other instabilities are present, such as, for examples, a weak economy or strained international relations. Cf. K. Phillips, *American Theocracy: The Peril and Politics of Radical Religion, Oil, and Borrowed Money in the 21st Century* (New York: Viking, 2006). Yet, as a politically thematic issue of *Discipleship Journal* (165, May/June 2008) suggests, many Christians remain convinced that their basic religious beliefs should impact their political practices (R. Sider, "Big Picture Politics," 34-43), and though admitting that historically Christians have not always done well with politics (R.D. Hughes, "What's History Got to Do with It?" 44-50), they still feel biblical values should influence voting (G. Wolfaardt, "Voting by the Book, 52-61). Wisely, and refreshingly too, Sider, Hughes, and Wolfaardt all admit applying spirituality to politics is complex business and they allow ample room for diversity among the faithful—even while advocating that faith does make a definitive difference.

45. This section dialogues with the work of Philip Jenkins.

46. Jenkins, *Next Christendom*, 1-3 (1). Cf. T. Richie's reviews of *The Next Christendom* in *PR* 11:4 (Fall 2008), 68-71, and of Jenkins' "Companions of Life: A Supple Faith," Christian Vision Project, *Books & Culture* 13:2 (March/April 2007), 9-18, *PR* 10:3 (Summer 2007), 71-74.

47. Jenkins, *Next Christendom*, 3-6.

48. Jenkins, *Next Christendom*, 6-9, 78, 80 (6).

49. Wills, *Under God,* remarks that while some have thought religious liberalism more true to the American experience, others have certainly disagreed, 88. In fact, Evangelical discontent with Jimmy Carter's liberalism would ultimately be his undoing in presidential politics, and harness the power needed for propelling the Reagan revolution, 119-20. Battles between fundamentalism and liberalism have also raged in America's highest and most hallowed academies, 320. See Jenkins, *Next Christendom*, 9.

50. Jenkins, *Next Christendom*, 12-15.

51. Jenkins, *Next Christendom*, 31.

52. Jenkins, *Next Christendom*, 184. Cf. 189-222. Cf. A. Yong's review of Jenkins' *The New Faces of Christianity: Reading the Bible in the Global South* (Oxford: Oxford University Press, 2006) and *God's Continent: Christianity, Islam, and Europe's Religious Crisis* (Oxford: Oxford University Press, 2007) in *PR* 11:4 (Fall 2008), 65-68.

53. This section dialogues with the work of Allan Anderson.

54. North American Pentecostalism tends to be much more heavily influenced by its heritage of revivalism than does its global counterpart. E.g., see S. Rabey, *Revival in Brownsville: Pensecola, Pentecostalism, and the Power of American Revivalism* (Nash-

ville, TN: Thomas Nelson, 1998). For a brief but fascinating look at revialism's early influence, see S. Comstock, "Aimee Semple MacPherson: Prima Dona of Revivalism," *Harper's Monthly Magazine* (December 1927), 16-17.

55. A. Anderson, *An Introduction to Pentecostalism: Global Charismatic Christianity* (New York: Cambridge University Press, 2004, 2007 pr.), xiii.

56. Anderson, *Introduction,* 1-15 (15).

57. Anderson, *Introduction,* 249-53. Anderson is convinced that Pentecostalism, especially when broadly defined as a diverse movement unified by an experience of the power of the Spirit emphasizing spiritual manifestations and gifts, may be a potent force for "genuine ecumenical co-operation" (258).

58. Veteran Roman Catholic missionary, theologian, historian, and Orbis book editor W.R. Burrows who persuasively posits an increasingly global Christian movement involving ecumenical interaction between Catholics and Evangelicals, Pentecostals, and others as an exciting new "world Christianity" is being birthed. See "From a Roman Catholic 'Mission Church' to a Catholic 'World Christianity' Paradigm: A Personal Pilgrimage," *U.S. Catholic Historian,* 23 (Summer 2006), 165-79. Cf. Anderson, *Introduction,* 253-56.

59. Anderson, *Introduction,* 256-60. G.M. Marsden, *Fundamentalism and American Culture* (Oxford/New York: Oxford University Press, 2006), calls Pentecostals "close cousins to the original fundamentalists" (236), but then notes the ambiguity of their relations contributed to the rise of the Neo-Evangelicals, 236. Others, such as, e.g., Bill Bright of Campus Crusade for Christ, became increasingly open to Pentecostals as they became decreasingly fundamentalist in their theology, 326 (Fn 31).

60. Anderson, *Introduction,* 282-85 (283). Cf., however, with more exclusive, less effective approaches of Western mission programs of Pentecostals, 215. Pentecostals tend to be more effective when adopting a pragmatic and sympathetic approach to local customs and culture, including pre/non-Christian religions, an approach utilized more often by indigenous representatives, 223.

61. Anderson, *Introduction,* 202-03.

62. N. Anderson, *Christianity and World Religions: The Challenge of Pluralism* (Downer's Grove, IL: InterVarsity Press, 1970, rev. ed., 1984), distinguishes between religious pluralism (affirming multiple religions) and religious syncretism (integrating multiple religions) but admits frequent overlap, 15-16 (e.g., 38). See A. Anderson, *Introduction,* 235-42 (237).

63. Anderson, *Introduction,* 283, 286.

64. This section dialogues with the collaborative work of Donald Miller and Tetsunao Yamamori.

65. D.E. Miller and T. Yamamori, *Global Pentecostalism: The New Face of Christian Social Engagement* (Los Angeles: University of California Press, 2007), 1-3.

66. Miller, *Global Pentecostalism,* 5-6. Significantly, in his study of politics and religion in USA, *American Theocracy,* Phillips usually lumps Evangelicals and Pentecostals together with hardline Fundamentalists in a quite different evaluative outcome more representative of "radicalized religion". See 99-131 (106-07 and 112-121). Admittedly, enough truth is there to warrant that general charge. However, Phillips seems either unaware of or uninterested in serious rifts between Evangelicals/Pentecostals and Fundamentalists or of the existence of more moderate-minded Evangelicals and Pentecostals considerably qualifying his incautious over identification. Cf. Chapter 1 of this study.

67. Marsden, *Fundamentalism,* explains that for Evangelicals "the menace of atheistic secularism" has been grouped with the likes of communism, totalitarianism, and imminent nuclear threat, 239. Moreover, a perceived drift toward secularism continues to be

one of Evangelicalism's (including Pentecostals) abiding concerns in spite of their own increasingly close ties to mainstream culture, 242 and 255. See Miller, *Global Pentecostalism*, 36-37.

68. Miller, *Global Pentecostalism*, 23-25.

69. Miller, *Global Pentecostalism*, 94-95, 59-62 (cf. 50 and 123). However, this does not deny or diminish the continuing and sometimes contentious reality of religious oppression or the role of competition among religions, 204-07. Cf. 54 and 124.

70. Miller, *Global Pentecostalism*, 67.

71. Miller, *Global Pentecostalism*, 211. No wonder H. Cox, *Fire From Heaven: The Rise of Pentecostal Spirituality and the Reshaping of Religion in the 21st Century* (New York: Addison-Wesley, 1995), says, "The great strength of the Pentecostal impulse is the power to combine, its aptitude for adopting the language, the music, the cultural artifacts, the religious tropes, even the demigods and the wraiths of the setting in which it lives" (259). However, he adds that "this very flexibility can also be, at times, its most dangerous quality as well" (259; referencing its failure to "exorcise" "the demon of race" in S. Africa). Nevertheless, this untamed vitality brings an overflowing freshness with it too. Cf. 248 and 319.

72. Miller, *Global Pentecostalism*, 212.

73. Cf. A.G. Miller, "Pentecostalism as a Social Movement: Beyond the Theory of Deprivation," *JPT* 9 (1996), 97-114. D. Miller, *Global Pentecostalism*, 219-21.

74. Miller, *Global Pentecostalism*, 108-10 and 20-22.

75. Miller, *Global Pentecostalism*, 224 and 19. Yet Cox, *Fire*, thinks that "recovery of primal spirituality" is an important underlying element of the appeal of Pentecostalism everywhere, 132 and 203.

76. Miller, *Global Pentecostalism*, 127 and 212. Important to remember is that large-scale change is taking place among many conservative Christians suffering "disappointments". Clearly, "some sort of realignment is underway." See J. Stout, "2007 Presidential Address: The Folly of Secularism," *JAAR* 76:3 (September 2008), 533-44 (541).

77. Notably, Pannenberg, in an essay on "The Future and the Unity of Mankind," *Ethics,* 175-97, argues for an eschatological orientation toward the future that includes both secular and theological anticipatory aspects of the future through extrapolations from and continuations with the past and present but also the newness made possible by the reality of independent activity of God, expressing apparent discontinuity but actually in authentic continuity with history through eternity, and that the latter confront the present with the future, directing and shaping it accordingly, 175-78. Still more notably, Pannenberg argues that this envisioned future includes a movement toward human unity that inevitably invites ecumenical and interfaith dialogue in the present. Cf. 184-86 and 193-97. The present study concerns itself with the appropriate role of Pentecostalism in this movement toward unity and its accompanying process of dialogue.

78. This section enters draws on the work Jerry Redman and Fleming Rutledge.

79. Of course, Classical Pentecostal denominations have long expressed interest and encouraged activity regarding the social issues of the day. E.g., see the Church of God (Cleveland, TN) official website's "Resolutions" on various "Social Concerns" over the last several decades at http://www.churchofgod.org/resolutions/index.cfm. However, increasingly noticeable is an openness to and emphasis on wider involvement and deeper commitment.

80. Evidence increasingly indicates global Evangelicals, including Pentecostals, exhibit more diversity politically and socially than counterparts in North America. Cf. M.A. Noll, "Early Returns are Mixed," *CT* 52:6 July 1, 2008), 1-3, at

http://www.christianitytoday.com/ct/2008/june/31.53.html?start=1. Noll's tagline is "Global evangelicals don't necessarily vote like American evangelicals."

81. See J. Redman, "A Theology of Social Action," 1-7, Faith News Network (4/14/08) at http://www.faithnews.cc/articles.cfm?sid=8827.

82. See Redman, "Social Action," 2.

83. Redman, "Social Action," 4-6.

84. Redman, "Social Action," 7. Redman's stirring essay, originally written as part of his master's work in the Transformational Leadership program at Bethel Seminary (St. Paul, MN), appeared in the "Opinion and Commentary" section of Faith News Network. Other essays on such topics have also appeared in this section recently. E.g., see on exploitation of children, "Who Will Cry for the Children" 4/22/08, on racism "Race, Religion, and the Roots of Obama's Faith," 3/31/08, both by L.J. Grady, and on ethical implications of steroid use by professional athletes, "Perspectives: Of Steroids and Sin," B. Locke, 1/21/08.

85. E.g., *AJ* 62:1 (Spring 2007) recently devoted an entire issue to "Wesleyan Thinking about the Environment". A notable contribution by H. Snyder, "Salvation Means Creation Healed: Creation, Cross, Kingdom, and Mission," 9-47, illustrates the movement's directional momentum. *The Holiness Manifesto,* ed. K.W. Mannoia and D.Thorsen (Grand Rapids: Eerdmans, 2008), assertively integrates individual and social holiness. On pluralism, cf. J.L. Walls, *The Problem of Pluralism: Recovering United Methodist Identity* (Wilmore, KY: Good News, 1986).

86. Neither do these appear to be isolated incidents. Other Evangelicals are moving in similar directions. "An Evangelical Manifesto: A Declaration of Evangelical Identity and Public Commitment," May 7, 2008, Washington, D. C., signed by several Evangelical leaders and thinkers, among other things, enumerates concerns for political and social action, ecological awareness, and ecumenical openness and even interreligious engagement. Its tone is quite positive, though just a bit defensive at points, and well-balanced. Most of all, it is an intelligent and articulate presentation of Evangelical concerns for a wider arena of issues than previously typical. See http://www.anevangelicalmanifesto.com/docs/Evangelical_Manifesto.pdf.

87. See F. Rutledge, "When God Disturbs the Peace," *CT* 52:6 (June 2008) at http://www.christianitytoday.com/ct/2008/june/13.30.html. Cf. "About the Reverend Fleming Rutledge," on the Generous Orthodoxy website at http://www.generousorthodoxy.org/about.aspx. Cf. internationally known Charismatic speaker and writer Cindy Jacobs's emphasis on working to achieve social transformation through intercession and prophetic ministry. See *The Reformation Manifesto: Your Part in God's Plan to Change Nations Today* (Minneapolis: Bethany House, 2008).

88. Indeed, Cizik, "Public Policy Resolutions of NAE," argues that for the last several decades the NAE has been slowly but surely moving toward building coalitions with non-evangelicals, including non-Christians, and initiating interfaith dialogue and cooperation, 59-60, 62. For him, a fruitful future for the NAE will necessarily include "constructing meaningful coalitions with non-evangelicals, including leaders of other faith traditions" (63). He points out Pentecostal denominations comprise the majority of NAE membership, 44.

89. This section dialogues with the work of Jon Meacham, Jim Wallis, Martin E. Marty, and Jonathan Moore.

90. Meacham, *American Gospel*, 237. However, Cox, *Fire*, claims Pentecostals have been especially adept at combining and integrating vastly different traditions in widely varying settings, 259.

91. J. Wallis, *God's Politics: Why the Right Gets It Wrong and the Left Doesn't Get It* (New York: HarperSanFrancisco, 2005), 87-107.
92. Marty, *Politics, Religion, and the Common Good*, 161-62.
93. E.g., C. Hitchens, *God is not Great: How Religion Poisons Everything* (New York: Twelve, 2007).
94. E.g., see R. Stark, *Discovering God: The Origins of the Great Religions and the Evolution of Belief in God* (New York: HarperOne, 2007). Interestingly, Cox, *Fire*, previously one of the leading "death of God" theologians convinced contemporary society would finally become completely secularized, not only has reversed that fatalistic view, but has attributed the rise of Pentecostalism with playing a major role in the actual global reversal of that previously apparently inexorable trend, xvi-xvii and 104-05.
95. "Ask tough questions about religion, says Vatican cardinal," Ecumenical News International, 9 April 2008, at http://www.ekklesia.co.uk/node/7017. Cf. Y. Congar, *I Believe in the Holy Spirit* (*IBHS*) 3 vols. trans. David Smith (New York: Seabury, 1983), a Catholic thinker willing at least at the *intra*-faith level of ecumenism to takle tough questions, such as e.g., the possible usurpation by substitution of the Holy Spirit by traditional commitments to the Eucharist, the Pope, and the Virgin Mary, 1:159-66.
96. Discussion partners for this section are Dale Coulter, Simon Chan, Shane Clifton, and Clark Pinnock.
97. E.g., P. Tillich, *Christianity and the Encounter of World Religions* (NY: Columbia, 1961, 1963) and J.H. Berthrong, *The Divine Deli: Religious Identity in the North American Cultural Mosaic* (Maryknoll, NY: Orbis, 1999).
98. D. Coulter, "The Development of Ecclesiology in the Church of God (Cleveland, TN): A Forgotten Contribution?" *Pneuma* 29:1 (2007), 59-85. Cf. V.M. Kärkkäinen, "Church as Charismatic Fellowship: Ecclesiological Reflections from Pentecostal-Roman Catholic Dialogue," *JPT* 18 (2001), 100-21. "Baptism, Conversion, and Grace: Reflections on the 'Underlying Realities' Between Pentecostals, Methodists, and Catholics," *Pneuma* 31:2 (2009), 189-212, indicates Coulter's continuing insights in theological and soteriological intersections in ecclesiology and ecumenism.
99. See Coulter, "Development of Ecclesiology," 82. Cf. M. Volf, *After Our Likeness: The Church as the Image of the Trinity* (Grand Rapids: Eerdmans, 1998).
100. S. Chan, "The Church and the Development of Doctrine," *JPT* 13:1 (October 2004), 57-77.
101. Chan, "Development of Doctrine," 75-77.
102. E.g., cf. S. Dove, "Wesley's Sanctification Narrative: A Tool for Understanding the Holy Spirit's Work in a More Physical Soul," *Pneuma* 31:2 (2009), 225-41.
103. S. Clifton, "Pentecostal Ecclesiology: A Methodological Proposal for a Diverse Movement," *JPT* 15:2 (April 2007), 213-32. For further reflection on Pentecostal ecclesiology, see J. Sepúlveda, "Reflections on the Pentecostal Contribution to the Mission of the Church in Latin America," *JPT* 1 (1992), 93-108.
104. Impetus for this discussion arose out of Pinnock's keynote speech to the Society for Pentecostal Studies at Regent University in Virginia Beach, VA (March 10-12, 2005).
105. C.H. Pinnock, "The Church in the Power of the Spirit: The Promise of Pentecostal Ecclesiology," *JPT* 14:2 (April 2006), 147-65. For an interesting look at ecclesiology by a Pentecostal from a definitive ecumenical perspective, see W. Vondey, People of Bread: Rediscovering Ecclesiology (Mahwah, NJ: Paulist Press, 2008).
106. F.D. Macchia, "Pinnock's Pneumatology: A Pentecostal Appreciation," *JPT* 14:2 (April 2006), 167-73.
107. T.L. Cross, "A Response to Clark Pinnock's 'Church in the Power of the Spirit,'" *JPT* 14:2 (April 2006), 175-82. Cf. Congar, *IBHS*, who is sharply critical of

classical ecclesiologies he thinks are guilty of "forgetting the Holy Spirit" and thus failing to be truly trinitarian (1:159-60).

108. R.H. Gause, "A Pentecostal Response to Pinnock's Proposal," *JPT* 14:2 (April 2006), 183-88.

109. The following draws on Richard Bauckham's insightful study of Moltmann as well as Moltmann himself.

110. R. Bauckham, *The Theology of Jürgen Moltmann* (Edinburgh: T & T Clark, 1995, 1996), 13-14; cf. 126.

111. R. Diprose, *Israel and the Church* (Waynesville, GA: Authentic Media, 2000), argues that ignoring Israel's significance has harmful affects for Christian theology, 1-3. C.A. Blaising and D.L. Bock, *Dispensationalism, Israel and the Church: The Search for Definition* (Grand Rapids, MI: Zondervan, 1992), claim the relation between Israel and the Church is a crucial reference point for Christian theology for distinguishing between dispensational and non-dispensational thought. It presents Israel and the Church as distinct theological institutions in the history of divine revelation related as successive phases of the redemptive program. Cf. Bauckham, *Moltmann,* 131.

112. Bauckham, *Moltmann,* 149-50.

113. Bauckham, *Moltmann,* 18. Cf. G. McFarlane, "Atonement, Creation, and Trinity," 192-207, gen. eds. D. Tidball, D. Hilborn, & J. Thacker, *The Atonement Debate: Papers from the London Symposium on the Theology of the Atonement* (Grand Rapids, MI: Zondervan, 2008).

114. J. Moltmann, *The Church in the Power of the Spirit: A Contribution to Messianic Ecclesiology* (*London*: SCM Press, 1977), 64-65.

115. Moltmann, *The Church in the Power of the Spirit,* 64-65. Congar, *IBHS,* proposes viewing the Church as performing a special doxological role gathering up everything the Spirit is doing in the world, i.e., beyond the Church, and offering it up to glory of the Father, 2:218-24. Accordingly, jealousy or rivalry would be most inappropriate.

116. J. Moltmann, "Hope", in *NHCT,* eds. D.W. Musser and J.L. Price (Nashville: Abingdon, 1992), 239-41 (240).

117. This section draws on the solid work of J.N.D. Kelly and Mary Ann Donovan on Irenaeus.

118. I still remember Professor Hollis Gause telling his Church of God Theological Seminary class (early 1990s) that Irenaeus generally provides Pentecostals an example of sound theology.

119. Irenaeus, *Against Heresies,* in *Ante-Nicene Fathers,* Volume 1 (PC Study Bible formatted electronic database Copyright © 2003 by Biblesoft, Inc.), 3:24:1. D.J. Unger, *Irenaeus of Lyons: Against Heresies: Book I,* Ancient Christian Writers 15 (Mahwah, NJ: Paulist Press, 1992), gives this statement as an example of "many concise statements that have become classic, many of them jewels", 7-8 (7).

120. J.N.D. Kelly, *Early Christian Beliefs* (New York: HarperSanFrancisco, 1978 ed.), 192.

121. F.D. Macchia, *Baptized in the Spirit: A Global Pentecostal Theology* (Grand Rapids: Zondervan, 2006), 188.

122. M.A. Donovan, *One Right Reading? A Guide to Irenaeus* (Collegeville, Minnesota: Liturgical Press, 1997), 93. Cf. J.P. Smith, *St. Irenaeus: Proof of Apostolic Preaching,* Ancient Christian Writers 16 (Mahwah, NJ: Paulist Press, 1978), 19, 21, and 43-44, who argues that Irenaeus transmits what he considers the substance of truth passed down from the original Apostles.

123. Donovan, *One Right Reading?* 94. Original italics. Thus Congar, *IBHS,* suggests that for Ireneaus the Church and the Spirit "conditioned each other" (1:68). For Congar,

"this dialectical tension" of pneumatological ecclesiology is "too divine for us to be able to break it without betraying some aspect of it" (1:68).

124. This section is indebted to the work of David M. Griffis.

125. E.g., see J. Almand and J. Wooderson, *Establishing Values* (Cleveland: Pathway, 1976), 139). Of course, there are interesting exceptions where Pentecostal and Charismatic type groups promoted interpersonal, international, and interracial peace. E.g., see S. Dupree, *African-American Holiness-Pentecostal Movement: Annotated Bibliography* (London/New York: Routledge, 1995), 369, 371, and D.A. Hoekema, "Black Churches, the Third World, and Peace (Conference Held in Atlanta)," *The Christian Century* 100 (November 30, 1983), 1100-01.

126. Cf. D.M. Griffis, *Spirit Wars: The Power of His Might Against the Rulers of The Darkness of This World* (Cleveland: Pathway, 1994).

127. An intriguing question is whether Pentecostals, and other conservatives and evangelicals, have similarly misunderstood the teaching of *jihad* among moderate Muslims, who often see it as signifying spiritual struggle, though undeniably Islamic extremists have applied it literally and radically to justify physical violence.

128. See J. Beaman, *Pentecostal Pacifism: The Origin, Development, and Rejection of Pacific Belief among the Pentecostals* (Hillsboro, Kansas: Center for Mennonite Brethren Studies, 1989) and J. Shuman, "Pentecost and the End of Patriotism: A Call for the Restoration of Pacifism among Pentecostal Christians," *JPT* 9 (1996), 70-96.

129. See J.E. Adams, *Sibling Rivalry in the Household of God* (Denver: Accent, 1988). Adams recommends giving in to the Spirit's conviction over this sin, repenting and confessing, and beginning to treat one another with love. See 133-35.

130. Lauree Hersch Meyer and Jeffrey Gros, "Introduction," eds. Lauree Hersch Meyer and Jeffrey Gros, *The Fragmentation of the Church and Its Unity in Peacemaking* (Grand Rapids: Eerdmans, 2001), 1-15, suggest the gospel places peacemaking at the center of the identity of the Christian church, but over the centuries, however, churches have divided over the specific place of this peacemaking imperative in their lives and teachings. The Pentecostal contributor to this volume, Murray W. Dempster, "Pacifism in Pentecostalism: The Case of the Assemblies of God," 137-55, laments the loss of pacifism in Pentecostalism, 139, suggests its sectarian development may explain the change and regrets the concomitant loss of social conscience it may signify, 141-42. Pacifism may have been a signifier of Pentecostalism's restorationist concrete moral practice, 146. Cf. 152-53. Arguably, whether contemporary Pentecostals adopt pacifism per se or not, they may nevertheless applaud and possibly extend their heritage of peacemaking through ecumenical and interfaith dialogue and cooperation.

131. This section builds on the work of Mark Ellingsen.

132. E.g., M. Ellingsen, *The Evangelical Movement: Growth, Impact, Controversy, Dialog* (Minneapolis: Augsburg, 1988), 23-44 (37-39). Of course, Pentecostals, for example, the Church of God (Cleveland, TN), are aware of trends toward inclusivism and even pluralism. See "Survey: 'My Faith Isn't the Only Way,'" (June 24, 2008), http://www.faithnews.cc/articles.cfm?sid=9041.

133. Ellingsen, *Evangelical Movement*, 37, 129-32, and 387. In fact, I have been personally part of an organized and ongoing dialogue between Mennonites (Mennonite Church USA) and Pentecostals in the Church of God (Cleveland, TN) from 2005 to the present (2008).

134. Ellingsen, *Evangelical Movement*, 293-94. I question the truly dialogical character of dispensationalism's eschatological fascination with modern Israel and with the Middle East, including to some extents Jews, as not necessarily attention to Judaism per

se, but concedes that it at least shows interest beyond its own ecclesial borders. See Ellingsen, *Evangelical Movement*, 55-56, 62.

135. This section draws on the work of Donald Miller and Tetsunao Yamamori, and Hollis Gause.

136. See S.J. Land, *Pentecostal Spirituality: A Passion for the Kingdom* JPTSup 1 (Sheffield: Sheffield Academic Press, 1993). The essentially eschatological character of the gift of the Spirit has been argued by Congar, *IBHS*, e.g., 2:69-70. Further, like Land, Congar sets discussion of the eschatological Spirit in the context of an "already-not yet" theology of the Kingdom of God, 2:106-11. See fn. 130 and 141 below. Cf. H. Jurgenson, "Awaiting the Return of Christ: A Re-Examination of 1 Thessalonians 4.13-5.11 from a Pentecostal Perspective," *JPT* 4 (1994), 81-113.

137. Miller, *Global Pentecostalism*, 182. Eschatology is an area some Charismatics tend to be more open and less adamant about that Classical Pentecostals. E.g., see L.D. Hart, *Truth Aflame: Theology for the Church in Renewal* (Grand Rapids: Zondervan, 1999, 2005 rev. ed.), 508-17.

138. Anderson, *Introduction*, 218. The work of R.H. Gause, *Revelation: God's Stamp of Sovereignty on History* (Cleveland: Pathway, 1983), indicates that for quite a time some Pentecostals scholars have been well aware of issues in this area, and working to revisit Pentecostal eschatology from a firmer position.

139. Anderson, *Introduction*, 219. For in depth study, see D. William Faupel, *The Everlasting Gospel: The Significance of Eschatology in the Development of Pentecostal Thought*, JPTS Series 10 (Sheffield, UK: Sheffield Academic, 1996).

140. Gause, *Revelation*, 18-21. Significantly, Pathway Press is his denomination's publishing house.

141. Gause, *Revelation*, 20. Noteworthy is that some contemporary dispensationalist theologians are attempting to address such concerns with their system, revising and developing it into what is coming to be called "progressive dispensationalism" as a result. E.g. see C.A. Blaising and D.L. Bock, *Progressive Dispensationalism* (Grand Rapids: Baker, 1993) and R.L. Saucy, *The Case for Progressive Dispensationalism: The Interface Between Dispensational & Non-Dispensational Theology* (Grand Rapids: Zondervan, 1993).

142. Gause, *Revelation*, 20-21.

143. E.g., Gause specifically affirms his beliefs that the Church will be taken away in the Rapture before the Great Tribulation begins and that the Millennium involves the literal reign of Christ, *Revelation*, 120, 173 and 253-55. Presumably, however, progressive revelation calls for serious rethinking and substantial revision of political and theological ideologies inordinately tied to dispensationalism.

144. Discussion resources for this section include the work of Allan Anderson, Steven J. Land, John Christopher Thomas, and Andrew Lincoln.

145. Anderson, *Introduction*, 219-20. For a fuller treatment, see Land, *Pentecostal Spirituality*. This approach is otherwise technically known as inaugurated eschatology (the kingdom is present but remains to be consummated) vis-à-vis either realized (the kingdom is now) or unrealized (the kingdom is future) eschatology.

146. Cf. J.C. Thomas, 'Max Turner's *The Holy Spirit and Spiritual Gifts: Then and Now* (Carlisle: Paternoster Press, 1996): An Appreciation and Critique,' *JPT* 6:12 (1998), 3-21 (17).

147. Referring to God's redemptive blessings in Christ and the gift of the Spirit, G.D. Fee, *God's Empowering Presence: The Holy Spirit in the Letters of Paul* (Peabody, Massachusetts: Hendrickson, 1994, 2005), describes this passage as pointing to "God's authentication and guarantee of their existence both now and forever" (661-62).

148. Cf. T. Richie, "Eschatological Inclusivism: Exploring Early Pentecostal Theology of Religions in Charles Fox Parham," *JEPTA* 27:2 (2007), 138-52.

149. Arrington, "Luke," observes that Jesus' command requires one to "fulfill the commandment to love God and neighbor by meeting the needs of others regardless of race, color, or gender" (454). One might add, or of creed. Indeed, C.A. Evans, *NIBC: Luke* (1990), asserts that "The Parable of the Good Samaritan contributes significantly to Luke's overall concern to show that foreigners, outcasts, poor, and humble may all receive God's mercy" (177).

150. Interestingly, Y. Tesfai, *Liberation and Orthodoxy: The Promise and Failures of Interconfessional Dialogue* (New York: Orbis, 1996), uses the Roman Catholic/Pentecostal dialogue as an example, 26. He notes that "the forum of the dialogues is more or less interested in fostering cordial relations" with "no intention" to move beyond the maintenance of useful and constructive contacts" (26). Significantly, the Pentecostal participants are not even official representatives but serve as respected members of the movement, and the conversations are very broad and general, 26. At times, quite contentious has been the case in contexts involving encounters between Pentecostal missionaries and indigenous religions. See R. Marshall, *Political Spiritualities: The Pentecostal Revolution in Nigeria* (Chicago: University of Chicago, 2009), 54.

151. Arrington, "Luke," observes that Jesus is emphasizing "the disciples' stewardship between his death and return to earth" (500). In other words, "Each of Jesus' servants will be judged for how well he or she served him and his cause" (501). As a "day is coming when we must give an account of our stewardship", "All Christians ought to strive to be useful to their Lord" (501).

152. A.T. Lincoln, *Paradise Now and Not Yet: Studies in the Role of the Heavenly Dimension in Paul's Thought with Special Reference to His Eschatology* (Grand Rapids; Baker, 1981).

153. Lincoln, *Now and Not Yet*, 178-79 and 195.

154. Lincoln, *Now and Not Yet*, 187.

155. For Paul, this pneumatological fusing arising out of the biblical tradition itself, Lincoln, *Now and Not Yet*, 161. Cf. A.T. Lincoln and A.J.M. Wedderburn, *The Theology of the Later Pauline Letters* (Cambridge, UK: Cambridge University Press, 1993), 115, suggesting that talk of the Spirit "signals" joining of the already/not yet eschatological dimensions.

156. This section will dialogue with the work of Gordon D. Fee, Peter Althouse, Frank Macchia, and Andrew Lord.

157. Fee, *God's Empowering Presence*, 803-26. Interestingly, Fee describes the present life in the Spirit as paradoxical in that "the Spirit is both the fulfillment of the eschatological promises of God and the down payment on our certain future." He adds that, "We are both already and not yet. The Spirit is the evidence of the one, the guarantee of the other." See 826.

158. G.D. Fee, *Paul, the Spirit, and the People of God* (Peabody, Massachusetts: Hendrickson, 1996, 2005), 51-52 (52). E.g., 1 Co 7:31; 10:11; 2 Co 5:14-15, 17.

159. P. Althouse, *The Spirit of the Last Days: Pentecostal Eschatology in Conversation with Jürgen Moltmann* (London and New York: T & T Clark, 2003).

160. See Macchia, *Baptized*, 38-49, 85-88, 91-107, and 279-80. Cf. Macchia, "*Baptized in the Spirit:* Reflections in Response to My Reviewers," *JPT* 16:2 (April 2008), 14-20 (20). Fee, *God's Empowering Presence,* references 1 Co 15:20-28 in a context of "manifestation of the Spirit for the church's present eschatological existence" "between the inauguration of the End through the death and resurrection of Jesus with the subsequent outpouring of the Spirit and the final consummation when God will be 'all in all'"

(206). He observes further that this is a central part of Paul's abiding perspective on the kingdom in the eschaton, 805. Hagner, *NIBC: Hebrews* (1983, 1990), on Heb 6:5 explains that "the realized aspects of the new age presently enjoyed by the Christian church" are in view (91).

161. A. Lord, "Mission Eschatology: A Framework for Mission in the Spirit," *JPT* 11 (1997), 111-23.

162. E.g., Macchia, *Baptized*, 85-88 and 178-89.

163. Pannenberg, *Ethics,* stresses an eschatological movement toward human unity already becoming present in the Kingdom of God through Christ, 186-93. For him, this movement, involving a clear commitment to an eschatological anticipation, orientation, and devotion, is essentially "a religious question", 193. The almost entirely economic orientation of much of Western society renders it incapable of accomplishing the unity which is humanity's destiny, 194-95. Thus, Pannenberg poses, "the Western societies stand in desperate need of renewal and revision of their religious heritage," which, he is careful to point out, is "where the roots of their modern beginnings are found" in the first place, 195. Accordingly, he says "the problem of unity is ultimately a religions problem" (195). These observations issue in his assertion that religion must not be only a private matter but also public and that it must take into account considerations regarding "the general problem of pluralism in religious thought and life" (195). He recommends affirming a form of pluralism acknowledging the variety of religious experience and expression while asserting the unity of truth, 196. Therefore, ecumenical and interreligious dialogues are necessarily of public concern, 196, and Pannenberg passionately appeals for across the board participation in dialogue, 197. The appropriate role of Pentecostalism in this dialogue process is a primary concern of the present study.

164. I bring to the discussion nearly three decades of full-time vocational ministry to and for Pentecostals and over half a century of daily residing among them. Of course, sociological, psychological, and even, sometimes, theological studies of Pentecostals often depend on firsthand observational research. E.g., in an interesting integrative study ed., J.D. Photiadis, *Religion in Appalachia: Theological, Social, and Psychological Dimensions and Correlates* (Morgantown, WV: University of West Virginia, approx. 1977), T.D. Abell, "The Holiness-Pentecostal Experience in Southern Appalachia," 79-101, lived and worshiped among Appalachian Pentecostals for a year as the basis of his study. In fact, in the same volume L. Jones, "Mountain Religion: The Outsider's View," 401-07, roundly criticizes another contributor, N.L. Gerrard, "Churches of the Stationary Poor in Southern Appalachia," 271-84, for forming what he considered faulty conclusions failing to appreciate insider insights drawn from sustained, direct, personal observation and interaction, 402-03. He complains that "It is common for intellectual observers of all kinds to talk of religion only in clinical terms" (403).

165. At times, some Pentecostals tell of what might be described as a divine compulsion to testify for the glory of God, C.T. Gilkes, "'You've Got a Right to the Tree of Life': The Biblical Foundations of an Empowered Attitude Among Black Women in the Sanctified Church," Alexander and Yong, *Philip's Daughters,* 152-69, ed. Estrelda Alexander and Amos Yong, *Philip's Daughters: Women in Pentecostal-Charismatic Leadership*, Princeton Monograph Series (Eugene, OR: Pickwick, 2008), 161.

166. V. Johnson, "Romans," 693-797, *FLBCNT,* explains that Paul refers to daily living pleasing to God, 768, and J.R. Edwards, *NIBC: Romans* (1992), that such living is demonstrative approval of God's will through obedient behavior, 285-86.

167. Cf. B. Aker, "John," 1-118, *FLBCNT,* 93, demonstrating the multilayered aspects of the Spirit's convicting/convincing work. J.R. Michaels, *NIBC: John,* suggests

this is John's testimony to the basic Christian message in the form of the Spirit's witness to truth regarding sin, righteousness, and judgment, 282.

168. Pentecostals would agree with Hagner, *Hebrews,* that unpleasant as it may be, discipline is also a reassuring sign of authentic relation to God as Father, 216. J.W. Adams, "Hebrews," 1295-1399, would also perhaps receive an "Amen!" from Pentecostals with his stress on discipline as a means of sanctification and character development preparing God's authentic children for eternal fellowship with their holy Father, 1381-82. .

169. See G.P. Duffield and N.M. Van Cleave, *Foundations of Pentecostal Theology* (Los Angeles: L.I.F.E. Bible College, 1983, 1987), 402. Cf. T.D. Abell, *Better Felt Than Said: The Holiness-Pentecostal Experience in Southern Appalachia* (Waco, TX: Baylor University Press, 1982), 26, 199.

170. Pentecostals frequently have a strong sense of divine blessing, and for that matter, of divine cursing, and of the value of being available for God's abundant blessings. A perennially popular text on this topic is D. Prince, *Blessing or Curse: You Can Choose* (Grand Rapids: Chosen, 1990, 2000, 2006). See R. Hammons, *The Pentecostal Movement* (Bloomington, IN: AuthorHouse, 2009), 31, 50. In fact, the identifying experience of Spirit baptism is not uncommonly called "the Pentecostal blessing" or even just "the blessing". E.g. W.I. Goodall and R. Goodall, *The Blessing: Experiencing the Power of the Holy Spirit Today* (Lake Mary, FL: Creation House, 2005).

171. E.g., see P. Alexander, *Signs and Wonders: Why Pentecostalism is the World's Fastest Growing Faith* (San Francisco: Jossey-Bass, 2009), 117. Cf. M.W. Mittelstadt, "Spirit and Suffering in Contemporary Pentecostalism: The Lukan Epic Continues," 144-74, ed. Steven Studebaker, *Defining Issues in Pentecostalism: Classical and Emergent,* McMaster's Theological Studies (Eugene, OR: Pickwick, 2008), 144.

172. Indeed, as J.H. Sailhammer, *The Pentateuch as Narrative: A Biblical-Theological Commentary* (Grand Rapids: Zondervan, 1992), observes, Num 13 suggests that faithfulness to God in the face of unfaithfulness by others who trust more in appearances than in their covenant-keeping God is all the more commendable, 387-88. Cf. J. Harris, C. Brown, and M. Moore, *Joshua, Judges, Ruth* (2000), 27-31, on Rahab's incredibly adventurous faith.

173. G. Wacker, *Heaven Below: Early Pentecostals and American Culture* (London, Eng: Harvard University Press, 2001)*,* 58, and W.E. Warner, "Periodicals," *NIDPCM,* 974-82 (975).

174. See G. Niebuhr, *Beyond Tolerance: Searching for Interfaith Understanding in America* (New York: Viking, 2008), 80, 82 (cf. 183). Interfaith participation in, or at least, observation of, worship may be conducive to understanding and perhaps appreciation. As a Christian, I have experienced that affect when attending prayer and/or worship services and fellowship events with Jews or Muslims. Though obviously not as common, as pastor I have had those of other faiths attend Pentecostal worship services at intervals and a few on a regular basis, including several Muslims and a Buddhist.

175. This shows where Pentecostals have had little or no engaging dialogue with those of other religions. See D. Westerlund, "Introduction," 1-26, D. Westerlund, ed. *Global Pentecostalism: Encounters with Other Religious Traditions* (New York: I. B. Tauris, 2009), 12. The lack of serious engagement or dialogue, due in part to Pentecostalism's missionary identity, with adherents of other religions continues to challenge Pentecostals, A. Anderson, "Pentecostalism in India and China in the Early Twentieth Century and Inter-Religious Relations," 117-36, Westerlund, *Global Pentecostalism,* 132. Unfortunately, Pentecostal theology has not always been strong in the area of interreligious dialogue, J.A. Alvarsson, "Traditional AmerIndian Religion: In the Eyes of an Indigenous Pentecostal Church," 277-94, Westerlund, *Global Pentecostalism* (277).

176. A. Jacobs, *Looking Before and After: Testimony and the Christian Life* (Grand Rapids: Eerdmans, 2008), 19.

177. C.B. Johns, *Pentecostal Formation: A Pedagogy among the Oppressed* JPTSup 2 (Sheffield, England: Sheffield Academic Press, 1993, 1998), 131.

178. R.D. McCall, "Storytelling and Testimony: Reclaiming a Pentecostal Distinctive," unpublished Doctor of Ministry Dissertation, Columbia Theological Seminary, 1998, 52.

179. The unique Pentecostal tradition of testimony is perhaps in part indebted to the influence of its Pietist heritage. See D.D. Bundy, "European Pietist Roots of Pentecostalism," *NIDPCM*, 610-13. C. Bunners, "Paul Gerhardt (1607-1676)," ed., C. Linberg, *The Pietist Theologians: An Introduction to Theology in the Seventeenth and Eighteenth Centuries* (Malden, Massachusetts: Wiley-Blackwell, 2004), 68-83, explains that though usually stressing the inward life of Christ, the Pietistic tradition has also sometimes emphasized "a more lively form" expressed "in vigorous testimony" (81). In fact, testimony became an important part of Pietist conversion and autobiography, M. Matthias, "August Hermanne Franke (1663-1727)," Linberg, *The Pietist Theologians*, 100-14 (110). Nevertheless, Pietists tend to lay heavier emphasis on "the internal testimony" of the Holy Spirit. See D.W. Brown, *Understanding Pietism* (Nappanee, IN: Evangel, 1996), 25, 46, 48-51, 72-73. Thus, religious experience and warmth tend to characterize the tradition's unique testimony, not necessarily verbal expression of it, 78, 96. Evangelicalism has also utilized testimonies to some extent, I. Randall, *What a Friend We Have in Jesus: The Evangelical Tradition*, Traditions of Christian Spirituality Series (New York: Orbis, 2005), 39, 48. Evangelicalism, however, tends to focus almost entirely on conversion and its nature as encounter with Christ, 33. Yet Pentecostal/Charismatic spirituality gives unique place to testimony—even a central significance, M.J. Cartledge, *Encountering the Spirit: The Charismatic Tradition*, Traditions of Christian Spirituality (New York: Orbis, 2007), 83. As Cartledge notes, testimony, like speaking in tongues, prophecy, preaching, words of wisdom and knowledge, etc., is inspired speech, 32, 58, 69, and 119. Pentecostals consider such inspired speech completely consistent with the inspiration and authority of Scripture and the illumination of the Holy Spirit, existing quite comfortably alongside each other without competition or contradiction, 47, 78. One's personal experience of the Holy Spirit can thus serve as an enduring basis for possible testimony, 77. Of course, the involvement and assessment of the faith community are essential, 124-25. Cf. Mark J. Cartledge, *Testimony: Its Importance, Place, and Potential* (Cambridge: Grove, 2002).

180. Cf. J.E. Hartley, *NIBC: Genesis* (2000), 192-97 and 202-04, and J. Ellicott, *Ellicott's Bible Commentary in One Volume*, D. Bowdle, editor (Grand Rapids: Zondervan, 1971, 1980), 48-49 and 50-51,

181. E.g., F.W. Jordan, "At Arms Length: The First Presbyterian Church, Pittsburg, and Kathryn Kuhlman," ed., E.L. Blumhoffer, R.P. Spittler, G.A. Wacker, *Pentecostal Currents in American Protestantism* (Champaign, IL:University of Illinois, 1999), 188-208, reports an impromptu 'testimony meeting' that completely changed perceptions of Pentecostals, helping establish lasting personal friendships, 193.

182. Much of the descriptive logic behind this mindset arises from a view of Christianity as either entirely or primarily "other-worldly," or of another, i.e., heavenly, world. Everything or everyone else is by default "this-worldly," or of this world. See W.G. Boulton, T.D. Kennedy, Allen Verhey, ed., *From Christ to the World: Introductory Readings in Christian Ethics* (Grand Rapids: Eerdmans, 1994): W.G. Boulton, "The Riddle of Romans 13," 288-93 (289), M.L. King, Jr., "Letter from Birmingham Jail," 427-35 (434), and S. McFague, "God and the World," 501-13 (505). Cf. C. Plantinga, *Engaging*

God's World: A Christian Vision of Faith, Learning, and Living (Grand Rapids: Eerdmans, 2002), 56, 68, 96. However, the very definition of "world" can be surprisingly complex, "World," P. Sheldrake, *NWDCS*, 652.

183. On uncommitted as a categorical concept, see W.C. Smith, *Faith and Belief: The Difference Between Them* (Oxford: Oneworld, 1998), 13, 65, 239. Contrariwise, on faith as committed loyalty, see Smith: 4, 6, 73, 77, and 103. Traditionally, Pentecostals, especially *Classical* Pentecostals, who have deep roots in the Holiness Movement, describe those who pursue a life of physicality, sensuality, and temporality as "worldly" in contrast with those who pursue spirituality, morality, and eternity (cf. 1 John 2:15-17). Cf. Abell, *Better Felt*, 191 (cf. 6, 13, 54, 78, etc.). While not exclusive of that application, the present definition embraces all the non-religious, including those who may live comparably more or less moral lives. Nevertheless, Pentecostals do tend to stress a high degree of religious commitment. See V. Synan, *The Holiness-Pentecostal Movement in the United States* (Grand Rapids: Eerdmans, 1971), 228, 258.

184. Subjection to such ridicule has been a common testimony among many Pentecostals. E.g., see Abell, *Better Felt*, 37, 87, and 199. Abell explains that many critics simply do not understand the worldview of Holiness-Pentecostals in Southern Appalachia, but he endeavors to recount how they "make sense out of life" as it "centers around their God" (6). At times, the criticism and ridicule amounted to outright persecution, but often served as a consolidating rather than discouraging force. See Synan, *Holiness-Pentecostal Movement*, 72, 124, 137, 195, 226, and 233.

185. The Azusa Street Mission during the cataclysmic revival it birthed in the early 20th century was especially vulnerable to these kinds of critical attacks. In addition to the obvious factor of the rise of a different religious phenomenon, the egalitarian nature of early Pentecostalism also invited anger and outrage from a society infected with rampant racism, class prejudice, and gender wars. These factors frequently came to the fore in testimonials because all were expected to speak a word in the Spirit regardless of such societal distinctions. Cf. C.M. Robeck, *The Azusa Street Mission & Revival: The Birth of the Global Pentecostal Movement* (Nashville: Nelson, 2006), 1-4.

186. E.g., Abell, *Better Felt*, 4, 35.

187. Albeit, Ellicott, *Ellicott's*, explains that Agrippa's words "are the expression, not of a half-belief, but of a cynical sneer" (914).

188. Accordingly, some graphically describe the danger of rejecting the power of God for too long, Abell, *Better Felt*, 20. Synan *Holiness-Pentecostal Movement*, who suggests the Church of God (Cleveland, TN) interpreted its mission in comparable eschatological terms, 76. Further, "harvest" terminology, with its implicit ideas of sowing and reaping, in relation salvation of souls is also common. E.g. J.R. Goff, Jr., *Fields White Unto Harvest: Charles F. Parham and the Missionary Origins of Pentecostalism* (Fayetteville: University of Arkansas, 1988). Cf. John 4:34-38.

189. See Synan, *Holiness-Pentecostal Movement*, 46-47, 207, and 289. Cf. Robeck, *Azusa Street*, 88.

190. Ellicott, *Ellicott's*, describes the love mentioned in John 13:35 as "the distinctive Christian mark" by which Christ's disciples "always should be linked to Him and to each other" (840). In the unity mentioned in 17:20-23, the world would see "a proof of the divine origin of Christianity" (847).

191. Admittedly, acceptance and affirmation by others is a thorny issue for thoughtful Pentecostals. There are those who fear, perhaps not altogether inappropriately, that as members of a typically marginalized sect Pentecostals are motivated psychologically, at least subliminally, to seek acceptance and affirmation from former critics possibly to the point of risking compromise of their authentic identity. See D.C. Warrington, a Pentecos-

tal (Church of God, Cleveland, TN), "The Strange Missiology of Tony Richie," 1 September 2007, http://www.vulcanhammer.org/?p=310. Cf. with Warrington's follow ups, "Pentecostal Perspectives on World Religions: A Response to an Earlier Post," 8 September 2007, http://www.vulcanhammer.org/?p=318, "More on the Fairness of God," 24 September 2007, http://www.vulcanhammer.org/?p=338, "Secularists Accuse Evangelical of Being Un-Christian," 15 November 2007, http://www.vulcanhammer.org/?p=388, and, though less directly, "Reply to Jonathan Stone on the Possibility of Dialogue between Pentecostals and the LBGT Community," 27 March 2008, http://www. vulcanhammer.org/?p=578. Conversely, I consider the subliminal psychological motif a legitimate but not determinative point in the discussion. Rather, I judge expanding Pentecostal engagement of others as a mark of the movement's maturation from sectarian to establishment status in agreement with Christ's imperative to seek to influence the world positively (Matt 5:16).

192. Strictly speaking, human acts and words do not "affect" God according to the impassibility theology proper of classical theism. However, this dynamic terminology used here indicates how Pentecostal involvement in interreligious dialogue through testimony relates to God.

193. See L. Martin, *Holy Ghost Revival on Azusa Street: The True Believers: Eyewitness Accounts of the Revival that Shook the World* (Pensacola, FL: Christian Life, 1998), 53, 76, 129. Cf. L. Martin, William J. Seymour, *The Words That Changed the World: Azusa Street Sermons* (Pensacola, FL: Christian Life, 1999), 33, 35, 37, and also 69, 87, 89.

194. Ellicott, *Ellicott's*, explains that "The link between human nature and the divine spirit is the human spirit, which is the shrine of the Holy Spirit" and that true worship "is in harmony with the nature of the God we worship" (813). Pentecostal worship, therefore, strives to be primarily a spiritual action and relation.

195. See Johns, *Pentecostal Formation*, 126-27.

196. One even hears the language of how the Holy Ghost "shines" on the countenances of Spirit-filled believers. Cf. E. Hyatt, *Fire on the Earth: Eyewitness Reports Azusa Street Revival* (Lake Mary, FL: Creation House, 2006), 47. The terminology of light coming to or showing through Pentecostal believers is quite common, e.g., 52, 57, 89, 98, 132-33, 136-137, 148, and 161.

197. See *CWJW* (Rio, WI: Ages Software, Inc., 2002), 6:340-41. As biblical support Wesley quotes Psalm 145:9. Cf. L. Martin, *The Topeka Outpouring of 1901* (Pensacola, FL: Christian Life, 1997), 64, 113.

198. Pentecostal teaching tends to emphasize God's love for all as well as Christ's offer of life to all. E.g., see L.E. Martin and W.J. Seymour, *The Doctrines and Discipline of the Azusa Street Apostolic Faith Mission of Los Angeles,* The Complete Azusa Street Library (Pensacola, FL: Christian Life, 2000), 49, 55 (cf. 54, 66, 74, 151, 153). Cf. Martin and Seymour, *Words That Changed the World,* 31, 44, 94. Cf. 59 and 85.

199. Cf. J. Shelton, "Matthew," 119-253, *FLBCNT,* 204, and Arrington, "Acts," 555-56. Noticeable is how often even written testimonial accounts of Pentecostals spontaneously break out into praising the Lord and glorifying God. Cf. Hyatt, *Fire on the Earth*, 145, 150, 151, 153, 154, 155, 158, 163, 167, 169, 170, etc.

Conclusion

Introduction

The final chapter of this work endeavors to pull together its several strands in summary form. A brief survey of its contents, accompanied by succinct explanatory statements, intends to place in the most concise and concrete structure possible the main ideas of the entire work. It is therefore necessarily repetitive by nature. However, it also introduces an illustrious example of how the testimonial paradigm may work at its best in the engagement of Pentecostal Christians with religious others through interreligious encounter and dialogue, a few words of warning for participating Pentecostals, a last mild attempt at assessment, and, perhaps appropriately enough, a personal testimony. This chapter, and therefore the entire work, closes with a prayer for peace and progress among the religions.

Overview and Summary

The present study has focused on developing a Classical Pentecostal theology of religions that utilizes their tradition of testimony as a pneumatological paradigm for interreligious encounter and dialogue. Therefore, the Introduction gave attention to a historical-terminological, theological-pneumatological, and sociological-doctrinal sketch of Classical Pentecostalism. Ultimately, the present work draws on biblical, theological, and practical resources of a Pentecostal and pneumatological theology of religions (always endeavoring to be faithfully christological and ecclesiological) to provide a praxis-oriented approach for actual interreligious encounter and dialogue. The desire has been to hear authentically the Holy Spirit's voice in a process or experience of interreligious dialogue and encounter through the Pentecostal tradition of testimony for the glory of God.

Chapter 1 assessed the contemporary context of religious pluralism in terms of both problem and opportunity. Focus was on religious pluralism in the sense of the reality of different faiths and their adherents co-existing in close proximity in contemporary society. It utilized a wide array of resources, but included Pentecostal critiques. It suggested that a biblically, practically, and theologically informed approach to interreligious encounter, dialogue, and cooperation is appropriate for Pentecostals. Yet it advanced that a Pentecostal theology of religions adequate for the contemporary task of interreligious coexistence ought to be faithful to its own inherent values. It judged that the challenge of Pentecostal theology of religions today is to utilize its distinctive pneumatology for developing a theology of religions that effectively addresses the current situation of religious pluralism in a manner avoiding the pitfalls of pluralism that is faithful to Pentecostal identity and ethos.

Chapter 2 surveyed contemporary Pentecostal theology of religions with a view toward assessing progress on preparedness for dealing with religious pluralism, especially in its radical versions. Overall, it endeavored as concisely and yet completely as possible to give an indication of the current state of Pentecostal theology of religions. It showed that certain elements of the general Christian tradition, the Evangelical and Wesleyan movements, and key interactive theologians are playing an important role in Pentecostal self-understanding and development. Pentecostalism itself appears to be advancing in constructive and distinctive directions, forming an inclusive Pentecostal theology of religions that endeavors to be true to its roots in creative ways adequate for its present and its future. Neither lax pluralism nor strict exclusivism comfortably fit with Pentecostal values properly understood or sufficiently face contemporary societal pluralistic realities. Increasingly clear is that Pentecostal spirituality and theology contains rich reserves for utilization in theology of religions.

Chapter 3 surveyed the subjects of interreligious encounter and dialogue through what is currently underway in the field. Throughout, it made an effort to understand and articulate the significance and nature of interreligious encounter and dialogue in order to further inform and develop Pentecostal theology of religions and dialogue praxis. It concluded that Pentecostal theology of religions and thought and practice of interreligious dialogue are at an early and exciting stage of formation and development. Pentecostals are beginning to marshal rich resources of their pneumatic experience and teaching for application in dialogue with religious others. However, Pentecostalism needs a model for dialogue with familiarity and specificity from within the movement. This chapter suggested the category of testimony would serve well.

Chapter 4 argued that regarding response to religious pluralism the situation is critical though Pentecostalism possesses reservoirs of resources for addressing it because these are not being sufficiently plumbed at a satisfactory rate matching the need of the hour. However, Pentecostal pneumatology as experienced and expressed in the practice of personal testimony specifically provides space and support as well as substantive direction for understanding and engaging in contemporary interreligious encounter and dialogue. Pentecostal testimony is part of a distinctive overall oral and narrative tradition that is far reaching in its power. Energy and vitality are its obvious characteristics. Moreover, testimony presupposes an ability to communicate through inspired (and inspiring) speech that is supra rational. It is not dogmatic. It is emotive. It is engaging. It can easily address a wide audience. These and other qualities appear to qualify testimony as a possible medium for encounter and dialogue beyond the confines of Pentecostal congregations

Chapter 5 specifically explored the tradition of testimony as a resource for interreligious dialogue by mining the major implications of the last chapter on testimony for application at the dialogue table. It addressed practical as well as theological issues. This chapter, as the most constructive and creative endeavor of this overall study, is of critical and pivotal significance. It presented Pentecostal testimony as a feasible and viable resource for interreligious encounter and dialogue. It insisted that the broad contours of this study suggest testimony authentically connects Pentecostal tradition with the goals of contemporary interreligious dialogue. It thus embraces an environment of constructive continuity and creative connectivity promising great potential for progress in the current crisis of relations among the world religions.

Chapter 6 attempted to anticipate some of the more obvious objections possibly raised against the hypothesis of this project. The approach taken was to look first at possible objections based on biblical interpretation, and then at those regarding suspected betrayal of the Pentecostal tradition or a stealthy minimization of Christian ecclesial mission. It also addressed questions of competing interreligious truth claims from the perspective of a concern for relativization of religious truth and whether interfaith conflict is practically resolvable and the role that dialogue may play therein. This chapter did not purport to give an exhaustive apology for this project's approach to interreligious encounter and dialogue. However, it endeavored to demonstrate that the approach presented herein does offer defensible and reasonable support for itself against a selection of possible objections. The aim was to exhibit congruence with the historic pattern of biblical and theological faith consciously prevalent in Pentecostalism.

Chapter 7 turned to an attempt at envisioning future developments through the anticipated application of the study's prescriptive insights. More than a way forward this chapter was perhaps somewhat of a hypothetical or prognosticative "what if". It concentrated on the increasingly complex qualities of religion as it co-exists and overlaps with other disciplines of corporate human life such as economics and politics as well as national and international attitudes and ideologies. Always the accent was on better understanding Pentecostalism and its place in relation to interreligious dialogue. Throughout, the suggestion seemed clearly justified that Pentecostal involvement in interreligious dialogue, in general and in testimonial mode, could and would indeed contribute significantly to the status of interreligious relations and global harmony and stability along with distinctively fulfilling Pentecostalism's own authentic spiritual and theological destiny.

An Illustrious Example: E. Stanley Jones in India

E. Stanley Jones (1884-1973) was a Methodist missionary and theologian. During the first decades of the twentieth century, he held thousands of surprisingly effective and influential interreligious lectures across the subcontinent of India.

His support for the cause of Indian self-determination won him many friends with leaders of the then up-and-coming Indian National Congress party. He was well acquainted with Mahatma Gandhi, and with the Nehru family. Gandhi's life and thought challenged Jones. Therefore, through his writing Jones helped thousands of Western missionaries during the last decades of the British Raj gain greater respect for the Indian character of their work. In his seminal work, *The Christ of the Indian Road,* Jones attempted to contextualize Christianity for India.[1]

Jones well exemplifies important elements of the present work. Phenomenally effective, some describe him as the "Missionary Extraordinary."[2] Jones inaugurated 'round table conferences' at which Christians and non-Christians alike sat down as equals to "share their testimonies as to how their religious experiences helped them to live better."[3] He himself spoke of the immense importance of testimony in his personal experience as a minister and as a missionary. His very first sermon ended dismally until he turned to telling what God had done for him. Traveling around India debating got him nowhere until he started telling what God had done for him, and then the results were dramatic indeed.[4] Interestingly, he was convinced that spiritual experience shared through interreligious testimony opens the way for appreciation and respect between religious others.[5] He even shares specific testimonies of how the power of Pentecost is discernible and recognizable to religious others, arguing that a "new Pentecost" along the lines of the Book of Acts is the need of contemporary Christian missions. Along with the experienced presence and power of the Holy Spirit, for Jones one of the chief features of apostolic preaching is that it was "throbbing with testimony." He carefully recounted how "a rich testimony from a very Christian life, simply told and meaning much" is often unanswerable where the finest arguments were unsuccessful.[6]

The amazing example of E. Stanley Jones illustrates how well wisely used testimony may work in interreligious contexts. He used it primarily as a missionary, yet, for him, that included rather then excluded interreligious dialogue. Jones realized that contemporary Christian missions and interreligious relations require contextualization and innovation as well as developing deep personal relations.[7] Further, his ecumenical orientation and social activism make him a natural resource for today's context of global pluralism.[8] Ecclesial mission today that rightly understands interreligious dialogue to be part of its task can also well utilize testimony. Jones boldly coupled breaking new ground in the area of ecclesial mission and interreligious relations with clear testimony of his commitment to Christ and to Christianity.[9] Here grateful Pentecostals should stand on the shoulders of a great Wesleyan leader.

A Few Words of Warning

Veli-Matti Kärkkäinen notes that Lesslie Newbigin became increasingly critical of the WCC, a leading organization in the world regarding ecumenical and interreligious dialogue, for what he saw as their capitulation to a 'secular agenda'.[10] Newbigin, himself a leader in the ecumenical movement and participant in WCC programs, particularly pointed out he felt this secular agenda was usurping legitimate Christian mission, social action, and interfaith dialogue.[11] Newbigin especially worked to counteract a secular and postmodern cultural and societal distortion of Christian identity.[12] Kärkkäinen's succinct summary of Newbigin's theology of religion shows its significance for interfaith dialogue.

> Newbigin's theology of religions is firmly rooted in the uniqueness of Jesus Christ and Christian rationality. It is explicitly antipluralistic, but it cannot be regarded as exclusive or ecclesiocentric. The church plays a crucial role as the bearer of the truth and its witness, but Newbigin does not engage the speculation as to the destiny of those who have not heard the gospel. What he makes clear is that salvation is to be found in Christ and has to be proclaimed to all—that salvation comes in and through his cross and resurrection. While missionary, it also gives space to other traditions with their truth claims.... Christians are entitled to argue for the validity of their truth claims in the public arena of religions and ideologies; the eschaton gives the final ratification of whose rationality is the true one.[13]

However, essential to understanding Newbigin is his uncompromising commitment to the fundamental missionary character of the Church.[14] Any departure from or dilution of the Church's missionary identity is simply unacceptable.[15] In his judgment, the WCC sometimes struggles to maintain its Christian witness in the face of other factors.[16] He particularly questions it's relation with or reaction to the concept of culture, especially if it may move toward resulting privatization of Christian faith and values.[17] Arguably, therefore, even as this study suggests more ecumenical and interreligious involvement by Pentecostals, one may infer from Newbigin's example that such an approach need not be naïve or uncritical. Interreligious dialogue is more than merely addressing current topics from a particular religious perspective. The world cannot call the cadence for the Church.[18] Christians and non-Christian alike will likely wish to assure that dialogue directly and discriminately addresses the issues existing between them and in their contexts. For Pentecostal Christians, this means that Christ's uniqueness and the Church's Spirit-led mission will be in the forefront of conversations.[19] For others, perhaps there will be specific topics they too will want to insist are included. The point is that Pentecostals need not avoid any involvement with organizations like the WCC but that they will likely need to guard against a co-opted agenda.

Furthermore, Kärkkäinen observes that Sri Lankan theologian Vinoth Ramachandra's work of careful interaction with his Asian context, in which dealing with religious pluralism is a major element, enriches his theology significantly.[20] Ramachandra wishes to restore "a creative balance" between what he calls "indigenous and pilgrim principles", both springing from the gospel, with an evangelical orientation.[21] Convinced of the need for committed dialogue, he nonetheless warns against efforts at dialogue that are inadequate due to subtle arrogance, spineless convictions, or abstract theorizing.[22] Critical of pluralism, he desires to move beyond pluralist paradigms in doing Christian mission.[23] Yet genuine dialogue and faithful Christian witness are nonetheless important.[24] Ramachandra's theology of religions appears incapable of simple classification. For example, it does not neatly fit into the now traditional categories of exclusivism, pluralism, and inclusivism. Rather, it exhibits traits common to each while also extending beyond any of them.[25] Interestingly, he is able to focus on "establishing a foundation for Christian uniqueness and thus Christian mission, all the while giving credence to religions than join forces in the common search for truth."[26]

Drawing from the preceding, ever rapidly expanding Pentecostalism ought to be particularly sensitive to global contexts. Therefore, Pentecostal articulation of theology of religions and participation in interreligious dialogue would do well pay heed to dangers of over conceptualizing and over classification through over reliance on Western rationalist categories. Perhaps it is not impertinent to imply that the West may have something to learn from the East here. Oriental Christians have long had to deal daily with the realities of existence in a cultural context characterized by multiple religions.[27] That Occidental Christians now experiencing a cultural shift in the same direction may benefit from their already established experience and expertise seems sensible enough.

For Classical Pentecostals watching out for over conceptualization and over classification on Christian theology of religions and interreligious encounter and dialogue likely will have at least two important elements. First, it will mean simultaneously avoiding the rigidity of fundamentalists and the elasticity of liberals.[28] Second, it will mean it will mean relying on the true distinctives of Pentecostalism.[29] As for the first, Pentecostals will wish to allow ample room for freedom of the Spirit in faith and in life in order for real progress to occur.[30] This means no attempt to force themselves, or others, into preconceived, and perhaps, ill-conceived, categories that may be culturally or geographically shaped and sized. However, Pentecostals refuse to abandon biblical, classical, and historical Christianity. These are the boundary guidelines for credible development.

As for the second, Pentecostals have an invaluable resource for interreligious engagement within their own pneumatologically rich tradition. Building upon their own unique experience and understanding of the Holy Spirit enables Pentecostals to discern the Spirit's presence and power in others. Pentecostals do not need to superimpose creedal or dogmatic formulations on everyone.[31] They recognize that the Spirit often works at a supra rational level or plane. One of their favorite biblical texts compares the mystery of the Spirit to the moving of the wind (John 3:8).[32] Therefore, Pentecostals can perhaps best appreciate fruit and gifts of the Spirit appearing in and active among other cultures and traditions in surprising places.[33] Applying this insight to theology of religions and interreligious encounter and dialogue opens up incredible possibilities.[34]

A Mild Attempt at Self-Assessment: Moderately Radical and Radically Moderate

Somewhat in the spirit of Ovid's ancient adage, "You will go most safely in the middle,"[35] this project has argued that inclusivism is a balanced and best middle way between unfortunate extremes of exclusivism and pluralism.[36] Furthermore, the argument has been made that at least a substantial strain of inclusivism is traceable in early Pentecostalism. Therefore, a theology of interreligious dialogue derived from an inclusivist theology of religions is viewed as a retrieval of an original Pentecostal value. Yet this does not detract from the difficulty of persuading and applying inclusivism and dialogue in the modern context. As Virgil wisely but regretfully reflected, at times getting back to where one started is much more difficult, and even dangerous, than the original departure.[37] Nevertheless, encouraging is that Wesley scholars appropriately describe John Wesley's theological resiliently amazing approach to Christian truth and practice holistically as *via media,* or the "middle way."[38] Therefore, perhaps it is not overly optimistic to conclude that though sensationalizing extremes may capture the crowd's attention temporarily balance and moderation more often than not win the day.

Of course, part of the problem with moderation is correctly identifying the boundaries of extremities. In the present work, judged extreme are the kinds of exclusivism that limit Christ's lordship to the Christian religion with its spires and steeples and the kinds of pluralism that lose Christ's lordship among a host of world religions with their founders, leaders, and teachers. Emphatically, it desires neither to limit nor to lose Christ. Accordingly, on the one hand, neither compromising biblical and historic Christianity nor aggrandizing other religions, or on the other hand, neither absolutizing Christianity nor demonizing other religions is acceptable. Dialogue is necessary to help work out these intricacies and their consequences. In all of this, it is radically moderate. It tirelessly tries to achieve a delicate, elusive equilibrium.

Yet, for full-fledged pluralists this work will still be too exclusive, too elitist, for full-fledged exclusivists, still too plural, too broad. That is the perennial hurdle of inclusivism. However, in a real way the present proposal is at least moderately radical. It unstintingly challenges Pentecostals to review and revise their assumptions regarding theology of religions and interreligious encounter and dialogue, and appreciatively advises them to utilize their own rich resources for intentional engagement. As many Pentecostals adamantly and aggressively have taken quite the opposite course, it is reaching for a radical response—a theological version of the Pentecostal altar invitation.[39] Nevertheless, it is only moderately radical after all. It only reaches its radical hands so far forth as it can do while still feeling its moderate feet firmly planted on Pentecostal ground.[40] Ardently hoped for is that attentive Pentecostals will understand that point whether or not they accept everything else about this particular proposal.

A Tone Setting Personal Pentecostal Testimony[41]

Prior to entering this investigation regarding interreligious dialogue, I had an experience that effectively moved me onto a trajectory eventually directing me into this field of endeavor. Long fascinated with the Church Fathers, mostly due to Wesley's influence, I had been reading Irenaeus on Gnosticism with particular attention.[42] Finally, having finished his five volumes of *Adversus Heresies,* the significance seized upon me of Irenaeus' heroic work against the Gnostics for having safeguarded early and historical Christian faith and life for centuries. One day shortly thereafter, during a time of personal prayer with a strong devotional element, this theme once again exercised itself upon my imagination. Immediately and fervently, I began to pray for God to help me thus to stand against any contemporary heresies or aberrations of truth and righteousness. As I did so, the clear voice of the Spirit spoke to my own spirit in a commanding fashion. I heard simply, "Pluralism is the Gnosticism of your day." There and then, I pledged to God in prayer to combat pluralism just as persistently as Irenaeus had prevailed against Gnosticism.[43]

Continuing prayer and in depth study over a prolonged period convinced me further that the best counterpoint to pluralism is a pneumatological theology of inclusivism, and that interreligious dialogue can actually help in combating concerns over rampant pluralism. Though for years I had given my primary attention to pastoral ministry, this dialogical directive dovetailed nicely with my own earlier struggles with religious diversity and plurality on the way to conversion to Christ. I became increasingly involved in speaking and writing on theology of religions and in engaging in ecumenical and interreligious dialogue. Again, this time one night late and a few years hence as well, in prayer I felt a flash of inspiration, or perhaps better, illumination, regarding the role Pentecostal testimony should play in the dialogical process. Although by no means confessing any claim to an infallible divine inspiration, I feel convinced that these developments might evolve into helpful contributions for the current crisis brought on in large part by radical religious pluralism, God willing.

Conclusion/Summary

The final chapter of this work has endeavored to pull together its several strands in summary form. After briefly surveying its contents, it also gave an illustrious historical example of the testimonial paradigm at work in the engagement with religious others. Then, a few words of warning for Pentecostals to stay on course with their conviction were necessary, followed by some overall assessment. Appropriately enough, a personal testimony put the work in devotional context.

How might this research be further developed in the future? One certainly hopes these ideas will be refined and developed through continuing research and also through lessons learned in the actual practice of dialogue with others. Some of these directions or developments may not be presently anticipated. However, even at this time I can see that the two chapters specifically on testimony could be expanded into full length monographs developing further the key themes articulated. Probably as part of that process, rather than focusing as here on suggestions for how testimony can be appropriated for dialogical purposes, one might set forth other leading models for comparison and contrast while explicating further inherent themes in testimony. I see what I have done already as a basic starting point, although obviously building upon existing theology and praxis, for a new and dynamic approach, particularly for Pentecostals, which should be systematically extended beyond these parameters. Perhaps more importantly, as other theologians review and respond to the present work it will assuredly be refined in its present composition as well as in areas possibly hitherto unexpected as these are brought forth for discussion and application.

Now, this chapter and therefore the entire work, close with a prayer for the Holy Spirit and for peace and progress among the religions.[44]

Prayer to the Holy Spirit

Spirit of truth, you who search the depths of God,
memory and prophecy in the Church,
lead humankind to recognize in Jesus of Nazareth the Lord of Glory,
the Savior of the world,
the supreme fulfillment of history.

Come Spirit of Love and Peace!

Spirit of holiness, divine breath that moves the universe,
come and renew the face of the earth.
Awaken in Christians a desire for full unity,
that they may be for the world an effective sign and instrument
of intimate union with God and of the unity of the whole human race.

Come Spirit of Love and Peace!

Spirit of wisdom, inspiration of minds and hearts,
direct science and technology
to the service of life, justice and peace.
Render fruitful our dialogue with the followers of other religions,
lead the different cultures to appreciate the values of the Gospel.

Come Spirit of Love and Peace!

To you, Spirit of love,
with the Almighty Father and the Only-Begotten Son,
be praise, honor and glory
for ever and ever. AMEN.[45]

Notes

1. See E.S. Jones, *The Christ of the Indian Road* (Nashville: Abingdon, 1925) and P.A.J. Martin, *Missionary of the Indian Road: The Theology of Stanley Jones* (Koramangala, Bangalore: Theological Book Trust, 1996).
2. Cf. S.A. Graham, *Ordinary Man, Extraordinary Mission: The Life and Work of E. Stanley Jones* (Nashville: Abingdon, 2005).
3. See "Eli Stanley Jones: Missionary Extraordinary," http://vaxxine.com/eves/jones.htm. Cf. E. Stanley Jones, *Christ at the Round Table* (Whitefish, MT: Kessinger, 2004).
4. Jones, *The Indian Road*, 138-53 (141-44).

5. Admittedly, discussing spiritual experience in interfaith settings can be a difficult task theologically for Christians, but it can have its benefits also. See M. Barnes, "Spirituality and the Dialogue of Religions," *NWDCS*, ed. Philip Sheldrake (Louisville, KY: Westminster John Knox Press, 2005), 32-37.

6. Jones, *The Indian Road,* 148-52 (151-52). Unaware of this aspect of Jones' approach when starting this research, I have been thrilled to discover its testimonial dynamic present and awaiting exploitation.

7. See R.W. Taylor, "E. Stanley Jones 1884-1973: Following the Christ of the Indian Road," 339-48, G.H. Anderson and R.T. Coote, *Mission Legacies: Biographical Studies of Leaders of the Modern Missionary Movement,* American Society of Missiology Series (New York: Orbis, 1995), 340-43. See also ibid, Clinton Bennett, "Lewis Bevan Jones 1880-1960: Striving to Touch Muslim Hearts," 283-89 (esp. 284-85).

8. Taylor, "E. Stanley Jones," 340, 344.

9. S.B. Bevans and R.P. Schroeder, *Constants in Context: A Theology of Mission for Today,* American Society of Missiology Series (New York: Orbis, 2004), 258. Yet Jones always insisted on the priority of the Kingdom of God in the Church's mission, 310. Cf. argument of J.R. Williams, *Renewal Theology: Systematic Theology from a Charismatic Perspective* (*RT*), three volumes in one (Grand Rapids: Zondervan, 1996), that Christ's fullness is only manifested in the Church but Christ's headship is nonetheless truly universal, 3:71-72.

10. See L. Newbigin, "Ecumenical Amnesia," *IBMR* 18 (January 1994), 2-5. K. Raiser, the General Secretary of the WCC, responded with "Is Ecumenical Apologetics Sufficient? A Response to Lesslie Newbigin's 'Ecumenical Amnesia,'" *IBMR* 18 (April 1994), 50-51. Newbigin felt an ancient tendency toward secularism has come to a head with the rise of Cartesian skepticism and the subsequent capitulation to modernism. See his *Foolishness to the Greeks: The Gospel and Western Culture* (Geneva: World Council of Churches, 1986), esp. 1-19, 34-37.

11. Conversely, Newbigin argued for a philosophy of faith undergirding a distinctively Christian worldview as a basis for Christian mission. See a series of works by Newbigin, including, *The Gospel in a Pluralist Society* (Grand Rapids: Eerdmans, 1989); *Truth to Tell: The Gospel as Public Truth* (Grand Rapids: Eerdmans, 1991); *A Word in Season: Perspectives on Christian World Missions* (Grand Rapids: Eerdmans, 1995); and, *Truth and Authority in Modernity* (Valley Forge, PA: Trinity, 1996).

12. V.M. Kärkkäinen, *An Introduction to Theology of Religions: Biblical, Historical, & Contemporary Perspectives* (Downer's Grove: InterVarsity Press, 2003), 245-46. Another longtime insider who criticizes WCC "ambivalent theology and ambivalent policy" regarding interfaith dialogue is K. Cracknell, *In Good and Generous Faith: Christian Responses to Religious Pluralism* (Peterborough: Epworth, 2005), 180-209.

13. Kärkkäinen, *Theology of Religions,* 256.

14. L. Newbigin, *The Open Secret: An Introduction to the Theology of Mission* (Grand Rapids: Eerdmans, 1995), 1-2.

15. Cf. Newbigin, *Open Secret,* 9-10.

16. Cf. Newbigin, *Open Secret,* 112. Cf. Williams' discussion of tensions between the ecumenical and evangelical movements, *RT,* 3:43-48. Although Williams expresses concerns similar to Newbigin, he concludes that there is overlapping concern and increasing convergence between the two movements, 3:46. However, for existential affinity to occur evangelicals expect that "The primary concern in the ecumenical movement should be with the spiritual vitality of the churches seeking to unite" (3:47). Thus, unity apart from vitality is not an attainable or even desirable aspiration.

17. Newbigin, *Gospel in Pluralist Society,* 198.

18. E.g., when Nicaraguan Sandinistas, at least some of whom apparently were anti-Semitic and had ties with communism, blatantly attempted to co-opt Christian faith and values in support of their revolutionary political platform, local Pentecostals reacted strongly and negatively. See C.L. Smith, "Revolutionaries and Revivalists: Pentecostal Eschatology, Politics and the Nicaraguan Revolution," *Pneuma* 30:1 (2008), 55-82.Cf. I.C. Rottenberg's analysis, in *The Promise and the Presence: Toward a Theology of the Kingdom of God* (Grand Rapids: Eerdmans, 1980), of WCC's dangerous tendency to 'let the world set the agenda' and of typical evangelical overreaction, 71-72.

19. Thus Newbigin, *Gospel in a Pluralist Society,* affirmed "the unique decisiveness of God's action in Christ" (166), and the primacy of the Holy Spirit's power in doing Christian mission, 117-18. H. Netland, *Encountering Religious Pluralism: The Challenge to Christian Faith & Mission* (Downer's Grove, IL: InterVarsity Press, 2201), also notes Newbigin's sharp criticism of WCC because of its perceived "drift away from theological orthodoxy toward relativism and pluralism" (47). According to Netland, Newbigin's concerns centered on "his insistence on Jesus Christ, the incarnate Son of God, as the one Lord and Savior for all humankind, and upon the continuing need for the church to share the gospel with those of other religions, even as he was careful not to limit the activity of the Holy Spirit among religious others" (48).

20. Kärkkäinen, *Theology of Religions,* 333. E.g., V. Ramachandra, *Faiths in Conflict: Christian Integrity in a Multicultural World* (Downer's Grove, IL: InterVarsity Press, 1999).

21. Ramachandra, *Faiths in Conflict,* 138. Thus, the Evangelical theologian Netland, *Encountering,* frequently quotes Ramachandra approvingly. See 31, 32n, 215-16, 285n, 336n, and 341-42.

22. Ramachandra, *Faiths in Conflict,* 45, 74-75, 162.

23. V. Ramachandra's *The Recovery of Mission: Beyond the Pluralist Paradigm* (Carlisle, UK: Paternoster, 1996), 13, 99, 101.

24. Ramachandra, *Recovery,* 270.

25. Kärkkäinen, *Theology of Religions,* 340-41.

26. Kärkkäinen, *Theology of Religions,* 333. Cf. Vinoth Ramachandra's *Recovery* and *Gods That Fail: Modern Idolatry and Christian Mission* (Downer's Grove: InterVarsity, 1996).

27. See L.O. Sanneh, *Disciples of All Nations: Pillars of World Christianity,* Studies in World Christianity (New York: Oxford University Press, 2007), 61, 65, 231. Cf. C. Baumer, M. Dinkha IV, *The Church of the East: An Illustrated History of Assyrian Christianity* (Ney York: I. B. Tauris, 2006), 137-68.

28. See V. Synan, "Fundamentalism," *NIDPCM,* 655-58, and M. Crews, *The Church of God: A Social History* (Knoxville: University of Tennessee, 1990), 172, 175-76 (Cf. 1-18). B.D. McLaren, *A Generous Orthodoxy: Why I Am a Missional, Evangelical, Post/Protestant, Liberal/Conservative, Mystical/Poetic, Biblical, Charismatic/Contemplative, Fundamentalist/Calvinist, Anabaptist/Anglican, Methodist, Catholic, Green, Incarnational, Depressed-yet-Hopeful, Emergent, Unfinished CHRISTIAN* (Grand Rapids: Zondervan, 2004), represents a popular attempt to transcend such typical divides (esp. 131-44).

29. E.g., see J.R. Goff, Jr., *Fields White Unto Harvest: Charles F. Parham and the Missionary Origins of Pentecostalism* (Fayetteville: University of Arkansas, 1988), 4-5 (Cf. 164-65). See also: F.D. Macchia, "Theology, Pentecostal," *NIDPCM,* 1120-40 (1121); K. Warrington, *Pentecostal Theology: A Theology of Encounter* (New York: T & T Clark, 2008), 84-95 and 119-23; M.R. Hathaway, in "The Elim Pentecostal Church: Origins, Development and Distinctives," *Pentecostal Perspectives,* ed. K. Warrington

(Carlisle: Paternoster, 1998), 1-39; D. Petts, "The Baptism in the Holy Spirit: The Theological Distinctive," 98-119; and V.M. Kärkkäinen, *Pneumatology: The Holy Spirit in Ecumenical, International, and Contextual Perspective* (Grand Rapids: Baker, 2002), 92-94.

30. W.J. Hollenweger, *The Pentecostals* (London: SCM, 1972/Peabody: Hendrickson, 1988), 298-99.

31. Hollenweger, *Pentecostals,* 506. Cf. W. Kay, "Do Doctrinal Boundaries Protect Our Identity or Prevent Fellowship," *EPTA Bulletin* 12 (1993), 38-41.

32. Emphasis on the mystery of the Spirit's work is common. E.g., see G.P. Duffield and N.M. Van Cleave, *Foundations of Pentecostal Theology* (Los Angeles: L.I.F.E. Bible College, 1983, 1987), 111, 129, 229, 233. Furthermore, Duffield and Van Cleave explain that wind in John 3:8 "symbolizes the invisible, everywhere present, power and life-sustaining influence of the Spirit" (114) and that John 3:8 points to inexplicable experience of the Holy Spirit, 251. F.L. Arrington, *Encountering the Holy Spirit: Paths of Christian Growth and Service* (Cleveland: Pathway, 2003), references John 3:8 as part of a pattern in both Old and New Testaments indicating *"the Spirit's work is marked by mystery and power"* (28; italics original). He insists it indicates that "The mysterious wind of God has incomparable power and can never be controlled by man" (28). Furthermore, Arrington argues that John 3:8 indicates the Spirit's gifts have an illimitable and open-ended character because of the Spirit's own sovereign nature, 243. W. Hildebrandt, *An Old Testament Theology of the Spirit of God* (Peabody, Massachusetts: Hendrickson, 1995/1999), uses John 3:8 to summarize the complexity and variety of Israelite pneumatology, 1. S.M. Horton, *What the Bible Says about the Holy Spirit* (Springfield, MO: Gospel Publishing, 1976/1992), says of this text that the wind of the Spirit "has a way of blowing in the most unexpected, wonderful, and mysterious ways" (115). For him, it also signifies the sovereignty and variety of the Spirit and of the Spirit's ways, 261. J.C. Thomas, *The Spirit of the New Testament* (Leiderdorp, The Netherlands: Deo, 2004), in a chapter on "The Spirit in the Fourth Gospel: Narrative Explorations," suggests that this text is part of a narrative that not only indicates the mystery of the Spirit but also the multidimensionality of Christ as "Spirit agent", 159-60 (160).

33. A. Yong, "'Not Knowing Where the Wind Blows...': On Envisioning a Pentecostal-Charismatic Theology of Religions," *JPT* 14 (April 1999), 81-112, explicitly applies John 3:8 to theology of religions.

34. According to J. Sepúlveda in "Indigenous Pentecostalism and the Chilean Experience," A. Anderson and W.J. Hollenweger, eds., *Pentecostals after a Century: Global Perspective son a Movement in Transition.* (JSup Series 15 (Sheffield, England: Sheffield Academic Press, 1999), 111-34, Chilean Pentecostals have instinctively but effectively demonstrated the potential of this approach in their synthesis of Protestant (Methodist) and "the *mestizo* lower classes of Chilean society"—and this has been crucial to their growth, 132. It results in a non-"Classical" version of Pentecostalism. Sepúlveda argues for a broader definition of Pentecostalism, stressing that, "the rediscovery of pneumatology by modern Pentecostalism has to do mainly with the spiritual freedom to 'incarnate' the gospel anew in diverse cultures," 133.

35. T. Bulfinch, *Bulfinch's Mythology: A Modern Abridgement* by Edmund Fuller (New York: Dell, 1959, 1967), 268 (cf. 43).

36. On the one hand, Pentecostals tend to see religious pluralism as suffering from Christological defectiveness and overall lack of biblical and theological integrity, e.g., A. Yong, *Discerning of the Spirit(s): A Pentecostal-Charismatic Contribution to the Christian Theology of Religions* JSup 20 (Sheffield: Sheffield Academic, 2000), 46, 47, *Beyond the Impasse: Toward a Pneumatological Theology of Religions* (Grand Rapids:

Baker, 2003), 24, 109-110, 123, V.M. Kärkkäinen, *An Introduction to Theology of Religions: Biblical, Historical, & Contemporary Perspectives* (Downer's Grove: InterVarsity Press, 2003), 25, 171, 292-93, but on the other hand, religious exclusivism shuts out pneumatological and soteriological possibilities, as well as dialogue and cooperation, more in tune with developing Pentecostal theology of religions, e.g., F.D. Macchia, *Baptized in the Spirit: A Global Pentecostal Theology* (Grand Rapids: Zondervan, 2006), 178-90, A. Yong, "Can We Get 'Beyond the Paradigm' in Christian Theology of Religions? A Response to Terry Muck," Interpretation 61:1 (January 2007), 28-32.

37. See *Bulfinch's Mythology,* 269 (cf. 211-12). The actual quote, placed on the Sibyl's lips, is, "The descent to Avernus is easy; the gate of Pluto stands open night and day; but to retrace one's steps and return to the upper air, that is the toil, that the difficulty."

38. E.g., see *CWJW* (Rio, WI: Ages Software, Inc., 2002), 7:67, 58; 6:340-41, 45; 7:216, 377. Cf. "Mr. Wesley and Mohammed: A Contemporary Inquiry Concerning Islam," *ATJ* 58:2 (Fall 2003), 79-99. R.L. Maddox in "Wesley and the Question of Truth or Salvation in Other Religions," *WTJ* 27 (1992), 9-29. See also R.A. Mattke, "Integration of Truth in John Wesley," May 13, 2008, http://wesley.nnu.edu/wesleyan theology/theojrnl/06-10/08-1.htm. Cf. M.D. Hughes, "The Holistic Way: John Wesley's Practical Piety as a Resource for Integrated Healthcare," *Journal of Religion & Health,* 47:2 (June 2008), 237-52. Many of Wesley's comments on the religions are incidentally scattered throughout his vast corpus. Occasionally, however, he approaches the topic more systematically. In these sections his inclusivism and moderation are most evident. E.g., see his "On Divine Providence," *CWJW* (The Wesleyan Heritage Collection; Ages Software, Inc. Rio, WI: 2002), 6:335-47 (esp. 340-42), or "On Faith," 7:214-21 (216-17, 220), and "On Charity," 7:56-67 (58, 67).

39. Thankfully, that many first-rate Pentecostal scholars are becoming more ecumenically open is increasingly clear. See "Ecumenical Dialogue/Ecumenism" bibliography at: http://artsweb.bham.ac.uk/aanderson/Pentecost/ecumenical. Yet even at that, the move into interfaith dialogue is still a challenge.

40. In all of this Pentecostalism potentially transcends the tired but typical conservative-liberal debate. Pentecostals wed respect for the inspiration and authority of Scripture to the liberating dynamic of the Spirit. Always authentic Pentecostalism's clarion cry is that the letter without the Spirit kills (cf. 2 Co 3:1-6). Comparably, there seems to be a recent spate of books attempting transcendence of the debilitating conservative-liberal divide (both politically and theologically). E.g., R.E. Olson, *How to Be Evangelical Without Being Conservative* (Grand Rapids: Zondervan, 2008), O. Guinness, *The Case for Civility: And Why Our Future Depends on It* (New York: HarperCollins, 2008), A.E. Black, *Beyond Left and Right: Helping Christians Make Sense of American Politics* (Grand Rapids: Baker, 2008), and R.J. Sider, *The Scandal of Evangelical Politics: Why Are Christians Missing the Change to Change the World* (Grand Rapids: Baker, 2008).

41. Saying that, "testimony is the poetry of Pentecostal experience," Pentecostal philosopher-theologian J.K.A. Smith, "Teaching a Calvinist to Dance," *CT* (May 2008), http://www.christianitytoday.com/ct/2008/may/25.42.html?start=1, uses his and his wife's testimonies to frame his own spiritual, philosophical, theological journey.

42. Irenaeus, *Against Heresies, ANF,* Volume 1 (PC Study Bible formatted electronic database Copyright © 2003 by Biblesoft, Inc.).

43. The battle of Irenaeus against what E. Osborn, *Irenaeus of Lyons* (New York: Cambridge University Press, 2001), calls the chameleon-like quality of the Gnostic heresy is well documented, 22. Cf. Colin E. Gunton, "Historical and Systematic Theology," 3-20, C.E. Gunton, ed., *The Cambridge Companion to Christian Doctrine* (New York:

Cambridge University Press 1997). J.N.D. Kelly, *Early Christian Doctrines* (New York: HarperCollins, revised ed., 1978), explains that the eclectic amalgam of magic, pagan philosophy, Greek mystery religions, astrology, and Judaism and Christianity known as Gnosticism was one of "the most potent forces operating in the Church's environment", and that, in addition to Irenaeus, other patristic leaders such as Tertullian and Hippolytus also took issue with it, 22-28 (22). This description may not sound too incomparable with modern pluralism. M.A. Donovan, *One Right Reading? A Guide to Irenaeus* (Collegeville, Minnesota: Liturgical, 1997), notes that Irenaeus concludes that Gnosticism is inherently inconsistent and contradictory to Scripture, 54-55.

44. Pentecostal pragmatism, G. Wacker, *Heaven Below: Early Pentecostals and American Culture* (London, Eng: Harvard University Press, 2001), 10-14 (cf. 266-69), does seem to suggest that peace and progress among the religions would be a not undesirable development. Cf. A. Yong, *Discerning*, 227-34. However, contra E. Patterson, "Conclusion: Back to the Future: U. S. Pentecostalism in the 21st Century," *The Future of Pentecostalism in the United States,* eds., E. Patterson and E. Rybarczyk (Lanham, MD: Rowman and Littlefield, 2007), 189-210 (esp. 196-98).

45. Condensed and adapted from the "Prayer for the Year of the Holy Spirit," Pope John Paul II (2000), http://www.domestic-church.com/CONTENT.DCC/19980101/ARTICLES/HLYSPIRIT.HTM. Despite some disagreement, the long tenure of John Paul II had a significant and positive impact on Pentecostal/Charismatic and Roman Catholic relations on both professional and popular levels. See C.M. Robeck's eulogistic, "John Paul II: A Personal Account of His Impact and Legacy," *Pneuma* 27:1 (2005), 3-34. Also see S. Mansfield, "Keeper of the Flame," *Charisma* (June 2005). (http://www.charismamag.com/display.php?id=11134), and R. Martin's cover story, "A Man of the Spirit," *Charisma* (June 2005), 46 (http://www.charismamag.com /display.php?id=11135).

Afterword
by Cheryl Bridges Johns

Tony Richie takes those of us seeking a way to live and witness in a religiously pluralistic world into a new, yet unexplored realm. As readers we journey past the "Evidence that Demands a Verdict"[1] form of Christian apologetics and past the "no witness" of radical pluralism. We even journey beyond the rationalistic and document based form of dialogue so common in the West. We are taken into a dimension of Spirit-enlivened testimony.

In this dimension evangelism and inclusiveness are woven together to form a tapestry that includes the values of charity, hospitality, availability, certainty and humility. This tapestry is rich in pneumatology and has the beauty of epistemic humility. And it is covered in prayer.

It is this rich reality that offers us hope for a viable future. More and more we are seeing the rise of forms of religious fundamentalism that are accompanied by shrill rhetoric and harsh actions. Sometimes these actions escalate to the point of violence. Pentecostals, in particular, need a way forward without becoming captive to this reality. The Pentecostal tradition is an ever-increasing globalized culture. Its strength has been a Spirit-inspired ability to relate to many tongues and cultures without losing the distinctiveness of the gospel. I believe that one way Pentecostalism has been able to have such a broad impact is its practice of Spirit-enlivened testimony.

As Richie aptly observes, "Pentecostal testimony accesses spiritual experience as much as it expresses it." This spiritual reality is one in which God is at work in the world. Testimony as doxology offers praise and worship to this wonder working God!

The form of testimonial witness that Richie offers is not a rigid stylized formula. Rather, it is fluid, taking into account by the one speaking and well as the one listening. It is based upon a relational view of all knowledge. The face of the "other" thus becomes iconic for truth rather than a threat to a truth system.

I believe that Richie's model for inter-faith dialogue is pregnant with possibilities. Inherent within the model is a firm belief in the biblical imperative of hospitality as central to the Christian witness. On the larger scale we can see the world as God's hospitable *oikoumene*. Here God is the host and we are all guests. On a smaller scale, human interactions can mirror the grace that flows from and through the economy of God's household. At this hospitable table stories are told, food is prepared and people look into the faces of others. At this table there is no platform for the tyranny of words found in sheer monologue. At this table there is both the telling and the listening.

It is at this table that we can offer the taste of the new wine of the Spirit. We can tell stories of how and when Christ's empowering presence broke into our lives. It is at this table that we can listen to the other and discern the Spirit at work in the world. Richie gives us the ways and manners of such table talk. He helps us to see how important it is to create hospitable environments. Such places are not optional for the Christian witness.

Unfortunately, hospitable space is rare these days. It seems that we are ever increasingly tribal. That is why Richie's words to us are so important. He carefully analyzes the biblical, theological and philosophical foundations for his model of inter-religious encounter and dialogue. As a result, he helps readers understand how to have both clear boundaries and a dialectical attitude of openness. He strips away fear that encountering the faith of the other will somehow diminish one's own passion for the kingdom. He carefully works through how the Holy Spirit is distinctively present in the Christian witness and yet at work in all of creation.

This model of inter-faith witness offers us hope for the future. As we look ahead, over the far horizon of time, there portends a landscape that is filled with complexities of culture, religion, ethnic and tribal identities. These complexities can either overwhelm us or we can see them as opportunities for witness. Richie's model of testimony is a way to seize this opportune time for both the proclamation of the gospel and the common good among all people.

It is my hope that Richie's work will be taken seriously, not only by Pentecostals, but by other faith traditions. It is a viable ecumenical and inter-faith paradigm that gives us all hope.

Notes

1. See Josh McDowell, *Evidence that Demands a Verdict* (San Bernardino, CA: Here's Life Publishers, 1972).

Appendix:
Introducing (but Not Necessarily Explaining) Pentecostalism

Classical Pentecostalism is the religious tradition and affiliation out of which I worship and work. Accordingly, a brief survey of Classical Pentecostalism may be helpful for purposes of clarity. Perhaps interested non-Pentecostals will benefit most from this brief appendix. However, possibly Pentecostals themselves may also find it beneficial. Essentially it gives a brief historical-terminological, theological-pneumatological, and sociological-doctrinal sketch of Classical Pentecostalism. It is not intended as an exhaustive analysis, nor is it an apologetic or polemic effort; it only serves as a means of orienting others to the basic context of the research of chapters of this book. Therefore, the relationship of the present appendix to the remainder of this work is indirect but nevertheless indispensable.

A Brief Historical-Terminological Sketch of Classical Pentecostalism

Within the last century, the Classical Pentecostal movement has grown to be the largest family of Protestant Christians in the world.[1] Formerly known simply as Pentecostals (cf. Acts 2:1-4), the adjective "Classical" was added around 1960 to distinguish those who had their origins in the United States around the turn of the twentieth century, many of whom established denominational organizations with Pentecostal distinctives, from so-called "neo-Pentecostals" arising about that time in other non-Pentecostal Protestant denominations and even in Roman Catholicism. The latter soon came to be called "Charismatics".[2] Classical Pentecostal historian and theologian Vinson Synan identifies the roots of modern Pentecostalism in the nineteenth century Holiness and Higher Life movements in England and America.[3] These groups stressed "second blessing" sanctification and Holy Spirit baptism as empowerment for divine service. Pentecostals, however, emphasized a post-conversion experience of Spirit baptism accompanied by speaking in tongues (or glossolalia). This teaching came to be known as the doctrine of "initial evidence", for which explicit support was found in Acts 2, 10, and 19, and implicit in Acts 8 and 9. Tongues were expected to continue to be manifested in a believer's life and sometimes other spiritual gifts, especially divine healing, occurred as well.[4] Pentecostals understood divine healing as a provision of the atonement of Christ. Pentecostalism, therefore, ardently denies the teaching of cessation of spiritual gifts that had been standard in Western churches since Augustine. Pentecostals also taught the restoration of other spiritual gifts to the Church (cf. 1 Co 12:8-10). They understood the outpouring of the Holy Spirit and consequent restoration of spiritual gifts as a kind of "latter rain" signifying the imminence of Christ's second coming and supplying an urge to evangelize prior to that event.[5]

However, both historical and theological variations on Pentecostal self-understanding inevitably appear.[6] For example, historian Paul King recounts the more "cautiously charismatic" history of the Christian and Missionary Alliance founded by A. B. Simpson and later led by A. W. Tozer.[7] Although open to spiritual gifts, including speaking in tongues, the Alliance rejected the doctrine of initial evidence, arguing that speaking in tongues is normal but not normative and adopting the pithy formula "seek not, forbid not" as a guide.[8]

Furthermore, from the United Kingdom contemporary theologian Keith Warrington argues that the movement exhibits a great deal of diversity regarding speaking in tongues in general and tongues as initial evidence in particular.[9] He suggests Pentecostal theology has a good deal of fluidity regarding beliefs and doctrines but that a commitment to experientially encountering God's presence and power centrally characterizes all Pentecostals.[10] Although Warrington warns against possible unevenness in an overly experiential theology, he nonetheless affirms the essential importance of personally experiencing the life of the Spirit vis-à-vis a disproportionately rationalist approach. For him, "That which is central to being a Pentecostal is the desire to encounter the Spirit."[11]

Arguably, the work of King and Warrington indicates greater diversity in Pentecostal self-understanding than may come across in Synan. Nevertheless, personally experiencing the Spirit and spiritual gifts, including but not entirely speaking in tongues, seems consistently characteristic of the movement's adherents.[12] Awareness of underlying similarity amidst overall diversity appears important for understanding the movement.

Although there were multiple outpourings of the Holy Spirit in not only North America but also globally, Pentecostalism received its greatest impetus from the Azusa Street revival of 1906-09 in Los Angeles, California.[13] William J. Seymour, an African American Holiness preacher from Texas, led the Azusa revival.[14] However, Pentecostalism soon spread beyond the Wesleyan-Holiness movement to practically every Protestant denomination in America. In time, Pentecostals formed new denominations.[15] These denominations include the Assemblies of God, the Church of God (Cleveland, TN), the Church of God in Christ, the Pentecostal Holiness Church, the Pentecostal Church of God, the International Church of the Foursquare Gospel, and others. Because of their teachings and expressive worship, Pentecostals were heavily criticized by other

Christian groups, especially the older Holiness and Fundamentalist churches—those most similar to them. Consequently, growth was slow until after World War II when unprecedented growth resulted from the impetus of divine healing and deliverance ministries of Oral Roberts, Tommy Hicks, Jack Coe, William Branham, and others. Modern media, especially television, though a "mixed blessing," seemed almost tailor made to Pentecostal presentation.[16] Pentecostalism began to spread widely at the popular level.[17]

A word needs said about Pentecostals' close association with Fundamentalists and Evangelicals. Fundamentalism arose as a reaction to liberalism and modernism, which espoused higher criticism of the biblical text and subsequent denials of cherished teachings of historical Christianity, and reached it height in America during the 1920s.[18] A rigorous, rigid movement, Fundamentalism heavily influenced early Pentecostalism simply because it presented itself as an alternative to liberalism's touted compromises.[19] However, Fundamentalists were dispensationalist cessationists, that is, they denied the continuing possibility and validity of the miraculous, including spiritual gifts or charismata, for the present age, setting them in diametric opposition to Pentecostals. Fundamentalists insisted Pentecostals were apostates. Eventually, that Pentecostals were not inherently Fundamentalists became increasingly clear. In fact, the more moderate elements within Fundamentalism finally moved away from what they perceived as a censorious and sectarian spirit to form what has become known as Evangelicalism. Pentecostals were accepted by and in turn embraced the Evangelical movement. Synan opines that the break with Fundamentalism "turned out to be a blessing that freed Pentecostals from the cultural and theological baggage of a discredited movement and opened up the way for unparalleled influence and growth".[20]

An example of an arguably negative impact of Fundamentalism and Evangelicalism, at least in a certain dogmatic reactionary form, might be visible in changing attitudes among Pentecostals toward Scripture, particularly in the understanding of inspiration. Warrington and others suggest that the inerrancy and infallibility issue so prominent and problematic in Fundamentalism and Evangelicalism was not an issue for early Pentecostals.[21] In fact, apparently Pentecostals did not sense a need to draw up a statement on these matters until they began close association with the NAE, and even then some reticent revisionism may have been occurring.[22] Although Pentecostals typically exhibit a high degree of respect for the inspiration and authority of Scripture, they also tend to exercise a high degree of personal application of the biblical text, a practical position that is not as rigid as that of Fundamentalists or even of many Evangelicals.[23] One might therefore not unreasonably inquire as to whether Pentecostals may have curtailed their own liberty for the sake of unity with those not entirely likeminded in such areas.

Basic Theological-Pneumatological Orientation of Classical Pentecostalism

Though doctrinally similar in several ways, the greater ecumenical openness and social involvement of Evangelicalism, contra Fundamentalism, more accurately characterizes the majority of contemporary Pentecostals.[24] However, neither are Evangelicalism and Pentecostalism necessarily synonymous. For example, the openness to spiritual experience and spiritual gifts of Pentecostals points to a pneumatological aspect not present in non-Pentecostal or non-Charismatic Evangelicals. Moreover, Evangelicalism as a whole tends to be more rationalistic and propositional than does Pentecostalism.[25] Harvard theologian and analyst of Pentecost Harvey Cox thus observes that many Pentecostals today are trying to restore their roots in original pre-Fundamentalist, and even to some extent pre-Evangelical, days.[26]

Certainly Hollenweger has argued that an almost fanatical form of fundamentalism has plagued the historical and theological development of Pentecostalism.[27] Nevertheless, he insists that a minority of Pentecostal leaders and thinkers have long been uncomfortable with the modern Fundamentalist movement. In fact, he is convinced that important early Pentecostal leaders and teachers such as Donald Gee of Britain and others were never comfortable with the Fundamentalist fit.[28] At least some Pentecostals instinctively identified fundamentalist rigidity as at odds with Pentecostal liberty.[29]

Throughout the present study, remembering that Pentecostalism is characterized by great variety resisting easy categorization will be helpful. Its multicultural and multinational beginnings and growth within many different cultures partly explains its variety. Pentecostal ecumenist and theologian Veli-Matti Kärkkäinen even suggests speaking of "Pentecostalisms", that is, in the plural, rather than of Pentecostalism in the singular. Nonetheless, he observes that a dynamic charismatic spirituality is at the center of the Pentecostal way of life. For Pentecostals, experiencing the presence of God in worship includes "an interesting mixture" of Spirit-inspired spontaneity, exercise of spiritual gifts such as speaking in tongues, prophesying, and prayer for healing, and "attentiveness to the mystical encounter with God."[30] In the power of the Holy Spirit, the focus is on Jesus Christ and God. Enthusiastic, expressive worship is the norm. Pentecostals emphasize the Holy Spirit's empowerment for witness and service, and Pentecostal worship emphasizes the supernatural element. For Pentecostals, unity is based more on shared experience than on doctrine.[31]

Pentecostals understand themselves first and foremost on the basis of their distinctive spirituality.[32] A look at their distinctive pneumatology, therefore, enlightens one as to the nature of the movement itself. Pentecostal identity runs counter to the modernist and rationalist denial of the supernatural, pointedly stressing the miraculous and paranormal. Pentecostalism specifically espouses what they call the "full gospel".[33] Five points comprise the full gospel. First is justification by faith in Christ. Second is sanctification by faith as a second definite work of grace. Third is healing of the body as provided for all in the atonement. Fourth is the premillennial return of Christ. Fifth is the baptism in the

Holy Spirit evidenced by speaking in tongues.[34] Sometimes Pentecostals stress their christological center by referring to this series as, "Jesus is savior, sanctifier, Spirit baptizer, healer, and soon coming king." Some Pentecostals of a less Wesleyan or more Baptistic orientation collapse sanctification and Spirit baptism into one and speak of a fourfold full gospel. In any case, Spirit baptism accompanied by speaking in tongues came to be the most distinctive motif. Some suggest adding the "prophethood" of all believers, or the belief that the Spirit forms the Church as a prophetic community capable of and called to speak under the Spirit's inspiration, as a sixth motif.[35] Arguably, however, one might assert that the prophethood of believers is a developmental extension of the doctrine and experience of Spirit baptism. Then again, others suggest that, generally, the orality of Pentecostal worship, its narrative nature, maximum level of participation for all members, inclusion of dreams and visions, and an experiential understanding of the mind/body relationship are most descriptive of Pentecostal spirituality and theology.[36] Again, arguably, one might assert that this last description of Pentecostal distinctiveness is largely and simply more of a focus on functions of Pentecostalism's spirituality and theology in corporate beliefs and practices.

Kärkkäinen admits that the universal applicability of the preceding categorizations may be open to question for some. However, for him these categories are not what are most important. What is "important to note is that Pentecostalism emphasizes lived charismatic spirituality rather than discursive theology."[37] At this point, Kärkkäinen appears to have put his finger on the core distinctiveness of the movement.[38] However, observing closely that he does not suggest Pentecostalism is unaware of the importance of doing "discursive theology", but that it *emphasizes* "lived charismatic experience" is significant. Indeed, Kärkkäinen's own vocation as a Pentecostal theologian flies in the face of easy assumptions about anti-intellectualism among Pentecostals. Rather, the crucial point is that Pentecostalism is dissatisfied with an intellectual faith bereft of spiritual fervor. On this score, Pentecostals often quote the Pauline saying concerning those who "having a form of godliness but denying its power" are to be avoided (2 Tim 3:5).[39]

Warrington apparently affirms this same avenue of thought regarding Pentecostal theological identity, and adds important implications for the practice of the life of faith.

> Pentecostals (traditionally) do not think theologically so much as live out their theology practically. Pentecostalism is not just distinctive because of its belief base but also because of the worldview it owns. The latter is based on a certainty that a religion that does not work is not worth much. Consequently, they look for expressions of life and vitality in their faith. The sense of the immediate, the God of the now, not the distant past, are characteristics that underlie how they do theology. Pentecostal theology tends to be seen through the eyes of people, not theologians; through the faith and worship of their community, not ancient or modern creeds.[40]

Warrington goes on to describe Pentecostal theology as "a theology of the dynamic, seen through the lens of experience", and as "a functional theology that exists to operate in life and to incorporate an experiential dimension."[41] He insists that "Pentecostal theology does not operate as other theologies", by which he means those that "only detail a list of beliefs"; rather, though it does do this and more, "it insists on exploring them in the context of praxis."[42] Interestingly, a Pentecostal approach to experience appears to have much in common with the cultural shift from modernist to postmodernist conceptual paradigms.[43]

Finally, Pentecostalism represents a revival movement with a strong restorationist element that tends to take a low view of history, institutions, and tradition. However, interaction with Charismatics (and, admittedly, increasing scholarship) is perhaps partly modifying that tendency.[44] Though interpreted variously, beyond reasonable doubt the distinctive experience and teaching of Pentecostal Christianity is Spirit baptism as distinct from and subsequent to conversion-initiation and accompanied by speaking in tongues. Spirit baptism accompanied by speaking in tongues is not peripheral but central to Pentecostal identity.[45] Classical Pentecostalism, therefore, is best understood as a conservative orthodox Christian movement with a pneumatological orientation resulting in strong emphases on fervent personal piety and expressive corporate worship in a context of the miraculous manifestation and experience of the divine presence.[46]

However, Warrington warns that although there certainly have been legitimate attempts to become more culturally relevant, some contemporary Pentecostals have largely become much more accommodating to culture and, for example, in the United States, identify closely with its economic and social values.[47] Consequently, they are "less radical and less restorationist" than they once were.[48] There are less taboos than there were once were too, and though Warrington admits that sometimes this has been a healthy development, there are occasions when a reluctance to critique popular behavior has been detrimental or destructive.[49] One wonders how much concession is possible before restorationism cools—including Pentecostalism's acclaimed fervency and piety.[50]

Worth remembering is that the Classical Pentecostal movement has within recent decades entered a new phase of maturation theologically through increased scholarship. Contemporary Pentecostal theology is challenging, developing, and extending itself in fresh ways.[51] The preoccupation of this study with a theology of interreligious encounter and dialogue is perhaps one example of fresh vistas that are unfolding. Also worth remembering, is that while Spirit baptism, speaking in tongues, and charismata are the central distinctives of Pentecostalism, other emphases are often included. For examples, Pentecostal systematic theologian Frank Macchia notes Pentecostal theologian Cheryl Johns' emphasis on Pentecostalism as a movement among the marginalized and the argument of some that Pentecostalism is a more or less grassroots interpretation of the gospel or popular form of non-academic theology.[52] He highlights its exceptionally and ardently biblical-based theology and its eschatological orientation, for example, in the thought of Pentecostal theologian Steven Land, with emphasis on a sanctified and empowered life in the light of the coming kingdom.[53] Macchia also mentions Cecil Robeck's insistence that Pentecostalism is really an ecumenical and multicultural movement and the cultural contextualization insights of Wonsuk Ma and Julie Ma.[54] Moreover, contemporary Pentecostals

Murray Dempster and Douglas Peterson draw attention to the profound social implications of Pentecostal belief and practice.[55] This mere sampling suggests there are many, many other important emphases as well. However, important to note is that the preceding emphases, or others like them, do not deny the centrality of Spirit baptism, glossolalia, or charismata, but rather exhibit differing ways of interpreting and applying these values. Perhaps the following representative words of Macchia are the best summation of the present state and future vision of Pentecostal theology.

> The gospel that stands at the center of this koinoniac and doxological context of theology for pentecostals is the "full gospel," which has not been occupied fundamentally by an idea but a (sic) by a person—Jesus. The living figure of Jesus as Savior, Sanctifier, Spirit baptizer, Healer, and Coming King is the core of pentecostal theological reflection, meaning that pentecostal theology, to be true to itself, would not be ideological or dogmatic but dialogical and humble, open to legitimate pluralism. At stake from such a center of concern is the ongoing validity of Jesus' experience of the Spirit for the expectations of the churches today with regard to Jesus' ministry among them and through them to the world. This is a promising point of departure for future reflection.[56]

Throughout the present study of constructing and developing a Pentecostal pneumatological theology of interreligious encounter and dialogue based on testimony, one should keep in mind the preceding frame of reference. The historical-terminological and theological-pneumatological background and basis of Classical Pentecostalism is fundamentally important for establishing and extending its central thrust.

Beginning Sociological-Doctrinal Analysis of Classical Pentecostalism

Alternative versions of Pentecostalism are available. Robert Mapes Anderson, in *Vision of the Disinherited: the Making of American Pentecostalism*, began one of the first and most thorough analyses of Pentecostalism incorporating insights from social sciences, including economic and political factors. Anderson claims Pentecostalism is "a specific form of a general class of ecstatic religions" and "of a general class of millenarian movements" (at least initially), "each of which classes includes a very wide spectrum of Christian and non-Christian religions", having both "similarities and dissimilarities" with these.[57] He argues for Pentecostalism's close connections with parts of Fundamentalism but admits contradictory confluences.[58] More so, Anderson suggests there is a mystical, ecstatic, orgiastic element in Christianity and other religions with a pneumatic basis that Pentecostalism exemplifies, including first century Judaism and Gentile religions their environment.[59] He notes that early Pentecostals were often critical of what they considered cold, dead forms of Christianity, including both Protestants and Roman Catholics, as well as of cults and the occult.[60] Perhaps surprisingly, they were more usually tolerant of Jews, who were considered non-Christians but not anti-Christian as some other religions were.[61] Significantly, Anderson suggests Pentecostal aggression against other religions (mostly other

Christian denominations) may have been due to unvoiced political and economical grievances, and says that with increasing prosperity came increasing tolerance.[62] In fact, Anderson rooted the rising popularity of Pentecostalism primarily in class struggles in ways very much indebted to social deprivation theory.[63]

Subsequently, however, as historian of the Holiness and Pentecostal movements Randall J. Stephens has pointed out, several scholars, while acknowledging Anderson's contributions, have concluded that he overdid his emphasis on economic and political factors and inordinately downplayed the importance of doctrinal and theological issues.[64] Arguably, understanding Classical Pentecostalism is much more than a sociological study of history, though this is also an important component. Therefore, Pentecostalism is only accurately understood on its own terms, that is, as a religious movement with clear doctrinal and theological origins and developments, especially regarding experiential pneumatology. Yet, as will become apparent in later chapters in this work, the traditional and developing social status and insights of Pentecostalism is a factor in its interreligious engagement. Accordingly, remembering that Pentecostal praxis is to an extent affected by sociological, including economical and political, factors, along with its spirituality and theology, may be conducive to understanding.[65]

Additionally, Shepperd has analyzed Pentecostalism sociologically according to contributions of modernization and secularization, relative deprivation, symbolic interaction theory, and globalization.[66] Apparently, each of these theories provides some answers but do not alone appear to offer satisfactory solutions for interpreting the historical origins and sociological structures of Pentecostalism.[67] Pentecostalism defies but exemplifies the overall complexity of these constructs. For example, Shepperd complains that deprivation theory relies too heavily on unsubstantiated stereotypes of Pentecostals, and argues for "a combination religious interpretation and dynamic social-movement theory."[68] He suggests that when "the focus is on the religious experience rather than the social origins of [Pentecostalism's] adherents," a theory such as "relative deprivation loses much of its power."[69] Also difficult is determining precisely when Pentecostalism is being influenced by or influencing developing factors, such as, for example, globalization.[70]

Notes

1. H. V. Synan, "Classical Pentecostalism," *NIDPCM* (Grand Rapids: Zondervan, 2002), 553-55.

2. J.R. Goff, Jr., *Fields White Unto Harvest: Charles F. Parham and the Missionary Origins of Pentecostalism* (Fayetteville: University of Arkansas, 1988), argues that a chief distinguishing characteristic between Pentecostalism and the Charismatic movement is the latter's lack of emphasis on tongues as initial evidence. For him, both movements are distinguishable parts of a broader "Pneumatic, or Spirit, age" arising in the late nineteenth century, 4-5. Cf. also to Goff, 164-65.

3. Synan, "Classical," 553.

4. Synan, "Classical," 553.

5. Synan, "Classical," 553-55 (553). Interestingly, M.S. Clark, "Pentecostalism's Anabaptist Roots: Hermeneutical Implications," *The Spirit and Spirituality: Essays in*

Honor of Russell P. Spittler, ed. W. Ma and R.P. Menzies (New York: T & T Clark, 2004), 194-211, investigates an alternative and radical influence on Pentecostalism that may further inform its self-understanding and ecumenical relations, "a remarkable omission" persistent in studies of the movement (194). Cf. esp. 210-11.

6. E.L. Blumhofer, *Restoring the Faith* (Urbana and Chicago: University of Illinois Press, 1993), admits "Pentecostalism comes in a bewildering variety of forms, each marked by tremendous internal diversity" (1).

7. P.L. King, *Genuine Gold: The Cautiously Charismatic History of the Early Christian and Missionary Alliance* (Tulsa: Word & Spirit, 2006).

8. King, *Gold,* 283-96. In general, early Alliance leadership struggled to be open but balanced regarding the Pentecostal movement and its charismatic manifestations. Cf. 265-74.

9. K. Warrington, *Pentecostal Theology: A Theology of Encounter* (New York: T & T Clark, 2008), 84-95 and 119-23. M.R. Hathaway, in "The Elim Pentecostal Church: Origins, Development and Distinctives," in *Pentecostal Perspectives*, ed. K. Warrington (Carlisle: Paternoster, 1998), shows how a leading Pentecostal denomination in the United Kingdom struggled with the doctrine of initial evidence even in the early days of the movement, and finally adopted a mediating position, 1-39 (36). However, in the same volume, speaking of the overall movement and not the Elim group only, D. Petts argues that belief in Spirit baptism as an experience subsequent to and distinct from regeneration and that it is accompanied by tongues is hermeneutically and exegetically defensible. See "The Baptism in the Holy Spirit: The Theological Distinctive," 98-119 (101-15). However, in a sensitive section on "Pastoral Guidelines," Petts suggests some may receive Spirit baptism without manifesting the evidence of tongues, possibly due to some deficiency of understanding or desire, but that this is not an adequate basis for denying either the authenticity of their experience or of the doctrine of initial evidence, 115-19 (116-17). Obviously, unanimity on initial evidence even among Pentecostals does not exist. Important to remember, especially for non-Pentecostals seeking to understand Pentecostalism, is that their "in house" debate over tongues is an effort to articulate the way tongues work and not whether they could or should in fact work today. On that, Pentecostals indeed appear unanimously affirmative.

10. Warrington, *Encounter,* 17-27. T.L. Cross, *Answering the Call in the Spirit: Pentecostal Reflections on a Theology of Vocation, Work and Life* (Cleveland: Lee University Press, 2007), explains that Pentecostal experiences of encountering God's presence and power in the Spirit include expectations of personal and moral transformation, 14-16. Accordingly, Pentecostal theology and spirituality resolutely require "radical openness" to God and to God's presence and power (14, 107).

11. Warrington, *Encounter,* 130. Blumhoffer agrees that there is diversity of opinion among Pentecostals regarding glossolalia, adding that "two suppositions" undergird the movement: the gifts of the Spirit should operate today, and there is a distinct baptism in the Holy Spirit, *Restoring,* 1-2.

12. In a somewhat different vein, Goff, *Fields,* proposes both that Parham is the legitimate founder of Pentecostalism and that "the essential character of this new faith revolved around an intense millenarian-missions emphasis" (15). This claim is consistent with Goff's conclusion that Parham uniquely impacted the early formation of the movement, and that one of the key features of that impact was an ardent emphasis on evangelistic mission with eschatological underpinnings, 164-65.

13. Pentecostal professor of religious studies S.M. Burgess points out that Pentecostalism is part of a continuing stream of Christian traditions throughout Church history accenting ecstatic experience. See his "The Pentecostal Tradition," *CHB* 58:17:2 (1998),

40-41. G. Strachen argues in *The Pentecostal Theology of Edward Erving* (Peabody: Hendrickson, 1973, 1988) that, though certainly not exact parallels theologically, many consider the controversial 1830s British pastor and theologian and his congregation as early precedents for later Pentecostal approaches to pneumatology and charismata.

14. In their "Introduction" Goff and Wacker, J.R. Goff, Jr. and G. Wacker, eds., *Portraits of a Generation: Early Pentecostal Leaders* (Fayetteville: University of Arkansas, 2002), xi-xviii, note that one of the idiosyncratic features of early Pentecostalism was its adamant denial of the role of human leadership, xv-xviii. For them, "The Holy Ghost ran everything" (xv). Thus, powerful personalities who might have been considered by outsider observers as founders/cofounders of the movement, such as itinerant Holiness preacher and teacher Charles Fox Parham, African American pastor William J. Seymour, or flaming female evangelist Aimee Semple McPherson, were only agents of the Spirit in the eyes Pentecostals (xvi). Nevertheless, Goff and Wacker think "we dare not take Pentecostals solely at their word" (xvii). I.e., leaders did play an important part in the movement, and these leaders included both clergy and laity, and both male and female, of varying levels of influence, xvii-xviii.

15. Synan, "Classical," 554.

16. Synan, "Classical," 554. Cf. D.J. Hedges, "Television," *NIDPCM,* 1118-20.

17. G. Wacker, *Heaven Below: Early Pentecostals and American Culture* (Cambridge: Harvard University Press, 2001), argues that Pentecostalism has uniquely harnessed and exhibited dual emphases of primitivism (idealism, restorationism, otherworldliness) and pragmatism (practicality, adaptability, this worldliness), 10-14. Cf. 266. Wacker even goes so far as to say that Pentecostals thus instinctively transcended one of the most difficult and longstanding hurdles in historic Christianity: how to relate the natural and the supernatural in everyday faith and life, 268-69. He calls this "the 'Mary and Martha' problem" or simultaneously negotiating spiritual and material wellbeing (268).

18. See V. Synan, "Fundamentalism," *NIDPCM,* 655-58.

19. Synan, "Fundamentalism," 655-58.

20. Synan, "Fundamentalism," 655-58 (58). Cf. V. Synan, "Evangelicalism," *NIDPCM,* 613-16.

21. Warrington, *Encounter,* 182. Cf. W. Kay, "Do Doctrinal Boundaries Protect Our Identity or Prevent Fellowship," *EPTA Bulletin* 12 (1993), 38-41, and S. Ellington, "Pentecostals and the Authority of Scripture," *JPT* 9 (1996), 16-38.

22. Warrington, *Encounter,* 182-84.

23. Warrington, *Encounter,* 188-91. Wacker, *Heaven Below,* suggests Pentecostalism is perhaps best understood as an outgrowth of a tradition of particularly radical forms of evangelicalism, 1-6.

24. Synan, "Evangelicalism," 613-16.

25. Synan, "Evangelicalism," 613-16.

26. H. Cox, *Fire From Heaven: The Rise of Pentecostal Spirituality and the Reshaping of Religion in the Twenty-First Century* (New York: Addison-Wesley, 1995), 74-76.

27. See W.J. Hollenweger, *The Pentecostals* (London: SCM, 1972/Peabody: Hendrickson, 1988), 291-310.

28. Hollenweger, *Pentecostals,* 297.

29. Hollenweger, *Pentecostals,* 298-99.

30. V.M. Kärkkäinen, *Pneumatology: The Holy Spirit in Ecumenical, International, and Contextual Perspective* (Grand Rapids: Baker, 2002), 87-98 (89-92). However, M.W. Mittelstadt, *The Spirit and Suffering in Luke-Acts: Implications for a Pentecostal Pneumatology* (London and New York: T & T Clark, 2004), illuminates a tension between divine empowering and the neglected element of the work of the Spirit in contexts of

opposition defying and debunking earlier pneumatological oversimplification by or about Pentecostals. Accordingly, Jesus not only lives and ministers in the power of the Holy Spirit, but he also experiences opposition and persecution as a man of the Spirit. And he transfers the Spirit to his disciples in anticipation of a similar fate for his followers. The Lukan material forecasts that this divine enablement of the Spirit also available for future witnesses brings with it a similar anticipation of the same rejection and opposition as experienced by Jesus and his earliest disciples.

31. Kärkkäinen, *Pneumatology*, 87-98.
32. Kärkkäinen, *Pneumatology*, 92-93.
33. Kärkkäinen, *Pneumatology*, 92-93.
34. Kärkkäinen, *Pneumatology*, 92-93. Works such as S. Solivan, *The Spirit, Pathos and Liberation: Toward an Hispanic Pentecostal Theology*, JSup 14 (Sheffield: Sheffield Academic Press, 1998) and Cross, *Answering*, suggest some contemporary Pentecostal theologians are thinking about creatively fresh ways of appropriating their heritage of a pneumatological hermeneutic.
35. Kärkkäinen, *Pneumatology*, 93.
36. Kärkkäinen, *Pneumatology*, 93-94. Additionally, E. Villafañe, *The Liberating Spirit: Toward an Hispanic American Pentecostal Social Ethic* (Grand Rapids: Eerdmans, 1993), demonstrates that Pentecostalism, including its distinctive charismatic and pneumatological thought and experience, is clearly capable of decisive social development and application.
37. Kärkkäinen, *Pneumatology*, 94.
38. A look at M. Wilkinson's "When is a Pentecostal a Pentecostal? The Global Perspective of Allan Anderson," *Pneuma* 28:2 (Fall 2006), 278-82, demonstrates something of the complexity of determining Pentecostal identity. Wilkinson admits that the precise nature of Pentecostal and Charismatic Christianity is "hotly debated" (278). Thus, he commends an approach that "attempts to understand the diversity of forms and expression of the movement" (278). For him, of key importance is giving adequate attention to both local and global dynamics, 278-79. Pentecostalism's "identity, origins, and boundaries" are difficult to pin down with precision but may be best attempted through a perspective that is "historical, inclusive, and crosscultural" in its vision (282). Of course, there are those, e.g., John F. MacArthur, Jr., *Charismatic Chaos* (Grand Rapids: Zondervan, 1992), who simply sees Pentecostals and Charismatics as examples of seriously aberrational Christianity due to their interest in spiritual experience.
39. Cf. C.W. Conn, *Like a Mighty Army: A History of the Church of God: Definitive Edition* (Cleveland: Pathway, 1996), xxv-xxix.
40. Warrington, *Encounter*, 16. Of course, Warrington is being consistent with his conviction, previously noted above, that Pentecostalism is essentially about actually encountering God in the context of lived life. See Warrington, 20-27.
41. Warrington, *Encounter*, 16. Contemporary Pentecostal theologian T.L. Cross, "The Divine-Human Encounter: Towards a Pentecostal Theology of Experience," *Pneuma* 31:1 (Spring 2009), 3-34, is not unaware of special challenges that spiritual experience presents the modern mind. Cross forthrightly confronts contemporary psychological and philosophical concerns, arguing for a careful theological explication of healthy religious experience, 3-8. For Cross, this explication is not an articulation of a different theology beginning altogether anew with the advent of Pentecostalism so much as it is a cultivation of the experiential dimension in biblical and historic Christian theology as a whole, 8-10. He convincingly contends that a Pentecostal theology of experience can contribute much to the traditional categories of classic Christian theology—and that these in their turn can helpfully inform Pentecostal faith and life, 8-34.

42. Warrington, *Encounter*, 16. Garnet Parris, Director of the Centre for Black Theology at Birmingham University, England, describes Pentecostal spirituality as emphasizing a piety of divine immanence penetrating and permeating all of life with "the personal and direct awareness of and experiencing of the Holy Spirit" as being especially critical. The significance of experiencing the Holy Spirit includes the centrality of the Spirit's charismatic gifts and the presence and power of the Holy Spirit. Parris focuses on Spirit baptism and speaking in tongues for the empowerment of individuals for the edification of the whole church in a context of the priority of worship. See Parris, "Pentecostal Spirituality," *NWDCS*, ed. P. Sheldrake (Louisville, KY: Westminster John Knox Press, 2005), 485-86.

43. E.g., Cross claims his heritage of Pentecostalism and his developing postmodernism have proven to be mutually informative and supportive, "Divine-Human Encounter," 31-32.

44. Kärkkäinen, *Pneumatology*, 94-95.

45. Kärkkäinen, *Pneumatology*, 95-98. See G.B. McGee, ed., *Initial Evidence: Historical and Biblical Perspectives on the Pentecostal Doctrine of Spirit Baptism* (Peabody, MA: Hendrickson, 1191). Cf. W.W. and R. Menzies, *Spirit and Power: Foundations of Pentecostal Experience* (Grand Rapids: Zondervan, 2000). Also, see R.P. Spittler, "The Pentecostal View," *Christian Spirituality: Five Views of Sanctification*, ed. D.L. Alexander (Downer's Grove, IL: InterVarsity Press, 1988), 133-54, S.M. Horton, "The Pentecostal Perspective," *Five Views on Sanctification*, M.E. Dieter, S.M. Horton, et al (Grand Rapids; Zondervan, 1987), 105-135, and Horton, "Spirit Baptism: A Pentecostal Perspective," *Perspectives on Spirit Baptism; Five Views*, ed. C.O. Brand (Nashville: Broadman & Holman, 2004), 47-94.

46. Admittedly, a comparatively small wing of Pentecostals is "unorthodox" by creedal standards because of their rejection of the traditional doctrine of the Trinity. See D.A. Reed, "Oneness Pentecostalism," *NIDPCM*, 936-44.

47. Warrington, *Encounter*, 211-12. Goff, "Thomas Hampton Gourley: Defining the Boundaries," Goff and Wacker, *Portraits*, speculates that Pentecostals struggled with an "innate inferiority complex" due to humble social origins leading to "reverse conceit" in their movement's growth outstripping others more "socially prominent and powerful"; in effect, this turned "social outcasts into a spiritual elite" but conversely fueled an inordinate desire for social respectability, 143-44 (143).

48. Warrington, *Encounter*, 213. Along this line, M. Crews, *The Church of God: A Social History* (Knoxville: University of Tennessee, 1990), argues that the historical development of one of the most conservative and radical of the Classical Pentecostal denominations displays a gradual but consistent movement into mainstream Evangelicalism and North American mores, 172, 175-76. However, he concedes that the denomination began out of a strong a populist impulse with a moderate countercultural identity, 1-18. Furthermore, though Crews concurs on the unique importance of glossolalia as a distinctive trademark of the Church of God, 174, he also contends for its egalitarian nature, 11, 14, pacifist character, especially early on, 108-37, and on the supreme importance of its literalist biblical hermeneutic, 174.

49. Warrington, *Encounter*, 213-14. Cf. Blumhofer, *Restoring*, 6-9, who suggests this is a major issue for the largest of all the Classical Pentecostal denominations, the Assemblies of God. That makes difficult a dual task of simultaneously "conserving and expanding", 264-74.

50. Cf. Blumhofer, *Restoring*, 4-5.

51. See J.C. Thomas, 1998 Presidential Address, "Pentecostal Theology in the Twenty-First Century," *Pneuma* 20 (Spring 1998), 3-19.

52. F.D. Macchia, "Theology, Pentecostal," *NIDPCM,* 1120-40 (1121). Cf. C.B. Johns, *Pentecostal Formation: A Pedagogy among the Oppressed* JPTSup 2 (Sheffield, England: Sheffield Academic Press, 1993, 1998).
53. Macchia, "Theology," 1122. Cf. S.J. Land, *Pentecostal Spirituality: A Passion for the Kingdom* JPTSup 1 (Sheffield: Sheffield Academic Press, 1993).
54. Macchia, "Theology," 1125. Cf. C.M. Robeck, Jr. "Taking Stock of Pentecostalism: The Personal Reflections of a Retiring Editor," *Pneuma,* 15:1 (Spring 1993), 35-60. Also cf. W. Ma and R.P. Menzies, *Pentecostalism in Context: Essays in Honor of William W. Menzies* JPTSup 11 (Sheffield: Sheffield Academic Press, 1997).
55. Macchia, "Theology," 1139. Cf. M.A. Dempster, B.D. Klaus, D. Petersen, eds. *Called and Empowered: Global Mission in Pentecostal Perspective* (Grand Rapids: Hendrickson, 1991).
56. Macchia, "Theology,"1140.
57. R.M. Anderson, *Vision of the Disinherited: the Making of American Pentecostalism* (New York: Oxford University, 1979), 4. Goff, *Fields,* suggests Anderson's approach is indebted to Marxist methodology and, while helpful in raising important complex questions, too simplistic, 9-10. He also suggests Anderson's thesis fails to take into adequate account theological and sociological diversity within Pentecostalism, thus allowing important themes to become misplaced or missed altogether, 10-13, 15-16.
58. Anderson, *Vision,* 5-6.
59. Anderson, *Vision,* 10-12, 21-22.
60. Anderson, *Vision,* 212-18,
61. Anderson, *Vision,* 218-20.
62. Anderson, *Vision,* 220-22. Cf. Goff, 8-9. However, several studies indicate a variety of social, racial, economic, and, of course, religious factors in the rise and spread of Pentecostalism. E.g., see J.T. Nichol, *The Pentecostals* (New York: Harper & Row, 1966, repr. 1971), K. Poewe, ed., *Charismatic Christianity as a Global Culture* (Columbia: University of South Carolina, 1994), and A. Cerillo, Jr. "Interpretative Approaches to the History of American Pentecostal Origins," *Pneuma* 19:1 (1997), 29-52.
63. Anderson, *Vision,* 108, 136. For sociologists like C.Y. Glock and H. Ellinson, religion served as an escape mechanism for the deprived and was unable actually to alter social status. See Glock, "The Role of Deprivation in the Origin and Evolution of Religious Groups," in *Religion and Social Conflict,* R. Lee and M.E. Marty eds. (New York: Oxford University Press, 1964), 27, 29. Also see, H. Elinson, "The Implications of Pentecostal Religion for Intellectualism, Politics, and Race Relations," *AJS* 70 (1965): 403-415. For a counter view, see, H.G. Lefever, "Religion of the Poor: Escape or Creative Force?" *JSSR* 16:3 (September 1977), 525-534.
64. R.J. Stephens, "Assessing the Roots of Pentecostalism: A Historiographic Essay," at American Religious Experience, http://are.as.wvu.edu/pentroot.htm (n.d.; site last modified October 2007). See also his *The Fire Spreads: Holiness and Pentecostalism in the American South* (Boston: Harvard University Press, 2007).
65. N.O. Hatch, *The Democratization of American Christianity* (New Haven: Yale, 1989), argues that Pentecostalism's success in the United States is in part due to its instinctive and convictive populist impulse in a culture deeply shaped historically and politically by a democratization aspiration. See 208, 212, and 214-19.
66. J.W. Shepperd, "Sociology of World Pentecostalism," *NIDPCM,* 1083-90 (84-89). L. Guy, Introducing Early Christianity: A Topical Survey of Its Life, Beliefs & Practices (Downer's Grove: InterVarsity Press, 2004), suggests yet another possible distinction between Pentecostalism and other forms of Christianity: ecclesiastical authority, 41. Guy notes that church history has drawn up three main responses to the issue of church

authority: the Church, Scripture, and the guidance of the Spirit. Roman Catholicism represents the first response, Protestantism the second, and Pentecostalism the third, 41. According to Guy, Ignatius, set an early precedent for placing authority primarily in the bishop, and thus in the Church, as the ecclesial authority in spite of his serious consideration of Scripture and stated dependence on the demonstration of the Spirit, 41-43. Thus, ecclesiology might be an especially interesting point of comparison for Pentecostalism and other forms of Christianity. Cf. W. Vondey, People of Bread: Rediscovering Ecclesiology (Mahwah, NJ: Paulist Press, 2008). Incidentally, Guy approaches this topic in a context of an increasing de-charismatization of the Early Church and its concomitant progressive institutionalization, 87-90. A Pentecostal might therefore argue for a charismatic Church and ministry as more faithful to the primitive Church.

67. Although too far afield for the present investigation, indeed extensive research exists indicating that deep and profound sociological (e.g., G. Lenski, *The Religious Factor; A Sociologist's Inquiry* (New York: Anchor, 1963) and P.L. Berger, *The Sacred Canopy: Elements of a Sociological Theory of Religion* (New York: Anchor, 1969, 1990), psychological (e.g., C.G. Jung, *Modern Man in Search of a Soul* (New York: Harcourt, 1933), and, yes, spiritual (e.g., M. Kelsey, *Discernment: A Study in Ecstasy and Evil* (New York: Paulist, 1978) and W. Proudfoot, *Religious Experience* (Los Angeles: University of California, 1985), factors may be contributing to dramatic developments such as, for instance, the rise and spread of the Pentecostal and Charismatic movements.

68. Shepperd, "Sociology," 1085.

69. Shepperd, "Sociology," 1086.

70. Shepperd, "Sociology," 1088. An interesting integrative study edited by J.D. Photiadis, *Religion in Appalachia: Theological, Social, and Psychological Dimensions and Correlates*, (Morgantown, WV: University of West Virginia, 1977), adds suggestive insights. Photiadis, in "A Theoretical Supplement," 7-27, suggests that in anxiety-ridden cultures, such as isolated and impoverished areas of Appalachia, charismatic and spiritual renewal movements offer relief (and release) through "the joy of being touched" (by the divine that is), and that the presence or absence of "anxiety reducing mechanisms" may be expected to influence the rise or fall of such movements (26-27). However, M.O. Meitzen, "The Background and Content of Twentieth Century American Theology and Religious Experience," 33-64, argues that charismatic movements, which he admits have "a great deal of influence on the American people", "reflect the long-time suppression of the Holy Spirit by main line churches", and therefore transcend denominational boundaries, including even Protestant and Roman Catholic groups (63-64). T.D. Abell, "The Holiness-Pentecostal Experience in Southern Appalachia," 79-101, who lived and worshiped among Appalachian Pentecostals for a year, found nothing "suggesting psychological deprivation on the part of persons who speak in tongues" (101). He added that "a social deprivation conclusion is possible" based on "situational variables" (101). Although recognizing the feasibility of an alternative conclusion, he nevertheless concluded, "that much of Holiness-Pentecostal membership, ideology, and behavior is due to socialization" (101). However, he frankly admitted this amounted to little more than observing that "Children everywhere learn how to perceive, behave, and value in accordance with their cultural setting" (101). N.L. Gerrard, "Churches of the Stationary Poor in Southern Appalachia," 271-84, suggests that abject, unalleviated, and inescapable poverty can lead to religious emphases, and perhaps excesses, of fundamentalism, otherworldliness, and perfectionism that may be expressed in terms of ecstatic behavior interpreted as the control of the Holy Spirit and including glossolalia and similar phenomena, 277-80. For him, such churches are "viable" because they "alleviate anxieties generated by status deprivation, guilt, illness," and also, "supply recreation ...where recreational

facilities are scarce" (281). However, L. Jones, "Mountain Religion: The Outsider's View," 401-07, roundly criticizes Gerrard for failing to appreciate the viability of religious beliefs and spiritual practices shared by the Pentecostal Holiness Church with many religious groups in other regions, and which are therefore not only a part of a pattern of regional poverty (402-03). He adds: "Now it is quite likely that the churches do serve the needs Gerrard lists, but it is strange that he did not also list something having to do with the spiritual needs of the people, beyond normal guilt and anxieties about life and morality that all of humankind feel. It is common for intellectual observers of all kinds to talk of religion only in clinical terms" (403). Of course, the Appalachian connection becomes of special concern when it is remembered that the region played a significant role in the early development of certain branches of Pentecostalism. E.g., see Conn, *Army*, 6, 8, 60, 75, 84, 132, and 535.

Bibliography

Abell, T.D. "The Holiness-Pentecostal Experience in Southern Appalachia," J.D. Photiadis, ed. *Religion in Appalachia: Theological, Social, and Psychological Dimensions and Correlates*, (Morgantown, WV: University of West Virginia, approx. 1977), 79-101.

_____. *Better Felt Than Said: The Holiness-Pentecostal Experience in Southern Appalachia* (Waco, TX: Baylor University Press, 1982).

Accad, F.E. *Building Bridges: Christianity and Islam* (Colorado Springs, Colorado: NavPress, 1997).

Adams, A. "*Bricando el Charco*/Jumping the Puddle: A Case Study of Pentecostalism's Journey from Puerto Rico to New York to Allentown, Pennsylvania," Cleary, E.L. and H. Stewart, ed. *Power, Politics, and Pentecostals in Latin America* (Boulder, Colorado: Westview, 1996), 163-78.

Adams, J.W. "Hebrews," F.L. and R. Stronstad, eds. *FLBCNT*, (Grand Rapids: Zondervan, 1999), 1295-1399.

Adler, A. *Understanding Human Nature: The Psychology of Personality* (Center City, Montana: Hazeldon, 1998 repr).

Aikman, D. *Jesus in Beijing: How Christianity is Transforming China and Changing the Global Balance of Power* (Washington, DC: Regenery, 2003).

Aker, B. "John," Arrington, F.L. and R. Stronstad, eds. *FLBCNT*, (Grand Rapids: Zondervan, 1999), 1-118.

Albright, M. *The Mighty & the Almighty: Reflections on America, God, and World Affairs* (New York: Harper, 2006).

Alexander, D.L. ed. *Christian Spirituality; Five Views of Sanctification* (Downer's Grove: InterVarsity Press, 1988).

_____. R.P. Spittler, "The Pentecostal View," 133-54.

Alexander, K.E. *Pentecostal Healing: Models in Theology and Practice* Journal of Pentecostal Theology Supplement Series (DEO, 2006).

Alexander, P. *Signs & Wonders: Why Pentecostalism is the World's Fastest Growing Faith* (San Francisco: Jossey-Bass, 2009).
_____. *Peace to War: Shifting Allegiances in the Assemblies of God* (Telford, PA: Cascadia, 2009).
Alford, D. "Music, Pentecostal and Charismatic," *NIDPCM,* 911-20.
Al-Sammak, M. "The Culture of Dialogue in Islam; Freedom of Choice and the Right to Differ," *CD* 48 (December 2006), 20-25.
Althouse, P. *The Spirit of the Last Days: Pentecostal Eschatology in Conversation with Jürgen Moltmann* (London and New York: T & T Clark, 2003).
Alvarsson, J.A. "Traditional AmerIndian Religion: In the Eyes of an Indigenous Pentecostal Church," 277-94, D. Westerlund, ed., *Global Pentecostalism: Encounters with Other Religious Traditions* (New York: I. B. Tauris, 2009).
Anderson, A. *An Introduction to Pentecostalism: Global Charismatic Christianity* (Cambridge: Cambridge University Press, 2004).
_____. with W.J. Hollenweger, editors, *Pentecostals after a Century: Global Perspectives on a Movement in Transition,* JSup Series 15 (Sheffield, England: Sheffield Academic Press, 1999).
_____. *Spreading Fires: The Missionary Nature of Early Pentecostalism* (New York: Orbis, 2007).
_____. "Pentecostalism in India and China in the Early Twentieth Century and Inter-Religious Relations," 117-36, D. Westerlund, ed., *Global Pentecostalism: Encounters with Other Religious Traditions* (New York: I. B. Tauris, 2009).
Anderson, N. *The Mystery of the Incarnation* (London: Hodder & Stoughton, 1978).
_____. *Christianity and World Religions: The Challenge of Pluralism* (Downer's Grove, IL: InterVarsity Press, 1970, rev. ed., 1984).
Anderson, N.D. *A Definitive Study of Evidence Concerning John Wesley's Appropriation of the Thought of Clement of Alexandria* (Lampeter, Ceredigion, Wales: Edwin Mellen, 2004).
Anderson, R.M. *Vision of the Disinherited: the Making of American Pentecostalism* (New York: Oxford University, 1979).
Apprill, E.D. "The New Pentecostal Networks of Brazzaville," A. Corten and R.R. Marshall-Fratani, eds. *Between Babel and Pentecost: Transnational Pentecostalism in Africa and Latin America* (Bloomington, Indiana: Indiana Univesity Press, 2001), 293-308.
Archer, K.J. "Pentecostal Story: the Hermeneutical Filter for Producing Meaning," *JPT* 26:1 (2004), 36-59.
_____. *Pentecostal Hermeneutics: Spirit, Scripture, and Community* (Cleveland, TN: CPT, 2009)
Arinze, R. *Religions for Peace: A Call for Solidarity to the Religions of the World* (New York: Random House, 2002).
Arrington, F.L. *The Acts of the Apostles: Introduction, Translation, and Commentary* (Peabody: Hendrickson, 1988).
_____. *Christian Doctrine: A Pentecostal Perspective: Volume One, Two, Three* (Cleveland: Pathway, 1993).

_____. "Luke," Arrington, F.L. and R. Stronstad, eds. *FLBCNT*, (Grand Rapids: Zondervan, 1999), 375-534.

_____. "The Acts of the Apostles," F.L. and R. Stronstad, eds. *FLBCNT*, (Grand Rapids: Zondervan, 1999), 535-692.

_____. *Encountering the Holy Spirit: Paths of Christian Growth and Service* (Cleveland: Pathway, 2003).

Asani, A.S. "So That You May Know One Another," *Annals*, AAPSS 58 (July 2003), 40-51.

Austin-Broos, D.J. "Jamaican Pentecostalism: Transnational Relations and the Nation-State," A. Corten and R.R. Marshall-Fratani, eds. *Between Babel and Pentecost: Transnational Pentecostalism in Africa and Latin America* (Bloomington, IN: Indiana University Press, 2001), 142-62.

Ayers, E.L. and B.C. Mittendorf, eds., *The Oxford Book of the American South: Testimony, Memory, and Fiction*, (New York/Oxford: Oxford University Press, 1997).

Bailey, R. "Telling Your Faith Story," *COGE*, 99:9 (September 2009), 20.

Balmer, R. and Lauren F. Winner, *Protestantism in America* (New York: Columbia University Press, 2002).

Bandow, D. *Beyond Good Intentions: A Biblical View of Politics* (Wheaton, ILL: Crossway, 1988).

Barnes, D.C. "Is There a Difference?" *COGE*, (August 12, 1944), 6-7.

Barnes, M. "Spirituality and the Dialogue of Religions," *NWDCS*, 32-37.

Bartleman, *Azusa Street* (originally *Another Wave Rolls In*) (New Kensington, PA: Whitaker, 1982).

Bastian, J-P. "Pentecostalism, Market Logic and Religious Transnationalisation in Costa Rica," A. Corten and R.R. Marshall-Fratani, eds. *Between Babel and Pentecost: Transnational Pentecostalism in Africa and Latin America* (Bloomington, IN: Indiana University Press, 2001), 163-80.

Bauckham, R. *The Theology of Jürgen Moltmann* (Edinburgh: T & T Clark, 1996).

_____. *Jesus and the Eyewitnesses: The Gospels as Eyewitness Testimony* (Grand Rapids: Eerdmans, 2006).

Beaman, J. *Pentecostal Pacifism: The Origin, Development, and Rejection of Pacific Belief among the Pentecostals* (Hillsboro, Kansas: Center for Mennonite Brethren Studies, 1989).

Bendix, R. *Max Weber: An Intellectual Portrait* (New York: Doubleday, 1960, 1962).

Berger, P.L. *The Sacred Canopy: Elements of a Sociological Theory of Religion* (New York: Anchor, 1969, 1990).

Bergunder, M. *The South Indian Pentecostal Movement in the Twentieth Century*, Studies in the History of Christian Missions (Grand Rapids: Eerdman, 2008).

Berthrong, J.H. *The Divine Deli: Religious Identity in the North American Cultural Mosaic* (Orbis: NY, 1999).

Biallas, L.J. "Dogmatic Theology," Musser, D.W. and J.L. Price, eds. *NHCT* (Nashville: Abingdon, 1992), 127-30.

Bigner, J. and R. Steitmatter, *From "Perverts" to "Fab Five": The Media's Changing Depiction of Gay Men and Lesbians* (New York: Taylor & Francis, 2009).
Black, A.E. *Beyond Left and Right: Helping Christians Make Sense of American Politics* (Grand Rapids: Baker, 2008).
Blackaby, H. *Chosen to be God's Prophet: Lessons from the Life of Samuel* (Nashville: Nelson, 2003).
Blair, T. (about), "Blair Faith Foundation launches in New York," by staff writers of *Ekklesia* (30 May 2008), http://www.ekklesia.co.uk/node/7235.
_____. "Yale and Tony Blair Launch Faith and Globalization Initiative" (September 18, 2008), http://opa.yale.edu/news/article.aspx?id=6040.
Blaising, C.A. and D.L. Bock, *Dispensationalism, Israel and the Church: The Search for Definition* (Grand Rapids, MI: Zondervan, 1992).
_____. *Progressive Dispensationalism* (Grand Rapids, MI: Baker, 1993).
Blumhoffer, E.L., *The Assemblies of God: A Chapter in the Story of American Pentecostalism* (Springfield, MO: 1989).
_____. *Restoring the Faith* (Urbana and Chicago: University of Illinois Press, 1993).
_____ and C.R. Armstrong, "Assemblies of God," *NIDPCM,* 333-40.
Boa, K. *Augustine to Freud: What Theologians & Psychologist Can Teach Us About Human Nature* (Nashville: Broadman, 2004).
Boone, R.J. "Community and Worship: Key Components of Pentecostal Christian Formation," *JPT* 8 (1996), 129-42.
Boyd G.A. & P.R. Eddy, *Across the Spectrum: Understanding Issues in Evangelical Theology* (Grand Rapids: Baker Academic, 2002).
Boys, M.C. *Jewish-Christian Dialogue: One Woman's Experience* (New York: Paulist, 1997).
Bowdle, D. editor, *Ellicott's Bible Commentary in One Volume* (Grand Rapids: Zondervan, 1971, 1980).
Bowers, J. "A Wesleyan-Pentecostal Approach to Christian Formation," *JPT* 6 (1995), 55-86.
Braaten, C. *No Other Gospel: Christianity among the World's Religions* (Minneapolis, MN: Fortress, 1992).
Brown, D.W. *Understanding Pietism* (Nappanee, IN: Evangel, 1996).
Brown, S.A. and P.D. Miller, eds., *Lament: Reclaiming Practices in Pulpit, Pew, and Public Square* (Louisville, KY: Westminster John Knox, 2005).
_____. B.K. Blount, "Breaking Point: A Sermon," 145-54.
Bruce, F.F., gen. ed. *New International Commentary on the New Testament* (Grand Rapids, MI: Eerdmans).
_____. F.F. Bruce, *The Book of Acts* (1988).
_____. L. Morris, *The Gospel According to John* (1971, 1987).
Buckwalter, H.D. "Testimony," Elwell, W.A. ed. *BTDB* (Grand Rapids: Baker, 1996), 765-69.
Bundy, D.D. "Boddy, Alexander Alfred," *NIDPCM,* 436-37.
_____. "Gee, Donald," 662-63.
_____. "European Pietist Roots of Pentecostalism," 610-13.

_____. "Hollenweger, Walter Jacob," 7729.
_____. "Paul, Jonathan Anton Alexander," 958.
_____. "United Methodist Charismatics," 1158-60.
Bunners, C. "Paul Gerhardt (1607-1676)," Linberg, C., ed. *The Pietist Theologians: An Introduction to Theology in the Seventeenth and Eighteenth Centuries* (Malden, Massachusetts: Wiley-Blackwell, 2004), 68-83.
Burgess, S.M. "The Pentecostal Tradition," *CHB* 58:17:2 (1998), 40-41.
_____. "Holy Spirit, Doctrine of Reformation Traditions," *NIDPCM*, 763-69.
Burridge, R.A. *Imitating Jesus: An Inclusive Approach to New Testament Ethics* (Grand Rapids: Eerdmans, 2007).
Burrows, W.R. "From a Roman Catholic 'Mission Church' to a Catholic 'World Christianity' Paradigm: A Personal Pilgrimage," *U.S. Catholic Historian*, 23 (Summer 2006), 165-79.
Burton, K.A. *The Blessing of Africa* (Downer's Grove: InterVarsity Press, 2007).
Callen, B.L. *Clark H. Pinnock: Journey Toward Renewal* (Nappanee: Evangel, 2000).
_____. *Discerning the Divine: God in Christian Theology* (Louisville, KY: Westminster John Knox, 2004).
Campbell, P.B., SJ, "Blessed and Broken: How Religion Infuses and Confuses American Presidential Politics," *Thinking Faith: The Online Journal of the British Jesuits*, 22 April 2008,
http://www.thinkingfaith.org/articles/20080422_1.htm.
Carroll, J.T. and J.B. Green et al, *The Death of Jesus in Early Christianity* (Peabody: Hendrickson, 1995).
Carpenter, H. "Tolerance or Irresponsibility: The Problem of Pluralism in Missions," *Advance*, 31:2 (1995), 19.
Catherwood, C. *A Brief History of the Middle East: From Abraham to Arafat* (New York: Carroll & Graf, 2006).
Carter, J. *Palestine: Peace Not Apartheid* (New York: Simon & Schuster, 2006).
Cartledge, M.J. *Testimony: Its Importance, Place, and Potential* (Cambridge: Grove, 2002).
_____. *Encountering the Spirit: The Charismatic Tradition*, Traditions of Christian Spirituality (New York: Orbis, 2007).
Cerillo, Jr. A. "Frank Bartleman: Pentecostal 'Lone Ranger' and Social Critic," Goff, J.R., Jr. and G. Wacker, eds., *Portraits of a Generation: Early Pentecostal Leaders* (Fayetteville: University of Arkansas, 2002).
César, W. "From Babel to Pentecost: A Social-Historical- Theological Study of the Growth of Pentecostalism," A. Corten and R.R. Marshall-Fratani, eds. *Between Babel and Pentecost: Transnational Pentecostalism in Africa and Latin America* (Bloomington, IN: Indiana University Press, 2001), 22-40.
Chan, S. "An Asian Response," *JPT* 4 (1994), 35-40.
_____. *Spiritual Theology: A Systematic Study of the Christian Life* (Downer's Grove: IVP, 1998).
_____. *Pentecostal Theology and the Christian Spiritual Tradition* JPTS 21 (Sheffield: Sheffield Academic Press, 2000, 2003).

_____. "The Church and the Development of Doctrine," *JPT* 13:1 (October 2004), 57-77.
Chappell, E.B. *Studies in the Life of John Wesley* (Salem, OH: Schmul, 1991 [1911]).
Cheetham, D. *John Hick: A Critical Introduction and Reflection* (Abingdon, UK, & Brookfield, VT: Ashfield, 2002).
Chia, R. *Hope for the World: A Christian Vision of the Last Things,* Christian Doctrine in Global Perspective, series editor, David Smith, consulting editor, John Stott (Downer's Grove: InterVarsity Press, 2005).
Chilton, B. "Judaism, Christianity, and Islam in Their Contemporary Encounters: Christianity Meets Other Religions," ed., Jacob Neusner, *Religious Foundations of Western Civilization: Judaism, Christianity, and Islam,* (Nashville: Abingdon, 2006), 609-19.
Chossudovsky, M. *America's "War on Terrorism"* (Quebec: Global Research, 2005).
Clark, M.S., "Pentecostalism's Anabaptist Roots: Hermeneutical Implications," *The Spirit and Spirituality: Essays in Honor of Russell P. Spittler,* ed. W. Ma and R.P. Menzies (New York: T & T Clark, 2004).
Clarke, A. *Clarke's Commentary: Malachi,* Wesleyan Heritage Collection (Rio, WI: Ages Software, 2002).
Cleary, E.L. and H. Stewart, "Chilean Pentecostalism: Coming of Age," Cleary, E.L. and H. Stewart, ed. *Power, Politics, and Pentecostals in Latin America* (Boulder, Colorado: Westview, 1996), 97-122.
Clemmons, I.C. "Mason, Charles Harrison," *NIDPCM,* 865-67.
Clifton, S. "Experience in Australian Pentecostalism Pragmatic Ecclesiology: What have Australian Pentecostals gained and lost in the search for a contemporary church?" http://www.anchist.mq.edu.au/CTE/Documents/Shane%20Clifton%20 on %20experience.doc.
_____. "Pentecostal Ecclesiology: A Methodological Proposal for a Diverse Movement," *JPT* 15:2 (April 2007), 213-32.
Clouse, R.G. "Francis of Assisi," *Eerdmans' Handbook to the History of Christianity* (Grand Rapids: Eerdmans, 1977, 1988), 264-65.
Cobb, J.B. Jr., *Christ in a Pluralistic Age* (Philadelphia: Westminster, 1975).
_____. *Grace & Responsibility: A Wesleyan Theology for Today* (Nashville: Abingdon, 1995).
Cobban, H. "Religion and Violence," *JAAR* 73:4 (Dec 2005), 1121-39.
Collins, K.J., ed. *Exploring Christian Spirituality: An Ecumenical Reader* (Grand Rapids: Baker, 2000).
_____. *"The Evangelical Moment: The Promise of an American Religion* (Grand Rapids: Baker Academic, 2005).
Comstock, S. "Aimee Semple MacPherson: Prima Dona of Revivalism," *Harper's Monthly Magazine* (December 1927), 16-17.
Congar, Yves. *I Believe in the Holy Spirit* 3 vols. trans. David Smith (New York: Seabury, 1983).

_____. *The Word and the Spirit*, trans. David Smith (San Francisco: Harper & Row, 1986).

Conn, C.W. *Like a Mighty Army: A History of the Church of God: Definitive Edition* (Cleveland: Pathway, 1996).

Conn, S. *Growing Up Pentecostal* (Xulon Press, 2006).

Cook, M.L. "Confessional Theology," Musser, D.W. and J.L. Price, eds. *NHCT* (Nashville: Abingdon, 1992), 96-98.

Copan, P. *"True for You, But Not for Me" Overcoming Objections to Christian Faith* (Bloomington, Minnesota: Bethany House, 2009).

Copleston, F.C. *Religion and the One: Philosophies East and West* (New York: Crossroad, 1982).

Corten, A. and R.R. Marshall-Fratani, eds. *Between Babel and Pentecost: Transnational Pentecostalism in Africa and Latin America* (Bloomington, IN: Indiana University Press, 2001), 106-23.

Cossey, J.E. "The State of the Church 2008: An Interview with G. Dennis McQuire," *COGE* (January 2008), 24-26.

Coulter, D. "The Development of Ecclesiology in the Church of God (Cleveland, TN): A Forgotten Contribution?" *Pneuma* 29:1 (2007), 59-85.

_____. "Baptism, Conversion, and Grace: Reflections on the 'Underlying Realities' Between Pentecostals, Methodists, and Catholics," *Pneuma* 31:2 (2009), 189-212.

Cox, H. *Fire From Heaven: The Rise of Pentecostal Spirituality and the Reshaping of Religion in the Twenty-First Century* (New York: Addison-Wesley, 1995).

Cracknell, K. *In Good and Generous Faith: Christian Responses to Religious Pluralism* (Peterborough: Epworth, 2005).

Crews, M. *The Church of God: A Social History* (Knoxville: University of Tennessee Press, 1990).

Crockett, W.V. and James G. Sigountos, eds., *Through No Fault of Their Own? The Fate of Those Who Have Never Heard* (Grand Rapid: Baker, 1991).

Cross, T.L. "A Proposal to Break the Ice: What Can Pentecostal Theology Offer Evangelical Theology?" *JPT* 10:2 (2002), 44-73.

_____. "A Response to Clark Pinnock's 'Church in the Power of the Holy Spirit," *JPT* 14:2 (April 2006), 175-82.

_____. *Answering the Call in the Spirit: Pentecostal Reflections on a Theology of Vocation, Work and Life* (Cleveland: Lee University Press, 2007).

_____. "The Divine-Human Encounter: Towards a Pentecostal Theology of Experience," *Pneuma* 31:1 (Spring 2009), 3-34.

Culpepper, R.F. *The Great Commission: The Solution...* (Cleveland, TN: Pathway Press, 2009).

Currie, D.A. "Moltmann, Jürgen," *EDT,* 784.

The Dalai Lama, *The Four Noble Truths,* trans. Geshe Thupten Jinpa and ed. Dominque Side (London: Thorsens, 1997).

Danaher, J. "Our Journey into the Truth, Beauty, and Holiness of the Gospel," *ERT* 32:1 (January 2008), 56-64.

Dayton, D.W. *Theological Roots of Pentecostalism,* Foreword by M.E. Marty (Grand Rapids: Zondervan, 1987).
D'Costa, G. *John Hick's Theology of Religions* (New York: University Press of America, 1987).
_____. "Christian Theology and Other Religions: An Evaluation of John Hick and
Paul Knitter," *Studia Missionalia* 42 (1993), 161-78.
_____. *The Meeting of Religions and the Trinity* (Maryknoll, New York: Orbis, 2000).
_____. *Christianity and the World Religions: Disputed Questions in the Theology of Religions* (West Sussex, UK: Wiley-Blackwell, 2009).
Donovan, M.A. *One Right Reading? A Guide to Irenaeus* (Collegeville, Minnesota: Liturgical Press, 1997).
Daniels, III, D.D. "'Gotta Moan Sometime': A Sonic Exploration of Earwitnesses to Early Pentecostal Sound in North America," *Pneuma* 30:1 (2008), 5-32.
Daugherty, K. "*Missio Dei:* The Trinity and Christian Missions," *ERT Theology* 31:2 (April 2007), 151-68.
DeArtega, W. *Quenching the Spirit: Examining Centuries of Opposition to the Moving of the Holy Spirit* (Lake Mary, FL: Creation House, 1992).
Deiros, P.A. and E.A. Wilson, "Hispanic Pentecostalism in the Americas," V. Synan, ed., *The Century of the Holy Spirit: 100 Years of Pentecostal and Charismatic Renewal* (Nashville, TN: Nelson, 2001), 293-324.
Dempster, M.A. and B.D. Klaus, D. Petersen, eds. *Called and Empowered: Global Mission in Pentecostal Perspective* (Grand Rapids: Hendrickson, 1991).
Diprose, R. *Israel and the Church* (Waynesville, GA: Authentic Media, 2000).
Dove, S. "Wesley's Sanctification Narrative: A Tool for Understanding the Holy Spirit's Work in a More Physical Soul," *Pneuma* 31:2 (2009), 225-41.
Dryness, W.A., *Invitation to Cross-Cultural Theology: Case Studies in Vernacular Theology* (Grand Rapids, MI: Zondervan, 1992).
_____. Ed. with V.M. Kärkkäinen, assoc. ed., et al, *GDT* (Downer's Grove, IL: IVP Academic, 2008).
Duffield, G.P. and N. M. Van Cleave, *Foundations of Pentecostal Theology* (Los Angeles: L.I.F.E. Bible College, 1983, 1987).
Dupree, S. *African-American Holiness-Pentecostal Movement: Annotated Bibliography* (London/New York: Routledge, 1995).
Eck, D.L. *A New Religious America: How A "Christian Country" Has Become the World's Most Religiously Diverse Nation* (New York: HarperCollins, 2001).
Edwards, J.R. *Is Jesus the Only Savior?* (Grand Rapids: Eerdmans, 2005).
_____. *Romans,* W.W. Gasque, NT editor, *NIBC* (Peabody, MA: Hendrickson, 1992).
Elinson, H. "The Implications of Pentecostal Religion for Intellectualism, Politics, and Race Relations," *AJS* 70 (1965): 403-415.

Ellingsen, m. *The Evangelical Movement: Growth, Impact, Controversy, Dialog* (Minneapolis: Augsburg, 1988).

Ellington, S.A. "Pentecostals and the Authority of Scripture," *JPT* 9 (1996), 16-38.

_____. "The Costly Loss of Testimony," *JPT* 16 (2000), 48-59.

_____. "History, Story, and Testimony: Locating Truth in a Pentecostal Hermeneutic," *Pneuma* 23:2 (2001), 245-63.

_____. "The Reciprocal Reshaping of History and Experience in the Psalms: Interactions with Pentecostal Testimony," *JPT* 16:1 (2007), 18-31.

Erickson, M.J. *How Shall They Be Saved? The Destiny of Those Who Do Not Hear of Jesus* (Grand Rapids: Baker, 1996).

_____. *The Evangelical Left: Encountering Postconservative Evangelical Theology* (Grand Rapids: Baker, 1997).

_____. "Postmodernity and Theology," *Christian Theology* (Grand Rapids: Baker, 1998, 2nd ed.), 158-74.

Estep, W.R. *The Anabaptist Story: An Introduction to Sixteenth Century Anabaptism* (Grand Rapids: Eerdmans, 1975, 1996).

Evans, C.A. *Luke*, W.W. Gasque, NT editor, *NIBC* (Peabody, MA: Hendrickson, 1990).

Ezzat, H.R. "Dialogue with Passion," H. Ucko, ed. *Changing the Present, Dreaming the Future: A Critical Moment in Interreligious Dialogue,* ed. Hans Ucko (Geneva: World Council of Churches, 2006), 22-27.

Fackre, G., R.H. Nash, and J. Sanders, *What About Those Who Have Never Heard: Three Views on the Destiny of the Unevangelized* (Downer's Grove: InterVarsity, 1995).

Faupel, D.W. *The Everlasting Gospel: The Significance of Eschatology in the Development of Pentecostal Thought,* JPTS Series 10 (Sheffield, UK: Sheffield Academic, 1996).

Fee, G.D. *God's Empowering Presence: The Holy Spirit in the Letters of Paul* (Peabody, Massachusetts: Hendrickson, 1994, 2005).

_____. *Paul, the Spirit, and the People of God* (Peabody, Massachusetts: Hendrickson, 1996, 2005).

Finger, T "A Mennonite Theology for Interfaith Relations," S.M. Heim, Ed., *Grounds for Understanding: Ecumenical Responses to Religious Pluralism* (Grand Rapids: Eerdmans, 1998), 69-92.

Fisher, F.L. "Witness, Testimony," E.F. Harrison, G.W. Bromiley, and C.F.H. Henry, eds. (Grand Rapids: Baker, 1960, 1987), 555-56.

Fisher, O.L. *The Role of the Spirit in the World and Life: How God is Immanent in His Creation* (USA: Xulon Press, 2004).

Fitzgerald, M.L. and John Borelli, *Interfaith Dialogue: A Catholic View* (New York: Orbis, 2006).

Flannery, A. Gen. Ed., *Nostra aetate* in "Declaration on the Relations of the Church to Non-Christian Religions," *Vatican Council II: The Conciliar and Post-Conciliar Documents*, vol. one (Collegeville, MN: Liturgical Press, 1992).

Flint, C. *Introduction to Geopolitics: Tensions, Conflicts and Resolutions* (New York: Routledge, 2006).
Florence, A.C. *Preaching as Testimony* (Louisville, KY: John Knox Westminster, 2007).
Ford, D.F. "Paul Ricoeur: A Biblical Philosopher on Jesus," ed. P.K. Koser, *Jesus and Philosophy: New Essays* (New York: Cambridge University Press, 2009), 169-98.
Fox, R.W. *Jesus in America: Personal Savior, Cultural Hero, National Obsession* (New York: HarperSanFrancisco, 2005).
Fredericks, J.L. *Buddhists and Christians: Through Comparative Theology to Solidarity* (Mary Knoll: Orbis, 2004).
Freeman, B. *The Triune God in Experience (The Testimony of Church History)* (Spokane, WA: Ministry, 1992).
Frei, H.W. *The Eclipse of Biblical Narrative: A Study in Eighteenth and Nineteenth Century Hermeneutics* (New Haven: Yale Press, 1974).
Freston, P. "The Transnationalisation of Brazilian Pentecostalism: The Universal Church of the Kingdom of God," A. Corten and R.R. Marshall-Fratani, eds. *Between Babel and Pentecost: Transnational Pentecostalism in Africa and Latin America* (Bloomington, IN: Indiana University Press, 2001), 196-215.
Fritsch, C.T. *Genesis,* Kelly, B.H. et al, Ed., *The Layman's Bible Commentary: Genesis*, (Richmond, VA: John Knox Press, 1959, 1963).
Fuller, R.H., "Matthew," J.L. Mays, gen. ed. *Harper's Bible Commentary,* (San Francisco, CA: Harper & Row, 1988), 951-82.
Gallagher, R.L. "The Holy Spirit in the World: In Non-Christians, in Creation, and Other Religions," *Asian Journal of Pentecostal Studies* 9:1 (2006), 17-33.
Gause, R.H. *Living in the Spirit: The Way of Salvation* (Cleveland: Pathway, 1980).
_____. *Revelation: God's Stamp of Sovereignty on History* (Cleveland: Pathway, 1983).
_____. "A Pentecostal Response to Pinnock's Proposal," *JPT* 14:2 (April 2006), 183-88.
Gaustad, E.S. and L.E. Schmidt, *The Religious History of America: The Heart of the American Story from Colonial Times to Today* (New York: HarperCollins, rev. ed., 2002).
Gbuji, A.O. "Evangelization and Other Living Faiths: A Roman Catholic Perspective", H.D. Hunter and P.D. Hocken, eds. *All Together in One Place: Theological Papers from the Brighton Conference on World Evangelization* (JPTSup 4, Sheffield, Eng: Sheffield Academic Press, 1993), 215-18.
George, T. "Evangelical Theology in North American Contexts," Larsen, T. and D.J. Treier, ed., *The Cambridge Companion to Evangelical Theology,* (Cambridge: Cambridge University Press, 2007), 275-92.
Gerrard, N.L. "Churches of the Stationary Poor in Southern Appalachia," ed., J.D. Photiadis, *Religion in Appalachia: Theological, Social, and Psychologi-*

cal Dimensions and Correlates (Morgantown, WV: University of West Virginia, approx. 1977), 271-84.

Gilkes, C.T. "'You've Got a Right to the Tree of Life': The Biblical Foundations of an Empowered Attitude Among Black Women in the Sanctified Church," Alexander, E. and A. Yong, *Philip's Daughters: Women in Pentecostal-Charismatic Leadership,* Princeton Monograph Series (Eugene, OR: Pickwick, 2008), 152-69.

Gill, J.H. *Faith in Dialogue: A Christian Apologetic* (Waco: Word, 1985).

Gilmore, L. *The Limits of Autobiography: Trauma and Testimony* (New York: Cornell University Press, 2001).

Glock, C.Y. "The Role of Deprivation in the Origin and Evolution of Religious Groups," in *Religion and Social Conflict,* R. Lee and M.E. Marty eds., (New York: Oxford University Press, 1964).

Goff, J.R., Jr. *Fields White Unto Harvest: Charles F. Parham and the Missionary Origins of Pentecostalism* (Fayetteville: University of Arkansas, 1988).

_____ and G. Wacker, eds., *Portraits of a Generation: Early Pentecostal Leaders* (Fayetteville: University of Arkansas, 2002).

Goldingay, J. *Models for Scripture* (Grand Rapids: Eerdmans, 1994).

Gonzalez, J.L. *A History of Christian Thought: From the Beginnings to the Council of Chalcedon* (Nashville: Abingdon, 1970, 1978).

_____. *A History of Christian Thought: From Augustine to the Eve of the Reformation* (Nashville: Abingdon, 1971, 1988)

_____. *The Crusades: Piety Misguided* (Nashville: Graded Press, 1988).

Graham, B. *The Holy Spirit: Activating God's Power in Your Life* (Nashville, TN: Thomas Nelson, 1978, 1988).

Graham, S.A. *Ordinary Man, Extraordinary Mission: The Life and Work of E. Stanley Jones* (Nashville: Abingdon, 2005).

Gray T. & C. Sinkinson, eds., *Reconstructing Theology: A Critical Assessment of the Theology of Clark Pinnock* (Waynesboro: Paternoster, 2000).

Green, M. *"But Don't All Religions Lead to God?" Navigating the Multi-Faith Maze* (Baker: Grand Rapids), 2002.

Grele, R.J., ed., *Envelopes of Sound: Six Practitioners Discuss the Method, Theory and Practice of Oral History and Oral Testimony* (Chicago: Precedent, 1975).

Grenz, S.J. *Renewing the Center: Evangelical Theology in a Post-Theological Era* (Grand Rapids: Baker, 2000).

_____, with Olson, R.E. *20th Century Christian Theology: God & the World in a Transitional Age* (Downer's Grove, IL: InterVarsity Press, 1992).

Griffis, D.M. *Spirit Wars: The Power of His Might Against the Rulers of The Darkness of This World* (Cleveland: Pathway, 1994).

Griffith, R.M. "A Network of Praying Women: Women's Aglow Fellowship and Mainline American Protestantism," Blumhoffer, E.L., with R.P. Spittler, G.A. Wacker, *Pentecostal Currents in American Protestantism* (Champaign, IL: University of Illinois, 1999), 131-51.

Griffith, R.M. and D. Roebuck, "Women, Role of," *NIDPCM,* 1203-09.

Gros, J., "A Pilgrimage in the Spirit: Pentecostal Testimony in the Faith and Order Movement," *Pneuma* 25:1 (2003), 29-53.
_____. with L.H. Meyer, eds., *The Fragmentation of the Church and Its Unity in Peacemaking* (Grand Rapids: Eerdmans, 2001).
_____ with L.F. Fuchs, and T.F. Best, eds. *Growth in Agreement III: International Dialogue, Texts, and Agreed Statements, 1998-2005,* (Geneva: WCC, 2007).
Gross, R.M. and T.C. Muck, eds., *Christians Talk about Buddhist Mediation, Buddhists Talk about Christian Prayer* (New York: Continuum, 2003).
Guidelines on Dialogue with Men of Living Faiths and Ideologies (Geneva: World Council of Churches Publications, 1979).
Guinness, O. *The Case for Civility: And Why Our Future Depends on It* (New York: HarperCollins, 2008).
Guy, L. Introducing Early Christianity: A Topical Survey of Its Life, Beliefs & Practices (Downer's Grove: InterVarsity Press, 2004).
Habets, M. "Spirit Christology: Seeing in Stereo," *JPT* 11:2 (2003), 199-234.
Hagen, M.A. *Whores of the Court: The Fraud of Psychiatric Testimony and the Rape of American Justice* (New York: HarperCollins, 1997).
Hagner, D.A. *Hebrews,* W.W. Gasque, NT editor, *NIBC* (Peabody: Hendrickson, 1983, 1990).
Harrell, Jr., D.E. "Healers and Televangelists after World War II," V. Synan, ed. *The Century of the Holy Spirit: 100 Years of Pentecostal and Charismatic Renewal* (Nashville, TN: Nelson, 2001), 325-48.
Hart, L.D. *Truth Aflame: Theology for the Church in Renewal* (Grand Rapids: Zondervan, 1999, 2005 rev. ed.).
Hartley, J.E., *Genesis,* R.L. Hubbard, Jr., and R.K. Johnston, OT editors, *NIBC* (Peabody, MA: Hendrickson, 2000).
Harnack, A. von. *The History of Dogma, Volume I* (New York: Dover, 1961).
Harris, J., C. Brown, and M. Moore, *Joshua, Judges, Ruth,* Hubbard, R.L., Jr., and R.K. Johnston, OT editors, *NIBC* (Peabody, MA: Hendrickson, 2000).
Hatch, N.O. *The Democratization of American Christianity* (New Haven: Yale, 1989).
Hathaway, M.R., "The Elim Pentecostal Church: Origins, Development and Distinctives," *Pentecostal Perspectives,* ed. K. Warrington (Carlisle: Paternoster, 1998).
Hay, D. "Experience, Religious," *NWDCS,* 295-97.
Hayford, J.W. with G. Howse and M. Posey, *Race and Reconciliation: Healing the Wounds, Winning the Harvest* Spirit-Filled Life Kingdom Dynamics Study Guides (Nashville, TN: Nelson, 1996).
Hedlund, R.E. "Apostolic Christian Assembly (India)," *NIDPCM,* 322.
_____. "Indigenous Churches," *NIDPCM,* 779-84.
Heim, S.M. *Salvations: Truth and Difference in Religion* (New York: Orbis, 1995, 1997).
_____. Ed., *Grounds for Understanding: Ecumenical Responses to Religious Pluralism* (Grand Rapids: Eerdmans, 1998).

Heinz H. and Michael A. Signer, *Coming Together for the Sake of God: Contributions to Jewish-Christian Dialogue from Post-Holocaust Germany* (Collegeville, Minnesota: Michael Glazier, 2007).

Helmick, R. and R.L. Petersen, ed., *Forgiveness and Reconciliation* (Radnor, PA: Templeton Foundation, 2001).

_____. M. Volf, "Forgiveness, Reconciliation, and Justice: A Christian Contribution to a More Peaceful Social Environment," 27-49.

Hesselgrave, D.J. in *Paradigms in Conflict: 10 Key Questions in Christian Missions Today* (Grand Rapids: Kregel, 2005).

Hick, J. *The Metaphor of God Incarnate Christology in a Pluralistic Age* (Louisville: Westminster John Knox, 1993).

_____. "A Pluralist View," S.N. Gundry, D.L. Okholm, and T.R. Phillips, eds., *Four Views on Salvation in a Pluralistic World* (Grand Rapids: Zondervan, 1995), 27-59.

_____. "The Possibility of Religious Pluralism: A Reply to Gavin D'Costa," *Religious Studies* 33 (1997), 161-66.

_____. "The Theological Challenge of Religious Pluralism," *Christianity and Other Religions: Selected Readings*, ed. J. Hick and B. Hebblethwaite (Oxford: Oneworld, 2001), 156-71.

Higgins, J.R., M.L. Dusing, and F.D. Tallman, *An Introduction to Theology: A Classical Pentecostal Perspective* (Dubuque, Iowa: Kendall/Hunt, 1993, 1994).

Hildebrandt, W. *An Old Testament Theology of the Spirit of God* (Peabody, Massachusetts: Hendrickson, 1995/1999).

Hinn, B. *The Anointing* (Nashville, TN: Thomas Nelson, 1992, 1997).

Hocken, P. "Charismatic Movement," *NIDPCM,* 477-519.

_____. "Dalliere, Louis," 569-70.

_____. "House Church Movement," 773-74.

_____. "Montague, George T.," 903.

_____. "The Catholic Charismatic Renewal," V. Synan, *Voices of Pentecost: Testimonies of Lives Touched by the Holy Spirit* (Ann Arbor, Michigan: Servant Books, 2003), 209-32.

Hodge, C. *Systematic Theology, vol. 1* (Peabody: Hendrickson, 2003).

Hoekema, D.A. "Black Churches, the Third World, and Peace (Conference Held in Atlanta)," *The Christian Century* 100 (November 30, 1983), 1100-01.

Holdcroft, L.T. *The Holy Spirit: A Pentecostal Interpretation* (Sumas, WA: CeeTec, 1999).

Hollenweger, W.J. *The Pentecostals* (London: SCM, 1972/Peabody: Hendrickson, 1988).

_____. "Evangelism: A Non-Colonial Model," *JPT* 7 (1995), 107-28.

_____. "After Twenty Years of Research on Pentecostalism," *IRM* (January 1986), 3-12.

_____. "Pentecostals and Charismatics," *The Study of Spirituality*, eds. C. Jones, G. Wainwright, and E. Yarnold, SJ (New York: Oxford University Press, 1986), 549-54.

_____. "From Azusa Street to the Toronto Phenomenon: Historical Roots of the Pentecostal Movement," *Pentecostal Movements as an Ecumenical Challenge,* eds. Moltmann and K.J. Kuschel, *Concilium* 1996/3 (Maryknoll, NY: Orbis, 1996), 3-14.
_____. *"Fire from Heaven:* A Testimony by Harvey Cox," *Pneuma* 20:2 (1998), 197-204.
_____, with A. Anderson editors, *Pentecostals after a Century: Global Perspective son a Movement in Transition,* JSup Series 15 (Sheffield, England: Sheffield Academic Press, 1999).
_____. "Biblically Justified Abuse: A Review of Stephen Parson's *Ungodly Fear: Fundamentalist Christianity and the Abuse of Power,*" *JPT* 10:2 (2002), 129-35.
Hollingsworth, A. "Spirit and Voice: Toward a Feminist Pentecostal Pneumatology," *Pneuma* 29:2 (2007), 189-213.
Holstein, J.A. and J.F. Gubrium. *The Self We Live By: Narrative Identity in a Postmodern World* (Oxford/New York: Oxford University Press, 2000).
Homerin, Th.E. "Judaism, Christianity, and Islam in Their Contemporary Encounters: Islam and Pluralism," ed., Jacob Neusner, *Religious Foundations of Western Civilization: Judaism, Christianity, and Islam,* (Nashville: Abingdon, 2006), 621-37.
Horton, S.M. *What the Bible Says about the Holy Spirit* (Springfield, MO: Gospel Publishing, 1976/1992).
_____. "The Pentecostal Perspective," *Five Views on Sanctification,* M.E. Dieter, S.M. Horton, et al (Grand Rapids; Zondervan, 1987), 105-135.
_____. "Spirit Baptism: A Pentecostal Perspective," *Perspectives on Spirit Baptism;Five Views,* ed. C.O. Brand (Nashville: Broadman & Holman, 2004), 47-94.
Hubron, L. "Pentecostalism and Transnationalisation in the Caribbean," A. Corten and R.R. Marshall-Fratani, eds. *Between Babel and Pentecost: Transnational Pentecostalism in Africa and Latin America* (Bloomington, IN: Indiana University Press, 2001), 124-41.
Hughes, R.H. *Church of God Distinctives* (Cleveland: Pathway, 1968, 1989).
_____. *Pentecostal Preaching* (Cleveland: Pathway, 1981).
Hunter, H.D. "We are the Church: A New Congregationalism—a Pentecostal Perspective," *Pentecostal Movements as an Ecumenical Challenge,* ed. J. Moltmann and K-J. Kuschel (London: SCM; Maryknoll, NY: Orbis, 1996), 17-21.
Huntingdon, S.P. *The Clash of Civilizations and the Remaking of World Order* (New York: Touchstone, 1996).
Hurtado, L.W., *Mark,* W.W. Gasque, NT editor, *NIBC* (Peabody, MA: Hendrickson, 1983, 1989).
_____. *How on Earth Did Jesus Become a God: Historical Questions about Earliest Devotion to Jesus* (Grand Rapids/Cambridge: Eerdmans, 2005).
Hutchinson, W.R. *Religious Pluralism in America: The Contentious History of a Founding Idea* (New Haven: Yale, 2003).

Hyatt, E. *Fire on the Earth: Eyewitness Reports Azusa Street Revival* (Lake Mary, FL: Creation House, 2006).
Hyatt, S.C. "Spirit-Filled Women," V. Synan, ed., *The Century of the Holy Spirit: 100 Years of Pentecostal and Charismatic Renewal* (Nashville, TN: Nelson, 2001), 233-64.
Irenaeus, *Against Heresies, ANF,* Volume 1 (PC Study Bible formatted electronic database Copyright © 2003 by Biblesoft, Inc.).
Jacobs, A. *Looking Before and After: Testimony and the Christian Life* (Grand Rapids: Eerdmans, 2008).
Jacobs, C. *The Reformation Manifesto: Your Part in God's Plan to Change the Nations Today* (Bloomington, Minnesota: Bethany House, 2008).
Jacobsen, D. *Thinking in the Spirit: Theologies of the Early Pentecostal Movement* (Bloomington & Indianapolis: Indiana University Press, 2003).
Jacques-Suurmond, J. *Word and Spirit at Play: Towards a Charismatic Theology,* trans. John Bowden (Grand Rapids: Eerdmans, 1995).
Jakes, T.D. *Release Your Anointing: Tapping the Power of the Holy Spirit in You* (Shippensburg, PA: Destiny Image, 2008).
James, W. *The Varieties of Religious Experience* (New York: Triumph, 1902, 1991).
Jameson, Faussett, and Brown. *Jameson, Fausset, and Brown Commentary* (Electronic Database, 1997, 2003, Biblesoft, Inc).
Jenkins, P. "Companions for Life: A Supple Faith," Christian Vision Project, *Books & Culture* 13:2 (March/April 2007), 9-18.
_____. *The Next Christendom: The Coming of Global Christianity,* revised and expanded edition (New York: Oxford, 2007).
Jervis, L.A. *Galatians,* W.W. Gasque, NT editor, *NIBC* (Peabody, MA: Hendrickson, 1999).
Johns, C.B. *Pentecostal Formation: A Pedagogy among the Oppressed* JPTSup 2 (Sheffield, England: Sheffield Academic Press, 1993, 1998).
_____. "The Adolescence of Pentecostalism: In Search of a Legitimate Sectarian Identity," *Pneuma* 17:1 (1995), 3-17.
Johns, J.D. "Pentecostalism and the Postmodern Worldview," *JPT* 7 (1995), 73-96.
Johnson, V. "Romans," F.L. and R. Stronstad, eds. *FLBCNT,* (Grand Rapids: Zondervan, 1999), 693-797.
Jones, C.B. *The View from Mars Hill: Christianity in the Landscape of World Religions* (Cambridge, MA: Cowley, 2005).
Jones, C.E. "Holiness Movement," *NIDPCM,* 726-28.
Jones, E.S. *The Christ of the Indian Road* (New York: Abingdon, 1925).
_____. *Christ at the Round Table* (Whitefish, MT: Kessinger, 2004).
Jones, J.W. *Blood that Cries Out from the Earth: The Psychology of Religious Terrorism* (Oxford/New York: Oxford University Press, 2008).
Jones, L. "Mountain Religion: The Outsider's View," J.D. Photiadis, ed. *Religion in Appalachia: Theological, Social, and Psychological Dimensions and Correlates,* (Morgantown, WV: University of West Virginia, approx. 1977), 401-07.

Jordan, F.W. "At Arms Length: The First Presbyterian Church, Pittsburg, and Kathryn Kuhlman,"Blumhoffer, E.L., with R.P. Spittler, G.A. Wacker, *Pentecostal Currents in American Protestantism* (Champaign, IL:University of Illinois, 1999), 188-208.

Juergensmeyer, M. *The New Cold War? Religious Nationalism Confronts the Secular State* (Los Angeles, CA: University of California, 1993, 1994).

_____. *Terror in the Mind of God: The Global Rise of Religious Violence* (Berkeley and Los Angeles: University of California, 2001).

_____. *Global Rebellion: Religious Challenges to the Secular State from Christian Militias to Al Qaeda* (Los Angeles, CA: University of California, 2009).

Jung, C.G. *Modern Man in Search of a Soul* (New York: Harcourt, 1933).

_____. *Memories, Dreams, Reflections,* ed. A. Jaffé; trans. R. and C. Winston (New York: Pantheon, 1963).

Jurgenson, H. "Awaiting the Return of Christ: A Re-Examination of 1 Thessalonians 4.13-5.11 from a Pentecostal Perspective," *JPT* 4 (1994), 81-113.

Kalu, O. *African Pentecostalism: An Introduction* (Oxford/New York: Oxford University Press, 2008).

_____. "*Sankofa:* Pentecostalism and African Cultural Heritage," Kärkkäinen, V.M., ed. *The Spirit in the World: Emerging Pentecostal Theologies in Global Contexts* (Grand Rapids: Eerdmans, 2009), 135-54.

Kärkkäinen, V.M. "Missiology, Pentecostal and Charismatic," *NIDPCM,* 877-85

_____. "Church as Charismatic Fellowship: Ecclesiological Reflections from Pentecostal-Roman Catholic Dialogue," *JPT* 18 (2001), 100-21.

_____. *Pneumatology: The Holy Spirit in Ecumenical, International, and Contextual Perspective* (Grand Rapids: Baker, 2002).

_____. *Toward a Pneumatological Theology: Pentecostal and Ecumenical Perspectives on Ecclesiology, Soteriology, and Theology of Missio*n, ed. Amos Yong (Lanham: University Press of America, 2002).

_____. "Toward a Pneumatological Theology of Religions: A Pentecostal-Charismatic Inquiry," *IRM* 91: 361 (2002), 187-98.

_____. *An Introduction to Ecclesiology: Ecumenical, Historical & Global Perspectives* (Downer's Grove, IL: InterVarsity Press, 2002).

_____. *An Introduction to Theology of Religions: Biblical, Historical, & Contemporary Perspectives* (Downer's Grove: InterVarsity Press, 2003).

_____. *Trinity and Religious Pluralism: The Doctrine of the Trinity in Christian Theology of Religions* (Burlington: Ashgate, 2004).

_____. "The Working of the Spirit of God in Creation and in the People of God: The Pneumatology of Wolfhart Pannenberg," *Pneuma* 26:1 (2004), 17-35.

_____. "The Uniqueness of Christ and the Trinitarian Faith", *Christ the One and Only: A Global Affirmation of the Uniqueness of Jesus Christ,* ed. Sung Wook Chung (Grand Rapids: Baker Academic, 2005), 111-35.

_____. "How to Speak of the Spirit among Religions: Trinitarian 'Rules' for a Pneumatological Theology of Religions," *IBMR* 30:3 (2006): 121-27.

_____. "A Response to Tony Richie's 'Azusa-era Optimism: Bishop J. H. King's Pentecostal Theology of Religions as a Possible Paradigm for Today," *JPT* 15:2 (October 2007), 263-68.

_____. "Evangelical Theology and the Religions," Larsen, T. and D.J. Treier, ed., *The Cambridge Companion to Evangelical Theology,* (Cambridge: Cambridge
University Press, 2007), 199-212.

_____. "Pentecostal Pneumatology of Religions: The Contribution of Pentecostalism to Our Understanding of the Work of God's Spirit in the World," Kärkkäinen, V.M., ed. *The Spirit in the World: Emerging Pentecostal Theologies in Global Contexts* (Grand Rapids: Eerdmans, 2009), 155-80.

Kateregga, B.D. and D.W. Shenk, *A Muslim and A Christian in Dialogue* (Scottsdale, PA: Herald, 1997).

Kay, W. "Do Doctrinal Boundaries Protect Our Identity or Prevent Fellowship," *Epta Bulletin* 12 (1993), 38-41.

Keefauver, L. *Receiving the Anointing of the Spirit* (Lake Mary, FL: Strang Communications, 1997).

Keener, C.S. "Why Does Luke Use Tongues as a Sign of the Spirit's Empowerment?" *JPT* 15:2 (April 2007), 177-84.

Kelly, J.N.D. *Early Christian Beliefs* (New York: HarperSanFrancisco, 1978 ed.).

Kelsey, M. *Discernment: A Study in Ecstasy and Evil* (New York: Paulist, 1978).

Kennedy, R. *A History of Reasonableness: Testimony and Authority in the Art of Thinking* (Rochester Studies in Philosophy) (Rochester, New York: University of Rochester, 2004).

King, J.H. *Yet Speaketh* (Franklin Springs, GA: Publishing House of the Pentecostal Holiness Church, 1949).

_____. *From Passover to Pentecost* (Franklin Springs, GA: Advocate, 1911, 1976 [fourth edition]).

King, P.L., *Genuine Gold: The Cautiously Charismatic Story of the Early Christian and Missionary Alliance* (Tulsa: Word & Spirit, 2006).

Kireopoulos, A. "Reflection on Pope Benedict XVI's Encyclical Letter, *Spe Salvi*"(November 30, 2007),
http://www.ncccusa.org/news/071217spesalvi.html.

Kim, K. *The Holy Spirit in the World: A Global Conversation* (Maryknoll, NY: Orbis, 2007).

Kimball, C. *When Religion Becomes Evil* (New York: HarperSanFrancisco, 2002).

King, J.H. *From Passover to Pentecost* (Franklin Springs, GA: Advocate, 1911, 1976 [fourth edition]).

_____. *Yet Speaketh* (Franklin Springs, GA: Publishing House of the Pentecostal Holiness Church, 1949).

Kinnamon, M. "Ecumenism," *NHCT,* eds. D.W. Musser & J.L. Price (Nashville: Abingdon, 1992), 142-45.

Kishkovsky, L. "Response to Miroslav Volf," *IBMR* 20:1 (Jan 1996), 31-36.

Kittle, G. and G. Friedrich, eds., *TDNT,* trans. and abridged by G.W. Bromiley, (Grand Rapids: Eerdmans, 1985, 1990).
Knight III, H.H. *A Future for Truth: Evangelical Theology in a Postmodern World* (Nashville: Abingdon, 1997).
Knitter, P.F. *Jesus and the Other Names: Christian Mission and Global Responsibility* (New York: Maryknoll, 1996).
_____. *Introducing Theology of Religions* (Maryknoll, New York: Orbis, 2002).
Koivisto, R.A. *One Lord, One Faith: A Theology for Cross-Denominational Renewal* (Wheaton: Bridgepoint/Victor, 1993),
Köstenberger, A.J. "'What is Truth?' Pilate's Question in Its Johannine and Larger Biblical Context," Mohler, R.A. and J.P. Moreland, et al, *Whatever Happened to Truth?* (Wheaton, IL: Crossway, 2005), 19-52.
Kramnik I. and R. Laurence Moore, *The Godless Constitution: A Moral Defense of the Secular State* (New York: W. W. Norton & Co, 2005).
Kselman, J.S. "Genesis," J.L. Mays, gen. ed. *Harper's Bible Commentary,* (San Francisco, CA: Harper & Row, 1988), 85-128.
Küng, H. *Christianity and World Religions: Paths to Dialogue with Islam, Hinduism, and Buddhism* (New York: Doubleday, 1986).
_____. *Theology for the Third Millennium: An Ecumenical View* (New York: Anchor Books, 1990).
_____ with K.-J. Kuschel, eds., *A Global Ethic: The Declaration of the World's Religions* (New York: Continuum, 1993).
_____. "Global Ethics and Education," *The Future of Theology: Essays in Honor of Jürgen Moltmann,* eds. Miroslav Volf, Carmen Krieg, Thomas Kucharz (Grand Rapids: Eerdmans, 1996), 267-83.
_____. *Islam: Past, Present, and Future,* trans. J. Bowden (Oxford: Oneworld, 2008).
Kuzmic, P. "A Croatian War-Time Reading," *JPT,* 4 (1994), 17-24.
Kydd, R.A.N. "Healing in the Christian Church," *NIDPCM,* 698-711.
Lambert, F. *The Founding Fathers and the Place of Religion in America* (Princeton: Princeton University Press, 2003).
Land, S.J. *Pentecostal Spirituality: A Passion for the Kingdom* JPTSup 1 (Sheffield: Sheffield Academic Press, 1993).
_____. . "The Nature and Evidence of Spiritual Fullness," ed. R. White, *Endued with Power: The Holy Spirit in the Church* (1995), 55-82.
Lapoorta, J.J. "An African Response," *JPT* 4 (1994), 51-58.
Laurent, P.J. "Transnationalisation and Local Transformations: The Example of the Church of the Assemblies of God in Burkina Faso," A. Corten and R.R. Marshall-Fratani, eds. *Between Babel and Pentecost: Transnational Pentecostalism in Africa and Latin America* (Bloomington, IN: Indiana University Press, 2001), 256-73.
Lefever, H.G. "Religion of the Poor: Escape or Creative Force?" *JSSR* 16:3 (September 1977), 525-534.
Leith, J.H. "Ecclesiology," Musser, D.W. and J.L. Price, eds. *NHCT* (Nashville: Abingdon, 1992), 135-38.

Lenski, G. *The Religious Factor; A Sociologist's Inquiry* (New York: Anchor, 1963).
Lewis, C.S. *Mere Christianity* (New York: Collier, 1960).
_____. *Miracles* (London: G. Bless, 1947; HarperCollins ed., 2001).
Levenson, J.D. "Judaism, Christianity, and Islam in Their Contemporary Encounters: Judaism Addresses Christianity," ed. Jacob Neusner, *Religious Foundations of Western Civilization: Judaism, Christianity, and Islam*, (Nashville: Abingdon, 2006), 581-608.
Liechty, J. "Migration in Northern Ireland: A Strategy for Living in Peace When Truth Claims Clash," D.R. Smock, ed., *Interfaith Dialouge and Peacebuilding* (Washington, DC: United States Institute for Peace, 2002), 89-102.
Lincoln, A.T. *Paradise Now and Not Yet: Studies in the Role of the Heavenly Dimension in Paul's Thought with Special Reference to His Eschatology* (Grand Rapids; Baker, 1981).
_____ with A.J.M. Wedderburn, *The Theology of the Later Pauline Letters* (Cambridge, UK: Cambridge University Press, 1993).
Lodahl, M. *The Story of God: Wesleyan Theology and Biblical Narrative* (Beacon Hill: Kansas City; 1994).
Long, T.G. *Testimony: Talking Ourselves into Being Christian*, Practice of Faith Series (San Francisco: Jossey-Bass, 2004).
Lord, A. "Mission Eschatology: A Framework for Mission in the Spirit," *JPT* 11 (1997), 111-23.
_____. "The Pentecostal-Moltmann Dialogue: Implications for Mission," *JPT* 11:2 (2003), 271-87.
Lovett, L. "Black Theology," *NIDPCM*, 428-32.
Loftus, E. and K. Ketcham, *Witness for the Defense: The Accused, The Eyewitness, and the Expert Who Puts Memory on Trial* (New York: St Martin's, 1991).
Ma W. and R.P. Menzies, eds., *Pentecostalism in Context: Essays in Honor of William W. Menzies* JPTSup 11 (Sheffield: Sheffield Academic Press, 1997).
_____. *The Spirit and Spirituality: Essays in Honor of Russell P. Spittler* (New York: T & T Clark, 2004).
_____. "'When the Poor are Fired Up': The Role of Pneumatology in Pentecostal Charismatic Mission," Kärkkäinen, V.M., ed., *The Spirit in the World: Emerging Pentecostal Theologies in Global Contexts* (Grand Rapids: Eerdmans, 2009), 40-52.
MacArthur, Jr., J.F. *Charismatic Chaos* (Grand Rapids: Zondervan, 1992).
Macchia, F.D. "A North American Response," *JPT* 4 (1994), 25-33.
_____. "The Spirit and Life: A Further Response to Jürgen Moltmann," *JPT* 5 (October 1994), 121-27.
_____. "Tradition and the Novum of the Spirit: A Review of Clark Pinnock's *Flame of Love*," *JPT* 13 (1998), 31-48.
_____. "Theology, Pentecostal," *NICPCM* (Grand Rapids: Zondervan, 2002).
_____. *Baptized in the Spirit: A Global Pentecostal Theology* (Grand Rapids: Zondervan, 2006).

_____. "Pinnock's Pneumatology: A Pentecostal Appreciation," *JPT* 14:2 (April 2006), 167-73.
_____. "Finitum Capax Infiniti: A Pentecostal Distinctive?" *Pneuma* 29:2 (2007), 185-87.
Maddox, R.L. "Wesley and the Question of Truth or Salvation in Other Religions," *WTJ* (27 1992), 9-29.
Mansfield, S. "Keeper of the Flame," *Charisma* (June 2005), at http://www.charismamag.com/display.php?id=11134.
Mariz, C.L. and M.D.C. Machado, "Pentecostalism and Women in Brazil," Cleary, E.L. and H. Stewart, ed. *Power, Politics, and Pentecostals in Latin America* (Boulder, Colorado: Westview, 1996), 41-54.
Marsden, G.M. *Fundamentalism and American Culture* (Oxford/New York: Oxford University Press, 2006).
Marshall-Fratani, R. "Mediating the Global and Local in Nigerian Pentecostalism," A. Corten and R.R. Marshall-Fratani, eds. *Between Babel and Pentecost: Transnational Pentecostalism in Africa and Latin America* (Bloomington, IN: Indiana University Press, 2001), 80-105.
Marshall, I.H. *New Testament Theology: Many Witnesses, One Gospel* (Downer's Grove: InterVarsity Press, 2004).
Marshall, R. *Political Spiritualities: The Pentecostal Revolution in Nigeria* (Chicago: University of Chicago, 2009).
Martin, D. *Tongues of Fire: The Explosion of Protestantism in Latin America* (Cambridge, Massachusetts: Wiley-Blackwell, 1993).
_____. *Pentecostalism: The World Their Parish* (Cambridge, Massachusetts: Wiley-Blackwell, 2008).
Martin, P.A.J. *Missionary of the Indian Road: The Theology of Stanley Jones* (Koramangala, Bangalore: Theological Book Trust, 1996).
Martin, L. *The Topeka Outpouring of 1901* (Pensacola, FL: Christian Life, 1997).
_____. *Holy Ghost Revival on Azusa Street: The True Believers: Eyewitness Accounts of the Revival that Shook the World* (Pensacola, FL: Christian Life, 1998).
_____, and W.J. Seymour, *The Words That Changed the World: Azusa Street Sermons* (Pensacola, FL: Christian Life, 1999).
_____, and W.J. Seymour, *The Doctrines and Discipline of the Azusa Street Apostolic Faith Mission of Los Angeles,* The Complete Azusa Street Library (Pensacola, FL: Christian Life, 2000).
Martin, R. "A Man of the Spirit," *Charisma* (June 2005), 46, at http://www.charismamag.com/display.php?id=11135).
Marty, M.E. *Pilgrims in Their Own Land: 500 Years of Religion in America* (New York: Penguin, 1984).
_____. *When Faiths Collide,* (Malden: Blackwell, 2005).
_____ with Jonathan Moore. *Politics, Religion, and the Common Good: Advancing a Distinctively American Conversation about Religion's Role in Our Shared Life* (San Francisco: Jossey-Bass, 2000).

Maslow, A.H. *Religions, Values, and Peak Experiences* (New York: Viking, 1964, 1970, 1973).

Matthias, M. "August Hermanne Franke (1663-1727)," Linberg, C., ed. *The Pietist Theologians: An Introduction to Theology in the Seventeenth and Eighteenth Centuries* (Malden, Massachusetts: Wiley-Blackwell, 2004), 100-14.

Mattke, R.A. "Integration of Truth in John Wesley," May 13, 2008, at http://wesley.nnu.edu/wesleyan_theology/theojrnl/06-10/08-1.htm.

May, F.J. *"The Book of Acts & Church Growth: Growth Through the Power of God's Holy Spirit* (Cleveland: Pathway, 1990).

Mayrargue, C. "The Expansion of Pentecostalism in Benin: Individual Rationales and Transnational Dynamics," A. Corten and R.R. Marshall-Fratani, eds. *Between Babel and Pentecost: Transnational Pentecostalism in Africa and Latin America* (Bloomington, IN: Indiana University Press, 2001), 274-92.

McAdams, D.P., R. Josselson, and A. Lieblich, eds. *Identity and Story: Creating Self in Narrative* (American Psychological Association, 2006).

McCall, R.D. "Storytelling and Testimony: Reclaiming a Pentecostal Distinctive," unpublished Doctor of Ministry Dissertation, Columbia Theological Seminary, 1998.

McClung, G.L., Jr., ed. *Azusa Street and Beyond: Pentecostal Missions and Church Growth* (South Plainfield, NJ: Logos, 1986).

_____. McClung, "Introduction: Spontaneous Strategy of the Spirit: Pentecostal Missionary Practices," 71-81.

_____. D. Gee, "Spiritual Gifts and World Evangelization," 113.

_____. P.A. Pomerville, "The Pentecostals and Growth,"151-55.

McClung, G.L., Jr. "Evangelism," *NIDPCM,* 617-20.

McDaniel, J.B. *Gandhi's Hope: Learning from World Religions as a Path to Peace* (Maryknoll, New York: Orbis, 2005).

McDermott, G.R. *Can Evangelicals Learn from World Religions: Jesus, Revelation, & Religious Traditions* (Downer's Grove: InterVarsity Press, 2000).

_____. *God's Rivals: Why Has God Allowed Different Religions? Insights from the Bible and the Early Church* (Downer's Grove: IVP Academic, 2007).

McDonnell, K. *Charismatic Renewal and the Churches* (New York: Seabury Press, 1976).

McFarlane, G. "Atonement, Creation, and Trinity, 192-207, gen. eds. D. Tidball, D. Hilborn, & J. Thacker, *The Atonement Debate: Papers from the London Symposium on the Theology of the Atonement* (Grand Rapids, MI: Zondervan, 2008).

_____. *Why Do You Believe What You Believe About the Holy Spirit?* (Theological Foundations), (Eugene, OR: Wipf & Stock, 2009).

McGee, G.B., ed., *Initial Evidence: Historical and Biblical Perspectives on the Pentecostal Doctrine of Spirit Baptism* (Peabody, MA: Hendrickson, 1991).

_____. "Ball, Henry Cleopas," *NIDPCM,* 354.

_____. "Initial Evidence, *NIDPCM,* 784-91.

_____. "Missions, Overseas (N. American Pentecostal)," *NIDPCM,* 885-901.

_____. "Moss, Virginia E.," *NIDPCM,* 909.

_____. "To the Regions Beyond: The Global Expansion of Pentecostalism," V. Synan, ed., *The Century of the Holy Spirit: 100 Years of Pentecostal and Charismatic Renewal* (Nashville, TN: Nelson, 2001), 69-96.

McGonigle, H.B. *Sufficient Saving Grace: John Wesley's Evangelical Arminianism* (Waynesboro, GA: Paternoster, 2001).

McGrath, A.E. *The Future of Christianity,* Blackwell Manifesto (Malden, Massachusetts: Wiley-Blackwell, 2002).

McGraw, B.A. and R. Formicola, *Taking Religious Pluralism Seriously: Spiritual Politics on America's Sacred Ground* (Waco, TX: Baylor University Press, 2005).

_____. M.A. Muqtedar Khan, "American Muslims and the Rediscovery of America's Sacred Ground," 127-48.

McGuire, M.B. "Testimony as a Commitment Mechanism in Catholic Pentecostal Prayer Groups," *JSSR* 16:2 (June 1977), 165-68.

Meacham, J. *American Gospel: God, the Founding Fathers, and the Making of a Nation* (New York: Random House, 2006).

Meitzen, M.O. "The Background and Content of Twentieth Century American Theology and Religious Experience," J.D. Photiadis, ed. *Religion in Appalachia: Theological, Social, and Psychological Dimensions and Correlates,* (Morgantown, WV: University of West Virginia, approx. 1977), 33-64.

Mellor, G.H. "Evangelism and Religious Pluralism in the Wesleyan Tradition," *Theology and Evangelism in the Wesleyan Heritage,* ed. James C. Logan (Nashville: Kingswood Books, 1994), 109-26.

Menzies, W.W. and R. Menzies, *Spirit and Power: Foundations of Pentecostal Experience* (Grand Rapids: Zondervan, 2000).

Merrick, J.R.A. "The Spirit of Truth as Agent in False Religions? A Critique of Amos Yong's Pneumatological Theology of Religions with Reference to Current Trends," *TJ* 29:1 (Spring 2008), 107-25.

Meyer, J.F. *Inaccuracies in Children's Testimony* (New York/London: The Haworth Press, 1997).

Miller, A.G. "Pentecostalism as a Social Movement: Beyond the Theory of Deprivation," *JPT* 9 (1996), 97-114.

Miller D.E. and T. Yamamori, *Global Pentecostalism: The New Face of Christian Social Engagement* (Los Angeles: University of California Press, 2007).

Miller, K. *Surrender to the Spirit: The Limitless Possibilities of Yielding to the Spirit* (Shippensburg, PA: Destiny Image, 2006).

Mittelstadt, M.W. *The Spirit and Suffering in Luke-Acts: Implications for a Pentecostal Pneumatology* (London and New York: T & T Clark, 2004).

_____. "Spirit and Suffering in Contemporary Pentecostalism: The Lukan Epic Continues," 144-74, ed. Steven Studebaker, *Defining Issues in Pentecostalism: Classical and Emergent,* McMaster's Theological Studies (Eugene, OR: Pickwick, 2008).

Moltmann, J. *Theology of Hope: On the Ground and the Implications of a Christian Eschatology,* trans. J.W. Leitch (London: SCM, 1967).

_____. *The Church in the Power of the Spirit: A Contribution to Messianic Ecclesiology,* trans. Margaret Kohl (London: SCM Press, 1977).

_____. "Hope," *NHCT,* eds. D.W. Musser and J.L. Price (Nashville: Abingdon, 1992), 239-41.

_____. "A Response to My Pentecostal Dialogue Partners," *JPT* 4 (1994), 59-70.

_____. *The Spirit of Life: A Universal Affirmation,* trans. Margaret Kohl (Minneapolis, MN: First Fortress, 1991, 2001).

_____. *A Broad Place: An Autobiography* (Minneapolis: Fortress, 2008).

Moon, T. "J.H. King's Theology of Religions: 'Magnanimous Optmism?' *JPT* 16:1 (2007), 112-32.

Moran, G. *Uniqueness: Problems or Paradox in Jesus and Christian Traditions* (Maryknoll, New York: Orbis, 1992).

Morgan, L.F. "The Flame Still Burns," *Charisma* (November 2007), 42-48, 50, 52, 54, 56, and 58.

Mounce, R.H. *Matthew,* W.W. Gasque, NT editor, *NIBC* (Peabody, MA: Hendrickson, 1985, 1991).

Muck, T.C. *Alien Gods on American Turf,* Christianity Today Series (Wheaton, IL: Scripture Press Publications, Inc., Victor Books, 1990).

Mulholland, M.R. *Invitation to a Journey: A Roadmap for Spiritual Formation* (Downer's Grove, IL: InterVarsity, 1993).

Murphy, E. *The Handbook for Spiritual Warfare,* revised and updated (Nashville, TN: Nelson, 1992, 1996, 2003).

Nash, R.H. *Is Jesus the Only Savior?* (Grand Rapids: Zondervan, 1994).

Neal, R.A. *Theology as Hope: On the Ground and Implications of Jürgen Moltmann's Doctrine of Hope,* Princeton Theological Monograph Series (Eugene, OR: Wipf & Stock, 2008).

Neill, S. *Christianity and Other Faiths: Christian Dialogue with Other Religions,* second edition (New York: Oxford University Press, 1961, 1970).

_____. *Colonialism and Christian Missions* (New York: McGraw-Hill, 1966).

_____. *Christian Faith and Other Faiths* (Downer's Grove: InterVarsity Press, 1984).

_____. *A History of Christian Missions,* rev. ed. (Hammondsworth, UK: Penguin, 1986).

Netland, H. *Encountering Religious Pluralism: The Challenge to Christian Faith & Mission* (Downer's Grove, ILL: InterVarsity, 2001).

Neusner, J., ed., *Religious Foundations of Western Civilization: Judaism, Christianity, and Islam,* (Nashville: Abingdon, 2006).

Neville, R.C. ed., *The Comparative Religious Ideas Project,* 3 vols. (Albany: SUNY Press, 2001).

Newbigin, L. *The Household of God: Lectures on the Nature of the Church* (London: SCM, 1953).

_____. *A Faith for this One World* (London, 1961).

_____. *The Finality of Christ* (London, 1969).

_____. *The Open Secret* (Grand Rapids, 1978).

_____. *The Gospel in a Pluralist Society* (London: SPCK, 1989).

_____. *Truth to Tell: The Gospel as Public Truth* (Grand Rapids: Eerdmans, 1991).
_____. "Ecumenical Amnesia," *IBMR* 18 (January 1994), 2-5.
_____. *A Word in Season: Perspectives on Christian World Missions* (Grand Rapids: Eerdmans, 1995).
_____. *Truth and Authority in Modernity* (Valley Forge, PA: Trinity, 1996).
Niebuhr, G. *Beyond Tolerance: Searching for Interfaith Understanding in America* (New York: Viking, 2008).
Niebuhr, R. *Moral Man and Immoral Society* (New York: Charles Scribner's Sons, 1932, 1960).
_____. *The Children of Light and The Children of Darkness: A Vindication of Democracy and A Critique of Its Traditional Defense* (New York: Charles Scribner's Sons, 1944, 1960).
_____. *Pious and Secular America* (New York: Charles Scribner's Sons, 1958).
_____. *The Nature and Destiny of Man: A Christian Interpretation, I and II* (Louisville, KY: Westminster John Knox, 1996).
_____. *The Irony of American History: With a New Introduction by Andrew J. Bacevich* (Chicago: University of Chicago Press, 1952, 2008).
Nkansah-Obrempong, J. "The Contemporary Theological Situation in Africa: An Overview", *ERT* 31:2 (April 2007), 140-50.
Noll, M.A. *The Scandal of the Evangelical Mind* (Grand Rapids: Eerdmans, 1994).
_____. "The History of an Encounter: Roman Catholics and Protestant Evangelicals," *Evangelicals & Catholics Together: Toward a Common Mission*, ed. Charles Colson and Richard John Neuhaus (Dallas: Word, 1995), 81-114.
_____. *Turning Points: Decisive Moments in the History of Christianity* (Grand Rapids: Baker Academic, 1997).
_____. "Early Returns are Mixed," *CT* 52:6 (July 1, 2008), 1-3, http://www.christianitytoday.com/ct/2008/june/31.53.html?start=1.
O'Connor, E.D. *The Pentecostal Movement in the Catholic Church* (Notre Dame: Ave Maria Press, 1971).
Oden, T.C. *John Wesley's Scriptural Christianity: A Plain Exposition of His Teaching on Christian Doctrine* (Grand Rapids: Zondervan, 1994).
_____. *The Living God: Systematic Theology: Volume One* (Prince: Peabody, MA. 2001).
Ogden, S.M. *Is There Only One True Religion or Are There Many?* (Dallas: Southern Methodist University Press, 1992).
Olson, R.E. *The Story of Christian Theology: Twenty Centuries of Tradition & Reform* (Downer's Grove: InterVarsity, 1999).
_____. *How to Be Evangelical Without Being Conservative* (Grand Rapids: Zondervan, 2008).
Omar, I.R. "Pope Benedict XVI's Comments on Islam in Regensburg: A Muslim Response," *Current Dialogue* 48 (December 2006), 16-19.
O'Neal, S.S. *Bridges to People: Communicating Jesus to People and Growing Missional Churches in a Multi-Ethnic World* (USA: Xulon Press, 2007).

_____. "Sharing the Gospel in a Postmodern World," *COGE,* 99:9 (September 2009), 14-15.

Orr, J. *Biblical Faith and Natural Theology* (New York: Oxford, 1993).

Onyinah, O. "Deliverance as a Way of Confronting Witchcraft in Contemporary Africa: Ghana as a Case Study,"Kärkkäinen, V.M., ed. *The Spirit in the World: Emerging Pentecostal Theologies in Global Contexts* (Grand Rapids: Eerdmans, 2009), 181-202.

Osborne, E. *Irenaeus of Lyons* (New York: Cambridge University Press, 2001).

Oswalt, J.N. "The Mission of Israel to the Nations," *Through No Fault of Their Own,* ed. W. V. Crockett and J. Sigountos (Grand Rapids: Baker, 1991), 85-95.

_____. *The New International Commentary on the Old Testament: The Book of Isaiah: Chapters 1-39* (Grand Rapids: Eerdmans, 1986).

_____. *The New International Commentary on the Old Testament: The Book of Isaiah: Chapters 40-66* (Grand Rapids: Eerdmans, 1998).

Otto, R. *The Idea of the Holy,* trans. John Harvey, (New York: Oxford University Press, 1958).

Owens, R. "The Azusa Street Revival: The Pentecostal Movement Begins in America," V. Synan, ed., *The Century of the Holy Spirit: 100 Years of Pentecostal and Charismatic Renewal* (Nashville, TN: Nelson, 2001), 39-68.

Padgett, A.G. and P.R. Keifert, eds. *But Is It All True? The Bible and the Question of Truth* (Grand Rapids, MI: Eerdmans, 2006).

_____. E.T. Charry, "Walking in the Truth: On Knowing God," 144-69.

Palma, A. "1 Corinthians," F.L. and R. Stronstad, eds. *FLBCNT,* (Grand Rapids: Zondervan, 1999), 799-913.

Palmer, M.D. "Ethics in the Classical Pentecostal Tradition," *NIDPCM,* 605-10.

Pannenberg, W. *Human Nature, Election, and History* (Philadelphia: Westminster, 1977).

_____. *Ethics,* trans. K. Crim (Philadelphia: Westminster, 1981).

_____. *An Introduction to Systematic Theology* (Grand Rapids: Eerdmans, 1991).

Panikkar, R. *The Unknown Christ of Hinduism* (London: Darton, Longman, & Todd, 1964, 1981).

Parham, C.F. *The Sermons of Charles F. Parham* (NY: Garland, 1985 pr). This is a collection of earlier and separate publications by Parham previously published as *A Voice Crying in the Wilderness* (1902) and *The Everlasting Gospel* (1919).

Park, M.S. "David Yonggi Cho and International Pentecostal/Charismatic Movements," *JPT* 12:1 (2003), 107-28.

_____. "Korean Pentecostal Spirituality as Manifested in the Testimonies of Believers of the Yoido Full Gospel Church," *AJPS* 7:1 (2004), 35-56.

Parris, G. "Pentecostal Spirituality," *NWDCS,* 485-86.

Pedro A. and P. Semán, "Brazilian Pentecostalism Crosses National Borders," A. Corten and R.R. Marshall-Fratani, eds. *Between Babel and Pentecost: Transnational Pentecostalism in Africa and Latin America* (Bloomington, IN: Indiana University Press, 2001), 181-95.

Pettite, P., ed. *Foundations of Spiritual Formation: A Community Approach to Becoming Like Christ* (Grand Rapids: Kregel, 2008).
Petts, D., "The Baptism in the Holy Spirit: The Theological Distinctive," *Pentecostal Perspectives*, ed., K. Warrington (Carlisle: Paternoster, 1998).
Philips, T.R. "Christianity and Religions," *EDT*, 231-34.
Pickett, F. *Walking in the Anointing of the Holy Spirit: Book II* (Lake Mary, FL: Charisma House, 2004).
Photiadis, J.D. "A Theoretical Supplement," J.D. Photiadis, ed. *Religion in Appalachia: Theological, Social, and Psychological Dimensions and Correlates*, (Morgantown, WV: University of West Virginia, approx. 1977), 7-27.
Pinnock, C.H. "Toward an Evangelical Theology of Religions," *JETS* 33:3 (1990), 359-68.
_____. *A Wideness in God's Mercy: The Finality of Jesus Christ in a World of Religions* (Grand Rapids: Zondervan, 1992)
_____. "The Work of the Holy Spirit in Hermeneutics," *JPT* 2 (April 1993), 3-23.
_____. "Evangelism and Other Living Faiths: An Evangelical Charismatic Perspective", 208-14, H.D. Hunter and P.D. Hocken, eds. *All Together in One Place: Theological Papers from the Brighton Conference on World Evangelization* (JPTSup 4, Sheffield, Eng: Sheffield Academic Press, 1993).
_____. *Flame of Love: A Theology of the Holy Spirit* (InterVarsity Press: Downer's Grove, IL. 1994).
_____. "Response to John Hick," Gundry, S.N., D.L. Okholm, and T.R. Phillips, eds., *Four Views on Salvation in a Pluralistic World* (Grand Rapids: Zondervan, 1995), 60-64.
_____. "The Holy Spirit in the Theology of Donald G. Bloesch," *Evangelical Theology in Transition: Theologians in Dialogue with Donald Bloesch* (Downer's Grove, IL: InterVarsity, 1999), 119-35.
_____. "The Church in the Power of the Holy Spirit: The Promise of a Pentecostal Ecclesiology," *JPT* 14:2 (April 2006), 147-65.
_____. "A Review of Frank D. Macchia's *Baptized in the Spirit: A Global Theology,*" *JPT* 16:2 (April 2008), 1-4.
Pittman, D.A., Ruben L. F. Habito, and Terry Muck, eds., *Ministry and Theology in Global Perspective: Contemporary Challenges for the Church* (Grand Rapids: Eerdmans, 1996.
_____. D.J. Hesselgrave, "Evangelicals and Interreligious Dialogue," 425-28.
Plüss, J.D. "Testimony," *GDT,* 877-79.
Poirier, J.C. "Narrative Theology and Pentecostal Commitments," *JPT* 16:2 (April 2008), 69-85.
Poloma, M.M. "Divine Healing, Religious Revivals, and Contemporary Pentecostalism: A North American Perspective," Kärkkäinen, V.M., ed. *The Spirit in the World: Emerging Pentecostal Theologies in Global Contexts* (Grand Rapids: Eerdmans, 2009), 21-39.
Pope, L. *Millhands and Preachers* (New Haven: Yale University Press, 1942, 1958).

Powers, J.E. "Pentecostalism 101: Your Daughters Shall Prophesy," Alexander, E. and A. Yong, *Philip's Daughters: Women in Pentecostal-Charismatic Leadership,* Princeton Monograph Series (Eugene, OR: Pickwick, 2008), 133-51.

Price, L. *Theology Out of Place: A Theological Biography of Walter J. Hollenweger* (J Sup Series, (Sheffield, Eng: Sheffield Academic Press, 2002).

Propp, V. *Morphology of the Folktale* (2nd ed., Austin, TX: University of Texas Press, 1968).

Proudfoot, W. *Religious Experience* (Berkley, CA: University of California, 1985).

Quebedeaux, R. *The New Charismatics II: How a Christian Renewal Movement Became Part of the American Religious Mainstream* (San Francisco: Harper & Row, 1976, 1983).

Rabinowitz, D. *No Crueler Tyrannies: Accusation, False Witness, and Other Terrors of Our Times* (New York: Free Press, 2003).

Race, A. *Christians and Religious Pluralism: Patterns in the Theology of Religions* (Maryknoll: Orbis, 1983).

Rahner, K. *Foundations of Christian Faith: An Introduction to the Idea of Christianity,* trans. William V. Dych (New York: Crossroad, 1978, 2002).

Raiser, K. "Is Ecumenical Apologetics Sufficient? A Response to Lesslie Newbigin's 'Ecumenical Amnesia,'" *IBMR* 18 (April 1994), 50-51.

Ramachandra, V. *The Recovery of Mission: Beyond the Pluralist Paradigm* (Carlisle, UK: Paternoster, 1996).

_____. *Gods That Fail: Modern Idolatry and Christian Mission* (Downer's Grove: InterVarsity, 1996).

_____. *Faiths in Conflict: Christian Integrity in a Multicultural World* (Downer's Grove, IL: InterVarsity Press, 1999).

Rambachan, A. and A.R. Omar, and M.T. Thangaraj, eds. *Hermeneutical Explorations in Dialogue: Essays in Honor of Hans Ucko,* eds. (Dehli: ISPCK, 2007).

Raser, R.E. *Phoebe Palmer: Her Life and Thought* (Lewiston, NY: Mellen, 1987).

Reddie, A.G. *Black Theology in Transatlantic Dialogue* (New York: Palgrave MacMillan, 2006).

Redman, J. "A Theology of Social Action," 1-7, Faith News Network (4/14/08) at http://www.faithnews.cc/articles.cfm?sid=8827.

Reed, D.A. "Oneness Pentecostalism," *NIDPCM,* 936-44.

Rentoul, J. *Tony Blair: Prime Minister* (London: Time Warner, 2003).

Reynolds, T. "Reconsidering Schleiermacher and the Problem of Religious Diversity: Toward a Dialectical Pluralism," *JAAR* 73:1 (Mar 2005), 151-81.

Rheenen, G.V. "Changing Motivations for Missions: From "Fear of Hell" to "the Glory of God," M. Pocock, G.V. Rheenen, and D. McConnell *The Changing Face of World Missions: Engaging Contemporary Issues and Trends,* (Grand Rapids: Baker, 2005), 161-81.

Rice, C. "America's Confidence in Freedom," *RFIA,* 4:2 (Fall 2002), 37-40.

Richard, R.P. *The Population of Heaven: A Biblical Response to the Inclusivist Position on Who will be Saved* (Chicago: Moody, 1994).

Richardson, A. *An Introduction to the Theology of the New Testament* (New York:

Harper & Brothers, 1958).
_____. *Religion in Contemporary Debate* (London: SCM, 1966).
Richie, T. "Mr. Wesley and Mohammed: A Contemporary Inquiry Concerning Islam," *ATJ* 58:2 (Fall 2003), 79-99.
_____. "Awe-full Encounters: A Pentecostal Conversation with C. S. Lewis Concerning Spiritual Experience," *JPT* 14:1 (October 2005), 99- 122.
_____. "Neither Naïve nor Narrow: A Balanced Approach to Christian Theology of Religions," *CPCR* 15 (Feb. 2006), http://www.pctii.org/cyberj/cyber15.html.
_____. "God's Fairness to People of All Faiths: A Respectful Proposal to Pentecostals for Discussion Regarding World Religions," *Pneuma* 28:1 (2006), 105-19.
_____. "'The Unity of the Spirit': Are Pentecostals Inherently Ecumenists and Inclusivists?" *JEPTA* 26 (2006), 21-35.
_____. "Azusa-era Optimism: Bishop J. H. King's Pentecostal Theology of Religions as a Possible Paradigm for Today," *JPT* 14:2 (April 2006), 247-60.
_____. "Being Faithfully Pentecostal in a World of Pluralistic Faiths," *COGE* (August 2006), 6-7.
_____. "Is Pentecostalism Just Another American Success Story? A Response to Jürgen Moltmann on the Place of Optimism in the Pentecostal Tradition," *Refleks* 5:2 (2006), 77-93.
_____. "A Pentecostal in Sheep's Clothing: an Unlikely Participant but Hopeful Partner in Interreligious Dialogue," *CD* 48 (December 2006), 9-15.
_____. "Eschatological Inclusivism: Exploring Early Pentecostal Theology of Religions in Charles Fox Parham," *JEPTA* 27:2 (2007), 138-52.
_____. "Revamping Pentecostal Evangelism: Appropriating Walter J. Hollenweger's Radical Proposal", *IRM* 96:382-83 (July-October 2007), 343-54.
_____. "Healing Fire from Heaven: A Wesleyan-Pentecostal Approach to Interfaith Forgiveness and Reconciliation", *WTJ* 42:2 (Fall 2007), 136-54.
_____. "Effectively Engaging Pluralism and Postmodernism in a So-Called Post-Christian Culture: A Review Essay of Lesslie Newbigin's *The Gospel in a Pluralist Society*", *PR* (Fall 2007), 27-39.
_____. "Much More than a Man among Men: The Supreme Significance of Jesus Christ," *COGE* (December 2007), 6-7.
_____"Hints from Heaven: Can C. S. Lewis Help Evangelicals Hear God in Other Religions?" *ERT* 32:1 (January 2008), 38-55.
_____. "A Threefold Cord: Weaving Together Pentecostal Ecumenism, Ethics, and
Evangelism in Conversion," *CD* 50 (January 2008), 47-54.
_____. "Approaching the Problem of Religious Truth in a Pluralistic World: A Pentecostal-Charismatic Contribution," *JES* 43:3 (Summer 2008), 351-69.
_____. "Pentecostal Spirituality Politically Applied," *Pax Pneuma* 5:1 (Spring 2009), 28-33.
_____. "Azusa-Era Optimism: Bishop J.H. King's Pentecostal Theology of Religions as a Possible Paradigm for Today,"Kärkkäinen, V.M., ed. *The Spirit in the World: Emerging Pentecostal Theologies in Global Contexts* (Grand Rapids: Eerdmans, 2009), 227-43.
Ricoeur, P. *Essays on Biblical Interpretation,* ed. L.S. Mudge (Philadelphia, PA:

Fortress, 1974, 1980).

———. *Oneself as Another,* trans. Kathleen Blamey (Chicago, IL: University of Chicago Press, 1992, 1994).

——— and M.I. Wallace. *Figuring the Sacred* (Minneapolis, MN: Augsburg, 1995).

Ritchie, D.A. *Doing Oral History: Using Interviews to Uncover the Past and Preserve it for the Future* (New York: Oxford University Press, 2003).

Robeck, C.M., Jr. "David du Plessis and the Challenge of Dialogue," *Pneuma* 9 (Spring 1987), 1-4.

———. "Pentecostals and the Apostolic Faith: Implications for Ecumenism," *Pneuma* 9 (Spring 1987), 61-84.

———. "Pentecostals and Social Ethics," *Pneuma* 9 (Fall 1987), 103-07.

———. "Taking Stock of Pentecostalism: The Personal Reflections of a Retiring Editor," *Pneuma,* 15:1 (Spring 1993), 35-60.

———. "When Being a 'Martyr' is not Enough: Catholics and Pentecostals," *Pneuma* 21 (1999), 3-10.

———. "Farrow, Lucy F.," *NIDPCM,* 632-33.

———. "Junk, Thomas," *NIDPCM,* 814.

———. "Pike, John Martin," *NIDPCM,* 988-89.

———, with J.L. Sandidge, "World Council of Churches," *NIDPCM,* 1213-17.

———, with J.L. Sandidge, "Dialogue, Roman Catholic and Classical Pentecostal," *NIDPCM.* 576-82.

———. "John Paul II: A Personal Account of His Impact and Legacy," *Pneuma* 27:1 (2005), 3-34.

———. *The Azusa Street Mission & Revival: The Birth of the Global Pentecostal Movement* (Nashville: Nelson, 2006).

Robinson, E.B. "Johnson, Bernard, Jr.," *NIDPCM,* 812-13.

Rock, J. "Resources in the Reformed Tradition for Responding to Religious Plurality," S.M. Heim, Ed., *Grounds for Understanding: Ecumenical Responses to Religious Pluralism* (Grand Rapids: Eerdmans, 1998), 46-58.

Roebuck, D. "'Cause He's My Chief Employer': Hearing Women's Voices in a Classical Pentecostal Denomination,"Alexander, E. and A. Yong, *Philip's Daughters: Women in Pentecostal-Charismatic Leadership,* Princeton Monograph Series (Eugene, OR: Pickwick, 2008), 38-60.

Rogers, C.R. *On Becoming a Person* (Boston: Houghton Mifflin, 1961).

Rollins, W.G. *Jung and the Bible* (Atlanta: John Knox Press, 1983).

Rosenberg, D. *Testimony: Contemporary Writers Make the Holocaust Personal* (New York: Time/Random House, 1989).

Rottenberg, I.C. *The Promise and the Presence: Toward a Theology of the Kingdom of God* (Grand Rapids: Eerdmans, 1980).

Rubenstein, M.A. "Taiwan," *NIDPCM,* 259-64.

Rutledge, F. "When God Disturbs the Peace," *Christianity Today* 52:6 (June 2008) at http://www.christianitytoday.com/ct/2008/june/13.30.html.

Runyon, T. *The New Creation: John Wesley's Theology Today* (Nashville: Abingdon, 1998).

Sailhammer, J.H. *The Pentateuch as Narrative: A Biblical-Theological Commentary* (Grand Rapids: Zondervan, 1992).
Samartha, S.J. *One Christ, Many Religions: Toward a Revised Christology* (New York: Maryknoll, 1991).
Sanders, C.J. *Saints in Exile: The Holiness-Pentecostal Experience in African American Religion and Culture* (Religion in America) (New York: Oxford University Press, 1999).
Sanders, J. *No Other Name: An Investigation into the Destiny of the Unevangelized* (Grand Rapids: Eerdmans, 1992).
Saucy, R.L. *The Case for Progressive Dispensationalism: The Interface Between Dispensational & Non-Dispensational Theology* (Grand Rapids: Zondervan, 1993).
Schmidt-Leukel, P. "Exclusivism, Inclusivism, Pluralism: The Tripolar Typology—Clarified and Reaffirmed," *The Myth of Religious Superiority: Multifaith Explorations of Religious Pluralism,* ed., P.F. Knitter (Maryknoll, New York: Orbis, 2005), 13-27.
_____. "Chalcedon Defended: A Pluralistic Re-Reading of the Two Natures Doctrine," *ET* 118:3 (2006), 113-19.
Schroeder, D.E. *Walking in Your Anointing: Knowing that You are Filled with the Spirit* (Bloomington, IN: AuthorHouse, 2007).
Scott, J.M. *2 Corinthians*, Gasque, W.W., NT editor, *NIBC* (Peabody, MA: Hendrickson, 1988).
Seager, R. *The Dawn of Religious Pluralism: Voices from the World's Parliament of Religions, 1893* (Peru, IL: Open Court, 1993, 1999).
Seldon, A. *Blair* (Sidney, Australia: Simon & Schuster, 2004, 2005).
Sepúlveda, J. "Reflections on the Pentecostal Contribution to the Mission of the Church in Latin America," *JPT* 1 (1992), 93-108.
_____. "The Perspective of Chilean Pentecostalism," *JPT* 4 (1994), 41-49.
_____. "Characteristics of Indigenous Pentecostalism: Chile," *In the Power of the Spirit,* eds. D.A. Smith and B.F. Guiterrez, http://www.religion-online.org/showchapter.asp?title=374&C=9 (downloaded November 7, 2007).
Shaw, B.J. "Habermas and Religious Inclusion: Lessons from Kant's Moral Theology," *PT* 27:5 (October 1999), 634-66.
Sheard, R.B. *Interreligious Dialogue in the Catholic Church Since Vatican II: An Historical and Theological Study* Toronto Studies in Theology vol. 31 (Lewiston/Queenston: Edwin Mellen Press, 1987).
Sheldrake, P. "Postmodernity," *NWDCS,* 498-500.
Shelton, J. "Matthew," Arrington, F.L. and R. Stronstad, eds. *FLBCNT,* (Grand Rapids: Zondervan, 1999), 119-253.
Shenk, C.E. *Who Do You Say That I Am? Christians Encounter Other Religions* (Scottsdale, PA: Herald, 1997).
Shepperd, J.W. "Sociology of World Pentecostalism," *NIDPCM,* 1083-90.
Shuman, J. "Pentecost and the End of Patriotism: A Call for the Restoration of Pacifism Among Pentecostal Christians," *JPT* 9 (1996), 70-96.

Siddiqui, M. "When Reconciliation Fails: Global Politics and the Study of Religion," *JAAR* 73:4 (Dec 2005), 1141-53.
Sider, R.J. *The Scandal of Evangelical Politics: Why Are Christians Missing the Change to Change the World* (Grand Rapids: Baker, 2008).
Sims, J. *Power with Purpose: The Holy Spirit in Historical and Contemporary Perspective* (Cleveland: Pathway, 1984).
Simut, C.C. *A Critical Study of Hans Küng's Ecclesiology*, (New York: Palgrave MacMillan, 2008).
Sinkinson, C. "In Defense of the Faith: Clark Pinnock and the World Religions," *Reconstructing Theology: A Critical Assessment of the Theology of Clark Pinnock,* eds. T. Gray & C. Sinkinson (Waynesboro, GA: Paternoster, 2000), 155-83.
Smart, N. "Pluralism," *NHCT*, eds. D.W. Musser and J.L. Price (Nashville: Abingdon, 1992), 360-64.
Smith, B.G. "Attitudes toward Religious Pluralism: Measurements and Consequences," *Social Compass,* 54:2 (2007), 333-53.
Smith, C.L. "Revolutionaries and Revivalists: Pentecostal Eschatology, Politics and the Nicaraugan Revolution," *Pneuma* 30:1 (2008), 55-82.
Smith, D.M. "John," J.L. Mays, gen. ed. *Harper's Bible Commentary,* (San Francisco, CA: Harper & Row, 1988), 1044-76.
Smith, J.K.A. "Teaching a Calvinist to Dance," *Christianity Today* (May 2008), http://www.christianitytoday.com/ct/2008/may/25.42.html?start=1.
Smith, J.P. *St. Irenaeus: Proof of Apostolic Preaching,* Ancient Christian Writers 16 (Mahwah, NJ: Paulist Press, 1978).
Smith, S.M. "Hope, Theology of," *EDT,* 577-79.
Smith, W.C. *Faith and Belief: The Difference Between Them* (Oxford: Oneworld, 1998).
Smock, D.R. "Conclusion," D.R. Smock, ed., *Interfaith Dialouge and Peacebuilding* (Washington, DC: United States Institute for Peace, 2002), 127-32.
Snell, J.T. "Beyond the Individual and Into the World: A Call to Participate in the Larger Purposes of the Spirit on the Basis of Pentecostal Theology", *Pneuma* 14:1 (Spring 1992), 43-57.
Snyder, H. "Salvation Means Creation Healed: Creation, Cross, Kingdom, and Mission," *AJ* 62:1 (Spring 2007), 9-47.
Soards, M.L. *1 Corinthians*, W.W. Gasque, NT editor, *NIBC* (Peabody, MA: Hendrickson, 1999).
Solivan, S. "Interreligious Dialogue: An Hispanic American Pentecostal Perspective," S.M. Heim, Ed., *Grounds for Understanding: Ecumenical Responses to Religious Pluralism* (Grand Rapids: Eerdmans, 1998), 37-45.
_____. *The Spirit, Pathos and Liberation: Toward an Hispanic Pentecostal Theology,* Journal of Pentecostal Theology Supplement Series 14 (Sheffield: Sheffield Academic Press, 1998).
Spero, J.E. and J.A. Hart, *The Politics of International Economic Relations* (Boston, MA: Wadsworth, 2003).
Spina, F.A. *The Faith of the Outsider: Exclusion and Inclusion in the Biblical Story* (Grand Rapids: Eerdmans, 2005).

Spittler, R.P. ed. *Perspectives on the New Pentecostalism* (Grand Rapids: Baker, 1976).
_____. W.G. MacDonald, "Pentecostal Theology: A Classical Viewpoint," 58-75.
Spittler, R.P. "Du Plessis, David Johannes," *NIDPCM,* 589-93.
_____. "Robeck, Cecil Melvin, Jr.," *NIDPCM,* 1023-24.
_____. "Spirituality, Pentecostal," *NIDPCM,* 1096-1102.
_____. "Glossolalia," *NIDPCM,* 670-76.
Stackhouse, J.G., Jr., ed., *No Other Gods Before Me? Evangelicals and the Challenge of World Religions* (Grand Rapids: Baker Academic, 2001).
Stamps, D.C., gen. ed., and J.W. Adams, assoc. ed., *The Full Life Study Bible,* assoc. ed. J.W. Adams (Grand Rapids, MI: Zondervan, 1992).
Stanley, S.C. "Wesleyan/Holiness and Pentecostal Women Preachers: Pentecost as the Pattern for Primitivism," Alexander, E. and A. Yong, *Philip's Daughters: Women in Pentecostal-Charismatic Leadership,* Princeton Monograph Series (Eugene, OR: Pickwick, 2008), 19-37.
Stephens, R.J. "Assessing the Roots of Pentecostalism: A Historiographic Essay," at American Religious Experience, http://are.as.wvu.edu/pentroot.htm (n. d.; site last modified October 2007).
_____. *The Fire Spreads: Holiness and Pentecostalism in the American South* (Boston: Harvard University Press, 2007).
Sterling, L. Jr., "Our Only Hope in a Pluralistic World," *COGE* (December 2007), 8-9.
Stibbe, M.W.G. "A British Appraisal," *JPT,* 4 (1994), 5-16.
Stone, B. *Evangelism after Christendom: The Theology and Practice of Christian Witness* (Grand Rapids: Brazos, 2007).
Stott, J.R. "Dialogue, Encounter, Even Confrontation," D.A. Pittman, R.L.F. Habito, and T. Muck, eds., *Ministry and Theology in Global Perspective: Contemporary Challenges for the Church* (Grand Rapids: Eerdmans, 1996), 408-414.
Stout, J. "2007 Presidential Address: The Folly of Secularism," *JAAR* 76:3 (September 2008), 533-44.
Strachen, G. *The Pentecostal Theology of Edward Erving* (Peabody: Hendrickson, 1973, 1988).
Strang, S. "Gimenez, John," *NIDPCM,* 668.
Stronstad, R. *The Charismatic Theology of St. Luke* (Peabody: Hendrickson, 1984).
Studebaker, S. ed., *Defining Issues in Pentecostalism: Classical and Emergent,* McMaster's Theological Studies (Eugene, OR: Pickwick, 2008).
Summer, L. "Non-Christian Religions," *The C.S. Lewis Readers' Encyclopedia,* eds.
  Jeffrey D. Schultz and John G. West Jr. (Grand Rapids: Zondervan, 1998), 294-95.
Sumner, G.R. *The First & the Last: The Claim of Jesus Christ and the Claims of OtherReligions* (Grand Rapids: Eerdmans, 2004).

Synan, V. *The Holiness-Pentecostal Movement in the United States* (Grand Rapids: Eerdmans, 1971).
_____. *In the Latter Days: The Outpouring of the Holy Spirit in the Twentieth Century* (Ann Arbor: Servant, 1974)
_____. "Classical Pentecostalism," *NIDPCM,* 553-55.
_____. "Fundamentalism," *NIDPCM,* 655-58.
_____. "Evangelicalism," *NIDPCM,* 613-16.
_____. "International Pentecostal Holiness Church," *NIDPCM,* 798-801.
Synan, V. "Streams of Renewal at the End of the Century," V. Synan, ed. *The Century of the Holy Spirit: 100 Years of Pentecostal and Charismatic Renewal* (Nashville, TN: Nelson, 2001), 349-80.
Swearer, D.K. 's *Dialogue: The Key to Understanding Other Religions* (Philadelphia: Westminster, 1977), *Biblical Perspectives on Current Issues* series, H.C. Kee, Gen. Ed.
Swindler L. and P. Mojzes, ed., *The Uniqueness of Jesus: A Dialogue with Paul Knitter,* (Maryknoll, New York: Orbis, 1997).
Tan-Chow, M.L. *Pentecostal Theology for the Twenty-First Century* (Burlington, VT: Ashgate, 2007).
Telushkin, J. *Biblical Literacy* (New York: William Morrow, 1997).
Tennent, T.C. *Christianity at the Religious Roundtable: Evangelicalism in Conversation with Hinduism, Buddhism, and Islam* (Grand Rapids: Baker Academic, 2002).
Tesfai, Y. *Liberation and Orthodoxy: The Promise and Failures of Interconfessional Dialogue* (New York: Orbis, 1996).
Thangaraj, M.T. *Relating to People of Other Religions: What Every Christian Needs to Know* (Nashville: Abingdon, 1997).
Thigpen, T.P. "Catholic Charismatic Renewal," *NIDPCM,* 460-65.
Thomas, A. "Everyone Has a Story to Tell," *AARP* (July/August 2008), 30-34.
_____. *Thinking About Memoir* (AARP Books/Sterling, 2008).
Thomas, J.C. 1998 Presidential Address, "Pentecostal Theology in the Twenty-First Century," *Pneuma* 20 (Spring 1998), 3-19.
_____. "The Charismatic Structure of Acts," *JPT* 13:1 (October 2004), 19-30.
_____. *The Spirit of the New Testament* (Netherlands: Deo, 2005).
Thorsen, D.A.D. *The Wesleyan Quadrilateral: Scripture, Tradition, Reason, & Experience as a Model of Evangelical Theology* (Grand Rapids: Zondervan, 1990).
_____, with Kevin W. Mannoia, eds., *The Holiness Manifesto,* (Grand Rapids: Eerdmans, 2008).
Tillich , P. *Christianity and the Encounter of World Religions* (NY: Columbia, 1961, 1963).
_____. *The Future of Religions* (New York:: Harper & Row, 1966).
Toynbee, A. *Christianity Among the Religions of the World* (New York: Scribner's, 1957).
Tozer, A.W. *The Best of Tozer: Book One* (Camp Hill, PA: Wingspread, 2007; repr. Baker, 1978).

_____. *The Best of Tozer: Book Two* (Camp Hill, PA: Wingspread, 2007; repr. Baker, 1980, 1995).
Tracy, D. *Dialogue with the Religious Other: The Inter-Religious Dialogue* (Grand Rapids: Eerdmans, 1990).
Turner, B.S. "Sovereignty and Emergency: Political Theology, Islam and American Conservatism," *Theory, Culture & Society,* 19:4 (2002), 103-19.
Turner, H.L. "Pentecostal Currents in SBC: Divine Intervention, Prophetic Preachers, and Charismatic Worship," Blumhoffer, E.L., with R.P. Spittler, G.A. Wacker, *Pentecostal Currents in American Protestantism* (Champaign, IL:University of Illinois, 1999), 209-28.
Turner, Jr., W.C. *The United Holy Church of America: A Study in Black Holiness-Pentecostalism* (New Jersey: Gorgias, 2006).
Ucko, H. "Testimonies from a Multifaith Hearing on Conversion, Lariano (Italy), May 12-16, 2006" in *CD* 50 (February 2008), 20-37.
Unger, D.J. *Irenaeus of Lyons: Against Heresies: Book I,* Ancient Christian Writers Series (Mahwah, NJ: Paulist Press, 1992).
Vaihinger, H. "Fictionalism and Finalism," Ansbacher, H. and R.R. Ansbacher, ed. *The Individual Pschology of Alfred Adler* (New York: Harper & Rox, 1956), 76-100.
Villafañe, E. *The Liberating Spirit: Toward an Hispanic American Pentecostal Social Ethic* (Grand Rapids: Eerdmans, 1993).
Volf, M. *Exclusion and Embrace: A Theological Exploration of Identity, Otherness, and Reconciliation* (Nashville: Abingdon, 1994).
_____. *After Our Likeness: The Church as the Image of the Trinity* (Grand Rapids: Eerdmans, 1998).
Vondey, W. People of Bread: Rediscovering Ecclesiology (Mahwah, NJ: Paulist Press, 2008).
Von Harnack, A. *The History of Dogma, Volume I* (New York: Dover, 1961).
Wacker, G. *Heaven Below: Early Pentecostals and American Culture* (London: Harvard University Press, 2001).
Wallis, J. *God's Politics: Why the Right Gets It Wrong and the Left Doesn't Get It* (New York: HarperSanFrancisco, 2005).
Walker, P.L. *Is Christianity the Only Way?* (Cleveland, TN: Pathway, 1975).
Walls, J.L. *The Problem of Pluralism: Recovering United Methodist Identity* (Wilmore, KY: Good News, 1986).
Walsh, A.S. *Latino Pentecostal Identity* (New York: Columbia University Press, 2003).
Ware, F.L. "Spiritual Egalitarianism, Ecclesial Egalitarianism, and the Status of Women in Ordained Ministry," Alexander, E. and A. Yong, *Philip's Daughters: Women in Pentecostal-Charismatic Leadership,* Princeton Monograph Series (Eugene, OR: Pickwick, 2008), 215-34.
Warner, W.E. "Montgomery, Carrie Judd," *NIDPCM,* 904-06.
_____. "Pentecostal Fellowship of North America," *NIDPCM,* 968-69.
_____. "Periodicals," *NIDPCM,* 974-82.
Warrington, K. *Pentecostal Theology: A Theology of Encounter* (New York: T & T

Clark, 2008).

Webber, R.E., ed., *The Complete Library of Christian Worship: Volume 1, The Biblical Foundations of Christian Worship*, (Nashville: StarSong, 1993).

_____. *Ancient-Future Faith: Rethinking Evangelicalism for a Postmodern World* (Grand Rapids: Baker, 1999).

_____. *The Divine Embrace: Recovering the Passionate Spiritual Life* (Grand Rapids: Baker, 2006).

Webster, D.D. "Liberation Theology, *EDT,* 686-88.

Weems, A. *Psalms of Lament* (Louisville, KY: Westminster John Knox, 1995).

Weibe, R.H. *Self-Rule: A Cultural History of American Democracy* (Chicago, IL: University of Chicago, 1995).

Welker, M. *God the Spirit*, trans. John F. Hoffmeyer (Minneapolis: Fortress, 1994).

_____, ed., *The Work of the Spirit: Pneumatology and Pentecostalism* (Grand Rapids: Eerdmans, 2006).

Wesley, J. *CWJW* (Rio, WI: Ages Software, Inc., 2002).

Westerlund, D., ed., *Global Pentecostalism: Encounters with Other Religious Traditions* (New York: I.B. Tauris, 2009).

White, C.E. *The Beauty of Holiness: Phoebe Palmer as Theologian, Revivalist, Feminist, and Humanatarian* (Grand Rapids: Asbury/Zondervan, 1986).

White, J.F. *Roman Catholic Worship: Trent to Today* (Collegeville, Minnesota: Liturgical Press, 2003).

White, J.R. "Political Eschatology: A Theology of Antigovernment Extremism," *ABS,* 44:6 (February 2001), 937-56.

White, V.L., Jr., *Inside the Nation of Islam: A Historical and Personal Testimony by a Black Muslim* (Gainesville, FL: University of Florida Press, 2001).

Whitney, D.S. *Spiritual Disciplines for the Christian Life* (Colorado Springs, CO: NavPress, 1991).

Wilkinson, M. "When is a Pentecostal a Pentecostal? The Global Perspective of Allan Anderson," *Pneuma* 28:2 (Fall 2006), 278-82.

Williams, C.W. *John Wesley's Theology Today: A Study of the Wesleyan Tradition in the Light of Current Theological Dialogue* (Nashville: Abingdon, 1960, 1990).

Williams, J.R. Williams, *Renewal Theology: Systematic Theology from a Charismatic Perspective*, three volumes in one (Grand Rapids: Zondervan, 1996).

_____. "Baptism in the Holy Spirit," *NIDPCM,* 354-63.

Wills, G. *Under God: Religion and American Politics* (New York: Simon & Schuster, 1990).

Wilson, D.J. "Church Membership," *NIDPCM,* 529-30.

Wingate, A. *The Church and Conversion: A Study of Recent Conversions to and from Christianity in the Tamil Area of South India* (Kashmere Gate, Delhi: ISPCK, 1997).

Witherington III, B. *The Problem with Evangelical Theology: Testing the Exegetical Foundations of Calvinism, Dispensationalism, and Wesleyanism* (Waco, TX: Baylor University Press, 2005),

Wood, L.W. *Pentecostal Grace* (Grand Rapids: Zondervan, 1984).

_____. *The Meaning of Pentecost in Early Methodism: Rediscovering John Fletcher as John Wesley's Vindicator and Designated Successor* (Lanham: Scarecrow, 2002).

_____. *Theology as History and Hermeneutics: A Post-Critical Conversation with Contemporary Theology* (Lexington, KY: Emeth, 2005).

Wright, C. *Deuteronomy,* R.L. Hubbard, Jr., and R.K. Johnston, OT editors, *NIBC* (Peabody, MA: Hendrickson, 1996, 2003).

Wright, N.T. *Surprised by Hope: Rethinking Heaven, the Resurrection, and the Mission of the Church* (New York: HarperCollins, 2008).

Young, R.D. *Encounter with World Religions* (Philadelphia: Westminster, 1970).

Yong, A. ""Tongues of Fire" in the Pentecostal Imagination: The Truth of Glossolalia in   Light of R. C. Neville's Theory of Religious Symbolism", *JPT* 12 (1998), 39-65.

_____. "'Not Knowing Where the Wind Blows...': On Envisioning a Pentecostal-Charismatic Theology of Religions," *JPT* 14 (April 1999), 81-112.

_____. "Whither Theological Inclusivism? The Development and Critique of an Evangelical Theology of Religions," *EQ* 71:4 (October 1999), 327-48.

_____. *Discerning of the Spirit(s): A Pentecostal-Charismatic Contribution to the Christian Theology of Religions* JSup 20 (Sheffield: Sheffield Academic, 2000).

_____. *Beyond the Impasse: Toward a Pneumatological Theology of Religions* (Grand Rapids: Baker, 2003).

_____. "'As the Spirit Gives Utterance...': Pentecost, Intra-Christian Ecumenism, and the Wider Oekumene," IRM 92:366 (July 2003), 299-314.

_____. "The Spirit Bears Witness: Pneumatology, Truth, and the Religions," SJT 57:1 (2004), 14-38.

_____. *The Spirit Poured Out on All Flesh: Pentecostalism and the Possibility of Global Theology* (Grand Rapids: Baker, 2005).

_____. "Whither Evangelical Theology? The Work of Veli-Matti Kärkkäinen as a Case Study of Contemporary Trajectories," *ERT* 30:1 (2006), 60-85.

_____. "From Azusa Street to the Bo Tree and Back: Strange Babblings and Interreligious Interpretations in the Pentecostal Encounter with Buddhism," Kärkkäinen, V.M., ed. *The Spirit in the World: Emerging Pentecostal Theologies in Global Contexts* (Grand Rapids: Eerdmans, 2009), 203-226.

_____. "Can We Get 'Beyond the Paradigm' in Christian Theology of Religions? A Response to Terry Muck," Interpretation 61:1 (January 2007), 28-32.

_____. "The Spirit, Christian Practices, and the Religions: Theology of Religions in Pentecostal and Pneumatological Perspective," *AJ* 62:2 (2007): 5-31.

_____, with T. Richie, "Bearing Witness in a Religiously Pluralistic World: Pentecostal Missiology, the Religions, and Interreligious Encounter," *Studying Global Pentecostalism: Theories and Methods*, eds. A. Anderson, M. Bergunder, A Droogers & C. van der Laan (Berkeley, CA: University of California Press, 2010).

_____. "Guests, Hosts, and the Holy Ghost: Pneumatological Theology and Christian Practices in a World of Many Faiths," D. Jensen, ed., *Lord and Giver of Life: A Constructive Pneumatology* (Louisville: Westminster John Knox Press, 2008).

_____. *Hospitality and the Other: Pentecost, Christian Practices, and the Neighbor* (Maryknoll: Orbis, 2008).

Yun, K.D. "Pentecostalism from Below: *Minjung* Liberation and Asian Pentecostal Theology," Kärkkäinen, V.M., ed. *The Spirit in the World: Emerging Pentecostal Theologies in Global Contexts* (Grand Rapids: Eerdmans, 2009), 89-114.

Zacharias, R. *Jesus Among Other Gods: The Absolute Claims of the Christian Message* (Nashville: W Publishing/Thomas Nelson, 2000).

Zeigler, J.R. "Full Gospel Business Men's Fellowship," *NIDPCM*, 653-54.

_____. "Shakarian, Demos," *NIDPCM*, 1058.

Scripture Index

Genesis
General (100)
1-2 (229)
1:3, 6, 9, 14, 20, 24, 26, 29 (164)
12 (208-209, 278)
12:2-4 (228)
12:3 (208, 211)
14 (211)
14:18-20 (230)
16 (228)
18 (211, 230)
19 (208)
20 (207-211, 226, 227, 228, 278)
20:11-13 (211)
21 (221, 228)
21:1-20 (226)
21:22-34 (207-211, 226, 227, 228, 229)
45:5-8 (228)
50:20 (228)
Exodus
General (71, 171, 191, 226, 228, 271)
19:6 (228)
23:23 (211)
Numbers
16:22 (104)
27:16 (104, 230)
33:52, 53 (211)
Deuteronomy
4:15-20 (230)
20:16, 17 (211)
1 Samuel
17:38-40 (105)
2 Chronicles
35:20-27 (231)
35:21-27 (231)
Nehemiah
8:10 (28)

Book of Job
General (230)
Psalm
General (139, 155, 156, 161, 185)
19 (51)
23:5-6 (113)
27:11 (204)
51:12 (28)
96:3 (174)
102:27 (190)
145:9 (51, 280)
Proverbs
16:9 (228)
19:21 (228)
Isaiah
General (185, 214, 233, 237)
44:28 (230)
45:1, 13 (230)
48:12 (190)
57:15 (214)
Book of Jonah
General (208)
Malachi
3:6 (171, 190)
Matthew
General (114, 151, 230, 232-33)
2:1-2 (51)
5:8 (40)
5:9 (255)
5:16 (261, 280)
11:27 (48)
15:21-28 (230)
15:31 (261)
18:28 (204, 213)
18:28-35 (224)
24:14 (81)
25:31-46 (90)

Mark
11:20-25 (164)
16:9-20 (224)
16:15 (204, 213)
Luke
General (63, 77, 88, 108, 160, 306)
4:16-21 (241, 263)
6:21 (87)
9:58 (88)
10:25 (86, 89)
10:25-37 (89, 113)
10:37 (257, 275)
19:13 (257, 275)
John
1:1, 14, 18 (261)
1:9 (51, 227)
3:8 (205, 286, 292)
3:16 (261)
3:16-21 (223)
3:18 (204, 224)
3:18-21 (224)
4:1-42 (230)
4:21-24 (167)
4:24 (261)
5:23 (215, 233)
10:8 (48)
10:10 (171)
13:35 (261, 279)
14:6 (48, 204, 222, 223, 235)
14:17 (104)
15:26 (139)
15:26, 27 (218, 230)
16:5-11 (258)
17:20-23 (80, 261, 279)
Acts
General (153, 284)
1:8 (102, 230)
2 (24, 62, 76, 151, 184, 298)
2:1-4 (169, 297)
2:4 (230)
2:14-21 (210)
2:17 (62)
4:12 (47, 48, 204, 205, 224, 225)
4:21 (261)
8:26-40 (220, 236)
9:2 (204)
10 (86, 94, 230)
17:22-31 (230)
17:31 (81)
19:9, 23 (204)
24:14, 22 (204)
26:28 (260)
28:2 (89)
Romans
1:18-23 (226)
1:19-21 (51)
1:21-23 (206)
2:12-16 (51, 230)
3:25 (48)
4:7 (48)
8:16 (139)
12:2 (258, 274)
13 (278)
1 Corinthians
12:3 (230)
12:7 (87)
12:7, 11 (167)
12:8-10 (210, 298)
13:9 (86, 216)
14:8 (86)
14:29 (63)
14:40 (167)
15:20-28 (257, 275)
2 Corinthians
General (225)
3:6 (205)
4:5 (98)
Galatians
3:7 (211, 231)
3:10-14 (229)
4:1-6 (51)
4:28-31 (211, 231)
Ephesians
1:3 (259)
1:13-14 (256)
2 Timothy
3:5 (301)
Hebrews
2:3-4 (139)
6:5 (257, 276)
9:15 (48)
12:4-13 (259)
12:14 (29, 40, 238)
13:8 (139, 170, 190)
1 Peter
1:8 (28)
1:9 (261)
2:9 (228)
3:15 (86, 195)
4:9-10 (86)
1 John
2:23 (48)
3:24 (139)
5:6-12 (139)

General Index

Abell, Troy D., 276, 277, 310
Abimelech, 207, 208, 209, 210, 211, 226, 227, 228, 229, 260
Abraham, 34, 35, 207, 208, 209, 210, 211, 226, 227, 228, 229, 230, 231, 260, 266, 316
Adams, John Wesley, 40, 190, 263, 277, 343
Adler, Alfred, 262, 345
Africa, 16, 65, 69, 96, 158, 182, 206, 244, 245, 269, 313, 314, 316, 318, 321, 325, 329, 331, 332, 335, 336
African American, 65, 111, 114, 144, 167, 180, 183, 213, 298, 306, 341
Aker, Benny, 235, 276
Albright, Madeline, 21, 35
Alexander, Estrelda, 276
Alexander, Kimberly Ervin, 154
Alexander, Paul, 157, 159, 237, 277
Al-Sammak, Mohammad, 12
Althouse, Peter, 235, 275
American experiment, 264
Anderson, Allan, 6, 41, 44, 65, 71, 82, 83, 107, 111, 112, 184, 192, 245, 267, 268, 274, 277, 292, 307, 325, 346, 347
Anderson, Norman, 30, 46, 66, 67, 92, 94, 111, 117
Aquinas, 45, 66, 69
Archer, Kenneth, 141
Arminian, 3, 57, 69

Arminius, 51
Arrington, French, 26, 133, 205
Asani, Ali s., 240, 262
Asia, 16, 33, 38, 96, 142
Assemblies of God, 39, 40, 43, 65, 108, 146, 157, 182, 196, 224, 273, 298, 308, 313, 315, 329
Augustine, 66, 112, 125, 205, 206, 225, 227, 262, 298, 315, 322
Azusa, 39, 74, 75, 108, 110, 111, 115, 136, 153-155, 158, 160, 178, 182, 183, 186, 188, 189, 192-194, 232, 279, 280, 298, 314, 325, 326, 328, 331, 332, 336, 339, 340, 347
baptism in the Holy Spirit, 301, 305
Barth, Karl, 12
Bartleman, Frank, 7, 316
Bauckham, Richard, 54, 131, 252, 272
Bede, 225
black, 32, 37, 87, 107, 135, 192, 199
Blair, Tony, 21, 36, 315, 338
Blumhoffer, Edith L., 152, 188, 196, 278
Boone, Jerome, 134, 152, 159
Bowdle, Donald, 40, 226, 278
Brown, Cheryl, 230, 277, 323
Bruce, F. F., 205, 315
Buddhism, 8, 12, 13, 34, 35, 65, 67, 95, 96, 118, 121, 158, 198, 329, 344, 347

351

Buddhists, 15, 52, 93, 99, 123, 230, 247, 259, 321, 323
Bundy, David D., 107, 110, 151, 152, 183, 193, 232, 278
Callen, Barry, 56
Calvinism, 68, 69, 291, 293, 342, 347
Carter, Jimmy, 21, 35, 267
Cartledge, Mark J., 150, 278
Catholic, 2, 15, 17, 53, 60, 73, 76, 86, 96, 105, 106, 107, 111, 122, 123, 146, 161, 185, 189, 193, 195, 213, 220, 237, 251, 268, 271, 275, 291, 294, 316, 320, 321, 324, 327, 333, 335, 340, 341, 344, 346
Catholicism, 7, 12, 80, 81, 243, 264, 297, 310
Chan, Simon, 142, 151, 156, 251, 271
Charismatic, 2, 46, 53, 54, 72, 73, 76, 103, 124, 126, 164, 177, 183, 197, 198, 224, 251, 253, 298, 300, 301, 305, 307, 308, 310
Chilton, Bruce, 240, 262
China, 45, 66, 142, 247, 277, 312, 313
Cho, David, 159
Christian mission, 32, 56, 59, 92, 98, 113, 115, 120, 121, 285, 290, 291
Christianity,
  historic or traditional, 43, 44, 50, 95, 96, 237, 287, 306
  scriptural or biblical, 46, 126, 171, 206, 220, 222, 248, 287, 292, 307, 335
Christology, 23, 24, 26, 30, 31, 38, 50, 61, 75, 84, 87, 92, 102, 109, 110, 121, 191, 205, 254, 323, 324, 341
Chrysostom, 208, 226, 227
Church of God in Christ, 298
Church of God, 2, 34, 39, 40, 43, 65, 68, 120, 138, 142, 143, 153, 158, 182, 192, 196, 248, 249, 251, 256, 269, 271, 272, 273, 279, 280, 291, 298, 307, 308, 318, 325
civic pluralism, 18
civil pluralism, 25, 26
civil religion, 34
Classical Pentecostalism, 6, 61, 297, 302
Clement of Alexandria, 51, 70, 227, 228, 313
Clifton, Shane, 146, 160, 251, 271
Cobb, Jr, John B., 39, 70
Collins, Kenneth, 52

Cone, James, 192
Congar, Yves, 67, 73, 110, 120, 152, 154, 187, 230, 271
Conn, Charles W., 65, 158, 307
continuity, 3, 5, 8, 44, 55, 57, 100, 105, 181, 204, 213, 252, 264, 269, 283
conversation, 3-8, 18, 25, 53, 73, 80, 84, 91, 98, 104, 105, 121, 126, 147, 165, 168, 179, 198, 216-222, 239, 240-244, 247, 249, 250-255, 257, 261, 262, 267
conversion, 1, 12, 28, 32, 40, 73, 86, 92, 98, 99, 100, 101, 104, 115, 116, 124, 125, 141, 144, 154, 166, 167, 174, 181, 185, 186, 191, 194, 199, 213, 224, 234, 247, 250, 259, 278, 288, 297, 302
cooperation, 3, 7, 12, 30, 54, 79, 80, 97, 101, 221, 246-248, 254, 257, 270, 273, 282, 293
Coulter, Dale, 251, 271
Cox, Harvey, 135, 142, 153, 300, 325
creativity, 3, 5, 8, 57, 91
Crews, Mickey, 192, 291, 308
Cross, Terry L., 73, 191, 251, 271, 305, 307
Culpepper, Raymond F., 34, 153, 189
Culture, 11, 17, 25, 29, 44, 45, 51, 58, 87, 99, 101, 111, 117, 121, 142, 178, 192, 198, 219, 221, 226, 231, 239, 241-243, 248, 265, 268, 269, 285, 295, 296, 302, 309
Donald A. Hagner, D. A., 40, 190
D'Costa, Gavin, 31, 37
Dalai Lama, 12, 31, 318
Daniels, David D., 159
Dayton, Donald W., 71
dialogue,
  definition and nature, 79-81; ecumenical, 80, 81, 83, 106, 107, 246, 255, 257, 293; interfaith or interreligious, 1, 2, 3, 4-7, 11, 12, 17, 18, 35, 45, 58, 68, 72, 79-126, 147, 163-199, 204-207, 211, 213, 215, 216, 218-222, 224, 233, 236-239, 240-250, 252, 254-258, 261, 262, 264, 269, 270, 273, 276, 277, 280-285, 286-288, 290, 293, 320, 337, 339, 341, 342
diplomacy, 65, 180
diplomatic, 21, 240
Donovan, Mary Ann, 253, 272

doxological, 4, 138, 144, 159, 178, 193, 228, 261, 272, 303
Dryness, William A., 121, 147
du Plessis, David, 2, 6, 82, 107, 340
Duffield, Guy P., 39, 151, 182, 277, 292
Ecclesial Mission, 28
ecclesiology, 30, 55, 61, 73, 76, 102, 138, 146, 251, 252, 253, 254, 271, 273, 310
Eck, Diana 15, 19, 25, 30, 34
economics, 241, 262, 283
economy, 75, 241, 267, 296
ecumenical, 2, 3, 7, 17, 23, 29, 50, 53, 60, 72, 75, 76, 79, 85, 101, 104, 108, 125, 134, 169, 174, 178, 179, 189, 193, 196, 197, 206, 212, 213, 221, 224, 227, 231, 245, 247, 250-259, 267, 268, 269, 270, 271, 273, 276, 284, 285, 288, 290, 296, 300, 302, 305
ecumenism, 2, 53, 75, 77, 79, 80, 81, 82, 83, 92, 105-108, 212, 213, 224, 246, 271
Edwards, James R., 225, 226, 276
Elim Pentecostal Church, 291, 305, 323
Ellicott, Charles J., 40
Ellingsen, Mark, 255, 273
Ellington, Scott, 139, 146, 160
empowerment, 16, 20, 89, 113, 169, 197, 297, 300, 308
engagement, 5-7, 18, 38, 58, 63, 84, 85, 88, 91, 93, 105, 106, 117, 134, 164, 181, 184, 191, 203, 206, 213, 218, 219, 245, 247, 248, 250, 251, 255, 257, 270, 277, 280, 281, 286-288, 304
Erickson, Millard J., 69, 73, 225, 235
eschatology, 49, 54, 71, 124, 189, 218, 255-258, 274
Ethics, 110, 122, 156, 220, 237, 238, 263, 269, 276, 278, 316, 329, 336, 339, 340
Europe, 25, 33, 45, 82, 111, 206, 244, 267
Evangelical, 7, 43, 44, 46, 49, 53, 64-69, 71, 73-75, 94-96, 111, 116-118, 123-125, 132, 144, 151, 157, 185, 191, 205, 212, 215, 225, 235, 248, 249, 251, 255, 265, 267, 270, 273, 278, 280, 282, 291, 293, 299, 300, 315, 317, 318, 320, 321, 322, 328, 329, 333, 335, 337, 342, 344, 347
evangelism, 3, 45, 49, 50-52, 68, 85, 87, 92, 94, 96-98, 100, 102, 104, 110, 111, 117, 120, 123, 125, 139, 141, 152, 155, 192, 204, 206, 213, 214, 215, 224, 232, 233, 247, 255, 257, 295
exclusivism, 12, 13, 49, 50, 52, 53, 59, 60, 61, 64, 71, 75, 90, 91, 95, 100, 117, 204, 212, 223, 224, 282, 286, 287, 293
experience
  Charismatic or Pentecostal, 24, 26, 27, 44, 53, 58, 77, 102, 111, 133, 137, 140, 147, 173, 183, 190, 193, 276, 277, 293, 301, 305, 308, 310, 312, 333, 341; general religious, 57, 67, 131, 147, 149, 168, 183, 185, 223, 234, 236, 276, 278, 284, 304, 307, 309, 310, 326, 333, 338, 343; theology of, 307, 318
extremism, 103, 250
extremists, 265, 273
faiths, 11, 12, 13, 14, 15, 17, 18, 19, 21, 25, 26, 28, 29, 46, 52, 59, 60, 61, 62, 63, 65, 68, 80, 84, 85, 86, 90, 91, 92, 93, 101, 115, 119, 124, 163, 164, 165, 168, 169, 170, 179, 182, 190, 191, 198, 207, 210, 211, 215, 224, 231, 234, 239, 240, 245, 246, 247, 255, 260, 263, 264, 266, 277, 281
familiarity, 3, 104, 105, 106, 163, 240, 282
Faupel, D. William, 274
Fee, Gordon D., 225, 274, 275
Finger, Thomas, 96
Fletcher, John, 50, 51, 69, 347
Ford, David F., 148
Fox, Richard, 243
Francis of Assisi, 66, 317
freedom *of* religion, 119, 241, 264, 265
Fritsch, Charles Theodore, 226
Fuller, R. H., 232
fundamentalism, 2, 15, 16, 32, 68, 221, 267, 295, 300, 310
Gallagher, Robert L., 39, 75
Gandhi, 34, 67, 284, 332
Gause, R. Hollis, 39, 50, 68, 69, 73, 184, 251, 256, 272, 274
Gee, Donald, 82, 107, 300

Gill, Jerry, 219
globalization, 3, 5, 11, 14, 16, 17, 29, 81, 304
glossolalia, 4, 136, 146, 191, 194, 298, 303, 305, 308, 310
Goff, James R., 279, 291, 304, 306
Gonzalez, Justo L., 33, 227
Green, Michael, 70
Grenz, Stanely J., 74, 117, 234, 235
Griffis, David M., 273
Gros, Jeff, 106, 155
Hagar, 226, 228
Harris, J., 230, 277
Hart, Larry D., 107, 274
Hartley, John, 209, 226
Healing, 20, 110, 114, 132, 153, 154, 158, 185, 189, 231, 312, 323, 329, 337, 339
Heim, S. Mark,37, 189, 320, 340, 342
Hesselgrave, David J., 66, 118, 124, 186, 337
Hick, John, 31, 38, 324
Hildebrandt, Wilf, 292
Hinduism, 8, 13, 31, 34, 65, 67, 96, 99, 118, 121, 198, 329, 336, 344
History, 33, 35, 36, 65, 66, 68, 79, 115, 119, 124, 130, 148-151, 155, 158, 160, 185, 192, 195, 197, 218, 227, 235, 263, 265, 266, 267, 274, 291, 305, 307-309, 314, 316, 317, 318, 320, 321, 322, 323, 325, 328, 334, 335, 336, 340, 345, 346, 347
Hocken, Peter D., 123, 183, 193, 195, 232, 321, 337
Holiness, 3, 6, 43, 50, 57, 65, 74, 114, 183, 187, 191, 195, 232, 243, 266, 270, 273, 276, 277, 297, 304, 306, 309, 310, 312, 318, 319, 328, 341, 343, 344, 345, 346; movement, 2, 29, 71, 193, 213, 279, 298, 326
Hollenweger, Walter, 2, 82, 154, 212, 232
Hollingsworth, Andrea, 193
Holocaust, 44, 130, 148, 161, 194, 199, 240, 324, 340
Holy Spirit
  in the Church, 55, 77, 103, 241, 329
  in the world, 39, 66, 75, 110, 113, 124, 125, 153, 157, 158, 159, 320, 321, 327, 328, 330, 336, 337, 339, 347, 348; of Christ, 58, 103, 164, 261; of God, 2, 24, 175, 234, 253, 292, 324, 327
Homerin, Th. Emil, 240, 262
Horton, Stanely M., 40, 292, 308, 325
hospitality, 15, 17, 18, 25, 32, 34, 38, 59, 88, 89, 90, 91, 92, 104, 114, 115, 295, 296
Hughes, Ray H., 40, 160
Hunter, Harold D., 76, 123, 321, 337
Huron, 46
Hurtado, Larry W., 37, 224
imperialism, 37, 99
inclusivism, 12, 13, 49, 51, 52, 56, 57, 59, 60, 61, 63, 64, 67, 68, 71, 75, 83, 90, 91, 95, 99, 117, 118, 203, 204, 205, 209, 212, 213, 214, 224, 227, 233, 273, 286, 287, 288, 293
inclusivist, 8, 12, 31, 49, 50, 51, 53, 56, 57, 59, 60, 61, 67, 73, 83, 90, 119, 120, 203, 206, 207, 210, 212, 213, 214, 227, 251, 287
India, 99, 116, 184, 206, 215, 224, 277, 283, 284, 313, 323, 346
Indians, 46
initial evidence, 77, 83, 154, 245, 298, 304, 305
inspiration, 13, 27, 30, 39, 61, 68, 102, 145, 150, 174, 225, 256, 259, 278, 288, 289, 293, 299, 301
inspired speech, 1, 137, 145, 150, 153, 164, 169, 278
Interfaith Relations, 7, 119, 195, 320
International Church of the Foursquare Gospel, 298
Irenaeus, 114, 227, 253, 272, 287, 293, 319, 326, 336, 342, 345
Ishmael, 226, 231
Islam, 8, 12, 13, 15, 31, 34, 36, 45, 50, 65, 67, 70, 96, 99, 118, 119, 130, 149, 180, 198, 211, 214, 226, 231, 233, 240, 245, 263, 267, 293, 312, 313, 317, 325, 329, 330, 334, 335, 339, 344, 345, 346
Israel, 51, 54, 55, 68, 99, 122, 138, 156, 171, 185, 190, 214, 227, 228, 229, 230, 233, 236, 252, 256, 272, 273, 315, 319, 336
Jacobs, Cindy, 224, 270
Jacobsen, Douglas, 213, 232
Jenkins, Philip, 45, 244, 267
Jervis, L. Ann, 231
Jesus Christ, 1, 14, 24, 26, 28, 29, 31, 47, 52, 55, 56, 57, 61, 67, 69, 74,

83, 86, 87, 88, 91, 93, 94, 95, 97, 99, 100, 104, 109, 110, 118, 122, 138, 139, 170, 185, 190, 195, 214, 215, 217, 224, 227, 233, 237, 244, 252, 285, 291, 300, 327, 337, 339, 343
Jews, 12, 16, 38, 44, 45, 48, 51, 52, 93, 115, 119, 123, 185, 199, 215, 220, 228, 231, 236, 242, 259, 263, 273, 277, 303
Johns, Cheryl Bridges, 133, 151, 159, 295
Johns, Jackie D., 235
Johnson, Van, 226, 276
Jones, Charles, 100, 123
Jones, E. Stanley, 283, 284, 289, 290, 322
Judaism, 8, 13, 44, 51, 65, 211, 214, 222, 226, 231, 240, 245, 255, 263, 264, 273, 294, 303, 317, 325, 330, 334
Juergensmeyer, Mark, 16, 20, 30, 33, 35
Julie Ma, 302
Jung, Carl G., 310
Justin Martyr, 51, 227
Kalu, Ogbu, 185
Kärkkäinen, Veli-Matti, 23, 37, 57, 74, 75, 84, 109, 110, 153, 212, 217, 232, 284, 300, 347
Kay, William, 292, 306
Kelly, J. N. D., 272, 294
Kimball, Charles, 22, 35, 37
King, J. H., 74, 110, 122, 158, 191, 232, 334, 339
King, Paul, 298
Kinnamon, Michael, 106
Kireopoulos, Antonios, 195
Knight, H. H., 74, 235
Knitter, Paul, 114, 126, 319, 344
Koran, 12, 31, 45, 51, 96, 231
Kraemer, Hendrick, 12
Kselman, J. S., 226
Küng, Hans, 17, 30, 47, 220, 221, 236, 237, 263, 342
Land, Steven J., 40, 69, 77, 152, 187, 232, 274, 309
Latin America, 40, 140, 150, 151, 157, 182, 184, 186, 189, 191, 197, 244, 271, 312, 313, 314, 316, 317, 318, 321, 325, 329, 331, 332, 336, 341
Latin American, 33, 82, 87, 140

Levenson, Jon D., 240, 262
Lewis, C. S., 66, 197, 227, 343
liberation, 13, 54, 157, 174, 192
liberty, 21, 28, 38, 87, 103, 106, 137, 145, 169, 180, 208, 209, 242, 243, 244, 299, 300
Lincoln, Andrew, 257, 274
liturgical, 13
liturgy, 45, 133, 135, 137, 152, 174
Lord, Andrew, 55, 257, 275
love, 26, 28, 34, 52, 61, 86, 92, 94, 95, 108, 125, 137, 144, 198, 210, 223, 226, 232, 243, 247, 261, 273, 275, 279, 280, 289
Lovett, L., 192
Ma, Wonsuk, 302
Macchia, Frank, 24, 37, 59, 135, 251, 253, 275, 302
MacDonald, William, 140, 156
Marshall, I. H., 40, 182
Martin, David, 111, 186
Martin, Larry, 280
Marty, Martin E., 14, 25, 30, 34, 105
McCall, Robert, 142
McClung, L. Grant, 155, 182
McDermott, Gerald, 94, 117
McFarlane, Graham, 67, 69, 112, 272
McGee, Gary B., 77, 154, 187, 193, 196, 308
McGuire, Meredith B., 161
Meacham, Jon, 241, 249, 264, 270
Mennonite, 96, 97, 119, 120, 273, 314, 320
Menzies, R., 77, 308, 333
Menzies, William W., 309
Michaels, J. R., 224, 276
Miracles, 197, 330
miraculous, 29, 82, 90, 133, 144, 160, 177, 178, 182, 183, 186, 194, 196, 197, 224, 259, 299, 300, 302
missio Dei, 91, 115
missiology, 73, 91, 96, 102
Mittelstadt, Martin., 277, 306
modernism, 183, 290, 299
modernity, 121, 236
Mohammed, 31, 51, 52, 70, 233, 263, 293, 339
Moltmann, Jürgen, 34, 40, 53, 54, 71, 72, 73, 109, 155, 187, 191, 232, 235, 237, 241, 252, 264, 272, 275, 313, 314, 329, 330, 334, 339
Moon, Tony, 74, 110

Moore, Jonathan, 270, 331
Moore, M., 230, 277, 323
Morris, Leon,222, 315
Mounce, Robert H.,224
Muck, Terry, 75, 293, 337, 347
Muslims, 15, 16, 36, 38, 45, 51, 52, 93, 99, 100, 110, 111, 119, 182, 215, 220, 231, 242, 245, 259, 273, 277, 333
narrative theology, 136
narrative, 62, 76, 77, 130, 136, 140, 141, 142, 143, 144, 146, 147, 152, 156, 161, 165, 168, 173, 195, 208, 210, 226, 282, 292, 301; autobiographical or personal, 139, 170, 171; biblical, 70, 132, 153, 171, 211, 216, 231, 321, 330; historical, 218; Pentecostal, 134, 135, 137, 142
Nationalism, 33, 327
Netland, Harold, 49
Neusner, Jacob, 239, 262, 317, 325, 330
Newbigin, Lesslie, 47, 61, 76, 92, 284, 290, 338, 339
Niebuhr, Reinhold, 32, 115, 116, 185, 234, 237, 238, 265, 266
Noll, Mark, 44, 125
Oden, Thomas C., 69, 126, 190, 227
Olson, Roger E., 66, 120, 228, 234, 293
Omar, A. Rashied, 12
Oneness Pentecostalism, 308, 338
Oral Tradition, 135
Origen, 190, 208, 209, 226
Oswalt, John, 214
Otto, Rudolf, 147
Palestine, 21, 36, 236, 316
Palma, A. 234
Palmer, Michael D., 263
Palmer, Phoebe, 195, 338, 346
Panikkar, Raimon, 31, 121
Pannenberg, Wolfhart, 216, 218, 225, 234, 263, 266, 327
parable, 89, 90
Parham, Charles F. 50, 57, 74, 232, 275, 279, 291, 304, 306, 322, 336, 339
Park, Myung Soo, 144, 159
pastoral, 137, 142, 147, 173, 178, 195, 258, 288
peace, 1, 17, 20, 25, 29, 34, 40, 84, 85, 125, 137, 157, 180, 181, 189, 191, 212, 220, 221, 236, 237, 238, 241, 245, 248, 249, 254, 258, 263, 273, 281, 289, 294
Pentecostal Church of God, 298
Pentecostal distinctiveness, 134, 301
Pentecostal Holiness Church, 298, 311
Pentecostal Missions, 155, 332
Pentecostal spirituality, 3, 32, 64, 125, 133, 134, 136, 137, 142, 144, 172, 234, 256, 258, 282, 301, 308
Pentecostalism
   Classical, 2, 29, 31, 50, 53, 81, 82, 146, 212, 213, 239, 274, 279, 286; conservative, 38; contemporary, 5, 43, 57, 60, 61, 64, 66, 83, 136, 143, 153, 158, 159, 213, 241, 254, 256, 273, 277, 282, 300, 302, 307, 333, 337; global, 37, 41, 44, 65, 71, 75, 83,107, 112, 125, 153, 160, 182, 184, 188, 189, 192, 234, 245, 246, 264, 268, 269, 272, 274, 277, 279, 293, 313, 330, 333, 340, 346, 347; historic, 53, 254; Holiness, 6, 50, 57, 65, 183, 191, 266, 273, 276, 277, 279, 310, 312, 319, 341, 344, 345; indigenous, 157, 251, 277, 292, 313, 341; Neo- or new, 2, 6, 7, 156, 196, 297, 313, 343; North American, 44, 87, 157, 255, 267; progressive, 246, 247; traditional, 3, 113, 141, 168, 255, 355
Pinnock, Clark, 53, 56, 71, 73, 141, 153, 156, 184, 223, 232, 251, 271, 318, 322, 330, 342
pluralism, 11-14, 17-19, 22-38, 43, 47, 49, 50-53, 57-61, 64, 68, 70, 71, 75, 79, 83, 90, 91, 95, 96, 99, 117, 118, 120, 126, 204, 206, 209, 219, 230, 242, 251, 264, 270, 273, 276, 281-288, 291, 294, 295, 303
Plüss, J. D., 147
pneumatic, 52, 59, 106, 125, 163, 183, 204, 251, 282, 303
pneumatology, 4, 30, 53-56, 60, 72, 73, 74, 75, 84-88, 102, 103, 104, 109, 110, 121, 124-126, 129, 157, 189, 191, 203, 212, 213, 216, 217, 230, 251, 252, 254, 257, 282, 292, 295, 300, 304, 306
Poirier, John, 136
political theology, 237, 241
Poloma, Margaret M., 153, 158

Pope John Paul II, 125, 294
postmodern, 20, 92, 142, 218, 226, 234, 236, 285
postmodernism, 96, 234, 308
power, 20, 24, 27, 28, 29, 36, 44, 53, 54, 58, 60, 62, 71, 77, 81, 83, 89, 91, 94, 101, 102, 111, 133, 134, 135, 136, 140, 144, 145, 147, 155, 158, 160, 164, 165, 168, 170, 171, 174, 175, 180, 184, 191, 192, 193, 194, 196, 205, 215, 218, 223, 226, 228, 229, 236, 237, 243, 249, 251, 260, 262, 267, 268, 269, 279, 282, 284, 286, 292, 298, 300, 301, 304, 305, 307, 308; divine, 95, 172; of faith, 86; spiritual, 7, 125, 143, 291; supernatural, 38
prayer, 14, 133, 134, 135, 136, 144, 146, 152, 153, 154, 159, 161, 167, 168, 169, 177, 178, 182, 183, 186, 187, 188, 193, 194, 197, 208, 209, 210, 211, 228, 230, 232, 277, 281, 287, 288, 289, 295, 300
prevenient grace, 52, 56, 73, 104, 126
Price, J. Lynn, 30, 106, 111, 154, 225, 272, 314, 318, 328, 329, 334, 342
prophetic, 68, 103, 118, 143, 145, 158, 173, 188, 208, 226, 233, 236, 256, 270, 301
Protestantism, 50, 145, 151, 152, 184, 186, 188, 194, 243, 244, 264, 278, 310, 314, 322, 327, 331, 345
psychology, 32, 37, 131, 220
Race, Alan, 71
Rahner, Karl, 31
Raiser, Konrad, 290
Ramachandra, Vinoth, 987, 120, 285, 291
reciprocity, 55, 165, 252
Reddie, Anthony G., 107
Redman, Jerry, 248, 269
relativism, 23, 34, 37, 54, 62, 64, 122, 219, 291
relativistic, 23, 149, 215, 236, 253
religious diversity, 16, 17, 19, 32, 33, 38, 83, 242, 265, 288
religious pluralism, 1, 11, 12, 14, 17, 21, 24, 26, 27, 28, 29, 30, 31, 35, 38, 43, 49, 50, 57, 64, 79, 96, 98, 99, 105, 113, 121, 163, 219, 222, 230, 244, 246, 251, 268, 281, 282, 285, 288, 292

Republic, 241, 242, 263
revelation, 12, 27, 47, 48, 51, 52, 56, 57, 61, 68, 89, 90, 95, 97, 118, 119, 121, 126, 131, 138, 148, 170, 177, 178, 217, 218, 219, 227, 256, 272, 274
Ricci, Matteo, 45
Rice, Condoleezza, 21, 35
Richard, Ramesh, 49, 204
Richardson, Alan, 206, 225, 230
Richie, Tony, 31, 33, 37, 39, 70, 74, 75, 76, 77, 108-112, 158, 191, 231, 232, 267, 275, 280, 295, 328, 347
Ricoeur, Paul, 130, 148, 236, 321
Robeck, Jr. Cecil M., 41, 82, 106-108, 123, 136, 153, 160, 182, 183, 186, 188, 193, 196, 197, 263, 279, 294, 309
Robuck, David, 193
Rogers, Carl, 194
Runyon, Theodore, 70
Rutledge, Fleming, 249, 269, 270
sacred texts, 14, 100
Sailhammer, John H., 228, 277
Salvation, 12, 27, 31, 32, 39, 69, 70, 90, 121, 187, 270, 293, 321, 324, 331, 337, 342
Sanders, Cheryl J., 183
Sanders, John, 69, 227, 320
Sandidge, Jerry L., 106, 107, 123, 193, 197, 340
Sarah, 207, 210, 226, 227
Scripture, 13, 27, 29, 30, 33, 48, 61, 68, 102, 113, 114, 117, 121, 133, 138, 141, 148, 150, 152, 155, 156, 159, 165, 184, 185, 190, 194, 197, 198, 203-207, 211, 223, 231, 256, 278, 293, 294, 299, 306, 310, 313, 320, 322, 334, 344
Sepúlveda, Juan, 73, 140, 150, 156, 157, 184, 189, 271, 292
Seymour, William J., 111, 136, 153, 280, 298, 306, 331
Shelton, James, 280
Shenk, Calvin, 96, 119
Shepperd, J. W., 309
Sims, John, 40
Simut, C. C., 237, 263
Smith, D. M., 223
Smith, Jane I., 110
Smith, Jamie K. A., 293
Smith, Wilfred Cantrell, 12, 279

Soards, Marion L., 234
social justice, 58, 90, 92, 125, 248
Society for Pentecostal Studies, 7, 271
Sociology, 16, 309, 310, 341
Solivan, Samuel, 126, 307
Soteriology, 27, 75, 231, 327
specificity, 3, 25, 26, 52, 105, 106, 132, 163, 282
Spina, Frank A., 225
Spirit baptism, 7, 24, 50, 75, 102, 136, 140, 142, 144, 147, 153, 157, 167, 177, 186, 188, 191, 197, 277, 297, 301, 302, 305, 308
spiritual gifts, 1, 27, 82, 136, 144, 167, 168, 178, 188, 191, 194, 234, 256, 298, 299, 300
spiritual warfare, 144, 172, 254
Spirituality, 6, 70, 120, 150, 182, 183, 187, 188, 194, 196, 245, 278, 290, 304, 312, 314, 316, 317, 324, 330, 336, 343; Pentecostal, 3, 32, 40, 64, 69, 125, 133, 134, 136, 137, 142, 144, 152, 153, 157, 159, 172, 182, 187, 191, 232, 234, 256, 258, 269, 274, 282, 301, 306, 308, 309, 318, 329, 336, 339
Spittler, Russell P., 7, 107, 108, 152, 183, 188, 191, 278, 308, 312, 322, 327, 345
Stackhouse, Jr., John G., 67
Stephen Neill, 92, 94, 115
Stephens, Randall J., 183, 304, 309
Stott, John, 68, 116, 317
Stronstad, Roger, 40, 160, 187, 188, 312, 314, 326, 336, 341
Studebaker, Steven, 277, 333
Suurmond, Jean-Jacques, 76, 77, 326
Synan, Vinson, 2, 6, 7, 65, 69,71, 155, 157, 161, 184, 185, 191, 192, 193, 197, 279, 291, 297—99, 304, 306, 319, 323, 324, 326, 333, 336, 344
Tan-Chow, MayLing, 7, 75, 156, 181, 185, 188, 189, 192, 195, 198, 344
Telushkin, Joseph Rabbi, 209, 226, 229, 244
Tennent, Timothy, 67, 69, 94, 95, 96, 118, 119, 121, 198, 344
terrorism or terrorists, 15-21, 32, 33, 36, 91, 249-250, 317, 326
testimonies or testimony, 1, 3-4, 5-6, 62, 72, 259, 260, 261, 293, 324, 336; dialogical, 63, 163-199, 284, 345; evangelical, 147, 278; paradigmatic, 1, 4-6, 7, 79, 104-105, 129-161, 169, 171, 196, 230, 245, 281, 288, 296; Pentecostal distinctive of, 134, 142, 167, 170, 186, 278, 332; personal, 1, 12, 129, 138, 149, 151, 153, 157, 159, 178, 189, 191, 194, 199, 211, 281, 282, 288, 346; public, 146, 176, 193
theology
  Christian, 21, 66, 91, 95, 98, 114, 117, 120, 125, 212, 216, 228, 234, 235, 237, 272, 307, 316, 320, 322, 335; Pentecostal/Charismatic/ Renewal, 7, 21, 37, 39, 40, 55, 66, 67, 75, 107, 111, 112, 122, 126, 135, 136, 140-142, 146, 153, 156, 157, 158, 160, 176, 183, 188, 189, 191, 198, 226, 251, 256, 277, 290, 292, 298, 301-303, 305, 306, 307, 308, 326, , 343, 346
theology of religions
  biblical, 205, 227; Christian, 44, 57, 60; Christological, 3, 23, 75, 121, 205; definition and purpose, 57-58; multifaceted and complex, 33, 285; Pentecostal, 43-77, 287; pneumatological, 75, 84-85, 85-86, 103; trinitarian, 7, 57-60, 84, 126
Thomas, John Christopher, 138, 139, 154, 155, 156, 190, 224, 274, 292, 308, 344
Thorsen, Don, 185, 270, 344
Tillich, Paul, 8, 47, 271, 344
Tozer, A.W., 150, 185, 187, 192, 298, 344
transformation, 13, 21, 50, 84. 90-91, 93, 94, 100, 122, 133-134, 140, 151, 158, 165, 166, 182, 184, 190, 192, 224, 270, 305
transnationalism, 182, 186, 187, 189, 196
truth
  absolute, 22-23, 203, 220, 283; dialogical, 84, 94, 98, 101, 102, 116, 118, 180, 181, 214, 218-220, 233; dynamic, 88, 235, 236; experience oriented, 141-144, 148, 157, 182, 187, 276; Holy Spirit, 39, 109, 194, 204-205, 215, 218, 230, 235, 253, 277, 289; honesty and humility of, 86, 118, 185, 195, 218; lifestyle of,

221, 223; methaphorical, 26; provisional and eschatological, 215-218, 287; religions and, 11-12, 18, 37, 48, 70, 72, 95, 103, 114, 117, 199, 206-207, 214, 234, 286; scriptural, 27, 118, 141, 156, 272; struggle for, 93; supernatural and natural, 54; tested, 50, 227; and testimony or narrative, 130, 136, 138, 140, 148, 158, 175, 179, 288, 295; tolerance and, 39; unique and ultimate in Christ, 61, 76, 97, 170, 204, 228, 230, 233, 285

Ucko, Hans, 7, 115, 116, 345

uniqueness
Christian, 26-27, 28, 39, 47, 51, 56, 61, 99, 101, 204, 223, 254, 285-286; compatible with diversity and inclusivism, 24, 46-48, 52, 57, 231; counter to pluralism, 14, 23, 32, 68, 114, 116; revealed in testimonies, 182, 188; Wesleyan-Pentecostal theologies, 50-51

United Kingdom, 12, 21, 46, 50, 60, 72, 107, 182, 297, 213, 245, 257, 284, 298, 305, 306, 308

United States of America, 2, 6, 15-16, 19-20, 21, 25, 33, 34, 36, 38, 44-46, 65, 73, 82, 87, 108, 109, 113, 126, 135, 143, 153, 154, 157, 167, 178, 191, 192, 220, 241-244, 245, 264, 265, 267, 279, 294, 297, 302, 309

unity
Christian, 40, 80-81, 122, 273, 279, 289; human and interreligous, 21, 212, 249, 269, 276; Pentecostals on, 7, 44, 58, 74, 81-83, 105, 107, 108, 134, 188, 231-232, 255, 261, 290, 299, 300

universalism, 48, 66, 70, 99, 103, 118

universality
dialectic with particularity, 56, 81, 120; distinct from universalism, 48, 66, 118; of the Holy Spirit, 84, 254; Pentecostal tradition of, 28, 33; regarding conflicting truth claims, 93; rooted in nature of God and Christ, 228-229, 233; toward religious others, 61, 68, 150, 204-205

Van Cleave, N. M., 39, 126, 132-133, 151, 182, 277, 292

Violence
contribution of secularism, 32; global challenge of, 221; jihad, 15, 273; mission of churches regarding, 237; politics and psychology of, 32, 220, 236; religions and interreligious relations, 14-22, 25, 33, 35, 36, 37, 99, 212, 295; role of hospitality, 91, 114; responsibility of Pentecostals, 29-30, 237

Vitality, 27, 134, 142, 147, 156, 163, 164, 215, 249, 253, 269, 282, 290, 301

Volf, Miroslav, 37, 212, 231, 271

Von Harnack, Adolf, 195, 345

Wacker, Grant, 7, 146-147, 154, 159, 161, 183, 185, 186, 189, 192, 193, 195, 198, 277, 294, 306

Wagner, Peter, 224

Walker, Paul, 39, 345

Wallis, Jim, 250, 270

War, 2, 16, 20, 22, 33, 36, 45, 73, 155, 157, 161, 211, 212, 220, 221, 237, 240, 241, 245, 299

Warner, W.E., 108, 186, 193, 196, 277

Warrington, Keith, 2, 7, 46, 66, 158, 298, 299, 301, 302, 307

Webber, Robert, 154, 159, 234

Weber, Max, 182

Wesley, John, 12, 31, 44, 49, 50-52, 56, 69-70, 73, 116, 125, 126, 144, 209, 214-15, 226, 227, 229, 233, 280, 287

Wesleyanism, 3, 28, 43, 44, 49, 50, 52, 53, 56, 57, 60, 61, 64, 70, 111, 125, 126, 152, 159, 213, 214, 218, 213, 248, 270, 282, 284, 298, 301

White, James, 161

White, Robert, 77

White, Vilbert L., Jr., 130, 149

Williams, J. Rodman, 40, 67, 107, 194, 226, 231-232, 237, 290

Wingate, Andrew, 116

Witherington, Ben III, 68

Witness
Christian, 80, 155, 285; Church's mission, 28-29, 72, 91, 120, 164, 285; compatible with dialogue, 96, 98, 100, 118, 187, 199; compatible with inclusivism, 49, 51, 119; expe-

riential, 140, 148, 150, 151, 152, 155; interreligious, 52-53, 71, 76, 84-86, 88, 96, 211; in power of Holy Spirit, 60, 76, 77, 89, 91, 102, 111, 113, 122, 136, 139, 145, 172, 187, 194, 197, 215, 230, 277; labor of love, 94, 96; through testimonies, 62, 130, 131, 132, 135, 136, 139, 143, 195, 197, 236; word and deed, 102-103, 261

Wood, Laurence, 50, 69, 126, 148, 218, 235

World Council of Churches, 41, 80, 106, 197, 290

World Religions, 12, 13, 20, 21, 30, 33, 34, 36, 37, 46, 54-55, 57, 72, 121, 168, 174, 181, 205, 209, 216, 219, 221, 223, 249-250, 252, 253, 268, 283, 287

Worship, 13, 16, 26, 37, 118, 134-135, 136, 137, 142, 143-144, 145, 146, 147, 154, 156, 159, 161, 166-167, 174, 183, 186-187, 188, 192, 193-194, 195, 199, 213, 237, 247, 258-261, 276, 277, 280

Wright, Christopher, 121, 230

Wright, N.T., 231

Yamamori, Tetsunao, 125, 189, 246-247, 255-256, 268, 274

Yoder, John Howard, 92, 115, 120

Yong, Amos, 7, 23, 30, 32, 35, 37, 38, 56, 58-59, 60, 71, 73, 74, 75, 76, 77, 84, 88-92, 103, 104, 109, 111, 112, 113, 114, 118, 124, 141, 142, 184, 186, 188, 191, 203-206, 222, 292, 294

www.ingramcontent.com/pod-product-compliance
Lightning Source LLC
Chambersburg PA
CBHW021816300426
44114CB00009BA/198